INTERNATIONAL AWARD W~~~~~~
HARRIS REFERE~~~
CATALOG

SO-AUC-020

1985 SPRING/SUMMER
EDITION

Postage Stamp Prices

OF THE

UNITED STATES
UNITED NATIONS
AND
CANADA AND PROVINCES

Plus: Confederate States, U. S. Possessions,
Albums and Accessories, Comprehensive U. S. Stamp Identifier.

SCOTT CATALOG NUMBERS ARE USED WITHIN THIS PUBLICATION
WITH THE PERMISSION OF SCOTT PUBLISHING CO.

H.E. Harris & Co., Inc.®
The World's Largest Stamp Firm — Founded in 1916
BOSTON, MASS. 02117

28600
International Standard Book Number ISBN: 0-937458-39-2

Continued support by thousands of collectors from the United States and abroad has built...

The World's Largest Stamp Firm
. . . doing business for over 69 years!

HEADQUARTERS AND MAIN BOSTON PLANT

Serving our customers from the world's largest and most modern stamp headquarters, H.E. Harris & Co., Inc., constantly strives to provide collectors with the things that have made us famous:

- **Extensive inventories**
- **Unique skills**
- **Fair dealing**
- **Honest value**

When you buy Harris supplies from your local dealer, or directly from us, you call upon an organization dedicated to the stamp hobby for over 69 years.

HARRIS ® The Sign of Satisfaction ... Guaranteed.

H.E. Harris & Co., Inc. ®

World's Largest Stamp Firm — founded in 1916

Foreword

Dear Collector:

Thank you for purchasing our catalog. In its pages you will find a complete listing (except for a few of the greatest rarities) of all United States, Canada and United Nations stamps. This catalog is a meaningful reference guide and price list - meaningful, because the prices listed herein are not arbitrary "catalog values" assigned by firms that neither buy nor sell stamps; -- they are our actual selling prices at the time this catalog went to press.

For your convenience, stamps are listed in several different grades of condition; a handy U. S. Stamp Identifier section is included; and at the back of the book, you will find a comprehensive price list of our stamp collecting supplies.

Many Harris products are available through stamp and hobby shops; chain and department store hobby centers; bookstores and other hobby outlets, or you may order directly from us.

When you buy a Harris product, you reap the fruits of 69 years of accumulated expertise in serving the needs of stamp collectors all over the world.

When you order from Harris, you are fully protected by our 30-day money-back Guarantee of Satisfaction.

Use this catalog. Enjoy it. May it bring you many hours of philatelic pleasure!

Cordially yours,

Wesley Mann

Wesley P. Mann, Jr.
President

Street Address	Mailing Address
	(For fastest service)
H.E. Harris & Co., Inc.	H.E. Harris & Co., Inc.
645 Summer Street	Boston, MA 02117
Boston, MA 02210	

INTRODUCTION

Published for over 54 years, the Harris "US/BNA Catalog" as it is usually called, lists (with the exception of the great rarities) all stamps of United States, United Nations and British North America--that is, Canada and Provinces -- and shows our current prices for each, for ordering and for reference purposes. Our stamp listings use, with permission, the numbering system according to the Scott Standard Postage Stamp Catalog, the most widely-used stamp cataloguing system in North America.

Underneath each illustration is the Scott Catalog number of the one or more stamps having that particular design. When more than one issue features the same design, exact identification may be determined by referring to the descriptive text of each number or to the Stamp Identifier section near the back of this catalog.

How to begin...

You can save stamps from your own correspondence, and ask relatives and friends to save theirs for you. Business people, members of the Armed Forces, and persons who travel or have relatives overseas are excellent sources of foreign stamps.

All stamps have value, so long as they are not torn or otherwise damaged. You will want the best possible copy of each stamp for your collection. Other copies that you may acquire -- "duplicates" -- are useful for trading with other collectors or with pen pals. A packet of duplicates and an inexpensive album make an excellent gift for a new collector.

Keeping Stamps...

Until they are properly mounted in an album, (see "Mounting Stamps") stamps should be kept in glassine envelopes, paper envelopes or in stock books (several are listed in the "Supplies" section at the back of this catalog.) Do *not* jam them into a small box or other container that could cause them to get torn, creased or wrinkled. Treat them as you would any special collectible object -- very carefully!

Choosing an Album...

Select an album according the the amount of time and money you anticipate spending on your hobby. It is better to start with a modest-sized album and "graduate" to a more comprehensive one later. We offer an excellent choice of world-wide and United States albums and stamp collecting kits (see back of this catalog) for beginning and intermediate collectors.

Most people start by collecting stamps of the world, and then later narrow their collecting interest to a particular country or topic. The true "romance of stamp collecting" that has given the hobby its wide appeal over the hundred and forty years people have been collecting stamps, however, is in acquiring these fascinating pieces of paper from distant lands -- from "far-away places with strange sounding names", as a popular song once called them. Areas for later specialization are about as diverse as the subjects portrayed on postage stamps. They can include a single country such as United States or Canada, France or Israel, Vatican City or any other stamp-issuing entity; the British Empire; airmails; topicals such as "art on stamps," "ships on stamps," "sports on stamps" or any of hundreds of other topics, or First Day Covers. Every one of these specialties has its own unique appeal, and Harris is prepared to help you enjoy the specialty of your choice.

Mounting Stamps...

NEVER USE TAPE OR GLUE FOR MOUNTING STAMPS. Always use an approved stamp mounting. The most widely-used method over the years has been stamp hinges, little pieces of gummed glassine which are folded, moistened lightly and attached to the stamp and to the album. In recent years, however, there has been a decided trend toward preserving the gum of unused stamps in "unhinged" condition by using so-called "hingeless" mounts such as Harris' Crystal-Mount. When buying older stamps, those which have never been hinged and still have the gum in "mint" condition command premium prices, as can be seen by studying the prices in this catalog.

Accessories...

There are a few basic accessories that every stamp collector should have. *Tongs*, which are like household tweezers except that they have smooth inside tips, are used for handling stamps so that they are protected from any moisture due to body oils or perspiration; *Magnifier,* for ease in seeing minor differences, such as those described in our Stamp Identifier; *Perforation Gauge,* for determining the number of perforations in two centimeters, often an important identifying feature in earlier issues; *Watermark Detector and Fluid,* necessary to identify those issues which can be told apart only by whether they are printed on watermarked paper or not.

Types of stamps...

There are a number of different types of stamps among which are the following:

- Definitives, or Regular Postage Issues — These are the "ordinary" stamps issued in very large quantities to handle all basic postal needs. They are usually sold at the post office over a period of several years, or until the next definitive issue comes out.

- Commemoratives — These are stamps, often larger in size than definitives, issued to commemorate a specific event, person or group of persons, historical anniversary or forthcoming special happening (such as Olympic Games). They are generally on sale for a fairly limited period of time.

- Airmails, Special Deliveries, Postage Dues — These are all special-purpose stamps, as their names imply.

- Revenues — Stamps issued for non-postal use, "revenues" are or have been required on certain items as a means of collecting a government tax. These include Hunting Permit stamps, playing cards, tobacco, documents, wines, etc.

- Coils — are stamps issued in rolls for use in stamp vending machines. They may be horizontal coils (perforations vertically) or vertical coils (having horizontal perforations).

- **Plate Blocks** — These are blocks of four, six or more stamps having the printing plate number or numbers in the attached selvage edge. Each printing plate carries its own number, and every sheet of stamps printed from that plate will carry that same number. Where two or more plates are used, as for multicolored printings, there will probably be additional plate numbers, one for each plate used.

- **First Day Cover** — An envelope, or "cover", postmarked on the first day of issue of the stamp used thereon. Most recent FDC's make use of privately printed envelopes which carry an attractive design, called a "cachet", from the French word meaning "official seal," appropriate to the person or event honored by the stamp.

About our Prices:

We reasonably expect the prices in this catalog to be valid for the entire life of this edition, but once in a while, an unusually active market may force us to increase a few prices. In all such instances, however, you are fully protected by our Harris guarantee of satisfaction, and you may return within thirty days (original order blank **must** be included) any item that is not fully satisfactory at the price charged.

Whether using the catalog for ordering or for reference, **condition** is an important consideration. Our catalog gives prices for unused original gum (o.g.); unused, and used stamps. Generally speaking, unused stamps from 1900 on will have gum, although they may have been hinged. Pre-1900 issues, even though unused, usually have little or no gum.

Condition is relative. In the case of certain issues, especially older stamps printed before the days of electronic centering, the very best obtainable copies (which command premium prices) may appear poor by today's centering standards, and yet be very desirable to knowledgeable collectors. Centering on most recent issues is excellent.

"Unused" and "used" stamps are just what their names imply, while "mint" stamps are unused stamps that have never been hinged; that is, are in "mint" condition, just as they came from the printer. If you require stamps in this condition, please specify "N.H." Never-hinged stamps generally command premium prices, and for issues prior to 1940, may be difficult to obtain.

Harris grading is extremely strict. Only the very best obtainable copies of each issue rate Harris' "very fine" grading level.

How to use this catalog...

Here is a sample page from the US/BNA illustrating the meaning of the various column headings.

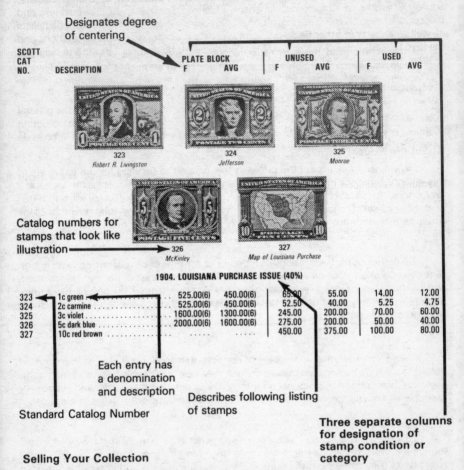

Designates degree of centering

SCOTT CAT NO.	DESCRIPTION	PLATE BLOCK F	AVG	UNUSED F	AVG	USED F	AVG

323
Robert R. Livingston

324
Jefferson

325
Monroe

Catalog numbers for stamps that look like illustration

326
McKinley

327
Map of Louisiana Purchase

1904. LOUISIANA PURCHASE ISSUE (40%)

Scott No.	Description	Plate Block F	Avg	Unused F	Avg	Used F	Avg
323	1c green	525.00(6)	450.00(6)	65.00	55.00	14.00	12.00
324	2c carmine	525.00(6)	450.00(6)	52.50	40.00	5.25	4.75
325	3c violet	1600.00(6)	1300.00(6)	245.00	200.00	70.00	60.00
326	5c dark blue	2000.00(6)	1600.00(6)	275.00	200.00	50.00	40.00
327	10c red brown	......	......	450.00	375.00	100.00	80.00

Each entry has a denomination and description

Describes following listing of stamps

Standard Catalog Number

Three separate columns for designation of stamp condition or category

Selling Your Collection

We recommend that every serious collector keep a copy of our little booklet "When You Have Stamps to Sell" with his or her collection, for there may come a time when the collector (or his heirs) may wish to dispose of all or a portion of the collection, and many persons do not know where to begin. This booklet (which can be ordered directly from us for $.75 postage and handling) explains the various ways of disposing of a stamp collection and the pros and cons of each, together with helpful information as to how to go about it.

Paying the Easy Way...

For your convenience, Harris accepts MasterCard, Visa and American Express credit cards (please be sure to give your correct number and expiration date) and our own Harris Credit Plan, for which you will find an application form in the back of this catalog. Otherwise, please enclose check or money order -- never cash. Our friends outside the United States should remit in bank draft or international money order payable in U. S. funds.

The Harris Guarantee...

All our stamps are guaranteed genuine, and we also stand behind every product that we sell. We are members in good standing with the Better Business Bureau, American Stamp Dealer's Association, International Federation of Stamp Dealers, Boston Chamber of Commerce, American Philatelic Society and other business and professional organizations. Our staff of employees includes many qualified philatelists as well as experts in other fields--accounting, data processing, customer relations and the like. It is our collective desire to serve you in any way that we can, and to help you get the maximum pleasure out of the world's greatest hobby--stamp collecting.

An Invitation...

In addition to its retail line, Harris also serves the wholesale trade and the general public with an extensive line of stamp albums and packets, stamp and coin collecting supplies, and books. Store managers and buyers are invited to contact our Wholesale Sales Division for further information.

Business firms interested in premium promotions are invited to contact our Premium Promotions Manager.

TERMS AND GENERAL INFORMATION

SPRING/SUMMER 1985

PRICES in this edition will generally be effective until September 30, 1985, subject to conditions mentioned under 'Our Prices Are Net', below.

OUR GUARANTEE PROTECTS YOU. All stamps are guaranteed genuine; and in addition, any purchases which for any reason whatsoever would prove unsatisfactory upon receipt and examination may be returned for prompt and cheerful exchange, credit or cash refund. Our only stipulation is that returns should be made within thirty days, **in the original envelope or container, and accompanied by the original order form.**

EACH CASH ORDER MUST TOTAL AT LEAST $5.00, CHARGE ORDERS $15.00. Due to present day handling costs, and because of our continuing desire to keep prices as low as possible, it is necessary to require that individual cash orders must total at least $5.00, and charge orders $15.00. Also, please see 'How To Write Your Order.'

PAYMENT should be enclosed with your order (unless you now have or wish to open a charge account with us) in any form that is most convenient for you: check, money order, or — by registered mail only — currency.

MASTER CARD, VISA and AMERICAN EXPRESS ARE ACCEPTED.

Canada customs duties are extra and must be paid by the customer.

OUR PRICES ARE NET. It will be our policy, during the life of this catalog edition, to try and maintain the quotations published herein — even though the market (over which we have no control) has been volatile for a number of years. Occasional price increases during the life of this edition may be absolutely unavoidable; but in such cases if they occur, you are always fully protected by our guarantee that anything you order may be returned — because of price or any other reason. We also reserve the right to limit quantities on certain items if necessary.

INQUIRIES OR REMARKS should be made on a separate sheet of paper, addressed to Customer Relations Dept. This will help us; and more importantly, it will insure prompt attention to your orders and inquiries.

THIS LIST SUPERSEDES PREVIOUS LISTS.

QUALITY AND CONDITION DEFINITIONS

Never Hinged (N.H.)—This simply means that the stamps have never been hinged (Post Office or Mint condition). From 1847 through 1869 please send a want list. From 1870-1900 add 40% to the Unused O.G. price. From 1901-1940 add the percentage in parentheses to the desired condition price. From 1941-1963 use the appropriate column. From 1964 to date all stamps will be never hinged

Original Gum (O.G.)—from 1900 to date, unused stamps will have (where issued with gum) full gum, although the stamp may have been hinged or have a hinge remnant. Prior to 1900, stamps normally will have partial gum or no gum — if you require full gum, use the appropriate pricing columns.

Average (AVG.)—The normal quality for earlier issues, generally acceptable to the majority of collectors. Perforations frequently would touch or slightly cut into stamp design. Before 1941, this is the quality provided at the prices given in the average column of our catalog. This is the condition that Harris has supplied to its customers for many years. On these earlier issues, if you require better than average quality, order the desired premium quality.

Pre 1900 Average

Perfs may touch or slightly cut into design.

Color should not be faded, but reasonable for the issue; slight oxidation or a light impression is acceptable.

Unused copies need not have original gum (if O.G. is present, the stamp is considered premium).

Used copies may have moderately heavy cancellations as long as important features of the design are not obscured.

1900-1940 Average

Perfs may touch or slightly cut into design.

Color not faded, but reasonable for the issue; slight oxidation or a light impression is acceptable.

Used copies may have moderately heavy cancellations as long as the important features of the design are not obscured.

Fine—Stamps of this quality would have perforations clear of the design, although stamps may not be "well centered." From 1941 to date, this is the quality provided at the prices given in the fine column of our catalog. On some extremely poorly centered issues perforations may touch the design on "Fine" quality. These are indicated by an "†" after the heading above the section. If you require "well centered" stamps please order " Very Fine."

Pre 1900 Fine

Perfs clear of the design (with the exception of a few varieties with difficult centering); the stamp need not be well centered.

Good color, unfaded, and clean impression; no oxidizing.

Unused copies need not have original gum.

Used copies should have moderately light, readable, unsmeared cancellations.

1900-1940 Fine

Perfs clear of the design; on some normally poorly centered issues, perfs may barely touch.

Unfaded, clean; good, clear impression.

Unused copies must have original gum if so issued; may be lightly hinged or have hinge remnants.

Used copies must have a clean, readable cancellation.

1941 to date Fine

Perfs must be clear of design.

Unfaded, clean; good, clear impression.

Unused copies must have original gum and must be lightly hinged or NH. Stamps issued in 1964 and later will be N.H.

Used copies must have a clean, readable cancellation.

Very Fine—Stamps of Very Fine quality are "well centered" which simply means the stamp design is close to or is evenly positioned between the four edges. Stamps of this quality are difficult to find, particularly on earlier issues, reflected in the considerably higher retail price. If Very Fine is desired use the following guidelines:

From 1847 to 1940 add the difference between the Average price and the Fine price to the Fine price.

From 1941 to date add 15% to the Fine price. The minimum extra charge per item is 3c. Note that all VF stamps from 1941 to 1963, and all Fine or better stamps from 1964 to date, will be Never Hinged.

Pre 1900 Very Fine

Perfs well clear of the design or stamp design reasonably well positioned within the margins or perforations.

Generally better color than usual; good, clear impression.

Unused copies need not have original gum.

Used copies must have light, unsmeared cancellations.

1900-1940 Very Fine

Perfs well clear of design; well centered, but need not be *perfectly* centered.

Full color; neat, clear impression

Unused copies must be NH, lightly hinged, or no more than ½ hinge remnant.

Used copies must have neat, clean readable cancellations.

1941 to date Very Fine

Perfs well clear of design; well centered, but need not be *perfectly* centered.

Full color; neat, clear impression.

Unused copies must be NH in order to be given a VF grade.

Used copies must have neat, clean, readable cancellations.

NOTES

GENERAL ISSUES

1,3,948a
Franklin

2,4,948b
Washington

1847.

SCOTT CAT NO.	DESCRIPTION	UNUSED O.G. F	AVG	UNUSED F	AVG	USED F	AVG
1	5c red brown	.....	.....	.....	.....	1150.00	850.00
2	10c black	.....	.....	.....	.....	2900.00	2200.00

1875. Reprints of 1847 Issues

3	5c red brown	.....	.....	1950.00	1600.00	———	———
4	10c black	.....	.....	2500.00	1900.00	———	———

5-9,18-24,40
Franklin

10,11,25,26,41
Washington

12,27-30A,42
Jefferson

13-16,31-35,43

17,36,44

Washington

1851-56. Imperforate

5A	1c blue (Ib)	.....	.....	.....	.....	3450.00	2800.00
6	1c blue (Ia)					4295.00	3650.00
7	1c e (II)	950.00	700.00	600.00	450.00	125.00	90.00
8	1c blue (III)	8100.00	6500.00	5900.00	4400.00	1900.00	1200.00
8A	1c blue (IIIa)	2500.00	1975.00	1800.00	1450.00	725.00	550.00
9	1c blue (IV)	600.00	475.00	425.00	325.00	125.00	85.00
10	3c orange brown (I)	2150.00	1800.00	1625.00	1300.00	80.00	65.00
11	3c dull red (I)	275.00	200.00	175.00	125.00	13.00	8.75
12	5c red brown (I)	14,300.00	12,200.00	9750.00	7750.00	1450.00	1100.00
13	10c green (I)	11,500.00	10,000.00	8700.00	7000.00	875.00	650.00
14	10c green (II)	2250.00	1900.00	1700.00	1400.00	350.00	250.00
15	10c green (III)	2200.00	1850.00	1650.00	1450.00	360.00	260.00
16	10c green (IV)	15,175.00	14,250.00	11,150.00	9500.00	1500.00	1200.00
17	12c black	2750.00	2350.00	2250.00	1800.00	325.00	240.00

NOTE: To determine the VF price for stamps issued from 1847 to 1900, add the difference between the Avg. and F prices to the F price. To determine the NH price for stamps 134 through 293, add 40% to the appropriate condition price. If you desire NH prior to 134 please send a want list.

SCOTT CAT NO.	DESCRIPTION	UNUSED O.G.		UNUSED		USED	
		F	AVG	F	AVG	F	AVG

37,45	38,46	39,47
Washington	*Franklin*	*Washington*

1857-61. Same design as preceding Issue, Perf. 15 (†)

18	1c blue (I)	1100.00	850.00	900.00	625.00	475.00	325.00
19	1c blue (Ia)	13,600.00	10,650.00	11,075.00	8500.00	2350.00	1850.00
20	1c blue (II)	775.00	625.00	625.00	425.00	175.00	125.00
21	1c blue (III)	5725.00	4775.00	4950.00	2800.00	995.00	850.00
22	1c blue (IIIa)	925.00	685.00	725.00	550.00	225.00	175.00
23	1c blue (IV)	2575.00	1950.00	2050.00	1425.00	300.00	250.00
24	1c blue (V)	235.00	175.00	175.00	125.00	42.50	30.00
25	3c rose (I)	1100.00	825.00	875.00	650.00	32.00	27.00
26	3c dull red (II)	150.00	90.00	90.00	50.00	7.25	5.00
26a	3c dull red (IIa)	200.00	145.00	165.00	125.00	25.00	20.00
27	5c brick red (I)	9250.00	7000.00	7500.00	6250.00	1150.00	850.00
28	5c red brown (I)	2400.00	1800.00	1900.00	1300.00	350.00	250.00
28A	5c Indian red (I)	11,800.00	9250.00	9800.00	7250.00	1350.00	1000.00
29	5c brown (I)	1125.00	875.00	900.00	675.00	250.00	175.00
30	5c orange brown (II)	1275.00	975.00	1075.00	725.00	1175.00	825.00
30A	5c brown (II)	725.00	550.00	525.00	400.00	210.00	150.00
31	10c green (I)	6800.00	5400.00	5475.00	4000.00	550.00	400.00
32	10c green (II)	1950.00	1475.00	1575.00	1200.00	200.00	150.00
33	10c green (III)	2075.00	1600.00	1700.00	1250.00	200.00	150.00
34	10c green (IV)	18,000.00	14,500.00	14,000.00	11,000.00	1425.00	1175.00
35	10c green (V)	315.00	230.00	255.00	170.00	95.00	70.00
36	12c black	500.00	375.00	400.00	285.00	100.00	75.00
37	24c grey lilac	995.00	725.00	775.00	600.00	265.00	165.00
38	30c orange	1240.00	925.00	975.00	750.00	350.00	275.00
39	90c blue	2300.00	1700.00	1800.00	1300.00	3600.00	2600.00

1875. Reprints of 1857-61 Issue. Perf. 12 Without Gum

40	1c bright blue	———	———	625.00	450.00	———	———
41	3c scarlet	———	———	3100.00	2650.00	———	———
42	5c orange brown	———	———	1000.00	800.00	———	———
43	10c blue green	———	———	2575.00	2100.00	———	———
44	12c greenish black			2900.00	2300.00	———	———
45	24c blackish violet	———	———	3400.00	2600.00	———	———
46	30c yellow orange	———	———	3450.00	2700.00	———	———
47	90c deep blue	———	———	4875.00	3775.00	———	———

55,63,85A 86,92,102	56,64-66,74,79,82, 83,85,85C,88,94,104	57,67,75,76, 80,95,105	58, 62B, 68 85D, 89, 96, 106
Franklin	*Washington*	*Jefferson*	*Washington*

59,69,85E,90,97,107	60,70,78,99,109	61,71,81,100,110	62,72,101,111
Washington	*Washington*	*Franklin*	*Washington*

SCOTT CAT NO.	DESCRIPTION	UNUSED O.G.		UNUSED		USED	
		F	AVG	F	AVG	F	AVG
	1861. First Designs (†)						
56	3c brown red	1300.00	1000.00	1000.00	700.00	.....	
62B	10c dark green	6950.00	5550.00	5600.00	4300.00	600.00	400.00
	1861-62. Second Designs (†)						
63	1c blue.....................	225.00	165.00	150.00	100.00	35.00	30.00
64	3c pink....................	4800.00	3900.00	3975.00	3100.00	295.00	250.00
65	3c rose....................	120.00	95.00	100.00	65.00	4.25	2.85
66	3c lake....................	2375.00	1850.00	1850.00	1275.00		
67	5c buff....................	5650.00	4650.00	4600.00	3700.00	450.00	325.00
68	10c yellow green	390.00	315.00	315.00	250.00	45.00	35.00
69	12c black...................	725.00	600.00	600.00	425.00	60.00	45.00
70	24c red lilac................	740.00	615.00	615.00	435.00	95.00	70.00
71	30c orange..................	740.00	615.00	615.00	435.00	95.00	70.00
72	90c blue....................	1700.00	1350.00	1350.00	1000.00	275.00	200.00

Below each illustration we list all catalog numbers of stamps that resemble it. If a particular number, under an illustration is not listed with a quotation it is a very scarce variety; reference to a Scott Catalog will give you further information.

73,84,85B,87,93,103
Jackson

77,85F,91,98,108
Lincoln

	1861-66 (†)						
73	2c black	235.00	175.00	175.00	110.00	45.00	25.00
74	3c scarlet	5500.00	4200.00	4200.00	3200.00	1750.00	1300.00
75	5c red brown	1925.00	1525.00	1525.00	1200.00	245.00	180.00
76	5c brown	400.00	335.00	335.00	250.00	65.00	50.00
77	15c black	800.00	650.00	650.00	450.00	90.00	65.00
78	24c lilac...................	400.00	325.00	325.00	225.00	75.00	65.00

1867. Grill with Points Up
A. Grill Covering Entire Stamp (†)

79	3c rose.....................	2800.00	2100.00	2100.00	1500.00	550.00	375.00

C. Grill About 13x16 mm. (†)

83	3c rose.....................	2200.00	1750.00	1750.00	1300.00	425.00	275.00

1867. Grill with Points Down
D. Grill About 12x14 mm. (†)

84	2c black	3425.00	2725.00	2725.00	2300.00	875.00	675.00
85	3c rose....................	1645.00	1285.00	1285.00	1000.00	365.00	300.00

Z. Grill About 11x14 mm. (†)

85B	2c black	1295.00	1095.00	1095.00	875.00	325.00	250.00
85C	3c rose....................	3400.00	2500.00	2500.00	2350.00	975.00	700.00
85E	12c black	2225.00	1775.00	1775.00	1300.00	570.00	475.00

E. Grill About 11x13 mm. (†)

86	1c blue....................	950.00	750.00	800.00	600.00	240.00	195.00
87	2c black	445.00	365.00	370.00	275.00	85.00	60.00
88	3c rose....................	365.00	250.00	260.00	195.00	12.50	9.50
89	10c green	1650.00	1325.00	1345.00	1000.00	180.00	135.00
90	12c black	1725.00	1375.00	1375.00	1225.00	180.00	150.00
91	15c black	3450.00	2725.00	2725.00	2200.00	450.00	360.00

SCOTT CAT NO.	DESCRIPTION	UNUSED O.G.		UNUSED		USED	
		F	AVG	F	AVG	F	AVG

F. Grill About 9x13 mm. (†)

SCOTT CAT NO.	DESCRIPTION	F	AVG	F	AVG	F	AVG
92	1c blue	425.00	325.00	325.00	225.00	100.00	70.00
93	2c black	325.00	225.00	225.00	150.00	45.00	30.00
94	3c red	165.00	120.00	100.00	75.00	5.95	4.95
95	5c brown	1365.00	1050.00	1050.00	750.00	250.00	175.00
96	10c yellow green	875.00	685.00	685.00	565.00	95.00	80.00
97	12c black	900.00	725.00	725.00	600.00	100.00	85.00
98	15c black	900.00	725.00	725.00	600.00	110.00	95.00
99	24c gray lilac	1625.00	1375.00	1350.00	1100.00	600.00	400.00
100	30c orange	1825.00	1475.00	1450.00	1250.00	450.00	300.00
101	90c blue	4650.00	3900.00	3900.00	2800.00	995.00	785.00

1875. Re-issue of 1861-66 Issue

SCOTT CAT NO.	DESCRIPTION	F	AVG	F	AVG	F	AVG
102	1c blue	725.00	570.00	575.00	475.00	700.00	600.00
103	2c black	3950.00	3075.00	3150.00	2500.00	3850.00	3000.00
104	3c brown red	4350.00	3400.00	3650.00	2900.00	4200.00	3600.00
105	5c light brown	2400.00	1925.00	1925.00	1625.00	1850.00	1600.00
106	10c green	3350.00	2700.00	2800.00	2100.00	2775.00	2200.00
107	12c black	4775.00	3675.00	3750.00	2950.00	4150.00	3350.00
108	15c black	4775.00	3675.00	3750.00	2950.00	4400.00	3500.00
109	24c deep violet	5100.00	4050.00	4200.00	3250.00	5400.00	4800.00
110	30c brownish orange	6025.00	4725.00	4725.00	4000.00	6500.00	5800.00
111	90c blue	7200.00	6400.00	6400.00	5200.00	8500.00	8000.00

NOTE: For further detail on the various types of similar appearing stamps please refer to our U.S. Stamp Identifier.

112,123,133
Franklin

113,124
Pony Express Rider

114,125
Locomotive

115,126
Washington

116,127
Shield and Eagle

117,128
S.S. Adriatic

118,119,129
Landing of Columbus

120,130
Signing of Declaration

121,131
Shield, Eagle & Flags

122,132
Lincoln

1869. Grill measuring 9½x9½ mm. (†)

SCOTT CAT NO.	DESCRIPTION	F	AVG	F	AVG	F	AVG
112	1c buff	450.00	350.00	350.00	225.00	110.00	80.00
113	2c brown	340.00	240.00	240.00	165.00	35.00	25.00
114	3c ultramarine	250.00	210.00	195.00	145.00	8.50	6.00
115	6c ultramarine	1300.00	1025.00	1025.00	775.00	125.00	90.00
116	10c yellow	1450.00	1175.00	1200.00	850.00	130.00	95.00
117	12c green	1150.00	925.00	950.00	750.00	135.00	90.00
118	15c brown & blue (I)	2775.00	2175.00	2200.00	1750.00	375.00	275.00
119	15c brown & blue (II)	1375.00	1100.00	1100.00	850.00	175.00	125.00
120	24c green & violet	3275.00	2750.00	2800.00	2375.00	625.00	475.00
121	30c blue & carmine	3200.00	2600.00	2675.00	2250.00	375.00	250.00
122	90c carmine & black	13,500.00	9600.00	9500.00	7500.00	1650.00	1150.00

**(†) means issue is usually very poorly centered.
Perforations may touch the design on "Fine" quality.**

SCOTT CAT NO.	DESCRIPTION	UNUSED O.G. F	AVG	UNUSED F	AVG	USED F	AVG

1875. Re-issue of 1869 Issue. Hard White Paper. Without Grill.

SCOTT CAT NO.	DESCRIPTION	UNUSED O.G. F	AVG	UNUSED F	AVG	USED F	AVG
123	1c buff	525.00	400.00	425.00	300.00	275.00	175.00
124	2c brown	625.00	500.00	525.00	375.00	360.00	300.00
125	3c blue	4150.00	3495.00	3450.00	2795.00	1550.00	1200.00
126	6c blue	1175.00	1025.00	1100.00	800.00	575.00	450.00
127	10c yellow	1975.00	1500.00	1550.00	1300.00	1200.00	975.00
128	12c green	2100.00	1650.00	1775.00	1400.00	1200.00	975.00
129	15c brown & white (III)	2100.00	1650.00	1775.00	1275.00	600.00	475.00
130	24c green & violet	2000.00	1500.00	1500.00	1200.00	600.00	475.00
131	30c blue & carmine	2600.00	2000.00	2250.00	1650.00	1200.00	975.00
132	90c carmine & black	7500.00	5975.00	6250.00	5000.00	8500.00	7500.00

1880. Same as above. Soft Porous Paper

SCOTT CAT NO.	DESCRIPTION	UNUSED O.G. F	AVG	UNUSED F	AVG	USED F	AVG
133	1c buff	375.00	275.00	295.00	195.00	195.00	130.00

134,145,156,167, 182,192,206
Franklin

135,146,157,168,178 180,183,193,203
Jackson

136,147,158,169 184,194,207,214
Washington

137,148,159,170, 186,195,208
Lincoln

138,149,160, 171,196
Stanton

139,150,161,172, 187,188,197,209
Jefferson

140,151,162, 173,198
Clay

141,152,163, 174,189,199
Webster

142,153,164, 175,200
Scott

143,154,165,176, 190,201,217
Hamilton

144,155,166,177, 191,202,218
Perry

1870-71. Printed by National Bank Note Co. with Grill

SCOTT CAT NO.	DESCRIPTION	UNUSED O.G. F	AVG	UNUSED F	AVG	USED F	AVG
134	1c ultramarine	725.00	595.00	650.00	425.00	80.00	55.00
135	2c red brown	525.00	400.00	425.00	300.00	55.00	40.00
136	3c green	360.00	285.00	310.00	210.00	12.50	9.50
137	6c carmine	1775.00	1375.00	1500.00	1275.00	310.00	230.00
138	7c vermilion	1750.00	1300.00	1350.00	950.00	310.00	225.00
139	10c brown	2275.00	1675.00	1750.00	1375.00	525.00	375.00
141	15c orange	2350.00	1850.00	1925.00	1500.00	835.00	635.00
143	30c black	5850.00	4800.00	4975.00	3775.00	1050.00	750.00
144	90c carmine	7250.00	5775.00	6000.00	4500.00	915.00	665.00

1870-71. Same as above, without Grill

SCOTT CAT NO.	DESCRIPTION	UNUSED O.G. F	AVG	UNUSED F	AVG	USED F	AVG
145	1c ultramarine	250.00	195.00	185.00	135.00	12.50	8.50
146	2c red brown	140.00	95.00	85.00	60.00	9.00	7.00
147	3c green	175.00	130.00	140.00	100.00	.80	.60
148	6c carmine	360.00	285.00	275.00	200.00	16.50	12.50
149	7c vermilion	565.00	425.00	450.00	325.00	75.00	55.00
150	10c brown	360.00	260.00	260.00	185.00	20.00	15.00
151	12c dull violet	825.00	600.00	625.00	450.00	75.00	55.00
152	15c bright orange	775.00	575.00	635.00	450.00	80.00	60.00
153	24c purple	750.00	625.00	650.00	500.00	100.00	75.00
154	30c black	1600.00	1250.00	1275.00	900.00	135.00	95.00
155	90c carmine	1725.00	1300.00	1400.00	1050.00	215.00	155.00

NOTE: To determine the VF price for stamps issued from 1847 to 1900, add the difference between the Avg. and F prices to the F price. If Never Hinged is desired on stamps 134 through 293 add 40% to the Unused O.G. price. If you desire NH prior to 134 please send a want list.

SCOTT CAT NO.	DESCRIPTION	UNUSED O.G.		UNUSED		USED	
		F	AVG	F	AVG	F	AVG

1873. Same designs as 1870-71 with Secret Marks
Printed by Continental Bank Note Co. Thin hard grayish white paper.

156	1c ultramarine	85.00	65.00	70.00	50.00	3.00	2.25
157	2c brown	245.00	185.00	190.00	145.00	9.75	7.25
158	3c green	70.00	55.00	55.00	40.00	.30	.20
159	6c dull pink	290.00	220.00	240.00	165.00	14.50	11.00
160	7c orange vermilion	675.00	500.00	550.00	400.00	85.00	65.00
161	10c brown	350.00	265.00	275.00	200.00	16.50	12.00
162	12c black violet	800.00	600.00	675.00	500.00	80.00	60.00
163	15c yellow orange	750.00	575.00	635.00	450.00	80.00	60.00
165	30c gray black	750.00	575.00	635.00	450.00	80.00	60.00
166	90c rose carmine	1625.00	1275.00	1375.00	1100.00	210.00	175.00

NOTE: 167-77, 180-81, 192-204, 205C, 211B, 211D, are rare special printings.

179,181,185,204
Taylor

205,205C,216
Garfield

210,211B,213
Washington

211,211D,215
Jackson

212
Franklin

1875

178	2c vermilion	245.00	185.00	195.00	135.00	6.50	5.00
179	5c blue	250.00	190.00	200.00	140.00	12.50	10.00

1879. Same Type as 1870-75 Issues.
Printed by the American Bank Note Co. soft porous yellowish paper.

182	1c dark ultramarine	185.00	140.00	150.00	110.00	2.00	1.50
183	2c vermilion	110.00	80.00	85.00	60.00	2.00	1.50
184	3c green	100.00	70.00	75.00	55.00	.35	.25
185	5c blue	285.00	225.00	250.00	175.00	13.50	10.00
186	6c pink	725.00	525.00	575.00	425.00	18.50	12.50
187	10c brn. (no secret mark)	1050.00	850.00	850.00	600.00	19.00	15.00
188	10c brn. (secret mark)	675.00	525.00	565.00	400.00	23.50	18.50
189	15c red orange	260.00	200.00	220.00	160.00	23.50	19.50
190	30c full black	725.00	575.00	625.00	425.00	32.50	24.50
191	90c carmine	1575.00	1175.00	1275.00	900.00	210.00	150.00

1882

205	5c yellow brown	160.00	120.00	140.00	95.00	6.50	5.00

1881-82. Designs of 1873 Issue, Re-engraved.

206	1c gray blue	57.50	45.00	47.50	35.00	1.00	.80
207	3c blue green	65.00	52.50	57.50	42.50	.40	.30
208	6c rose	390.00	290.00	340.00	240.00	65.00	45.00
209	10c brown	130.00	95.00	110.00	75.00	3.50	2.50
209b	10c black brown	160.00	120.00	140.00	100.00	10.00	7.00

1883

210	2c red brown	52.50	40.00	45.00	32.50	.23	.18
211	4c blue green	245.00	175.00	210.00	150.00	10.25	7.25

1887

212	1c ultramarine	95.00	75.00	80.00	60.00	1.00	.75
213	2c green	40.00	30.00	35.00	25.00	.22	.18
214	3c vermilion	80.00	60.00	70.00	50.00	50.00	37.50

SCOTT CAT NO.	DESCRIPTION	UNUSED O.G.		UNUSED		USED	
		F	AVG	F	AVG	F	AVG

1888

215	4c carmine	250.00	190.00	210.00	150.00	15.00	10.00
216	5c indigo	215.00	165.00	200.00	135.00	10.00	7.50
217	30c orange brown	600.00	450.00	525.00	375.00	89.50	70.00
218	90c purple	1150.00	850.00	1000.00	700.00	200.00	140.00

219 Franklin	219D, 220 Washington	221 Jackson	222 Lincoln	223 Grant	224 Garfield

225 Sherman	226 Webster	227 Clay	228 Jefferson	229 Perry

1890-93(†)

219	1c dull blue	42.50	30.00	35.00	25.00	.20	.15
219D	2c lake	235.00	180.00	200.00	150.00	.80	.60
220	2c carmine	33.50	25.00	28.00	20.00	.12	.08
220a	"Cap on left 2"	70.00	50.00	60.00	40.00	1.65	1.20
220c	"Cap on both 2's"	200.00	150.00	175.00	125.00	12.75	8.00
221	3c purple	110.00	80.00	95.00	65.00	7.00	5.00
222	4c dark brown	100.00	70.00	85.00	55.00	2.75	2.00
223	5c chocolate	100.00	70.00	85.00	55.00	2.75	2.00
224	6c brown red	100.00	70.00	85.00	55.00	21.00	16.50
225	8c lilac	80.00	60.00	90.00	50.00	14.50	10.00
226	10c green	180.00	125.00	155.00	100.00	2.75	2.25
227	15c indigo	275.00	195.00	230.00	160.00	26.00	18.50
228	30c black	415.00	285.00	360.00	235.00	28.50	20.00
229	90c orange	675.00	475.00	600.00	400.00	135.00	100.00

230 In Sight of Land	231 Landing of Columbus	232 Flagship	233 Fleet of Columbus

234 Soliciting Aid	235 At Barcelona	236 Restored To Favor	237 Presenting Natives

238
Discovery

239
At La Rabida

240
Recall of Columbus

241
Pledging Jewels

242
Columbus in Chains

243
Describing 3rd Voyage

244
Isabella & Columbus

245
Portrait of Columbus

1893. COLUMBIAN ISSUE

Scott No.	Description	Unused O.G. F	Unused O.G. AVG	Unused F	Unused AVG	Used F	Used AVG
230	1c blue	47.50	35.00	40.00	28.50	.50	.35
231	2c violet	47.50	35.00	38.00	25.00	.12	.08
231c	2c "broken hat"	100.00	72.50	85.00	60.00	.80	.60
232	3c green	100.00	72.50	85.00	60.00	26.50	20.00
233	4c ultramarine	135.00	100.00	115.00	79.50	9.50	7.00
234	5c chocolate	165.00	115.00	130.00	90.00	10.50	8.00
235	6c purple	160.00	110.00	120.00	80.00	42.50	33.50
236	8c magenta	110.00	80.00	85.00	55.00	12.50	9.00
237	10c black brown	250.00	190.00	210.00	145.00	11.50	7.50
238	15c dark green	425.00	315.00	380.00	265.00	110.00	80.00
239	30c orange brown	610.00	435.00	535.00	365.00	160.00	120.00
240	50c slate blue	740.00	540.00	625.00	425.00	210.00	160.00
241	$1 salmon	2150.00	1500.00	1750.00	1150.00	850.00	575.00
242	$2 brown red	2275.00	1675.00	1900.00	1300.00	750.00	550.00
243	$3 yellow green	4450.00	3250.00	3850.00	2650.00	1350.00	925.00
244	$4 crimson lake	5400.00	4200.00	5000.00	3500.00	1900.00	1300.00
245	$5 black	6300.00	4500.00	5500.00	3750.00	2125.00	1500.00

246,247, 264,279
Franklin

248-252,265-267,279B
Washington

253,268
Jackson

254,269,280
Lincoln

255,270,281
Grant

256,271,282
Garfield

257,272
Sherman

258,273,282C,283
Webster

259,274,284
Clay

260,275,
Jefferson

261,261A,276,276A
Perry

262,277
Madison

263, 278
Marshall

SCOTT CAT NO.	DESCRIPTION	UNUSED O.G.		UNUSED		USED	
		F	AVG	F	AVG	F	AVG

1894 Unwatermarked

SCOTT CAT NO.	DESCRIPTION	F	AVG	F	AVG	F	AVG
246	1c ultramarine	38.50	28.50	33.50	22.50	5.25	4.00
247	1c blue	80.00	55.00	73.50	51.00	2.25	1.50
248	2c pink, Type I	32.00	24.00	28.50	20.00	3.25	2.50
249	2c carmine lake, Type I	200.00	150.00	175.00	125.00	2.00	1.50
250	2c carmine, Type I	37.50	29.00	33.00	22.00	.35	.25
251	2c carmine, Type II	285.00	210.00	250.00	170.00	3.75	2.50
252	2c carmine, Type III	140.00	110.00	115.00	85.00	4.50	3.25
253	3c purple	140.00	110.00	125.00	90.00	12.25	9.25
254	4c dark brown	160.00	120.00	140.00	100.00	5.50	4.50
255	5c chocolate	120.00	95.00	100.00	75.00	6.45	4.85
256	6c dull brown	220.00	170.00	190.00	135.00	23.00	18.00
257	8c violet brown	165.00	120.00	140.00	100.00	20.00	16.50
258	10c dark green	300.00	225.00	260.00	185.00	11.00	8.00
259	15c dark blue	450.00	325.00	400.00	275.00	75.00	55.00
260	50c orange	625.00	450.00	545.00	365.00	100.00	75.00
261	$1 black (I)	1675.00	1325.00	1325.00	475.00	310.00	210.00
261A	$1 black (II)	3250.00	2400.00	2850.00	2000.00	675.00	475.00
262	$2 blue	3950.00	2900.00	3350.00	2400.00	775.00	550.00
263	$5 dark green	5975.00	4250.00	5275.00	3500.00	1425.00	975.00

1895. Double Line Watermark "USPS" (†)

SCOTT CAT NO.	DESCRIPTION	F	AVG	F	AVG	F	AVG
264	1c blue	10.50	7.75	9.25	6.50	.20	.15
265	2c carmine, Type I	42.50	30.00	37.00	25.00	1.25	.90
266	2c carmine, Type II	48.00	35.00	42.50	30.00	4.50	3.25
267	2c carmine, Type III	8.50	6.50	7.50	5.50	.12	.08
268	3c purple	55.00	42.00	47.50	35.00	1.75	.125
269	4c dark brown	55.00	42.00	47.50	35.00	2.25	1.75
270	5c chocolate	55.00	42.00	47.50	35.00	2.95	2.15
271	6c dull brown	125.00	95.00	115.00	80.00	5.00	4.25
272	8c violet brown	55.00	42.00	47.50	35.00	2.25	1.75
273	10c dark green	120.00	90.00	100.00	75.00	2.45	2.00
274	15c dark blue	325.00	240.00	285.00	200.00	13.50	10.00
275	50c dull orange	450.00	325.00	400.00	275.00	32.50	25.00
276	$1 black (I)	1100.00	800.00	950.00	650.00	110.00	85.00
276A	$1 black (II)	3200.00	1600.00	2000.00	1300.00	210.00	150.00
277	$2 blue	1600.00	1150.00	1400.00	950.00	400.00	275.00
278	$5 dark green	3200.00	2400.00	2800.00	2000.00	550.00	375.00

1898 (†)

SCOTT CAT NO.	DESCRIPTION	F	AVG	F	AVG	F	AVG
279	1c deep green	17.50	12.50	14.50	9.50	.15	.10
279B	2c red	15.50	11.00	13.50	9.00	.14	.08
280	4c rose brown	52.50	40.00	45.00	32.50	1.50	1.20
281	5c dark blue	57.50	45.00	48.00	36.00	1.50	1.20
282	6c lake	75.00	55.00	65.00	45.00	4.50	3.50
282C	10c brown (I)	265.00	190.00	230.00	160.00	4.50	3.50
283	10c orange brown (II)	170.00	120.00	150.00	99.50	3.75	3.00
284	15c olive green	190.00	140.00	170.00	120.00	13.00	10.00

285
Marquette on the Mississippi

286
Farming in the West

287
Indian Hunting Buffalo

SCOTT CAT NO.	DESCRIPTION	UNUSED O.G.		UNUSED		USED	
		F	AVG	F	AVG	F	AVG

288
Fremont on the Rocky Mountains

289
Troops Guarding Train

290
Hardships of Emigration

291
Western Mining Prospector

292
Western Cattle in Storm

293
Eads Bridge over Mississippi River

1898. TRANS-MISSISSIPPI EXPOSITION ISSUE

Scott No.	Description	F	AVG	F	AVG	F	AVG
285	1c yellow green	60.00	45.00	50.00	37.50	9.00	6.50
286	2c copper red	55.00	40.00	41.00	29.00	2.25	1.75
287	4c orange	265.00	210.00	225.00	175.00	47.50	37.00
288	5c dull blue	265.00	210.00	225.00	175.00	35.00	27.50
289	8c violet brown	345.00	250.00	270.00	190.00	80.00	65.00
290	10c gray violet	380.00	285.00	310.00	210.00	42.50	32.50
291	50c sage green	1375.00	975.00	1150.00	775.00	245.00	180.00
292	$1 black	3200.00	2400.00	2800.00	2000.00	875.00	625.00
293	$2 orange brown	4800.00	3500.00	4200.00	2900.00	1150.00	800.00

		PLATE BLOCK		UNUSED		USED	
		F	AVG	F	AVG	F	AVG

294
Fast Lake Navigation

295
Fast Express

296
Automobile

297
Bridge at Niagara Falls

298
Canal at Sault Ste. Marie

299
Fast Ocean Navigation

1901. PAN-AMERICAN ISSUE (40%)

Scott No.	Description	F	AVG	F	AVG	F	AVG
294	1c green & black	450.00 (6)	350.00 (6)	40.00	30.00	8.00	6.00
295	2c carmine & black	450.00 (6)	350.00 (6)	40.00	30.00	2.00	1.50
296	4c chocolate & black	3050.00 (6)	2800.00 (6)	160.00	110.00	32.50	25.00
297	5c ultramarine & black	3500.00 (6)	3200.00 (6)	175.00	125.00	32.50	25.00
298	8c brown violet & black	......	......	235.00	160.00	125.00	95.00
299	10c yellow brown & black	......	......	330.00	230.00	65.00	55.00

NOTE: To determine the VF price for stamps issued from 1901 to 1940, add the difference between the Avg. and F prices to the F price. To determine the NH price for these issues, add the percentage in parentheses to the appropriate condition price.

SCOTT CAT NO.	DESCRIPTION	PLATE BLOCK F	AVG	UNUSED F	AVG	USED F	AVG

300,314,316,318
Franklin

301
Washington

302
Jackson

303,314A
Grant

304,315,317
Lincoln

305
Garfield

306
Martha Washington

307
Webster

308
Harrison

309
Clay

310
Jefferson

311
Farragut

312,479
Madison

313,480
Marshall

319-22
Washington

1902-03. Perf. 12 (40%) (†)

300	1c blue green	225.00 (6)	200.00 (6)	17.00	12.00	.14	.10
301	2c carmine	220.00 (6)	195.00 (6)	18.00	13.00	.15	.11
302	3c violet	1195.00 (6)	1095.00 (6)	90.00	60.00	4.75	3.95
303	4c brown	1195.00 (6)	1095.00 (6)	90.00	60.00	1.85	1.50
304	5c blue	1500.00 (6)	1275.00 (6)	110.00	75.00	1.85	1.50
305	6c claret	1500.00 (6)	1275.00 (6)	110.00	75.00	4.00	3.00
306	8c violet black	1075.00 (6)	950.00 (6)	65.00	45.00	3.85	3.00
307	10c red brown	1750.00 (6)	1500.00 (6)	110.00	80.00	2.50	2.00
308	13c purple black	875.00 (6)	750.00 (6)	65.00	45.00	15.00	11.00
309	15c olive green			270.00	180.00	11.00	8.50
310	50c orange			810.00	535.00	42.50	30.00
311	$1 black			1760.00	885.00	90.00	65.00
312	$2 dark blue			1850.00	1250.00	280.00	200.00
313	$5 dark green			4000.00	2800.00	900.00	600.00

1906-08. Imperforate (40%)

This and all subsequent imperforate issues can usually be supplied in unused pairs at double the single price

314	1c blue green	350.00 (6)	300.00 (6)	46.00	36.00	32.50	25.00
315	5c blue			825.00	625.00	375.00	275.00

1903. Perf. 12 (40%) (†)

319	2c carmine	160.00 (6)	125.00 (6)	13.00	9.50	.13	.10
319f	2c lake			11.50	8.00	.35	.30

1906. Imperforate (40%)

320	2c carmine	450.00 (6)	375.00 (6)	45.00	35.00	35.00	30.00
320a	2c lake			110.00	90.00	43.50	35.00

SCOTT CAT NO.	DESCRIPTION	PLATE BLOCK F	AVG	UNUSED F	AVG	USED F	AVG

323
Robert R. Livingston

324
Jefferson

325
Monroe

326
McKinley

327
Map of Louisiana Purchase

1904. LOUISIANA PURCHASE ISSUE (40%)

323	1c green	415.00 (6)	340.00 (6)	60.00	45.00	7.00	5.00
324	2c carmine	415.00 (6)	340.00 (6)	45.00	32.50	2.70	1.95
325	3c violet	1250.00 (6)	950.00 (6)	150.00	110.00	52.50	38.50
326	5c dark blue	1525.00 (6)	1125.00 (6)	175.00	125.00	31.00	21.00
327	10c red brown			350.00	250.00	52.00	37.50

328
Capt. John Smith

329
Founding of Jamestown

330
Pocahontas

1907. JAMESTOWN EXPOSITION ISSUE (40%) (†)

328	1c green	775.00 (6)	350.00 (6)	40.00	25.00	7.25	4.25
329	2c carmine	975.00 (6)	550.00 (6)	46.50	31.50	4.75	2.75
330	5c blue	5000.00 (6)	3350.00 (6)	230.00	150.00	45.00	30.00

331-392
Franklin

332-393,519

333-541

Washington

1908-09. Double Line Watermark. "U.S.P.S." (40%)

331	1c green	140.00 (6)	95.00 (6)	12.50	8.50	.12	.09
332	2c carmine	140.00 (6)	95.00 (6)	12.00	8.00	.12	.09
333	3c violet	500.00 (6)	350.00 (6)	45.00	32.50	6.25	5.00
334	4c orange brown	550.00 (6)	400.00 (6)	47.50	35.00	2.50	2.00
335	5c blue	875.00 (6)	650.00 (6)	60.00	45.00	3.00	2.50
336	6c red orange	1275.00 (6)	975.00 (6)	75.00	55.00	7.50	5.50

NOTE: For identification of the similar appearing Washington-Franklin issues see the chart in the Stamp Identifier section.

SEE PAGE X FOR CONDITION DEFINITIONS

SCOTT CAT NO.	DESCRIPTION	PLATE BLOCK F	PLATE BLOCK AVG	UNUSED F	UNUSED AVG	USED F	USED AVG
337	8c olive green	785.00 (6)	560.00 (6)	55.00	40.00	4.25	3.25
338	10c yellow	1475.00 (6)	1075.00 (6)	100.00	70.00	2.65	2.00
339	13c blue green	765.00 (6)	540.00 (6)	80.00	65.00	47.50	35.00
340	15c pale ultramarine	1025.00 (6)	725.00 (6)	95.00	70.00	12.50	10.00
341	50c violet	. . . . .	. . . . .	475.00	350.00	27.00	20.00
342	$1 violet black	. . . . .	. . . . .	680.00	480.00	120.00	85.00

1908-09. Imperforate (38%)

SCOTT CAT NO.	DESCRIPTION	PLATE BLOCK F	PLATE BLOCK AVG	UNUSED F	UNUSED AVG	USED F	USED AVG
343	1c green	130.00 (6)	110.00 (6)	14.00	12.00	5.75	5.00
344	2c carmine	200.00 (6)	175.00 (6)	18.50	15.00	6.75	5.00
345	3c deep violet	390.00 (6)	340.00 (6)	35.00	30.00	35.00	30.00
346	4c orange brown	600.00 (6)	500.00 (6)	60.00	50.00	30.00	25.00
347	5c blue.	950.00 (6)	800.00 (6)	90.00	75.00	50.00	45.00

1908-10. Coil Stamps. Perf. 12 Horizontally (40%)

LINE PAIR

SCOTT CAT NO.	DESCRIPTION	F	AVG	UNUSED F	UNUSED AVG	USED F	USED AVG
348	1c green	275.00	175.00	35.00	25.00	28.50	18.50
349	2c carmine	295.00	220.00	75.00	52.50	9.00	6.75
350	4c orange brown	975.00	750.00	175.00	125.00	90.00	65.00
351	5c blue.	975.00	750.00	200.00	140.00	115.00	85.00

1909. Perf. 12 Vertically

SCOTT CAT NO.	DESCRIPTION	F	AVG	UNUSED F	UNUSED AVG	USED F	USED AVG
352	1c green	400.00	250.00	85.00	60.00	27.50	20.00
353	2c carmine	325.00	250.00	75.00	52.50	9.50	6.75
354	4c orange brown	925.00	700.00	195.00	135.00	70.00	50.00
355	5c blue.	1000.00	775.00	200.00	140.00	95.00	75.00
356	10c yellow	. . . . .	. . . . .	1650.00	1100.00	600.00	350.00

NOTE: Coil Pairs can be supplied at two times the singles price.

1909. Bluish Grey paper. Perf. 12 (40%)

SCOTT CAT NO.	DESCRIPTION	F	AVG	UNUSED F	UNUSED AVG	USED F	USED AVG
357	1c green	. . . . .	. . . . .	160.00	110.00	140.00	100.00
358	2c carmine	. . . . .	. . . . .	165.00	115.00	115.00	85.00
359	3c violet	. . . . .	. . . . .	1950.00	1450.00	1450.00	1000.00
360	4c orange brown	. . . . .	. . . . .	16,000.00	12,000.00	. . . . .	. . . . .
361	5c blue.	. . . . .	. . . . .	4900.00	3400.00	4900.00	3700.00
362	6c orange	. . . . .	. . . . .	1275.00	950.00	775.00	550.00
363	8c olive green	. . . . .	. . . . .	16,500.00	12,000.00	. . . . .	. . . . .
364	10c yellow	. . . . .	. . . . .	1450.00	950.00	850.00	600.00
365	13c blue green	. . . . .	. . . . .	2750.00	1900.00	1400.00	1000.00
366	15c pale ultramarine	. . . . .	. . . . .	1350.00	950.00	875.00	600.00

367-369
Lincoln

370,371
William H. Seward

372,373
S.S. Clermont

1909. LINCOLN MEMORIAL ISSUE (35%)

SCOTT CAT NO.	DESCRIPTION	F	AVG	UNUSED F	UNUSED AVG	USED F	USED AVG
367	2c carmine	280.00 (6)	180.00 (6)	12.00	8.50	5.25	4.00
368	2c carmine imperf.	500.00 (6)	400.00 (6)	75.00	60.00	50.00	40.00
369	2c carmine (on b.g. paper)	6150.00 (6)	4700.00 (6)	475.00	350.00	300.00	225.00

1909. ALASKA YUKON ISSUE (35%)

SCOTT CAT NO.	DESCRIPTION	F	AVG	UNUSED F	UNUSED AVG	USED F	USED AVG
370	2c carmine	575.00 (6)	325.00 (6)	20.00	15.00	4.75	3.75
371	2c carmine imperf.	550.00 (6)	450.00 (6)	85.00	60.00	50.00	40.00

SCOTT CAT NO.	DESCRIPTION	PLATE BLOCK F	PLATE BLOCK AVG	UNUSED F	UNUSED AVG	USED F	USED AVG
		1909. HUDSON-FULTON ISSUE (35%)					
372	2c carmine	545.00 (6)	370.00 (6)	24.00	17.50	8.25	6.50
373	2c carmine, imperf.	770.00 (6)	595.00 (6)	90.00	70.00	47.50	40.00

NOTE: To determine the VF price for stamps issued from 1901 to 1940, add the difference between the Avg. and F prices to the F price. To determine the NH price for these issues, add the percentage in parentheses to the appropriate condition price.

SCOTT CAT NO.	DESCRIPTION	PLATE BLOCK F	PLATE BLOCK AVG	UNUSED F	UNUSED AVG	USED F	USED AVG
		1910-11. Single Line Watermark. "U.S.P.S." Perf. 12 (40%)					
374	1c green	155.00 (6)	105.00 (6)	12.50	9.00	.12	.09
375	2c carmine	125.00 (6)	90.00 (6)	11.00	8.00	.12	.09
376	3c deep violet	300.00 (6)	220.00 (6)	25.00	18.50	3.25	2.50
377	4c brown	425.00 (6)	300.00 (6)	37.50	27.50	.95	.75
378	5c blue	540.00 (6)	350.00 (6)	37.50	27.50	.95	.75
379	6c red orange	820.00 (6)	595.00 (6)	55.00	40.00	1.50	1.25
380	8c olive green	2000.00 (6)	1475.00 (6)	175.00	125.00	25.00	17.50
381	10c yellow	2000.00 (6)	1475.00 (6)	160.00	110.00	6.25	5.00
382	15c ultramarine	3775.00 (6)	2875.00 (6)	385.00	260.00	25.00	18.00
		191-1. Imperforate (30%)					
383	1c green	135.00 (6)	125.00 (6)	7.00	6.00	6.25	5.50
384	2c carmine	310.00 (6)	270.00 (6)	11.00	9.00	3.60	3.25
		COIL STAMPS					
		1910. Perf. 12 Horizontally (40%)					
		LINE PAIR					
385	1c green	210.00	150.00	45.00	32.50	17.50	12.50
386	2c carmine	300.00	200.00	55.00	42.50	15.00	11.00
		1910-11. Perf. 12 Vertically (40%)					
387	1c green	425.00	325.00	115.00	80.00	35.00	25.00
388	2c carmine	. . . . .	. . . . .	725.00	525.00	110.00	75.00
		1910. Perf. 8½ Horizontally (40%)					
390	1c green	37.50	35.00	9.25	7.00	6.25	5.00
391	2c carmine	325.00	225.00	50.00	45.00	15.00	12.00
		1910-13. Perf 8½ Vertically					
392	1c green	155.00	120.00	35.00	25.00	26.50	20.00
393	2c carmine	275.00	200.00	67.00	45.00	11.25	9.00
394	3c violet	455.00	330.00	85.00	60.00	50.00	35.00
395	4c brown	455.00	330.00	85.00	60.00	50.00	35.00
396	5c blue	455.00	330.00	85.50	60.00	50.00	35.00

NOTE: Coil pairs can be supplied at two times the singles price.

397,401
Balboa

398,402
Panama Canal

399,403
Golden Gate

400,400A,404
Discovery of San Francisco Bay

SCOTT CAT NO.	DESCRIPTION	PLATE BLOCK F	AVG	UNUSED F	AVG	USED F	AVG

Plate blocks will be blocks of 4 stamps unless otherwise noted.

PANAMA-PACIFIC ISSUE (40%)
1913 Perf. 12

397	1c green	325.00 (6)	200.00 (6)	33.00	23.00	2.60	2.00
398	2c carmine	525.00 (6)	400.00 (6)	35.00	25.00	1.00	.75
399	5c blue	.....	.....	155.00	115.00	19.00	14.00
400	10c orange yellow	.....	.....	290.00	190.00	50.00	40.00
400A	10c orange	.....	.....	410.00	285.00	32.50	25.00

1914-15 Perf. 10

401	1c green	670.00 (6)	495.00 (6)	50.00	35.00	11.00	9.00
402	2c carmine	.....	.....	160.00	115.00	3.65	3.00
403	5c blue	.....	.....	330.00	230.00	37.50	30.00
404	10c orange	.....	.....	2175.00	1575.00	120.00	90.00

405-545   406-546   414-518

1c-7c Washington   *8c-$1 Franklin*

1912-14 Perf. 12 (40%)

405	1c green	165.00 (6)	120.00 (6)	12.50	8.75	.12	.10
406	2c carmine	210.00 (6)	150.00 (6)	11.50	8.50	.12	.10
407	7c black	.....	.....	160.00	115.00	11.75	8.75

1912 Imperforate (30%)

408	1c green	42.50 (6)	35.00 (6)	2.50	2.00	1.25	1.00
409	2c carmine	95.00 (6)	75.00 (6)	3.50	2.85	1.50	1.25

COIL STAMPS
1912 Perf. 8½ Horizontally (40%)

LINE PAIR

410	1c green	50.00	35.00	11.00	8.00	6.75	5.50
411	2c carmine	60.00	45.00	14.00	10.00	7.25	6.00

1912 Perf. 8½ Vertically (40%)

412	1c green	125.00	95.00	40.00	27.50	10.25	8.00
413	2c carmine	265.00	210.00	65.00	45.00	1.20	.85

NOTE: Coil pairs can be supplied at two times the singles price.

1912-14 Perf. 12 Single Line Watermark

414	8c olive green	770.00 (6)	570.00 (6)	55.00	40.00	3.00	2.50
415	9c salmon red	1100.00 (6)	800.00 (6)	70.00	50.00	26.50	20.00
416	10c orange yellow	915.00 (6)	650.00 (6)	55.00	40.00	.50	.40
417	12c claret brown	825.00 (6)	535.00 (6)	55.00	40.00	7.75	6.50
418	15c gray	1275.00 (6)	925.00 (6)	125.00	95.00	7.75	6.50
419	20c ultramarine	.....	.....	275.00	200.00	26.50	20.00
420	30c orange red	.....	.....	195.00	135.00	26.50	20.00
421	50c violet	.....	.....	765.00	540.00	26.50	20.00

1912. Double line watermark "U.S.P.S." (40%)

422	50c violet	.....	.....	425.00	300.00	26.50	20.00
423	$1 violet black	.....	.....	850.00	600.00	130.00	100.00

SCOTT CAT NO.	DESCRIPTION	PLATE BLOCK F	AVG	UNUSED F	AVG	USED F	AVG

NOTE: To determine the VF price for stamps issued from 1901 to 1940, add the difference between the Avg. and F prices to the F price. To determine the NH price for these issues, add the percentage in parentheses to the appropriate condition price.

1914-15. Single line watermark, "U.S.P.S." Perf. 10 (40%)

No.	Description	PB F	PB AVG	Unused F	Unused AVG	Used F	Used AVG
424	1c green	90.00 (6)	60.00 (6)	6.15	4.50	.13	.10
425	2c carmine	70.00 (6)	49.50 (6)	5.25	4.25	.13	.10
426	3c deep violet	200.00 (6)	150.00 (6)	22.50	17.50	3.65	3.00
427	4c brown	625.00 (6)	450.00 (6)	52.50	40.00	.90	.75
428	5c blue	485.00 (6)	350.00 (6)	47.50	35.00	.90	.75
429	6c orange	575.00 (6)	400.00 (6)	57.50	45.00	2.75	2.25
430	7c black	1450.00 (6)	1075.00 (6)	140.00	100.00	9.50	7.50
431	8c olive green	600.00 (6)	450.00 (6)	55.00	42.50	3.25	2.75
432	9c salmon red	775.00 (6)	575.00 (6)	75.00	55.00	23.50	20.00
433	10c orange yellow	870.00 (6)	620.00 (6)	72.50	52.50	.65	.55
434	11c dark green	335.00 (6)	210.00 (6)	40.00	27.50	14.50	11.50
435	12c claret brown	390.00 (6)	250.00 (6)	42.50	30.00	8.00	6.50
437	15c gray	1300.00 (6)	900.00 (6)	200.00	150.00	11.50	9.00
438	20c ultramarine	.....	.....	350.00	250.00	8.75	7.00
439	30c orange red	.....	.....	435.00	295.00	25.00	20.00
440	50c violet	.....	.....	1050.00	850.00	35.00	28.50

COIL STAMPS (40%)
1914. Perf. 10 Horizontally

LINE PAIR

No.	Description	F	AVG	Unused F	Unused AVG	Used F	Used AVG
441	1c green	16.00	12.00	2.45	1.95	2.00	1.60
442	2c carmine	70.00	55.00	16.50	12.50	13.00	10.00

1914. Perf. 10 Vertically (40%)

No.	Description	F	AVG	Unused F	Unused AVG	Used F	Used AVG
443	1c green	120.00	100.00	37.50	27.50	12.50	10.50
444	2c carmine	225.00	175.00	55.00	40.00	2.50	2.00
445	3c violet	.....	.....	350.00	225.00	175.00	125.00
446	4c brown	775.00	650.00	225.00	165.00	70.00	55.00
447	5c blue	295.00	210.00	80.00	55.00	40.00	30.00

ROTARY PRESS COIL STAMPS
1915-16. Perf. 10 Horizontally (40%)

No.	Description	F	AVG	Unused F	Unused AVG	Used F	Used AVG
448	1c green	60.00	50.00	10.00	7.50	7.50	5.00
449	2c red (I)	.....	.....	.....	.....	200.00	125.00
450	2c carmine (III)	125.00	80.00	20.00	15.75	8.95	6.00

1914-16. Perf. 10 Vertically (40%)

No.	Description	F	AVG	Unused F	Unused AVG	Used F	Used AVG
452	1c green	110.00	80.00	22.50	12.50	3.35	2.00
453	2c red (I)	800.00	680.00	210.00	150.00	7.50	5.50
454	2c carmine (II)	1075.00	825.00	225.00	160.00	27.50	15.00
455	2c carmine (III)	130.00	90.00	20.50	16.50	1.75	1.25
456	3c violet	1525.00	1175.00	450.00	325.00	235.00	130.00
457	4c brown	240.00	180.00	55.00	40.00	40.00	25.00
458	5c blue	240.00	180.00	55.00	40.00	38.00	25.00

1914 Imperforate

No.	Description	F	AVG	Unused F	Unused AVG	Used F	Used AVG
459	2c carmine	———	———	700.00	500.00	.....	.....
459	2c pair	———	———	1525.00	1100.00	.....	.....

NOTE: Coil pairs can be supplied at two times the singles price.

1915 Flat Plate Printing-Double Line Watermark Perf. 10 (40%)

No.	Description	F	AVG	Unused F	Unused AVG	Used F	Used AVG
460	$1 violet black	.....	.....	1150.00	900.00	130.00	90.00

SCOTT CAT NO.	DESCRIPTION	PLATE BLOCK F	PLATE BLOCK AVG	UNUSED F	UNUSED AVG	USED F	USED AVG

1915 Single Line watermark. "U.S.P.S." Perf. 11 (40%)

461	2c pale carmine red			120.00	95.00	110.00	80.00

1916-17 Unwatermarked. Perf. 10 (40%)

462	1c green	185.00 (6)	165.00 (6)	12.50	9.50	.65	.55
463	2c carmine	140.00 (6)	110.00 (6)	9.00	7.00	.20	.15
464	3c violet	1600.00 (6)	1400.00 (6)	135.00	100.00	25.00	20.00
465	4c orange brown	1025.00 (6)	900.00 (6)	75.00	55.00	3.25	2.75
466	5c blue	1250.00 (6)	1100.00 (6)	125.00	90.00	3.25	2.75
467	5c carmine (error)	———	———	1375.00	775.00	750.00	500.00
468	6c red orange			150.00	110.00	13.00	10.00
469	7c black			175.00	125.00	25.00	20.00
470	8c olive green	645.00 (6)	595.00 (6)	80.00	60.00	10.00	8.00
471	9c salmon red	825.00 (6)	675.00 (6)	80.00	60.00	30.00	25.00
472	10c orange yellow	1675.00 (6)	1500.00 (6)	155.00	110.00	2.15	1.70
473	11c dark green	400.00 (6)	350.00 (6)	47.50	35.00	36.50	30.00
474	12c claret brown	700.00 (6)	600.00 (6)	70.00	50.00	11.00	9.00
475	15c gray			250.00	175.00	25.00	20.00
476	20c ultramarine			400.00	275.00	25.00	20.00
477	50c light violet			1975.00	1425.00	90.00	65.00
478	$1 violet black			1300.00	925.00	30.00	25.00

Design of 1902-03

479	$2 dark blue			800.00	525.00	65.00	50.00
480	$5 light green			650.00	425.00	100.00	80.00

1916-17 Imperforate

481	1c green	23.00 (6)	18.00 (6)	2.85	2.50	1.20	1.10
482	2c carmine	45.00 (6)	35.00 (6)	3.45	3.00	2.60	2.25
483	3c violet (I)	250.00 (6)	225.00 (6)	30.00	25.00	17.00	15.00
484	3c violet (II)	175.00 (6)	150.00 (6)	20.00	15.00	12.00	10.00

ROTARY PRESS COIL STAMPS
1916-19 Perf. 10 Horizontally

		LINE	PAIR				
486	1c green	6.00	4.50	1.60	1.25	.35	.30
487	2c carmine (II)	220.00	170.00	35.00	25.00	9.25	8.00
488	2c carmine (III)	42.00	28.00	6.25	4.25	2.50	2.25
489	3c violet	52.50	45.00	8.50	6.00	2.50	2.25

1916-22 Perf. 10 Vertically

490	1c green	5.75	4.50	1.25	.95	.30	.25
491	2c carmine (II)	. . . .	. . . .	. . . .	. . . .	260.00	185.00
492	2c carmine (III)	80.00	60.00	17.50	12.50	.16	.12
493	3c violet (I)	230.00	170.00	50.00	35.00	3.50	2.50
494	3c violet (II)	200.00	150.00	30.00	22.00	1.60	1.30
495	4c orange brown	200.00	150.00	30.00	22.00	7.25	5.75
496	5c blue	35.00	27.50	6.75	5.00	1.70	1.40
497	10c orange yellow	195.00	150.00	42.50	35.00	21.50	15.00

1917-19. Flat Plate Printing Perf. 11 (40%)

498	1c green	28.00 (6)	18.00 (6)	1.35	1.00	.10	.07
499	2c rose (I)	22.00 (6)	15.00 (6)	1.35	1.00	.10	.07
500	2c deep rose (Ia)			400.00	275.00	175.00	125.00
501	3c violet (I)	250.00 (6)	190.00 (6)	26.50	20.00	.15	.12
502	3c violet (II)	350.00 (6)	250.00 (6)	26.50	20.00	.45	.35
503	4c brown	285.00 (6)	200.00 (6)	26.50	20.00	.30	.25
504	5c blue	325.00 (6)	175.00 (6)	18.50	13.50	.20	.15

NOTE: Coil pairs can be supplied at two times the singles price.

SCOTT CAT NO.	DESCRIPTION	PLATE BLOCK F	AVG	UNUSED F	AVG	USED F	AVG
505	5c rose (error)			800.00	535.00	575.00	400.00
506	6c red orange	350.00 (6)	250.00 (6)	27.50	20.00	.45	.40
507	7c black	525.00 (6)	375.00 (6)	50.00	40.00	2.10	1.60
508	8c olive bistre	400.00 (6)	250.00 (6)	25.00	18.50	1.45	1.15
509	9c salmon red	400.00 (6)	250.00 (6)	30.00	23.50	4.00	3.00
510	10c orange	475.00 (6)	375.00 (6)	35.00	25.00	.20	.15
511	11c light green	225.00 (6)	150.00 (6)	20.00	15.00	5.75	4.75
512	12c claret brown	225.00 (6)	150.00 (6)	20.00	15.00	1.10	.85
513	13c apple green	225.00 (6)	150.00 (6)	23.50	18.50	12.75	10.00
514	15c gray	1150.00 (6)	800.00 (6)	80.00	60.00	1.85	1.35
515	20c ultramarine	1225.00 (6)	875.00 (6)	115.00	85.00	.40	.30
516	30c orange red	1150.00 (6)	750.00 (6)	90.00	65.00	1.90	1.40
517	50c red violet	2350.00 (6)	1700.00 (6)	150.00	100.00	1.15	.85
518	$1 violet black	1900.00 (6)	1250.00 (6)	160.00	110.00	3.35	2.75

1917. Design of 1908-09
Double Line Watermark. Perf 11 (40%)

519	2c carmine	. . . . .	. . . . .	335.00	240.00	300.00	220.00

523, 524, 547
Franklin

537
"Victory" and Flags

1918. Unwatermarked (40%)

523	$2 orange, red & black	. . . . .	. . . . .	1900.00	1200.00	250.00	180.00
524	$5 deep green & black	. . . . .	. . . . .	750.00	475.00	42.50	30.00

1918-20 Offset Printing. Perf. 11 (40%)

525	1c gray green	50.00 (6)	35.00 (6)	6.00	5.00	1.25	.95
526	2c carmine (IV)	350.00 (6)	250.00 (6)	50.00	28.00	5.75	4.25
527	2c carmine (V)	225.00 (6)	175.00 (6)	32.50	25.00	1.75	1.25
528	2c carmine (Va)	165.00 (6)	110.00 (6)	25.00	20.00	.35	.25
528A	2c carmine (VI)	575.00 (6)	400.00 (6)	75.00	55.00	2.00	1.50
528B	2c carmine (VII)	295.00 (6)	195.00 (6)	40.00	30.00	.20	.15
529	3c violet (III)	90.00 (6)	60.00 (6)	3.40	3.25	.25	.20
530	3c purple (IV)	27.00 (6)	17.00 (6)	2.75	2.25	.20	.15

Imperforate (30%)

531	1c gray green	150.00 (6)	125.00 (6)	24.00	20.00	20.00	17.50
532	2c carmine (IV)	630.00 (6)	550.00 (6)	92.50	80.00	80.00	70.00
533	2c carmine (V)			380.00	280.00	100.00	80.00
534	2c carmine (Va)	200.00 (6)	150.00 (6)	30.00	22.50	18.00	15.00
534A	2c carmine (VI)	525.00 (6)	450.00 (6)	65.00	50.00	45.00	35.00
534B	2c carmine (VII)			2300.00	1700.00	550.00	400.00
535	3c violet	165.00 (6)	115.00 (6)	25.00	20.00	12.00	10.00

1919. Perf. 12½ (40%)

536	1c gray green	275.00 (6)	200.00 (6)	27.50	20.00	20.00	16.00

1919. VICTORY ISSUE (40%)

537	3c violet	250.00 (6)	175.00 (6)	15.75	13.00	7.75	6.00

SEE PAGE X FOR CONDITION DEFINITION

SCOTT CAT NO.	DESCRIPTION	PLATE BLOCK F	AVG	UNUSED F	AVG	USED F	AVG
		1919-21 (†)					
		Rotary Press Printings					
		Perf. 11 x 10 (40%)					
538	1c green	175.00	125.00	17.50	12.00	14.00	10.00
538a	Same, imperf. horizontally			125.00	90.00	. . . . .	. . . . .
539	2c carmine rose (II)	. . . . .	. . . . .	2700.00	2000.00	975.00	625.00
540	2c carmine rose (III)	210.00	135.00	17.50	12.00	16.00	11.00
540a	Same, imperf. horizontally			125.00	90.00		
541	3c violet	800.00	475.00	57.50	37.50	56.00	36.50
		Perf. 10 x 11 (40%)					
542	1c green	150.00 (6)	135.00 (6)	13.00	9.00	1.40	1.00
		Perf. 10 x 10 (40%)					
543	1c green	21.00	19.00	1.50	.90	.17	.13
		Perf. 11 x 11 (40%)					
545	1c green	. . . . .	. . . . .	175.00	125.00	150.00	90.00
546	2c carmine rose	. . . . .	. . . . .	160.00	100.00	100.00	67.50
		1920 Flat Plate Printing. Perf. 11 (40%)					
547	$2 carmine & black	. . . . .	. . . . .	675.00	425.00	55.00	40.00

548	**549**
The "Mayflower"	Landing of the Pilgrims

550
Signing of the Compact

1920. PILGRIM TERCENTENARY ISSUE (40%)

SCOTT CAT NO.	DESCRIPTION	PLATE BLOCK F	AVG	UNUSED F	AVG	USED F	AVG
548	1c green	155.00 (6)	95.00 (6)	10.00	7.00	5.00	3.75
549	2c carmine rose	190.00 (6)	125.00 (6)	15.00	10.00	3.50	2.50
550	5c deep blue	1400.00 (6)	900.00 (6)	95.00	65.00	29.50	21.00

NOTE: To determine the VF price for stamps issued from 1901 to 1940, add the difference between the Avg. and F prices to the F price. To determine the NH price for these issues, add the percentage in parentheses to the appropriate condition price.

551,653	**552,575,578,581,594,**	**553,576,582,598,**	**554,577,579,583,595,**	**555,584,**	**556,585**
Nathan Hale	596,597,604,632	599-99A,606,634-34A	599-99A,606,634-34A	600,635	601,636
	Franklin	Harding	Washington	Lincoln	Martha Washington

557,586,602,637	**558,587,638,723**	**559,588,639**	**560,589,640**	**561,590,641**	**562,591,603,642**
Roosevelt	Garfield	McKinley	Grant	Jefferson	Monroe

SCOTT CAT NO.	DESCRIPTION	PLATE BLOCK F	AVG	UNUSED F	AVG	USED F	AVG

563,692
Hayes

564,693
Cleveland

565,695
American Indian†

566,696
Statue of Liberty

567,698
Golden Gate

568,699
Niagara Falls

569,700
Bison

570,701
Arlington Amphitheatre

571
Lincoln Memorial

572
U.S. Capitol

573
"America"

Flat Plate Printings
1922-25 Perf. 11 (30%)

Scott	Description	Plate Block F	AVG	Unused F	AVG	Used F	AVG
551	½c olive brown	14.00 (6)	9.00 (6)	.40	.30	.13	.10
552	1c deep green	55.00 (6)	40.00 (6)	4.75	3.50	.15	.12
553	1½c yellow brown	75.00 (6)	55.00 (6)	7.25	6.00	.75	.60
554	2c carmine	50.00 (6)	40.00 (6)	3.25	2.00	.11	.08
555	3c violet	450.00 (6)	350.00 (6)	33.00	25.00	2.50	1.95
556	4c yellow brown	450.00 (6)	350.00 (6)	30.00	22.50	.48	.40
557	5c dark blue	475.00 (6)	375.00 (6)	30.00	22.50	.22	.18
558	6c red orange	800.00 (6)	650.00 (6)	60.00	45.00	2.75	1.95
559	7c black	175.00 (6)	125.00 (6)	18.00	12.00	2.00	1.50
560	8c olive green	1600.00 (6)	1100.00 (6)	80.00	60.00	2.75	1.95
561	9c rose	400.00 (6)	275.00 (6)	30.00	22.50	3.00	2.25
562	10c orange	650.00 (6)	450.00 (6)	37.50	27.50	.24	.18
563	11c blue	90.00 (6)	65.00 (6)	3.50	2.50	.65	.55
564	12c brown violet	225.00 (6)	175.00 (6)	17.50	12.00	.24	.18
565	14c dark blue	127.50 (6)	97.50 (6)	12.75	9.75	2.75	2.25
566	15c gray	500.00 (6)	350.00 (6)	50.00	35.00	.50	.25
567	20c carmine rose	500.00 (6)	350.00 (6)	50.00	35.00	.19	.15
568	25c green	500.00 (6)	350.00 (6)	50.00	35.00	1.60	1.50
569	30c olive brown	700.00 (6)	575.00 (6)	80.00	55.00	.80	.65
570	50c lilac	1895.00 (6)	1450.00 (6)	120.00	95.00	.32	.25
571	$1 violet black	1000.00 (6)	700.00 (6)	110.00	80.00	1.05	.90
572	$2 deep blue	2900.00 (6)	2000.00 (6)	275.00	200.00	19.50	16.00
573	$5 carmine & blue			675.00	425.00	30.00	23.00

1923-25 Imperforate (20%)

Scott	Description	Plate Block F	AVG	Unused F	AVG	Used F	AVG
575	1c green	185.00 (6)	160.00 (6)	17.50	14.00	9.00	8.00
576	1½c yellow brown	60.00 (6)	50.00 (6)	3.50	3.00	4.00	3.75
577	2c carmine	55.00 (6)	45.00 (6)	3.75	3.25	4.25	4.00

(†) means an issue is usually very poorly centered. Perforations may touch the design on "Fine" quality.

SCOTT CAT NO.	DESCRIPTION	PLATE BLOCK F	AVG	UNUSED F	AVG	USED F	AVG
		Rotary Press Printings 1923-26. Perf. 11 x 10 (30%) (†)					
578	1c green	1050.00	850.00	145.00	95.00	120.00	85.00
579	2c carmine	575.00	450.00	105.00	75.00	99.50	75.00
		1923-26 Perf. 10 (30%) (†)					
581	1c green	145.00	110.00	11.00	8.00	1.60	1.20
582	1½c brown	75.00	45.00	11.50	8.50	1.60	1.20
583	2c carmine	65.00	42.50	5.75	4.50	.16	.13
584	3c violet	425.00	375.00	60.00	45.00	4.00	3.25
585	4c yellow brown	350.00	250.00	30.00	22.50	.80	.60
586	5c blue	350.00	250.00	31.00	23.50	.80	.60
587	6c red orange	150.00	115.00	17.75	12.75	1.20	1.00
588	7c black	215.00	175.00	22.50	17.50	11.00	9.00
589	8c olive green	450.00	325.00	70.00	55.00	6.00	4.25
590	9c rose	80.00	60.00	13.00	10.00	6.00	4.25
591	10c orange	1025.00	775.00	117.50	87.50	.18	.15
		Perf. 11 (†)					
595	2c carmine			320.00	220.00	235.00	160.00
		1923-29 Rotary Press Cell Stamps (30%)					
		LINE PAIR					
597/606	(597-99,600-06) 10 vars.	200.00	165.00	25.00	19.50	2.90	2.50
		Perf. 10 Vertically					
597	1c green	5.00	4.50	.70	.60	.13	.10
598	1½c deep brown	11.00	8.50	1.65	1.40	.20	.17
599	2c carmine (I)	4.00	3.50	.60	.50	.10	.07
599A	2c carmine (II)	1050.00	850.00	200.00	160.00	17.50	15.00
600	3c deep violet	75.00	65.00	11.75	9.75	.16	.12
601	4c yellow brown	60.00	50.00	7.50	6.00	1.10	1.00
602	5c dark blue	18.00	15.00	2.50	2.00	.30	.25
603	10c orange	42.50	35.00	8.00	5.50	.30	.25
		Perf. 10 Horizontally					
604	1c green	8.00	6.00	.40	.30	.15	.12
605	1½c yellow brown	5.50	4.00	.40	.30	.48	.40
606	2c carmine	4.25	3.00	.50	.40	.24	.20

NOTE: Pairs of the above can be supplied at two times the single price.

610-613 Harding	614 Ship "New Netherlands"	615 Landing at Fort Orange	616 Monument at Mayport Fla.

1923. HARDING MEMORIAL ISSUE (30%)

610	2c black, pf. 11 flat	70.00 (6)	50.00 (6)	1.75	1.25	.13	.10
611	2c black, imperf.	250.00 (6)	225.00 (6)	21.50	19.50	10.25	9.50
612	2c black, pf. 10 rotary	575.00	375.00	38.50	28.50	4.50	3.50

1924. HUGUENOT-WALLOON ISSUE (30%)

614	1c green	105.00 (6)	80.00 (6)	10.50	8.50	8.25	6.75
615	2c carmine rose	185.00 (6)	150.00 (6)	15.00	12.00	5.00	4.00
616	5c dark blue	800.00 (6)	600.00 (6)	78.50	58.50	46.50	36.50

SCOTT CAT NO.	DESCRIPTION	PLATE BLOCK F	AVG	UNUSED F	AVG	USED F	AVG

617
Washington at Cambridge

618
Birth of Liberty

619
The Minute Man

1925. LEXINGTON-CONDORD SESQUICENTENNIAL (30%)

617	1c green	100.00 (6)	80.00 (6)	9.50	7.50	10.50	8.75
618	2c carmine rose	185.00 (6)	150.00 (6)	17.00	14.00	12.50	10.00
619	5c dark blue	725.00 (6)	550.00 (6)	85.00	65.00	48.50	38.50

620
Sloop "Restaurationen"

621
Viking Ship

622,694
Harrison

623,697
Wilson

1925. NORSE-AMERICAN ISSUE (30%)

620	2c carmine & black	450.00 (8)	350.00 (8)	15.00	12.00	12.95	10.95
621	5c dk. blue & black	1300.00 (8)	950.00 (8)	60.00	45.00	51.00	41.00

1925-26 Flat Plate Printings. Perf. 11 (30%)

622	13c green	325.00 (6)	250.00 (6)	35.00	25.00	1.25	1.00
623	17c black	385.00 (6)	295.00 (6)	39.50	29.50	.65	.50

627
Liberty Bell

628
John Ericsson Statue

629
Hamilton's Battery

1926-27.	COMMEMORATIVES						(30%)
627/644	(627-29, 43-44)5 vars cpl	. . . . .	. . . . .	40.00	32.50	24.50	20.00

1926. SESQUINCENTENNIAL EXPOSITION (30%)

627	2c carmine rose	135.00 (6)	110.00 (6)	7.75	6.50	1.10	.90

1926. ERICSSON MEMORIAL ISSUE (30%)

628	5c gray lilac	250.00 (6)	200.00 (6)	17.00	13.50	9.75	7.75

1926. BATTLE OF WHITE PLAINS (30%)

629	2c carmine rose	110.00 (6)	90.00 (6)	5.50	4.75	4.75	4.00
630	Souvenir Sheet of 25	_____	_____	775.00	575.00	. . . . .	. . . . .

FOR YOUR CONVENIENCE IN ORDERING, COMPLETE SETS ARE LISTED BEFORE SINGLE STAMP LISTINGS

SCOTT CAT NO.	DESCRIPTION	PLATE BLOCK F	AVG	UNUSED F	AVG	USED F	AVG

NOTE: To determine the VF price for stamps issued from 1901 to 1940, add the difference between the Avg. and F prices to the F price. To determine the NH price for these issues, add the percentage in parentheses to the appropriate condition price.

Rotary Press Printings Designs of 1922-25
1926. Imperforate (20%)

631	1½c brown	130.00	115.00	6.00	4.50	3.00	2.75

1926-28 Perf. 11 x 10½ (30%)

632/42	1c-10c (632-34, 635-42) 11 Vars.	.....	.....	50.00	35.00	1.10	.80
632	1c green	5.75	5.00	.30	.25	.10	.07
633	1½c yellow brown	150.00	125.00	6.25	4.50	.13	.10
634	2c carmine (I)	5.00	4.50	.40	.35	.10	.07
634	Electric Eye Plate	9.50 (10)	7.50 (10)	⸺	⸺		
634	Electric Eye Plate	6.00 (6)	4.75 (6)				
634A	2c carmine (II)	.....	.....	575.00	375.00	27.50	20.00
635	3c violet	12.50	10.50	.85	.70	.11	.08
636	4c yellow brown	200.00	150.00	6.00	4.75	.15	.12
637	5c dark blue	35.00	25.00	5.25	4.00	.10	.07
638	6c red orange	35.00	25.00	6.25	4.50	.10	.07
639	7c black	35.00	25.00	6.25	4.50	.13	.10
640	8c olive green	35.00	25.00	6.50	4.75	.10	.07
641	9c orange red	35.00	25.00	6.25	4.50	.10	.07
642	10c orange	70.00	50.00	9.50	7.00	.10	.07

643	644	645	646	647	648

1927 (30%)

643	2c Vermont	110.00 (6)	90.00 (6)	2.85	2.50	3.75	3.35
644	2c Burgoyne	130.00 (6)	110.00 (6)	10.00	8.00	7.25	6.25

1928 (30%)

645	2c Valley Forge	90.00 (6)	75.00 (6)	2.75	2.25	1.40	1.25
646	2c Monmouth	125.00	100.00	3.75	3.00	4.00	3.25
647	2c Hawaii	350.00	250.00	15.00	11.00	11.00	9.25
648	5c Hawaii	725.00	500.00	45.00	35.00	40.00	30.00
649	2c Aeronautics	45.00 (6)	35.00 (6)	3.75	3.00	3.00	2.50
650	5c Aeronautics	185.00 (6)	135.00 (6)	17.50	10.00	8.25	7.25

U.S. COMMEMORATIVES
ISSUED PRIOR TO 1941

In one moderate purchase, you can obtain these desirable commemoratives at a considerable savings from the individual retail prices.

#A146 100 Unused Commemoratives Save over $14.00 .... $68.50
#A147 130 Used Commemoratives Save over $17.83 .... $45.50

SCOTT CAT NO.	DESCRIPTION	PLATE BLOCK F	AVG	UNUSED F	AVG	USED F	AVG

| 649 | 650 | 651 | 654-656 | 657 |

1929 (30%)

| 651 | 2c George R. Clark | 37.50 (6) | 30.00 (6) | 1.60 | 1.25 | 1.30 | 1.00 |

1929. Design of 1922-25
Rotary Press Printing. Perf. 11 x 10½ (30%)

| 653 | ½c olive brown | 3.00 | 2.50 | .23 | .20 | .11 | .08 |

1929. EDISON COMMEMORATIVE (30%)
Flat Plate Printing. Perf. 11

| 654 | 2c carmine rose | 82.50 (6) | 62.50 (6) | 2.60 | 2.25 | 2.60 | 2.25 |

Rotary Press Printing. Perf. 11 x 10½

| 655 | 2c carmine rose | 120.00 | 85.00 | 2.00 | 1.90 | .50 | .40 |

Rotary Press Coil. Perf. 10 Vertically

LINE PAIR

656	2c carmine rose	————	————	40.00	35.00	3.50	2.75
656	Same, pair	160.00	125.00	80.00	70.00	. . . . .	. . . . .
657	2c Sullivan Expedition	75.00 (6)	60.00 (6)	1.85	1.50	1.85	1.50

1929
632-42 Overprinted Kans. (30%)

658-68	1c-10c, 11 Vars. cpl.	. . . . .	. . . . .	490.00	385.00	. . . . .	. . . . .
658	1c green	70.00	55.00	5.00	4.00	4.25	3.50
659	1½c brown	95.00	80.00	9.25	7.75	8.75	7.50
660	2c carmine	110.00	80.00	9.25	7.75	2.10	1.25
661	3c violet	310.00	220.00	42.50	32.50	37.00	30.00
662	4c yellow brown	375.00	275.00	42.50	32.50	16.50	13.00
663	5c deep blue	325.00	250.00	30.00	22.00	20.50	16.00
664	6c red orange	775.00	600.00	47.50	35.00	37.50	30.00
665	7c black	675.00	500.00	70.00	55.00	50.00	40.00
666	8c olive green	1350.00	1000.00	190.00	150.00	140.00	110.00
667	9c light rose	350.00	250.00	32.50	25.00	27.50	22.50
668	10c orange yellow	625.00	475.00	50.00	40.00	25.00	20.00

1929
632-42 Overprinted Nebr. (30%)

669-79	1c-10c 11 Vars. cpl.	. . . . .	. . . . .	650.00	525.00	. . . . .	. . . . .
669	1c green	65.00	50.00	6.25	5.25	5.75	4.75
670	1½c brown	80.00	60.00	8.00	6.50	6.00	5.00
671	2c carmine	90.00	70.00	7.00	6.00	2.00	1.65
672	3c violet	350.00	250.00	45.00	35.00	32.00	28.00
673	4c brown	375.00	275.00	45.00	35.00	30.00	25.00
674	5c blue	450.00	325.00	45.00	35.00	40.00	32.50
675	6c orange	900.00	675.00	80.00	60.00	52.50	45.00
676	7c black	450.00	325.00	55.00	45.00	48.00	37.50
677	8c olive green	450.00	275.00	75.00	60.00	60.00	50.00
678	9c rose	725.00	500.00	90.00	75.00	65.00	55.00
679	10c orange yellow	1500.00	1100.00	250.00	200.00	55.00	45.00

SCOTT CAT NO.	DESCRIPTION	PLATE BLOCK F	AVG	UNUSED F	AVG	USED F	AVG

680   681   682   683

1929 (30%)

Scott	Description	Plate Block F	AVG	Unused F	AVG	Used F	AVG
680	2c Fallen Timbers	97.50 (6)	80.00 (6)	4.25	3.75	4.00	3.50
681	2c Ohio River	70.00 (6)	60.00 (6)	2.40	2.20	2.35	2.15

1930-31 COMMEMORATIVES (20%)

Scott	Description	Plate Block F	AVG	Unused F	AVG	Used F	AVG
682/703	(682-83, 688-90, 702-03) 7 Vars., cpl	. . . . .	395.00	14.25	12.50	13.25	11.75

1930 (20%)

Scott	Description	Plate Block F	AVG	Unused F	AVG	Used F	AVG
682	2c Massachusetts Bay	80.00 (6)	60.00 (6)	2.25	2.00	1.50	1.25
683	2c Carolina-Charleston	150.00 (6)	120.00 (6)	4.50	4.00	4.50	4.00

684,686   685,687   688   689   690

Scott	Description	Plate Block F	AVG	Unused F	AVG	Used F	AVG
684-87	4 Vars. cpl., ...	———	———	14.15	12.15	1.50	1.15

Rotary Press Printing. Perf. 11 x 10½ (20%)

Scott	Description	Plate Block F	AVG	Unused F	AVG	Used F	AVG
684	1½c Harding	8.50	7.00	1.00	.85	.12	.08
685	4c Taft	24.00	20.00	2.45	2.00	.12	.08

Rotary Press Coil Stamps. Perf. 10 Vertically (20%)

LINE PAIR

Scott	Description	Plate Block F	AVG	Unused F	AVG	Used F	AVG
686	1½c Harding	———	———	4.75	4.25	.15	.11
686	Same, pair	23.50	20.00	9.50	8.50		
687	4c Taft	———	———	6.75	5.75	1.20	1.00
687	Same, pair	35.00	30.00	13.50	11.50	. . . . .	. . . . .
688	2c Braddock's Field	125.00 (6)	100.00 (6)	4.25	3.75	4.25	3.75
689	2c Von Steuben	80.00 (6)	65.00 (6)	1.75	1.50	1.75	1.50

1931 (20%)

Scott	Description	Plate Block F	AVG	Unused F	AVG	Used F	AVG
690	2c Pulaski	65.00 (6)	55.00 (6)	.90	.75	.55	.50

1931. Designs of 1922-26. Rotary Press Ptg. (20%)

Scott	Description	Plate Block F	AVG	Unused F	AVG	Used F	AVG
692-701	11c to 50c 10 Varieties cpl., ...	. . . . .	1595.00	350.00	285.00	3.00	2.50

Perf. 11 x 10½

Scott	Description	Plate Block F	AVG	Unused F	AVG	Used F	AVG
692	11c light blue	55.00	45.00	8.50	7.00	.20	.15
693	12c brown violet	85.00	70.00	14.50	12.00	.13	.10
694	13c yellow green	55.00	45.00	6.25	5.25	.50	.45
695	14c dark blue	82.50	70.00	10.25	8.75	.95	.80
696	15c gray	125.00	100.00	26.50	22.00	.15	.12

Plate blocks will be blocks of 4 stamps unless otherwise noted.

SCOTT CAT NO.	DESCRIPTION	PLATE BLOCKS F	AVG	UNUSED F	AVG	USED F	AVG
			Perf 10½ x 11				
697	17c black	90.00	75.00	14.50	12.00	.60	.50
698	20c carmine rose	215.00	175.00	37.50	30.00	.15	.12
699	25c blue green	275.00	140.00	30.00	25.00	.22	.17
700	30c brown	325.00	275.00	50.00	40.00	.18	.15
701	50c lilac	845.00	685.00	170.00	140.00	.18	.15

702   703

702	2c Red Cross	7.00	6.00	.45	.40	.45	.40
703	2c Yorktown	10.00	9.00	1.00	.90	1.10	1.00

704   705   706   707   708   709

710   711   712   713   714   715

Various Portraits of Washington

1932 WASHINGTON BICENTENNIAL (20%)

704-15	½c to 10c 12 Vars. cpl.	.....	1350.00	90.00	70.00	4.85	4.00
704	½c olive brown	23.00	20.00	.22	.17	.22	.17
705	1c green	20.50	17.50	.35	.30	.12	.08
706	1½c brown	70.00	55.00	.90	.75	.19	.14
707	2c carmine	7.25	6.00	.16	.12	.12	.08
708	3c purple	75.00	60.00	1.75	1.25	.15	.12
709	4c light brown	27.50	22.50	.85	.70	.18	.13
710	5c blue	90.00	75.00	7.25	6.00	.20	15
711	6c orange	275.00	225.00	14.00	11.00	.22	.16
712	7c black	42.50	35.00	1.10	.90	.55	.50
713	8c olive bistre	325.00	275.00	14.00	11.00	2.50	2.25
714	9c pale red	195.00	150.00	11.75	9.25	.45	.40
715	10c orange yellow	550.00	450.00	50.00	40.00	.20	.15

716   717   718   719   720-722   724

NOTE: To determine the VF price for stamps issued from 1901 to 1940, add the difference between the Avg. and F prices to the F price. To determine the NH price for these issues, add the percentage in parentheses to the appropriate condition price.

SCOTT CAT NO.	DESCRIPTION	PLATE BLOCKS F	AVG	UNUSED F	AVG	USED F	AVG
	1932. COMMEMORATIVES (20%)						
716/25	(716-19, 724-25) 6 Varieties	.....	275.00	14.25	12.50	2.20	2.00
716	2c Winter Olympics	50.00 (6)	40.00 (6)	1.35	1.20	.75	.65
717	2c Arbor Day	30.00	25.00	.42	.35	.25	.20
718	3c Summer Olympics	60.00	50.00	4.25	3.75	.13	.10
719	5c Summer Olympics	85.00	70.00	6.75	5.75	.45	.40
720-23	4 Vars. cpl.	——	——	47.95	39.95	1.95	1.65
720	3c deep violet	5.50	4.75	.75	.70	.10	.07
	Rotary Press Coil Stamps						
	Perf. 10 Vertically						
	LINE PAIR						
721	3c deep violet	——	——	7.50	6.50	.14	.11
721	Same, pair	23.50	20.00	15.00	13.00	.....	.....
	Perf. 10 Horizontally						
722	3c deep violet	——	——	4.75	4.00	1.45	1.25
722	Same, pair	18.00	15.00	9.50	8.00	.....	.....
	Design of 1922-25. Perf. 10 Vertically						
723	6c deep orange	——	——	42.50	35.00	.35	.30
723	Same, pair	125.00	110.00	85.00	70.00	.....	.....
724	3c Penn	50.00	40.00	1.00	.90	.40	.35

725   726   727,752   728,730,766   729,731,767   732

725	3c Webster	90.00 (6)	75.00 (6)	1.45	1.25	.60	.50
	1933. COMMEMORATIVES (20%)						
726//34	(726-29, 732-34) 7 Varieties	.....	285.00	6.25	5.50	3.25	2.75
726	3c Oglethorpe	60.00 (6)	50.00 (6)	.95	.85	.45	.35
727	3c Washington Hdqrs	18.00	15.00	.45	.35	.20	.15
	1933. CENTURY OF PROGRESS EXPOSITION						
728	1c Fort Dearborn	9.00	7.75	.32	.27	.11	.08
729	3c Federal Bldg	13.00	11.00	.35	.30	.10	.07
	Special Printing for A.P.S. Convention						
	Imperforate: without Gum						
730	1c yellow green, Sheet of 25	——	——	100.00	——	.....	.....
730a	1c yellow green single	——	——	2.00	——	1.10	.95
731	3c violet, Sheet of 25	——	——	85.00	——	.....	.....
731a	3c violet, single	——	——	1.80	——	1.10	.95
732	3c N.R.A.	8.00	7.00	.32	.27	.10	.07

733,735,753,768   734   736   737,738, 754   739,755

SCOTT CAT NO.	DESCRIPTION	PLATE BLOCKS F	AVG	UNUSED F	AVG	USED F	AVG
733	3c Byrd	75.00 (6)	65.00 (6)	1.95	1.75	1.95	1.75
734	5c Kosciuszko	175.00 (6)	150.00 (6)	2.25	2.00	.60	.55

1934. NATIONAL PHILATELIC EXHIBITION
Imperf. Without Gum

735	3c dark blue, Sheet of 6	—	—	55.00	—	. . . . .	. . . . .
735a	3c dark blue, single	—	—	7.75	—	5.00	4.50

1934. COMMEMORATIVES (20%)

736-39	4 Varieties	84.95	71.95	1.80	1.55	1.25	1.05

736	3c Maryland	42.50 (6)	35.00 (6)	.40	.35	.40	.35

1934. MOTHER'S DAY ISSUE
Rotary Press Printing. Perf. 11 x 10½

737	3c Mother's Day	5.50	4.75	.40	.35	.10	.07

Flat Plate Printing Perf. 11

738	3c Mother's Day	21.00 (6)	18.25 (6)	.65	.55	.60	.55
739	3c Wisconsin	20.50 (6)	17.75 (6)	.47	.40	.22	.18

740,751,756,769

741,757   742,750,758,770

744,760

743,759

745,761

747,763

746,762   748,764   749,765,797

SCOTT CAT NO.	DESCRIPTION	PLATE BLOCK F	AVG	UNUSED F	AVG	USED F	AVG

1934. NATIONAL PARKS ISSUE (20%)

SCOTT CAT NO.	DESCRIPTION	PLATE BLOCK F	AVG	UNUSED F	AVG	USED F	AVG
740-49	1c-10c 10 Vars. cpl., ...	565.00	485.00	38.75	33.95	19.95	16.95
740	1c Yosemite	5.00 (6)	4.25 (6)	.25	.20	.18	.15
741	2c Grand Canyon	5.25 (6)	4.50 (6)	.30	.25	.18	.15
742	3c Mt. Rainier	10.75 (6)	9.50 (6)	.47	.40	.18	.15
743	4c Mesa Verde	45.00 (6)	40.00 (6)	1.60	1.35	1.50	1.25
744	5c Yellowstone	52.50 (6)	45.00 (6)	2.85	2.50	1.50	1.25
745	6c Crater Lake	95.00 (6)	80.00 (6)	5.75	5.00	2.75	2.20
746	7c Acadia	60.00 (6)	50.00 (6)	3.75	3.25	2.75	2.25
747	8c Zion	82.50 (6)	70.00 (6)	8.50	7.50	7.00	6.00
748	9c Glacier	95.00 (6)	80.00 (6)	7.00	6.00	1.65	1.35
749	10c Great Smoky Mts.	155.00 (6)	130.00 (6)	10.50	9.50	3.75	3.25

Special Printing for the A.P.S. convention & Exhibition of Atlantic City
Imperforate Souvenir Sheet

SCOTT CAT NO.	DESCRIPTION	PLATE BLOCK F	AVG	UNUSED F	AVG	USED F	AVG
750	3c deep violet, sheet of 6	—	—	80.00	—	......	......
750a	3c deep violet, single	—	—	9.50	—	6.25	......

Special Printing for TransMississippi Philatelic Expostion and Convention at Omaha
Imperforate Souvenir Sheet

SCOTT CAT NO.	DESCRIPTION	PLATE BLOCK F	AVG	UNUSED F	AVG	USED F	AVG
751	1c green, sheet of 6	—	—	40.00	—	......	......
751a	1c green, single	—	—	4.50	—	3.25	......

	PLATE BLOCK	CENTER-LINE BLOCK	ARROW BLOCK	V. LINE BLOCK	H. LINE BLOCK	V. LINE PAIR	H. LINE PAIR	FINE UNUSED	FINE USED

1935 "FARLEY SPECIAL PRINTINGS" Designs of 1933-34

		PLATE BLOCK	CENTER-LINE BLOCK	ARROW BLOCK	V. LINE BLOCK	H. LINE BLOCK	V. LINE PAIR	H. LINE PAIR	FINE UNUSED	FINE USED
752-71	20 Vars. cpl		.....	.....	.....	.....	.....	.....	75.00	.....

Perf. 10½ x 11 Ungummed

		PLATE BLOCK	CENTER-LINE BLOCK	ARROW BLOCK	V. LINE BLOCK	H. LINE BLOCK	V. LINE PAIR	H. LINE PAIR	FINE UNUSED	FINE USED
752	3c Newburgh 40.00		100.00	32.50	28.00	17.00	14.00	8.50	.40	.40

Perf. 11 Ungummed

		PLATE BLOCK	CENTER-LINE BLOCK	ARROW BLOCK	V. LINE BLOCK	H. LINE BLOCK	V. LINE PAIR	H. LINE PAIR	FINE UNUSED	FINE USED
753	3c Byrd .... 50.00(6)		225.00	125.00	170.00	10.00	85.00	5.00	1.25	.90

Imperforate Ungummed

		PLATE BLOCK	CENTER-LINE BLOCK	ARROW BLOCK	V. LINE BLOCK	H. LINE BLOCK	V. LINE PAIR	H. LINE PAIR	FINE UNUSED	FINE USED
754	3c Mothers' Day .... 70.00(6)		18.50	12.50	10.00	10.00	5.00	5.00	2.25	1.50
755	3c Wisconsin ...... 70.00(6)		18.50	12.50	10.00	10.00	5.00	5.00	2.25	1.50

NATIONAL PARKS Imperforate, Ungummed

		PLATE BLOCK	CENTER-LINE BLOCK	ARROW BLOCK	V. LINE BLOCK	H. LINE BLOCK	V. LINE PAIR	H. LINE PAIR	FINE UNUSED	FINE USED
756-65	1c-10c 10 Vars. cpl 765.00		440.00	360.00	335.00	335.00	175.00	169.95	44.75	36.95
756	1c Yosemite ...... 20.00(6)		9.00	6.00	5.00	5.00	2.50	2.50	.45	.45
757	2c Grand Canyon .... 22.50(6)		15.00	4.75	4.50	4.50	2.25	2.25	.95	.60
758	3c Mt. Rainier ...... 47.50(6)		20.00	8.50	7.50	7.50	3.75	3.75	1.75	1.75
759	4c Mesa Verde...... 70.00(6)		35.00	28.00	28.00	28.00	14.00	14.00	3.50	3.50
760	5c Yellowstone .....75.00(6)		40.00	34.00	34.00	34.00	17.00	17.00	6.00	6.00
761	6c Crater Lake ..... 105.00(6)		63.00	55.00	50.00	50.00	25.00	25.00	6.00	5.00
762	7c Acadia ...... 95.00(6)		65.00	57.50	50.00	50.00	25.00	25.00	5.00	4.25
763	8c Zion .... 120.00(6)		59.50	52.50	50.00	50.00	25.00	25.00	5.65	4.25
764	9c Glacier ...... 125.00(6)		59.50	50.00	50.00	50.00	25.00	25.00	6.00	4.25
765	10c Gt. Smoky Mts. ...... 135.00(6)		90.00	85.00	80.00	80.00	50.00	40.00	12.00	9.00

SCOTT CAT NO.	DESCRIPTION	PLATE BLOCK	CENTER-LINE BLOCK	ARROW BLOCK	V. LINE BLOCK	H. LINE BLOCK	V. LINE PAIR	H. LINE PAIR	FINE UNUSED	FINE USED
			Imperforate. Ungummed							
766a-70a	5 Vars. cpl . . . . _____		220.00	. . . . .	185.00	160.00	85.00	75.00	22.95	. . . . .
766a	1c Ft. Dearborn . . . . . _____		40.00	. . . . .	30.00	24.00	15.00	12.00	1.75	1.00
767a	3c Federal Building . . . _____		40.00	. . . . .	30.00	26.00	15.00	13.00	2.00	1.00
768a	3c Byrd . . . . _____		42.50	. . . . .	40.00	35.00	20.00	15.75	7.50	4.75
769a	1c Yosemite . . . . _____		40.00	. . . . .	37.00	25.00	12.00	9.50	3.75	3.75
770a	3c Mt. Rainier . . . . . . _____		70.00	. . . . .	60.00	56.00	30.00	28.00	9.50	8.00
			Design of CE1							
771	16c Airmail Spec. Deliv. . . . . . . 250.00(6)		175.00	44.00	36.00	38.00	17.00	18.00	8.00	5.25

	PLATE BLOCKS		UNUSED		USED	
	F	AVG	F	AVG	F	AVG

772,778a

773,778b

775,778C

776,778d

774

778

777

	1935-36. COMMEMORATIVES (10%)						
772//84	(772-77, 782-84) 9 Varieties	43.50	38.75	2.95	2.50	.90	.65
772	3c Connecticut	5.75	5.00	.45	.40	.13	.10
773	3c San Diego	5.00	4.50	.30	.25	.10	.07
774	3c Boulder Dam	5.75	5.25	.30	.25	.13	.10
775	3c Michigan	5.75	5.00	.30	.25	.10	.07
	1936						
776	3c Texas	5.75	5.00	.30	.25	.10	.07
777	3c Rhode Island	5.75	5.25	.45	.40	.10	.07

SCOTT CAT NO.	DESCRIPTION	PLATE BLOCK		UNUSED		USED	
		F	AVG	F	AVG	F	AVG

1936. 3rd INT'L PHILATELIC EXHIBITION (10%)
"TIPEX" Imperforate Souvenir Sheet
Designs of 772, 773, 775, 776

778	red violet, sheet of 4	——	——	10.00	——	10.00	——
778a	3c Connecticut	——	——	2.50	——	2.50	——
778b	3c San Diego	——	——	2.50	——	2.50	——
778c	3c Michigan	——	——	2.50	——	2.50	——
778d	3c Texas	——	——	2.50	——	2.50	——

782

783

784

782	3c Arkansas Statehood	5.00	4.50	.35	.30	.11	.08
783	3c Oregon Territory	4.75	4.25	.35	.30	.11	.08
784	3c Suffrage for Women	2.50	2.25	.35	.30	.10	.07

785

786

787

788

789

790

791

792

793

794

1936-37. ARMY AND NAVY ISSUE (10%)

785-94	10 Vars., cpl.	180.00	160.00	10.50	9.25	2.80	2.25

ARMY COMMEMORATIVES

785	1c green	4.25	3.75	.18	.15	.12	.09
786	2c carmine	4.25	3.75	.33	.28	.12	.09
787	3c purple	4.50	4.00	.40	.35	.15	.12
788	4c gray	40.00	35.00	1.60	1.40	.55	.45
789	5c ultramarine	45.00	40.00	3.00	2.70	.55	.45

NAVY COMMEMORATIVES

790	1c green	4.25	3.75	.18	.15	.12	.09
791	2c carmine	4.25	3.75	.33	.28	.12	.09
792	3c purple	4.50	4.00	.38	.35	.15	.12
793	4c gray	40.00	35.00	1.60	1.40	.55	.45
794	5c ultramarine	45.00	40.00	3.00	2.70	.55	.45

NOTE: To determine the VF price for stamps issued from 1901 to 1940, add the difference between the Avg. and F prices to the F price. To determine the NH price for these issues, add the percentage in parentheses to the appropriate condition price.

SCOTT CAT NO.	DESCRIPTION	PLATE BLOCKS F	AVG	UNUSED F	AVG	USED F	AVG

SPECIAL OFFER
U.S. COMMEMORATIVES
COMPLETE FROM 1941-50

In one money-saving purchase, you acquire all the perforated commemoratives
issued from 1941 through 1950. The souvenir sheet (#948)
is included. 95 different varieties.

DON'T MISS THIS SPECIAL OPPORTUNITY!

#A151 Unused 1941-50 (SAVE $8.96) **$20.75**
#A161 Used 1941-50 (SAVE $4.11) **$12.25**

1937. COMMEMORATIVES (10%)

795//802	(795-96, 798-802) 7 vars.	49.75	42.95	2.50	2.20	1.10	.85

795

796

797

795	3c N.W. Ordinance	4.50	4.00	.30	.27	.10	.07
796	5c Virginia Dare	25.00(6)	21.00(6)	.65	.60	.50	.45

1937. S.P.A. CONVENTION ISSUE (10%)
Design of 749 Imperforate Souvenir Sheet

797	10c blue green	—	—	2.75	—	1.35	

798

800

801

799

802

798	3c Constitution	4.00	3.50	.28	.25	.11	.08
799	3c Hawaii	4.75	4.25	.35	.30	.11	.08
800	3c Alaska	4.75	4.25	.35	.30	.11	.08
801	3c Puerto Rico	4.75	4.25	.35	.30	.11	.08
802	3c Virgin Islands	4.75	4.25	.35	.30	.11	.08

SCOTT CAT NO.	DESCRIPTION	PLATE BLOCKS F	AVG	UNUSED F	AVG	USED F	AVG

803   804,839,848   805,840,849   806,841,850   807,842,851   808,843   809,844

810,845   811,846   812   813   814   815,847   816

817   818   819   820   821   822   823

824   825   826   827   828   829   830

831   832   833   834

1938. PRESIDENTIAL SERIES (10%)

Scott No.	Description	PB F	PB AVG	Unused F	Unused AVG	Used F	Used AVG
803-34	½c-$5, 32 Varieties, cpl.	2550.00	2150.00	540.00	450.00	33.50	28.50
803-31	½c-50c, 29 Varieties	500.00	495.00	113.00	95.00	6.95	5.95
803	½c Franklin	1.65	1.50	.11	.08	.10	.07
804	1c G. Washington	.65	.55	.11	.08	.10	.07
805	1½c M. Washington	.70	.60	.11	.08	.10	.07
806	2c J. Adams	.85	.75	.18	.15	.10	.07
807	3c Jefferson	.90	.80	.21	.18	.10	.07
808	4c Madison	5.75	5.00	1.00	.85	.10	.07
809	4½c White House	5.50	5.00	.42	.35	.15	.12
810	5c J. Monroe	5.25	4.75	1.05	.95	.10	.07
811	6c J.Q. Adams	5.25	4.75	.75	.65	.10	.07
812	7c A. Jackson	5.50	5.00	.95	.85	.10	.07
813	8c Van Buren	5.50	5.00	.95	.85	.10	.07
814	9c Harrison	5.75	5.25	1.05	.90	.11	.08
815	10c Tyler	5.50	5.00	.85	.70	.10	.07
816	11c Polk	11.25	10.00	2.10	1.80	.13	.10
817	12c Taylor	20.50	18.00	4.50	4.00	.11	.08
818	13c Fillmore	20.50	18.00	3.40	3.00	.21	.18
819	14c Pierce	20.50	18.00	4.40	4.00	.21	.18
820	15c Buchanan	9.00	8.00	2.00	1.75	.11	.08
821	16c Lincoln	21.00	18.50	3.75	3.25	.90	.85
822	17c Johnson	20.00	17.50	3.75	3.25	.17	.14
823	18c Grant	29.50	25.00	6.25	5.50	.17	.14

SCOTT CAT NO.	DESCRIPTION	PLATE BLOCKS F	AVG	UNUSED F	AVG	USED F	AVG
824	19c Hayes	23.00	20.00	5.00	4.50	1.25	1.05
825	20c Garfield	11.00	9.50	2.50	2.20	.10	.07
826	21c Arthur	23.50	20.00	5.00	4.50	.28	.25
827	22c Cleveland	30.00	25.00	3.75	3.25	1.70	1.50
828	24c B.Harrison	75.00	65.00	16.00	14.00	.40	.35
829	25c McKinley	17.00	15.00	3.50	3.00	.10	.07
830	30c T. Roosevelt	95.00	80.00	21.50	18.00	.11	.08
831	50c Taft	130.00	110.00	27.00	22.00	.11	.08

Flat Plate Printing. Perf. 11

SCOTT CAT NO.	DESCRIPTION	PLATE BLOCKS F	AVG	UNUSED F	AVG	USED F	AVG
832	$1 Wilson	160.00	135.00	35.00	30.00	.20	.16
832b	$1 Watermarked "USIR"	......	......	425.00	350.00	120.00	95.00
832c	$1 dry print thick paper	160.00	135.00	35.00	30.00	.20	.17
833	$2 Harding	450.00	375.00	85.00	70.00	14.00	12.00
834	$5 Coolidge	1450.00	1200.00	325.00	275.00	13.00	11.00

| 835 | 836 | 837 | 838 |

1938-39. COMMEMORATIVES (10%)

SCOTT CAT NO.	DESCRIPTION	PLATE BLOCKS F	AVG	UNUSED F	AVG	USED F	AVG
835/58	(835-38, 852-58) 11 Vars. cpl.,	112.50	99.50	4.75	4.25	1.40	1.10
835	3c Ratification	11.50	10.00	.45	.40	.13	.10
836	3c Swedes-Finns	9.75 (6)	8.50 (6)	.45	.40	.15	.12
837	3c North West Territory	28.50	25.00	.45	.40	.13	.10
838	3c Iowa Territory	18.00	16.00	.45	.40	.16	.13

1939. Rotary Press Coil (10%)

LINE PAIR

SCOTT CAT NO.	DESCRIPTION	F	AVG	UNUSED F	AVG	USED F	AVG
839-51	13 Vars. cpl.	275.00	225.00	91.50	78.50	7.75	6.65

Perf. 10 Vertically

SCOTT CAT NO.	DESCRIPTION	F	AVG	UNUSED F	AVG	USED F	AVG
839	1c G. Washington	2.65	2.20	.70	.60	.10	.07
840	1½c M. Washington	4.00	3.25	.90	.80	.10	.07
841	2c J. Adams	4.00	3.25	.90	.80	.10	.07
842	3c T. Jefferson	5.00	4.25	1.45	1.25	.10	.07
843	4c J. Madison	55.00	45.00	19.00	16.50	.90	.80
844	4½c White House	11.00	9.00	1.75	1.50	1.10	.95
845	5c J. Monroe	55.00	45.00	15.50	13.50	.70	.60
846	6c J.Q. Adams	15.00	12.50	3.10	2.50	.30	.25
847	10c J. Tyler	95.00	80.00	35.00	30.00	.90	.75

Perf. 10 Horizontally

SCOTT CAT NO.	DESCRIPTION	F	AVG	UNUSED F	AVG	USED F	AVG
848	1c G. Washington	5.75	5.00	3.15	1.85	.18	.15
849	1½c M. Washington	9.50	8.25	2.00	1.50	1.25	1.10
850	2c J. Adams	17.50	15.00	6.75	6.25	1.25	1.10
851	3c T. Jefferson	16.50	14.00	6.50	6.00	1.25	1.10

NOTE: Coils pairs can be supplied at two times the single price.

SEE PAGE X FOR CONDITION DEFINITIONS

SCOTT CAT NO.	DESCRIPTION	PLATE BLOCKS F	AVG	UNUSED F	AVG	USED F	AVG

NOTE: Plate blocks will be blocks of 4 stamps unless otherwise noted.

852   853   854   857

855   856   858

1939 (10%)

Scott	Description	PB F	PB AVG	Unused F	Unused AVG	Used F	Used AVG
852	3c Golden Gate	4.25	3.75	.28	.25	.11	.08
853	3c World's Fair	6.50	6.00	.28	.25	.11	.08
854	3c Inauguration	10.75(6)	9.50(6)	.80	.75	.15	.12
855	3c Baseball	9.00	8.00	.75	.70	.13	.10
856	3c Panama Canal	11.25(6)	10.00(6)	.45	.40	.15	.12
857	3c Printing	4.50	4.00	.28	.25	.13	.10
858	3c Four States	4.50	4.00	.40	.35	.13	.10

859   860   861   862   863

1940
FAMOUS AMERICANS ISSUES (10%)

Scott	Description	PB F	PB AVG	Unused F	Unused AVG	Used F	Used AVG
859-93	35 Vars., cpl	1350.00	1175.00	78.95	68.95	32.95	27.75
859//91	All 1c, 2c, 3c values. 21 Vars.	.....	.....	4.95	4.25	2.40	1.80

American Authors (10%)

Scott	Description	PB F	PB AVG	Unused F	Unused AVG	Used F	Used AVG
859	1c Washington Irving	3.50	3.25	.16	.13	.12	.09
860	2c James F. Cooper	3.75	3.50	.19	.16	.12	.09
861	3c Ralph W. Emerson	6.25	5.75	.21	.18	.11	.08
862	5c Louisa May Alcott	40.00	35.00	.80	.70	.55	.45
863	10c Samuel L. Clemens	140.00	120.00	5.00	4.50	4.00	3.50

NOTE: To determine the VF price for stamps issued from 1901 to 1940, add the diference between the Avg. and F prices to the F price. To determine the NH price for these issues, add the percentage in parentheses to the appropriate condition price.

SCOTT CAT NO.	DESCRIPTION	PLATE BLOCKS F	AVG	UNUSED F	AVG	USED F	AVG

864   865   866   867   868

American Poets (10%)

864	1c Henry W. Longfellow	7.00	6.00	.18	.15	.17	.14
865	2c John Whittier	7.25	6.25	.30	.25	.12	.09
866	3c James Lowell	11.00	9.50	.30	.25	.11	.08
867	5c Walt Whitman	45.00	40.00	1.10	1.00	.60	.50
868	10c James Riley	140.00	120.00	7.00	6.00	5.15	4.50

869   870   871   872   873

American Educators (10%)

869	1c Horace Mann	6.50	5.75	.28	.25	.12	.09
870	2c Mark Hopkins	6.50	5.75	.28	.25	.12	.09
871	3c Charles W. Eliot	10.00	8.50	.55	.50	.11	.08
872	5c Frances Willard	45.00	40.00	1.70	1.50	.60	.50
873	10c Booker T. Washington	125.00	110.00	6.25	5.75	3.60	3.00

874   875   876   877   878

American Scientists (10%)

874	1c John J. Audubon	5.25	4.75	.15	.12	.13	.10
875	2c Dr. Crawford Long	4.00	3.50	.20	.17	.15	.12
876	3c Luther Burbank	6.25	5.50	.24	.21	.13	.10
877	5c Dr Walter Reed	30.00	25.00	.70	.60	.45	.35
878	10c Jane Addams	90.00	75.00	5.50	5.00	2.75	2.35

SCOTT CAT NO.	DESCRIPTION	PLATE BLOCKS F	AVG	UNUSED F	AVG	USED F	AVG

879   880   881   882   883

American Composers (10%)

879	1c Stephen Foster	3.65	3.25	.19	.16	.11	.08
880	2c John Philip Sousa	4.25	3.75	.29	.25	.11	.08
881	3c Victor Herbert	4.50	4.00	.35	.30	.13	.10
882	5c Edward A. MacDowell	45.00	40.00	1.30	1.10	.55	.45
883	10c Ethelbert Nevin	150.00	125.00	13.50	12.00	3.25	2.75

884   885   886   887   888

American Artists (10%)

884	1c Gilbert Stuart	3.50	3.00	.16	.13	.11	.08
885	2c James Whistler	3.75	3.25	.19	.16	.11	.08
886	3c A. Saint-Gaudens	4.50	4.00	.24	.20	.12	.09
887	5c Daniel C. French	38.00	32.50	1.55	1.40	.55	.45
888	10c Frederic Remington	125.00	110.00	6.25	5.50	3.75	3.25

889   890   891   892   893

American Inventors (10%)

889	1c Eli Whitney	9.75	8.75	.23	.20	.12	.09
890	2c Samuel Morse	5.50	5.00	.23	.20	.11	.08
891	3c Cyrus McCormick	6.25	5.50	.50	.45	.11	.08
892	5c Elias Howe	65.00	55.00	3.50	3.00	.85	.75
893	10c Alexander G. Bell	275.00	230.00	32.00	27.00	5.75	4.75

NOTE: To determine the VF price for stamps issued from 1901 to 1940, add the difference between the Avg. and F prices to the F price. To determine the NH price for these issues, add the percentage in parentheses to the appropriate condition price.

SCOTT
CAT
NO.   DESCRIPTION

894

896

898

895

897

		PLATE BLOCKS F	AVG	UNUSED F	AVG	USED F	AVG
1940. COMMEMORATIVES (10%)							
894-902	9 Vars., cpl	66.75	58.50	4.50	3.95	1.35	1.10
894	3c Pony Express	11.50	9.75	.85	.75	.27	.25
895	3c Pan-Am.Union	15.50	14.00	1.05	.90	.20	.17
896	3c Idaho Statehood	7.50	6.50	.58	.50	.15	.12
897	3c Wyoming Statehood	7.00	6.00	.63	.55	.15	.12
898	3c Coronado Expedition	6.00	5.25	.63	.55	.15	.12

899

900

901

NATIONAL DEFENSE ISSUE (10%)

899	1c Liberty	2.00	1.75	.13	.10	.10	.07
900	2c Gun	2.00	1.75	.15	.12	.10	.07
901	3c Torch	2.00	1.75	.23	.20	.10	.07

902

902	3c Emancipation	17.00	15.00	.55	.50	.30	.25

NOTE: First Day Covers prior to #903 can be found in the special First Day Cover section of this catalog.

SCOTT CAT. NO.	DESCRIPTION	FIRST DAY COVERS SING. PL BLK		MINT SHEET	PLATE BLOCKS F/NH	F	UNUSED F/NH	F	USED F

903

904

905

906

907

908

1941-43 COMMEMORATIVES

SCOTT CAT. NO.	DESCRIPTION	SING.	PL BLK	MINT SHEET	F/NH	F	F/NH	F	USED F
903-08	6 Varieties	.....	.....	.....	59.50	52.95	1.95	1.65	.85
				1941					
903	3c Vermont	7.50	10.00	22.95(50)	7.50	6.75	.42	.37	.12
				1942					
904	3c Kentucky	5.00	8.00	20.75(50)	5.25	4.75	.42	.37	.12
905	3c Win The War	5.00	8.00	16.75(100)	1.35	1.25	.20	.17	.07
906	5c China Resistance	9.00	12.00	66.75(50)	45.00	40.00	.75	.65	.45
				1943					
907	2c Allied Nations	5.00	8.00	15.00(100)	1.55	1.40	.18	.15	.07
908	1c Four Freedoms	7.50	10.00	10.75(100)	2.00	1.75	.13	.10	.07

909

910

911

912

913

914

915

916

917

918

919

920

921

NOTE: To determine the VF price on stamps issued from 1941 to date, add 15% to the F/NH or F (used) price (minimum .03 per item). All VF unused stamps from 1941 to date will be NH.

SCOTT CAT. NO.	DESCRIPTION	FIRST DAY COVERS SING.	FIRST DAY COVERS PL BLK	MINT SHEET	PLATE BLOCKS F/NH	PLATE BLOCKS F	UNUSED F/NH	UNUSED F	USED F

1943-44. OVERRUN COUNTRIES SERIES

SCOTT CAT. NO.	DESCRIPTION	SING.	PL BLK	MINT SHEET	F/NH	F	F/NH	F	F
909-21	13 Vars. cpl	95.00	230.00	.....	265.00	235.00	9.25	8.50	6.50
909	5c Poland	9.00	22.50	54.75(50)	35.00	30.00	.65	.60	.45
910	5c Czechoslovakia	7.50	18.00	34.95(50)	12.00	10.00	.60	.55	.40
911	5c Norway	7.50	18.00	22.50(50)	6.50	5.50	.45	.40	.30
912	5c Luxembourg	7.50	18.00	20.50(50)	6.00	5.50	.40	.35	.30
913	5c Netherlands	7.50	18.00	22.50(50)	6.00	5.50	.45	.40	.30
914	5c Belgium	7.50	18.00	20.50(50)	6.00	5.50	.40	.35	.30
915	5c France	7.50	18.00	20.50(50)	6.00	5.50	.40	.35	.30
916	5c Greece	7.50	18.00	122.50(50)	60.00	55.00	1.90	1.75	1.25
917	5c Jugoslavia	7.50	18.00	69.00(50)	35.00	30.00	1.05	.95	.65
918	5c Albania	7.50	18.00	69.00(50)	35.00	30.00	1.05	.95	.65
919	5c Austria	7.50	18.00	42.00(50)	17.00	14.00	.75	.70	.65
920	5c Denmark	7.50	18.00	72.50(50)	30.00	27.00	1.20	1.10	.80
921	5c Korea(1944)	9.00	22.50	45.00(50)	27.50	25.00	.55	.50	.65

922　　　923　　　924　　　925

1944. COMMEMORATIVES

SCOTT CAT. NO.	DESCRIPTION	SING.	PL BLK	MINT SHEET	F/NH	F	F/NH	F	F
922-26	5 Varieties	.....	.....	.....	20.50	18.50	1.70	1.50	1.05
922	3c Railroad	6.00	10.00	20.95(50)	5.00	4.50	.45	.40	.22
923	3c Steamship	5.00	8.00	18.95(50)	5.00	4.50	.40	.35	.25
924	3c Telegraph	3.00	5.00	12.95(50)	2.75	2.50	.28	.25	.22
925	3c Corregidor	3.00	5.00	17.25(50)	5.25	4.75	.35	.30	.22
926	3c Motion Picture	3.25	5.50	15.75(50)	3.75	3.25	.35	.30	.22

926　　　927　　　928　　　929

1945. COMMEMORATIVES

SCOTT CAT. NO.	DESCRIPTION	SING.	PL BLK	MINT SHEET	F/NH	F	F/NH	F	F
927-38	12 Varieties, cpl.	.....	.....	.....	16.85	14.95	2.95	2.65	.85
927	3c Florida	5.65	7.75	13.50(50)	2.65	2.50	.28	.25	.11
928	5c Peace Conference	3.00	4.50	14.50(50)	1.65	1.50	.33	.30	.10
929	3c Iwo Jima	3.25	5.00	11.95(50)	1.40	1.25	.28	.25	.07

930　　　931　　　932　　　933

SCOTT CAT. NO.	DESCRIPTION	SING.	PL BLK	MINT SHEET	F/NH	F	F/NH	F	F
930	1c FDR & Hyde Park	5.50	7.50	4.85(50)	.65	.50	.13	.10	.07
931	2c FDR & "Little White House"	5.50	7.50	6.15(50)	1.05	.90	.15	.12	.08
932	3c FDR & White House	5.50	7.50	12.15(50)	1.40	1.25	.28	.25	.08
933	5c FDR & Globe(1946)	5.50	7.50	17.00(50)	1.90	1.75	.38	.35	.08

SCOTT CAT. NO.	DESCRIPTION	FIRST DAY COVERS		MINT SHEET	PLATE BLOCKS			UNUSED	USED
		SING.	PL BLK		F/NH	F	F/NH	F	F

934	3c Army	3.00	4.50	11.95(50)	1.40	1.25	.28	.25	.08
935	3c Navy	3.00	4.50	11.95(50)	1.40	1.25	.28	.25	.08
936	3c Coast Guard	3.00	4.50	11.95(50)	1.40	1.25	.28	.25	.07
937	3c Al Smith	3.00	4.50	23.85(100)	1.40	1.25	.28	.25	.07

| 938 | 3c Texas Statehood .... | 3.00 | 4.50 | 11.95(50) | 1.40 | 1.25 | .28 | .25 | .07 |

1946-47. COMMEMORATIVES

939//52	(939-47, 949-52) 13 Vars	.....	.....	.....	14.95	13.75	2.70	2.35	.85
939	3c Merchant Marine	3.00	4.50	9.85(50)	1.25	1.15	.23	.20	.07
940	3c Honorable Discharge	3.00	4.50	17.50(100)	1.25	1.15	.21	.18	.07
941	3c Tennessee Statehood	3.00	4.50	8.95(50)	1.25	1.15	.21	.18	.07

942	3c Iowa Statehood	3.00	4.50	9.85(50)	1.25	1.15	.23	.20	.07
943	3c Smithsonian Institute	3.00	4.50	8.95(50)	1.25	1.15	.21	.18	.07
944	3c Kearny Expedition	4.50	5.95	9.85(50)	1.25	1.15	.23	.20	.07

1947

| 945 | 3c Thomas A. Edison........ | 4.50 | 5.95 | 12.25(70) | 1.10 | 1.00 | .21 | .18 | .07 |

BUY COMPLETE SETS AND SAVE

SCOTT CAT. NO.	DESCRIPTION	FIRST DAY COVERS SING.	PL BLK	MINT SHEET	PLATE BLOCKS F/NH	F	UNUSED F/NH	F	USED F

946

947

948

949

950

| 946 | 3c Joseph Pulitzer . . . . | 3.00 | 4.50 | 8.95(50) | 1.20 | 1.10 | .21 | .18 | .07 |
| 947 | 3c Stamp Centenary . . . . | 3.00 | 4.50 | 8.95(50) | 1.20 | 1.10 | .21 | .18 | .07 |

"CIPEX" SOUVENIR SHEET

948	5c & 10c Sheet of 2	4.50	—	—	—	—	2.50	—	1.90
948a	5c blue, single stamp	. . . .	—	—	—	—	1.15	—	.90
948b	10c brown orange, single stamp	. . . .	—	—	—	—	1.20	—	.90
949	3c Doctors	1.75	3.25	8.75(50)	1.05	.95	.21	.18	.07
950	3c Utah Centennial	1.75	3.25	9.95(50)	1.40	1.25	.23	.20	.07

951

952

953

954

| 951 | 3c "Constitution" . . . . | 2.50 | 4.75 | 11.95(50) | 1.40 | 1.25 | .28 | .25 | .07 |
| 952 | 3c Everglades Nt'l. Park . . . . . | 1.75 | 3.25 | 8.75(50) | 1.05 | .95 | .21 | .18 | .07 |

1948. COMMEMORATIVES

953-80	28 Vars. cpl	. . . .	. . . .	. . . .	54.95	50.50	6.50	5.75	2.20
953	3c George Washington Carver . .	1.75	3.25	10.45(70)	1.15	1.05	.18	.15	.07
954	3c Gold Rush	1.75	3.25	11.95(50)	1.40	1.25	.28	.25	.07

955

956

957

958

955	3c Mississippi Territory	1.75	3.25	12.95(50)	1.25	1.15	.30	.27	.07
956	3c Chaplains	1.75	3.25	7.60(50)	1.15	1.05	.18	.15	.07
957	3c Wisconsin Statehood	1.75	3.25	7.60(50)	1.15	1.05	.18	.15	.07
958	5c Swedish Pioneers	1.75	3.25	17.50(50)	2.50	2.25	.38	.35	.15

SCOTT CAT. NO.	DESCRIPTION	FIRST DAY COVERS SING.	PL BLK	MINT SHEET	PLATE BLOCKS F/NH	F	UNUSED F/NH	F	USED F

959   960   961   962

963   964   965   966

Scott	Description	Sing.	Pl Blk	Mint Sheet	F/NH	F	F/NH	F	Used F
959	3c Women's Progress	1.75	3.25	7.60(50)	1.15	1.05	.18	.15	.07
960	3c William White	1.75	3.25	17.35(50)	1.95	1.75	.28	.25	.07
961	3c U.S. Canada Friendship	1.75	3.25	8.75(50)	1.05	.95	.21	.18	.07
962	3c Francis S. Key	1.75	3.25	8.75(50)	1.05	.95	.21	.18	.07
963	3c Salute to Youth	1.75	3.25	8.75(50)	1.05	.95	.21	.18	.07
964	3c Oregon Territory	1.75	3.25	8.00(50)	1.85	1.50	.18	.15	.10
965	3c Harlan Stone	1.75	3.25	22.50(70)	4.00	3.75	.33	.30	.10
966	3c Mt. Palomar	2.75	4.50	25.75(70)	7.50	7.00	.33	.30	.10

967   968   969   970

971   972   973

Scott	Description	Sing.	Pl Blk	Mint Sheet	F/NH	F	F/NH	F	Used F
967	3c Clara Barton	1.75	3.25	7.50(50)	1.05	.95	.18	.15	.08
968	3c Poultry	1.75	3.25	12.50(50)	1.75	1.65	.28	.25	.10
969	3c Gold Star Mothers	1.75	3.25	7.50(50)	1.05	.95	.18	.15	.08
970	3c Fort Kearny	1.75	3.25	11.95(50)	1.40	1.25	.28	.25	.08
971	3c Volunteer Firemen	1.75	3.25	14.50(50)	1.55	1.45	.33	.30	.08
972	3c Indian Centennial	1.75	3.25	12.50(50)	1.55	1.45	.28	.25	.08
973	3c Rough Riders	1.75	3.25	10.75(50)	2.25	2.00	.23	.20	.10

SEE PAGE X FOR CONDITION DEFINITIONS

974   975   976   977

978   979   980

SCOTT CAT. NO.	DESCRIPTION	FIRST DAY COVERS SING.	PL BLK	MINT SHEET	PLATE BLOCKS F/NH	F	UNUSED F/NH	F	USED F
974	3c Juliette Low	1.75	3.25	11.95(50)	1.40	1.25	.28	.25	.08
975	3c Will Rogers	1.75	3.25	14.25(70)	1.95	1.80	.23	.20	.08
976	3c Fort Bliss	3.50	5.50	31.25(50)	10.50	9.50	.40	.35	.08
977	3c Moina Michael	1.75	3.25	7.50(50)	1.05	.95	.18	.15	.08
978	3c Gettysburg Address	1.75	3.25	11.95(50)	1.40	1.25	.28	.25	.10
979	3c American Turners	1.75	3.25	7.75(50)	1.40	1.25	.18	.15	.10
980	3c Joel C. Harris	1.75	3.25	11.50(70)	2.45	2.25	.18	.15	.10

981   982   983   984

985   986   987   988

SCOTT CAT. NO.	1949-50 COMMEMORATIVES DESCRIPTION	SING.	PL BLK	MINT SHEET	F/NH	F	F/NH	F	USED F
981-97	17 Vars. cpl.				18.75	16.95	3.70	3.25	1.10
981	3c Minnesota Territory	1.75	3.25	8.75(50)	1.05	.95	.21	.18	.07
982	3c Wash. & Lee University	1.75	3.25	9.85(50)	1.20	1.10	.23	.20	.07
983	3c Puerto Rico	1.75	3.25	8.75(50)	1.05	.95	.21	.18	.07
984	3c Annapolis	1.75	3.25	8.75(50)	1.05	.95	.21	.18	.07
985	3c G.A.R.	1.75	3.25	8.75(50)	1.05	.95	.21	.18	.07
986	3c Edgar A. Poe	1.75	3.25	12.35(70)	1.25	1.15	.21	.18	.07

SCOTT CAT. NO.	DESCRIPTION	FIRST DAY COVERS SING.	PL BLK	MINT SHEET	PLATE BLOCKS F/NH	F	UNUSED F/NH	F	USED F
				1950					
987	3c Bankers Association	1.75	3.25	8.75(50)	1.05	.95	.21	.18	.07
988	3c Samuel Gompers	1.75	3.25	8.75(50)	1.05	.95	.21	.18	.07

989 990 991 992

989-92	Set on 1 cover	7.50	___	___	___	___	___	___	___
989	3c Statue of Freedom	2.25	3.75	11.95(50)	1.40	1.25	.28	.25	.07
990	3c Executive Mansion	2.25	3.75	11.95(50)	1.40	1.25	.28	.25	.07
991	3c Supreme Court	2.25	3.75	11.95(50)	1.40	1.25	.28	.25	.07
992	3c United States Capitol	2.25	3.75	11.95(50)	1.40	1.25	.28	.25	.07

993 994 995 996

993	3c Railroad	2.25	3.75	8.75(50)	1.05	.95	.21	.18	.07
994	3c Kansas City	1.75	3.25	8.75(50)	1.05	.95	.21	.18	.07
995	3c Boy Scouts	1.75	3.25	8.75(50)	1.05	.95	.21	.18	.07
996	3c Indiana Territory	1.75	3.25	8.75(50)	1.05	.95	.21	.18	.07

997 998 999

997	3c California Statehood	1.75	3.25	11.95(50)	1.40	1.25	.28	.25	.07
				1951-52. COMMEMORATIVES					
998-1016	19 Vars. cpl.	. . . . .	. . . . .	. . . . .	22.25	20.25	3.95	3.50	1.25
998	3c Confederate Veterans	1.75	3.25	8.85(50)	1.10	1.00	.21	.18	.07
999	3c Nevada Settlement	1.75	3.25	8.85(50)	1.10	1.00	.21	.18	.07

FOR YOUR CONVENIENCE IN ORDERING, COMPLETE SETS ARE LISTED BEFORE SINGLE STAMP LISTINGS

1000

1001

1002

1003

SCOTT CAT. NO.	DESCRIPTION	FIRST DAY COVERS SING.	PL BLK	MINT SHEET	PLATE BLOCKS F/NH	F	UNUSED F/NH	F	USED F
1000	3c Landing of Cadillac	1.75	3.25	8.85(50)	1.10	1.00	.21	.18	.07
1001	3c Colorado Statehood	2.50	4.50	8.95(50)	1.40	1.25	.21	.18	.07
1002	3c Chemical Society	1.75	3.25	8.85(50)	1.10	1.00	.21	.18	.07
1003	3c Battle of Brooklyn	1.75	3.25	11.95(50)	1.40	1.25	.28	.25	.07

1004

1005

1006

1007

1008

1009

1952

1004	3c Betsy Ross	2.25	4.50	8.95(50)	1.25	1.15	.21	.18	.07
1005	3c 4-H Club	1.75	3.25	8.85(50)	1.10	1.00	.21	.18	.07
1006	3c B. & O. Railroad	2.25	3.75	12.65(50)	1.85	1.75	.28	.25	.07
1007	3c AAA	2.25	3.75	9.75(50)	1.10	1.00	.23	.20	.07
1008	3c NATO	2.25	3.75	17.25(100)	1.10	1.00	.21	.18	.07
1009	3c Grand Coulee Dam	2.25	3.75	8.85(50)	1.10	1.00	.21	.18	.07

1010

1011

1012

1013

1010	3c Lafayette	1.75	3.25	8.95(50)	1.40	1.25	.21	.18	.07
1011	3c Mt. Rushmore	2.25	3.75	11.95(50)	1.40	.1.25	.28	.25	.07
1012	3c Civil Engineers	1.75	3.25	8.95(50)	1.40	1.25	.21	.18	.07
1013	3c Service Women	2.25	3.75	11.95(50)	1.40	1.25	.28	.25	.07

NOTE: To determine the VF price on stamps issued from **1941** to date, add **15%** to the F/NH or F (used) price (minimum .03 per item). All VF unused stamps from 1941 to date will be NH.

SCOTT CAT. NO.	DESCRIPTION	FIRST DAY COVERS SING.	FIRST DAY COVERS PL BLK	MINT SHEET	PLATE BLOCKS F/NH	PLATE BLOCKS F	UNUSED F/NH	UNUSED F	USED F

1014

1015

1016

1017

1014	3c Gutenberg Press	2.25	3.75	8.85(50)	1.10	1.00	.21	.18	.07
1015	3c Newspaper Boys	1.75	3.25	8.85(50)	1.10	1.00	.21	.18	.07
1016	3c Red Cross	1.75	3.25	8.85(50)	1.10	1.00	.21	.18	.07

1953-54. COMMEMORATIVES

| 1017/63 | (1017-29, 1060-63) 17 Vars., cpl. .... | ..... | ..... | ..... | 24.25 | 21.95 | 4.15 | 3.65 | 1.15 |
| 1017 | 3c National Guard .... | 1.75 | 3.25 | 11.95(50) | 1.40 | 1.25 | .28 | .25 | .07 |

1018

1019

1020

1021

1018	3c Ohio Statehood	1.75	3.25	16.95(70)	1.60	1.45	.28	.25	.07
1019	3c Washington Territory	1.75	3.25	11.95(50)	1.40	1.25	.28	.25	.07
1020	3c Louisiana Purchase	2.00	3.50	8.85(50)	1.10	1.00	.21	.18	.07
1021	5c Opening of Japan	1.75	3.25	17.95(50)	4.50	4.00	.35	.32	.10

1022

1023

1024

1025

1022	3c American Bar Assoc.......	1.75	3.25	11.95(50)	1.40	1.25	.28	.25	.07
1023	3c Sagamore Hill	1.75	3.25	11.95(50)	1.40	1.25	.28	.25	.07
1024	3c Future Farmers..........	1.75	3.25	8.85(50)	1.10	1.00	.21	.18	.07
1025	3c Trucking Industry	1.75	3.25	8.85(50)	1.10	1.00	.21	.18	.07
1026	3c Gen. George S. Patton.....	1.75	3.25	8.95(50)	1.40	1.25	.21	.18	.07

1026

1027

1028

1029

| 1027 | 3c New York City .... | 1.75 | 3.25 | 14.50(50) | 1.60 | 1.45 | .33 | .30 | .07 |
| 1028 | 3c Gadsden Purchase .... | 1.75 | 3.25 | 11.95(50) | 1.40 | 1.25 | .28 | .25 | .07 |

1954

| 1029 | 3c Columbia University ...... | 1.75 | 3.25 | 9.75(50) | 1.10 | 1.00 | .23 | .20 | .07 |

| SCOTT CAT. NO. | DESCRIPTION | FIRST DAY COVERS SING. | PL BLK | MINT SHEET | PLATE BLOCKS F/NH | F | UNUSED F/NH | F | USED F |

1030   1031, 1054   1031A, 1054A   1032   1033, 1055   1034, 1056

1035, 1057, 1075a   1036, 1058   1037, 1059   1038   1039   1040

1041, 1075b   1042 (re-engraved)   1042A   1043   1044   1044A

1045   1046   1047   1048, 1059A   1049   1050

1051

1052

1053

1954-61. LIBERTY SERIES

SCOTT CAT. NO.	DESCRIPTION	FDC SING.	FDC PL BLK	MINT SHEET	PL BLK F/NH	PL BLK F	UNUSED F/NH	UNUSED F	USED F
1030-53	½c-$5, 27 Varieties, cpl.	150.00	330.00	.....	1275.00	1050.00	275.00	240.00	15.95
1030-51	1c-50c, 25 Varieties	55.95	115.00	.....	195.00	180.00	38.95	35.95	1.75
1030	½c Benjamin Franklin	1.75	3.25	6.95(100)	.70	.60	.10	.07	.07
1031	1c George Washington	1.75	3.25	6.85(100)	.60	.50	.10	.07	.07
1031A	1¼c Palace of Governors	1.75	3.25	9.25(100)	2.25	2.00	.11	.08	.08
1032	1½c Mt. Vernon	1.75	3.25	19.00(100)	12.00	10.50	.13	.10	.08
1033	2c Thomas Jefferson	1.75	3.25	9.65(100)	.65	.50	.13	.10	.07
1034	2½c Bunker Hill	2.25	4.65	15.75(100)	2.50	2.25	.18	.15	.08
1035	3c Statue of Liberty	1.75	3.25	14.50(100)	.90	.75	.18	.15	.07
1036	4c Abraham Lincoln	1.75	3.25	18.95(100)	1.10	.95	.23	.20	.07
1037	4½c Hermitage	1.75	3.25	29.50(100)	2.35	2.10	.33	.30	.08
1038	5c James Monroe	1.75	3.25	37.95(100)	2.00	1.80	.45	.40	.07
1039	6c Theodore Roosevelt	1.75	3.25	100.00(100)	6.00	5.50	1.20	1.10	.07
1040	7c Woodrow Wilson	1.75	3.25	38.75(100)	3.00	2.75	.45	.40	.07
1041	8c Statue of Liberty	2.95	6.95	42.50(100)	6.75	6.25	.45	.40	.08
1042	8c Liberty re-engraved	1.75	3.25	50.00(100)	3.25	3.00	.65	.55	.07
1042A	8c John J. Pershing	1.75	3.25	52.50(100)	2.95	2.50	.65	.55	.07
1043	9c Alamo	1.75	3.25	53.50(100)	4.75	4.50	.65	.55	.07
1044	10c Independence Hall	1.95	4.15	81.00(100)	3.75	3.60	.90	.85	.07
1044A	11c Statue of Liberty	1.75	3.50	52.50(100)	2.95	2.65	.65	.55	.08

SCOTT CAT. NO.	DESCRIPTION	FIRST DAY COVERS SING.	PL BLK	MINT SHEET	PLATE BLOCKS F/NH	F	UNUSED F/NH	F	USED F
1045	12c Benjamin Harrison	1.75	3.25	79.50(100)	6.50	6.00	.90	.80	.08
1046	15c John Jay	1.75	3.25	115.00(100)	7.00	6.50	1.40	1.25	.07
1047	20c Monticello	2.25	5.50	190.00(100)	9.50	9.00	2.25	2.00	.07
1048	25c Paul Revere	3.00	6.50	540.00(100)	32.50	28.00	6.50	6.00	.07
1049	30c Robert E. Lee	4.00	7.00	370.00(100)	18.50	18.00	4.35	4.00	.08
1050	40c John Marshall	6.00	13.75	.....	43.00	38.00	8.50	8.00	.12
1051	50c Susan B. Anthony	8.00	17.00	.....	43.00	38.00	8.50	8.00	.08
1052	$1 Patrick Henry	15.00	30.00	.....	140.00	130.00	32.50	30.00	.08
1053	$5 Alexander Hamilton	90.00	200.00	.....	995.00	900.00	225.00	200.00	15.00

1954-65. COIL STAMPS
Perf. 10 Vertically or Horizontally

SCOTT CAT. NO.	DESCRIPTION	SING.	PL BLK	MINT SHEET	LINE PAIR		F/NH	F	USED F
1054-59A	1c-25c, 8 Varieties, cpl	____	.....	____	63.95	58.75	9.60	8.75	3.70
1054	1c George Washington	1.75	____	____	2.75	2.50	.80	.75	.12
1054A	1¼c Palace of Governors	1.75	____	____	6.50	6.00	.70	.65	.25
1055	2c Thomas Jefferson	1.75	____	____	.80	.75	.13	.10	.07
1056	2½c Bunker Hill Monument	1.75	____	____	11.75	11.00	.90	.85	.37
1057	3c Statue of Liberty	1.75	2.25	____	1.35	1.25	.35	.30	.07
1058	4c Abraham Lincoln	1.75	2.25	____	1.50	1.40	.40	.35	.07
1059	4½c Hermitage	2.50	4.50	____	38.50	35.00	5.50	5.00	2.50
1059A	25c Paul Revere	2.50	3.50	____	4.35	4.00	1.35	1.25	.45

NOTE: Pairs of the above can be supplied at two times the single price.

1060

1061

1062

1063

1060	3c Nebraska Territory	1.75	3.25	9.65(50)	1.40	1.25	.23	.20	.07
1061	3c Kansas Territory	1.75	3.25	9.65(50)	1.40	1.25	.23	.20	.07
1062	3c George Eastman	1.75	3.25	13.35(70)	1.10	1.00	.23	.20	.07
1063	3c Lewis & Clark	1.75	3.25	11.95(50)	1.40	1.25	.28	.25	.07

1064

1065

1066

1067

1068

DON'T FORGET CRYSTAL MOUNTS

SCOTT CAT. NO.	DESCRIPTION	FIRST DAY COVERS SING.	PL BLK	MINT SHEET	PLATE BLOCKS F/NH	F	UNUSED F/NH	F	USED F
1955. COMMEMORATIVES									
1064-72	9 Vars., cpl.	——	——	——	13.25	12.00	2.35	2.10	.60
1064	3c Pennsylvania Academy	1.75	3.25	11.95(50)	1.40	1.25	.23	.20	.07
1065	3c Land Grant Colleges	1.75	3.25	9.65(50)	1.10	1.00	.23	.20	.07
1066	8c Rotary International	1.75	3.25	22.25(50)	3.00	2.75	.48	.45	.12
1067	3c Armed Forces Reserves	3.25	4.50	9.65(50)	1.40	1.25	.23	.20	.07
1068	3c Great Stone Face	1.75	3.25	11.95(50)	1.40	1.25	.28	.25	.07

1069   1070   1071   1072

1069	3c Soo Locks	1.75	3.25	9.65(50)	1.10	1.00	.23	.20	.07
1070	3c Atoms For Peace	1.75	3.25	12.75(50)	1.90	1.75	.28	.25	.07
1071	3c Ft. Ticonderoga	2.25	3.50	11.95(50)	1.40	1.25	.28	.25	.07
1072	3c Andrew Mellon	1.75	3.25	16.75(70)	1.40	1.25	.28	.25	.07

1073   1074   1075

1073//85	(1073-74,76-85)12 Vars.	. . . . .	. . . . .	. . . . .	15.75	14.25	2.85	2.50	.70
1956. COMMEMORATIVES									
1073	3c Benjamin Franklin	1.75 —	3.25	11.95(50)	1.40	1.25	.28	.25	.07
1074	3c Booker T. Washington	1.75	3.25	11.95(50)	1.40	1.25	.28	.25	.07
1075	3c & 8c FIPEX Sheet of 2	12.95	——	——	——	——	12.00	——	12.00
1075a	3c deep violet, single	. . . . .	——	——	——	——	5.25	——	5.25
1075b	8c violet blue & carmine, single . .	. . . . .	——	——	——	——	5.25	——	5.25

1076   1077   1078   1079

1076	3c FIPEX	1.75	3.25	11.95(50)	1.40	1.25	.28	.25	.07
1077	3c Wild Turkey	2.25	3.50	12.25(50)	1.60	1.45	.28	.25	.07
1078	3c Antelope	2.25	3.50	12.25(50)	1.60	1.45	.28	.25	.07
1079	3c Salmon	2.25	3.50	12.25(50)	1.60	1.45	.28	.25	.07

SCOTT CAT. NO.	DESCRIPTION	FIRST DAY COVERS SING.	PL BLK	MINT SHEET	PLATE BLOCKS F/NH	F	UNUSED F/NH	F	USED F
1080	3c Pure Food & Drug Act	1.75	3.25	7.95(50)	1.10	1.00	.19	.16	.07
1081	3c "Wheatland"	1.75	3.25	8.00(50)	1.15	1.05	.19	.16	.07
1082	3c Labor Day	1.75	3.25	8.20(50)	1.40	1.25	.19	.16	.07
1083	3c Nassau Hall	1.75	3.25	8.00(50)	1.15	1.05	.19	.16	.07
1084	3c Devil's Tower	1.75	3.25	11.95(50)	1.40	1.25	.28	.25	.07
1085	3c Children of the World	2.25	3.50	11.95(50)	1.40	1.25	.28	.25	.07

1957. COMMEMORATIVES

SCOTT CAT. NO.	DESCRIPTION	FIRST DAY COVERS SING.	PL BLK	MINT SHEET	PLATE BLOCKS F/NH	F	UNUSED F/NH	F	USED F
1086-99	14 Vars. cpl	. . . .	. . . .	. . . .	17.50	15.95	3.00	2.60	1.00
1086	3c Alexander Hamilton	1.75	3.25	9.75(50)	1.10	1.00	.23	.20	.07
1087	3c Polio	1.75	3.25	7.50(50)	1.10	1.00	.18	.15	.07
1088	3c Coast and Geodetic Survey . . .	1.75	3.25	7.50(50)	1.10	1.00	.18	.15	.07
1089	3c Architects	1.75	3.25	9.75(50)	1.10	1.00	.23	.20	.07
1090	3c Steel Industry	1.75	3.25	7.50(50)	1.10	1.00	.18	.15	.07
1091	3c Int'l Naval Review	1.75	3.25	9.85(50)	1.25	1.15	.23	.20	.07
1092	3c Oklahoma Statehood	1.75	3.25	11.95(50)	1.40	1.25	.28	.25	.07

1093

1094

1095

1096

1097

SCOTT CAT. NO.	DESCRIPTION	FIRST DAY COVERS SING.	PL BLK	MINT SHEET	PLATE BLOCKS F/NH	F	UNUSED F/NH	F	USED F
1093	3c School Teachers	1.75	3.25	9.75(50)	1.10	1.00	.23	.20	.07
1094	4c 48-Star Flag	2.25	3.50	11.25(50)	1.40	1.25	.26	.23	.08
1095	3c Shipbuilding Anniv	1.75	3.25	10.35(70)	1.10	1.00	.18	.15	.07
1096	8c Ramon Magsaysay	2.50	3.95	20.00(48)	3.50	3.25	.43	.40	.20
1097	3c Birth of Lafayette	1.75	3.25	9.75(50)	1.10	1.00	.23	.20	.07

1098	3c Whooping Cranes	1.75	3.25	7.50(50)	1.10	1.00	.18	.15	.07
1099	3c Religious Freedom	1.75	3.25	7.50(50)	1.10	1.00	.18	.15	.07

1958. COMMEMORATIVES

1100-23	21 Vars. cpl.	.....	.....		35.50	32.50	5.35	4.75	1.65
1100	3c Gardening & Horticulture	1.75	3.25	7.50(50)	1.10	1.00	.18	.15	.07
1104	3c Brussels Exhibition	2.25	3.50	7.50(50)	1.10	1.00	.18	.15	.07
1105	3c James Monroe	1.75	3.25	10.35(70)	1.10	1.00	.18	.15	.07

1106	3c Minnesota Statehood	1.75	3.25	7.50(50)	1.10	1.00	.18	.15	.07
1107	3c Intl. Geophysical Year	1.75	3.25	10.50(50)	1.75	1.50	.23	.20	.07
1108	3c Gunston Hall	1.75	3.25	11.95(50)	1.40	1.25	.28	.25	.07
1109	3c Mackinac Bridge	1.75	3.25	7.50(50)	1.10	1.00	.18	.15	.07

SCOTT CAT. NO.	DESCRIPTION	FIRST DAY COVERS SING.	PL BLK	MINT SHEET	PLATE BLOCKS F/NH	F	UNUSED F/NH	F	USED F

1110,1111   1113   1114   1117,1118

1112   1115   1116

1110	4c Simon Bolivar	1.95	3.25	13.35(70)	1.10	1.00	.23	.20	.07
1111	8c Simon Bolivar	2.50	3.95	46.75(72)	8.75	8.00	.63	.60	.22
1112	4c Atlantic Cable Centenary	1.75	3.25	9.85(50)	1.40	1.25	.23	.20	.07
1113	1c Abraham Lincoln (1959)	1.75	3.25	3.60(50)	.60	.55	.10	.07	.07
1114	3c Bust of Lincoln (1959)	1.75	3.25	9.15(50)	1.05	.90	.22	.19	.07
1115	4c Lincoln-Douglas Debates	1.75	3.25	13.50(50)	1.50	1.35	.31	.28	.07
1116	4c Statue of Lincoln (1959)	1.75	3.25	13.50(50)	1.50	1.35	.31	.28	.07
1117	4c Lajos Kossuth	4.00	8.00	13.35(70)	1.10	1.00	.23	.20	.07
1118	8c Lajos Kossuth	1.95	3.25	44.50(72)	6.50	6.00	.63	.60	.20

1119   1120   1121   1122   1123

1119	4c Freedom of Press	2.25	3.50	13.50(50)	1.50	1.35	.31	.28	.07
1120	4c Overland Mail	1.75	3.25	10.95(50)	1.15	1.05	.26	.23	.07
1121	4c Noah Webster	1.75	3.25	15.45(70)	1.15	1.05	.26	.23	.07
1122	4c Forest Conservation	1.75	3.25	10.95(50)	1.15	1.05	.26	.23	.07
1123	4c Ft. Duquesne	1.75	3.25	10.95(50)	1.15	1.05	.26	.23	.07

1124   1125,1126   1127   1128

SCOTT CAT. NO.	DESCRIPTION	FIRST DAY COVERS SING.	PL BLK	MINT SHEET	PLATE BLOCKS F/NH	F	UNUSED F/NH	F	USED F
		1959. COMMEMORATIVES							
1124-38	15 Vars	.....	.....	.....	24.95	23.25	4.40	3.95	1.25
1124	4c Oregon Statehood	1.75	3.25	9.65(50)	1.10	1.00	.23	.20	.07
1125	4c Jose de San Martin	1.75	3.25	16.75(70)	1.40	1.25	.28	.25	.07
1126	8c Jose de San Martin	2.50	3.95	42.75(72)	4.50	4.25	.63	.60	.20
1127	4c NATO	1.75	3.25	13.35(70)	1.10	1.00	.23	.20	.07
1128	4c Arctic Exploration........	1.75	3.25	9.85(50)	1.40	1.25	.23	.20	.07

	1129			1130		1131		1132	
1129	8c World Peace & Trade	1.75	3.25	29.25(50)	3.50	3.25	.63	.60	.12
1130	4c Silver Centennial	1.75	3.25	9.65(50)	1.10	1.00	.23	.20	.07
1131	4c St. Lawrence Seaway	1.75	3.25	9.65(50)	1.10	1.00	.23	.20	.07
1132	4c 49-Star Flag	1.75	3.25	9.65(50)	1.10	1.00	.23	.20	.07

	1133		1134		1135		1136, 1137		1138
1133	4c Soil Conservation	1.75	3.25	9.65(50)	1.10	1.00	.23	.20	.07
1134	4c Petroleum Industry	1.75	3.25	9.85(50)	1.40	1.25	.23	.20	.07
1135	4c Dental Health	1.75	3.25	9.65(50)	1.10	1.00	.23	.20	.07
1136	4c Ernst Reuter	1.75	3.25	13.35(70)	1.10	1.00	.23	.20	.07
1137	8c Ernst Reuter	2.35	3.75	43.25(72)	4.50	4.25	.63	.60	.20
1138	4c Dr. Ephraim McDowell	1.75	3.25	13.35(70)	1.10	1.00	.23	.20	.07

1139   1140   1141

1142   1143   1144

SCOTT CAT. NO.	DESCRIPTION	FIRST DAY COVERS SING.	FIRST DAY COVERS PL BLK	MINT SHEET	PLATE BLOCKS F/NH	PLATE BLOCKS F	UNUSED F/NH	UNUSED F	USED F
	1960-61. CREDO OF AMERICA SERIES								
1139-44	4c cpl, 6 Vars.	. . . . .	. . . . .	. . . . .	10.75	9.95	2.10	1.90	.35
1139	4c Credo-Washington	2.50	4.50	11.85(50)	1.65	1.50	.28	.25	.07
1140	4c Credo-Franklin	2.50	4.50	11.85(50)	1.65	1.50	.28	.25	.07
1141	4c Credo-Jefferson	2.50	4.50	14.00(50)	1.90	1.75	.33	.30	.07
1142	4c Credo-Key	2.50	4.50	14.00(50)	1.90	1.75	.33	.30	.07
1143	4c Credo-Lincoln	2.50	4.50	20.50(50)	2.20	2.00	.48	.45	.07
1144	4c Credo-Henry (1961)	2.50	4.50	20.50(50)	2.20	2.00	.48	.45	.07

1145   1149   1150   1152

1146   1147,1148   1151   1153

SCOTT CAT. NO.	DESCRIPTION	FIRST DAY COVERS SING.	FIRST DAY COVERS PL BLK	MINT SHEET	PLATE BLOCKS F/NH	PLATE BLOCKS F	UNUSED F/NH	UNUSED F	USED F
	1960. COMMEMORATIVES								
1145-73	29 Varieties	. . . . .	. . . . .	. . . . .	47.95	44.25	8.30	7.60	2.40
1145	4c Boy Scouts	1.75	3.25	9.95(50)	1.10	1.00	.24	.21	.07
1146	4c Winter Olympics	1.75	3.25	9.65(50)	1.35	1.25	.23	.20	.07
1147	4c Thomas Masaryk	1.95	3.25	13.35(70)	1.10	1.00	.23	.20	.07
1148	8c Thomas Masaryk	2.50	3.95	29.75(72)	4.50	4.25	.43	.40	.20
1149	4c World Refugee Year	1.75	3.25	9.65(50)	1.10	1.00	.23	.20	.07
1150	4c Water Conservation	1.75	3.25	9.65(50)	1.10	1.00	.23	.20	.07
1151	4c SEATO	1.75	3.25	13.65(70)	1.40	1.25	.23	.20	.07
1152	4c American Women	1.75	3.25	9.65(50)	1.10	1.00	.23	.20	.07
1153	4c 50-Star Flag	1.75	3.25	9.85(50)	1.40	1.25	.23	.20	.07

FOR YOUR CONVENIENCE IN ORDERING, COMPLETE SETS ARE LISTED BEFORE SINGLE STAMP LISTINGS

SCOTT CAT. NO.	DESCRIPTION	FIRST DAY COVERS SING.	PL BLK	MINT SHEET	PLATE BLOCKS F/NH	F	UNUSED F/NH	F	USED F

1154

1155

1156

1157

1158

1154	4c Pony Express	1.75	3.25	19.25(50)	1.65	1.50	.43	.40	.07
1155	4c Employ the Handicapped . . .	1.75	3.25	9.85(50)	1.40	1.25	.23	.20	.07
1156	4c World Forestry Congress . . .	2.25	3.75	15.35(50)	1.55	1.40	.35	.32	.07
1157	4c Mexican Independence	1.75	3.25	9.65(50)	1.10	1.00	.23	.20	.07
1158	4c U.S.-Japan Treaty	1.75	3.25	9.65(50)	1.10	1.00	.23	.20	.07

1159, 1160

1161

1162

1163

1164

1159	4c Ignacy Paderewski	1.75	3.25	13.35(70)	1.10	1.00	.23	.20	.07
1160	8c Ignacy Paderewski	2.35	3.75	29.50(72)	4.00	3.75	.43	.40	.20
1161	4c Robert A. Taft	1.75	3.25	13.35(70)	1.10	1.00	.23	.20	.07
1162	4c Wheels of Freedom	1.75	3.25	9.65(50)	1.10	1.00	.23	.20	.07
1163	4c Boys' Clubs of America	1.75	3.25	9.75(50)	1.20	1.10	.23	.20	.07
1164	4c Automated Post Office	1.75	3.25	9.65(50)	1.10	1.00	.23	.20	.07

1165, 1166

1167

1168, 1169

1170

1171

1172

1165	4c Gustaf Mannerheim	1.75	3.25	13.35(70)	1.10	1.00	.23	.20	.07
1166	8c Gustaf Mannerheim	2.35	3.75	29.95(72)	4.25	4.00	.43	.40	.20
1167	4c Camp Fire Girls	1.75	3.25	9.65(50)	1.10	1.00	.23	.20	.07
1168	4c Giuseppe Garibaldi	1.75	3.25	13.35(70)	1.10	1.00	.23	.20	.07
1169	8c Giuseppe Garibaldi	2.50	4.50	35.25(70)	4.00	3.75	.53	.50	.20
1170	4c Walter George	1.75	3.25	13.35(70)	1.10	1.00	.23	.20	.07
1171	4c Andrew Carnegie	1.75	3.25	32.95(70)	1.90	1.75	.53	.50	.07
1172	4c John Foster Dulles	1.75	3.25	13.35(70)	1.10	1.00	.23	.20	.07

SCOTT CAT. NO.	DESCRIPTION	FIRST DAY COVERS SING.	FIRST DAY COVERS PL BLK	MINT SHEET	PLATE BLOCKS F/NH	PLATE BLOCKS F	UNUSED F/NH	UNUSED F	USED F

1173
1174, 1175
1176
1177

| 1173 | 4c "ECHO!" Satellite .... | 4.75 | 12.50 | 34.25(50) | 4.25 | 4.00 | .75 | .70 | .12 |

1961. COMMEMORATIVES

1174//90	(1174-77, 83-90) 12 Vars....	.....	.....		17.25	15.95	2.95	2.65	.90
1174	4c Mahatma Gandhi	1.95	3.25	13.35(70)	1.10	1.00	.23	.20	.07
1175	8c Mahatma Gandhi	2.50	5.00	36.50(72)	4.50	4.25	.53	.50	.20
1176	4c Range Conservation	3.00	5.00	12.25(50)	1.40	1.25	.28	.25	.07
1177	4c Horace Greeley	3.00	5.00	12.25(70)	1.40	1.25	.28	.25	.07

1178
1179
1183
1180
1181
1182
1184

1961-65. CIVIL WAR CENTENNIAL SERIES

1178-82	5 Vars., cpl	.....	.....		9.25	8.50	1.50	1.35	.30
1178	4c Fort Sumter	5.00	6.50	14.45(50)	2.20	2.00	.31	.28	.07
1179	4c Shiloh (1962)	5.00	6.50	12.85(50)	1.90	1.75	.28	.25	.07
1180	5c Gettysburg (1963)	5.00	6.50	14.75(50)	1.90	1.75	.33	.30	.07
1181	5c Wilderness (1964)	5.00	6.50	14.75(50)	1.90	1.75	.33	.30	.07
1182	5c Appomattox (1965)	5.00	6.50	14.75(50)	1.90	1.75	.33	.30	.07
1183	4c Kansas Statehood	1.75	3.25	9.65(50)	1.10	1.00	.23	.20	.07
1184	4c George W. Norris	1.75	3.25	9.65(50)	1.10	1.00	.23	.20	.07

1185
1186
1187
1188
1189
1190

| 1185 | 4c Naval Aviation .... | 2.95 | 4.25 | 9.65(50) | 1.10 | 1.00 | .23 | .20 | .07 |
| 1186 | 4c Workmens' Compensation .. | 1.75 | 3.25 | 9.85(50) | 1.30 | 1.15 | .23 | .20 | .07 |

SCOTT CAT. NO.	DESCRIPTION	FIRST DAY COVERS SING.	FIRST DAY COVERS PL BLK	MINT SHEET	PLATE BLOCKS F/NH	PLATE BLOCKS F	UNUSED F/NH	UNUSED F	USED F
1187	4c Frederic Remington	1.75	3.25	10.45(50)	1.85	1.75	.23	.20	.07
1188	4c Sun Yat-sen	1.75	3.25	9.95(50)	1.40	1.25	.23	.20	.07
1189	4c Basketball	3.00	4.25	9.95(50)	1.40	1.25	.23	.20	.07
1190	4c Nursing	2.25	3.75	9.65(50)	1.10	1.00	.23	.20	.07

1191　　　1192　　　1193　　　1194

1962. COMMEMORATIVES

1191-1207 17 Vars.		.....	.....		30.25	27.25	4.75	4.50	1.35
1191	4c New Mexico Statehood	1.75	3.25	12.25(50)	1.40	1.25	.28	.25	.07
1192	4c Arizona Statehood	1.75	3.25	12.25(50)	1.40	1.25	.28	.25	.07
1193	4c Project Mercury	3.50	6.50	16.75(50)	2.75	2.45	.38	.35	.15
1194	4c Malaria Eradication	1.75	3.25	12.25(50)	1.40	1.25	.28	.25	.07

1195　　　1196　　　1197　　　1198

1199　　　1200　　　1201　　　1202

1195	4c Charles Evans Hughes	1.75	3.25	12.25(50)	1.40	1.25	.28	.25	.07
1196	4c Seattle World's Fair	2.25	3.50	12.25(50)	1.40	1.25	.28	.25	.07
1197	4c Louisiana Statehood	1.75	3.25	14.50(50)	1.60	1.45	.33	.30	.07
1198	4c Homestead Act	3.00	5.00	12.50(50)	1.60	1.45	.28	.25	.07
1199	4c Girl Scouts	1.75	3.25	12.25(50)	1.40	1.25	.28	.25	.07
1200	4c Brien McMahon	1.75	3.25	12.50(50)	1.60	1.45	.28	.25	.07
1201	4c Apprenticeship	1.75	3.25	14.50(50)	1.60	1.45	.28	.30	.07
1202	4c Sam Rayburn	1.75	3.25	12.25(50)	1.40	1.25	.28	.25	.07

NOTE: To determine the VF price on stamps issued from 1941 to date, add 15% to the F/NH or F (used) price (minimum .03 per item). All VF unused stamps from 1941 to date will be NH.

SCOTT CAT. NO.	DESCRIPTION	FIRST DAY COVERS SING.	FIRST DAY COVERS PL BLK	MINT SHEET	PLATE BLOCKS F/NH	PLATE BLOCKS F	UNUSED F/NH	UNUSED F	USED F

1203   1204   1205   1206

1203	4c Dag Hammarshjold	1.95	3.75	14.50(50)	1.60	1.45	.33	.30	.07
1204	4c Hammarskjold Inverted	7.95	13.50	23.75(50)	7.00	6.75	.43	.40	.30
1205	4c Christmas '62	1.75	3.25	23.75(100)	1.40	1.25	.28	.25	.07
1206	4c Higher Education	1.75	3.25	12.25(50)	1.40	1.25	.28	.25	.07

1207   1208   1209, 1225   1213, 1229

| 1207 | 4c Winslow Homer . . . . | 2.25 | 3.50 | 16.50(50) | 1.80 | 1.65 | .38 | .35 | .07 |

1962-63. REGULAR ISSUE

1208-29	cpl., 5 Vars.	. . . . .	. . . . .		3.10(3)	2.65(3)	3.60	3.45	.30
1208	5c Flag & White House	1.75	3.25	23.75(100)	1.40	1.25	.28	.25	.07
1209	1c Andrew Jackson	1.75	3.25	6.25(100)	.50	.35	.10	.07	.07
1213	5c Washington	1.75	3.25	23.75(100)	1.40	1.25	.28	.25	.07

1962-63. COIL STAMPS Perf. 10 Vertically

					LINE PAIRS				
1225	1c Andrew Jackson	___	Pair	___	1.65	1.50	.30	.25	.07
1229	5c George Washington	2.25	3.75	___	5.50	5.25	3.00	2.90	.07

NOTE: Pairs of the above are available at two times the singles price. For Line Pair FDC's please send Want List.

1230   1231   1232   1233

1963. COMMEMORATIVES

1230-41	12 Varieties	. . . . .	. . . . .		17.65	15.95	3.50	3.15	.80
1230	5c Carolina Charter	1.75	3.25	13.95(50)	1.65	1.50	.33	.30	.07
1231	5c Food for Peace	1.75	3.25	13.95(50)	1.65	1.50	.33	.30	.07
1232	5c West Virginia Statehood . . .	2.25	3.75	13.95(50)	1.65	1.50	.33	.30	.07
1233	5c Emancipation Proclamation .	1.75	3.25	13.95(50)	1.65	1.50	.33	.30	.07

SCOTT CAT. NO.	DESCRIPTION	FIRST DAY COVERS SING. PL BLK		MINT SHEET	PLATE BLOCKS F/NH F		UNUSED F/NH F		USED F

1234

1235

1236

1237

1238

1239

1240

1241

1242

Scott	Description	Sing.	Pl Blk	Mint Sheet	F/NH	F	F/NH	F	Used F
1234	5c Alliance for Progress	1.75	3.25	12.25(50)	1.40	1.25	.28	.25	.07
1235	5c Cordell Hull	1.75	3.25	13.95(50)	1.65	1.50	.33	.30	.07
1236	5c Eleanor Roosevelt	1.75	3.25	12.25(50)	1.40	1.25	.28	.25	.07
1237	5c The Sciences	2.25	3.75	12.25(50)	1.65	1.50	.28	.25	.07
1238	5c City Mail Delivery	1.75	3.25	12.25(50)	1.40	1.25	.28	.25	.07
1239	5c Int'l Red Cross	1.75	3.25	12.25(50)	1.40	1.25	.28	.25	.07
1240	5c Christmas '63	3.25	4.75	23.75(100)	1.40	1.25	.28	.25	.07
1241	5c John J. Audubon	2.25	3.75	15.95(50)	1.75	1.60	.38	.35	.07

1243

1244

1246

1248

1245

1247

1249

1250

1251

1960 through 1965 COMMEMORATIVES

Every commemorative stamp (116 different) issued from 1960 to 1965 at a special price.

#A153 Unused (SAVE $6.82) $31.95
#A163 Used (SAVE $2.70) $6.95

SCOTT CAT. NO.	DESCRIPTION	FIRST DAY COVERS		MINT SHEET	ZIP	PLATE BLOCK	UN-USED	USED
		SING.	PL. BLK.					
		1964 COMMEMORATIVES						
1242-60	19 Varieties	——	——	——	——	30.50(16)	10.75	1.25
1242	5c Sam Houston	1.75	3.25	14.25(50)	1.25	1.35	.30	.07
1243	5c Charles M. Russell	1.75	3.25	21.50(50)	2.00	2.25	.45	.07
1244	5c New York World's Fair	1.75	3.25	13.25(50)	2.20	2.20	.25	.07
1245	5c John Muir	1.75	3.25	12.25(50)	——	1.25	.25	.07
1246	5c John F. Kennedy	2.25	3.75	12.25(50)	——	1.25	.25	.07
1247	5c New Jersey Tercentenary . .	1.75	3.25	14.25(50)	1.40	1.50	.30	.07
1248	5c Nevada Statehood	1.75	3.25	12.25(50)	1.25	1.25	.25	.07
1249	5c Register and Vote	1.75	3.25	12.25(50)	1.25	1.25	.25	.07
1250	5c Shakespeare	1.75	3.25	12.25(50)	1.25	1.25	.25	.07
1251	5c Mayo Brothers	1.75	3.25	12.25(50)	1.25	1.25	.25	.07

1252   1253   1254   1255   1256   1257

1252	5c American Music	1.75	3.25	12.25(50)	1.25	1.25	.25	.07
1253	5c Homemakers	1.75	3.25	12.25(50)	1.50	1.50	.25	.07
1254-57	5c Xmas, 4 Vars., attd	5.50	9.00	230.00(100)	10.00	10.00	7.25	. . . .
1254	5c Holly	3.00	——	——		——	1.75	.07
1255	5c Mistletoe	3.00	——	——		——	1.75	.07
1256	5c Poinsettia	3.00	——	——		——	1.75	.07
1257	5c Pine Cone	3.00	——	——		——	1.75	.07

1258   1260   1262   1263   1264

1259   1261   1265   1266

1258	5c Verrazano-Narrows Bridge . .	1.75	3.25	12.25(50)	1.25	1.50	.25	.07
1259	5c Modern Art	1.75	3.25	12.25(50)	1.25	1.50	.25	.07
1260	5c Radio Amateurs	1.75	3.25	14.25(50)	1.50	1.50	.30	.07

SCOTT CAT. NO.	DESCRIPTION	FIRST DAY COVERS		MINT SHEET	ZIP	PLATE BLOCK	UN-USED	USED
		SING.	PL. BLK.					
	1965 COMMEMORATIVES							
1261-76	16 Varieties	.....	.....	.....	29.75	44.75	4.85	1.55
1261	5c Battle of New Orleans	2.75	3.25	16.25(50)	1.40	1.50	.35	.07
1262	5c Physical Fitness	1.75	3.25	12.25(50)	1.25	1.50	.25	.07
1263	5c Crusade Against Cancer ...	1.75	3.25	12.25(50)	1.25	1.50	.25	.07
1264	5c Winston Churchill	1.75	3.25	12.25(50)	1.25	1.50	.25	.07
1265	5c Magna Carta	1.75	3.25	12.25(50)	1.25	1.50	.25	.07
1266	5c Int'l Cooperation Year	1.75	3.25	18.25(50)	1.25	1.50	.38	.07

1267   1268   1269   1271   1273   1275

1270   1272   1274   1276

1267	5c Salvation Army	1.75	3.25	12.25(50)	1.25	1.50	.25	.07
1268	5c Dante Alighieri	1.75	3.25	12.25(50)	1.25	1.50	.25	.07
1269	5c Herbert Hoover	1.75	3.25	13.25(50)	1.25	1.50	.27	.07
1270	5c Robert Fulton	1.75	3.25	13.25(50)	1.25	1.50	.27	.07
1271	5c Florida Settlement	1.75	3.25	12.25(50)	1.25	1.50	.25	.07
1272	5c Traffic Safety	1.75	3.25	13.25(50)	1.25	1.25	.27	.07
1273	5c John S. Copley	1.75	3.25	13.25(50)	1.50	1.50	.27	.07
1274	11c Telecommunication	1.75	3.25	65.00(50)	15.00	25.00	1.00	.60
1275	5c Adlai Stevenson	1.75	3.25	16.25(50)	____	1.50	.35	.07
1276	5c Christmas '65	1.75	3.25	33.25(100)	1.25	1.50	.35	.07

– SUPPLIES –

See our complete line of supplies for all your collecting needs
at the back of this catalog.

**FOR YOUR CONVENIENCE IN ORDERING, COMPLETE
SETS ARE LISTED BEFORE SINGLE STAMP LISTINGS**

SCOTT CAT. NO.	DESCRIPTION	FIRST DAY COVERS SING.	FIRST DAY COVERS PL. BLK.	MINT SHEET	MAIL EARLY	ZIP	PLATE BLOCK	UN-USED	USED

1278,1299   1279   1280   1281,1297   1282,1303

1283,1304   1283B, 1304C   1284,1298   1285   1286

1286A   1287   1288, 1288B, 1288D / 1305E, 1305 I   1289   1290

1291   1292   1293   1294,1305C   1295   1305

1965-79. PROMINENT AMERICANS SERIES

Scott No.	Description	FDC Sing.	FDC Pl. Blk.	Mint Sheet	Mail Early	Zip	Plate Block	Unused	Used
1278-95	1c-$5, 21 Vars., cpl.	.....	.....	.....	.....	.....	215.00(20)	36.25	7.25
1278-93	1c-50c, 19 Vars.	.....	.....	.....	.....	.....	113.50(18)	13.10	1.50
1278	1c Thomas Jefferson	1.95	3.25	6.50(100)	.50	.35	.35	.07	.07
1279	1¼c Albert Gallatin	1.95	4.00	99.95(100)			50.00	.30	.30
1280	2c Frank L. Wright	1.95	3.25	9.50(100)	.75	.55	.55	.10	.07
1281	3c Francis Parkman	1.95	3.25	14.50(100)	1.40	.90	.90	.15	.07
1282	4c Abraham Lincoln	1.95	4.65	18.95(100)			1.00	.20	.07
1283	5c George Washington	1.95	3.25	36.50(100)			1.90	.38	.07
1283B	5c Wash., redrawn	1.95	3.25	29.00(100)			1.80	.30	.07
1284	6c Franklin D. Roosevelt	1.95	3.25	35.00(100)	10.65	10.00	1.50	.30	.07
1285	8c Albert Einstein	1.95	3.25	57.50(100)	4.25	3.00	3.00	.60	.07
1286	10c Andrew Jackson	1.95	4.25	48.50(100)	4.50	3.50	3.00	.50	.07
1286A	12c Henry Ford	2.25	4.25	57.00(100)	3.75	2.60	2.60	.60	.07
1287	13c John F. Kennedy	3.00	3.75	85.00(100)			3.75	.90	.07
1288	15c Oliver W. Holmes, die I	2.25	5.95	71.50(100)	5.00	3.50	3.50	.75	.07
1288B	Same, from Booklet Pane	2.00						.75	.07
1289	20c George C. Marshall	2.35	5.75	95.00(100)	6.25	4.50	4.50	1.00	.07
1290	25c Frederick Douglass	2.75	5.95	120.00(100)	7.75	6.50	6.50	1.25	.07
1291	30c John Dewey	2.75	5.50	142.50(100)	9.25	8.00	8.00	1.50	.08
1292	40c Thomas Paine	3.25	7.25	189.00(100)	12.65	8.25	8.25	2.00	.10
1293	50c Lucy Stone	4.25	8.00	240.00(100)	15.50	11.25	12.50	2.50	.10
1294	$1 Eugene O'Neill	9.50	30.00	475.00(100)	32.00	21.00	21.00	5.00	.12
1295	$5 John Bassett Moore	70.00	125.00	2350.00(100)			85.00	20.00	5.95

NOTE: All stamps from #1242 to date are priced for F/NH condition. For VF/NH price, add 15% (minimum .03 per item) to listed price.

SCOTT CAT. NO.	DESCRIPTION	FIRST DAY COVERS SING.	PL. BLK.	MINT SHEET	ZIP	PLATE BLOCK	UN-USED	USED

1966-81. COIL STAMPS

		PAIR				LINE PAIR		
1297-1305I	1c-$1, 9 Vars., (No 1305E) .	.....	.....	___	___	20.25	5.25	2.25

Perf. 10 Horizontally

1297	3c Francis Parkman . . . . (1975)	1.75	___	___	___	1.00	.15	.07
1298	6c Franklin D. Roosevelt (1967)	1.75	2.00	___	___	3.00	.50	.07

Perf. 10 Vertically

1299	1c Thomas Jefferson . . . (1968)	1.75	___	___	___	.35	.07	.07
1303	4c Abraham Lincoln	1.75	2.00	___	___	2.00	.27	.10
1304	5c George Washington	1.75	2.00	___	___	1.20	.37	.07
1304C	5c Washington, redrawn (1981)	.....	.....	___	___	.95	.15	.07
1305	6c Franklin D. Roosevelt (1968)	1.75	2.00	___	___	1.90	.60	.07
1305C	$1 Eugene O'Neill (1973)	6.50	8.50	___	___	8.00	3.00	1.85
1305E	15c Oliver W. Holmes, die I (1978)	1.75	2.00	___	___	5.00	1.25	.....
1305I	15c O.W. Holmes, die II (1979)	.....	.....	___	___	1.25	.45	.07

NOTE: Pairs of the above can be supplied at two times the single price. For FDC Line Pairs—please send want list.

1306   1307   1310, 1311   1314

1308   1309   1312   1313   1315

1966. COMMEMORATIVES

1306/22	(1306-10,1312-22) 16 Vars. .	.....	.....	.....	21.95	22.25	4.10	1.00
1306	5c Migratory Bird Treaty	1.75	3.25	13.25(50)	1.35	1.35	.27	.07
1307	5c A.S.P.C.A.	1.75	3.25	13.25(50)	1.35	1.35	.27	.07
1308	5c Indiana Statehood	1.75	3.25	13.25(50)	1.35	1.35	.27	.07
1309	5c American Circus	2.50	4.00	13.25(50)	1.35	1.35	.27	.07
1310	5c SIPEX, (single)	1.75	3.25	13.25(50)	1.35	1.35	.27	.07

SCOTT CAT. NO.	DESCRIPTION	FIRST DAY COVERS SING.	FIRST DAY COVERS PL. BLK.	MINT SHEET	ZIP	PLATE BLOCKS	UN-USED	USED
	Imperforate Souvenir Sheet							
1311	5c SIPEX	1.75	———	———	———	———	.60	.60
1312	5c Bill of Rights	1.75	3.25	13.25(50)	1.35	1.50	.27	.07
1313	5c Polish Millenium	1.75	3.25	13.25(50)	1.35	1.35	.27	.07
1314	5c Natl. Park Service	1.75	3.25	13.25(50)	1.35	1.50	.27	.07
1315	5c Marine Corps Reserve	1.75	3.25	13.25(50)	1.35	1.50	.27	.07

1316

1318

1321

1322

1317

1319

1320

1323

1316	5c Womens' clubs	1.75	3.25	13.25(50)	1.35	1.50	.27	.07
1317	5c Johnny Appleseed	1.95	3.50	13.25(50)	1.35	1.50	.27	.07
1318	5c Beautification	1.75	3.25	13.75(50)	1.50	2.00	.27	.07
1319	5c Great River Road	1.75	3.25	13.25(50)	1.35	1.50	.27	.07
1320	5c Servicemen—Bonds	1.75	3.25	12.95(50)	1.35	1.35	.27	.07
1321	5c Christmas '66	1.75	3.25	25.50(100)	1.35	1.35	.27	.07
1322	5c Mary Cassatt	1.75	3.25	17.50(50)	3.00	3.25	.30	.07

	1967.COMMEMORATIVES							
1323-37	15 Vars, cpl.	. . . . .	. . . . .	. . . . .	40.95(13)	44.75(14)	9.75	1.35
1323	5c National Grange	1.75	3.25	13.25(50)	1.50	1.50	.27	.07

1324

1325

1326

1324	5c Canada Centennial	1.75	3.25	13.50(50)	1.65	2.00	.27	.07
1325	5c Erie Canal	1.75	3.25	13.25(50)	1.65	1.65	.27	.07
1326	5c Search for Peace	1.75	3.25	13.25(50)	1.65	1.65	.27	.07

SCOTT CAT. NO.	DESCRIPTION	FIRST DAY COVERS SING.	PL. BLK.	MINT SHEET	ZIP	PLATE BLOCK	UN-USED	USED
1327	5c Henry D. Thoreau	1.75	3.25	16.75(50)	1.65	1.80	.35	.07
1328	5c Nebraska Statehood	1.75	3.25	16.75(50)	1.65	1.80	.35	.07
1329	5c Voice of America	1.75	3.25	11.95(50)	1.65	1.65	.27	.07
1330	5c Davy Crockett	1.75	3.25	16.75(50)	1.65	1.80	.35	.07

1331-32	Space, att'd., 2 Vars.	12.65	22.00	210.00(50)	21.50	22.50	6.50	. . . . .
1331	5c Astronaut	2.25	—	—	—	—	1.75	.27
1332	5c Gemini 4 Capsule	2.25	—	—	—	—	1.75	.27

1333	5c Urban Planning	1.75	3.25	13.25(50)	2.50	2.50	.27	.07
1334	5c Finnish Independence	1.75	3.25	13.25(50)	2.50	2.50	.27	.07

1335	5c Thomas Eakins	1.75	3.25	14.50(50)	—	2.50	.30	.07
1336	5c Christmas '67	1.75	3.25	11.95(50)	1.25	1.25	.27	.07
1337	5c Mississippi Statehood	1.95	4.50	13.25(50)	2.50	2.50	.27	.07

SCOTT CAT. NO.	DESCRIPTION	FIRST DAY COVERS SING. PL. BLK.		MINT SHEET	MAIL EARLY	ZIP	PLATE BLOCK	UN-USED	USED

1339

1340

1338, 1338A-G

1968-71. REGULAR ISSUES

SCOTT CAT. NO.	DESCRIPTION	SING.	PL. BLK.	MINT SHEET	MAIL EARLY	ZIP	PLATE BLOCK	UN-USED	USED
1338/41	(1338-38G, 1341) 6 Vars., cpl.	. . . . .	. . . . .	. . . . .	. . . . .	. . . . .	78.95(4)	14.00	6.50

GIORI PRESS
1968, Design size: 18½ x 22 mm Perf. 11

1338	6c Flag & White House	1.75	3.25	28.50(100)	2.20	1.60	1.60	.30	.07

HUCK PRESS Design Size: 18 x 21 mm
1969 Coil Stamp Perf. 10 Vertically

1338A	6c Flag & White House	1.75	—	—	—	—	—	.40	.07
1338A	same, pair	2.00	—	—	—	—	—	.80	. . . . .

1970. Perf. 11 x 10½

1338D	6c Flag & White House	1.75	3.25	28.95(100)	—	—	6.50(20)	.30	.07

1971. Perf. 11 x 10½

1338F	8c Flag & White House	1.75	3.25	39.95(100)	—	—	10.00(20)	.40	.07

Coil Stamp Perf. 10 Vertically

1338G	8c Flag & White House	1.75	—	—	—	—	—	.60	.07
1338G	same, pair	2.00	—	—	—	—	—	1.20	. . . . .

1968 COMMEMORATIVES

1339//64	(1339-40,42,44,55,64) 15 Vars.	. . . . .	. . . . .	. . . . .	51.75(14)	31.50(14)	37.50	5.85	1.00
1339	6c Illinois Statehood	1.75	3.25	14.50(50)	—	1.90	2.00	.30	.07
1340	6c Hemisfair '68	1.75	3.25	14.50(50)	4.50	1.90	2.00	.30	.07

1341

1342

1343

1344

1341	$1 Airlift to Servicemen	9.75	27.50	625.00(50)	85.00	60.00	65.00	13.00	6.45
1342	6c Support our Youth	1.75	3.25	14.50(50)	4.50	1.80	2.00	.30	.07
1343	6c Law & Order	1.75	3.25	14.50(50)	4.50	1.80	2.00	.30	.07
1344	6c Register & Vote	1.75	3.25	14.50(50)	4.50	1.80	1.80	.30	.07

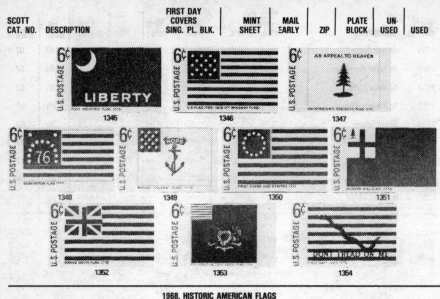

SCOTT CAT. NO.	DESCRIPTION	FIRST DAY COVERS SING. PL. BLK.	MINT SHEET	MAIL EARLY	ZIP	PLATE BLOCK	UN- USED	USED
		1968. HISTORIC AMERICAN FLAGS						
1345-54	10 Vars., cpl., att'd	19.50(1)	. . . . .	81.50(50)	____	____	32.50(20)	16.00	8.75
1345/54	Inscr.blks.	____	7.50	____	10.50	7.00	11.00		
1345	6c Fort Moultrie Flag	4.00	____	____	____	____		1.50	1.10
1346	6c Fort McHenry Flag	4.00	____	____	____	____		1.50	1.10
1347	6c Washington's Cruisers	4.00	____	____	____	____		1.50	1.10
1348	6c Bennington Flag	4.00	____	____	____	____		1.50	.90
1349	6c Rhode Island Flag	4.00	____	____	____	____		1.50	.90
1350	6c 1st Stars & Stripes	4.00	____	____	____	____		1.50	.90
1351	6c Bunker Hill Flag	4.00	____	____	____	____		1.50	.90
1352	6c Grand Union Flag	4.00	____	____	____	____		1.50	.90
1353	6c Philadelphia Light Horse	4.00	____	____	____	____		1.50	.90
1354	6c First Navy Jack	4.00	____	____	____	____		1.50	.90

NOTE: All 10 varieties of 1345-54 were printed on the same sheet; therefore, plate and regular blocks are not available for each variety separately. Plate blocks of 4 will contain two each of #1346, with number adjacent to #1345 only; Zip blocks will contain two each of #1353 and #1354, with inscription adjacent to #1354 only; Mail Early blocks will contain two each of #1347-49 with inscription adjacent to #1348 only. A plate strip of 20 stamps, with two of each variety will be required to have all stamps in plate block form and will contain all marginal inscription.

SCOTT CAT. NO.	DESCRIPTION	FIRST DAY COVERS SING. PL. BLK.		MINT SHEET	MAIL EARLY	ZIP	PLATE BLOCKS	UN-USED	USED
1355	6c Walt Disney	2.75	4.50	29.00(50)	3.95	3.00	3.50	.60	.07
1356	6c Father Marquette	2.00	3.50	19.25(50)	3.00	2.00	2.00	.40	.07
1357	6c Daniel Boone	1.75	3.25	14.75(50)	3.75	1.90	1.90	.30	.07
1358	6c Arkansas River	1.75	3.25	21.25(50)	3.50	2.25	2.25	.45	.07
1359	6c Leif Erikson	1.75	3.25	14.75(50)	4.50	2.30	1.90	.30	.07
1360	6c Cherokee Strip	1.75	4.50	23.75(50)	4.50	2.50	2.50	.50	.07
1361	6c Trumbull Art	1.75	4.50	17.75(50)	3.50	3.00	3.00	.35	.07
1362	6c Wildlife Conservation	1.75	4.50	29.00(50)	5.00	4.00	4.00	.60	.07
1363	6c Christmas '68	1.75	3.25	15.50(50)	____	____	4.50(10)	.30	.07
1364	6c Chief Joseph	2.25	3.75	40.00(50)	5.75	4.25	4.25	.85	.07

PLANT for more BEAUTIFUL CITIES   1365   PLANT for more BEAUTIFUL PARKS   1366   PLANT for more BEAUTIFUL HIGHWAYS   1367   PLANT for more BEAUTIFUL STREETS   1368

1969. COMMEMORATIVES

SCOTT CAT. NO.	DESCRIPTION	FDC SING.	PL. BLK.	MINT SHEET	MAIL EARLY	ZIP	PLATE BLOCKS	UN-USED	USED
1365-86	22 Vars., cpl.	.....	.....	.....	75.00(15)	58.95(15)	62.50(16)	30.25	2.00
1365-68	Beautification, 4 Vars., att'd.	5.25	8.50	95.00(50)	15.00	11.00	11.00	9.00	.....
1365	6c Azaleas & Tulips	3.25	____	____	____	____	____	2.00	.15
1366	6c Daffodils	3.25	____	____	____	____	____	2.00	.15
1367	6c Poppies	3.25	____	____	____	____	____	2.00	.15
1368	6c Crabapple Trees	3.25	____	____	____	____	____	2.00	.15

1369   1370   1371   1372

1369	6c American Legion	1.75	3.25	14.75(50)	2.25	1.90	1.90	.30	.07
1370	6c Grandma Moses	1.75	3.25	14.75(50)	2.25	1.90	1.95	.30	.07
1371	6c Apollo 8 Moon Orbit	4.75	10.00	28.75(50)	4.25	3.75	3.75	.60	.07
1372	6c W.C. Handy-Musician	1.75	3.25	14.75(50)	2.25	1.90	1.90	.30	.07

SCOTT CAT. NO.	DESCRIPTION	FIRST DAY COVERS SING. PL. BLK.		MINT SHEET	MAIL EARLY	ZIP	PLATE BLOCKS	UN-USED	USED

1373

1374

1375

Scott	Description	Sing.	Pl. Blk.	Mint Sheet	Mail Early	Zip	Plate Blocks	Unused	Used
1373	6c California Settlement	1.75	3.25	14.75(50)	2.25	1.90	2.00	.30	.07
1374	6c Major John W. Powell	1.75	3.25	23.50(50)	3.25	1.90	2.25	.50	.07
1375	6c Alabama Statehood	1.75	3.25	14.75(50)	2.25	1.90	1.90	.30	.07

1376

1377

1378

1379

Scott	Description	Sing.	Pl. Blk.	Mint Sheet	Mail Early	Zip	Plate Blocks	Unused	Used
1376-79	Botanical Congress, 4 Vars., Att'd	5.25	8.50	175.00(50)	27.00	20.00	22.50	18.00	. . . . .
1376	6c Douglas Fir	3.25	____	____			____	3.50	.15
1377	6c Ladyslipper	3.25	____	____			____	3.50	.15
1378	6c Ocotillo	3.25	____	____			____	3.50	.15
1379	6c Franklinia	3.25	____	____			____	3.50	.15

1380

1381

1382

Scott	Description	Sing.	Pl. Blk.	Mint Sheet	Mail Early	Zip	Plate Blocks	Unused	Used
1380	6c Dartmouth College	1.75	3.25	14.75(50)	2.25	1.90	1.90	.30	.07
1381	6c Professional Baseball	3.25	5.50	20.00(50)	3.50	2.75	3.00	.40	.07
1382	6c College Football	2.75	5.50	17.50(50)	3.00	2.25	2.50	.35	.07

SCOTT CAT. NO.	DESCRIPTION	FIRST DAY COVERS SING.	PL. BLK.	MINT SHEET	MAIL EARLY	ZIP	PLATE BLOCKS	UN- USED	USED

1383	6c Eisenhower	1.75	3.25	10.95(32)	3.75	3.50	1.95	.35	.07
1384	6c Christmas '69	1.75	3.25	14.75(50)			3.50(10)	.30	.07
1385	6c Rehabilitation	2.25	3.75	14.75(50)	2.25	1.90	1.90	.30	.07
1386	6c William M. Harnett	1.75	3.25	9.75(32)	2.25	1.90	1.90	.30	.07

1970. COMMEMORATIVES

1387/1422 (1387-92, 1405-22) 24 Vars. . . .		. . . . .	. . . . .	. . . . .	54.50(14)	41.95(14)	56.95(14)	17.75	2.25
1387-90	Natural History, 4 Vars., att'd. . . .	4.00	6.00	15.50(32)	4.00	3.25	3.75	2.00	. . . . .
1387	6c Bald Eagle	2.50	—	—	—	—	—	.45	.13
1388	6c Elephant Herd	2.50	—	—	—	—	—	.45	.13
1389	6c Haida Canoe	2.50	—	—	—	—	—	.45	.13
1390	6c Reptiles	2.50	—	—	—	—	—	.45	.13
1391	6c Maine Statehood	1.75	3.25	16.50(50)	2.75	1.90	.90	.35	.07
1392	6c Wildlife-Buffalo	2.25	3.75	12.95(50)	2.00	1.65	1.65	.30	.07

-SUPPLIES-

Don't forget that Harris offers a complete line of albums, supplies, and accessories for all your stamp collecting needs. See our supply section in the back of this catalog.

SCOTT CAT. NO.	DESCRIPTION	FIRST DAY COVERS SING.	PL. BLK.	MINT SHEET	MAIL EARLY	ZIP	PLATE BLOCK	UN-USED	USED

1393, 1401

1393D

1394

1395, 1402

1396

1397

1398

1399

1400

1970-74. REGULAR ISSUE

Scott	Description	FDC Sing.	PL. BLK.	Mint Sheet	Mail Early	ZIP	Plate Block	Unused	Used
1393-1402	6c-21c cpl., 11 Vars.	.....	.....	.....	30.50(8)	22.50(8)	30.50(8)	5.95	1.20
1393	6c Dwight Eisenhower	2.75	5.50	28.25(100)	2.00	1.35	1.35	.30	.07
1393D	7c Benjamin Franklin (1972)	2.75	3.00	33.25(100)	2.50	1.75	1.75	.35	.07
1394	8c Ike-black, blue, red (1971)	2.75	3.00	37.85(100)	2.65	1.85	1.85	.40	.07
1395	Same, rose violet (1971)	2.75						.45	.07
1396	8c Postal Service Emblem (1971)	2.75	3.25	41.95(100)	2.75(4)	2.75	9.50(12)	.40	.07
1397	14c Fiorello LaGuardia (1972)	2.75	3.50	66.75(100)	4.50	3.25	3.50	.70	.16
1398	16c Ernie Pyle (1971)	2.75	3.75	76.50(100)	5.00	3.75	4.25	.80	.07
1399	18c Elizabeth Blackwell (1974)	2.75	6.50	85.00(100)	5.85	4.50	5.00	.90	.17
1400	21c Amadeo P. Giannini (1973)	2.75	3.75	97.50(100)	6.75	4.50	5.15	1.00	.40

NOTE: #1395 was issued in booklet form, so all copies will have one or more straight edges.

1970-71 COIL STAMPS-Perf. 10 Vertically

							LINE PAIR		
1401	6c Dwight Eisenhower	1.75	pr.1.95	—	—	—	1.35	.45	.07
1402	8c Eisenhower, rose violet (1971)	1.75	pr. 1.95	—	—	—	1.40	.50	.07

NOTE: Pairs can be supplied at double the singles price. Send want list for FDC Line Pairs.

1405

1406

1407

1408

1409

1970

1405	6c Edgar L. Masters-Poet	1.75	3.25	14.25(50)	2.50	1.45	1.50	.30	.07
1406	6c Woman Suffrage	1.75	3.25	19.50(50)	2.75	1.75	1.75	.42	.07
1407	6c South Carolina Terc.	1.75	3.25	19.50(50)	2.75	1.75	1.75	.42	.07
1408	6c Stone Mt. Memorial	1.75	3.25	14.25(50)	2.50	1.45	1.50	.30	.07
1409	6c Fort Snelling	1.75	3.25	14.50(50)	2.50	1.50	1.75	.30	.07

SCOTT CAT. NO.	DESCRIPTION	FIRST DAY COVERS SING. PL. BLK.		MINT SHEET	MAIL EARLY	ZIP	PLATE BLOCKS	UN-USED	USED

SAVE OUR SOIL — UNITED STATES · SIX CENTS
1410

SAVE OUR CITIES — UNITED STATES · SIX CENTS
1411

SAVE OUR WATER — UNITED STATES · SIX CENTS
1412

SAVE OUR AIR — UNITED STATES · SIX CENTS
1413

SCOTT CAT. NO.	DESCRIPTION	SING.	PL. BLK.	MINT SHEET	MAIL EARLY	ZIP	PLATE BLOCKS	UN-USED	USED
1410-13	Anti-Pollution, 4 Vars., att'd.	7.50	9.50	39.75(50)	8.75	6.25	11.25(10)	4.00	.....
1410	6c Globe & Wheat	4.50	—	—	—	—	—	.75	.15
1411	6c Globe & City	4.50	—	—	—	—	—	.75	.15
1412	6c Globe & Bluegill	4.50	—	—	—	—	—	.75	.15
1413	6c Globe & Seagull	4.50	—	—	—	—	—	.75	.15

1415

1414

1416

1417

1418

SCOTT CAT. NO.	DESCRIPTION	SING.	PL. BLK.	MINT SHEET	MAIL EARLY	ZIP	PLATE BLOCKS	UN-USED	USED
1414	6c Nativity	1.75	3.25	14.75(50)	2.50	1.85	4.00(8)	.32	.07
1415-18	Christmas Toys, 4 Vars., att'd	5.75	8.50	83.50(50)	11.50	9.75	17.50(8)	8.75	.....
1415	6c Locomotive	3.50	—	—	—	—	—	1.50	.10
1416	6c Horse	3.50	—	—	—	—	—	1.50	.10
1417	6c Tricycle	3.50	—	—	—	—	—	1.50	.10
1418	6c Doll Carriage	3.50	—	—	—	—	—	1.50	.10

Precancelled.

SCOTT CAT. NO.	DESCRIPTION	SING.	PL. BLK.	MINT SHEET	MAIL EARLY	ZIP	PLATE BLOCKS	UN-USED	USED
1414a	6c Nativity (precancelled)	.....	.....	19.25(50)	3.50	3.00	4.75(8)	.37	.08
1415a-18a	Xmas Toys, precan. 4 Vars., att'd.	.....	.....	290.00(50)	32.00	28.00	55.00(8)	25.00	.....
1415a	6c Locomotive	—	—	—	—	—	—	3.50	.15
1416a	6c Horse	—	—	—	—	—	—	3.50	.15
1417a	6c Tricycle	—	—	—	—	—	—	3.50	.15
1418a	6c Doll Carriage	—	—	—	—	—	—	3.50	.15

Note: Unused precancels are with original gum while used are without gum.

UNITED STATES POSTAGE 6 CENTS — United Nations 25ᵗʰ Anniversary
1419

U.S. POSTAGE 6 CENTS
1420

50 years of service
1421

HONORING U.S. SERVICEMEN — PRISONERS OF WAR MISSING AND KILLED IN ACTION — UNITED 6 STATES
1422

UNITED STATES — AMERICA'S WOOL
1423

DOUGLAS MacARTHUR — 6c US
1424

SCOTT CAT. NO.	DESCRIPTION	SING.	PL. BLK.	MINT SHEET	MAIL EARLY	ZIP	PLATE BLOCKS	UN-USED	USED
1419	6c U.N. 25th Anniversary	1.75	3.25	16.00(50)	2.25	1.90	1.90	.32	.07
1420	6c Pilgrim Landing	1.75	3.25	16.75(50)	2.25	1.90	1.90	.35	.07
1421-22	D.A.V. Servicemen, 2 Vars., att'd	2.50	3.75	23.75(50)	8.50	8.00	8.00	.70	.....
1421	6c Disabled Vets	2.00	—	—	—	—	—	.35	.10
1422	6c Prisoners of War	2.00	—	—	—	—	—	.35	.10

SCOTT CAT. NO.	DESCRIPTION	FIRST DAY COVERS SING.	PL. BLK.	MINT SHEET	MAIL EARLY	ZIP	PLATE BLOCKS	UN-USED	USED
				1971. COMMEMORATIVES					
1423-45	23 Vars., cpl.	. . . . .	. . . . .	. . . . .	44.00(16)	32.50(16)	46.95(16)	9.95	2.00
1423	6c Sheep	1.75	3.25	16.00(50)	2.65	1.65	1.9007	.32	
1424	6c General D. MacArthur	1.75	3.25	16.00(50)	2.65	1.65	1.9007	.32	

1425

1427

1426

1428

1429

1430

1425	6c Blood Donors	1.75	3.25	16.00(50)	2.65	1.65	1.75	.32	.07
1426	8c Missouri Statehood	1.75	3.25	19.75(50)	1.85(4)	1.85	5.50(12)	.40	.07
1427-30	Wildlife Conserv. 4 Vars., att'd . . .	5.00	7.75	18.95(50)	3.50	2.50	2.75	2.25	. . . . .
1427	8c Trout	3.50	——				——	.55	.12
1428	8c Alligator	3.50	——				——	.55	.12
1429	8c Polar Bear	3.50	——				——	.55	.12
1430	8c Condor	3.50	——				——	.55	.12

1431

1433

UNITED STATES IN SPACE··· A DECADE OF ACHIEVEMENT

1434   1435

1432

1436

1437

1438

1439

1431	8c Antarctic Treaty	1.95	3.25	19.25(50)	2.75	2.00	2.25	.40	.07
1432	8c American Revolution	2.25	3.95	37.25(50)	6.50	5.00	5.25	.75	.07
1433	8c J. Sloan-Artist	1.75	3.25	19.25(50)	2.75	2.10	2.25	.40	.07
1434-35	Space Achievements, 2 Vars., att'd	3.50	6.50	19.75(50)	3.25	2.50	2.50	.80	
1434	8c Moon, Earth, Sun & Landing Craft	2.00	——				——	.40	.12
1435	8c Lunar Rover	2.00	——				——	.40	.12
1436	8c Emily Dickinson	1.75	3.25	19.25(50)	2.75	1.75	1.90	.40	.07

SCOTT CAT. NO.	DESCRIPTION	FIRST DAY COVERS SING.	PL. BLK.	MINT SHEET	MAIL EARLY	ZIP	PLATE BLOCKS	UN-USED	USED
1437	8c San Juan	1.95	3.50	19.25(50)	2.75	1.75	1.90	.40	.07
1438	8c Drug Addiction	1.75	3.25	19.50(50)	2.75	2.00	3.00(6)	.40	.07
1439	8c CARE	1.75	3.25	19.75(50)	2.75	2.00	3.75(8)	.40	.07

HISTORIC PRESERVATION 1440

HISTORIC PRESERVATION 1441

HISTORIC PRESERVATION 1442

Christmas 1444

1445

HISTORIC PRESERVATION 1443

1446

Peace Corps 8c United States 1447

Scott	Description	Sing.	Pl. Blk.	Mint Sheet	Mail Early	Zip	Plate Blocks	Unused	Used
1440-43	Historic Preservation, 4 Vars., att'd	3.50	6.25	16.50(32)	3.65	2.50	2.50	2.25	.....
1440	8c Decatur House	2.65	___	___	___	___	___	.55	.12
1441	8c Whaling Ship	2.65	___	___	___	___	___	.55	.12
1442	8c Cable Car	2.65	___	___	___	___	___	.55	.12
1443	8c Mission	2.65	___	___	___	___	___	.55	.12
1444	8c Christmas Nativity	3.25	4.95	19.50(50)	1.75(4)	1.75	5.25(12)	.40	.07
1445	8c Christmas Patridge	3.25	4.95	19.50(50)	1.75(4)	1.75	5.25(12)	.40	.07

	1972. COMMEMORATIVES								
1446//74	(1446-47,55-74)22 Vars.	.....	.....	.....	40.25(15)	31.25(16)	48.50(16)	9.75	2.50
1446	8c Sidney Lanier-Poet	1.75	3.25	25.95(50)	3.75	2.50	2.50	.55	.07
1447	8c Peace Corps	1.75	3.25	19.95(50)	2.85	1.75	3.00(6)	.40	.07

1448-51

National Parks Centennial 1452

National Parks Centennial 1454

1453

Family Planning UNITED STATES 1455

	1972. NATIONAL PARKS CENTENNIAL								
1448-54	cpl. 7 Vars.	.....	.....	.....	16.00(4)	10.25(4)	10.25(4)	2.00	1.30
1448-51	Cape Hatteras, 4 Vars., att'd	2.50	3.75	14.25(100)	5.50(8)	3.50	3.50	.48	.48
1448	2c Ship's Hull	___	___	___	___	___	___	.12	.12
1449	2c Lighthouse	___	___	___	___	___	___	.12	.12
1450	2c Three Seagulls	___	___	___	___	___	___	.12	.12
1451	2c Two Seagulls	___	___	___	___	___	___	.12	.12

SCOTT CAT. NO.	DESCRIPTION	FIRST DAY COVERS SING.	PL. BLK.	MINT SHEET	MAIL EARLY	ZIP	PLATE BLOCKS	UN-USED	USED
1452	6c Wolf Trap Farm Park	1.75	3.75	14.50(50)	2.65	1.50	1.50	.30	.18
1453	8c Yellowstone Park	1.75	3.75	22.65(50)	3.10	2.05	2.05	.48	.07
1454	15c Mt. McKinley	1.75	3.95	44.95(50)	6.00	4.00	4.00	.95	.70
1455	8c Family Planning	1.75	3.25	19.25(50)	2.75	1.75	1.75	.40	.07

1456

1457

1458

1459

1456-59	Colonial Craftsmen, 4 Vars., att'd .	5.50	8.50	32.50(50)		3.00	3.25	2.40	.....
1456	8c Glassmaker	3.75	——	——				.60	.12
1457	8c Silversmith	3.75	——	——				.60	.12
1458	8c Wigmaker	3.75	——	——				.60	.12
1459	8c Hatter	3.75	——	——				.60	.12

1460

1461

1462

1463

1460	6c Olympics-Cycling	3.25	5.50	14.50(50)	2.50	1.75	3.50(10)	.30	.20
1461	8c Olympics-Bob Sled Rcg.	3.25	5.50	19.25(50)	2.65	1.75	4.25(10)	.40	.07
1462	15c Olympics-Foot Racing	3.25	6.00	47.75(50)	6.25	4.25	10.25(10)	1.00	.95
1463	8c Parents-Teachers Assoc	1.75	3.25	19.25(50)	2.65	1.75	1.75	.40	.07
1463a	Same, Reversed Plate No.	——	——	20.00(50)			2.75	——	——

1464

1465

1466

1467

1468

1464-67	Wildlife conserv., 4 Vars., att'd.	4.50	6.00	15.25(32)	3.35	2.35	2.35	2.00	.....
1464	8c Fur Seal	2.50	——	——	——	——	——	.50	.12
1465	8c Cardinal	2.50	——	——	——	——	——	.50	.12
1466	8c Brown Pelican	2.50	——	——	——	——	——	.50	.12
1467	8c Bighorn Sheep	2.50	——	——	——	——	——	.50	.12
1468	8c Mail Order Business	1.75	3.25	19.50(50)	1.75(4)	1.75	5.25(12)	.40	.07

SCOTT CAT. NO.	DESCRIPTION	FIRST DAY COVERS SING. PL. BLK.		MINT SHEET	MAIL EARLY	ZIP	PLATE BLOCKS	UN-USED	USED

1469   1470   1471   1472

1469	8c Osteopathic Medicine	2.00	3.50	19.50(50)	2.75	1.75	2.75(6)	.40	.07
1470	8c Tom Sawyer-Folklore	1.75	3.25	19.25(50)	2.65	1.75	1.85	.40	.07
1471	8c Xmas-Virgin Mother	1.75	3.25	19.50(50)	1.75	1.75	5.25(12)	.40	.07
1472	8c Xmas-Santa Claus	1.75	3.25	19.50(50)	1.75	1.75	5.25(12)	.40	.07

1473   1474   1475

| 1473 | 8c Pharmacy .... | 2.25 | 3.75 | 19.25(50) | 2.65 | 1.75 | 1.75 | .40 | .07 |
| 1474 | 8c Stamp Collecting .... | 2.00 | 3.50 | 15.25(40) | 2.65 | 1.75 | 1.75 | .40 | .07 |

1973. COMMEMORATIVES

1475//1508 (1475-88,1488-1500, 1507-08) 22 Vars.	......	......	......	35.50(17)	31.25(17)	59.75(19)	8.95	2.40

| 1475 | 8c "Love" .... | 1.75 | 3.25 | 19.50(50) | 2.75 | 2.00 | 2.75(6) | .40 | .07 |

1476   1477   1478   1479   1480-83

COLONIAL COMMUNICATIONS

1476	8c Pamphlet Printing	2.25	3.75	19.25(50)	2.65	2.00	2.00	.40	.08
1477	8c Posting Broadside	2.25	3.75	19.25(50)	2.65	2.00	2.00	.40	.08
1478	8c Colonial Post Rider	2.25	3.75	19.25(50)	2.65	2.00	2.00	.40	.08
1479	8c Drummer & Soldiers	2.25	3.75	19.25(50)	2.65	2.00	2.00	.40	.08
1480-83	Boston Tea Party, 4 Vars., att'd. .	5.95	7.95	23.75(50)	3.35	2.25	2.35	2.00	....
1480	8c Throwing Tea	1.95	———	———	———	———	———	.50	.12
1481	8c Ship	1.95	———	———	———	———	———	.50	.12
1482	8c Rowboats	1.95	———	———	———	———	———	.50	.12
1483	8c Rowboats & Dock	1.95	———	———	———	———	———	.50	.12

SCOTT CAT. NO.	DESCRIPTION	FIRST DAY COVERS SING. PL. BLK.		MINT SHEET	MAIL EARLY	ZIP	PLATE BLOCKS	UN-USED	USED
1484	8c George Gershwin-Comp	1.75	3.25	15.75(50)	(combo)	1.75	5.35(12)	.40	.07
1485	8c Robinson Jeffers-Poet	1.75	3.25	15.75(50)	(combo)	1.75	5.35(12)	.40	.07
1486	8c Henry O. Tanner-Artist	1.75	3.25	15.75(50)	(combo)	1.75	5.35(12)	.40	.07
1487	8c Willa Cather-Novelist	1.75	3.25	15.75(50)	(combo)	1.75	5.35(12)	.40	.07
1488	8c Nicolaus Copernicus	2.75	4.25	19.25(50)	2.65	1.75	1.75	.40	.07

POSTAL SERVICE EMPLOYEES

1489-98	cpl., 10 Vars., att'd	7.25	10.50	25.00(50)	___	___	10.65(20)	5.20	. . . . .
1489-93	cpl., 5 Vars., att'd	___	___				5.45(10)	. . . . .	. . . . .
1494-98	cpl., 5 Vars., att'd	___	___				5.45(10)	. . . . .	. . . . .
1489	8c Window Clerk	2.50	___	___	___	___	___	.52	.15
1490	8c Mail Pickup	2.50	___	___	___	___	___	.52	.15
1491	8c Conveyor Belt	2.50	___	___	___	___	___	.52	.15
1492	8c Sacking Parcels	2.50	___	___	___	___	___	.52	.15
1493	8c Mail Cancelling	2.50	___	___	___	___	___	.52	.15
1494	8c Manual Sorting	2.50	___	___	___	___	___	.52	.15
1495	8c Machine Sorting	2.50	___	___	___	___	___	.52	.15
1496	8c Loading Truck	2.50	___	___	___	___	___	.52	.15
1497	8c Letter Carrier	2.50	___	___	___	___	___	.52	.15
1498	8c Rural Delivery	2.50	___	___	___	___	___	.52	.15

SCOTT CAT. NO.	DESCRIPTION	FIRST DAY COVERS SING. PL. BLK.		MINT SHEET	MAIL EARLY	ZIP	PLATE BLOCKS	UN-USED	USED

1500

1501

1502

1499

1504

1505

1506

1503

1499	8c Harry S. Truman	1.75	3.25	12.50(32)	——	——	1.75	.40	.07
1500	6c Electronics	2.25	4.75	14.95(50)	2.65	1.75	2.00	.30	.18
1501	8c Electronics	2.25	4.75	19.25(50)	2.65	1.75	1.75	.40	.07
1502	15c Electronics	2.25	6.50	36.95(50)	4.75	3.50	4.25	.75	.75
1503	8c Lyndon B. Johnson	1.75	3.25	12.75(32)	——	——	5.25(12)	.40	.07

1973-74. RURAL AMERICA

1504	8c Angus Cattle	1.75	3.25	19.25(50)	3.00	1.75	1.75	.40	.07
1505	10c Chautauqua(1974)	1.75	3.25	23.95(50)	3.25	2.25	2.50	.50	.07
1506	10c Winter Wheat (1974)	1.75	3.25	23.95(50)	3.25	2.25	2.50	.50	.07

1509, 1519

1510 ,1520

1511

1518

1507

1508

1973 CHRISTMAS

1507	8c Madonna	1.95	4.75	19.25(50)	2.65	1.75	5.15(12)	.40	.07
1508	8c Christmas Tree	1.95	4.75	19.25(50)	2.65	1.75	5.15(12)	.40	.07

1973-74. REGULAR ISSUES

1509-20	6 Vars., cpl.	.....	.....	.....	.....	.....	15.95(3)	2.75	.70
1509	10c Crossed Flags	1.75	3.25	47.50(100)	——	——	10.50(20)	.50	.07
1510	10c Jefferson Memorial	1.75	3.25	47.50(100)	3.25	2.25	2.25	.50	.07
1511	10c Zip Code Theme	1.75	3.25	47.50(100)	3.25	2.25	4.15(8)	.50	.07

COIL STAMPS Perf. 10 Vertically

			PAIR				LINE PR.		
1518	6.3c Liberty Bell	1.75	——	——	——	——	1.25	.40	.40
1519	10c Crossed Flags	1.75	1.95	——	——	——	——	.50	.07
1520	10c Jefferson Memorial	1.75	1.95	——	——	——	1.25	.50	.07

NOTE: Pairs of the above can be supplied at two times the single price. For FDC Line Pairs please send Want List.

SCOTT CAT. NO.	DESCRIPTION	FIRST DAY COVERS SING. PL. BLK.		MINT SHEET	MAIL EARLY	ZIP	PLATE BLOCK	UN-USED	USED

1525

1527

1528

Robert Frost
AMERICAN POET
1526

1529

1974. COMMEMORATIVES

SCOTT CAT. NO.	DESCRIPTION	SING.	PL. BLK.	MINT SHEET	MAIL EARLY	ZIP	PLATE BLOCK	UN-USED	USED
1505//52	(1505-06, 25-29, 38-52) 22 Vars.	.....	.....	.....	43.95(14)	39.25(17)	58.50(16)	11.25	1.80
1525	10c Veterans of Fgn. Wars	1.75	3.00	23.95(50)	3.25	2.25	2.50	.50	.07
1526	10c Robert Frost	1.75	3.00	23.95(50)	3.25	2.25	2.50	.50	.07
1527	10c Environment-Expo. 74	1.75	3.00	19.50(40)	(combo)	2.25	6.25(12)	.50	.07
1528	10c Horse Racing	1.75	3.00	23.95(50)	3.25	2.25	6.25(12)	.50	.07
1529	10c Skylab Project	2.00	3.95	23.95(50)	3.25	2.25	2.50	.50	.07

1530

1532

1533

1534

1535

1536

1537

1974. UNIVERSAL POSTAL UNION

1530-37	8 Vars., att'd	5.50	7.95(4)	14.95(32)			7.25(16)	4.25(8)	....
1530-37	6 Vars., att'd	---	---	---	(combo)	3.25(6)	6.00(10)	---	---

SCOTT CAT. NO.	DESCRIPTION	FIRST DAY COVERS		MINT SHEET	MAIL EARLY	ZIP	PLATE BLOCK	UN-USED	USED
		SING.	PL. BLK.						
1530	10c Raphael	1.75	———	———	———	———	———	.50	.40
1531	10c Hokusai	1.75	———	———	———	———	———	.50	.40
1532	10c J.F. Peto	1.75	———	———	———	———	———	.50	.40
1533	10c J.E. Liotard	1.75	———	———	———	———	———	.50	.40
1534	10c G. Terborch	1.75	———	———	———	———	———	.50	.40
1535	10c J.B.S. Chardin	1.75	———	———	———	———	———	.50	.40
1536	10c T. Gainsborough	1.75	———	———	———	———	———	.50	.40
1537	10c F. deGoya	1.75	———	———	———	———	———	.50	.40

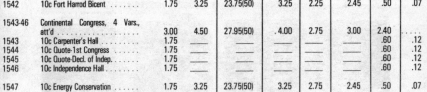

1538   1539   1540   1541

1538-41	Mineral Heritage 4 Vars., att'd . . .	4.00	5.25	26.95(48)	4.00	2.75	2.75	2.40	. . . .
1538	10c Petrified Wood	1.85	———	———	———	———	———	.60	.12
1539	10c Tourmaline	1.85	———	———	———	———	———	.60	.12
1540	10c Amethyst	1.85	———	———	———	———	———	.60	.12
1541	10c Rhodochrosite	1.85	———	———	———	———	———	.60	.12

1542   1543   1544   1545   1546   1547

1542	10c Fort Harrod Bicent	1.75	3.25	23.75(50)	3.25	2.25	2.45	.50	.07
1543-46	Continental Congress, 4 Vars., att'd	3.00	4.50	27.95(50)	.4.00	2.75	3.00	2.40	. . . .
1543	10c Carpenter's Hall	1.75	———	———	———	———	———	.60	.12
1544	10c Quote-1st Congress	1.75	———	———	———	———	———	.60	.12
1545	10c Quote-Decl. of Indep.	1.75	———	———	———	———	———	.60	.12
1546	10c Independence Hall	1.75	———	———	———	———	———	.60	.12
1547	10c Energy Conservation	1.75	3.25	23.75(50)	3.25	2.75	2.45	.50	.07

1549

1548

| 1548 | 10c Sleepy Hollow . . . . | 1.75 | 3.25 | 27.95(50) | 4.00 | 2.50 | 2.50 | .60 | .07 |
| 1549 | 10c Retarded Children . . . . | 1.75 | 3.25 | 23.75(50) | 3.25 | 2.25 | 2.45 | .50 | .07 |

SCOTT CAT. NO.	DESCRIPTION	FIRST DAY COVERS SING. PL. BLK.		MINT SHEET	MAIL EARLY	ZIP	PLATE BLOCK	UN-USED	USED
1550	10c Christmas-Angel	1.75	3.25	23.50(50)	3.25	2.25	5.25(10)	.50	.07
1551	10c Xmas-Currier & Ives	1.75	3.25	23.75(50)	2.25(4)	2.25	6.00(10)	.50	.07
1552	10c Xmas-Dove of Peace	1.75	3.25	27.50(50)	—	—	12.95(20)	.50	.07
1552	Same	—	—	—	—	—	9.90(12)	—	—

1553   1554   1555   1556   1557   1558

1975. COMMEMORATIVES

SCOTT CAT. NO.	DESCRIPTION	FIRST DAY COVERS SING. PL. BLK.		MINT SHEET	MAIL EARLY	ZIP	PLATE BLOCK	UN-USED	USED
1553-80	29 Vars. cpl.	.....	.....	.....	53.25(17)	46.95(20)	104.50(20)	14.95	2.95
1553	10c Benjamin West-Arts	1.75	3.25	26.00(50)	3.50	2.45	5.65(10)	.55	.07
1554	10c Paul Dunbar-Arts	1.75	3.25	23.50(50)	3.25	2.25	5.50(10)	.50	.07
1555	10c D.W. Griffith-Arts	1.75	3.25	23.75(50)	3.25	2.25	2.45	.50	.07
1556	10c Pioneer 10	2.50	4.25	23.75(50)	3.25	2.25	2.45	.50	.07
1557	10c Mariner 10	2.50	4.25	23.75(50)	3.25	2.25	2.45	.50	.07
1558	10c Collective Bargaining	1.75	3.25	23.50(50)	3.25	2.25	4.75	.50	.07

1559   1560   1561   1562

CONTRIBUTORS TO THE CAUSE

SCOTT CAT. NO.	DESCRIPTION	FIRST DAY COVERS SING. PL. BLK.		MINT SHEET	MAIL EARLY	ZIP	PLATE BLOCK	UN-USED	USED
1559	8c Sybil Ludington	1.85	3.50	20.25(50)	2.65	1.75	5.25(10)	.40	.27
1560	10c Salem Poor	1.85	3.50	23.95(50)	3.25	2.25	5.25(10)	.50	.07
1561	10c Haym Salomon	1.85	3.50	23.95(50)	3.25	2.25	5.25(10)	.50	.07
1562	18c Peter Francisco	1.95	4.25	46.75(50)	5.50	3.85	13.00(10)	.90	.85

SCOTT CAT. NO.	DESCRIPTION	FIRST DAY COVERS SING.	PL. BLK.	MINT SHEET	MAIL EARLY	ZIP	PLATE BLOCK	UN- USED	USED

1563   US Bicentennial 10 cents   1564   US Bicentennial 10c   1565   1566   1567   1568

1563	10c Lexington-Concord	1.75	3.50	21.00(40)	(combo)	2.35	6.75(12)	.55	.07
1564	10c Battle of Bunker Hill	1.75	3.50	21.00(40)	(combo)	2.35	6.75(12)	.55	.07
1565-68	Military Uniforms, 4 Vars., att'd. .	3.25	4.50	28.95(50)	2.85(4)	2.85	8.00(12)	2.40	. . . . .
1565	10c Continental Army	1.75	___	___	___	___	___	.60	.10
1566	10c Continental Navy	1.75	___	___	___	___	___	.60	.10
1567	10c Continental Marine	1.75	___	___	___	___	___	.60	.10
1568	10c American Militia	1.75	___	___	___	___	___	.60	.10

1569   1570

1569-70	Apollo-Soyuz Mission, 2 Vars., att'd	4.00	5.50	13.75(24)	(combo)	2.85	7.40(12)	1.16	. . . . .
1569	10c Docked	2.50	___	___	___	___	___	.58	.10
1570	10c Docking	2.50	___	___	___	___	___	.58	.10

1571   1572   1573   1574   1575   1576

| 1571 | 10c Int'l Womens' Year . . . . . . | 1.75 | 3.25 | 23.50(50) | 3.25 | 2.25 | 3.25(6) | .50 | .07 |
| 1572-75 | Postal Service Bicent., 4 Vars., att'd . . . . | 3.50 | 5.50 | 29.25(50) | 3.00(4) | 3.00 | 8.25(12) | 2.60 | . . . . |

NOTE: To determine the VF price on stamps issued from 1941 to date, add 15% to the F/NH or F (used) price (minimum .03 per item). All VF unused stamps from 1941 to date will be NH. From 1964 to date all unused stamps are F/NH.

SCOTT CAT. NO.	DESCRIPTION	FIRST DAY COVERS SING.	PL. BLK.	MINT SHEET	MAIL EARLY	ZIP	PLATE BLOCK	UN-USED	USED
1572	10c Stagecoach & Trailer	2.00	——	——	——	——	——	.65	.08
1573	10c Locomotives	2.00	——	——	——	——	——	.65	.08
1574	10c Airplanes	2.00	——	——	——	——	——	.65	.08
1575	10c Satellite	2.00	——	——	——	——	——	.65	.08
1576	10c World Peace thru Law	1.75	3.25	23.50(50)	3.25	2.25	2.25	.50	.07

1577

1578

1579

1580

SCOTT CAT. NO.	DESCRIPTION	FIRST DAY COVERS SING.	PL. BLK.	MINT SHEET	MAIL EARLY	ZIP	PLATE BLOCK	UN-USED	USED
1577-78	Banking & Commerce 2 Vars., att'd	2.00	3.50	24.50(40)	4.00	2.80	2.80	1.30	....
1577	10c Banking	1.75	——	——	——	——	——	.65	.08
1578	10c Commerce	1.75	——	——	——	——	——	.65	.08
1579	(10c) Madonna	1.75	3.25	26.25(50)	2.45(4)	2.45	6.75(12)	.55	.07
1580	(10c) Xmas Card	1.75	3.25	26.25(50)	2.45(4)	2.45	6.75(12)	.55	.07
1580b	(10c) Xmas Card. pf. 10½ x 11	......	......	80.95(50)	8.25(4)	8.25	22.50(12)	1.65	.15

1581, 1811   **1582**   **1584**   **1585**   **1590, 1591, 1616**

1592, 1617   **1593**   **1594, 1816**   **1595, 1618**   **1596**

1597, 1598, 1618C   **1599, 1619**   **1603**   **1604**   **1605**

1606   **1608**   **1610**   **1611**   **1612**

FOR YOUR CONVENIENCE IN ORDERING, COMPLETE SETS ARE LISTED BEFORE SINGLE STAMP LISTINGS

SCOTT CAT. NO.	DESCRIPTION	FIRST DAY COVERS SING.	PL. BLK.	MINT SHEET	COPY-RIGHT	ZIP	PLATE BLOCK	UN-USED	USED
	1975-81 AMERICANA ISSUE								
1581-1612	22 Vars., cpl (No. 1590a or bkIt. pairs)		.....	.....	125.00(18)	120.00(18)	150.00(19)	32.95	8.25
1581	1c Inkwell & Quill	2.00	4.75	2.75(100)	.55	.40	.40	.07	.07
1582	2c Speaker's Stand	2.00	4.75	6.75(100)	.55	.40	.55	.07	.07
1584	3c Ballot Box	2.00	4.75	7.75(100)	.65	.50	.60	.08	.07
1585	4c Books & Eyeglasses	2.00	4.75	10.25(100)	.75	.60	.60	.11	.07
1581-85	USPS Format FDC	2.75							
1590	9c Capitol, white paper, from b. pane	.....		———	———	———	———	2.75	.55
1590a	Same Pf. 10	.....		———	———	———	———	50.00	
1590,1623	Attd. Pr., from b. pane							3.50	
1590a, 1623b	Attd. Pr., Pf. 10							55.00	.....
1591	9c Capitol, grey paper	2.00	5.00	33.50(100)	2.75	1.80	2.25	.35	.07
1592	10c Justice	2.00	5.00	38.50(100)	2.65	1.75	2.55	.40	.07
1593	11c Printing Press	2.00	5.00	52.50(100)	3.45	2.35	2.55	.55	.07
1594	12c Torch	pr. 3.00	5.00	37.95(100)	2.65	1.75	1.95	.40	.15
1595	13c Liberty Bell	2.25						.65	.07
1596	13c Eagle & Shield	2.25	4.00	62.50(100)	2.65	2.65	8.30(12)	.65	.07
1597	15c Fort McHenry Flag	2.25	4.00	72.75(100)	———	———	15.95(20)	.75	.07
1598	Same, from blk. pane	2.25						.85	.07
1599	16c Statue of Liberty	2.75	7.50	77.00(100)	3.35	3.35	4.50	.80	.12
1603	24c Old North Church	2.75	7.50	115.00(100)	7.35	5.00	6.35	1.20	.09
1604	28c Fort Nisqually	2.75	11.00	134.00(100)	5.85	5.85	7.00	1.40	.10
1605	29c Lighthouse	3.75	11.00	140.00(100)	6.00	6.00	8.65	1.45	.15
1606	30c School House	4.00	11.50	92.50(100)	4.05	4.05	4.15	.95	.15
1608	50c "Betty" Lamp	4.25	15.00	130.00(100)	7.00	7.00	7.00	1.50	.30
1610	$1 Rush Lamp	7.25	20.00	225.00(100)	11.50	11.50	11.50	2.50	.30
1611	$2 Kerosene Lamp	11.50	50.00	450.00(100)	22.00	22.00	22.00	5.00	1.00
1612	$5 Conductor's Lantern	20.00	80.00	1150.00(100)	52.50	52.50	52.50	12.50	5.00

Copyright inscriptions replaced "Mail Early in the Day" inscriptions beginning in 1978; numbers 1599 and 1604-12 sheets all bear the Copyright inscription.

1613   1614   1615   1615C

1978-79. COIL STAMPS. Perforated Vertically
PAIR   **LINE PR.**

SCOTT CAT. NO.	DESCRIPTION						PLATE BLOCK	LINE PR.	USED
1613-19	9 Varieties, cpl	———	———	———	———	———	18.25(8)	4.50	1.15
1613	3.1c Guitar	2.00		———	———	———	1.85	.25	.15
1614	7.7c Saxhorns	2.00		———	———	———	2.95	.63	.20
1615	7.9c Drum	2.00		———	———	———	2.75	.65	.20
1615C	8.4c Piano	2.00		———	———	———	2.75	.42	.12
1616	9c Capitol	2.00		———	———	———	1.85	.45	.12
1617	10c Justice	2.00		———	———	———	1.65	.40	.10
1618	13c Liberty Bell	2.00		———	———	———	1.85	.45	.07
1618C	15c Fort McHenry	2.00		———	———	———	———	.75	.07
1619	16c Statue of Liberty	2.00	2.50	———	———	———	4.75	.80	.20

NOTE: Pairs of the above coils and #1625 can be supplied at two times the single price. For FDC Line Pairs send Want List.

SCOTT CAT. NO.	DESCRIPTION	FIRST DAY COVERS SING. PL. BLK.		MINT SHEET	MAIL EARLY	ZIP	PLATE BLOCK	UN-USED	USED

1622, 1622c, 1625   1623, 1623b

1975-81 REGULAR ISSUES

1622	13c Flag & Ind. Hall, pf 11 x 10½	1.75	3.25	78.00(100)	——	——	17.50(20)	.80	.07
1622c	13c Flag & Ind. Hall, pf 11	. . . . .	. . . . .	64.50(100)	——	——	15.50(20)	.65	.07
1623	13c Flag & Capitol	. . . . .	——	——	——	——	——	.75	.07
1623b	Same, from Bklt. Pane, perf. 10 . .	. . . . .	——	——	——	——	——	2.95	. . . . .

1975. COIL STAMP

1625	13c Flag & Ind. Hall	1.95	pr. 2.15	——	——	——	——	.95	.07

1629   1630   1631   1632

1976. COMMEMORATIVES

1629//1703	(1629-32, 83-85, 1690-1703) 21 Vars.	. . . . .	. . . . .		37.95(9)	39.50(13)	99.95(13)	16.75	1.65
1629-31	Spirit of '76, 3 Vars., att'd	2.50	4.50	35.95(50)	(combo)	6.50(8)	9.50(12)	2.25	. . . . .
1629	13c Boy Drummer	1.75	——	——	——	——	——	.75	.09
1630	13c Older Drummer	1.75	——	——	——	——	——	.75	.09
1631	13c Fifer	1.75	——	——	——	——	——	.75	.09
1632	13c Interphil	1.75	3.25	31.75(50)	4.15	2.85	3.45	.65	.07

1976 BICENTENNIAL STATE FLAGS

1633   1650

1633 Delaware	1650 Louisiana	1667 West Virginia
1634 Pennsylvania	1651 Indiana	1668 Nevada
1635 New Jersey	1652 Mississippi	1669 Nebraska
1636 Georgia	1653 Illinois	1670 Colorado
1637 Connecticut	1654 Alabama	1671 North Dakota
1638 Massachusetts	1655 Maine	1672 South Dakota
1639 Maryland	1656 Missouri	1673 Montana
1640 South Carolina	1657 Arkansas	1674 Washington
1641 New Hampshire	1658 Michigan	1675 Idaho
1642 Virginia	1659 Florida	1676 Wyoming
1643 New York	1660 Texas	1677 Utah
1644 North Carolina	1661 Iowa	1678 Oklahoma
1645 Rhode Island	1662 Wisconsin	1679 New Mexico
1646 Vermont	1663 California	1680 Arizona
1647 Kentucky	1664 Minnesota	1681 Alaska
1648 Tennessee	1665 Oregon	1682 Hawaii
1649 Ohio	1666 Kansas	

1638   1682

1633-82	State Flags 50 Vars., att'd	137.50(50)	——	45.00(50)	——	——	45.00(50)	45.00	32.95
	Singles of above	2.95	——	——	——	——	——	.90	.70
	Inscription Blocks				4.00(4)	4.00	11.50(12)		

NOTE: Plate, Zip, and Mail Early blocks are available with their respective marginal inscriptions in upper left, lower left, upper right, or lower right position in the block. Please specify UL, LL, UR, or LR when ordering.

SCOTT CAT. NO.	DESCRIPTION	FIRST DAY COVERS SING.	PL. BLK.	MINT SHEET	MAIL EARLY	ZIP	PLATE BLOCK	UN-USED	USED
		1683		1684			1685		
1683	13c Telephone	1.75	3.25	33.50(50)	4.45	3.00	3.25	.70	.07
1684	13c Aviation	1.75	3.25	31.25(50)	4.15	2.85	7.50(10)	.65	.07
1685	13c Chemistry	1.75	3.25	31.25(50)	2.85(4)	2.85	9.00(12)	.65	.07

1686

1687

1688

1689

		FIRST DAY COVERS	UNUSED	USED
1686-89	65c to 1.55, 4 Vars., complete	49.00	52.50	. . . . .
1686	65c Surrender of Cornwalis at Yorktown	10.00	7.75	. . . . .
1687	90c Signing of the Declaration of Independence	12.00	11.00	. . . . .
1688	$1.20 Washington Crossing the Delaware	12.00	15.00	. . . . .
1689	$1.55 Washington Reviewing Army at Valley Forge	15.00	19.00	. . . . .
1686a-89c	Set of 20 singles on 20 FDC	47.50	—	—

BICENTENNIAL EMBLEM BLOCKS OF 6

1456-59	8c Craftsmen	4.25	1479	8c Drummer	2.65
1477	8c Broadside	2.65	1480-83	8c Tea Party	3.45
1478	8c Post Rider	2.65	1543-46	10c Cont. Cong.	3.95

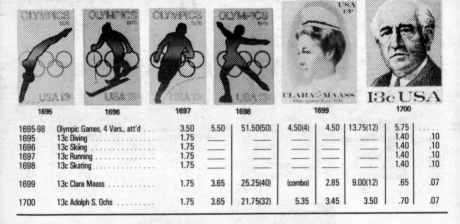

SCOTT NO.	DESCRIPTION	FIRST DAY COVERS SING.	PL. BLK.	MINT SHEET	MAIL EARLY	ZIP	PLATE BLOCK	UN-USED	USED
1690	13c Benjamin Franklin	1.75	3.25	35.50(50)	5.25	3.45	3.50	.75	.07
1691-94	Declaration of Independence 4 Vars., att'd	4.25	6.25	35.50(50)	(combo)	3.45	12.75(16)	3.12	. . . . .
1691	13c Delegation members	1.95	———	———	———	———	———	.78	.10
1692	13c Adams, etc	1.95	———	———	———	———	———	.78	.10
1693	13c Jefferson, Franklin etc.	1.95	———	———	———	———	———	.78	.10
1694	13c Hancock, Thomson etc.	1.95	———	———	———	———	———	.78	.10

NOTE: Specify Zip 1691-92 or 1693-94

SCOTT NO.	DESCRIPTION	FIRST DAY COVERS SING.	PL. BLK.	MINT SHEET	MAIL EARLY	ZIP	PLATE BLOCK	UN-USED	USED
1695-98	Olympic Games, 4 Vars., att'd . . .	3.50	5.50	51.50(50)	4.50(4)	4.50	13.75(12)	5.75	. . . . .
1695	13c Diving	1.75	———	———	———	———	———	1.40	.10
1696	13c Skiing	1.75	———	———	———	———	———	1.40	.10
1697	13c Running	1.75	———	———	———	———	———	1.40	.10
1698	13c Skating	1.75	———	———	———	———	———	1.40	.10
1699	13c Clara Maass	1.75	3.65	25.25(40)	(combo)	2.85	9.00(12)	.65	.07
1700	13c Adolph S. Ochs	1.75	3.65	21.75(32)	5.35	3.45	3.50	.70	.07

1976 through 1979 COMMEMORATIVES

Every commemorative postage stamp (160 different) issued from, 1976 through 1979 including State Flags and the popular Bicentennial Souvenir Sheets.

#A156 Unused $146.50 (SAVE $38.70)   #A166 Used $37.50 (SAVE $6.68)

NOTE: BICENTENNIAL & CAPEX S/S are not included in the used offer.

25 REGULAR ISSUE PLATE BLOCKS
All different issued from 1926 through 1974

Offer #A391 (SAVE $11.10) . . . . .Special Price $45.50

SCOTT CAT. NO.	DESCRIPTION	FIRST DAY COVERS SING. PL. BLK.		MINT SHEET	MAIL EARLY	ZIP	PLATE BLOCK	UN-USED	USED

1701

1702, 1703

1704

13

1705

1701	13c Nativity	1.75	3.65	30.95(50)	2.85(4)	2.85	9.00(12)	.65	.07
1702	13c "Winter Pastime"	1.75	3.65	30.95(50)	4.15	2.85	7.00(10)	.65	.07
1703	13c "Winter Pastime"(Gravure Int.)	1.75	3.65	33.75(50)			15.75(20)	.65	.07

1702: Marginal Inscription ½ millimeters below design. Black lettering.
1703: Marginal Inscription ¾ millimeters below design. Grey black lettering.

1977 COMMEMORATIVES

1704-30	27 Vars., cpl.	.....	.....	38.95(11)	47.75(16)	113.50(17)	18.95	2.10

Pueblo Art USA 13c

1706

Pueblo Art USA 13c

1707

Pueblo Art USA 13c

1708

Pueblo Art USA 13c

1709

1704	13c Princeton	1.75	3.65	28.95(40)	combo	3.25	8.00(10)	.75	.07
1705	13c Sound Recording	1.75	3.65	31.75(50	4.15	2.85	3.45	.65	.07
1706-09	Pueblo Art 4 Vars., att'd	5.00	6.50	31.95(40)	(combo)	5.25(6)	8.75(10)	3.12	.....
1706	13c Zia	1.75	___	___	___	___	___	.78	.10
1707	13c San Ildefonso	1.75	___	___	___	___	___	.78	.10
1708	13c Hopi	1.75	___	___	___	___	___	.78	.10
1709	13c Acoma	1.75	___	___	___	___	___	.78	.10

USA 13c

1710

COLORADO

1711

13c

SCOTT CAT. NO.	DESCRIPTION	FIRST DAY COVERS SING.	FIRST DAY COVERS PL. BLK.	MINT SHEET	MAIL EARLY	ZIP	PLATE BLOCK	UN-USED	USED
1710	13c Transatlantic Flight	1.75	3.65	31.25(50)	2.85(4)	2.85	9.00(12)	.65	.07
1711	13c Colorado Statehood	1.75	3.65	31.25(50)	2.85(4)	2.85	9.00(12)	.65	.07

1712    **1713**

1716

1714   **1715**

1712-15	Butterflies, 4 Vars., att'd	2.95	4.25	37.75(50)	3.40(4)	3.40	9.75(12)	3.20	. . . .
1712	13c Swallowtail	1.75						.80	.10
1713	13c Checkerspot	1.75						.80	.10
1714	13c Dogface	1.75						.80	.10
1715	13c Orange-Tip	1.75						.80	.10
1716	13c Lafayette	1.75	3.65	25.75(40)	4.15	2.85	3.45	.65	.07

1717    **1718**    **1719**    **1720**

1717-20	Skilled Hands, 4 Vars., att'd	2.95	4.25	37.75(50)	3.40(4)	3.40	9.75(12)	3.20	. . . .
1717	13c Seamstress	1.75						.80	.10
1718	13c Blacksmith	1.75						.80	.10
1719	13c Wheelwright	1.75						.80	.10
1720	13c Leatherworker	1.75						.80	.10

1721    **1722**    **1723**    **1724**

1721	13c Peace Bridge	1.75	3.65	31.75(50)	4.15	2.85	3.45	.65	.07
1722	13c Herkimer at Oriskany	1.75	3.65	25.95(50)	(combo)	2.85	7.50(10)	.65	.07
1723-24	Energy, 2 Vars.,att'd	2.35	3.95	29.75(40)	(combo)	3.45	9.75(12)	1.60	. . . .
1723	13c Conservation	1.75						.80	.08
1724	13c Development	1.75						.80	.08

1725    **1726**    **1727**    **1728**

SCOTT CAT. NO.	DESCRIPTION	FIRST DAY COVERS SING.	PL. BLK.	MINT SHEET	MAIL EARLY	ZIP	PLATE BLOCK	UN-USED	USED
1725	13c Alta California	1.75	3.65	31.75(50)	4.15	2.85	3.45	.65	.07
1726	13c Articles of Confederation ...	1.75	3.65	31.75(50)	4.15	2.85	3.45	.65	.07
1727	13c Talking Pictures	1.75	3.65	31.75(50)	4.15	2.85	3.45	.65	.07
1728	13c Surrender at Saratoga	1.75	3.65	26.25(40)	(combo)	2.85	8.00(10)	.65	.07

1729   1730   1731   1732   1733

1729	13c Washington, Xmas	1.75	3.65	64.50(100)	___	___	15.75(20)	.65	.07
1730	13c Rural Mailbox, Xmas	1.75	3.65	63.50(100)	4.15	2.85	7.00(10)	.65	.07

SCOTT CAT. NO.	DESCRIPTION	FIRST DAY COVERS SING.	PL. BLK.	MINT SHEET	COPY-RIGHT	ZIP	PLATE BLOCK	UN-USED	USED
		1978. COMMMEMORATIVES							
1731/69	(1731-33, 44-56, 58-69) 28 Vars.,.........	.....		.....	32.25(12)	48.95(16)	111.95(16)	21.75	2.20
1731	13c Carl Sandburg	1.75	3.45	31.50(50)	2.85	2.85	3.45	.65	.07
1732-33	Captain Cook, 2 Vars., att'd	2.50	___	33.95(50)			15.75(20)	1.35	.....
1732	13c Capt. Cook (Alaska)	1.75	3.45	___	2.85	2.85	3.45	.65	.08
1733	13c "Resolution"(Hawaii)	1.75	3.45	___	2.85	2.85	3.45	.65	.08

NOTE: The Plate Block set includes #1732 & 1733 P.B.'s of 4.

1734   1735, 1736, 1743   1737   1738   1739   1740   1741   1742

1978-80. Definitives

1734	13c Indian Head Penny	1.95	3.95	99.95(150)	4.50	4.50	8.75	.67	.10
1735	15c "A" Definitive (Gravure)	1.75	3.45	77.50(100)	5.25(M.E.)	3.45	3.50	.82	.07
1736	Same, (Intagio), from booklet pane	1.75						.75	.07
1737	15c Roses	1.75						.75	.07
1738-42	Windmills Strip of 5, att'd	5.00	___	___	___	___		3.75	
1738	15c Virginia Windmill	2.25	___	___				.75	.08
1739	15c Rhode Island Windmill	2.25	___	___				.75	.08
1740	15c Massachusetts Windmill	2.25	___	___				.75	.08
1741	15c Illinois Windmill	2.25	___	___				.75	.08
1742	15c Texas Windmill	2.25	___	___				.75	.08

1978. COIL STAMP

LINE PR.

1743	15c "A" Definitive	2.50		___	___	___		.75	.07
1743	Same, pair	3.00		___	___	___	1.95	1.50	.....

SCOTT CAT. NO.	DESCRIPTION	FIRST DAY COVERS SING.	PL. BLK.	MINT SHEET	COPY-RIGHT	ZIP	PLATE BLOCK	UN-USED	USED

1744

1745

1746

1747

1748

1744	13c Harriet Tubman	1.75	3.65	31.95(50)	2.85	2.85	9.00(12)	.65	.07
1745-48	Quilts, 4 Vars., att'd	3.00	4.25	37.50(48)	(combo)	3.55	10.00(12)	3.28	
1745	13c Flowers	1.75	———	———			———	.82	.10
1746	13c Stars	1.75	———	———			———	.82	.10
1747	13c Stripes	1.75	———	———			———	.82	.10
1748	13c Plaid	1.75	———	———			———	.82	.10

1749

1750

1751

1752

1749-52	American Dance 4 Vars., att'd ...	3.00	4.25	37.50(48)	(combo)	3.50	10.00(12)	3.28	.....
1749	13c Ballet	1.75	———	———			———	.82	.10
1750	13c Theatre	1.75	———	———			———	.82	.10
1751	13c Folk	1.75	———	———			———	.82	.10
1752	13c Modern	1.75	———	———			———	.82	.10

1753

1754

1755

1756

1753	13c French Alliance	1.75	3.75	25.25(40)	2.85	2.85	3.45	.65	.07
1754	13c Dr. Papanicolaou	1.75	3.75	31.50(50)	2.85	2.85	3.45	.65	.07
1755	13c Jimmie Rodgers	1.75	3.75	31.25(50)	2.85	2.85	9.00(12)	.65	.10
1756	15c George M. Cohan	1.75	3.75	36.75(50)	3.10	3.10	10.25(12)	.75	.07

SCOTT CAT. NO.	DESCRIPTION	FIRST DAY COVERS SING. PL. BLK.		MINT SHEET	COPY-RIGHT	ZIP	PLATE BLOCK	UN-USED	USED

Canadian International Philatelic Exhibition
Toronto

1757

Photography USA 15c
1758

Viking missions to Mars
1759

1978 CAPEX SOUVENIR SHEET

1757	$1.04 CAPEX	6.00	. . . .	29.75(6)	(combo)	5.35	5.35	5.20	. . . .
1757a-h	Same, 8 Vars., att'd	. . . .	. . . .	___	___	___	___	5.35	. . . .
1757a	13c Cardinal	1.75	___	___	___	___	___	.65	. . . .
1757b	13c Mallard	1.75	___	___	___	___	___	.65	. . . .
1757c	13c Canada Goose	1.75	___	___	___	___	___	.65	. . . .
1757d	13c Blue Jay	1.75	___	___	___	___	___	.65	. . . .
1757e	13c Moose	1.75	___	___	___	___	___	.65	. . . .
1757f	13c Chipmunk	1.75	___	___	___	___	___	.65	. . . .
1757g	13c Red Fox	1.75	___	___	___	___	___	.65	. . . .
1757h	13c Raccoon	1.75	___	___	___	___	___	.65	. . . .

NOTE: Singles are minor numbers starting with upper left stamp.

1758	15c Photography	1.75	3.85	29.50(40)	(combo)	3.10	10.00(12)	.75	.07
1759	15c Viking Mission	1.75	3.85	37.25(50)	3.15	3.15	5.00	.75	.07

1760

1761

1762

1763

1768

1769

1764

1765

1766

1767

NOTE: Plate, Zip, and Mail Early blocks are available with their respective marginal inscriptions in upper left, lower left, upper right, or lower right position in the block. Please specify UL, LL, UR, or LR when ordering.

SCOTT CAT. NO.	DESCRIPTION	FIRST DAY COVERS SING.	PL. BLK.	MINT SHEET	COPY- RIGHT	ZIP	PLATE BLOCK	UN- USED	USED
1760-63	American Owls, 4 vars. att'd.	2.75	4.00	47.50(50)	4.65	4.65	4.75	4.00	.....
1760	15c Great Gray	1.75	—	—	—	—	—	1.00	.09
1761	15c Saw-Whet	1.75	—	—	—	—	—	1.00	.09
1762	15c Barred Owl	1.75	—	—	—	—	—	1.00	.09
1763	15c Great Horned	1.75	—	—	—	—	—	1.00	.09
1764-67	Trees, 4 Vars., att'd	2.75	4.00	39.50(40)	(combo)	4.35	13.50(12)	4.00	.....
1764	15c Giant Sequoia	1.75	—	—	—	—	—	1.00	.09
1765	15c Pine	1.75	—	—	—	—	—	1.00	.09
1766	15c Oak	1.75	—	—	—	—	—	1.00	.09
1767	15c Birch	1.75	—	—	—	—	—	1.00	.09
1768	15c Madonna, Xmas	1.75	4.00	71.50(100)	3.10	3.10	9.75(12)	.75	.07
1769	15c Hobby Horse, Xmas	1.75	4.00	71.50(100)	3.10	3.10	9.75(12)	.75	.07

1770

1771

1772

1773

1774

1979. COMMEMORATIVES

1770/1802 (1770-94, 1799-1802) 29 Vars. cpl.					47.50(15)	54.50(16)	132.50(17)	21.50	2.50
1770	15c Robert F. Kennedy	1.75	4.00	32.25(48)	3.00	3.00	3.10	.70	.07
1771	15c Martin L. King Jr.	1.75	4.00	35.75(50)	3.00	3.00	10.50(12)	.70	.07
1772	15c Int'l. Year of the Child	1.75	4.00	33.50(50)	3.00	3.00	3.10	.70	.07
1773	15c John Steinbeck	1.75	4.00	33.50(50)	3.00	3.00	3.10	.70	.07
1774	15c Albert Einstein	1.75	4.00	33.50(50)	3.00	3.00	3.10	.70	.07

Folk Art USA 15c
1775

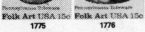
Folk Art USA 15c
1776

Architecture USA 15c
1779

Architecture USA 15c
1780

1783

1784

Folk Art USA 15c
1777

Folk Art USA 15c
1778

Architecture USA 15c
1781

Architecture USA 15c
1782

1785

1786

SCOTT CAT. NO.	DESCRIPTION	FIRST DAY COVERS SING.	PL. BLK.	MINT SHEET	COPY-RIGHT	ZIP	PLATE BLOCK	UN-USED	USED
1775-78	Pennsylvania Toleware, 4 Vars., att'd	2.75	4.00	32.50(40)	(combo)	7.50(6)	8.75(10)	3.40	.....
1775	15c Coffee Pot	1.75	___	___	___	___	___	.85	.09
1776	15c Tea Caddy	1.75	___	___	___	___	___	.85	.09
1777	15c Sugar Bowl	1.75	___	___	___	___	___	.85	.09
1778	15c Coffee Pot	1.75	___	___	___	___	___	.85	.09
1779-82	Architecture, 4 Vars., att'd	2.75	4.00	38.95(48)	4.00	4.00	4.00	3.40	.....
1779	15c Virginia Rotunda	1.75	___	___	___	___	___	.85	.09
1780	15c Baltimore Cathedral	1.75	___	___	___	___	___	.85	.09
1781	15c Boston State House	1.75	___	___	___	___	___	.85	.09
1782	15c Philadelphia Exchange	1.75	___	___	___	___	___	.85	.09
1783-86	Endangered Flora, 4 Vars., att'd	2.75	4.00	42.95(50)	3.75	3.75	12.75(12)	3.40	.....
1783	15c Trillium	1.75	___	___	___	___	___	.85	.09
1784	15c Broadbean	1.75	___	___	___	___	___	.85	.09
1785	15c Wallflower	1.75	___	___	___	___	___	.85	.09
1786	15c Primrose	1.75	___	___	___	___	___	.85	.09

1787   1788   1789, 1789a, 1789b   1790

1791   1792   1793   1794

1795   1796   1797   1798

1787	15c Guide Dog	1.75	4.25	39.95(50)	___	___	15.00(20)	.70	.07
1788	15c Special Olympics	1.75	4.25	33.95(50)	3.00	3.00	7.50(10)	.70	.07
1789	15c John P. Jones, Pf. 11 x12	1.75	4.25	33.95(50)	3.00	3.00	7.50(10)	.70	.07
1789a	Same, Pf. 11	.....	.....	33.95(50)	3.00	3.00	7.50(10)	.70	.12

NOTE: #1789a may be included in year date sets and special offers and not **1789**.

1790	10c Summer Olympics, Javelin Thrower	2.00	3.50	26.75(50)	2.60	2.60	7.25(12)	.55	.30
1791-94	Summer Olympics, 4 Vars., att'd	2.75	4.25	46.50(50)	4.00	4.00	14.50(12)	3.60	.....
1791	15c Runners	1.75	___	___	___	___	___	.90	.13
1792	15c Swimmers	1.75	___	___	___	___	___	.90	.13
1793	15c Rowers	1.75	___	___	___	___	___	.90	.13
1794	15c Equestrian	1.75	___	___	___	___	___	.90	.13

SCOTT CAT. NO.	DESCRIPTION	FIRST DAY COVERS SING.	PL. BLK.	MINT SHEET	COPY-RIGHT	ZIP	PLATE BLOCK	UN-USED	USED
		1980							
1795-98	Winter Olympics, 4 Vars., att'd ..	2.75	4.25	41.75 (50)	3.65	3.65	11.50(12)	3.40	.....
1795	15c Skater	1.75	——	——	——	——	——	.85	.10
1796	15c Downhill Skier	1.75	——	——	——	——	——	.85	.10
1797	15c Ski Jumper	1.75	——	——	——	——	——	.85	.10
1798	15c Hockey	1.75	——	——	——	——	——	.85	.10

| | | **1799** | | | | **1800** | | **1801** | | **1802** | | **1803** | | **1804** |

<table>
<tr><td colspan="10" align="center">1979</td></tr>
</table>

SCOTT CAT. NO.	DESCRIPTION	SING.	PL. BLK.	MINT SHEET	COPY-RIGHT	ZIP	PLATE BLOCK	UN-USED	USED
1799	15c Xmas-Madonna	1.75	4.25	68.50(100)	3.00	3.00	10.50(12)	.70	.07
1800	15c Xmas-Santa Claus	1.75	4.25	68.50(100)	3.00	3.00	10.50(12)	.70	.07
1801	15c Will Rogers	1.75	4.25	35.75(50)	3.00	3.00	10.50(12)	.70	.07
1802	15c Vietnam Veterans	1.75	4.25	33.95(50)	3.00	3.00	7.85(10)	.70	.07

1980 COMMEMORATIVES

1795/1843	(1795-98, 1803-10, 1821-43) 35 vars. cpl	.....	.....	.....	50.50(17)	50.50(17)	126.95(18)	22.75	2.75
1803	15c W.C. Fields	1.75	4.25	31.50(50)	2.85	2.85	8.25(12)	.65	.07
1804	15c Benjamin Banneker	1.75	4.25	31.50(50)	2.85	2.85	8.25(12)	.65	.07

| **1805** | | **1806** | | **1807** | | **1808** | | **1809** | | **1810** |

SCOTT CAT. NO.	DESCRIPTION	SING.	PL. BLK.	MINT SHEET	COPY-RIGHT	ZIP	PLATE BLOCK	UN-USED	USED
1805-10	6 Vars., att'd	5.25	.....	48.00(60)	11.00(12)	11.00(12)	32.50(36)	4.75	.....
1805-06	2 Vars., att'd	2.25	——	——	——	——	——	1.50	.....
1807-08	2 Vars., att'd	2.25	——	——	——	——	——	1.50	.....
1809-10	2 Vars., att'd	2.25	——	——	——	——	——	1.50	.....
1805	15c "Letters Preserve Memories".	.....	——	——	——	——	——	.75	.15
1806	15c claret & multicolor	.....	——	——	——	——	——	.75	.15
1807	15c "Letters Lift Spirits"	.....	——	——	——	——	——	.75	.15
1808	15c green & multicolor	.....	——	——	——	——	——	.75	.15
1809	15c "Letters Shape Opinions" ...	.....	——	——	——	——	——	.75	.15
1810	15c red, white & blue	.....	——	——	——	——	——	.75	.15

| **1813** | | **1818, 1819, 1820** |

SCOTT CAT. NO.	DESCRIPTION	FIRST DAY COVERS SING. PL. BLK.	MINT SHEET	COPY-RIGHT	ZIP	PLATE BLOCK	UN-USED	USED

1980-81 Coil Stamps. Perf. 10 Vertically

		PAIRS				LINE PR.		
1811	1c Inkwell & Quill	pr. 1.95	——	——		.55	.10	.10
1813	3.5c Two Violins	3.00	——	——		1.25	.15	.15
1816	12c Torch	3.00	——	——		1.75	.48	.18

1981

1818	18c "B" definitive	2.00	4.00	67.50(100)	4.45(ME)	3.00	3.00	.70	.07
1819	18c "8" Definitive, from Bklt. Pn.	2.00						.70	.07

1981 Coil Stamp Perf. Vertically

						LINE	PAIR	
1820	18c "B" definitive	2.25	——	——	——	4.25	.85	.07

| | **1821** | **1822** | **1823** | **1824** |

1821	15c Frances Perkins	1.75	4.00	30.95(50)	2.85	2.85	3.00	.65	.07
1822	15c Dolley Madison	1.75	4.00	79.75(150)	2.85	2.85	3.25	.65	.07
1823	15c Emily Bissell	1.75	4.00	30.95(50)	2.85	2.85	3.00	.65	.07
1824	15c H. Keller & A. Sullivan	1.75	4.00	30.95(50)	2.85	2.85	3.00	.65	.07

| **1825** | **1826** | **1827** | **1828** | **1829** | **1830** |

1825	15c Veterans Administration	1.75	4.00	30.95(50)	2.85	2.85	3.00	.65	.07
1826	15c Gen. B. de Galvez	1.75	4.00	30.95(50)	2.85	2.85	3.00	.65	.07
1827-30	Coral Reefs, 4 Vars., att'd	3.25	4.00	30.95(50)	2.85	2.85	8.25(12)	2.60	. . . . .
1827	15c Brain Coral, Virgin Is. . .	1.75	——	——	——	——	——	.65	.09
1828	15c Elkhorn Coral, Florida	1.75	——	——	——	——	——	.65	.09
1829	15c Chalice Coral, Am. Samoa . . .	1.75	——	——	——	——	——	.65	.09
1830	15c Finger Coral, Hawaii	1.75	——	——	——	——	——	.65	.09

NOTE: To determine the VF price on stamps issued from 1941 to date, add 15% to the F/NH or F (used) price (minimum .03 per item). All VF unused stamps from 1941 to date will be NH. From 1964 to date, all unused stamps are F/NH.

FOR YOUR CONVENIENCE IN ORDERING, COMPLETE SETS ARE LISTED BEFORE SINGLE STAMP LISTINGS

SCOTT CAT. NO.	DESCRIPTION	FIRST DAY COVERS SING. PL. BLK.		MINT SHEET	COPY-RIGHT	ZIP	PLATE BLOCK	UN-USED	USED

1831   **1832**   **1833**

1831	15c Organized Labor	1.75	4.00	30.95(50)	2.85	2.85	8.25(12)	.65	.07
1832	15c Edith Wharton	1.75	4.00	30.95(50)	2.85	2.85	3.00	.65	.07
1833	15c Education	1.75	4.00	30.95(50)	2.85	2.85	4.25(6)	.65	.07

1834   **1835**   **1836**   **1837**

1834-37	American Folk Art, 4 Vars., att'd	3.25	4.00	25.00(40)	2.85	2.85	6.85(10)	2.60	....
1834	15c Bella Bella Tribe	1.75						.65	.09
1835	15c Chilkat Tlingit Tribe	1.75						.65	.09
1836	15c Tlingit Tribe	1.75						.65	.09
1837	15c Bella Coola Tribe	1.75						.65	.09

1838   **1839**   **1840**   **1841**

1838-41	American Architecture, 4 Vars., att'd	3.25	4.00	25.00(40)	2.85	2.85	3.00	2.60	....
1838	15c Smithsonian Inst.	1.75						.65	.09
1839	15c Trinity Church	1.75						.65	.09
1840	15c Penn. Academy	1.75						.65	.09
1841	15c Lyndhurst	1.75						.65	.09

1842   **1843**

| 1842 | 15c Madonna | 1.75 | 4.00 | 30.95(50) | 2.85 | 2.85 | 8.25(12) | .65 | .07 |
| 1843 | 15c Xmas Wreath & Toy | 1.75 | 4.00 | 30.95(50) | | | 13.50(20) | .65 | .07 |

SCOTT CAT. NO.	DESCRIPTION	FIRST DAY COVERS SING. PL. BLK.		MINT SHEET	COPY-RIGHT	ZIP	PLATE BLOCK	UN-USED	USED

1843A   **1844**   **1844A**   **1845**   **1846**

1846A   **1847**   **1849**   **1850**   **1851**

1852   **1853**   **1854**   **1858**   **1859**   **1860**   **1861**

1980-84 GREAT AMERICANS

SCOTT CAT. NO.	DESCRIPTION	FDC SING.	PL. BLK.	MINT SHEET	COPY-RIGHT	ZIP	PLATE BLOCK	UN-USED	USED
1843A	1c Dorothea Dix	1.75	3.25	3.00(100)			1.50(20)	.07	.07
1844	2c Igor Stravinsky	1.75	3.25	6.75(100)	.37	.37	.37	.07	.07
1844A	3c Henry Clay	1.75	3.25	7.75(100)	.45	.45	.45	.08	.07
1845	4c Carl Schurz	1.75	3.25	9.95(100)	.55	.55	.55	.10	.07
1846	5c Pearl Buck	1.75	3.25	11.95(100)	.60	.60	.60	.12	.07
1846A	10c Richard Russell (1984)	1.75	3.25	22.50(100)			5.50(20)	.25	.07
1847	13c Crazy Horse	pr. 1.95	4.00	29.95(100)	1.55	1.55	1.55	.32	.07
1849	17c Rachel Carson	1.95	4.00	39.50(100)	2.00	2.00	2.00	.42	.07
1850	18c George Mason	1.95	4.00	42.50(100)	2.15	2.15	2.15	.45	.07
1851	19c Sequoyah	1.95	4.00	44.50(100)	2.30	2.30	2.30	.47	.10
1852	20c Ralph Bunche	1.95	4.00	49.75(100)	2.35	2.35	2.35	.50	.07
1853	20c Thomas Gallaudet	1.95	4.00	49.75(100)	2.35	2.35	2.35	.50	.07
1854	20c Harry Truman (1984)	1.95	4.00	49.75(100)			10.50(20)	.50	.07
1858	30c Frank C. Laubach	2.25	5.25	74.95(100)			16.50(20)	.75	.10
1859	35c Charles Drew	2.35	5.75	82.50(100)	4.20	4.20	4.20	.87	.10
1860	37c Robert Millikan	2.35	5.75	86.95(100)	4.40	4.40	4.40	.92	.12
1861	40c Lillian Gilbreth (1984)	2.50	6.00	89.95(100)			21.50(20)	.95	.15

1874   **1875**

1980 - 1983 COMMEMORATIVES

Every commemorative postage stamp (191 different) issued from 1980 through 1983 including the State Birds and Flowers, at a considerable savings from individual prices.

A157 Unused .... $99.95 .... Save $15.91
*A167 Used (191) .... $27.75 .... Save $ 3.19
*Does not include #1935

† Does not include #1927

1981 COMMEMORATIVES

				MINT SHEET	COPY-RIGHT	ZIP	PLATE BLOCK	UN-USED	USED
1874/1945 (1874-9, 1910-1945) 42 Vars., cpl.		.....	.....	55.50(20)	†60.50(21)	62.50(21)	26.50		3.20
1874	15c Everett Dirksen	1.75	3.25	28.50(50)	2.85	2.85	3.00	.60	.07
1875	15c Whitney M. Young	1.75	3.25	28.50(50)	2.85	2.85	3.00	.60	.07

SCOTT CAT. NO.	DESCRIPTION	FIRST DAY COVERS SING. PL. BLK.		MINT SHEET	COPY-RIGHT	ZIP	PLATE BLOCK	UN-USED	USED

Rose USA 18c
1876

Camellia USA 18c
1877

Dahlia USA 18c
1878

Lily USA 18c
1879

Scott	Description	FDC Sing.	FDC Pl. Blk.	Mint Sheet	Copy-right	Zip	Plate Block	Unused	Used
1876-79	Flowers, 4 vars., attd.	3.00	4.00	32.25(48)	3.00	3.00	3.10	2.80	——
1876	18c Rose	1.75	——	——	——	——	——	.70	.09
1877	18c Camelia	1.75	——	——	——	——	——	.70	.09
1878	18c Dahlia	1.75	——	——	——	——	——	.70	.09
1879	18c Lily	1.75	——	——	——	——	——	.70	.09

1880,1949

1881

1882

1883

1884

1885

1886

1887

1888

1889

1981 WILDLIFE DEFINITIVES

Scott	Description	FDC Sing.	FDC Pl. Blk.	Mint Sheet	Copy-right	Zip	Plate Block	Unused	Used
1880-89	Wildlife, Block of 10 attd. ...	9.75	——	——	——	——	7.45(10)	7.20	——
1880	18c Bighorned Sheep	1.75	——	——	——	——	——	.72	.10
1881	18c Puma	1.75	——	——	——	——	——	.72	.10
1882	18c Harbor Seal	1.75	——	——	——	——	——	.72	.10
1883	18c Bison	1.75	——	——	——	——	——	.72	.10
1884	18c Brown Bear	1.75	——	——	——	——	——	.72	.10
1885	18c Polar Bear	1.75	——	——	——	——	——	.72	.10
1886	18c Elk	1.75	——	——	——	——	——	.72	.10
1887	18c Moose	1.75	——	——	——	——	——	.72	.10
1888	18c White-tailed Deer	1.75	——	——	——	——	——	.72	.10
1889	18c Pronghorned Antelope	1.75	——	——	——	——	——	.72	.10

usa 18c
1890

USA 18c
1891

6c USA
1892

usa 18c
1893

USA 20c
1894, 1895, 1896

1981 FLAG AND ANTHEM ISSUE

Scott	Description	FDC Sing.	FDC Pl. Blk.	Mint Sheet	Copy-right	Zip	Plate Block	Unused	Used
1890	18c "Waves of Grain"	1.75	3.25	56.75(100)	——	——	12.50(20)	.60	.07

1981 Coil Stamp. Perf. 10 Vertically   PL.#PR.

Scott	Description	FDC Sing.	FDC Pl. Blk.	Mint Sheet	Copy-right	Zip	Plate Block	Unused	Used
1891	18c "Shining Sea"	1.75	pr.2.00	——	——	——	2.25	.60	.07

1981

Scott	Description	FDC Sing.	FDC Pl. Blk.	Mint Sheet	Copy-right	Zip	Plate Block	Unused	Used
1892	6c Stars, from booklet pane	1.75	——	——	——	——	——	3.25	.22
1893	18c "Purple Mountains" from bklt. pane	1.75	——	——	——	——	——	.65	.07
1892-93	6c & 18c as above, att'd pr. ...	....	——	——	——	——	——	3.95	.....
1894	20c Flag & Supreme Court	1.75	3.25	49.75(100)	——	——	10.50(20)	.50	.07

LINE PR.

Scott	Description	FDC Sing.	FDC Pl. Blk.	Mint Sheet	Copy-right	Zip	Plate Block	Unused	Used
1895	20c Flag & Supreme Court	1.75	pr.2.00	——	——	——	1.95	.50	.07

1981

Scott	Description	FDC Sing.	FDC Pl. Blk.	Mint Sheet	Copy-right	Zip	Plate Block	Unused	Used
1896	20c Flag & S.C., from bklt. Pane .	1.75	——	——	——	——	——	.50	.07

SCOTT CAT. NO.	DESCRIPTION	FIRST DAY COVERS SING. PL. BLK.	MINT SHEET	COPY-RIGHT	ZIP	PLATE BLOCK	UN-USED	USED

1896C   1897   1897A   1897B

1897C   1897D   1898   1899   1900

1901   1902   1905   1906   1907

1981-84, Perf. 10 Vertically
TRANSPORTATION COILS

SCOTT CAT. NO.	DESCRIPTION	PAIRS					LINE PAIRS	UN-USED	USED
1896C	1c Omnibus	1.75					.55	.07	.07
1897	2c Locomotive	1.95					.55	.07	.07
1897A	4c Stagecoach	1.75					.65	.14	.10
1897B	3c Handcar	1.75					.60	.09	.08
1897C	5c Motorcycle	1.75					.70	.17	.07
1897D	5.2c Sleigh	1.75					.65	.15	.10
1898	5.9c Bicycle	1.95					.80	.21	.15
1899	7.4 Baby Buggy (1984)	2.00					2.50	.26	.12
1900	9.3c Mail Wagon	2.15					1.40	.33	.15
1901	10.9c Hansom Cab	2.15					1.50	.38	.15
1902	11c Caboose (1984)	2.15					2.50	.38	.12
1905	17c Electric Car	1.95	2.25				2.25	.60	.10
1906	18c Surrey	1.95	2.25				2.25	.63	.07
1907	20c Fire Pumper	1.95	2.25				1.85	.50	.07

NOTE: Pairs of the above can be supplied at two times the singles price. For Line Pair FDC's please send Want List. Line Pair prices for #'s 1899 and 1902 are for number strips of three.

1909   1910   1911

1983 EXPRESS MAIL

SCOTT CAT. NO.	DESCRIPTION	FDC	PL. BLK.	MINT SHEET	COPY-RIGHT	ZIP	PLATE BLOCK	UN-USED	USED
1909	$9.35 Eagle & Moon	28.95						18.75	
1910	18c American Red Cross	1.75	3.25	30.50(50)	2.85	2.85	2.85	.65	.07
1911	18c Savings & Loan Assoc.	1.75	3.25	30.50(50)	2.85	2.85	2.85	.65	.07

SCOTT CAT. NO.	DESCRIPTION	FIRST DAY COVERS SING. PL. BLK.		MINT SHEET	COPY-RIGHT	ZIP	PLATE BLOCK	UN-USED	USED

1912

1913

1914

1915

1916

1917

1918

1919

Scott	Description	FDC Sing.	FDC Pl.Blk.	Mint Sheet	Copy-right	Zip	Plate Block	Unused	Used
1912-19	Space Achievement, 8 vars., att'd .	5.95	6.75	29.75(48)	(combo)	5.35(8)	5.35(8)	5.20	.....
1912	18c Exploring the Moon	1.75	___	___				.65	.10
1913	18c Releasing Boosters	1.75	___	___				.65	.10
1914	18c Cooling Electric Systems ...	1.75	___	___				.65	.10
1915	18c Understanding the Sun.....	1.75	___	___				.65	.10
1916	18c Probing the Planets	1.75	___	___				.65	.10
1917	18c Shuttle and Rockets	1.75	___	___				.65	.10
1918	18c Landing	1.75	___	___				.65	.10
1919	18c Comprehending the Universe .	1.75	___	___				.65	.10

1920

1921

1922

1923

1924

Scott	Description	FDC Sing.	FDC Pl.Blk.	Mint Sheet	Copy-right	Zip	Plate Block	Unused	Used
1920	18c Professional Management ...	1.75	3.25	30.50(50)	2.85	2.85	2.85	.65	.07
1921-24	Wildlife Habitats, 4 vars. att'd ...	3.00	4.00	30.50(50)	2.85	2.85	2.85	2.60	___
1921	18c Blue Heron	1.75	___	___				.65	.09
1922	18c Badger	1.75	___	___				.65	.09
1923	18c Grizzly Bear.............	1.75	___	___				.65	.09
1924	18c Ruffled Grouse	1.75	___	___				.65	.09

1925

1926

1927

SCOTT CAT. NO.	DESCRIPTION	FIRST DAY COVERS SING. PL. BLK.		MINT SHEET	COPY-RIGHT	ZIP	PLATE BLOCK	UN-USED	USED
1925	18c Disabled Persons	1.75	3.25	30.50(50)	2.85	2.85	2.85	.65	.07
1926	18c Edna St. Vincent Millay . . .	1.75	3.25	30.50(50)	2.85	2.85	2.85	.65	.07
1927	18c Alcoholism	1.75	3.25	40.00(50)	____	____	20.00(20)	.65	.07

1928   1929   1930   1931

1928-31	American Architecture, 4 vars., att'd.	3.00	4.00	25.00(40)	3.00	3.00	3.00	2.60	
1928	18c New York Univ. Library . . .	1.75	____					.65	.09
1929	18c Biltmore House	1.75	____					.65	.09
1930	18c Palace of the Arts	1.75	____					.65	.09
1931	18c National Farmers Bank . . .	1.75	____					.58	.09

1932   1933   1934

1932	18c Babe Zaharias	1.75	3.25	3.50(50)	2.85	2.85	2.85	.65	.07
1933	18c Bobby Jones	1.75	3.25	30.50(50)	2.85	2.85	2.85	.65	.07
1934	18c Coming Through the Rye . .	1.75	3.25	30.50(50)	2.85	2.85	2.85	.65	.07

1935   1936   1937   1938

1935	18c James Hoban	1.75	3.25	30.50(50)	2.85	2.85	2.85	.75	.60
1936	20c James Hoban	1.75	3.25	34.25(50)	3.10	3.10	3.10	.72	.07
1937-38	18c Yorktown/Virginia Capes, 2 vars., att'd	2.50	3.75	30.50(50)	2.85	2.85	2.85	1.30	
1937	18c Yorktown	1.75	____					.65	.08
1938	18c Virginia Capes	1.75	____					.65	.08

1939   1940   1941

SCOTT CAT. NO.	DESCRIPTION	FIRST DAY COVERS SING.	PL. BLK.	MINT SHEET	COPY-RIGHT	ZIP	PLATE BLOCK	UN-USED	USED
1939	(20c) Madonna & Child	1.75	4.25	67.95(100)	3.10	3.10	3.10	.72	.07
1940	(20c) Christmas Toy	1.75	4.25	34.25(50)	3.10	3.10	3.10	.72	.07
1941	20c John Hanson	1.75	3.75	34.25(50)	3.10	3.10	3.10	.72	.07

1943

1944

1945

1942

1942-45	Desert Plants, 4 vars, att'd . . .	3.00	4.00	28.75(40)	3.20	3.20	3.20	3.00	——
1942	20c Barrel Cactus	1.75	——	——				.75	.09
1943	20c Agave	1.75	——	——				.75	.09
1944	20c Beavertail Cactus	1.75	——	——				.75	.09
1945	20c Saguaro	1.75	——	——				.75	.09

1946, 1947, 1948

1946	(20c) "C" Eagle	1.75	3.75	67.95(100)	3.10	3.10	3.10	.72	.07

1981 Coil Stamp Perf. 10 Vertically

LINE PAIR

1947	(20c) "C" Eagle	1.75	Pr.2.00	——	——	——	2.25	.72	.07
1948	(20c) "C" Eagle, from bklt. pane	1.75		——	——	——		.72	.07

1982

1949	20c Bighorned Sheep, blue, from bklt. pane	1.75	——	——	——	——	——	.72	.07

1950   **1951**   **1952**

1982 COMMEMMORATIVES

1950/2030 (1950-52, 2003-04, 06-30) 30 Vars.		. . . . .	. . . . .	. . . . .	38.75(17)	40.75(17)	78.50(21)	16.95	2.15
1950	20c Franklin D. Roosevelt	1.75	3.75	26.25(48)	2.45	2.45	2.45	.55	.07
1951	20c LOVE	1.75	3.75	27.25(50)	2.45	2.45	2.45	.55	.07
1952	20c George Washington	1.75	3.75	27.25(50)	2.45	2.45	2.45	.55	.07

1982 STATE BIRDS AND FLOWERS

Alabama USA 20c

1953

Indiana USA 20c

1966

Massachusetts USA 20c

1973

Wyoming USA 20c

2002

1953	Alabama	1970	Louisiana	1987	Ohio
1954	Alaska	1971	Maine	1988	Oklahoma
1955	Arizona	1972	Maryland	1989	Oregon
1956	Arkansas	1973	Massachusetts	1990	Pennsylvania
1957	California	1974	Michigan	1991	Rhode Island
1958	Colorado	1975	Minnesota	1992	South Carolina
1959	Connecticut	1976	Mississippi	1993	South Dakota
1960	Delaware	1977	Missouri	1994	Tennessee
1961	Florida	1978	Montana	1995	Texas
1962	Georgia	1979	Nebraska	1996	Utah
1963	Hawaii	1980	Nevada	1997	Vermont
1964	Idaho	1981	New Hampshire	1998	Virginia
1965	Illinois	1982	New Jersey	1999	Washington
1966	Indiana	1983	New Mexico	2000	West Virginia
1967	Iowa	1984	New York	2001	Wisconsin
1968	Kansas	1985	North Carolina	2002	Wyoming
1969	Kentucky	1986	North Dakota		

Perf. 11; 10½x11

Description	SING.	PL. BLK.	MINT SHEET	COPY-RIGHT	ZIP	PLATE BLOCK	UN-USED	USED
1953-2002 50 Vars. att'd	115.00(50)	.....	28.00(50)	———		28.00(50)	28.00	18.95
Singles of above	2.50	———	———				.55	.40
Inscription Blocks	———		———	3.00	3.00	3.00(4)	———	———

NOTE: Plate, Zip, and Copyright blocks are available with their respective marginal inscriptions in upper left, lower left, upper right, or lower right positions. Please specify UL, LL, UR, or LR when ordering

2003

Library of Congress USA 20c
2004

Consumer Education
2005

	Description	SING.	PL. BLK.	MINT SHEET	COPY-RIGHT	ZIP	PLATE BLOCK	UN-USED	USED
2003	20c USA/Netherlands	1.75	3.75	24.95(50)	———		10.50(20)	.50	.07
2004	20c Library of Congress	1.75	3.75	24.95(50)	2.25	2.25	2.25	.50	.07
2005	20c Consumer Education, coil	1.75	pr.2.00	———			LINE PR. 1.95	.50	.07

USA 20c Solar energy · Knoxville World's Fair
2006

USA 20c Synthetic fuels · Knoxville World's Fair
2007

USA 20c Breeder reactor · Knoxville World's Fair
2008

USA 20c Fossil fuels · Knoxville World's Fair
2009

	Description	SING.	PL. BLK.	MINT SHEET	COPY-RIGHT	ZIP	PLATE BLOCK	UN-USED	USED
2006-09	World's Fair, 4 vars., att'd	3.00	4.00	31.25(50)	3.25	3.25	3.25	3.00	
2006	20c Solar Energy	1.75	———				———	.75	.09
2007	20c Synthetic Fuels	1.75	———				———	.75	.09
2008	20c Breeder Reactor	1.75	———				———	.75	.09
2009	20c Fossil Fuels	1.75	———				———	.75	.09

SCOTT CAT. NO.	DESCRIPTION	FIRST DAY COVERS SING. PL. BLK.		MINT SHEET	COPY-RIGHT	ZIP	PLATE BLOCK	UN-USED	USED

2010

2011

2012

2013

Scott	Description	Sing	Pl. Blk.	Mint Sheet	Copyright	Zip	Plate Block	Unused	Used
2010	20c Horatio Alger	1.75	3.75	24.95(50)	2.25	2.25	2.25	.50	.07
2011	20c Aging Together	1.75	3.75	24.95(50)	2.25	2.25	2.25	.50	.07
2012	20c Barrymores	1.75	3.75	24.95(50)	2.25	2.25	2.25	.50	.07
2013	20c Dr. Mary Walker	1.75	3.75	24.95(50)	2.25	2.25	2.25	.50	.07

2014

2015

2016

2017

Scott	Description	Sing	Pl. Blk.	Mint Sheet	Copyright	Zip	Plate Block	Unused	Used
2014	20c Peace Garden	1.75	3.75	24.95(50)	2.25	2.25	2.25	.50	.07
2015	20c America's Libraries	1.75	3.75	24.95(50)	2.25	2.25	2.25	.50	.07
2016	20c Jackie Robinson	1.75	3.75	29.95(50)	2.25	2.25	2.25	.50	.07
2017	20c Touro Synagogue	1.75	3.75	24.95(50)			10.50(20)	.50	.07

2018

Scott	Description	Sing	Pl. Blk.	Mint Sheet	Copyright	Zip	Plate Block	Unused	Used
2018	20c Wolf Trap Farm	1.75	3.75	24.95(50)	2.25	2.25	2.25	.50	.07

2019

2020

2021

2022

Scott	Description	Sing	Pl. Blk.	Mint Sheet	Copyright	Zip	Plate Block	Unused	Used
2019-22	American Architecture, 4 Vars., att'd.	3.00	4.00	28.75(40)	3.25	3.25	3.25	3.00	
2019	20c Falling Water Mill Run	1.75						.75	.09
2020	20c Illinois Inst. Tech	1.75						.75	.09
2021	20c Gropius House	1.75						.75	.09
2022	20c Dulles Airport	1.75						.75	.09

SCOTT CAT. NO.	DESCRIPTION	FIRST DAY COVERS SING. PL. BLK.		MINT SHEET	COPY-RIGHT	ZIP	PLATE BLOCK	UN-USED	USED

2023   2024   2025

SCOTT CAT. NO.	DESCRIPTION	SING.	PL. BLK.	MINT SHEET	COPY-RIGHT	ZIP	PLATE BLOCK	UN-USED	USED
2023	20c St. Francis of Assisi	1.75	3.75	24.95(50)	2.25	2.25	2.25	.50	.07
2024	20c Ponce de Leon	1.75	3.75	24.95(50)	____		10.50(20)	.50	.07
2025	13c Kitten & Puppy, Xmas....	1.75	3.75	15.95(50)	1.60	1.60	1.60	.32	.07

2026

2026	20c Madonna & Child, Xmas ..	1.75	3.75	24.95(50)	____	____	10.50(20)	.50	.07

2027   2028   2029   2030

2027-30	Winter Scenes, Xmas, 4 Vars., att'd.	3.00	4.00	31.25(50)	3.25	3.25	3.25	3.00	
2027	20c Sledding	1.75	____	____	____	____	____	.75	.09
2028	20c Snowman	1.75	____	____	____	____	____	.75	.09
2029	20c Skating	1.75	____	____	____	____	____	.75	.09
2030	20c Decorating	1.75	____	____	____	____	____	.75	.09

NOTE: To determine the VF price on stamps issued from 1941 to date, add 15% to the F/NH or F (used) price (minimum .03 per item). All VF unused stamps from 1941 to date will be NH. From 1964 to date, all unused stamps are F/NH.

1983 COMMEMORATIVES

2031-2065	35 Vars., cpl.	.....	.....	.....	41.25(18)	41.25(18)	91.00(23)	19.40	2.65

2031

2031	20c Science & Industry	1.75	3.75	24.95(50)	2.25	2.25	2.25	.50	.07

SCOTT CAT. NO.	DESCRIPTION	FIRST DAY COVERS SING. PL. BLK.		MINT SHEET	COPY-RIGHT	ZIP	PLATE BLOCK	UN-USED	USED

2032

2033

2034

2035

SCOTT CAT. NO.	DESCRIPTION	SING.	PL. BLK.	MINT SHEET	COPY-RIGHT	ZIP	PLATE BLOCK	UN-USED	USED
2032-35	20c Ballooning, 4 vars., att'd ..	3.00	4.00	28.75(40)	3.25	3.25	3.25	3.00	
2032	20c Intrepid	1.75	____	____	____	____	____	.75	.09
2033	20 Red, white, & blue balloon .	1.75	____	____	____	____	____	.75	.09
2034	20c Yellow, gold & gr. balloon .	1.75	____	____	____	____	____	.75	.09
2035	20c Explorer II	1.75	____	____	____	____	____	.75	.09

2036

2037

2038

2039

2036	20c USA/Sweden	1.75	3.75	24.95(50)	2.25	2.25	2.25	.50	.07
2037	20c Civilian Cons. Corps	1.75	3.75	24.95(50)	2.25	2.25	2.25	.50	.07
2038	20c Joseph Priestley	1.75	3.75	24.95(50)	2.25	2.25	2.25	.50	.07
2039	20c Volunteerism	1.75	3.75	24.95(50)	____		10.50(50)	.50	.07

2040

2041

2042

2043

2040	20c German Immigrants	1.75	3.75	24.95(50)	2.25	2.25	2.25	.50	.07
2041	20c Brooklyn Bridge	1.75	3.75	24.95(50)	2.25	2.25	2.25	.50	.07
2042	20c Tennessee Valley Auth. . . .	1.75	3.75	24.95(50)	____		10.50(20)	.50	.07
2043	20c Physical Fitness	1.75	3.75	24.95(50)	2.25	2.25	10.50(20)	.50	.07

2044

2045

2046

2047

2044	20c Scott Joplin	1.75	3.75	24.95(50)	2.25	2.25	2.25	.50	.07
2045	20c Medal of Honor	1.75	3.75	24.95(40)	2.25	2.25	2.25	.50	.07
2046	20c Babe Ruth	1.75	3.75	24.95(50)	2.25	2.25	2.25	.50	.07
2047	20c Nathaniel Hawthorne	1.75	3.75	24.95(50)	2.25	2.25	2.25	.50	.07

SCOTT CAT. NO.	DESCRIPTION	FIRST DAY COVERS SING. PL. BLK.		MINT SHEET	COPY-RIGHT	ZIP	PLATE BLOCK	UN-USED	USED

2048

2049

2050

2051

2048-51	13c Olympcis, 4 vars.,	3.00	4.00	22.75(50)	2.00	2.00	2.00	1.75	. . .
2048	13c Discus	1.75	___	___			___	.40	.25
2049	13c High Jump	1.75	___	___			___	.40	.25
2050	13c Archery	1.75	___	___			___	.40	.25
2051	13c Boxing	1.75	___	___			___	.40	.25

2052

2053

2054

2052	20c Treaty of Paris	1.75	3.75	19.95(40)	2.25	2.25	2.25	.50	.07
2053	20c Civil Service	1.75	3.75	24.95(50)	___		10.50(20)	.50	.07
2054	20c Metropolitan Opera	1.75	3.75	24.95(50)	2.25	2.25	2.25	.50	.07

2056

2057

2058

2055

2055-58	20c Inventors, 4 vars., attd.	3.00	4.00	31.25(50)	3.25	3.25	3.25	3.00	___
2055	20c Charles Steinmetz	1.75	___					.75	.09
2056	20c Edwin Armstrong	1.75	___					.75	.09
2057	20c Nikola Tesla	1.75	___					.75	.09
2058	20c Phil. T. Farnsworth	1.75	___					.75	.09

2059

2060

2061

2062

2059-62	20c Streetcars, 4 vars, attd.	3.00	4.00	31.25(50)	3.25	3.25	3.25	3.00	___
2059	20c First Streetcar	1.75	___					.75	.09
2060	20c Electric Trolly	1.75	___					.75	.09
2061	20c "Bobtail"	1.75	___					.75	.09
2062	20c St. Charles Streetcar	1.75	___					.75	.09

2063

2064

2065

2066

SCOTT CAT. NO.	DESCRIPTION	FIRST DAY COVERS SING. PL. BLK.		MINT SHEET	COPY-RIGHT	ZIP	PLATE BLOCK	UN-USED	USED
2063	20c Madonna	1.75	3.00	24.95(50)	2.25	2.25	2.25	.50	.07
2064	20c Santa Claus	1.75	3.00	24.95(50)			10.50(20)	.50	.07
2065	20c Martin Luther	1.75	3.00	24.95(50)	2.25	2.25	2.25	.50	.07

1984 COMMEMORATIVES

2066-2109	44 Varieties, cpl.				54.75(27)	57.50(28)	96.50(32)	20.50	3.15
2066	20c Alaska Statehood	1.75	3.75	24.95(50)	2.25	2.25	2.25	.50	.07

2067

2068

2069

2070

2067-70	20c Winter Olympics, 4 vars. att'd.	3.00	4.00	31.25(50)	3.25	3.25	3.25	3.00	
2067	20c Ice Dancing	1.75						.75	.0
2068	20c Downhill Skiing	1.75						.75	.0
2069	20c Cross Country Skiing	1.75						.75	.0
2070	20c Hockey	1.75						.75	.0

2071

2072

2073

2074

2071	20c FDIC	1.75	3.75	25.95(50)	2.25	2.25	2.25	.50	.07
2072	20c Love	1.75	3.75	25.95(50)			10.50(50)	.50	.07
2073	20c Carter G. Woodson	1.75	3.75	25.95(50)	2.25	2.25	2.25	.50	.07
2074	20c Conservation	1.75	3.75	25.95(50)	2.25	2.25	2.25	.50	.07

SCOTT CAT. NO.	DESCRIPTION	FIRST DAY COVERS SING.	PL. BLK.	MINT SHEET	COPY-RIGHT	ZIP	PLATE BLOCK	UN-USED	USED

2075   **2076**   **2077**   **2078**   **2079**

SCOTT CAT. NO.	DESCRIPTION	SING.	PL. BLK.	MINT SHEET	COPY-RIGHT	ZIP	PLATE BLOCK	UN-USED	USED
2075	20c Credit Union	1.75	3.75	25.95(50)	2.25	2.25	2.25	.50	.07
2076-79	20c Orchids, 4 vars., att'd	3.00	4.00	23.95(48)	2.25	2.25	2.25	2.00	
2076	20c Wild Pink	1.75	____	____	____	____		.50	.09
2077	20c Lady's Slipper	1.75	____	____	____	____		.50	.09
2078	20c Spreading Pogonia	1.75	____	____	____	____		.50	.09
2079	20c Pacific Calypso	1.75	____	____	____	____		.50	.09

2080   **2081**

2080	20c Hawaii Statehood	1.75	3.75	24.95(50)	2.25	2.25	2.25	.50	.09
2081	20c National Archives	1.75	3.75	24.95(50)	2.25	2.25	2.25	.50	.09

2082   **2083**   **2084**   **2085**

2082-85	20c Olympics, 4 vars., att'd.	3.00	4.00	24.95(50)	2.25	2.25	2.25	2.00	
2082	20c Men's Diving	1.75	—	—	—	—	—	.50	.09
2083	20c Long Jump	1.75	—	—	—	—	—	.50	.09
2084	20c Wrestling	1.75	—	—	—	—	—	.50	.09
2085	20c Women's Kayak	1.75	—	—	—	—	—	.50	.09

2087   **2086**

2086	20c Louisiana Exposition	1.75	3.75	19.95(40)	2.25	2.25	2.25	.50	.07
2087	20c Health Research	1.75	3.75	24.95(50)	2.25	2.25	2.25	.50	.07

SCOTT CAT. NO.	DESCRIPTION	FIRST DAY COVERS SING. PL. BLK.		MINT SHEET	COPY-RIGHT	ZIP	PLATE BLOCK	UN-USED	USED

2088

2089

2090

2088	20c Douglas Fairbanks	1.75	3.75	24.95(50)	———		10.50(20)	.50	.07
2089	20c Jim Thorpe	1.75	3.75	24.95(50)	2.25	2.25	2.25	.50	.07
2090	20c John McCormack	1.75	3.75	24.95(50)	2.25	2.25	2.25	.50	.07

2091

2092

2093

2094

2091	20c St. Lawrence Seaway	1.75	3.75	24.95(50)	2.25	2.25	2.25	.50	.07
2092	20c Preserving Wetlands	1.75	3.75	24.95(50)	2.25	2.25	2.25	.50	.07
2093	20c Roanoke Voyages	1.75	3.75	24.95(50)	2.25	2.25	2.25	.50	.07
2094	20c Herman Melville	1.75	3.75	24.95(50)	2.25	2.25	2.25	.50	.07

2095

2096

2097

2095	20c Horace Moses	1.75	3.75	24.95(50)	2.25	2.25	10.50(20)	.50	.07
2096	20c Smokey Bear	1.75	3.75	24.95(50)	2.25	2.25	2.25	.50	.07
2097	20c Roberto Clemente	1.75	3.75	24.95(50)	2.25	2.25	2.25	.50	.07

2098

2099

2100

2101

2098-101	**20c American Dogs, attch'd**	——	3.75	19.95(40)	2.25	2.25	2.25	2.00	——
2098	20c Beagle, Boston Terrier	1.75	——	——	——	——		.50	.09
2099	20c Chesapeake Bay Retriever, Cocker Spaniel	1.75	——	——	——	——		.50	.09
2100	20c Alaskan Malamute, Collie .	1.75	——	——	——	——		.50	.09
2101	20c Black & Tan Coonhound, American Foxhound	1.75	——	——	——	——		.50	.09

SCOTT CAT. NO.	DESCRIPTION	FIRST DAY COVERS SING. PL. BLK.		MINT SHEET	COPY-RIGHT	ZIP	PLATE BLOCK	UN-USED	USED

2102   2104

2102	20c Crime Prevention			'50)	2.25	2.25	2.25	.50	.09
2103	20c Hispanic Americans	1.75	3.75	15.. 3)	2.25	2.25	2.25	.50	.07
2104	20c Family Unity	1.75	3.75	24.95(50)	2.25	2.25	10.50(20)	.50	.09

2105   2106   2107

2105	20c Eleanor Roosevelt	1.75	3.75	19.95(40)	2.25	2.25	2.25	.50	.09
2106	20c Nation of Readers	1.75	3.75	24.95(50)	2.25	2.25	2.25	.50	.09
2107	20c Madonna & Child	1.75	3.75	24.95(50)	2.25	2.25	2.25	.50	.07

2108

| 2108 | 20c Santa Claus . . . . | 1.75 | 3.75 | 24.95(50) | 2.25 | 2.25 | 2.25 | .50 | .07 |
| 2109 | 20c Vietnam Veterans . . . . | 1.75 | 3.75 | 19.95(40) | (combo) | 3.25(6) | 2.25 | .50 | .07 |

SCOTT CAT. NO.	DESCRIPTION	PLATE BLOCK F	AVG	UNUSED F	AVG	USED F	AVG

AIR MAIL STAMPS

C1-C3 — *Curtiss Jenny Biplane*   C4 — *Airplane Propeller*   C5 — *Badge of Air Service*   C6 — *Airplane*   C7-C9 — *Map of U.S. and Airplanes*

1918 (40%)

C1	6c orange	2400.00 (6)	1900.00 (6)	190.00	140.00	65.00	50.00
C2	16c green	5250.00 (6)	3750.00 (6)	300.00	225.00	99.50	75.00
C3	24c carmine & blue	5400.00 (2)	3900.00 (2)	300.00	225.00	110.00	85.00

1923 (40%)

C4	8c dark green	1250.00 (6)	950.00 (6)	85.00	65.00	47.50	35.00
C5	16c dark blue	6450.00 (6)	4950.00 (6)	260.00	195.00	100.00	80.00
C6	24c carmine	7900.00 (6)	5950.00 (6)	345.00	245.00	80.00	65.00

1926-27 (30%)

C7	10c dark blue	150.00 (6)	100.00 (6)	10.00	7.50	.85	.65
C8	15c olive brown	200.00 (6)	140.00 (6)	10.75	7.75	5.25	4.25
C9	20c yellow green	340.00 (6)	250.00 (6)	22.50	15.00	4.50	3.50

C10 — *Lindbergh's Airplane "Spirit of St. Louis"*   C11 — *Beacon and Rocky Mountains*   C12,C16,C17,C19 — *Winged Globe*

1927. LINDBERGH TRIBUTE ISSUE (30%)

C10	10c dark blue	375.00 (6)	275.00 (6)	19.00	15.00	5.75	4.50

1928 (30%)

C11	5c carmine & blue	160.00 (6)	95.00 (6)	12.50	9.50	1.20	.95

1930. Flat Plate Printing. Perf. 11 (30%)

C12	5c violet	500.00 (6)	375.00 (6)	26.50	21.00	.90	.65

C13   C14 — *Graf Zeppelin*   C15

1930. GRAF ZEPPELIN ISSUE (30%)

C13-15	65c-$2.60 3 Vars. cpl.	.....	.....	4795.00	3795.00	3650.00	2850.00
C13	65c green	.....	.....	745.00	595.00	850.00	700.00
C14	$1.30 brown	.....	.....	1700.00	1350.00	1200.00	950.00
C15	$2.60 blue	.....	.....	2350.00	1850.00	1600.00	1200.00

Plate blocks will be blocks of 4 stamps unless otherwise noted.

See page X for Condition Definitions.

NOTE: To determine the VF price for stamps issued from 1901 to 1940, add the difference between the Avg. and F prices to the F price. To determine the NH price for these issues, add the percentage in parentheses to the appropriate condition price.

SCOTT CAT. NO.	DESCRIPTION	PLATE BLOCK		UNUSED		USED	
		F	AVG	F	AVG	F	AVG

1931-32 Rotary Press Printing. Perf. 10½ x 11 (20%)

C16	5c violet	325.00	250.00	16.00	12.50	1.10	.95
C17	8c olive bistre	100.00	75.00	7.25	5.75	.60	.50

C18
Graf Zeppelin

1933. CENTURY OF PROGRESS ISSUE (30%)

C18	50c green	2375.00 (6)	1950.00 (6)	250.00	200.00	250.00	195.00

1934. DESIGN OF 1930 (20%)

C19	6c orange	85.00	65.00	8.50	6.75	.25	.20

C20-C22
China Clipper

C23
Eagle

C24
Winged Globe

1935. TRANS-PACIFIC ISSUE (10%)

C20	25c blue	70.00 (6)	55.00 (6)	5.50	4.00	3.25	2.75

1937. Type of 1935 Issue, Date Omitted (10%)

C21	20c green	375.00 (6)	300.00 (6)	47.50	40.00	4.85	4.25
C22	50c carmine	375.00 (6)	300.00 (6)	47.50	40.00	12.50	11.00

1938 (10%)

C23	6c blue & carmine	28.00	24.00	1.30	1.10	.13	.10
C23c	6c ultramarine & carmine	.....	.....	300.00	250.00	.....	.....

1939. TRANS-ATLANTIC ISSUE (10%)

C24	30c dull blue	445.00 (6)	350.00 (6)	50.00	40.00	3.75	3.25

SCOTT CAT. NO.	DESCRIPTION	FIRST DAY COVERS SING. PL BLK		MINT SHEET	PLATE BLOCKS F/NH	F	UNUSED F/NH	F	USED F

C25-C31   C32

1941-44

C25-31	6c-50c 7 Vars. cpl.	.....	.....	.....	515.00	470.00	87.50	79.50	10.95
C25	6c Transport Plane	6.00	10.00	19.95(50)	2.60	2.25	.50	.45	.10
C26	8c Transport Plane	6.00	10.00	25.00(50)	4.50	4.00	.60	.55	.15
C27	10c Transport Plane	7.50	12.00	250.00(50)	52.50	42.50	5.50	5.00	.25
C28	15c Transport Plane	11.00	14.00	475.00(50)	60.00	50.00	10.75	10.00	.75
C29	20c Transport Plane	9.50	15.50	335.00(50)	50.00	45.00	7.75	6.75	.70
C30	30c Transport Plane	15.00	25.00	515.00(50)	60.00	55.00	12.00	11.00	.65
C31	50c Transport Plane	37.50	67.50	2400.00(50)	325.00	300.00	55.00	50.00	9.00

1946

C32	5c DC-4 Skymaster	1.75	4.50	15.65(50)	1.65	1.40	.35	.30	.07

C33,C37,C39,C41   C34   C35   C36

1947

C33-36	5c-25c 4 vars. cpl.	.....	.....	.....	34.75	32.25	6.95	6.25	.35
C33	5c DC-4 Skymaster	1.95	4.50	23.75(100)	1.65	1.50	.30	.25	.07
C34	10c Pan American Bldg.	2.25	4.50	44.50(50)	5.00	4.50	1.05	.95	.07
C35	15c New York Skyline	2.95	6.65	46.75(50)	5.00	4.50	1.10	1.00	.07
C36	25c Plane over Bridge	3.65	7.95	210.00(50)	25.00	23.50	5.00	4.50	.18

1948
Rotary Press Coil. Perf 10 Horiz.

LINE PAIR

C37	5c DC-4 Skymaster	3.95	pr.6.95	———	22.00	20.00	3.25	3.00	3.00

C38   C40

C38	5c New York Jubilee	3.00	6.00	57.50(100)	33.00	30.00	.32	.28	.25

1949
Design of 1947

C39	6c DC-4 Skymaster	1.75	3.25	37.75(100)	2.20	2.00	.45	.40	.07
C40	6c Alexandria, Va.	1.75	4.00	16.50(50)	1.90	1.75	.40	.35	.20

Design of 1947. Rotary Press Coil. Perf. 10 Horiz.
LINE PAIR

C41	6c DC-4 Skymaster	1.75	pr.2.00	———	35.00	32.50	11.50	11.00	.07

NOTE: Air Mail coil pairs can be supplied at two times the singles price.

SCOTT CAT. NO.	DESCRIPTION	FIRST DAY COVERS SING. PL BLK		MINT SHEET	PLATE BLOCKS F/NH F		UNUSED F/NH F		USED F

C42

C43

C44

1949 U.P.U ISSUES

C42	10c Post Office	3.00	6.25	41.95(50)	7.00	6.50	.85	.80	.80
C43	15c Globe & Dove	5.00	7.50	60.95(50)	6.50	6.00	1.40	1.30	1.30
C44	25c Plane & Globe	5.00	7.95	105.00(50)	35.00	28.00	2.00	1.85	1.50

C45

C46

C47

1949-58.

| C45-51 | 7 Varieties cpl . . . . | . . . . . | . . . . . | . . . . . | . . . . . | . . . . . | 28.95 | 26.25 | 3.60 |

1949

| C45 | 6c Wright Bros. . . . . | 3.00 | 4.00 | 27.95(50) | 3.00 | 2.75 | .65 | .60 | .27 |

1952

| C46 | 80c Hawaii . . . . | 22.50 | 67.50 | 1200.00(50) | 145.00 | 130.00 | 27.50 | 25.00 | 2.10 |

1953

| C47 | 6c Powered Flight . . . . | 2.00 | 3.50 | 15.75(50) | 1.90 | 1.75 | .38 | .33 | .22 |

C48, C50

C49

C51,C52,C60,C61

1954

| C48 | 4c Eagle . . . . | 1.75 | 3.25 | 34.50(100) | 8.00 | 7.50 | .33 | .30 | .17 |

1957

| C49 | 8c Air Force . . . . | 2.00 | 3.50 | 20.95(50) | 2.25 | 2.10 | .50 | .45 | .17 |

1958

| C50 | 5c Eagle . . . . | 1.75 | 5.25 | 55.00(100) | 8.00 | 7.50 | .55 | .50 | .50 |
| C51 | 7c Silhouette of Jet . . . . | 1.75 | 5.25 | 51.50(100) | 2.50 | 2.25 | .60 | .55 | .07 |

Rotary Press Coil. Perf. 10 Horiz.

					LINE	PAIR			
C52	7c Silhouette of Jet	1.75	pr.2.00	——	53.50	50.00	8.75	8.50	.20

C53

C54

C55

C56

1959 COMMEMORATIVES

| C53-56 | 4 Vars., cpl . . . . | . . . . . | . . . . . | . . . . . | 15.95 | 14.75 | 2.30 | 2.10 | 1.05 |

SCOTT CAT. NO.	DESCRIPTION	FIRST DAY COVERS SING.	PL BLK	MINT SHEET	PLATE BLOCKS F/NH	F	UNUSED F/NH	F	USED F
C53	7c Alaska Statehood	2.00	3.50	23.50(50)	2.75	2.50	.55	.50	.12
C54	7c Balloon Jupiter	1.75	3.25	23.50(50)	2.75	2.50	.55	.50	.12
C55	7c Hawaii Statehood	1.75	3.25	23.50(50)	2.75	2.50	.55	.50	.12
C56	10c Pan-Am Games	2.25	4.00	39.75(50)	8.50	8.00	.80	.75	.75

C57, C62   C58   C59   C63

1959-61. REGULAR ISSUES

C57/63	(C57-60,62-63) 6 Vars.				59.95	54.95	10.50	10.00	2.60

1959-60

C57	10c Liberty Bell	2.50	8.75	260.00(50)	33.00	30.00	5.50	5.35	2.00
C58	15c Statue of Liberty	2.65	4.50	66.50(50)	8.00	7.00	1.60	1.40	.18
C59	25c Abraham Lincoln	3.75	6.95	61.75(50)	6.25	6.00	1.40	1.30	.12

1960. Design of 1958

| C60 | 7c Jet Plane, carmine | 2.50 | 4.25 | 50.00(100) | 2.40 | 2.25 | .60 | .55 | .07 |

Rotary Press Coil—Perf. 10 Horiz.

					LINE PR.				
C61	7c Jet Plane, carmine	2.60	pr. 2.75		95.00	90.00	17.00	16.00	.70

1961

| C62 | 13c Liberty Bell | 2.50 | 4.75 | 59.75(50) | 9.50 | 9.00 | 1.30 | 1.20 | .25 |
| C63 | 15c Statue re-drawn | 2.50 | 4.75 | 40.00(50) | 4.00 | 3.65 | .90 | .85 | .12 |

C64, C65   C66   C67   C68   C69

1962-64

C64/69	(C64, 66-69) 5 Vars.				42.50	39.95	6.00	5.45	2.25

1962

| C64 | 8c Plane & Capitol | 1.95 | 3.35 | 50.00(100) | 2.45 | 2.25 | .60 | .55 | .07 |

Rotary Press Coil—Perf. 10 Horiz.

					LINE PR.				
C65	8c Plane & Capitol	2.00	pr. 2.25	——	9.50	9.00	.80	.75	.08

1963

C66	15c Montgomery Blair	2.50	6.00	149.00(50)	17.75	16.75	2.90	2.75	1.45
C67	6c Bald Eagle	2.25	5.65	51.50(100)	8.50	8.25	.50	.45	.30
C68	8c Amelia Earhart	3.25	5.00	32.25(50)	5.50	5.00	.65	.60	.30

1964

| C69 | 8c Dr. Robert H. Goddard | 3.50 | 13.50 | 146.50(50) | 10.50 | 10.00 | 1.75 | 1.50 | .30 |
| C69 | Zip Block | | | | 10.00 | 9.50 | | | |

SCOTT CAT. NO.	DESCRIPTION	FIRST DAY COVERS SING. PL. BLK.		MINT SHEET	MAIL EARLY	ZIP	PLATE BLOCK	UN-USED	USED

C70   C71   C72,C73   C74   C75,C81

		1967-69							
C70/76	(C70-72, 74-76) 6 Vars.	. . . .		. . . . .	48.95(4)	73.75	67.95	9.85	1.30
		1967							
C70	8c Alaska Purchase	1.75	3.25	58.95(50)	___	10.00	10.75	1.10	.35
C71	20c "Columbia" Jays	2.75	5.35	216.50(50)	___	22.00	22.00	4.50	.17
C72	10c 50-Stars	2.15	4.75	83.75(100)	12.50	12.50	5.00	.85	.08
		1968 Rotary Press Coil—Perf. 10 Vert.							
							LINE PR.		
C73	10c 50-Stars	1.95	pr.2.15	___		___	4.25	1.10	.08
C74	10c Air Mail Anniversary	3.65	5.50	60.95(50)	20.00	18.00	18.00	1.00	.33
C75	20c "USA" & Plane	2.35	4.25	110.00(50)	13.00	10.25	10.75	2.25	.17
		1969							
C76	10c Man on The Moon	3.50	5.65	22.25(32)	6.25	5.00	5.00	.65	.35

C76   C77   C78,C82   C79,C83   C80

		1971-73							
C77-81	9c-21c, 5 Vars. cpl.	. . . . .	. . . . .	. . . . .	25.25	16.50	16.50	3.65	.90
C77	9c Delta Winged Plane	1.95	3.35	42.75(100)	3.25	2.50	2.50	.45	.40
C78	11c Silhouette of Plane	1.95	3.35	51.95(100)	3.50	2.50	2.50	.55	.08
C79	13c Letter	1.95	3.95	61.75(100)	6.55	3.25	3.25	.65	.10
C80	17c Liberty Head	2.15	3.95	56.75(50)	7.35	5.00	5.00	1.20	.25
C81	21c "USA" & Plane	2.35	8.50	47.50(50)	6.15	4.35	4.35	1.00	.15
		Rotary Press Coils—Perf. 10 Vertically							
							LINE PR.		
C82	11c Silhouette of Jet	1.95	pr.2.15	___		___	2.45	.80	.08
C83	13c Letter	1.95	pr.2.15	___		___	2.75	.85	.10

NOTE: Air Mail coil pairs can be supplied at
two times the single price.

DON'T FORGET CRYSTAL MOUNT   **Inside Back Cover**

NOTE: To determine the VF price on stamps issued from 1941 to date, add 15% to the F/NH or F (used)
price (minimum .03 per item). All VF unused stamps from 1941 to date will be NH. From 1964 to
date, all will be F/NH.

SCOTT CAT. NO.	DESCRIPTION	FIRST DAY COVERS SING. PL. BLK.		MINT SHEET	MAIL EARLY	ZIP	PLATE BLOCK	UN-USED	USED

C84   C85   C86   C87

C88   C89   C90

Cat. No.	Description	Sing.	Pl. Blk.	Mint Sheet	Mail Early	Zip	Plate Block	Un-Used	Used
	1972-76								
C84-90	7 Vars. cpl.	.....		......	44.50	30.95	36.75	6.85	2.65
	1972								
C84	11c City of Refuge	2.25	4.50	29.25(50)	4.50	3.25	3.25	.60	.25
C85	11c Olympics	2.25	4.50	33.50(50)	5.50	3.50	7.50(10)	.70	.25
	1973								
C86	11c Electronics	2.25	4.50	35.25(50)	4.50	3.25	3.25	.75	.25
C87	18c Statue of Liberty	2.25	6.65	57.00(50)	7.25	5.00	5.00	1.20	1.30
C88	26c Mt. Rushmore	2.25	5.95	62.50(50)	8.00	5.50	5.75	1.30	.25
	1976								
C89	25c Plane & Globes	2.00	6.00	61.00(50)	7.75	5.35	7.00	1.25	.35
C90	31c Plane, Flag, & Globes	2.35	6.50	74.00(50)	9.50	6.75	7.00	1.55	.18

C91   C92   C93   C94   C95   C96

COPY-RIGHT

Cat. No.	Description	Sing.	Pl. Blk.	Mint Sheet	Mail Early	Zip	Plate Block	Un-Used	Used
	1978-79								
C91-97	7 Vars. cpl.	.....		......	27.95(4)	27.95(4)	51.75(4)	10.25	....
C91-92	2 Vars., att'd	4.95	6.75	150.00(100)	6.50	6.50	7.75	3.00	...
C91	31c Wright Bros. & Plane	2.75	———	———	———	———	———	1.50	.45
C92	31c Wright Bros. & Shed	2.75	———	———	———	———	———	1.50	.45
	1979								
C93-94	2 Vars., att'd	4.95	4.75	129.00(100)	5.65	5.65	7.50	2.70	...
C93	21c Chanute & Plane	2.75	———	———	———	———	———	1.35	.65
C94	21c Chanute & 2 Planes	2.75	———	———	———	———	———	1.35	.65
C95-96	2 Vars., att'd	4.95	6.25	158.00(100)	9.00	9.00	9.00	3.50	...
C95	25c Post & Plane	2.75	———	———	———	———	———	1.75	.65
C96	25c Plane & Post	2.75	———	———	———	———	———	1.75	.65

C97

| C97 | 31c High Jumper .... | 3.00 | 6.95 | 92.50(50) | 8.00 | 8.00 | 30.00(12) | 1.75 | .60 |

SCOTT CAT. NO.	DESCRIPTION	FIRST DAY COVERS SING. PL. BLK.		MINT SHEET	COPY-RIGHT	ZIP	PLATE BLOCK	UN-USED	USED

C99

C100

C98

1980

C98	40c Phillip Mazzei	2.00	6.00	59.95(50)	5.25	5.25	16.00(12)	1.20	.25
C99	28c Blanche S. Scott	1.95	4.95	45.00(50)	4.25	4.25	12.25(12)	.90	.30
C100	35c Glenn Curtiss	1.95	4.95	55.00(50)	4.75	4.75	14.75(12)	1.10	.35

C101

C102

C103

C104

1983

C101-104	4 Vars., att'd	5.50	6.75	33.50(50)	3.10	3.10	3.10	2.80	.....
C101	28c Womens Gymnastics .	2.25	—	—	—	—	—	.70	.....
C102	28c Hurdles	2.25	—	—	—	—	—	.70	.....
C103	28c Womens Basketball	2.25	—	—	—	—	—	.70	.....
C104	28c Soccer	2.25	—	—	—	—	—	.70	.....

C105

C106

C107

C108

C105-08	4 Vars., att'd.	6.75	8.00	45.50(50)	4.10	4.10	4.10	3.80	.....
C105	40c Shot Put	2.75	—	—	—	—	—	.95	.....
C106	40c Mens Gymnastics	2.75	—	—	—	—	—	.95	.....
C107	40c Womens Swimming	2.75	—	—	—	—	—	.95	.....
C108	40c Weight-Lifting	2.75	—	—	—	—	—	.95	.....

SAVE! See Special Offers On Next Page. And Don't Forget Our Complete Line Of Supplies Listed In The Back Of This Catalog.

SCOTT CAT. NO.	DESCRIPTION	FIRST DAY COVERS SING.	PL. BLK.	MINT SHEET	MAIL EARLY	ZIP	PLATE BLOCK	UN-USED	USED

C109

C110

C111

C112

SCOTT CAT. NO.	DESCRIPTION	SING.	PL. BLK.	MINT SHEET	MAIL EARLY	ZIP	PLATE BLOCK	UN-USED	USED
C109-12	35c Olympics, 4 vars., attd.	6.25	7.50	38.95(50)	3.75	3.75	3.75	3.40	
C109	35c Fencing	2.50						.85	
C110	35c Cycling	2.50						.85	
C111	35c Volleyball	2.50						.85	
C112	35c Pole Vault	2.50						.85	

U.S. COMMEMORATIVE STAMPS

U.S. COMMEMORATIVES ISSUED PRIOR TO 1941

In one moderate purchase, you can obtain these desirable commemoratives at a considerable savings from the individual retail prices.

#A146 100 Usnused Commemoratives
(Save over $14.00).........................$68.50
#A147 130 Used Commemoratives
(Save $17.83) $45.50

1941-1950 COMMEMORATIVES

In one money-saving purchase, you acquire all the perforated commemoratives issued from 1941 through 1950. The souvenir sheet #948 is included. 95 different varieties.

#A151 Unused (SAVE $8.96)...........$20.75
#A161 Used (SAVE $4.11) $12.25

1951-1959 COMMEMORATIVES

Every commemorative postage stamp (108 different) issued from 1951 through 1959 (including the souvenir sheet) at a special price.

#A152 Unused (SAVE $7.60)...........$28.95
#A162 Used (SAVE $2.87) $17.50

1960-1965 COMMEMORATIVES

Every commemorative postage stamp (116 different) issued from 1960 to 1965 at a special price.

#A153 Unused (SAVE $6.82)...........$31.95
#A163 Used (SAVE $2.70) $6.95

1966-1970 COMMEMORATIVES

Every commemorative postage stamp (97 different) issued from 1966 through 1970 including the souvenir sheet (no pre cancels) at a special price.

#A154 Unused (SAVE $25.16)...........$61.95
#A164 Used (SAVE $3.64) $14.75

1971-1975 COMMEMORATIVES

Every commemorative postage stamp (142 different) issued from 1971-1975 at a special price.

#A155 Unused (SAVE $13.39)...........$56.50
#A165 Used (SAVE $3.78) 14.95

1976-1979 COMMEMORATIVES

Every commemorative postage stamp (160 different) issued from 1976 through 1979 including State Flags and the popular Bicentennial Souvenir Sheets.

#A156 Unused (SAVE $38.70)..........$146.50
#A166 Used (SAVE $6.68) $37.50

NOTE: BICENTENNIAL & CAPEX S/S are not included in the used offer. Used A offer Contains 155 Stamps.

1980-1983 COMMEMORATIVES

Every commemorative postage stamp (192 different) issued from 1980 through 1983 including the popular State Birds and Flowers.

#A157 Unused (Save $22.36) $99.95
#A167 Used (Save $3.19) $27.75

SUPER SPECIAL—SAVE $165.07!
U.S. COMMEMORATIVES
COMPLETE—1941-1983

Save $165.07 on the unused collection, or $48.62 on the used. The collection includes every packet in this commemorative section except the #A146 and #A147. 910 Postage Commemoratives from 1941 through 1983 at a savings you can't afford to miss. Included are SOUVENIR SHEETS 948, 1075, 1311, 1686-89*, and 1757*. Don't miss this unusual opportunity.

(*Included in unused only)

#A158 Unused Commems...$395.00
#A168 904 Used Commems (#1935 not included)..................................$110.00

U.S. COMMEMORATIVE PLATE BLOCKS

30 UNUSED PLATE BLOCKS
1941-1952 — SAVE $9.50

#A382 Commem Pl. Blocks $32.95

30 UNUSED PLATE BLOCKS
1953-1959 — SAVE $5.50

#A383 Commem. Pl. Blocks............$28.95

25 UNUSED PLATE BLOCKS
1960-1967 — SAVE $8.35

#A384 Commem. Pl. Blocks...........$28.75

20 UNUSED PLATE BLOCKS
1968-1971 — SAVE $12.65

#A385 Commem. Pl. Blocks.............$38.75

20 UNUSED PLATE BLOCKS
1972-1975 — SAVE $8.35

#A386 Commem. Pl. Blocks............$37.95

15 UNUSED PLATE BLOCKS
1976-1979 — SAVE $19.80

#A387 Commem. Pl. Blocks...........$93.95

SUPER COLLECTION! 140 UNUSED PLATE BLOCKS 1941-1979—SAVE $89.20

Includes all Commemoratives Plate Block packets above. A tremendous beginning for a good plate block collection.

#A 389 Commem. Plate Blocks $225.00

U.S. REGULAR POSTAGE ISSUES

60 UNUSED REGULAR ISSUES—SAVE $5.24

Issued from 1917-1981; All unused; All face different; no Coils or imperforates. Several early issues included.

#A141 Unused 27.95

25 UNUSED COIL STAMPS
SAVE $6.99

Issues to 1971, all designs different, no current issues included.

#A144 Coils, unused $16.75

80 USED REGULAR ISSUES
SAVE OVER 35%

All face different, issued from 1938 through 1981. No Coils or imperfs.

#A143 Used $4.95

40 USED COIL STAMPS
SAVE $2.94

All different issued thru 1975. An excellent value of the popular category.

#A145 Coils, used $6.75

25 REGULAR ISSUE PLATE BLOCKS
ISSUED FROM 1926-1974 — BIG VALUE, SAVE $11.10!

Twenty five blocks from a 48-year period. Why not order this collection when you order the Commemorative blocks on opposite page?

#A391 Definitive Plate Blocks $45.00

U.S. AIRMAILS

55 UNUSED U.S. AIR MAILS
SAVE $12.91

The largest unused U.S. Air mail collection we have ever offered, this SPECIAL OFFER includes many of the more desirable issues such as the 1932 Winged Globe stamp and the complete Universal Postal Union Set.

#A271 Unused $57.95

40 UNUSED AIR MAILS
SAVE $6.11

A smaller collection designed to fit the more modest stamp budget. SAVE $6.11 OFF INDIVIDUAL PRICES.

#A272 Unused $19.95

60 USED AIR MAILS
SAVE $7.76

This is your chance to fill more than half of the spaces in the U.S. Air Post section of your album at considerable savings from individual prices. This offer contains the 5c Beacon, the 6c & 8c Winged Globes and other desirable items.

#A273. Used $12.95

25 AIR MAIL PLATE BLOCKS
SAVE $11.70

All different. All Unused. Issued from 1941-74. Save $11.70 off individual prices.

#A393 Air Mail PL. Block $61.95

U.S. "BACK-OF-THE-BOOK" ISSUES

25 UNUSED U.S.
SPECIAL ISSUES—SAVE $6.33

Included in this attractive collection are a fine section of Special Delivery and Postage Due stamps plus the popular Special Handling Stamp of 1928.

#A275 Unused $27.50

SAVE $4.30 — 30 UNUSED
20th Century Postal Stationery Entires

Both regular entires and air mail entires are contained in this special collection which is priced at a considerable savings from our individual prices. Included are many better varieties. All are obsolete issues no longer available at the the Post Office.

#A416 Unused $20.50

35 MINT U.S. POSTAL CARDS
SAVE $3.60

35 all different U.S. Postal Cards issued between 1914 and 1981. Includes the 1c Jefferson issue of 1913 as well as many popular air mail issues.

#A417 Postal Cards $17.95

You Save More Than 20% Off Individual Prices

25 UNUSED ZIP CODE BLOCKS SAVE $16.35

25 Unused Commemorative Zip Blocks issued between 1964 and 1969

#A401 .....Special Price $37.95

30 UNUSED ZIP CODE BLOCKS SAVE $15.05

30 Unused Commemorative Zip Blocks issued between 1970 and 1973.

#A402 .....Special Price $39.95

30 UNUSED ZIP CODE BLOCKS SAVE $11.55

30 Unused Commemorative Zip Blocks issued between 1974 and 1979.

#A403 .....Special Price $69.95

85 UNUSED ZIP CODE BLOCKS

A combination of the three Zip Block offers at an additional money saving price. Save over 24% off individual prices. Super Special Price

#A404 ....$145.00

25 MAIL EARLY AND EMBLEM BLOCKS SAVE $17.95

25 Unused Commemorative Mail Early and Emblem Blocks issued between 1968 and 1972.

#A405 .....Special Price $54.50

25 MAIL EARLY AND EMBLEM BLOCKS SAVE $30.70

25 Unused Commemorative Mail Early and Emblem Blocks Issued between 1973 and 1977.

#A406 .....Special Price $54.95

15 UNUSED COPYRIGHT BLOCKS SAVE $6.85

15 Unused Commemorative Copyright Blocks issued between 1978 and 1979.

#A407 .....Special Price $39.95

85 UNUSED MAIL EARLY AND COPYRIGHT BLOCKS

A combination of the three Mail Early and Copyright Offers. Save over 29% off individual prices Super Special Price.

#A408 ....$145.00

SCOTT CAT. NO.	DESCRIPTION	PLATE BLOCK F	AVG	UNUSED F	AVG	USED F	AVG

AIR MAIL SPECIAL DELIVERY STAMPS

771, CE1, CE2

1934

| CE1 | 16c dark blue . . . . | 70.00(6) | 60.00(6) | 3.75 | 3.50 | 3.75 | 3.50 |

1936

| CE2 | 16c red & blue . . . . | 35.00 | 30.00 | 1.20 | 1.00 | .55 | .50 |

NOTE: To obtain VF price, add the difference between the Avg. and F prices to the F price. For NH Price for CE1-2, add 15% to appropriate condition price.

---

60 DIFFERENT USED AIR MAILS

This is your chance to fill more than half of the spaces in the U.S. Air Post section of your album at considerable savings from individual prices: This offer contains the 5c Beacon, the 6c Winged Globes and other desireable items.

#A273 (SAVE $7.76) $12.95

25 AIR MAIL PLATE BLOCKS All different. All Unused. Issued from 1941-74
SAVE OVER $11.70 off individual prices.

#A393 . . . . $61.95

		UNUSED O.G. F	AVG	UNUSED F	AVG	USED F	AVG

SPECIAL DELIVERY STAMPS

E1

E2, E3

E4, E5

E6, E8-E11

1885
Inscribed "Secures Immediate Delivery at Special Delivery Office" Perf. 12

| E1 | 10c blue. . . . . | 525.00 | 400.00 | 450.00 | 325.00 | 100.00 | 85.00 |

1888
Inscribed "Secures Immediate Delivery at any Post Office"

| E2 | 10c blue. . . . . | 575.00 | 450.00 | 500.00 | 375.00 | 26.00 | 22.50 |

1893

| E3 | 10c orange . . . . | 350.00 | 275.00 | 300.00 | 225.00 | 42.00 | 35.00 |

1894
Same type as preceding issue, but with line under "Ten Cents" Unwatermarked.

| E4 | 10c blue. . . . . | 1275.00 | 925.00 | 1125.00 | 775.00 | 48.00 | 40.00 |

1895
Double Line Watermark

| E5 | 10c blue. . . . . | 320.00 | 240.00 | 275.00 | 200.00 | 7.50 | 6.25 |

E7

E12, E13, E15-E18   E14, E19

NOTE: To determine the VF price, add the difference between the Avg. and F prices to the F price. If NH is desired on back of the book stamps issued prior to 1900, add 50% to the Unused O.G. Price.

SCOTT CAT NO.	DESCRIPTION	PLATE BLOCK F	AVG	UNUSED F	AVG	USED F	AVG
		1902 (40%)					
E6	10c ultramarine	. . . . .	. . . . .	210.00	160.00	7.25	6.00
		1908 (40%)					
E7	10c green	. . . . .	. . . . .	145.00	110.00	95.00	80.00
		1911 Single Line Watermark (40%)					
E8	10c ultramarine	. . . . .	. . . . .	210.00	160.00	13.00	11.00
		1914 Perf. 10 (40%)					
E9	10c ultramarine	. . . . .	. . . . .	325.00	240.00	16.50	14.00
		1916 Unwatermarked. Perf. 10 (40%)					
E10	10c pale ultra.	. . . . .	. . . . .	565.00	400.00	53.50	45.00
		1917 Perf. 11 (40%)					
E11	10c ultramarine	600.00(6)	450.00(6)	55.00	48.50	.95	.80
		1922-25 Flat Plate Printing. Perf. 11 (30%)					
E12	10c deep ultra.	750.00(6)	600.00(6)	80.00	68.00	.40	.35
E13	15c deep orange	525.00(6)	425.00(6)	55.00	45.00	2.25	2.00
E14	20c black	125.00(6)	100.00(6)	8.00	6.50	4.50	4.00

NOTE: To determine the VF price for #E6-E14, add the difference between the Avg. and F prices to the F price. To determine the NH price, add the percentage in parentheses to the appropriate condition price.

		FIRST DAY COVERS SING.	PL. BLK.	PLATE BLOCK F/NH	F	UNUSED F/NH	F	USED F
		1927-51 Rotary Press Printing. Perf. 11 x 10½						
E15-19	10c-20c, 5 Vars	. . . . .	. . . . .	. . . . .	. . . . .	29.95	26.50	6.95
E15	10c gray violet (1927)	. . . . .	. . . . .	16.00	13.50	2.00	1.75	.08
E16	15c orange (1931)	. . . . .	. . . . .	14.50	12.50	2.25	2.00	.09
E17	13c blue (1944)	15.00	30.00	12.50	11.50	1.85	1.60	.10
E18	17c yellow (1944)	15.00	30.00	70.00	65.00	17.00	15.00	7.00
E19	20c black (1951)	12.00	25.00	35.00	30.00	9.00	7.75	.16

E20, E21

E22, E23

		1954-71						
E20-23	cpl., 4 Vars.	—	—	50.25	49.50	10.50	10.25	.70
E20	20c blue (1954)	3.50	6.00	8.75	8.25	1.75	1.60	.10
E21	30c maroon (1957)	3.50	6.00	7.25	6.75	1.50	1.40	.07
E22	45c red & blue (1969)	6.00	12.00	24.50	. . . . .	5.00	. . . . .	.42
	Zip Block	—	—	24.00	. . . . .	—		
	Mail Early Block	—	—	36.50	. . . . .	—		
E23	60c blue & red (1971)	6.00	12.00	12.50	. . . . .	2.75	. . . . .	.17
	Zip Block	—	—	12.50	. . . . .	—		
	Mail Early Block	—	—	17.00	. . . . .	—		

SCOTT CAT. NO.	DESCRIPTION	FIRST DAY COVERS SING.	PL. BLK.	PLATE BLOCK F/NH	F	UNUSED F/NH	F	USED F

CERTIFIED MAIL STAMP

FA1

POSTAL NOTE STAMPS

PN1-PN18
*All values printed
in black*

1955

| FA1 | 15 rose carmine . . . . | 4.25 | 8.25 | 16.00 | 15.00 | 1.20 | 1.10 | .55 |

1945

| PN1-18 | 1c to 90c 18 Vars. cpl. . . . . | —— | —— | 450.00 | 400.00 | 41.00 | 36.00 | 1.40 |

---

25 DIFFERENT UNUSED U.S. SPECIAL ISSUES

Included in this attractive collection are a fine selection of Special Delivery and Postage Due stamps plus a popular Special Handling Stamp of 1928.

Save $6.33 off individual retail prices.

#A275 . . . . **$27.50**

		UNUSED N.H. F	AVG	UNUSED F	AVG	USED F	AVG

REGISTRATION STAMP

F1

POSTAGE DUE STAMPS

J1-J28

1911

| F1 | 10c ultramarine . . . . | 280.00 | 235.00 | 215.00 | 165.00 | 12.00 | 10.00 |

		UNUSED O.G. F	AVG	UNUSED F	AVG	USED F	AVG

1879. Unwatermarked. Perf. 12

J1	1c brown	40.00	30.00	35.00	25.00	9.75	7.50
J2	2c brown	295.00	230.00	260.00	195.00	9.75	7.50
J3	3c brown	30.00	24.00	25.00	20.00	4.85	3.65
J4	5c brown	400.00	285.00	350.00	225.00	50.00	40.00
J5	10c brown	500.00	375.00	425.00	300.00	17.00	15.00
J6	30c brown	210.00	155.00	165.00	125.00	30.00	22.50
J7	50c brown	325.00	240.00	275.00	200.00	95.00	80.00

1884-89

| J15 | 1c red brown . . . . | 60.00 | 45.00 | 50.00 | 35.00 | 6.75 | 5.00 |
| J16 | 2c red brown . . . . | 65.00 | 50.00 | 55.00 | 40.00 | 7.75 | 6.00 |

SCOTT CAT. NO.	DESCRIPTION	UNUSED O.G. F	AVG	UNUSED F	AVG	USED F	AVG
J17	3c red brown	585.00	450.00	500.00	375.00	150.00	125.00
J18	5c red brown	325.00	240.00	275.00	200.00	21.00	17.50
J19	10c red brown	240.00	180.00	210.00	150.00	13.50	10.50
J20	30c red brown	210.00	160.00	175.00	135.00	45.50	35.00
J21	50c red brown	1325.00	925.00	1200.00	600.00	150.00	125.00

1891-93

J22	1c bright claret	14.75	11.50	13.50	10.00	1.10	.95
J23	2c bright claret	18.00	14.00	16.00	12.00	.95	.75
J24	3c bright claret	30.50	23.50	27.00	20.00	9.00	7.50
J25	5c bright claret	38.50	30.00	35.00	25.00	9.00	7.50
J26	10c bright claret	70.00	55.00	60.00	45.00	16.25	12.95
J27	30c bright claret	325.00	235.00	295.00	200.00	150.00	120.00
J28	50c bright claret	360.00	280.00	315.00	235.00	150.00	120.00

J29-J68

1894-95. Unwatermarked, Perf. 12 (†) 40%)

J29	1c pale vermillion	650.00	500.00	550.00	400.00	115.00	90.00
J30	2c dark vermillion	300.00	220.00	250.00	175.00	47.50	35.00
J31	1c deep claret	37.50	30.00	32.50	25.00	9.50	7.00
J32	2c deep claret	29.50	18.00	22.50	15.00	6.00	4.50
J33	3c deep claret	80.00	60.00	70.00	50.00	32.50	25.00
J34	5c deep claret	90.00	70.00	75.00	55.00	28.00	20.00
J35	10c deep claret	95.00	75.00	70.00	50.00	24.00	18.00
J36	30c deep claret	320.00	240.00	275.00	200.00	55.00	45.00
J36b	30c rose	290.00	210.00	240.00	175.00	52.50	42.50
J37	50c deep claret	550.00	425.00	475.00	350.00	150.00	110.00

1895-97. Double Line Watermark, Perf. 12 (40%) (†)

J38	1c deep claret	9.50	7.00	7.25	6.00	.95	.75
J39	2c deep claret	10.00	7.50	7.75	6.50	.32	.25
J40	3c deep claret	45.00	40.00	45.00	35.00	2.40	1.75
J41	50c deep claret	40.00	35.00	40.00	30.00	2.40	1.75
J42	10c deep claret	60.00	48.00	52.00	40.00	5.75	4.50
J43	30c deep claret	340.00	240.00	300.00	210.00	45.00	35.00
J44	50c deep claret	220.00	160.00	200.00	140.00	50.00	40.00

		PLATE BLOCK F	AVG	UNUSED F	AVG	USED F	AVG
		1910-12. Single Line Watermark, Perf. 12 (30%)					
J45	1c deep claret	450.00(6)	400.00(6)	28.00	22.50	3.25	2.50
J46	2c deep claret	425.00(6)	375.00(6)	28.00	22.50	.30	.25
J47	3c deep claret			400.00	300.00	17.50	13.50
J48	5c deep claret	650.00(6)	600.00(6)	60.00	45.00	3.75	3.00
J49	10c deep claret			95.00	75.00	18.75	15.75
J50	50c deep claret			725.00	525.00	95.00	70.00
		1914-15. Single Line Watermark, Perf. 10 (30%)					
J52	1c carmine lake	625.00(6)	550.00(6)	55.00	40.00	12.00	10.00
J53	2c carmine lake	400.00(6)	350.00(6)	28.00	20.00	.55	.45
J54	3c carmine lake			400.00	325.00	22.50	16.00
J55	5c carmine lake	350.00(6)	300.00(6)	30.00	20.00	2.75	2.25
J56	10c carmine lake	750.00(6)	650.00(6)	45.00	35.00	2.50	2.00
J57	30c carmine lake	2475.00(6)	2300.00(6)	185.00	140.00	22.00	18.00
J58	50c carmine lake			5450.00	4250.00	535.00	400.00
		1916. Unwatermarked, Perf. 10 (30%)					
J59	1c rose			1000.00	750.00	275.00	200.00
J60	2c rose			85.00	60.00	8.50	7.00

SCOTT CAT. NO.	DESCRIPTION	PLATE BLOCK F	AVG	UNUSED F	AVG	USED F	AVG

1917-23. Unwatermarked, Perf. 11 (30%)

J61	1c dull red	70.00(6)	55.00(6)	5.50	5.00	.28	.25
J62	2c dull red	55.00(6)	40.00(6)	5.50	5.00	.28	.25
J63	3c dull red	115.00(6)	90.00(6)	10.50	8.50	.28	.25
J64	5c dull red	115.00(6)	90.00(6)	10.50	8.50	.28	.25
J65	10c dull red	190.00(6)	140.00(6)	18.25	15.00	.60	.50
J66	30c dull red	675.00(6)	575.00(6)	80.00	65.00	1.30	1.25
J67	50c dull red	825.00(6)	750.00(6)	85.00	70.00	.35	.30

1925 (30%)

J68	½c dull red	15.00(6)	11.50(6)	1.25	1.00	.28	.25

J69-J76, J79-J86   J77, J78, J87   J88-J103

1930-31. Perf. 11 (30%)

J69	½c carmine	50.00(6)	40.00(6)	5.25	4.25	1.65	1.50
J70	1c carmine	40.00(6)	30.00(6)	4.00	3.00	.34	.30
J71	2c carmine	55.00(6)	45.00(6)	5.00	4.25	.34	.30
J72	3c carmine	325.00(6)	250.00(6)	27.00	20.00	2.15	1.95
J73	5c carmine	325.00(6)	250.00(6)	27.00	20.00	2.60	2.25
J74	10c carmine	500.00(6)	400.00(6)	47.50	32.50	.90	.75
J75	30c carmine	1100.00(6)	1000.00(6)	185.00	140.00	1.75	1.50
J76	50c carmine	1275.00(6)	1150.00(6)	195.00	150.00	.60	.50
J77	$1 scarlet	365.00(6)	275.00(6)	40.00	30.00	.25	.20
J78	$5 scarlet	500.00(6)	385.00(6)	75.00	60.00	.35	.25

1931-32. Rotary Press Printing, Perf. 11 x 10½ (20%)

J79-86	½c 50c 8 Vars. cpl.	.....	.....	48.95	42.50	.85	.60
J79	½c carmine	50.00	45.00	2.60	2.35	.15	.12
J80	1c carmine	4.50	3.75	.30	.25	.10	.07
J81	2c carmine	4.50	3.75	.35	.30	.10	.07
J82	3c carmine	8.00	7.50	.55	.45	.10	.07
J83	5c carmine	9.50	8.00	.75	.70	.10	.07
J84	10c carmine	15.25	13.50	2.35	2.00	.10	.07
J85	30c carmine	105.00	90.00	20.00	17.50	.13	.10
J86	50c carmine	140.00	125.00	25.00	22.00	.12	.08

SUPPLIES

Don't forget that Harris offers a complete line of albums, supplies, and accessories for all your stamp collecting needs. See our supply section in the back of this catalog.

See Page X For Condition Defintions.

NOTE: To determine the VF price for stamps issued from 1901 to 1940, add the difference between the Avg. and F prices to the F price. To determine the NH price for these issues, add the percentage in parentheses to the appropriate condition price.

SCOTT CAT. NO.	DESCRIPTION	PLATE BLOCK F/NH	F	UNUSED F/NH	F	USED F
		1956 Rotary Press Printing. Perf 10½ x 11				
J87	$1.00 scarlet	460.00	375.00	65.00	55.00	.25
		1959				
J88-101	½c-$5 14 Vars, cpl.	.....	.....	20.25	19.95	4.15
J88-97	½c-10c 10 Vars.	.....	.....	4.50	3.95	3.60
J88	½c red & black	295.00	275.00	3.15	3.00	3.00
J89	1c red & black	.60	.55	.10	.07	.07
J90	2c red & black	.65	.60	.10	.07	.07
J91	3c red & black	.75	.70	.12	.09	.07
J92	4c red & black	1.35	1.25	.13	.10	.07
J93	5c red & black	1.25	1.15	.15	.12	.07
J94	6c red & black	1.50	1.40	.18	.15	.11
J95	7c red & black	1.80	1.65	.21	.18	.18
J96	8c red & black	1.90	1.75	.23	.20	.09
J97	10c red & black	2.35	2.15	.28	.25	.07
J98	30c red & black	6.00	5.50	.80	.75	.09
J99	50c red & black	11.75	11.00	1.30	1.25	.07
J100	$1 red & black	12.50	12.00	2.60	2.50	.07
J101	$5 red & black	65.00	60.00	12.25	12.00	.20
		1978				
J102	11c red & black	3.25	.....	.28	.....	.17
J103	13c red & black	3.45	.....	.33	.....	.17

	UNUSED NH F	AVG	UNUSED F	AVG	USED F	AVG

OFFICES IN CHINA

1919

SHANGHAI
2¢
CHINA

K1-16: U.S. Postage
498-518 surcharged

1922

K17-18: U.S. Postage
498/528B with local surcharge

SHANGHAI
4Cts.
CHINA

		UNUSED NH F	AVG	UNUSED F	AVG	USED F	AVG
		1919					
K1	2c on 1c green	44.00	35.00	32.50	25.00	40.00	30.00
K2	4c on 2c rose	44.00	35.00	32.50	25.00	40.00	30.00
K3	6c on 3c violet	110.00	90.00	80.00	60.00	80.00	60.00
K4	8c on 4c brown	110.00	90.00	80.00	60.00	85.00	65.00
K5	10c on 5c blue	130.00	110.00	105.00	80.00	95.00	70.00
K6	12c on 6c red orange	145.00	120.00	105.00	80.00	100.00	75.00
K7	14c on 7c black	130.00	100.00	100.00	72.50	120.00	90.00
K8	16c on 8c olive	125.00	95.00	95.00	70.00	100.00	75.00
K8a	16c on 8c olive green	120.00	90.00	90.00	65.00	100.00	75.00
K9	18c on 9c salmon red	150.00	125.00	110.00	85.00	120.00	95.00
K10	20c on 10c orange yellow	145.00	120.00	105.00	80.00	120.00	95.00
K11	24c on 12c brown carmine	155.00	130.00	115.00	90.00	120.00	95.00
K11a	24c on 12c claret brown	165.00	140.00	125.00	100.00	115.00	90.00
K12	30c on 15c gray	150.00	125.00	110.00	85.00	115.00	90.00
K13	40c on 20c ultramarine	235.00	180.00	175.00	125.00	200.00	150.00
K14	60c on 30c orange red	235.00	180.00	175.00	125.00	200.00	150.00
K15	$1 on 50c light violet	1350.00	1050.00	1050.00	700.00	800.00	550.00
K16	$2 on $1 violet brown	900.00	700.00	675.00	485.00	675.00	485.00
		1922					
K17	2c on 1c green	175.00	140.00	125.00	95.00	110.00	80.00
K18	4c on 2c carmine	175.00	140.00	125.00	95.00	130.00	90.00

SCOTT CAT. NO.	DESCRIPTION	UNUSED O.G. F	AVG	UNUSED F	AVG	USED F	AVG

OFFICIAL STAMPS

O1-O9, O94, O95   O10-O14   O15-O24, O96-O103   O25-O34, O106, O107

Except for the Post Office Department, portraits for the various
denominations are the same as on the regular issues of 1870-73.

1873 Printed by the Continental Bank Note Co.
Thin hard paper

DEPARTMENT OF AGRICULTURE

		Unused O.G. F	AVG	Unused F	AVG	Used F	AVG
O1	1c yellow	85.00	60.00	70.00	50.00	45.00	32.50
O2	2c yellow	60.00	45.00	50.00	36.50	20.00	15.00
O3	3c yellow	50.00	35.00	40.00	30.00	6.00	4.00
O4	6c yellow	65.00	50.00	55.00	40.00	20.00	15.00
O5	10c yellow	150.00	110.00	125.00	90.00	70.00	50.00
O6	12c yellow	240.00	180.00	200.00	150.00	105.00	75.00
O7	15c yellow	150.00	110.00	125.00	90.00	70.00	50.00
O8	24c yellow	190.00	135.00	160.00	110.00	90.00	60.00
O9	30c yellow	240.00	165.00	200.00	140.00	130.00	90.00

EXECUTIVE DEPARTMENT

O10	1c carmine	325.00	240.00	275.00	200.00	135.00	95.00
O11	2c carmine	240.00	180.00	200.00	150.00	105.00	75.00
O12	3c carmine	275.00	210.00	225.00	175.00	95.00	70.00
O12a	3c violet rose	240.00	180.00	200.00	150.00	95.00	70.00
O13	6c carmine	420.00	320.00	350.00	260.00	210.00	150.00
O14	10c carmine	380.00	275.00	320.00	225.00	210.00	150.00

DEPARTMENT OF THE INTERIOR

O15	1c vermilion	23.00	17.00	19.00	14.00	4.00	3.00
O16	2c vermilion	20.00	15.00	16.00	12.00	3.25	2.75
O17	3c vermilion	32.50	25.00	27.50	20.00	3.25	2.75
O18	6c vermilion	23.50	17.25	18.50	13.50	3.25	2.75
O19	10c vermilion	18.00	13.75	15.00	11.00	7.00	5.00
O20	12c vermilion	32.00	24.00	27.50	20.00	4.50	3.50
O21	15c vermilion	65.00	50.00	55.00	40.00	13.50	10.00
O22	24c vermilion	50.00	35.00	42.50	30.00	9.50	7.00
O23	30c vermilion	60.00	42.00	50.00	35.00	13.00	7.50
O24	90c vermilion	130.00	95.00	110.00	80.00	20.00	15.00

DEPARTMENT OF JUSTICE

O25	1c purple	50.00	35.00	40.00	30.00	27.50	20.00
O26	2c purple	90.00	65.00	75.00	55.00	32.50	25.00
O27	3c purple	110.00	80.00	90.00	65.00	13.25	10.00
O28	6c purple	90.00	65.00	75.00	55.00	16.50	12.50
O29	10c purple	95.00	70.00	80.00	60.00	35.00	25.00
O30	12c purple	55.00	42.50	45.00	35.00	20.00	15.00
O31	15c purple	145.00	110.00	120.00	90.00	65.00	45.00
O32	24c purple	425.00	300.00	350.00	250.00	185.00	135.00
O33	30c purple	390.00	270.00	325.00	225.00	130.00	100.00
O34	90c purple	570.00	420.00	475.00	350.00	250.00	175.00

NOTE: To determine the VF price, add the difference between the Avg. and F prices to the F price. If
NH is desired, add 40% to the unused O.G. price.

SCOTT CAT.NO.	DESCRIPTION	UNUSED OG		UNUSED		USED	
		F	AVG	F	AVG	F	AVG

O35-O45   O47-O56, O108   O57-O67   O68-O71
Seward

NAVY DEPARTMENT

SCOTT CAT.NO.	DESCRIPTION	UNUSED OG F	AVG	UNUSED F	AVG	USED F	AVG
O35	1c ultramarine	45.00	35.00	40.00	30.00	20.00	16.00
O36	2c ultramarine	32.00	25.00	27.00	20.00	17.00	13.50
O37	3c ultramarine	35.00	26.50	30.00	22.00	7.75	6.50
O38	6c ultramarine	27.50	21.00	24.50	18.50	11.75	9.00
O39	7c ultramarine	230.00	180.00	200.00	150.00	100.00	75.00
O40	10c ultramarine	55.00	42.00	45.00	35.00	20.00	16.00
O41	12c ultramarine	70.00	55.00	60.00	45.00	16.00	12.50
O42	15c ultramarine	115.00	90.00	100.00	75.00	38.50	28.00
O43	24c ultramarine	115.00	90.00	100.00	75.00	55.00	40.00
O44	30c ultramarine	95.00	72.00	80.00	60.00	23.00	18.00
O45	90c ultramarine	425.00	325.00	375.00	275.00	160.00	125.00

POST OFFICE DEPARTMENT

SCOTT CAT.NO.	DESCRIPTION	UNUSED OG F	AVG	UNUSED F	AVG	USED F	AVG
O47	1c black	14.50	11.00	12.50	9.00	6.75	5.50
O48	2c black	14.50	11.00	12.50	9.00	5.75	4.50
O49	3c black	6.00	5.00	5.00	4.00	2.25	1.75
O50	6c black	15.00	12.00	13.00	10.00	3.75	2.00
O51	10c black	60.00	45.00	50.00	35.00	30.00	22.00
O52	12c black	27.50	20.00	22.00	16.50	7.00	5.00
O53	15c black	35.00	25.00	30.00	20.00	10.75	8.00
O54	24c black	40.00	30.00	35.00	25.00	14.00	10.00
O55	30c black	40.00	30.00	35.00	25.00	14.00	10.00
O56	90c black	62.50	48.00	55.00	40.00	20.00	15.00

DEPARTMENT OF STATE

SCOTT CAT.NO.	DESCRIPTION	UNUSED OG F	AVG	UNUSED F	AVG	USED F	AVG
O57	1c dark green	55.00	42.00	45.00	35.00	20.00	15.00
O58	2c dark green	120.00	90.00	105.00	75.00	45.00	35.00
O59	3c bright green	45.00	33.00	35.00	25.00	13.50	10.00
O60	6c bright green	45.00	33.00	35.00	25.00	13.50	10.00
O61	7c dark green	95.00	72.00	80.00	60.00	26.00	20.00
O62	10c dark green	55.00	42.00	45.00	35.00	20.00	15.00
O63	12c dark green	105.00	80.00	90.00	65.00	42.50	35.00
O64	15c dark green	75.00	55.00	65.00	45.00	26.50	20.00
O65	24c dark green	225.00	165.00	195.00	140.00	110.00	80.00
O66	30c dark green	205.00	155.00	180.00	130.00	80.00	60.00
O67	90c dark green	460.00	360.00	400.00	300.00	175.00	125.00
O68	$2 green & black	825.00	625.00	725.00	525.00	335.00	250.00
O69	$5 green & black	6300.00	4800.00	5500.00	4000.00	3000.00	2000.00
O70	$10 green & black	4000.00	3000.00	3450.00	2500.00	1900.00	1350.00
O71	$20 green & black	3500.00	2550.00	3000.00	2150.00	1500.00	1100.00

O72-O82, O109-O113   O83-O93, O114-O120

U.S. Official #072-0120

SCOTT CAT.NO.	DESCRIPTION	UNUSED O.G.		UNUSED		USED	
		F	AVG	F	AVG	F	AVG

TREASURY DEPARTMENT

072	1c brown	21.00	15.50	17.50	13.50	3.75	3.00
073	2c brown	30.00	24.00	26.00	20.00	3.75	3.00
074	3c brown	16.00	12.50	13.00	10.00	2.35	1.85
075	6c brown	29.50	22.00	25.00	18.00	2.35	1.85
076	7c brown	55.00	42.00	45.00	35.00	19.50	14.75
077	10c brown	55.00	42.00	45.00	35.00	9.00	5.00
078	12c brown	55.00	42.00	45.00	35.00	3.25	2.50
079	15c brown	55.00	42.00	45.00	35.00	6.00	4.50
080	24c brown	265.00	200.00	225.00	160.00	80.00	60.00
081	30c brown	70.00	55.00	60.00	45.00	7.00	5.00
082	90c brown	85.00	65.00	75.00	55.00	5.25	4.00

WAR DEPARTMENT

083	1c rose	80.00	60.00	70.00	50.00	6.00	4.75
084	2c rose	80.00	60.00	70.00	50.00	9.25	7.00
085	3c rose	70.00	55.00	60.00	45.00	3.00	2.50
086	6c rose	280.00	215.00	235.00	175.00	5.00	4.00
087	7c rose	70.00	55.00	60.00	45.00	38.50	27.50
088	10c rose	25.00	20.00	21.00	17.50	6.00	4.50
089	12c rose	65.00	50.00	57.50	42.00	4.50	3.50
090	15c rose	18.00	13.50	15.00	11.00	3.50	2.50
091	24c rose	19.00	14.50	16.00	12.00	4.00	3.00
092	30c rose	19.50	15.00	16.50	12.50	4.25	3.25
093	90c rose	55.00	42.00	45.00	35.00	17.00	13.00

1879 Printed by American Bank Note Co.
Soft Porous Paper.

DEPARTMENT OF AGRICULTURE

094	1c yellow	2100.00	1550.00	1800.00	1300.00	‒‒‒	‒‒‒
095	3c yellow	265.00	210.00	225.00	175.00	35.00	25.00

DEPARTMENT OF INTERIOR

096	1c vermilion	190.00	130.00	160.00	110.00	90.00	65.00
097	2c vermilion	4.50	3.50	4.00	3.00	1.65	1.35
098	3c vermilion	4.00	3.00	3.50	2.50	1.75	1.40
099	6c vermilion	6.00	4.25	4.75	3.50	2.25	1.75
0100	10c vermilion	48.00	36.00	40.00	30.00	25.00	18.00
0101	12c vermilion	75.00	55.00	62.50	45.00	41.50	30.00
0102	15c vermilion	170.00	130.00	145.00	110.00	90.00	65.00
0103	24c vermilion	1700.00	1250.00	1500.00	1050.00	. . . . .	. . . . .

DEPARTMENT OF JUSTICE

0106	3c bluish purple	62.50	48.50	55.00	40.00	27.50	20.00
0107	6c bluish purple	160.00	115.00	135.00	95.00	90.00	65.00

POST OFFICE DEPARTMENT

0108	3c black	9.50	7.25	8.00	6.00	2.60	2.00

TREASURY DEPARTMENT

0109	3c brown	32.50	24.00	27.00	20.00	4.75	3.50
0110	6c brown	70.00	55.00	60.00	45.00	30.00	22.00
0111	10c brown	105.00	80.00	90.00	65.00	26.00	20.00
0112	30c brown	1150.00	850.00	1000.00	700.00	210.00	150.00
0113	90c brown	1150.00	850.00	1000.00	700.00	210.00	150.00

WAR DEPARTMENT

0114	1c rose red	4.25	3.25	3.75	2.75	1.65	1.25
0115	2c rose red	5.50	4.25	4.75	3.50	2.50	1.75
0116	3c rose red	5.50	4.25	4.75	3.50	1.65	1.25
0117	6c rose red	5.25	4.00	4.75	3.25	1.75	1.35
0118	10c rose red	23.00	18.00	20.00	15.00	11.00	8.00
0119	12c rose red	20.00	15.00	18.50	12.50	3.50	2.75
0120	30c rose red	65.00	48.00	55.00	40.00	38.50	28.00

O121-O126   O127-O135

1910-11
Double Line Watermark.

SCOTT CAT.NO.	DESCRIPTION	UNUSED OG F	AVG	UNUSED F	AVG	USED F	AVG
O121	2c black	19.00	14.50	16.00	12.00	2.25	1.75
O122	50c dark green	170.00	130.00	150.00	110.00	55.00	40.00
O123	$1 ultramarine	170.00	130.00	150.00	110.00	17.00	12.00

Single Line Watermark.

O124	1c dark violet	8.50	6.00	6.50	5.00	2.25	1.75
O125	2c black	50.00	38.50	45.00	32.50	6.50	5.00
O126	10c carmine	15.50	12.00	13.00	9.75	2.25	1.75

1983

SCOTT CAT. NO.	DESCRIPTION	FIRST DAY COVERS SING.	PL. BLK.	MINT SHEET	COPY-RIGHT	BLOCK	PLATE USED	UN-USED
O127	1c Great Seal	1.75	3.25	2.95(100)	.35	.35	.07	.....
O128	4c Great Seal	1.75	3.25	9.95(100)	.50	.50	.10	.....
O129	13c Great Seal	1.75	3.25	30.95(100)	1.45	1.45	.32	.....
O130	17c Great Seal	1.75	3.25	39.95(100)	1.85	1.85	.42	.....
O132	$1.00 Great Seal	5.50	15.00	225.00(100)	11.00	11.00	2.50	.....
O133	$5.00 Great Seal	16.00	60.00	1100.00(100)	55.00	55.00	12.50	.....
O135	20c Great Seal, coil	1.75	2.00(pr)	—	—	4.95(pr)	.50	.....

NOTE: F.D.C. formats are: 3(1c), 1(4c), 1(13c) for #O127-29;   3(1c), 1(17c) for #O127 and O130.

PR1 (colored border)
PR4, PR5, PR8 (white border)

PR2, PR6
(colored border)

PR3, PR7
(colored border)

NEWSPAPER STAMPS

SCOTT CAT.NO.	DESCRIPTION	UNUSED	USED
	1865 Printed by the National Bank Note Co. No Watermark.		
PR1	5c dark blue	145.00	.....
PR2	10c blue green	75.00	.....
PR3	25c carmine red	70.00	.....
PR4	5c dark blue	40.00	30.00

1875 Reprints of 1865 Issue.
Printed by the Continental Bank Note Co.
Hard White Paper.

PR5	5c dull blue	60.00	—
PR6	10c dark bluish green	40.00	—
PR7	25c dark carmine	75.00	—

1880 Printed by the American Bank Note Co.
Soft Porous Paper

PR8	5c dark blue	125.00	

PR9-15, PR33-39, PR57-62
PR80-81, PR90-94
"Freedom"

PR16-23, PR40-47, PR63-70
PR82-89, PR95-99
"Justice"

PR24, PR48
PR71
"Ceres"

PR25, PR49
PR72, PR100
"Victory"

PR26, PR50,
PR73, PR101
"Clio"

PR27, PR51
PR74
"Minerva"

PR28, PR52
PR75
"Vesta"

PR29, PR53
PR76
"Peace"

PR30, PR54
PR77
"Commerce"

PR31, PR55,
PR78
"Hebe"

SCOTT CAT.NO.	DESCRIPTION	UNUSED	USED

PR32, PR36,
PR79
"Indian Maiden"

1875 Printed by the Continental Bank Note Co.
Thin Hard Paper.

		UNUSED	USED
PR9	2c black	8.00	7.75
PR10	3c black	15.00	15.00
PR11	4c black	15.00	15.00
PR12	6c black	16.50	16.50
PR13	8c black	20.00	20.00
PR14	9c black	35.00	25.00
PR15	10c black	25.00	20.00
PR16	12c rose	37.50	28.00
PR17	24c rose	55.00	40.00
PR18	36c rose	60.00	45.00
PR19	48c rose	100.00	60.00
PR20	60c rose	60.00	50.00
PR21	72c rose	125.00	95.00
PR22	84c rose	150.00	100.00
PR23	96c rose	110.00	90.00
PR24	$1.92 dark brown	130.00	95.00
PR25	$3 vermilion	175.00	115.00
PR26	$6 ultramarine	325.00	165.00
PR27	$9 yellow	425.00	195.00
PR28	$12 blue green	475.00	260.00
PR29	$24 gray violet	475.00	275.00
PR30	$36 brown rose	525.00	300.00
PR31	$48 red brown	675.00	425.00
PR32	$60 violet	650.00	400.00

Special Printing.
Hard White Paper, Without Gum.

PR33	2c gray black	65.00	
PR34	3c gray black	70.00	
PR35	4c gray black	90.00	
PR36	6c gray black	110.00	
PR37	8c gray black	125.00	
PR38	9c gray black	140.00	
PR39	10c gray black	195.00	
PR40	12c pale rose	225.00	
PR41	24c pale rose	250.00	
PR42	36c pale rose	350.00	
PR43	48c pale rose	400.00	
PR44	60c pale rose	525.00	
PR45	72c pale rose	625.00	
PR46	84c pale rose	650.00	
PR47	96c pale rose	825.00	

NOTE: Newspaper Stamps are very difficult to obtain in premium condition. If fine or better, or never hinged is desired, please write for availability and price.

SCOTT CAT.NO.	DESCRIPTION	UNUSED	USED

1879 Printed by the American Bank Note Co. Soft Porous Paper. No Watermark.

PR57	2c black	5.00	4.50
PR58	3c black	7.00	6.50
PR59	4c black	7.00	6.50
PR60	6c black	13.50	12.00
PR61	8c black	13.50	12.00
PR62	10c black	13.50	12.00
PR63	12c red	35.00	25.00
PR64	24c red	35.00	25.00
PR65	36c red	110.00	90.00
PR66	48c red	85.00	60.00
PR67	60c red	70.00	60.00
PR68	72c red	160.00	95.00
PR69	84c red	120.00	85.00
PR70	96c red	90.00	65.00
PR71	$1.92 pale brown	75.00	60.00
PR72	$3 red vermilion	75.00	60.00
PR73	$6 blue	120.00	85.00
PR74	$9 orange	85.00	60.00
PR75	$12 yellow green	120.00	80.00
PR76	$24 dark violet	160.00	110.00
PR77	$36 indian red	190.00	125.00
PR78	$48 yellow brown	250.00	160.00
PR79	$60 purple	275.00	160.00

1883 Special Printing.

PR80	2c intense black	135.00	

1885

PR81	1c black	5.75	3.65
PR82	12c carmine	14.50	10.00
PR83	24c carmine	18.00	15.00
PR84	36c carmine	35.00	20.00
PR85	48c carmine	40.00	30.00
PR86	60c carmine	55.00	35.00
PR87	72c carmine	65.00	50.00
PR88	84c carmine	125.00	90.00
PR89	96c carmine	100.00	75.00

1894 Printed by Bureau of Engraving and Printing. Soft Woven Paper. No Watermark.

PR90	1c intense black	25.00	
PR91	2c intense black	25.00	
PR92	4c intense black	35.00	
PR94	10c intense black	60.00	
PR95	12c pink	265.00	
PR96	24c pink	235.00	

PR102-05
PR114-17
"Freedom"

PR106, PR107
PR118, PR119
"Justice"

PR108, PR120
"Victory"

PR109, PR121
"Clio"

PR110, PR122
"Vesta"

PR111, PR123
"Peace"

PR112, PR124
"Commerce"

PR113, PR125
"Indian Maiden"

1895. No Watermark.

PR102	1c black	16.00	5.00
PR103	2c black	19.50	6.00
PR104	5c black	25.00	9.00
PR105	10c black	50.00	25.00
PR106	25c carmine	65.00	25.00
PR107	50c carmine	150.00	70.00
PR108	$2 scarlet	195.00	45.00
PR109	$5 ultramarine	325.00	145.00
PR110	$10 green	275.00	150.00
PR111	$20 slate	525.00	265.00
PR112	$50 dull rose	550.00	265.00
PR113	$100 purple	625.00	325.00

1895-97. Double Line Watermark. Yellowish Gum.

PR114	1c black	4.50	3.25
PR115	2c black	4.50	2.75
PR116	5c black	6.00	4.00
PR117	10c black	4.50	3.00
PR118	25c carmine	7.00	4.00
PR119	50c carmine	7.50	5.00
PR120	$2 scarlet	10.00	10.00
PR121	$5 dark blue	20.00	20.00
PR122	$10 green	17.50	25.00
PR123	$20 slate	20.00	25.00
PR124	$50 dull rose	25.00	25.00
PR125	$100 purple	25.00	35.00

PLATE BLOCKS CAT.NO.	DESCRIPTION	UNUSED NH F	AVG	UNUSED F	AVG	USED F	AVG

PARCEL POST STAMPS

Q1-Q12 Various Designs

PARCEL POST DUE STAMPS

JQ1-JQ5

SPECIAL HANDLING STAMPS

QE1-QE4

1912-13 All Printed in Carmine Rose (30%)

CAT.NO.	DESCRIPTION	NH F	AVG	UNUSED F	AVG	USED F	AVG
Q1-12	1c $1 12 Vars. cpl.	.....	.....	.....	.....	.....	220.00
Q1-9	1c-25c, 9 Vars.	.....	.....	.....	.....	.....	65.00
Q1	1c P.O. clerk		.....	7.00	5.00	2.60	2.20
Q2	2c City Carrier		.....	10.50	8.00	1.20	.95
Q3	3c Railway Clerk		.....	27.50	20.00	14.50	12.00
Q4	4c Rural Carrier		.....	60.00	48.00	4.00	3.00
Q5	5c Mail Train		.....	50.00	37.50	3.75	2.75
Q6	10c Steamship		.....	90.00	70.00	4.75	4.00
Q7	15c Auto Service		.....	125.00	100.00	16.00	12.50
Q8	20c Airplane		.....	250.00	190.00	28.50	22.50
Q9	25c Manufacturing		.....	120.00	90.00	12.00	10.00
Q10	50c Dairying		.....	350.00	300.00	80.00	65.00
Q11	75c Harvesting		.....	165.00	135.00	60.00	50.00
Q12	$1 Fruit Growing		.....	600.00	425.00	52.50	45.00

1912 (30%)

CAT.NO.	DESCRIPTION	NH F	AVG	UNUSED F	AVG	USED F	AVG
JQ1	1c dark green	800.00(6)	625.00(6)	20.00	15.00	6.75	5.50
JQ2	2c dark green	3800.00(6)	3000.00(6)	150.00	110.00	35.00	28.50
JQ3	5c dark green	1050.00(6)	800.00(6)	20.00	15.00	9.00	7.00
JQ4	10c dark green	.....	.....	275.00	210.00	100.00	85.00
JQ5	25c dark green	.....	.....	150.00	110.00	9.25	7.75

1925-29 (30%)

CAT.NO.	DESCRIPTION	NH F	AVG	UNUSED F	AVG	USED F	AVG
QE1	10c yellow green	50.00(6)	40.00(6)	4.50	3.75	2.25	2.00
QE2	15c yellow green	80.00(6)	65.00(6)	4.75	4.00	2.25	2.00
QE3	20c yellow green	80.00(6)	65.00(6)	9.50	8.00	4.25	3.75
QE4	25c yellow green	675.00(6)	575.00(6)	65.00	55.00	17.75	15.00
QE4a	25c deep green	750.00(6)	650.00(6)	72.50	60.00	12.50	10.50

NOTE: To obtain VF price, add the difference between the Avg. and F prices to the F price. For NH price for Q1-12, JQ1-5, and QE1-4a, add 30% to the appropriate condition price.

		UNUSED O.G. F	AVG	UNUSED F	AVG	USED F	AVG

OFFICIAL CARRIER STAMPS

LO1, LO3, LO4

Franklin

LO2, LO5, LO6

Eagle

1851

CAT.NO.	DESCRIPTION	O.G. F	AVG	UNUSED F	AVG	USED F	AVG
LO2	1c blue	57.50	40.00	45.00	30.00	45.00	30.00

1875 Reprints of 1851 Issues.

CAT.NO.	DESCRIPTION	O.G. F	AVG	UNUSED F	AVG	USED F	AVG
LO3	1c blue	___	___	65.00	50.00	___	___
LO5	1c blue, imperf.	___	___	35.00	25.00	___	___
LO6	1c blue, perforated	___	___	125.00	95.00	___	___

SCOTT CAT. NO.	DESCRIPTION	UNUSED ENTIRE	UNUSED CUT SQ.	USED CUT SQ.

ENVELOPES

U1-U18	U19-W25, U28, U29	U26-U33
Washington	*Franklin*	*Washington*

1853-55

Scott	Description	Unused Entire	Unused Cut Sq.	Used Cut Sq.
U1	3c red on white, die 1	550.00	95.00	6.00
U2	3c red on buff, die 1	375.00	50.00	4.00
U3	3c red on white, die 2	1400.00	400.00	18.50
U4	3c red on buff, die 2	725.00	95.00	9.25
U5	3c red on white, die 3	......	......	200.00
U6	3c red on buff, die 3	500.00	80.00	16.50
U7	3c red on white, die 4	2300.00	375.00	45.00
U8	3c red on buff, die 4	2200.00	650.00	70.00
U9	3c red on white, die 5	30.00	10.00	1.00
U10	3c red on buff, die 5	25.00	4.00	.85
U11	6c red on white	120.00	57.50	40.00
U12	6c red on buff	125.00	50.00	30.00
U13	6c green on white	200.00	135.00	65.00
U14	6c green on buff	180.00	130.00	57.50
U15	10c green on white, die 1	150.00	90.00	42.00
U16	10c green on buff, die 1	95.00	40.00	20.00
U17	10c green on white, die 2	175.00	125.00	60.00
U18	10c green on buff, die 2	95.00	52.50	25.00

1860-61

Scott	Description	Unused Entire	Unused Cut Sq.	Used Cut Sq.
U19	1c blue on buff, die 1	35.00	18.00	6.25
W20	1c blue on buff, die 1	70.00	40.00	35.00
W21	1c blue on manila, die 1	50.00	25.00	22.50
U23	1c blue on orange, die 2	300.00	245.00	250.00
U24	1c blue on buff, die 3	185.00	115.00	70.00
U26	3c red on white	25.00	15.00	8.50
U27	3c red on buff	19.00	12.50	6.50
U28	3c + 1c red & blue on white	300.00	230.00	175.00
U29	3c + 1c red & blue on buff	290.00	180.00	165.00
U30	6c red on white	1800.00	1100.00	875.00
U31	6c red on buff	1550.00	950.00	625.00
U32	10c green on white	3650.00	475.00	190.00
U33	10c green on buff	1250.00	425.00	110.00

U34-U39	*Washington*	U40-U45

1861

Scott	Description	Unused Entire	Unused Cut Sq.	Used Cut Sq.
U34	3c pink on white	20.00	10.00	2.50
U35	3c pink on buff	20.00	10.00	2.50
U36	3c pink on blue (letter sheet)	110.00	38.50	18.00
U38	6c pink on white	120.00	85.00	75.00
U39	6c pink on buff	85.00	55.00	55.00
U40	10c yellow green on white	33.00	18.00	19.00
U41	10c yellow green on buff	35.00	18.50	16.00
U42	12c brown & red on buff	220.00	120.00	100.00
U43	20c blue & red on buff	275.00	120.00	100.00

Scott	Description	Unused Entire	Unused Cut Sq.	Used Cut Sq.
U44	24c green & red on buff	385.00	140.00	110.00
U45	40c red & black on buff	425.00	185.00	180.00

U46-U49	*Jackson*	U50-W57

1863-64

Scott	Description	Unused Entire	Unused Cut Sq.	Used Cut Sq.
U46	2c black on buff, die 1	40.00	28.50	12.50
W47	2c black on dark manila, die 1	40.00	28.50	23.00
U48	2c black on dark manila, die 1	2000.00	850.00	
U49	2c black on orange, die 2	1300.00	725.00	
U50	2c black on orange, die 2	17.50	7.50	5.75
W51	2c black on buff, die 3	130.00	80.00	80.00
U52	2c black on buff, die 3	13.00	7.00	6.00
W53	2c black on dark manila, die 3	38.50	16.50	15.00
U54	2c black on buff, die 4	15.00	9.00	8.00
W55	2c black on buff, die 4	75.00	40.00	34.50
U56	2c black on orange, die 4	10.00	8.00	5.75
W57	2c black on light manila, die 4	14.00	7.50	7.50

U58-U65	*Washington*	U66-U73

1864-65

Scott	Description	Unused Entire	Unused Cut Sq.	Used Cut Sq.
U58	3c pink on white	4.50	3.00	1.35
U59	3c pink on buff	4.50	2.75	1.20
U60	3c brown on white	45.00	24.50	21.00
U61	3c brown on buff	40.00	22.50	17.50
U62	6c pink on white	46.50	27.50	20.00
U63	6c pink on buff	40.00	25.00	16.50
U64	6c purple on white	40.00	25.00	19.00
U65	6c purple on buff	40.00	25.00	16.50
U66	9c lemon on buff	375.00	180.00	130.00
U67	9c orange on buff	125.00	62.50	62.50
U68	12c brown on buff	350.00	150.00	130.00
U69	12c red brown on buff	90.00	65.00	50.00
U70	18c red on buff	155.00	60.00	45.00
U71	24c blue on buff	155.00	55.00	45.00
U72	30c green on buff	140.00	32.50	40.00
U73	40c rose on buff	180.00	50.00	100.00

U74-W77, U108-U121	U78-W81, U122-W158	U82-U84, U159-U169
Franklin	*Jackson*	*Washington*

SCOTT CAT. NO. DESCRIPTION	UNUSED ENTIRE	UNUSED CUT SQ.	USED CUT SQ.

U172-U180 *Taylor*

U85-U87, U181-U184 *Lincoln*

U88, U185, U186 *Stanton*

U89-U92, U187-U194 *Jefferson*

U93-U95, U195-U197 *Clay*

U96-U98, U198-U200 *Webster*

U99-U101, U201-U203 *Scott*

U102-U104, U204-U210, U336-U341 *Hamilton*

U105-U107, U211-U217, U342-U347 *Perry*

1870-71 REAY ISSUE

SCOTT CAT. NO. DESCRIPTION	UNUSED ENTIRE	UNUSED CUT SQ.	USED CUT SQ.
U74	1c blue on white	35.00	20.00	12.00
U74a	1c ultramarine on white . . .	52.00	30.00	17.00
U75	1c blue on amber	25.00	18.00	12.00
U75a	1c ultramarine on amber . . .	50.00	24.50	16.75
U76	1c blue on orange	15.00	8.25	8.25
W77	1c blue on manila	40.00	18.00	16.50
U78	2c brown on white	35.00	16.50	9.25
U79	2c brown on amber	20.00	10.00	6.25
U80	2c brown on orange	9.00	5.75	3.50
W81	2c brown on manila	20.00	8.00	8.00
U82	3c green on white	5.00	3.85	.65
U83	3c green on amber	6.25	3.75	1.35
U84	3c green on cream	10.00	6.50	2.25
U85	6c dark red on white	15.00	10.00	8.00
U86	6c dark red on amber	19.00	15.00	8.75
U87	6c dark red on cream	30.00	16.50	12.00
U88	7c vermilion on amber	30.00	17.50	90.00
U89	10c black on white	260.00	200.00	125.00
U90	10c olive black on amber . . .	260.00	200.00	125.00
U91	10c brown on white	52.50	37.50	37.50
U92	10c brown on amber	60.00	45.00	35.00
U93	12c plum on white	145.00	62.50	55.00
U94	12c plum on amber	150.00	55.00	45.00
U95	12c plum on cream	225.00	120.00	95.00
U96	15c red orange on white . . .	100.00	45.00	45.00
U97	15c red orange on amber . . .	275.00	95.00	100.00
U98	15c red orange on cream . . .	225.00	110.00	120.00
U99	24c purple on white	140.00	82.50	62.50
U100	24c purple on amber	220.00	92.50	110.00
U101	24c purple on cream	185.00	110.00	130.00
U102	30c black on white	150.00	52.50	60.00
U103	30c black on amber	300.00	110.00	140.00
U104	30c black on cream	190.00	100.00	175.00
U105	90c carmine on white	140.00	90.00	110.00
U106	90c carmine on amber	450.00	150.00	210.00
U107	90c carmine on cream	450.00	175.00	235.00

1874-86 PLIMPTION ISSUE

SCOTT CAT. NO. DESCRIPTION	UNUSED ENTIRE	UNUSED CUT SQ.	USED CUT SQ.
U108	1c dark blue on white, die 1	75.00	60.00	22.50
U109	1c dark blue on amber, die 1	70.00	65.00	45.00
U110	1c dark blue on cream, die 1	. . . . .	400.00	. . . . .
U111	1c dark blue on cream, die 1	20.00	12.00	8.00
U111a	1c dark blue on orange, die 1	18.00	12.00	7.50
W112	1c dark blue on manila, die 1	40.00	28.50	20.00
U113	1c light blue on white, die 2	1.10	.90	.60
U113a	1c light blue on white, die 2	10.00	5.75	3.00
U114	1c light blue on amber, die 2	2.50	1.75	1.35
U115	1c blue on cream, die 2 . . .	2.75	2.00	1.35
U115a	1c blue on cream, die 2	12.00	10.50	2.25
U116	1c light blue on orange, die 2	.80	.70	.25
U116a	1c blue on orange, die 2	4.25	1.00	.65
U117	1c blue on blue, die 2	4.00	3.00	2.35
U118	1c blue on fawn, die 2	3.75	3.00	2.35
U119	1c blue on manila, die 2 . . .	3.75	3.00	2.00
W120	1c light blue on manila, die 2	1.25	1.10	.85
W120a	1c dark blue on manila, die 2	4.00	3.00	1.75
U121	1c blue on amber manila, die 2	6.50	5.00	5.00
U122	2c brown on white, die 1 . . .	80.00	60.00	25.00
U123	2c brown on amber, die 1 . . .	50.00	24.50	18.00
U124	2c brown on cream, die 1 . . .	. . . . .	275.00	. . . . .
W126	2c brown on manila, die 1 . .	60.00	50.00	28.50
W127	2c vermilion on manila, die 1	1000.00	725.00	275.00
U128	2c brown on white, die 2 . .	40.00	26.50	14.50
U129	2c brown on amber, die 2 . .	40.00	30.00	16.50
W131	2c brown on manila, die 2 . .	8.25	6.25	6.25
U132	2c brown on white, die 3 . .	50.00	35.00	20.00
U133	2c brown on amber, die 3 . .	150.00	140.00	45.00
U134	2c brown on white, die 4 . .	450.00	400.00	85.00
U135	2c brown on amber, die 4 . .	300.00	240.00	75.00
U136	2c brown on orange, die 4 . .	40.00	25.00	18.00
W137	2c brown on manila, die 4 . .	45.00	35.00	22.50
U139	2c brown on white, die 5 . .	32.50	22.00	19.00
U140	2c brown on amber, die 5 . .	70.00	50.00	40.00
W141	2c brown on manila, die 5 . .	30.00	20.00	18.00
U142	2c vermilion on white, die 5 . .	4.00	3.00	1.75
U143	2c vermilion on amber, die 5 . .	4.00	3.50	1.75
U144	2c vermilion cream, die 5 . . .	8.00	6.00	5.50
U146	2c vermilion on blue, die 5 . .	115.00	65.00	25.00
U147	2c vermilion on fawn, die 5 . .	6.00	4.50	3.00
W148	2c vermilion on manila, die 5 . .	3.25	2.00	1.65
U149	2c vermilion on white, die 6 . .	35.00	25.00	15.00
U150	2c vermilion on amber, die 6 . .	17.00	14.00	10.00
U151	2c vermilion on blue, die 6 . .	7.00	5.50	3.75
U152	2c vermilion on fawn, die 6 . .	7.00	5.50	2.45
U153	2c vermilion on white, die 7 . .	40.00	30.00	18.00
U154	2c vermilion on amber, die 7 . .	175.00	150.00	50.00
W155	2c vermilion on manila, die 7 . .	12.00	7.50	5.75
U156	2c vermilion on white, die 8 . .	425.00	250.00	90.00
W158	2c vermilion on manila, die 8	80.00	50.00	35.00
U159	3c green on white, die 1 .	18.00	14.00	3.10
U160	3c green on amber, die 1 . .	20.00	17.00	5.00
U161	3c green on cream, die 1 . .	30.00	24.50	7.50
U163	3c green on white, die 2 . .	1.00	.60	.25
U164	3c green on amber, die 2 . .	1.50	.70	.30
U165	3c green on cream, die 2 . .	6.25	4.00	2.20
U166	3c green on blue, die 2 . .	7.00	4.00	2.50
U167	3c green on fawn, die 2 . .	4.00	2.00	1.25
U168	3c green on white, die 3 .	1200.00	275.00	30.00
U169	3c green on amber, die 3 .	175.00	125.00	65.00
U172	5c blue on white, die 1 . .	7.00	5.50	5.00
U173	5c blue on amber, die 1 . .	7.50	6.25	5.50
U174	5c blue on cream, die 1 . .	80.00	65.00	35.00
U175	5c blue on blue, die 1 . .	8.50	6.00	5.00
U176	5c blue on fawn, die 1 . .	145.00	65.00	40.00
U177	5c blue on white, die 2 . .	5.50	4.50	4.25
U178	5c blue on amber, die 2 . .	7.50	4.00	2.85
U179	5c blue on blue, die 2 . .	11.00	9.00	6.00
U180	5c blue on fawn, die 2 . .	75.00	60.00	30.00
U181	6c red on white	6.00	3.00	2.50
U182	6c red on amber	10.00	4.00	3.75

SCOTT CAT. NO.	DESCRIPTION	UNUSED ENTIRE	UNUSED CUT SQ.	USED CUT SQ.
183	6c red on cream	15.00	10.00	8.00
184	6c red on fawn	15.00	10.00	7.00
185	7c vermilion on white		550.00	
186	7c vermilion on amber	90.00	60.00	45.00
187	10c brown on white, die 1	30.00	14.00	10.00
188	10c brown on amber, die 1	50.00	35.00	20.00
189	10c chocolate on white, die 2	6.00	3.00	2.25
190	10c chocolate on amber, die 2	8.00	5.00	4.00
191	10c brown on buff, die 2	8.00	5.00	4.00
192	10c brown on blue, die 2	8.75	6.50	5.00
193	10c brown on manila, die 2	10.00	6.00	5.50
194	10c brown on amber manila, die 2	10.00	6.00	5.50
195	12c plum on white	110.00	90.00	45.00
196	12c plum on amber	140.00	110.00	75.00
197	12c plum on cream	500.00	135.00	80.00
198	15c orange on white	55.00	24.50	12.00
199	15c orange on amber	130.00	75.00	60.00
200	15c orange on cream	650.00	250.00	150.00
201	24c purple on white	150.00	110.00	50.00
202	24c purple on amber	165.00	110.00	65.00
203	24c purple on cream	500.00	90.00	70.00
204	30c black on white	45.00	30.00	19.00
205	30c black on amber	65.00	30.00	30.00
206	30c black on cream	575.00	225.00	160.00
207	30c black on oriental buff	95.00	50.00	45.00
208	30c black on blue	80.00	50.00	45.00
209	30c black on manila	75.00	40.00	40.00
210	30c black on amber manila	75.00	40.00	40.00
211	90c carmine on white	75.00	60.00	50.00
212	90c carmine on amber	140.00	75.00	90.00
213	90c carmine on cream	1200.00	750.00	
214	90c carmine on oriental buff	175.00	160.00	140.00
215	90c carmine on blue	150.00	100.00	125.00
216	90c carmine on manila	125.00	80.00	100.00
217	90c carmine on amber manila	135.00	75.00	90.00

U218-U221, U582
Pony Express Rider and Train

U222-U226
Garfield

ie 1. Single thick line under "POSTAGE"
ie 2. Two thin lines under "POSTAGE"

1876. CENTENNIAL ISSUE

218	3c red on white, die 1	70.00	60.00	20.00
219	3c green on white, die 1	60.00	50.00	14.00
221	3c green on white, die 2	80.00	50.00	12.00

1882-86

222	5c brown on white	3.00	2.25	1.10
223	5c brown on amber	4.50	2.25	1.50
224	5c brown on oriental buff	75.00	60.00	30.00
225	5c brown on blue	40.00	22.50	15.00
226	5c brown on fawn	165.00	125.00	

NOTE: For details on die or similar appearing varieties of envelopes, please refer to the Scott Specialized Catalogue.

U227-U230   U231-U249, U260-W292   U250-U259
Washington   Jackson

1883. OCTOBER

U227	2c red on white	3.00	2.25	.70
U228	2c red on amber	4.00	2.75	1.10
U229	2c red on blue	4.50	3.25	2.25
U230	2c red on fawn	4.25	3.00	1.35

1883. NOVEMBER
Four Wavy Lines in Oval.

U231	2c red on white	3.00	1.65	.45
U232	2c red on amber	3.50	2.25	.85
U233	2c red on blue	6.00	2.75	2.50
U234	2c red on fawn	4.00	2.25	.95
W235	2c red on manila	7.00	3.75	2.50

1884. JUNE

U236	2c red on white	5.00	3.25	1.35
U237	2c red on amber	9.00	6.25	3.00
U238	2c red on blue	12.00	7.50	4.25
U239	2c red on fawn	8.00	4.25	3.00
U240	2c red on white (3½ links)	30.00	26.00	15.00
U241	2c red on amber (3½ links)	400.00	350.00	190.00
U243	2c red on white (2 links)	50.00	30.00	25.00
U244	2c red on amber (2 links)	100.00	70.00	37.50
U245	2c red on blue (2 links)	150.00	120.00	50.00
U246	2c red on fawn (2 links)	150.00	110.00	60.00
U247	2c red on white (Round O)	600.00	425.00	150.00
U249	2c red on fawn (Round O)	375.00	250.00	130.00

1883-86

U250	4c green on white, die 1	3.00	2.00	1.50
U251	4c green on amber, die 1	3.50	2.25	1.50
U252	4c green on buff, die 1	7.25	4.00	3.00
U253	4c green on blue, die 1	7.00	4.25	3.00
U254	4c green on manila, die 1	7.00	5.25	3.75
U255	4c green on amber manila, die 1	15.00	12.00	6.00
U256	4c green on white, die 2	5.50	2.50	1.25
U257	4c green on amber, die 2	8.00	5.50	4.00
U258	4c green on manila, die 2	6.50	4.00	3.25
U259	4c green on amber manila, die 2	6.00	4.00	3.25

1884. MAY

U260	2c brown on white	8.75	6.50	2.00
U261	2c brown on amber	7.75	6.25	2.00
U262	2c brown on blue	9.50	6.50	4.00
U263	2c brown on fawn	7.75	6.25	3.00
W264	2c brown on manila	11.00	7.75	6.25

1884. JUNE

U265	2c brown on white	9.00	7.00	2.50
U266	2c brown on amber	27.50	25.00	11.00
U267	2c brown on blue	8.00	4.00	3.25
U268	2c brown on fawn	8.25	6.25	4.00
W269	2c brown on manila	14.50	12.00	8.00
U270	2c brown on white (2 links)	55.00	35.00	22.50
U271	2c brown on amber (2 links)	140.00	115.00	57.50
U273	2c brown on white (Round O)	95.00	80.00	40.00
U274	2c brown on amber (Round O)	95.00	85.00	40.00
U276	2c brown on fawn (Round O)	500.00	425.00	250.00

SCOTT CAT. NO. DESCRIPTION	UNUSED ENTIRE	UNUSED CUT SQ.	USED CUT SQ.
1884-86			
Two Wavy Lines in Oval.			
U277 2c brown on white, die 1	.55	.45	.25
U277a 2c brown lake on white, die 1	18.00	15.00	7.00
U278 2c brown on amber, die 1	.65	.60	.30
U279 2c brown on buff, die 1	3.25	2.50	1.35
U280 2c brown on blue, die 1	1.60	1.20	.80
U281 2c brown on fawn, die 1	2.00	1.35	.80
U282 2c brown on manila, die 1	7.00	6.25	2.65
W283 2c brown on manila, die 1	4.50	2.50	1.65
U284 2c brown on amber manila, die 1	5.00	3.25	2.25
U285 2c red on white, die 1	425.00	375.00	_____
U286 2c red on blue, die 1	145.00	130.00	_____
W287 2c red on manila, die 1	70.00	60.00	_____
U288 2c brown on white, die 2	225.00	85.00	13.00
U289 2c brown on amber, die 2	9.50	7.25	6.25
U290 2c brown on blue, die 2	230.00	275.00	80.00
U291 2c brown on fawn, die 2	20.00	14.75	12.00
W292 2c brown on manila, die 2	16.50	14.75	8.50

U293
Grant

U293 2c green on white	_____	4.00	3.50
Entire letter sheet		9.00	4.50

U294-U304, U352-W357
Franklin

U305-U323, U358-U370
Washington

U324-U329
Jackson

U330-U335, U377-U378
Grant

1887-94			
U294 1c blue on white	.65	.45	.12
U295 1c dark blue on white	5.50	4.50	1.65
U296 1c blue on amber	3.00	1.75	.70
U297 1c dark blue on amber	35.00	30.00	12.50
U300 1c blue on manila	.80	.65	.16

SCOTT CAT. NO. DESCRIPTION	UNUSED ENTIRE	UNUSED CUT SQ.	USED CUT SQ.
W301 1c blue on manila	.60	.30	.12
U302 1c dark blue on manila	20.00	16.00	5.25
W303 1c dark blue on manila	11.50	9.00	5.25
U304 1c blue on amber manila	3.25	2.00	1.65
U305 2c green on white, die 1	9.50	5.25	4.65
U306 2c green on amber, die 1	14.00	11.00	8.25
U307 2c green on buff, die 1	50.00	35.00	20.00
U308 2c green on blue, die 1		1500.00	350.00
U309 2c green on manila, die 1	2000.00	900.00	250.00
U311 2c green on white, die 2	.40	.35	.12
U312 2c green on amber, die 2	.50	.40	.12
U313 2c green on buff, die 2	.55	.45	.20
U314 2c green on blue, die 2	.65	.45	.20
U315 2c green on manila, die 2	.95	.75	.28
W316 2c green on manila, die 2	3.00	1.10	.70
U317 2c green on amber manila, die 2	2.00	1.00	.38
U318 2c green on white, die 3	60.00	55.00	8.00
U319 2c green on amber, die 3	85.00	75.00	11.00
U320 2c green on buff, die 3	90.00	80.00	18.00
U321 2c green on blue, die 3	110.00	95.00	22.50
U322 2c green on manila, die 3	95.00	80.00	35.00
U323 2c green on amber manila, die 3	180.00	165.00	40.00
U324 4c carmine on white	1.75	.95	.60
U325 4c carmine on amber	2.50	1.65	.95
U326 4c carmine on oriental buff	4.50	2.85	1.60
U327 4c carmine on blue	3.50	2.50	1.60
U328 4c carmine on manila	5.50	4.50	2.70
U329 4c carmine on amber manila	5.00	2.50	1.60
U330 5c blue on white, die 1	3.50	2.00	1.60
U331 5c blue on amber, die 1	5.00	2.50	1.30
U332 5c dark blue on buff, die 1	5.50	2.75	2.10
U333 5c dark blue on blue, die 1	5.75	3.25	3.00
U334 5c blue on white, die 2	9.25	6.75	5.20
U335 5c blue on amber, die 2	9.00	4.00	3.50
U336 30c brown on white	35.00	30.00	27.50
U337 30c brown on amber	30.00	25.00	19.00
U338 30c red on oriental buff	30.00	25.00	19.00
U339 30c red on blue	30.00	22.00	19.00
U340 30c red brown on manila	32.50	22.00	16.50
U341 30c red brown on amber manila	35.00	24.50	16.50
U342 90c purple on white	50.00	35.00	25.00
U343 90c purple on amber	60.00	35.00	25.00
U344 90c purple on oriental buff	60.00	45.00	30.00
U345 90c purple on blue	65.00	45.00	30.00
U346 90c purple on manila	65.00	35.00	30.00
U347 90c purple on amber manila	70.00	35.00	30.00

U348-U351
Columbus and Liberty, with
Shield and Eagle

1893. COLUMBIAN ISSUE			
U348 1c deep blue on white	2.85	2.50	
U349 2c violet on white	2.25	1.95	
U350 5c chocolate on white	12.50	9.00	6.00
U351 10c slate brown on white	50.00	40.00	20.00

SCOTT CAT. NO.	DESCRIPTION	UNUSED ENTIRE	UNUSED CUT SQ.	USED CUT SQ.

U371-U373　　**U374-W376**
Lincoln

1899

352	1c green on white	.55	.45	.22
353	1c green on amber	4.50	3.25	1.65
354	1c green on oriental buff	6.75	5.50	1.55
355	1c green on blue	7.00	5.50	2.30
356	1c green on manila	2.25	1.35	.45
W357	1c green on manila	2.00	1.35	.45
358	2c carmine on white, die 1	3.25	1.35	1.00
359	2c carmine on amber, die 1	14.00	9.00	6.75
360	2c carmine on buff, die 1	14.00	9.00	5.75
361	2c carmine on blue, die 1	35.00	30.00	15.00
362	2c carmine on white, die 2	.45	.35	.12
363	2c carmine on amber, die 2	1.25	.75	.12
364	2c carmine on buff, die 2	1.25	.60	.22
365	2c carmine on blue, die 2	2.00	1.00	.45
366	2c carmine on manila, die 2	3.25	3.00	1.25
367	2c carmine on white, die 3	4.00	2.00	.65
368	2c carmine on amber, die 3	8.00	5.25	2.75
369	2c carmine on buff, die 3	20.00	14.00	5.25
370	2c carmine on blue, die 3	11.00	5.75	3.75
371	4c brown on white, die 1	14.00	11.75	7.25
372	4c brown on amber, die 1	18.00	11.75	7.25
373	4c brown on white, die 2	3300.00	2800.00	250.00
374	4c brown on white, die 3	12.00	5.25	4.00
375	4c brown on amber, die 3	38.50	30.00	8.00
376	4c brown on manila, die 3	13.00	9.25	7.85
377	5c blue on white	9.00	7.00	4.00
378	5c blue on amber	11.00	9.25	5.75

U379-W384　　**U385-W389, U395-W399**
Franklin　　*Washington*

U390-W392　　**U393, U394**
Grant　　*Lincoln*

1903

79	1c green on white	.75	.60	.13
80	1c green on amber	10.00	7.25	1.25
81	1c green on oriental buff	9.50	7.00	1.25
82	1c green on blue	7.00	5.75	1.40
83	1c green on manila	3.00	2.15	.80
384	1c green on manila	.95	.60	.28

SCOTT CAT. NO.	DESCRIPTION	UNUSED ENTIRE	UNUSED CUT SQ.	USED CUT SQ.
U385	2c carmine on white	.40	.30	.13
U386	2c carmine on amber	1.95	1.50	.18
U387	2c carmine on oriental buff	1.75	1.25	.25
U388	2c carmine on blue	2.00	1.25	.22
W389	2c carmine on manila	13.75	12.00	5.50
U390	4c chocolate on white	16.50	13.00	4.00
U391	4c chocolate on amber	16.50	13.00	4.25
W392	4c chocolate on manila	14.00	10.50	4.50
U393	5c blue on white	12.00	10.00	4.00
U394	5c blue on amber	12.00	10.00	5.50

1904. RECUT DIE

U395	2c carmine on white	.60	.40	.15
U396	2c carmine on amber	6.25	5.25	.30
U397	2c carmine on oriental buff	4.50	4.00	.90
U398	2c carmine on blue	3.25	2.00	.90
W399	2c carmine on manila	13.00	9.00	4.00

U400-W405, U416 U417　　**U406-W415, U418 U419**
Franklin　　*Washington*

1907-16

U400	1c green on white	.40	.30	.12
U401	1c green on amber	.75	.55	.40
U402	1c green on oriental buff	1.00	.65	.40
U403	1c green on blue	3.00	2.50	1.00
U404	1c green on manila	2.50	2.00	.90
W405	1c green on manila	.70	.40	.20
U406	2c brown red on white	.60	.45	.13
U407	2c brown red on amber	4.50	3.25	1.25
U408	2c brown red on oriental buff	4.50	3.50	1.00
U409	2c brown red on blue	4.00	2.50	.90
W410	2c brown red on manila	30.00	22.50	14.00
U411	2c carmine on white	.40	.35	.12
U412	2c carmine on amber	.35	.25	.20
U413	2c carmine on oriental buff	.40	.25	.20
U414	2c carmine on blue	.45	.35	.18
W415	2c carmine on manila	3.50	1.75	1.25
U416	4c black on white	4.00	1.35	.50
U417	4c black on amber	5.00	3.25	2.25
U418	5c blue on white	5.50	3.25	2.25
U419	5c blue on amber	10.50	8.75	7.00

U420-U428, U440-U442　　**U429-U439, U443-U445, U481-W485, U529-U531**
Franklin　　*Washington*

1916-32

U420	1c green on white	.25	.15	.12
U421	1c green on amber	.50	.30	.28
U422	1c green on oriental buff	1.45	1.25	1.00
U423	1c green on blue	.55	.45	.20
U424	1c green on manila	4.00	3.25	2.50

SCOTT CAT. NO.	DESCRIPTION	UNUSED ENTIRE	UNUSED CUT SQ.	USED CUT SQ.
W425	1c green on manila	.25	.20	.18
U426	1c green on brown (glazed)	30.00	12.00	7.50
W427	1c green on brown (glazed)	50.00	45.00	
U428	1c green on brown (unglazed)	8.00	5.50	4.75
U429	2c carmine on white	.25	.15	.12
U430	2c carmine on amber	.40	.25	.12
U431	2c carmine on oriental buff	3.00	.50	.33
U432	2c carmine on blue	.50	.25	.12
W433	2c carmine on manila	.40	.30	.20
W434	2c carmin on brown (glazed)	60.00	50.00	30.00
W435	2c carmine on brown (unglazed)	70.00	60.00	35.00
U436	3c dark violet on white	.35	.25	.12
U436f	3c purple on white (1932)	.45	.20	.12
U436h	3c carmine on white (error)	20.00	15.00	15.00
U437	3c dark violet on amber	3.00	1.75	.55
U437a	3c purple on amber (1932)	.60	.35	.12
U437g	3c carmine on amber(error)	250.00	200.00	110.00
U437h	3c black on amber (error)	100.00	80.00	
U438	3c dark violet on buff	20.00	15.50	.90
U439	3c dark violet on blue	8.50	4.75	.95
U439a	3c purple on blue (1932)	.50	.35	.12
U439g	3c carmine on blue(error)	200.00	175.00	125.00
U440	4c black on white	2.00	.75	.40
U441	4c black on amber	3.25	2.00	1.10
U442	4c black on blue	3.50	2.50	.70
U443	5c blue on white	3.25	2.50	.95
U444	5c blue on amber	3.50	2.50	2.00
U445	5c blue on blue	3.50	2.50	2.00

1920-21. SURCHARGED

2 CENTS

Type 1

U446	2c on 3c violet on white (U436)	7.75	7.50	6.25

Type 2   **Type 3**

Surcharge on Envelopes of 1916-21. Type 2

U447	2c on 3c violet on white, rose (U436)	5.00	4.00	4.00
U448	2c on 3c violet on white (u436)	1.75	1.35	.75
U449	2c on 3c violet on amber (437)	4.50	3.75	3.50
U450	2c on 3c violet on buff (U438)	8.00	6.00	4.50
U451	2c on 3c violet on blue (U439)	8.00	6.50	3.00

Surcharge on Envelopes of 1874-1921. Type 3 Bars 2mm. apart.

U454	2c on 2c carmine on white (U429)	45.00	40.00	
U455	2c on 2c carmine on amber (U430)	450.00	375.00	
U456	2c on 2c carmine on buff (U431)	110.00	85.00	
U457	2c on 2c carmine on blue (U432)	110.00	90.00	

SCOTT CAT. NO.	DESCRIPTION	UNUSED ENTIRE	UNUSED CUT SQ.	USED CUT SQ.
U458	2c on 3c violet on white (U436)	.50	.25	.2
U459	2c on 3c violet on amber (U437)	2.50	1.50	.5
U460	2c on 3c violet on buff (38)	3.00	2.00	.6
U461	2c on 3c violet on blue (U439)	3.00	1.75	.7
U462	2c on 4c chocolate on white (U390)	200.00	150.00	55.00
U463	2c on 4c chocolate on amber (U391)	200.00	150.00	55.00
U464	2c on 5c blue on white (U443)	400.00	375.00	

Type 4 Like Type 3, but bars 1½ mm. apart.

U465	2c on 1c green on white (U420)	500.00	450.00	
U466A	2c on 2c carmine on white (U429)	130.00	100.00	
U467	2c on 3c green on white, die (U163)	160.00	135.00	
U468	2c on 3c violet on white (U436)	.75	.50	.3
U469	2c on 3c violet on amber (U437)	1.50	.90	.5
U470	2c on 3c violet on buff (U438)	4.00	2.50	2.0
U471	2c on 3c violet on blue (U439)	3.50	1.80	1.
U472	2c on 4c chocolate on white (U390)	11.00	5.50	3.
U473	2c on 4c chocolate on amber (U391)	14.00	6.50	3.
U474	2c on 1c on 3c violet on white (U436)	130.00	115.00	
U475	2c on 1c on 3c violet on amber (U437)	115.00	100.00	

Type 5   **Type 6**   **Type 7**

Surcharge on Envelope of 1916-21. Type 5

U476	2c on 3c violet on amber (U437)	60.00	55.00	

Surcharge on Envelope of 1916-21. Type 5

U477	2c on 3c violet on white (U436)	57.50	50.00	
U478	2c on 3c violet on amber (U437)	110.00	85.00	

Surcharge on Envelope of 1916-21. Type 7

U479	2c on 3c violet on white (black) (U436)	225.00	175.00	

1925-34

U481	1½c brown on white	.60	.25	
U481b	1½c purple on white (error)	55.00	50.00	
U482	1½c brown on amber	1.50	1.20	

SCOTT CAT. NO.	DESCRIPTION	UNUSED ENTIRE	UNUSED CUT SQ.	USED CUT SQ.
U483	1½c brown on blue	1.50	1.20	.65
U484	1½c brown on manila	6.00	3.50	2.25
W485	1½c brown on manila	1.10	.85	.22

1925

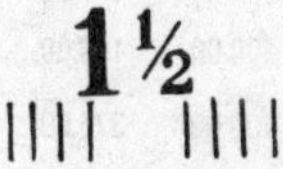

1½ Type 8   1½ Type 9

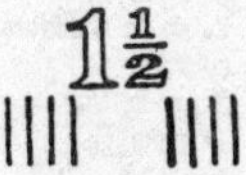

Surcharge on Envelopes of 1887 Type 8

U486	1½c on 2c green on white (U311)	225.00	200.00	
U487	1½c on 2c green on amber (U312)	375.00	350.00	

Surcharge on Envelopes of 1899 Type 8

U488	1½c on 1c green on white (U352)	300.00	250.00	.....
U489	1½c on 1c green on amber (U353)	45.00	40.00	28.50

Surcharge on Envelopes of 1907-10 Type 8

U490	1½c on 1c green on white (U400)	4.00	2.75	2.50
U491	1½c on 1c green on amber (U401)	6.00	3.25	1.75
U492	1½c on 1c green on oriental buff (U402)	135.00	110.00	30.00
U493	1½c on 1c green on blue (U403)	60.00	50.00	25.00
U494	1½c on 1c green on manila (U404)	170.00	150.00	50.00

Surcharge on Envelopes of 1916-21 Type 8

U495	1½c on 1c green on white (U420)	.50	.35	.22
U496	1½c on 1c green on amber (U421)	15.00	10.50	10.50
U497	1½c on 1c green on buff (U422)	3.50	2.55	1.25
U498	1½c on 1c green on blue (U423)	1.60	.70	.38
U499	1½c on 1c green on manila (U424)	10.00	6.00	3.50
U500	1½c on 1c green on brown (unglazed) (U428)	35.00	30.00	12.00
U501	1½c on 1c green on brown (glazed) (U426)	35.00	25.00	12.50
U502	1½c on 2c carmine on white (U429)	150.00	110.00	.....
U503	1½c on 2c carmine on buff (U431)	150.00	110.00	.....
U504	1½c on 2c carmine on blue (U432)	150.00	110.00	.....

Surcharge on Envelopes of 1925 Type 8

U505	1½c on 1½c brown on white (U481)	250.00	225.00	
U506	1½c on 1½c brown on blue (U483)	175.00	150.00	

SCOTT CAT. NO.	DESCRIPTION	UNUSED ENTIRE	UNUSED CUT SQ.	USED CUT SQ.

Surcharge on Envelope of 1899 Type 9

U508	1½c on 1c green on amber (U353)	35.00	30.00	

Surcharge on Envelope of 1903 Type 9

U508A	1½c on 1c green on white (U379)	700.00	650.00	
U509	1½c on 1c green on amber (U380)	8.50	3.25	2.25
U509B	1½c on 1c green on buff (U381)	25.00	20.00	9.00

Surcharge on Envelopes of 1907-10 Type 9

U510	1½c on 1c green on white (U400)	2.25	1.50	.90
U511	1½c on 1c green on amber (U401)	105.00	80.00	40.00
U512	1½c on 1c green on buff (U402)	4.50	2.75	1.90
U513	1½c on 1c green on blue (U403)	4.50	2.75	1.90
U514	1½c on 1c green on manila (U404)	22.75	11.00	4.75
US515	1½c on 1c green on white (U420)	.50	.30	.20
U516	1½c on 1c green on amber (U421)	35.00	26.50	15.00
U517	1½c on 1c green on buff (U422)	3.25	2.25	.65
U518	1½c on 1c green on blue (U423)	3.25	2.25	.65
U519	1½c on 1c green on manila (U424)	9.00	7.00	5.00
U520	1½c on 2c carmine on white (U429)	110.00	80.00	
U521	1½c on 1c green on white magenta surcharge (U420)	3.50	2.00	1.85

U522    U523-U528

U522: Die 1. "E" of "POSTAGE" has center bar shorter than top bar.
U522a: Die 2. "E" of "POSTAGE" has center and top bars same length.

U525: Die 1. "S" of "POSTAGE" even with "T".
U525a: Die 2. "S" of POSTAGE higher than "T".

1926. SESQUICENTENNIAL EXPOSITION

U522	2c carmine on white, die 1	2.50	1.90	.70
U522a	2c carmine on white, die 2	8.50	7.25	4.00

SCOTT CAT. NO.	DESCRIPTION	UNUSED ENTIRE	UNUSED CUT SQ.	USED CUT SQ.
1932. WASHINGTON BICENTENNIAL				
U523	1c olive green on white	2.00	1.75	.70
U524	1½c dark brown on white . . .	4.25	3.75	1.55
U525	2c carmine on white, die 1	.65	.55	.15
U525a	2c carmine on white, die 2	80.00	50.00	8.00
U526	3c violet on white	3.75	3.25	.35
U527	4c black on white	30.00	25.00	14.00
U528	5c dark blue on white	5.50	4.75	2.50
1932 Designs of 1916-32				
U529	6c orange on white	6.00	3.75	1.35
U530	6c orange on amber	10.00	8.25	4.25
U531	6c orange on blue	8.50	6.00	4.50

U532, U536	U533, U534	U535
Franklin	*Washington*	*Washington*

		1950		
U532	1c green	5.25	4.00	1.25
U533	2c carmine	1.35	1.25	.18
U534	3c dark violet	.55	.45	.18
		1951-58		
U535	1½c brown	4.75	3.75	2.15
U536	4c red violet	.65	.60	.12

U537, U538, U552, U566	U539, U540, U545, U553

Surcharges on Envelopes of 1916-32, 1950,1965, 1971

1958

U537	2c + 2c (4c) carmine (U429)	3.00	2.00	1.10
U538	2c + 2c (4c) carmine (U533)	1.10	.80	.33
U539	3c + 1c (4c) purple, die 1 . . . . (U436a)	14.00	13.00	. . . . .
U539a	3c + 1c (4c) purple, die 7 . . . . (U436e)	12.50	11.75	. . . . .
U539b	3c + 1c (4c) purple, die 9 . . . . (U436f)	20.00	16.50	. . . . .
U540	3c + 1c (4c) dark violet . . . . (U534)	.80	.60	.18

U541	U542	U544
Franklin	*Washington*	*Lincoln*

SCOTT CAT. NO.	DESCRIPTION	FIRST DAY COVER	UNUSED CUT SQ.	USED CUT SQ.
		U543		U546
1960				
U541	1¼c turquoise	1.75	.80	.8
U542	1½c blue	1.75	1.00	.8
U543	4c brown	2.00	.80	
1962				
U544	5c blue	1.25	.95	
Surcharged on envelope of 1958				
U545	4c + 1c red violet (U536)	_____	2.00	
1964				
U546	5c maroon	1.75	.70	

U547, U548, U548A, U556	U549

U550	U551

		1965-69		
U547	1¼c brown	1.75	1.00	
U548	1-4/10c brown	1.75	1.25	
U548A	1-6/10c orange	1.75	1.25	
U549	4c blue	1.75	1.00	
U550	5c purple	1.75	1.00	
U551	6c light green	2.00	1.10	

1968

1958 Type Surcharges on Envelopes of 1965

U552	4c + 2c (6c) blue . . . (U549)	_____	4.00	
U553	5c + 1c (6c) purple . (U550)	_____	2.50	1

U554	U555

NOTE: Entires after 1960 can be supplied at c[u] square price. Please specify your preference.

SCOTT CAT. NO.	DESCRIPTION	FIRST DAY COVER	UNUSED CUT SQ.	USED CUT SQ.
	1970			
U554	6c blue	1.75	.80	.20
	1971			
U555	6c light blue	1.75	1.00	.28

U557

U561, U562 (on U551, U555)

U556	1-7/10c purple	1.75	.45	.20
U557	8c ultramarine	1.75	.60	.10
U561	6c + 2c (8c) light green (on U551)	5.00	1.10	.25
U562	6c + 2c (8c)blue . (on U555)	5.00	2.50	.40

U563

U564

U565

U567

U563	8c crimson	1.75	.60	.15
U564	8c light blue	2.00	.60	.15
	1972			
U565	8c blue & red	1.75	.90	.12
	1973			
U566	8c+2c ultramarine . (onU557)	5.00	.55	.10
U567	10c green	1.75	.45	.10

U568

U569

	1974			
U568	1.8c turquoise	1.75	.40	.12
U569	10c blue, yellow & green .	2.00	.45	.15

SCOTT CAT. NO.	DESCRIPTION	FIRST DAY COVER	UNUSED CUT SQ.	USED CUT SQ.

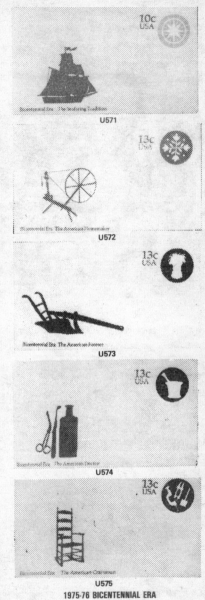

U571

U572

U573

U574

U575

1975-76 BICENTENNIAL ERA

U571	10c blue on brown, entire only	1.75	.60	.25
U572	13c blue green on brown, entire only	1.75	.65	.28
U573	13c green on brown, entire only	1.75	.65	.28
U574	13c orange on brown, entire only	1.75	.65	.28
U575	13c red on brown, entire only	1.75	.65	.25

SCOTT CAT. NO. DESCRIPTION	FIRST DAY COVER	UNUSED CUT SQ.	USED CUT SQ.

U576

U577

U578

U579

U580

U581

1975

U576	13c orange, brown	1.75	.65	.22

1976-78

U577	2c red	1.75	.35	.12
U578	2.1c green	1.75	.35	.12
U579	2.7c green	1.75	.30	.12
U580	15c "A" orange	1.75	.70	.22
U581	15c red & white	1.75	.70	.22

1976

U582	13c green (design of U218)	1.75	.65	.22

1977

U583	13c multicolored	1.75	.65	.22

U584

U585

SCOTT CAT. NO. DESCRIPTION	FIRST DAY COVER	UNUSED CUT SQ.	USED CUT SQ.
U584 13c multicolored	1.75	.65	.22
U585 13c multicolored	1.75	.65	.22

U586, U588

U586

1978

U586	15c on 16c blue & white	1.75	.75	.22

U587

1980

U587	15c red, white, blue & black	1.75	.65	.22
U588	15c on 13c white, brown .... (U576)	1.75	.65	.22

U589

U590

1979

U589	3.1c blue & white	1.75	.25	.15

1980

U590	3.5c purple	1.75	.30	.15

U591

U592

U593

U594

1981-82

U591	5.9c brown	1.75	.25	.....
U592	(18c) "B" purple & white	1.75	.65	.....
U593	18c white & dark blue	1.75	.65	.12
U594	(20c)"C" burnt orange & white	1.75	.65	.....

SCOTT CAT. NO.	DESCRIPTION	FIRST DAY COVER	UNUSED CUT SQ.	USED CUT SQ.

U595

U596

1979

| U595 | 15c brown & gray | 1.75 | .65 | .22 |
| U596 | 15c multicolored | 1.75 | .65 | .22 |

U597

U598   U599

1980

U597	15c maroon & brown	1.75	.60	.20
U598	15c America's Cup	1.75	.60	.....
U599	15c Honey Bee	1.75	.60	.20

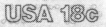

U600

1981

| U600 | 18c blue & white | 1.75 | .65 | .15 |

U601

U602

603   U604

| U601 | 20c plum & white | 1.75 | .60 | .12 |

1982

| U602 | 20c black, blue & red | 1.75 | .60 | .15 |
| U603 | 20c purple heart | 1.75 | .60 | .15 |

U605

1983

| U604 | 5.2 orange & white | 1.75 | .18 | ..... |
| U605 | 20c Paralyzed Veterans | 1.75 | .60 | ..... |

U606

1984

| U606 | 20c Small Business | 1.75 | .60 | ..... |

AN INTERESTING ERROR

Back in the 1920's, a quantity of 3c violet envelopes were surcharged with a "2" due to a reduction in postage rates. A small quantity were surcharged resulting in a "double surcharge" error that is readily apparent at a glance.

- U471b 2c on 3c violet,
  on blue, double surcharge, types 2 + 4,
  entire envelope only 85.00

SCOTT CAT. NO. DESCRIPTION	UNUSED ENTIRE	UNUSED CUT SQ.	USED CUT SQ.	SCOTT CAT. NO. DESCRIPTION	UNUSED ENTIRE	UNUSED CUT SQ.	USED CUT SQ.

AIR POST ENVELOPES

UC1

UC2-UC7

Airplane in Circle

Die 1. Vertical rudder not semi-circular, but slopes to left. Tall projects into "G".
Die 2. Vertical rudder is semi-circular. Tall only touches "G".
 Die 2a. "6" is 6½ mm. wide.
 Die 2b. "6" is 6 mm. wide.
 Die 2c. "6" is 5½ mm. wide.
Die 3. Vertical rudder leans forward. "5" closer to "O" than to "T" of "POSTAGE" and "E" has short center bar.

1929-44

UC1	5c blue, die 1	4.25	3.50	1.65
UC2	5c blue, die 2	11.00	9.00	3.00
UC3	6c orange, die 2a	1.75	1.35	.22
UC3n	6c die 2a, no border	2.00	1.75	.65
UC4	6c die 2b, with border	70.00	60.00	13.50
UC4n	6c die 2b, no border	2.75	2.50	1.35
UC5	6c die 2c, no border	.80	.65	.45
UC6	6c orange on white, die 3 . .	1.80	1.60	.70
UC6n	6c die 3, no border	2.25	2.00	.60
UC7	8c olive green	13.00	10.00	2.15

Envelopes of 1916-32 surcharged

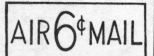
AIR 6¢ MAIL

1945

UC8	6c on 2c carmine on white . . . . (U429)	1.65	1.35	.80
UC9	6c on 2c carmine on white . . . . (U525)	50.00	35.00	30.00

UC10-13 Surcharged:

REVALUED
5¢
P.O. DEPT.

AIR MAIL
5¢   5¢
UNITED STATES · OF AMERICA
UC14, UC15, UC18, UC26
DC-4 Skymaster

UC14: Die 1. Small projection below rudder is rounded.
UC15: Die 2. Small projection below rudder is sharp pointed.

1946

UC10	5c on 6c, die 2a . . . . (UC3n)	3.50	2.75	1.50
UC11	5c on 6c, die 2b . . . . (UC4n)	10.00	8.50	3.50

UC12	5c on 6c, die 2c . . . (UC5)	1.00	.85	.65
UC13	5c on 6c, die 3 . . . . (UC6n)	1.20	.85	.50
UC14	5c carmine, die 1	1.25	1.00	.20
UC15	5c carmine, die 2	1.40	1.15	.28

UC16
DC-4 Skymaster

UC17
Washington and Franklin, Mail-carrying Vehicles

1947-55

UC16	10c rec on blue, cut square .		4.00	3.75
UC16	Entire "Air Letter" on face, 2-line inscription on back . . .		6.00	. . . . .
UC16a	Entire, "Air Letter" on face, 4-line inscription on back . . .		10.00	. . . . .
UC16c	Enire, "Air Letter" and "Aerogramme" on face, 4-line inscription on back . . .		40.00	. . . . .
UC16d	Entire, "Air Letter" and "Aerogramme" on face, 3-line inscription on back . . .		5.50	. . . . .

1947. CIPEX COMMEMORATIVE

UC17	5c carmine	.70	.60	.40

1950 Design of 1946

UC18	6c carmine	.70	.45	.20

Envelope of 1946 Surcharged

REVALUED
6¢
P. O. DEPT.

Envelope of 1946-47 Surcharged

REVALUED
6¢
P.O. DEPT.

1951 (Shaded Numeral)

UC19	6c on 5c, die 1 . . . (UC14)	1.50	1.20	.85
UC20	6c on 5c, die 2 . . . (UC15)	1.40	1.15	.85

1952 (Solid Numeral)

UC21	6c on 5c, die 1 . . . . (UC14)	20.00	18.00	13.00
UC22	6c on 5c, die 2 . . . . (UC15)	3.75	3.25	2.50
UC23	6c on 5c, entire . . . . (UC17)	450.00	. . . . .	

SCOTT CAT. NO.	DESCRIPTION	UNUSED ENTIRE	UNUSED CUT SQ.	USED CUT SQ.

UC25

Surcharge on Envelopes of 1934 to 1956

UC27-UC31

1956 FIPEX Commemorative

UC25	6c carmine		1.25	.80	.40

1958 Design of 1946

UC26	7c blue		.80	.60	.40

1958

UC27	6c * 1c (7c) orange, die 2a (UC3n)	130.00	110.00	.....
UC28	6c * 1c (7c) orange, die 2b (UC4n)	50.00	40.00	.....
UC29	6c * 1c(7c) orange, die 2c (UC5)	35.00	28.50	.....
UC30	6c * 1c (7c) carmine (UC18)	1.20	.90	.40
UC31	6c * 1c (7c) carmine (UC25)	1.50	1.15	.75

UC32

UC33, UC34

1958-59

UC32	10c blue & carmine		5.75	.80
	Entire letter sheet, 2-line inscription on back	8.25		
UC32a	Entire letter sheet, 3-line inscription on back	10.00		

1958 FIRST DAY COVER

UC33	7c blue		1.75	.85	.17

1960

UC34	7c red		1.75	.85	.15

UC35

UC36

1961

UC35	11c red & blue	5.00	3.00	1.60
	Entire Letter Sheet	4.00		

1962

UC36	8c red		2.00	1.10	.15

UC37

UC38, UC39

SCOTT CAT. NO.	DESCRIPTION	FIRST DAY COVER	UNUSED CUT SQ.	USED CUT SQ.

1965

UC37	8c red	1.75	.80	.12
UC38	11c blue & red		2.25	1.55
	Entire Letter sheet	2.00	3.25	

1967

UC39	13c blue & red		2.75	.85
	Entire letter sheet	2.00	3.25	

UC40

UC41 (on UC37)

1968

UC40	10c red	1.75	.85	.50
UC41	8c * 2c (10c) red		1.00	.28

UC42

UC42	13c multicolored		4.50	2.25
	Entire letter sheet	3.00	5.50	

UC43

1971

UC43	11c red & blue	1.75	.80	.18

UC44

UC44	15c gray, red blue		1.60	1.00
	Entire Letter Sheet	1.75	1.60	
UC44a	Aerogramme added Entire letter sheet	1.75	1.60	

UC45 (on UC40)

1971 Revalued

UC45	10 * 1c (11c) red	12.00	3.00	.40

SCOTT CAT. NO.	DESCRIPTION	FIRST DAY COVER	UNUSED CUT SQ.	USED CUT SQ.

UC46

UC47

1973

| UC46 | 15c red & blue, entire | 1.75 | .95 | .50 |
| UC47 | 13c red | 1.75 | .65 | .18 |

UC48

NATO

UC49

1974

| UC48 | 18c red & blue, entire | 1.75 | .85 | .35 |
| UC49 | 18c red, blue, & gray, entire | 1.75 | .85 | .30 |

usa/22c

UC50

1976

| UC50 | 22c red, white & blue, entire | 2.00 | 1.00 | .35 |

22c USA

UC51

1978

| UC51 | 22c blue | 2.00 | 1.00 | ..... |

UC52

1979

| UC52 | 22c multicolored, entire | 2.00 | 1.85 | ..... |

UC53, UC54

1980-81

| UC53 | 30c red, blue & brown, entire | 2.75 | .95 | ..... |
| UC54 | 30c yellow, magenta, blue & black, entire | 1.75 | .85 | ..... |

UC55

1982

| UC55 | 30c multicolored, entire | 1.75 | .75 | ..... |

SCOTT CAT. NO. DESCRIPTION	FIRST DAY COVER	UNUSED CUT SQ.	USED.

UC56

UC57

1983

UC56	30c Communications	..... 1.75	.75	.....
UC57	30c Olympics	.... 1.75	.75	.....

Don't forget Our Complete Line of Supplies and Albums in the Back of this Catalog.

SCOTT CAT. NO. DESCRIPTION	UNUSED ENTIRE	UNUSED CUT SQ.	USED CUT SQ.

OFFICIAL ENVELOPES

NOTE: For details on similar appearing varieties please refer to the Scott specialized Catalogue.

UO1-UO13   UO14-UO17

POST OFFICE DEPARTMENT

1873. SMALL NUMERALS

		Unused Entire	Unused Cut Sq.	Used Cut Sq.
UO1	2c black on lemon	10.50	5.50	2.75
UO2	3c black on lemon	6.00	2.00	1.75
UO4	6c black on lemon	10.50	6.00	5.00

1874-79. LARGE NUMERALS

UO5	2c black on lemon	4.25	1.90	1.20
UO6	2c black on white	35.00	25.00	16.50
UO7	3c black on lemon	.95	.65	.65
UO8	3c black on white	400.00	325.00	350.00
UO9	3c black on amber	30.00	22.00	16.50
UO12	6c black on lemon	2.25	1.10	1.00
UO13	6c black on white	500.00	350.00	

1877. POSTAL SERVICE

UO14	black on white	1.50	.80	.95
UO15	black on amber	75.00	12.00	7.00
UO16	blue on amber	60.00	13.00	9.00
UO17	blue on blue	2.50	1.90	1.65

UO18-UO69   UO70-UO72
Washington

Portraits for the various denominations are the same as on the regular issue of 1870-73.

WAR DEPARTMENT

1873. REAY ISSUE

UO18	1c dark red on white	325.00	260.00	120.00
UO19	2c dark red on white	350.00	325.00	115.00
UO20	3c dark red on white	32.50	22.00	12.50
UO22	3c dark red on cream	250.00	200.00	55.00
UO23	6c dark red on white	120.00	95.00	30.00
UO24	6c dark red on cream	850.00	750.00	150.00
UO25	10c dark red on white	2000.00	850.00	140.00
UO26	12c dark red on white	60.00	50.00	18.00
UO27	15c dark red on white	60.00	50.00	18.00
UO28	24c dark red on white	70.00	60.00	15.50
UO29	30c dark red on white	200.00	160.00	57.50

SCOTT CAT. NO. DESCRIPTION	UNUSED ENTIRE	UNUSED CUT SQ.	USED CUT SQ.
UO30	1c vermilion on white	175.00	95.00	
W031	1c vermilion on manila	8.00	5.00	4.00
UO32	2c vermilion on white	2000.00	85.00	
W033	2c vermilion on manila	100.00	80.00	
UO34	3c vermilion on white	85.00	25.00	13.50
UO35	3c vermilion on amber	130.00	42.50	
UO36	3c vermilion on cream	10.00	3.00	1.70
UO37	6c vermilion on white	50.00	35.00	
UO38	6c vermilion on cream	3250.00	165.00	
UO39	10c vermilion on white	220.00	85.00	
UO40	12c vermilion on white	120.00	50.00	
UO41	15c vermilion on white	1250.00	75.00	
UO42	24c vermilion on white	225.00	140.00	
UO43	30c vermilion on white	250.00	80.00	

1875. PLIMPTON ISSUE

UO44	1c red on white	60.00	50.00	50.00
UO45	1c red on amber		300.00	
W046	1c red on manila	1.75	.70	.55
UO47	2c red on white	45.00	40.00	
UO48	2c red on amber	20.00	14.00	2.75
UO49	2c red on orange	25.00	20.00	5.75
W050	2c red on manila	70.00	45.00	27.50
UO51	3c red on white	5.50	5.00	3.50
UO52	3c red on amber	5.00	3.25	2.25
UO53	3c red on cream	1.35	1.00	.60
UO54	3c red on blue	1.00	.70	.35
UO55	3c red on fawn	1.20	.90	.45
UO56	6c red on white	45.00	19.00	9.25
UO57	6c red on amber	45.00	30.00	11.50
UO58	6c red on cream	80.00	55.00	40.00
UO59	10c red on white	75.00	60.00	40.00
UO60	10c red on amber	525.00	450.00	
UO61	12c red on white	45.00	15.00	11.50
UO62	12c red on amber	350.00	300.00	
UO63	12c red on cream	350.00	225.00	
UO64	15c red on white	110.00	65.00	30.00
UO65	15c red on amber	375.00	325.00	
UO66	15c red on cream	375.00	325.00	
UO67	30c red on white	95.00	75.00	32.50
UO68	30c red on amber	475.00	425.00	
UO69	30c red on cream	550.00	425.00	

1911. POSTAL SAVINGS

UO70	1c green on white	50.00	40.00	6.00
UO71	1c green on oriental buff	120.00	100.00	30.00
UO72	2c carmine on white	6.25	4.50	.80

UO73

1983

			(F.D.C.)	
UO73	20c blue and white	1.75	.52	

SCOTT CAT. NO.	DESCRIPTION	MINT	UNUSED	USED	SCOTT CAT. NO.	DESCRIPTION	MINT	UNUSED	USED

POSTAL CARDS

Prices Are for Entire Cards

MINT: As issued, no printing or writing added.
UNUSED: Uncancelled, with printing or writing added.

UX1, UX3, UX65
Liberty

UX4, UX5, UX7
Liberty

UX6, UX13, UX16
Liberty

1873

UX1	1c brown, large watermark	250.00	40.00	19.00
UX3	1c brown, small watermark	80.00	15.00	2.25

1875 inscribed "Write the address," etc.

UX4	1c black, watermarked	1400.00	575.00	200.00
UX5	1c black unwatermarked	50.00	4.50	.55

1879

UX6	2c blue on buff	20.00	7.00	15.00

1881 inscribed "Nothing but the address." etc.

UX7	1c black on buff	50.00	4.00	.45

UX8   *Jefferson*   **UX9**

1885

UX8	1c brown on buff	35.00	5.00	1.10

1886

UX9	1c black on buff	12.00	1.50	.60

UX10, UX11
Grant

UX12
Jefferson

UX14

1891

UX10	1c black on buff	30.00	4.50	.80
UX11	1c blue on gray white	12.50	4.00	1.50

1894 Small wreath and name below.

UX12	1c black on buff	30.00	1.35	.40

1897 Large wreath and name below.

UX13	2c black on cream	95.00	45.00	65.00
UX14	1c black on buff	22.50	1.50	.40

UX15
John Adams

UX18   *McKinley*

UX19, UX20

1898

UX15	1c black on buff	35.00	7.00	12.00
UX16	2c black on buff	7.50	4.00	10.00

1902 Profile Background

UX18	1c black on buff	8.50	1.00	.45

1907

UX19	1c black on buff	30.00	1.50	.45

1908 Correspondence Space at Left

UX20	1c black on buff	45.00	5.50	3.25

UX21   **UX22, UX24**   **UX23, UX26**

UX25   **UX27**

1910 Background Shaded

UX21	1c blue on bluish	95.00	15.00	4.50

White Portrait Background.

UX22	1c blue on bluish	15.00	1.10	.40

1911

UX23	1c red on cream	6.50	1.85	5.00
UX24	1c red on cream	10.00	1.00	.40
UX25	2c red on cream	1.50	.35	8.00

SCOTT CAT. NO.	DESCRIPTION	MINT	UNUSED	USED
	1913			
UX26	1c green on cream	8.00	1.50	5.00
	1914			
UX27	1c green on buff	.40	.35	.30

UX28, UX43   UX29, UX30   UX32, UX33

NOTE: On UX29 end of queue slopes sharply down to right while on UX30 it extends nearly horizontally.

	1917-18			
UX28	1c green on cream	.80	.45	.40
UX29	2c red on buff, die 1	35.00	4.25	1.35
UX30	2c red on buff, die 2	22.50	3.75	1.35

1920. UX29 & UX30 Revalued

UX32	1c on 2c red, die 1	50.00	11.00	10.00
UX33	1c on 2c red, die 2	7.50	1.60	1.60

UX37   UX38   UX39-42

1926

UX37	3c red on yellow	2.75	.45	.40

1951

UX38	2c rose	.50	.40	.40

1952 UX27 & UX28 Surcharged by cancelling machine, light green

UX39	2c on 1c green	.75	.40	.40
UX40	2c on 1c green	.75	.45	.45

UX27 & UX28 Surcharge Typographed, dark green

UX41	2c on 1c green	5.00	1.25	2.25
UX42	2c on 1c green	6.00	3.00	3.00

1952 Design of 1917

UX43	2c rose	.40	.25	.30

UX44   UX45, UY16   UX46, UY17

SCOTT CAT. NO.	DESCRIPTION	FIRST DAY COVERS	MINT	USED
	1956. FIPEX COMMEMORATIVE			
UX44	2c magenta & blue	1.40	.40	.30
	1956. INTERNATIONAL CARD			
UX45	4c red & blue	1.50	1.10	.18
	1958			
UX46	3c purple	1.50	.45	.25
	As above. but with printed precancel lines			
UX46c	3c purple		4.00	2.75

UX47   UX48, UY18

1958 UX38 Surcharged

UX47	2c + 1c carmine rose		125.00	150.00

1962-66

UX48	4c red violet	1.60	.35	.30
UX48at	4c luminescent	50.00	.60	.30

UX49, UX54, UX59, UY19, UY20   UX50

1963

UX49	7c blue & red	1.60	1.80	1.10
UX50	4c red & blue	1.60	.60	.70

UX51

UX51	4c dull blue & red	1.60	.60	.30

1965

UX52	4c blue & red	1.60	.60	.30

UX53   UX55, UY21

SCOTT CAT. NO.	DESCRIPTION	FIRST DAY COVER	MINT	USED
UX53	4c bright blue & black	1.60	.50	.30

1967 Design of UX49

UX54	8c blue & red	1.60	1.50	.85

1968

UX55	5c emerald	1.60	.40	.25

UX56

UX58, UY22

UX57

1968

UX56	5c rose red & green	1.60	.60	.30

1970

UX57	5c multicolored	1.60	.60	.25

1971

UX58	6c brown	1.60	.35	.30

Design of UX49

UX59	10c blue & red	1.60	1.80	.70

UX60

UX60	6c multicolored	1.60	.40	.35

U.S. POSTAGE 6 CENTS
UX61

UX62
U.S. POSTAGE 6 CENTS

UX63
U.S. POSTAGE 6 CENTS

1972

UX61	6c black & dull orange	1.60	.55	.55
UX62	6c black & dull orange	1.60	.55	.55
UX63	6c black & dull orange	1.60	.55	.55

UX64, UY23

UX66, UY24

UX67

UX64	6c light blue	1.60	.35	.25

1973. Design of 1873

UX65	6c magenta	1.60	.35	.25
UX66	8c orange	1.60	.35	.25

1974

UX67	12c multicolored	1.60	.55	.35

UX68, UY25

SEE SPECIAL OFFERS FOR STATIONERY AND POSTAL CARDS IN THIS SECTION.

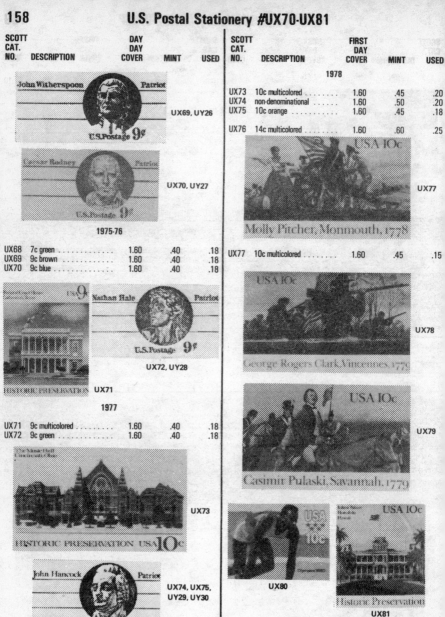

UX69, UY26

UX70, UY27

1975-76

UX68	7c green	1.60	.40	.18
UX69	9c brown	1.60	.40	.18
UX70	9c blue	1.60	.40	.18

UX72, UY28

HISTORIC PRESERVATION UX71

1977

UX71	9c multicolored	1.60	.40	.18
UX72	9c green	1.60	.40	.18

UX73

UX74, UX75, UY29, UY30

UX76

1978

UX73	10c multicolored	1.60	.45	.20
UX74	non-denominational	1.60	.50	.20
UX75	10c orange	1.60	.45	.18
UX76	14c multicolored	1.60	.60	.25

UX77

Molly Pitcher, Monmouth, 1778

UX77	10c multicolored	1.60	.45	.15

UX78

George Rogers Clark, Vincennes, 1779

UX79

Casimir Pulaski, Savannah, 1779

UX80

UX81

1979

UX78	10c multicolored	1.60	.45	.15
UX79	10c multicolored	1.60	.45	.15
UX80	10c multicolored	1.60	.65	.35
UX81	10c multicolored	1.60	.45	.15

SCOTT CAT. NO.	DESCRIPTION	FIRST DAY COVER	MINT	USED

UX82

HISTORIC PRESERVATION
UX83

Landing of Rochambeau, 1780
UX84

Battle of Kings Mountain, 1780
UX85

Drake's Golden Hinde 1580
UX86

USA 10c

Battle of Cowpens, 1781
UX87

1980

UX82	14c multicolored	1.60	.75	.35
UX83	10c multicolored	1.60	.40	.12
UX84	10c multicolored	1.60	.40	.10
UX85	10c multicolored	1.60	.40	.10
UX86	19c multicolored	1.60	.75	.35

SCOTT CAT. NO.	DESCRIPTION	FIRST DAY COVER	MINT	USED
UX87	10c muticolored	1.60	.40	.10

UX88, UY31   **UX89, UY32**

Nathanael Greene. Eutaw Springs, 1781
UX90

Lewis and Clark Expedition, 1806
UX91

UX92,UY33   **UX93, UY34**

"Swamp Fox" Francis Marion, 1782
UX94

1981

UX88	"B"(12c) purple & white ...	1.60	.40	....
UX89	12c white & lt. blue	1.60	.40	....
UX90	12c multicolored	1.75	.40	....
UX91	12c multicolored	1.75	.40	....
UX92	(13c)orange	1.75	.40	....
UX93	13c orange	1.75	.40	....
UX94	13c multicolored	1.75	.40	....

SCOTT CAT. NO.	DESCRIPTION	FIRST DAY COVER	MINT	USED

La Salle claims Louisiana, 1682

UX95

UX96

UX97

1982

UX95	13c multicolored	1.75	.33	.....
UX96	13c multicolored	1.75	.33	.....
UX97	13c multicolored	1.75	.33	.....

Landing of Oglethorpe, Georgia, 1733

UX98

1983

| UX98 | 13c multicolored | 1.75 | .33 | ..... |

SCOTT CAT. NO.	DESCRIPTION	FIRST DAY COVER	MINT	USED

UX99

Old Post Office, Washington, D.C.

UX100

| UX99 | 13c multicolored | 1.75 | .33 | ..... |
| UX100 | 13c multicolored | 1.75 | .33 | ..... |

UX101

Ark and Dove, Maryland, 1634

UX102

Historic Preservation USA 13

UX103

Frederic Baraga, Michigan, 1835

1984

UX101	13c multicolored	1.75	.33	.....
UX102	13c multicolored	1.75	.30	.....
UX103	13c multicolored	1.75	.30	.....

UX104

| UX104 | 13c multicolored | 1.75 | .30 | ...... |

SCOTT CAT. NO.	DESCRIPTION	MINT	UNUSED	USED

PAID REPLY POSTAL CARDS

UY1m, UY3m   UY2m, UY11m   UY4m

UY1r, UY3r   UY2r, UY11r   UY4r

1892 Card Framed

UY1	1c + 1c unsevered	35.00	10.00	4.50
UY1m	1c black . . . . (Message)	5.00	2.25	.95
UY1r	1c black . . . . (Reply)	5.00	2.25	.95

1893

UY2	2c + 2c unsevered	17.50	7.00	20.00
UY2m	2c blue . . . . (Message)	3.00	1.80	9.00
UY2r	2c blue . . . . (Reply)	3.00	1.65	12.00

1898 Designs of 1892. Card Unframed.

UY3	1c + 1c unsevered	50.00	15.00	8.50
UY3m	1c black . . . . (Message)	8.00	2.75	2.25
UY3r	1c black . . . . (Reply)	8.00	2.75	2.25

1904

UY4	1c + 1c unsevered	35.00	5.00	2.50
UY4m	1c black . . . . (Message)	6.50	1.50	.80
UY4r	1c black . . . . (Reply)	5.50	1.50	.80

UY5m, UY6m
UY7m, UY13m   UY8m   UY12m

UY5r, UY6r
UY7r, UY13r   UY8r

1910

UY5	1c + 1c unsevered	85.00	20.00	8.00
UY5m	1c blue . . . . (Message)	5.50	3.00	2.00
UY5r	1c blue . . . . (Reply)	5.50	3.00	2.50

SCOTT CAT. NO.	DESCRIPTION	MINT	UNUSED	USED

1911. Double Line Around Instructions

UY6	1c + 1c unsevered	95.00	35.00	20.00
UY6m	1c green . . . . (Message)	20.00	10.00	4.00
UY6r	1c green . . . . (Reply)	20.00	8.00	5.00

1915. Single Frame Line Around Instruction.

UY7	1c + 1c unsevered	1.35	.50	.40
UY7m	1c green . . . . (Message)	.35	.25	.30
UY7r	1c green . . . . (Reply)	.35	.25	.30

1918

UY8	2c + 2c unsevered	65.00	20.00	30.00
UY8m	2c red . . . . (Message)	12.00	7.00	4.00
UY8r	2c red . . . . (Reply)	12.00	7.00	4.00

1920 UY8 Surcharged

UY9	1c/2c + 1c/2c unsevered . .	18.50	5.00	7.00
UY9m	1c on 2c red . . . . (Message)	4.00	1.85	2.00
UY9r	1c on 2c red . . . . . (Reply)	4.00	1.65	2.25

1924 Designs of 1893

UY11	2c + 2c unsevered	2.25	1.40	1.50
UY11m	2c red . . . . (Message)	.80	.35	.85
UY11r	2c red . . . . (Reply)	.80	.35	.85

1926

UY12	3c + 3c unsevered	8.50	2.75	5.00
UY12m	3c red . . . . (Message)	2.25	1.35	2.00
UY12r	3c red . . . . (Reply)	2.25	1.35	2.00

		FIRST DAY COVER	MINT	USED

1951. Design of 1910 Single Line Frame.

UY13	2c + 2c unsevered	3.50	1.75	.80
UY13m	2c rose . . . . (Message)	____	.45	.30
UY13r	2c rose . . . . (Reply)	____	.45	.30

1952
UY7 Surcharged by cancelling machine, light green.

UY14	2c/1c + 2c/1c unsevered . .	____	1.25	.95
UY14m	2c on 1c green . . . (Message)	____	.60	.50
UY14r	2c on 1c green . . . . . (Reply)	____	.60	.50

1952. UY7 Surcharge Typographed, dark green.

UY15	2c/1c + 2c/1c unsevered . .	____	75.00	40.00
UY15m	2c on 1c green . . . (Message)	____	15.00	6.00
UY15r	2c on 1c green . . . . . (Reply)	____	15.00	6.00

1956. Design of UX45

UY16	4c + 4c unsevered	1.75	1.10	1.00
UY16m	4c red rose . . . . . (Message)	____	.60	.35
UY16r	4c red & blue . . . . . . (Reply)	____	.60	.35

1958. Design of UX46

UY17	3c + 3c purple, unsevered . .	1.60	3.50	.50

1962. Design of UX48

UY18	4c + 4c light purple, unseverd	2.50	3.00	.85

SCOTT CAT. NO.	DESCRIPTION	FIRST DAY COVER	MINT	USED
	1962. Design of UX49			
UY19	7c + 7c unsevered	1.75	2.50	1.35
UY19m	7c blue & red .. (Message)	____	.90	.65
UY19r	7c blue & red ..... (Reply)	____	.90	.65
	1967 Design of UX54			
UY20	8c + 8c unsevered	1.75	1.85	.75
UY20m	8c blue & red .. (Message)	____	.80	.80
UY20r	8c blue & red ..... (Reply)	____	.80	.80
	1968 Design of UX55			
UY21	5c + 5c emerald	1.75	1.75	.55
	1971 Design of UX58			
UY22	6c + 6c brown	1.60	1.00	.35
	1972 Design of UX64			
UY23	6c + 6c light blue	1.60	1.00	.35
	1973 Design of UX66			
UY24	8c + 8c orange	1.60	1.00	.35
	1975			
UY25	7c + 7c green, design of UX68	1.60	.95	.50
UY26	9c + 9c brown, design of UX69	1.60	.95	.35
	1976			
UY27	9c + 9c blue, design of UX70	1.60	.95	.35
	1977			
UY28	9c + 9c green, design of UX72	1.60	.95	.35
	1978			
UY29	(10c + 10c) orange, design of UX74	4.50	10.50	......
UY30	10c + 10c orange, design of UX75	1.75	.80	......
	1981			
UY31	(12c + 12c) "B" Eagle, design of UX88	1.75	.80	......
UY32	12c + 12c blue, design of UX89	1.75	.80	......
UY33	(13c + 13c) orange, design of UX92	2.00	.75	......
UY34	13c + 13c orange, design of UX93	2.00	.75	......

OFFICIAL POST CARD	UNUSED	USED

UZ1

UZ2

	1913		
UZ1	1c black	225.00	125.00
	1983		
UZ2	13c blue	1.75	.32	......

AIR POST POSTAL CARDS

UXC1

UXC2, UXC3

SCOTT CAT. NO.	DESCRIPTION	FIRST DAY COVER	MINT	USED
	1949			
UXC1	4c orange red	3.25	.60	.40
	1958 No border on card			
UXC2	5c red	3.25	2.25	.65
	1960 Type of 1958 re-engraved: with border on card			
UXC3	5c red	3.00	7.00	1.65

UXC4

UXC5, UXC8, UXC11

	1963			
UXC4	6c red	3.00	.70	.30
	1966			
UXC5	11c blue & red	2.25	.80	.40

UXC6

UXC7

	1967			
UXC6	6c multicolored	2.00	.50	.35
UXC7	6c blue, yellow, black, red.	1.75	.60	.25
UXC8	13c blue & red	2.00	1.50	.60

UXC9, UXC10

	1968-71			
UXC9	8c blue & red	1.75	1.10	.40
UXC9at	8c luminescent	17.00	2.00	2.75
UXC10	9c red & blue	2.25	.85	.40

SCOTT CAT. NO.	DESCRIPTION	FIRST DAY COVER	MINT	USED

1971. Inscribed U.S. Air Mail

| UXC11 | 15c blue & red | 2.00 | 1.50 | .65 |

UXC12

U.S. AIR MAIL 9 CENTS

UXC13

U.S. AIR MAIL 15 CENTS

1972
Issued with various designs on reverse

| UXC12 | 9c black & dull orange | 1.60 | .65 | .40 |
| UXC13 | 15c black & dull orange | 1.60 | .75 | .50 |

UXC14

UXC15

1974

| UXC14 | 11c red & blue | 1.60 | .60 | .30 |
| UXC15 | 18c multicolored | 1.60 | .80 | .40 |

UXC16

1975

| UXC16 | 21c multicolored | 1.60 | .95 | .50 |

UXC17

1978

| UXC17 | 21c multicolored | 2.00 | .95 | .... |

UXC18

1979

| UXC18 | 21c multicolored | 1.60 | 1.25 | .50 |

UXC19

1981

| UXC19 | 28c multicolored | 1.60 | .95 | .... |

UXC20

1982

| UXC20 | 28c multicolored | 1.75 | .75 | .... |

UXC21

1983

| UXC21 | 28c multicolored | 1.75 | .75 | .... |

REVENUE STAMPS
1863-71. FIRST ISSUE

When ordering from this issue be sure to indicate whether the "a", "b" or "c" variety is wanted. Example: R27c.

In the price columns below, a dash instead of a dotted line indicates that no stamp is known in that classification.

We can supply first-issue Revenue Stamps with the desirable hand-stamped cancellations. Send us your want list for these.

R102

R1-R4 R5-R15 R16-R42

R43-R53 R54-R65 R66-R76

R77-R80 R81-R87

R88-R96 *Washington* R97-R101

SCOTT CAT.NO.	Prices are for used single copies	IMPERF-ORATE a.	PART PERF. b.	PERF-ORATED c.
R1	1c Express	55.00	40.00	1.35
R2	1c Playing Cards	750.00	325.00	110.00
R3	1c Proprietary	500.00	105.00	.60
R4	1c Telegraph	175.00		9.25
R5	2c Bank Check, blue	1.00	1.25	.20
R6	2c Bank Check, orange		80.00	.15
R7	2c Certificate, blue	13.00		20.00
R8	2c Certificate, orange		20.00	
R9	2c Express, blue	12.00	14.00	.40
R10	2c Express, orange			6.50
R11	2c Playing Cards, blue		110.00	3.00
R12	2c Playing Cards, orange			25.00
R13	2c Proprietary, blue		90.00	.60
R14	2c Proprietary, orange			35.00
R15	2c U.S. Internal Revenue			.12
R16	3c Foreign Exchange		110.00	2.75
R17	3c Playing Cards	5000.00	110.00	120.00
R18	3c Proprietary		125.00	1.65
R19	3c Telegraph	37.50	20.00	2.00
R20	4c Inland Exchange			2.00
R21	4c Playing Cards		75.00	300.00
R22	4c Proprietry		135.00	2.50
R23	5c Agreement			.55
R24	5c Certificate	2.75	9.50	.35
R25	5c Express	3.75	4.50	.50
R26	5c Foreign Exchange			.50
R27	5c Inland Exchange	3.50	3.50	.30
R28	5c Playing Cards			12.00
R29	5c Proprietary			18.00
R30	6c Inland Exchange			1.10
R32	10c Bill of Lading	50.00	110.00	1.10
R33	10c Certificate	80.00	65.00	.60
R34	10c Contract, blue		70.00	.60
R34e	10c Contract. ultramarine		180.00	.90
R35	10c Foreign Exchange			3.75
R35e	10c Foreign Exchange, ultra			7.00
R36	10c Inland Exchange	95.00	3.00	.40
R37	10c Power of Attorney	290.00	22.50	.70
R38	10c Proprietary			15.00
R39	15c Foreign Exchange		20.00	14.00
R40	15c Inland Exchange	27.50	15.00	1.10
R41	20c Foreign Exchange	45.00		32.50
R42	20c Inland Exchange	20.00	17.50	.60

DON'T FORGET
CRYSTAL MOUNT

SCOTT	Prices are for	IMPERF-ORATE a.	PART PERF. b.	PERF-ORATED c.
CAT.NO.	used single copies			
R43	25c Bond	65.00	5.50	2.00
R44	25c Certificate	6.00	6.00	.25
R45	25c Entry of Goods	18.00	35.00	.80
R46	25c Insurance	10.00	11.00	.60
R47	25c Life Insurance	35.00	75.00	4.00
R48	25c Power of Attorney	5.50	18.00	.50
R49	25c Protest	23.50	125.00	4.50
R50	25c Warehouse Receipt	35.00	125.00	24.50
R51	30c Foreign Exhchange	45.00	150.00	40.00
R52	30c Inland Exchange	40.00	40.00	3.00
R53	40c Inland Exchange	400.00	4.00	2.50
R54	50c Conveyance, blue	11.50	1.50	.35
R54e	50c Conveyance, ultramarine			.50
R55	50c Entry of Goods		12.00	.65
R56	50c Foreign Exchange	40.00	35.00	3.75
R57	50c Lease	24.00	55.00	4.00
R58	50c Life Insurance	30.00	45.00	1.10
R59	50c Mortage	15.00	2.25	.70
R60	50c Original Process	3.00		.60
R61	50c Passage Ticket	60.00	90.00	.85
R62	50c Probate of will	35.00	45.00	20.00
R63	50c Surety Bond, blue	100.00	3.00	.50
R63e	50c Surety Bond, ultramarine			1.25
R64	60c Inland Exchange	75.00	40.00	5.50
R65	70c Foreign Exchange	250.00	75.00	6.00
R66	$1 Conveyance	12.00	250.00	3.00
R67	$1 Entry of Goods	30.00		2.00
R68	$1 Foreign Exchange	50.00		1.10
R69	$1 Inland Exchange	12.00	200.00	.90
R70	$1 Lease	35.00		1.40
R71	$1 Life Insurance	100.00		3.75
R72	$1 Manifest	50.00		22.50
R73	$1 Mortgage	20.00		125.00
R74	$1 Passage Ticket	125.00		125.00
R75	$1 Power of Attorney	60.00		2.50
R76	$1 Probate of Will	55.00		35.00
R77	$1.30 Foreign Exchange	1650.00		50.00
R78	$1.50 Inland Exchange	22.00		3.50
R79	$1.60 Foreign Exchange	500.00		70.00
R80	$1.90 Foreign Exchange	1500.00		55.00
R81	$2 Conveyance	80.00	375.00	3.00
R82	$2 Mortgage	70.00		3.00
R83	$2 Probate of Will	1700.00		45.00
R84	$2.50 Inland Exchange	850.00		4.50
R85	$3 Charter Party	85.00		5.00
R86	$3 Manifest	80.00		25.00
R87	$3.50 Inland Exchange	650.00		40.00
R88	$5 Charter Party	185.00		6.00
R89	$5 Conveyance	35.00		5.00
R90	$5 Manifest	75.00		80.00
R91	$5 Mortgage	80.00		20.00
R92	$5 Probate of Will	325.00		18.50
R93	$10 Charter Party	325.00		22.50
R94	$10 Conveyance	75.00		55.00
R95	$10 Mortgage	225.00		25.00
R96	$10 Probate of Will	650.00		25.00
R97	$15 Mortgage, blue	700.00		100.00
R97e	$15 Mortgage, ultramarine			125.00
R98	$20 Conveyance	50.00		30.00
R99	$20 Probate of Will	750.00		725.00
R100	$25 Mortgage	550.00		85.00
R101	$50 U.S. Internal Revenue	165.00		95.00
R102	$200 U.S. Internal Revenue	975.00		575.00

1871 SECOND ISSUE

NOTE: The individual denominations vary in design from the illustrations shown which are more typical of their relative size.

R103, R104, R134, R135, R151

R105-R111, R136-R139

R112-R114,

R115-R117, R142-R143

R118-R122, R144

R123-R126, R145-R147

R127, R128, R148, R149

R129-R131 R150

		USED
R103	1c blue and black	25.00
R104	2c blue and black	1.50
R105	3c blue and black	12.00
R106	4c blue and black	40.00
R107	5c blue and black	1.50
R108	6c blue and black	50.00
R109	10c blue and black	1.10
R110	15c blue and black	20.00
R111	20c blue and black	5.00
R112	25c blue and black	1.00
R113	30c blue and black	45.00
R114	40c blue and black	25.00
R115	50c blue and black	1.00

SCOTT CAT. NO.	DESCRIPTION	UNCANC. EACH	USED EACH
R116	60c blue and black	55.00	
R117	70c blue and black	25.00	
R118	$1 blue and black	3.00	
R119	$1.30 blue and black	200.00	
R120	$1.50 blue and black	12.00	
R121	$1.60 blue and black	275.00	
R122	$1.90 blue and black	110.00	
R123	$2.00 blue and black	12.00	
R124	$2.50 blue and black	20.00	
R125	$3.00 blue and black	25.00	
R126	$3.50 blue and black	95.00	
R127	$5 blue and black	18.00	
R128	$10 blue and black	95.00	
R129	$20 blue and black	275.00	
R130	$25 blue and black	275.00	
R131	$50 blue and black	300.00	

1871-72. THIRD ISSUE

SCOTT CAT. NO.	DESCRIPTION	UNCANC. EACH	USED EACH
R134	1c claret and black	20.00	
R135	2c orange and black		.15
R135b	2c orange and black (center inverted)	250.00	
R136	4c brown and black	30.00	
R137	5c orange and black		.50
R138	6c orange and black	25.00	
R139	15c brown and black	8.50	
R140	30c orange and black	10.00	
R141	40c brown and black	17.00	
R142	60c orange and black	45.00	
R143	70c green and black	30.00	
R144	$1 green and black	1.75	
R145	$2 vermilion and black	20.00	
R146	$2.50 claret and black	30.00	
R147	$3 green and black	32.50	
R148	$5 vermilion and black	18.00	
R149	$10 green and black	80.00	
R150	$20 orange and black	350.00	

1874 on greenish paper

SCOTT CAT. NO.	DESCRIPTION	UNCANC. EACH	USED EACH
R151	2c orange and black on green		.10
R151a	2c orange and black on green (center inverted)	325.00	

R152   R153   R154, R155
Liberty

1875-78

SCOTT CAT. NO.	DESCRIPTION	UNCANC. EACH	USED EACH
R152a	2c blue on blue, silk paper	.30	.12
R152b	2c watermarked ("USIR") paper	.30	.12
R152c	2c watermarked, rouletted		22.50

1898 Postage Stamps 279 & 267 Surcharged

SCOTT CAT. NO.	DESCRIPTION	UNCANC. EACH	USED EACH
R153	1c green, small I.R.	1.50	1.00
R154	1c green, large I.R.	.35	.25
R155	2c carmine, large I.R.	.35	.15

DOCUMENTARY STAMPS
Newspaper Stamp PR121 Surcharged
INT. REV.
$5.
DOCUMENTARY.

SCOTT CAT. NO.	DESCRIPTION	UNCANC. EACH	USED EACH
R159	$5 dark blue, red surcharge reading downwards	160.00	135.00
R160	$5 dark blue, red surcharge reading upwards	85.00	55.00

R161-R172   R173-R178, R182, R183

1898 Inscribed "Documentary"

SCOTT CAT. NO.	DESCRIPTION		UNCANC. EACH	USED EACH
R161	½c orange		2.50	6.00
R162	½c dark gray		.30	.25
R163	1c pale blue		.15	.10
R164	2c carmine		.15	.10
R165	3c dark blue		.80	.25
R166	4c pale rose		.50	.25
R167	5c lilac		.35	.15
R168	10c dark brown		.50	.15
R169	25c purple brown		.70	.15
R170	40c blue lilac	(cut cancel .30)	12.00	1.30
R171	50c slate violet		2.00	.20
R172	80c bistre	(cut cancel .15)	3.25	.65
R173	$1 dark green		1.50	.17
R174	$3 dark brown	(cut cancel .20)	3.25	
R175	$5 orange red	(cut cancel .30)		1.10
R176	$10 black	(cut cancel .70)		2.75
R177	$30 red	(cut cancel 25.00)	110.00	70.00
R178	$50 gray brown	(cut cancel 1.85)	45.00	3.00

R179, R225, R246, R248   R180, R226, R249   R181, R224, R227, R247, R250
Marshall   *Hamilton*   *Madison*

1899 Various Portraits. Inscribed "Series of 1898"

SCOTT CAT. NO.	DESCRIPTION		UNCANC. EACH	USED EACH
R179	$100 yellow brown & black	(cut cancel 11.00)	60.00	30.00
R180	$500 carmine lake & black	(cut cancel 190.00)		350.00
R181	$1000 green & blk.	(cut cancel 90.00)	400.00	300.00

1900

SCOTT CAT. NO.	DESCRIPTION		UNCANC. EACH	USED EACH
R182	$1 carmine	(cut cancel .20)	2.75	.60
R183	$3 lake	(cut cancel 6.25)	55.00	40.00

R184-R189   Designs of R173-78 surcharged   R190-R194

SCOTT CAT.NO.	DESCRIPTION	UNCANC. EACH	USED EACH
R184	$1 gray . . . . .(cut cancel, 10)	1.50	.25
R185	$2 gray . . . . .(cut cancel .10)	1.75	.25
R186	$3 gray . . . . .(cut cancel .75)	15.00	9.50
R187	$5 gray . . . . .(cut cancel .40)	5.50	3.00
R188	$10 gray . . .(cut cancel 2.50)	35.00	8.75
R189	$50 gray . .(cut cancel 65.00)	500.00	300.00
	1902		
R190	$1 green . . . . .(cut cancel .35)	2.95	1.60
R191	$2 green . . . . .(cut cancel .25)	2.75	1.10
R191a	$2 surcharged as R185	50.00	50.00
R192	$5 green . . . . .(cut cancel 1.50)	18.50	8.50
R192a	$5, surcharge omitted	50.00	
R193	$10 green . .(cut cancel 20.00)	200.00	135.00
R194	$50 green (cut cancel 200.00)	900.00	625.00

R195-R216

R217-R223

1914 Inscribed "Series of 1914." Single Line Watermark "USPS."

R195	½c rose	2.50	1.60
R196	1c rose	.85	.25
R197	2c rose	.85	.25
R198	3c rose	20.00	16.00
R199	4c rose	4.50	.80
R200	5c rose	1.35	.30
R201	10c rose	1.20	.20
R202	25c rose	6.00	.50
R203	40c rose	4.50	.70
R204	50c rose	1.50	.25
R205	80c rose	25.00	6.00

Double Line Watermark "USIR."

R206	½c rose	.80	.70
R207	1c rose	.10	.10
R208	2c rose	.15	.10
R209	3c rose	.80	.20
R210	4c rose	1.20	.30
R211	5c rose	.60	.12
R212	10c rose	.40	.10
R213	25c rose	2.50	.75
R214	40c rose . . . . .(cut cancel .75)	20.00	4.00
R215	50c rose . . . . .(cut cancel .60)	4.25	.18
R216	80c rose	25.00	7.00
R217	$1 green . . . .(cut cancel .10)	2.00	.20
R218	$2 carmine . . .(cut cancel .15)	5.00	.30
R219	$3 purple . . . .(cut cancel .30)	12.00	.95
R220	$5 blue . . . . .(cut cancel .70)	12.00	2.00
R221	$10 orange . .(cut cancel 1.00)	22.50	4.00
R222	$30 vermilion (cut cancel 2.75)	85.00	7.50
R223	$50 violet (cut cancel 200.00)	800.00	550.00

1914-15. Various Portraits
Inscribed "Series of 1914" or "Series of 1915"

R224	$60 brown .(cut cancel 45.00)	140.00	100.00
R225	$100 green .(cut cancel 15.00)	90.00	40.00
R226	$500 blue (cut cancel 200.00)	500.00	450.00
R227	$1000 orange		
	. . . .(cut cancel 200.00)	500.00	450.00

R228-239, R251-256, R260-263

R240-245, R257-259

SCOTT CAT.NO.	DESCRIPTION	UNCANC. EACH	USED EACH
	1917. Perf. 11.		
R228	1c carmine rose	.15	.15
R229	2c carmine rose	.10	.10
R230	3c carmine rose	.35	.30
R231	4c carmine rose	.25	.10
R232	5c carmine rose	.25	.10
R233	8c carmine rose	1.25	.18
R234	10c carmine rose	.30	.10
R235	20c carmine rose	.55	.15
R236	25c carmine rose	.80	.15
R237	40c carmine rose	.85	.15
R238	50c carmine rose	.90	.15
R239	80c carmine rose	2.75	.15
	Same design as issue of 1914-15. Without dates.		
R240	$1 green	2.25	.15
R241	$2 rose	5.00	.15
R242	$3 violet . . . . .(cut cancel .15)	12.00	.70
R243	$4 yellow brown (cut cancel .25)	5.50	2.25
R244	$5 blue, (cut cancel .15)		
	(perf. init. .20)	5.00	.25
R245	$10 orange . . .(cut cancel .25)	8.50	.75
	Types of 1899. Various Portraits. Perf. 12		
R246	$30 vermilion, Grant		
	. . . .(cut cancel .85)	30.00	2.75
R247	$60 brown, Lincoln		
	. . . .(cut cancel 1.25)	35.00	8.75
R248	$100 green, Washington		
	. . . .(cut cancel .65)	25.00	1.50
R249	$500 blue, Hamilton		
	. . . .(cut cancel 8.00)		32.50
R249a	$500 Numerals in orange		70.00
R250	$1000 orange, Madison		
	. . . .(Perf.Int. 3.50)		
	. . . .(cut cancel 3.75)	85.00	10.00
	1928-29 Perf. 10.		
R251	1c carmine rose	1.25	.65
R252	2c carmine rose	.30	.15
R253	4c carmine rose	3.50	2.35
R254	5c carmine rose	.80	.25
R255	10c carmine rose	.85	.70
R256	20c carmine rose	3.85	2.75
R257	$1 green . . . .(cut cancel 2.00)	40.00	25.00
R258	$2 rose	4.00	.30
R259	$10 orange (cut cancel 3.25)	25.00	8.00
	1929-30. Perf. 11 x 10.		
R260	2c carmine rose	1.85	1.35
R261	5c carmine rose	.95	.70
R262	10c carmine rose	5.00	4.25
R263	20c carmine rose	8.00	6.00

R733, R734

	UNUSED	USED (UNCUT)	USED (CUT CANC.)	USED (PERF INIT)
1962. CENTENNIAL INTERNAL REV.				
Inscribed "Established 1862"				
R733 10c	3.00	.45	.17	.15
(Plate Block 4)	20.00			
1964. Without Inscription Date				
R734 10c	6.50	.35	.12	.10
(Plate Block 4)	62.50			

HUNTING PERMIT STAMPS

RW1-RW5

RW6-RW49

SCOTT CAT.NO.	DESCRIPTION	PLATE BLOCK F	AVG	UNUSED F	AVG	USED F	AVG
	1934-1938						
	Inscribed: DEPARTMENT OF AGRICULTURE						
RW1	1934 $1 Mallards	7250.00	6250.00	435.00	350.00	95.00	80.00
RW2	1935 $1 Canvasbacks	9250.00	7750.00	650.00	550.00	235.00	200.00
RW3	1936 $1 Canada Geese	4750.00	4000.00	385.00	300.00	75.00	60.00
RW4	1937 $1 Scaup Ducks	2800.00	2200.00	225.00	175.00	35.00	30.00
RW5	1938 $1 Pintail Drake	2800.00	2200.00	225.00	175.00	35.00	30.00

NOTE: To obtain VF price, add the difference between the Avg. and F prices to the F price. For NH for #RW1-5, add 20% to the desired condition prices.

SCOTT CAT.NO.	DESCRIPTION	PLATE BLOCK F	AVG	UNUSED F	AVG	USED F
	1939-1982					
	Inscribed: DEPARTMENT OF INTERIOR					
RW6	1939 $1 Green-Winged Teal	1700.00(6)	1400.00(6)	155.00	125.00	18.50
RW7	1940 $1 Black Mallards	1600.00(6)	1300.00(6)	155.00	125.00	20.00
RW8	1941 $1 Ruddy Ducks	1275.00(6)	1000.00(6)	170.00	140.00	20.00
RW9	1942 $1 Baldpates	1275.00(6)	1000.00(6)	155.00	125.00	22.00
RW10	1943 $1 Wood Ducks	625.00(6)	500.00(6)	80.00	65.00	22.00
RW11	1944 $1 White Fronted Geese	535.00(6)	475.00(6)	80.00	65.00	18.00
RW12	1945 $1 Shoveller Ducks	485.00(6)	425.00(6)	60.00	50.00	15.00
RW13	1946 $1 Redhead Duck	485.00(6)	425.00(6)	60.00	50.00	12.00
RW14	1947 $1 Snow Geese	515.00(6)	450.00(6)	57.50	50.00	12.00
RW15	1948 $1 Buffleheads	550.00(6)	475.00(6)	65.00	55.00	12.00
RW16	1949 $2 Goldeneye Ducks	550.00(6)	475.00(6)	65.00	55.00	12.00
RW17	1950 $2 Trumpeter Swans	550.00(6)	475.00(6)	75.00	65.00	7.50
RW18	1951 $2 Gadwell Ducks	550.00(6)	475.00(6)	75.00	65.00	7.50
RW19	1952 $2 Harlequin Ducks	550.00(6)	475.00(6)	75.00	65.00	7.50
RW20	1953 $2 Blue-Winged Teal	550.00(6)	475.00(6)	75.00	65.00	7.50
RW21	1954 $2 Ring-Necked Ducks	575.00(6)	500.00(6)	80.00	70.00	7.50
RW22	1955 $2 Blue Geese	575.00(6)	500.00(6)	80.00	70.00	7.50
RW23	1956 $2 American Merganser	575.00(6)	500.00(6)	80.00	70.00	7.50
RW24	1957 $2 American Eider	575.00(6)	500.00(6)	80.00	70.00	7.50
RW25	1958 $2 Canada Geese	575.00(6)	500.00(6)	80.00	70.00	7.50
RW26	1959 $3 Dog & Mallard	675.00	600.00	95.00	85.00	7.50
RW27	1960 $3 Redhead Ducks	675.00	600.00	95.00	85.00	7.50
RW28	1961 $3 Mallard Hen & Ducklings	750.00	700.00	120.00	110.00	7.50
RW29	1962 $3 Pintail Drakes	750.00	700.00	135.00	125.00	10.00
RW30	1963 $3 Brant Landing Ducks	875.00	800.00	135.00	125.00	10.00

SCOTT CAT.NO.	DESCRIPTION	PLATE BLOCK F/NH	UNUSED F/NH	USED F
RW31	1964 $3 Hawaiian Nene Goose	4250.00(6)	145.00	8.00
RW32	1965 $3 Canvasback Drakes	575.00	120.00	7.00
RW33	1966 $3 Whistling Swans	600.00	120.00	7.00
RW34	1967 $3 Old Squaw Ducks	600.00	120.00	7.00
RW35	1968 $3 Hooded Mergansers	325.00	75.00	7.00
RW36	1969 $3 White-Winged Scoters	300.00	65.00	7.00
RW37	1970 $3 Ross' Goose	225.00	50.00	7.00
RW38	1971 $3 Three Cinnamon Teal	200.00	45.00	7.00
RW39	1972 $5 Emperor Geese	200.00	35.00	7.00
RW40	1973 $5 Steller's Eider's	150.00	30.00	7.00
RW41	1974 $5 Wood Ducks	125.00	25.00	7.00
RW42	1975 $5 Canvasbacks	125.00	25.00	7.00
RW43	1976 $5 Canada Geese	125.00	25.00	7.00
RW44	1977 $5 Pair of Ross' Geese	125.00	25.00	7.00
RW45	1978 $5 Hooded Merganser Drake	125.00	25.00	7.00
RW46	1979 $7.50 Green Winged Teal	135.00	30.00	7.00
RW47	1980 $7.50 Mallards	135.00	30.00	7.00
RW48	1981 $7.50 Ruddy Ducks	115.00	25.00	7.00
RW49	1982 $7.50 Canvasbacks	90.00	20.00	7.00
RW50	1983 $7.50 Pintails	80.00	18.75	....
RW51	1984 $7.50 Hunting & Conservation	80.00	18.75	....

SCOTT
CAT. NO. DESCRIPTION

U.S. Blocks #314-CE2

F UNUSED AVG |

F UNUSED AVG

171

703

CENTER LINE BLOCKS   ARROW BLOCKS

Scott Cat. No.	Description	Center F	Center AVG	Arrow F	Arrow AVG
314	1c Franklin	325.00	250.00	250.00	200.00
320	2c Washington	425.00	325.00	220.00	165.00
323	1c Louisiana Purchase			280.00	200.00
324	2c Louisiana Purchase			220.00	145.00
325	3c Louisisana Purchase			675.00	500.00
326	5c Louisiana Purchase			735.00	550.00
327	10c Louisiana Purchase			1600.00	1225.00
343	1c Franklin, imperf.	90.00	70.00	70.00	55.00
344	2c Washington, imperf.	120.00	85.00	95.00	65.00
345	3c Washington, imperf.,Type I	220.00	185.00	175.00	140.00
346	4c Washington, imperf.	400.00	310.00	350.00	275.00
347	5c Washington, imperf.	620.00	500.00	475.00	375.00
368	2c Lincoln, imperf.	385.00	300.00	350.00	265.00
371	2c Alaska-Yukon, imperf	425.00	310.00	400.00	285.00
373	2c Hudson-Fulton, imperf.	495.00	375.00	445.00	335.00
383	1c Franklin, imperf.	52.50	42.00	40.00	32.00
384	2c Washington, imperf	150.00	120.00	80.00	65.00
408	1c Washington, imperf.	20.00	16.00	13.00	9.50
409	2c Washington, imperf.	30.00	25.00	20.00	16.50
481	1c Washington, imperf.	19.50	15.00	13.50	11.00
482	2c Washington, imperf.,Type I	25.00	20.00	21.50	17.00
483	3c Washington, imperf.,Type I	185.00	135.00	135.00	105.00
484	3c Washington, imperf.,Type II	115.00	80.00	90.00	65.00
524	$5 Franklin	3950.00	2650.00	3800.00	2500.00
531	1c Washington, Offset, imperf.	175.00	145.00	110.00	85.00
532	2c Wash., Offset, imperf.,Type IV	475.00	400.00	400.00	335.00
533	2c Wash., Offset, imperf., Type V	2000.00	1500.00	1850.00	1350.00
534	2c Wash., Offset, imperf., Type Va	175.00	125.00	140.00	100.00
534A	2c Wash., Offset, imperf., Type VI	350.00	280.00	285.00	220.00
535	3c Washington, Offset, imperf.	200.00	120.00	175.00	95.00
547	$2 Franklin	3950.00	2750.00	3650.00	2575.00
571	$1 Lincoln Memorial			625.00	475.00
572	$2 U.S. Capitol			1625.00	1075.00
573	$5 "America"	3400.00	2200.00	3150.00	2100.00
575	1c Franklin, imperf.	125.00	100.00	105.00	85.00
576	1½c Harding, imperf.	37.00	30.00	22.00	18.50
577	2c Washington, imperf	40.00	32.50	23.00	19.50
611	2c Harding, imperf	200.00	160.00	140.00	115.00
620	2c Norse-American	90.00	70.00	85.00	65.00
621	5c Norse-American	350.00	260.00	320.00	250.00
631	1½c Harding, rotary, imperf.	62.50	50.00	42.50	35.00
702	2c Red Cross			2.25	2.00
703	2c Yorktown	5.00	4.25	4.75	4.00
832	$1 Wilson	245.00	200.00	165.00	135.00
833	$2 Harding	475.00	395.00	425.00	350.00
834	$5 Coolidge	1650.00	1375.00	1500.00	1250.00
C1	6c Curtiss Jenny Biplane	1075.00	850.00	1025.00	800.00
C2	16c Curtiss Jenny Biplane	1750.00	1350.00	1650.00	1275.00
C3	24c Curtiss Jenny Biplane	1800.00	1375.00	1675.00	1275.00
C23	6c Eagle	6.00	5.25	5.50	4.75
CE2	16c Coat of Arms	5.75	5.25	5.25	4.75

NOTE: For Never Hinged add the appropriate percentage as indicated in the listings.

U.S. BOOKLET PANES

Panes of 6 except as noted

C39a

SCOTT CAT.NO	DESCRIPTION	FIRST DAY COVER	UNUSED N.H. F	AVG	UNUSED F	AVG
		1903				
319g	2c carmine, Type I	.....	280.00	220.00	210.00	150.00
		1908				
331a	1c green	.....	250.00	210.00	210.00	165.00
332a	2c carmine	.....	260.00	220.00	220.00	175.00
		1910				
374a	1c green	.....	215.00	185.00	170.00	130.00
375a	2c carmine	.....	210.00	180.00	165.00	125.00
		1912				
405b	1c green	.....	140.00	110.00	100.00	75.00
406a	2c carmine	.....	200.00	150.00	140.00	110.00
		1914				
424d	1c green	.....	15.00	12.00	11.00	8.00
425e	2c carmine	.....	40.00	30.00	28.00	20.00
		1916				
462a	1c green	.....	27.50	22.00	20.00	15.00
463a	2c carmine	.....	190.00	160.00	150.00	120.00
		1917				
498e	1c green	.....	7.00	5.75	5.00	4.00
499c	2c rose	.....	8.00	6.75	5.75	4.50
		1917-18				
501b	3c violet, Type I	.....	195.00	150.00	150.00	110.00
502b	3c violet, Type II	.....	125.00	100.00	100.00	75.00
		1923				
552a	1c deep green	.....	11.50	9.00	9.00	6.50
554c	2c carmine	.....	13.00	10.00	10.00	7.00
		1926-27				
583a	2c carmine	.....	180.00	150.00	140.00	110.00
632a	1c green	.....	8.25	6.00	6.50	4.50
634d	2c carmine, Type I	.....	6.50	5.25	5.00	4.00
		1932				
720b	3c deep violet	200.00	90.00	65.00	70.00	50.00
		1939				
804b	1c green	25.00	6.00	4.75	5.00	4.00
806b	2c rose carmine	25.00	10.50	8.00	8.50	6.50
807a	3c deep violet	30.00	20.00	15.00	16.00	12.00
		AIR MAIL 1928				
C10a	10c dark blue	975.00	285.00	225.00	225.00	175.00

SLOGAN TYPES

I	-Your Mailman Deserves Your Help* Keep Harmful Objects out of . . .		IV	-Mail Early In The Day
			V	-Use Zip Code
II	-Add Zip to Your Mail* Use Zone Numbers for Zip Code.		VI	-Stamps In This Book . . .
			VII	-This Book Contains 25 . . .
III	-Add Zip to Your Mail* Always Use Zip Code		VIII	-Paying Bills? . . .

NOTE: Single Panes of Recent Issues May or May Not Have Selvege

SCOTT CAT.NO.	DESCRIPTION	FDC	F/NH	F
	1954-64			
1035a	3c Statue of Liberty	7.00	6.50	5.25
1036a	4c Lincoln	6.00	5.75	5.00
1213a	5c Washington (5)-I	6.00	13.00	12.00
1213a	5c Washington (5)-II	6.00	21.50	20.00
1213a	5c Washington (5)-III	6.00	4.50	4.00
	1967-78			
1278a	1c Jefferson	3.25	1.60	. . . . .
1278ae	1c Test gum.		4.50	
1278b	1c Jefferson (4)-IV & V . .	20.00	1.35	. . . . .
1280a	2c Wright (5)-IV	3.00	2.00	. . . . .
1280a	2c Wright (5)-V	3.00	2.00	. . . . .
1280c	2c Wright	20.00	2.00	. . . . .
1284b	6c F.D. Roosevelt (8)	4.00	2.75	. . . . .
1284c	6c F.D. Roosevelt (5)-IV	200.00	2.50	. . . . .
1284c	6c F.D. Roosevelt (5)-V	200.00	2.50	. . . . .
1288Bc	15c Holmes (8)	6.75	6.00	. . . . .
	1970-72			
1393a	6c Eisenhower (8)	4.50	2.50	. . . . .
1393ae	6c Test gum.		3.00	
1393b	6c Eisenhower (5)IV	4.00	2.25	. . . . .
1393b	6c Eisenhower (5)-V	4.00	2.25	. . . . .
1395a	8c Eisenhower (8)	5.00	4.50	. . . . .
1395b	8c Eisenhower	4.00	2.75	. . . . .
1395c	8c Eisenhower (4)-VI or VII .	3.00	2.25	. . . . .
1395d	8c Eisenhower (7)-IV	5.00	3.50	. . . . .
1395d	8c Eisenhower (7)-V	5.00	3.50	. . . . .
	1973-80			
1510a	10c Jefferson Memorial (5) .	4.00	2.50	. . . . .
1510c	10c Jefferson Memorial (8) .	6.00	4.00	. . . . .
1510d	10c Jefferson Memorial . . .	6.00	5.75	. . . . .
1595a	13c Liberty Bell	4.00	4.50	. . . . .

SCOTT CAT.NO.	DESCRIPTION	FDC	F/NH	F
1595b	13c Liberty Bell (7)-VIII	4.25	4.65	. . . . .
1595c	13c Liberty Bell (8)	4.50	5.35	. . . . .
1595d	13c Liberty Bell (5)	4.00	3.50	. . . . .
1598a	15c Fort McHenry (8)	4.50	7.00	. . . . .
1623a	13c & 9c Capitols (8)	110.00	8.25	. . . . .
1623c	13c & 9c Capitols, pf.10(8)	50.00	70.00	. . . . .
1736a	(15c) "A" Eagle (8)	6.75	6.00	. . . . .
1737a	15c Roses(8)	6.75	6.00	. . . . .
1742a	15c Windmills (10)	12.50	7.50	. . . . .
	1981-83			
1819a	(18c) "B" Eagle (8)	9.00	5.25	. . . . .
1889a	18c Wildlife (10)	11.50	7.20	. . . . .
1893a	6c & 18c Flags (8)	8.00	8.75	. . . . .
1896a	20c Flag & Sup. Ct. (6) . .	10.00	3.25	. . . . .
1896b	20c Flag & Sup. Ct. (10) . .	11.00	5.50	. . . . .
1909a	$9.35 Express Mail (3) . .	73.50	55.95	. . . . .
1948a	(20c) "C" Eagle (10)	10.00	7.00	. . . . .
1949a	20c Bighorned Sheep (10)	10.00	5.00	. . . . .
	AIR MAIL			
C25a	6c Twin-Motored Plane (3) .	30.00	9.75	8.00
C39a	6c DC-4 Skymaster	12.50	27.00	22.50
C51a	7c Silhouette of Jet	12.50	27.00	22.50
C60a	7c Silhouette of Jet	17.00	45.00	40.00
C64b	8c Plane & Capitol (5)-I	5.00	14.50	12.00
C64b	8c Plane & Capitol (5)-II		72.50	67.50
C64b	8c Plane & Capitol (5)-III		17.50	15.00
C72b	10c 50 Stars (8)	6.00	5.75	. . . . .
C72c	10c 50 Stars (5)-IV	200.00	22.50	. . . . .
C72c	10c 50 Strs (5)-V	200.00	6.00	. . . . .
C78a	11c Silhouette of Jet (4)-IV or V	4.00	2.15	. . . . .
C79a	13c Letter in Symbolic Flight (5)-VII	4.00	3.00	. . . . .

NO STAPLE HOLES

SCOTT CAT. NO.	DESCRIPTION	F/NH
	1954-62	
1035an	3c Statue of Liberty	8.00
1036an	4c Lincoln	7.50
1213an	5c Washington (5)-I	17.50
	1968-71	
1278an	1c Jefferson (8)	2.25
1278bn	1c Jefferson(4)-IV or V	1.65
1280an	2c Wright (5)-IV	3.00
1280an	2c Wright (5)-V	3.00
1280cn	2c Wright	3.00
1284bn	6c F.D. Roosevelt (8)	4.50
	1970-74	
1393an	6c Eisenhower (8)	3.75
1393bn	6c Eisenhower (5)-IV	3.50
1393bn	6c Eisenhower (5)-V	3.50

SCOTT CAT. NO.	DESCRIPTION	F/NH
1395an	8c Eisenhower (8)	6.00
1395bn	8c Eisenhower	3.50
1395cn	8c Eisenhower (4)-VI or VII	3.00
1395dn	8c Eisenhower (7)-IV	5.00
1395dn	8c Eisenhower (7)-V	5.00
1510bn	10c Jefferson Memorial (5)-VII	3.50
1510cn	10c Jefferson Memorial (8)	5.50
1510dn	10c Jefferson Memorial	7.75
	AIR MAIL	
C51an	7c Silhouette of Jet	32.50
C64bn	8c Plane & Capitol (5)-I	18.00
C72bn	10c 50 Stars (8)	8.50
C78an	11c Silhouette of Jet (4)-IV or V	3.25
C79an	13c Letter in Symbolic Fight (5)-VIII . . .	4.25

H.E.Harris & Co.,Inc.® UNITED STATES FIRST DAY COVER CLUB

Pictured above are covers in a recent club sending. Top cover with "Silk" cachet. Bottom cover with engraved cachet. Your new covers will have the same distinctive beauty and historical interest.

Get involved in today's most exciting collecting specialty!

A First Day Cover is created for every commemorative stamp issued by the U.S. Postal Service. Each cover bears the newly issued stamp, the official First Day of Issue Cancellation applied by the U.S. Post Office, and a beautiful cachet. By law, First Day Covers can not be re-issued or duplicated at a later date to meet new collector demands. Thus, they are true limited editions ... yet they are available at a very low cost!

Now you can start your exciting collection the easiest of all possible ways ... with a U.S. First Day Cover Club subscription. Your subscription guarantees that you will receive every new First Day Commemorative Cover issue, and selected additional covers, conveniently, at your home in fine condition. To enhance the beauty of the covers, all are unaddressed.

Here's All You Need Do, Choose Either or Both Cachets

There are two different cachets to choose from, each offering you a unique and exciting portrayal of the subject of the stamp.

Engraved -- Fine detailing and artistic excellence are the mark of the engraved cachet. Cachets are printed in a rich color complimentary to the colors of the stamp. The engraved cachet is one of the most popular at only $1.75 for a single stamp on cover; $3.00 for a "block-of-four" stamps on cover.

"SILK" -- Your First Day Cover comes alive with a rainbow of brilliance when full-color "silk" cachets are applied. Printed on a delightful silk-like fabric, these cachets are carefully mounted on your cover and framed with gold-colored embossing. Introduced to collectors in 1971, your covers will all have official "Colorano Silk" cachets. Priced at $2.25 for a single stamp on cover; $3.25 for each "block of four" cover, these covers are taking the world by storm.

Send no money! Your subscription will begin with the most recent issues and will include covers for all succeeding commemorative stamps. Covers will be sent in convenient groups every few weeks.

Pay For Your Covers upon receipt or conveniently charge them -- see details on subscription coupon on next page.

THE EASY, ECONOMICAL WAY TO COLLECT
U.S. FIRST DAY COVERS
BEGINNING WITH MOST RECENT ISSUES
Free Member's Album

included with your membership

As an introduction to the U.S. First Day Cover Subscription service, each new subscriber will receive a luxurious presentation Album absolutely free when they have purchased their second selection. For bookcase or coffee table, this elegant album is the perfect showcase for your First Day Cover collection. Each page in the Album has a special holder for the cover and the information card, custom designed to enhance and protect each issue. A handsome presentation piece you'll be proud to own.

SEND NO MONEY

Use This Coupon For Your Subscription—
H.E. Harris & Co./R & R, Box N, Boston, Mass. 02117

☐ Yes, start my membership in the R & R U.S. First Day Cover Club with the next sending. And . . . be sure to include a cover with a block-of-four when the Postal Service issues one.

☐ I'd like engraved cachets. (Bill me $1.75 for each single issue cover and $3.00 for each "block-of-four" cover).

☐ I'd like "silk" cachets. (Bill me $2.25 for each single issue cover and $3.25 for each "block-of-four" cover).

☐ I'd like to enroll in both programs.

☐ Bill me for each selection.

☐ Automatically charge my credit account for each selection.

    ☐ Visa   ☐ Master Card   ☐ American Express   ☐ Harris Credit Plan

Credit Card No. _____

Inter Bank No. _____ Exp. Date_____

Signature _____ or ☐ Send me an application

CUBNA1
Name_____

Address_____

City _____ State _____ Zip _____

(Note: Mass. residents will be billed 5% sales tax.)
MAIL COUPON TO: R & R, BOX N, BOSTON, MA 02117
SATISFACTION GUARANTEED OR YOUR MONEY BACK
(a division of H.E. Harris & Co., Inc., The World's Largest Stamp Firm)

UNITED STATES FIRST DAY COVERS

First Day covers are listed as Singles; ordinary Blocks of four and, on later issues Plate Blocks.

These covers are virtually all of standard size and will bear the proper first day cancel.

Before 1935 most First Day Covers did not bear cachets and these are listed first as "Uncacheted". All others listed will have appropriate cachets. For any items not listed herein, please send your want list to the attention of R & R Cover Division/H.E. Harris.

UNCACHETED

SCOTT CAT.NO.	DESCRIPTION	FIRST DAY SINGLE	COVERS BLOCK	SCOTT CAT.NO.	DESCRIPTION	FIRST DAY SINGLE	COVERS BLOCK
551	½c Hale	37.50	37.50	623	17c Wilson	45.00	70.00
552	1c Franklin	60.00	150.00	627	2c Sesquicentennial	30.00	45.00
553	1½c Harding	50.00	65.00	628	5c Ericsson	50.00	80.00
554	2c Washington	75.00	90.00	629	2c White Plains	17.50	30.00
555	3c Lincoln	75.00	90.00	630	2c White Plains SS	1800.00	——
556	4c M. Washington	75.00	90.00	630a	2c Same single	35.00	45.00
557	5c T. Roosevelt	175.00	215.00	631	1½c Harding	50.00	70.00
558	6c Garfield	250.00	——	632	1c Franklin	70.00	95.00
559	7c McKinley	150.00	850.00	633	1½c Harding	70.00	95.00
560	8c Grant	150.00	850.00	634	2c Washington	75.00	100.00
561	9c Jefferson	150.00	850.00	635	3c Lincoln	70.00	95.00
562	10c Monroe	175.00	850.00	635a	3c Lincoln	35.00	50.00
563	11c R.B. Hayes	700.00	2,000.00	636	4c Martha Washington	75.00	100.00
564	12c Cleveland	200.00	1,250.00	637	5c Roosevelt	75.00	100.00
565	14c American Indian	450.00	1,850.00	638	6c Garfield	85.00	110.00
566	15c Statue of Liberty	500.00	1,850.00	639	7c McKinley	90.00	115.00
567	20c Golden Gate	525.00	1,850.00	640	8c Grant	90.00	115.00
568	25c Niagra Falls	725.00	1,850.00	641	9c Jefferson	110.00	150.00
569	30c N. American Bison	825.00	1,850.00	642	10c Monroe	125.00	165.00
570	50c Arlington Amphitheatre	1050.00	1,900.00	643	2c Vermont	10.00	20.00
571	$1.00 Lincoln Memorial	5,000.00	9,700.00	644	2c Burgoyne	30.00	45.00
572	$2.00 U.S. Capitol Bldg.	12,500.00	——	645	2c Valley Forge	12.00	22.00
573	$5.00 Statue of Freedom	16,000.00		646	2c Molly Pitcher	25.00	45.00
576	1½c Harding	60.00	80.00	647	2c Hawaii	30.00	70.00
582	1½c Harding	70.00	95.00	648	5c Hawaii	75.00	200.00
584	3c Lincoln	75.00	115.00	647-48	2 on 1 cover	100.00	240.00
585	4c M. Washington	75.00	115.00	649	2c Aero Conf.	17.00	30.00
586	5c T. Roosevelt	75.00	115.00	650	5c Aero Conf.	25.00	50.00
587	6c Garfield	85.00	140.00	649-50	2 on 1 cover	40.00	65.00
588	7c McKinley	90.00	125.00	651	2c Clark	9.00	14.50
589	8c Grant	95.00	140.00	653	½c Hale	45.00	45.00
590	9c Jefferson	100.00	150.00	654	2c Electric Light	18.00	22.50
591	10c Monroe	125.00	175.00	655	2c Electric Light	90.00	115.00
597	1c Franklin	500.00	——	656	2c Electric Light	125.00	(pr.150.00)
598	1½c Harding	75.00	——	657	2c Sullivan	8.00	15.00
599	2c Washington	800.00	——	658	1c Kansas	35.00	60.00
600	3c Lincoln	95.00	——	659	1½c Kansas	35.00	60.00
602	5c T. Roosevelt	105.00	——	660	2c Kansas	35.00	60.00
603	10c Monroe	125.00	——	661	3c Kansas	50.00	150.00
604	1c Franklin	110.00	——	662	4c Kansas	40.00	95.00
605	1½c Harding	75.00	——	663	5c Kansas	40.00	95.00
606	2c Washington	110.00		664	6c Kansas	60.00	170.00
610	2c Harding (Marion)	35.00	70.00	665	7c Kansas	75.00	220.00
610	2c Harding (Washington)	65.00	95.00	666	8c Kansas	160.00	575.00
611	2c Harding	135.00	175.00	667	9c Kansas	90.00	150.00
612	2c Harding	160.00	220.00	668	10c Kansas	100.00	150.00
614	1c Huguenot-Walloon	85.00	105.00	658-68	11 on 1 Cover	1800.00	——
615	2c Huguenot-Walloon	115.00	135.00	669	1c Nebraska	35.00	60.00
616	5c Huguenot-Walloon	195.00	265.00	670	1½c Nebraska	35.00	60.00
614-16	3 on 1 cover	325.00	450.00	671	2c Nebraska	40.00	65.00
617	1c Lexington-Concord	75.00	95.00	672	3c Nebraska	60.00	150.00
618	2c Lexington-Concord	100.00	125.00	673	4c Nebraska	60.00	150.00
619	5c Lexington-Concord	160.00	275.00	674	5c Nebraska	65.00	160.00
617-19	3 on 1 cover	325.00	450.00	675	6c Nebraska	85.00	240.00
620	2c Norse-American	60.00	85.00	676	7c Nebraska	75.00	200.00
621	5c Norse-American	110.00	220.00	677	8c Nebraska	110.00	275.00
620-21	2 on 1 cover	150.00	240.00	678	9c Nebraska	110.00	275.00
622	13c Harrison	45.00	70.00	679	10c Nebraska	110.00	275.00

SCOTT CAT. NO.	DESCRIPTION	FIRST DAY COVERS SINGLE	BLOCK	SCOTT CAT. NO.	DESCRIPTION	FIRST DAY COVERS SINGLE	BLOCK
669-79	11 on 1 Cover	1800.00	———	746	7c Acadia	6.00	18.00
680	2c Fallen Timbers	7.00	20.00	747	8c Zion	10.00	50.00
681	2c Ohio River	7.00	20.00	748	9c Glacier Park	10.00	18.00
682	2c Mass. Bay Colony	7.00	20.00	749	10c Smoky Mountains	12.50	35.00
683	2c Carolina-Charleston	7.00	25.00	750	3c APS, Sheet of 6	85.00	
684	1½c Harding	6.00	8.00	750a	3c APS, single	18.50	45.00
	4c Taft	10.00	12.00	751	1c Yosemite, sheet of 6	65.00	
686	1½c Harding	8.00	(pr. 10.00)	751a	1c Same single	15.00	35.00
687	4c Taft	35.00	(pr.50.00)	752	3c Peace	18.00	40.00
688	2c Braddock	10.00	30.00	753	3c Byrd	20.00	40.00
689	2c von Steuben	8.50	20.00	754	3c Mothers of America	20.00	40.00
690	2c Pulaski	6.00	10.00	755	3c Wisconsin	20.00	40.00
692	11c Hayes	110.00	150.00	756	1c Yosemite	20.00	40.00
693	12c Cleveland	110.00	150.00	757	2c Grand Canyon	20.00	40.00
694	13c Harrison	110.00	150.00	758	3c Mount Rainier	20.00	40.00
695	14c Indian	110.00	120.00	759	4c Mesa Verde	20.00	40.00
696	15c Liberty	125.00	160.00	760	5c Yellowstone	20.00	40.00
697	17c Wilson	400.00	525.00	761	6c Crater Lake	25.00	45.00
698	20c Golden Gate	200.00	275.00	762	7c Acadia	25.00	45.00
699	25c Niagara Falls	450.00	625.00	763	8c Zion	25.00	45.00
700	30c Bison	300.00	485.00	764	9c Glacier Park	25.00	45.00
701	50c Arlington	450.00	575.00	765	10c Smoky Mountains	25.00	60.00
702	2c Red Cross	3.50	4.75	766a	1c Cent. of Progress	20.00	40.00
703	2c Yorktown	5.00	8.00	767a	3c Cent. of Progress	20.00	40.00
704	½c olive brown	10.00	10.00	768a	3c Byrd	20.00	40.00
705	1c green	10.00	15.00	769a	1c Yosemite	20.00	40.00
706	1½c brown	10.00	15.00	770a	3c Mount Rainier	20.00	45.00
707	2c carmine rose	10.00	15.00	771	16c Coat of Arms	35.00	50.00
708	3c deep violet	12.00	17.50				
709	4c light brown	12.00	17.50	C7	10c Map	150.00	210.00
710	5c blue	13.00	19.00	C8	15c Map	175.00	225.00
711	6c red orange	15.00	20.00	C9	20c Map	210.00	265.00
712	7c black	15.00	20.00	C10	10c Lindbergh	60.00	90.00
713	8c oliver bistre	20.00	28.50	C11	5c Beacon	(pr.)65.00	115.00
714	9c pale red	22.50	30.00	C12	5c Globe	25.00	37.50
715	10c orange yellow	25.00	33.50	C13	65c Graf Zeppelin	4,500.00	9,500.00
704-15	12 on 1 Cover	140.00	———	C14	$1.30 Graf Zeppelin	3,500.00	8,500.00
716	2c Olympic Winter Games	15.00	22.50	C15	$2.60 Graf Zeppelin	5,000.00	12,500.00
717	2c Arbor Day	7.00	9.00	C13-15	3 on one cover	30,000.00	
718	3c Olympic Summer Games	9.50	14.00	C16	5c Winged Globe	385.00	700.00
719	5c Olympic Summer Games	10.50	17.50	C17	8c Winged Globe	25.00	35.00
718-19	2 on 1 Cover	20.00	28.50	C18	50c Zeppelin	500.00	1,200.00
720	3c Washington	10.00	15.00	C19	6c Winged Globe	17.00	25.00
720b	3c Booklet pane	100.00		C20	25c China Clipper	60.00	80.00
721	3c Washington Coil	25.00	(pr.30.00)	C21	20c China Clipper	60.00	80.00
722	3c Washington Coil	25.00	(pr.30.00)	C22	50c China Clipper	60.00	90.00
723	6c Garfield Coil	25.00	(pr.30.00)	C21-C22	2 on one Cover	95.00	
724	3c William Penn	3.25	5.00	C23	6c Eagle	25.00	35.00
725	3c Daniel Webster	3.25	5.00	C24	30c Globe	50.00	65.00
726	3c Gen. Oglethorpe	3.25	5.00				
727	3c Peace Proclamation	3.50	5.00	CE1	16c Seal, dark blue	22.50	37.50
728	1c Century of Progress	3.30	5.00	CE2	16c Seal, red & blue	16.00	25.00
729	3c Century of Progress	3.40	5.00				
728-29	2 on 1 Cover	8.50	12.50	E12	10c Motorcycle Delivery	650.00	900.00
730	1c APS Sheet of 25	175.00	———	E13	15c Motorcycle Delivery	300.00	450.00
730a	1c APS single	3.75	5.75	E14	20c Mail Truck	175.00	265.00
731	3c APS Sheet of 25	175.00		E15	10c Motorcycle Delivery	115.00	180.00
731a	3c APS single	3.75	5.75	E16	15c Motorcycle Delivery	150.00	225.00
732	3c NRA	3.00	4.50				
733	3c Byrd	9.00	12.50	QE1	10c Special Handling	90.00	150.00
734	5c Kosciuszko	8.00	13.00	QE2	15c Special Handling	90.00	150.00
735	3c Nat'l Ex. sheet of 6	80.00	———	QE3	20c Special Handling	95.00	150.00
735a	3c Nat'l Ex. single	12.00	35.00	QE4	25c Special Handling	225.00	325.00
736	3c Maryland	3.00	6.00				
737	3c Mothers of America	3.50	6.00	U429	2c Washington	75.00	
738	3c Mothers of America	3.50	6.00	U436	3c Washington (size 7½)	35.00	———
739	3c Wisconsin	3.50	6.00	U437	3c Washington (Amber)	50.00	———
740	1c Yosemite	4.00	6.50	U439	3c Washington(Blue)	50.00	———
741	2c Grand Canyon	4.00	6.50	U522	2c Independence	35.00	———
742	3c Mt. Rainier	4.00	6.50	U523	1c Mount Vernon	20.00	———
743	4c Mesa Verde	4.00	6.50	U524	1½c Mount Vernon	20.00	———
744	5c Yellowstone	6.00	15.00	U525	2c Mount Vernon	18.00	———
745	6c Crater Lake	6.00	18.00	U526	3c Mount Vernon	18.00	———

SCOTT CAT.NO.	DESCRIPTION	FIRST DAY COVERS SINGLE		SCOTT CAT.NO.	DESCRIPTION	FIRST DAY COVERS SINGLE	BLOCK OF 4
U527	4c Mount Vernon	32.50		UC1	5c Monoplane (Size 5 & 8)	80.00	___
U528	5c Mount Vernon	20.00		UC3	6c Monoplane	18.00	___
U529	6c Washington (White)	15.00		UC7	8c Monoplane	18.00	___
U530	6c Washington (Amber)	15.00					
U531	6c Washington (Blue)	15.00		UX1	1c Liberty	1,850.00	___
UC1	5c Monoplane (Size 13)	35.00		UX37	3c William McKinley	350.00	___

CACHETED FIRST DAY COVERS

705	717	728

1923

610	2c Harding	450.00

1925

617	1c Lexington-Concord	150.00
618	2c Lexington-Concord	150.00
619	5c Lexington-Concord	200.00
620	2c Norse-American	125.00
621	5c Norse-American	200.00
620-21	2 on one cover	250.00

1925

623	17c Wilson	350.00

1926-34

627	2c Sesquicentennial	100.00
628	5c Ericsson	275.00
629	2c White Plains	80.00
630a	2c Same, single	150.00
635a	Lincoln	60.00
643	2c Vermont	75.00
644	2c Burgoyne	100.00
643-44	2 on one cover	250.00

1928

645	2c Valley Forge	75.00
646	2c Molly Pitcher	140.00
647	2c Hawaii	120.00
648	5c Hawaii	150.00
647-48	2 on one cover	295.00
649	2c Aero. Conf.	40.00
650	5c Aero. Conf.	60.00
649-50	2 on one cover	100.00

1929

651	2c Clark	50.00
654	2c Electric Light	65.00
655	2c Electric Light	225.00
656	2c Electric Light	200.00
657	2c Sullivan	50.00
680	2c Fallen Timbers	50.00
681	2c Ohio River	50.00

1930

682	2c Mass. Bay Colony	50.00
683	2c Carolina-Charleston	60.00

684	1½c Harding	40.00	.....
685	4c Taft	40.00	
686	1½ Harding	40.00	
687	4c Taft	75.00	
688	2c Braddock	50.00	
689	2c von Steuben	50.00	

1931

690	2c Pulaski	50.00	75.00
702	2c Red Cross	40.00	65.00
703	2c Yorktown	50.00	75.00

1932 WASHINGTON BICENTENNIAL ISSUE

704	½c olive brown	35.00	50.00
705	1c green	35.00	50.00
706	1½c brown	35.00	50.00
707	2c carmine rose	35.00	50.00
708	3c deep violet	35.00	50.00
709	4c light brown	38.00	55.00
710	5c blue	38.00	55.00
711	6c red orange	38.00	55.00
712	7c black	42.00	65.00
713	8c olive bistre	42.00	65.00
714	9c pale red	42.00	65.00
715	10c orange yellow	55.00	85.00
704-15	12 on one cover	285.00	

1932

716	2c Olympic Winter Games	40.00	65.00
717	2c Arbor Day	25.00	40.00
718	3c Summer Olympic Games	40.00	60.00
719	5c Summer Olympic Games	40.00	60.00
718-19	2 on one Cover	60.00	95.00
720	3c Washington	50.0	75.00
720b	3c Booklet pane	200.00	___
721	3c Washington Coil	50.00	___
722	3c Washington Coil	50.00	___
723	6c Garfield Coil	50.00	___
724	3c William Penn	30.00	45.00
725	3c Daniel Webster	30.00	45.00

1933

726	3c Gen. Oglethorpe	30.00	45.00
727	3c Peace Proclamation	30.00	45.00
728	1c Century of Progress	20.00	30.00

SCOTT CAT.NO.	DESCRIPTION	FIRST DAY COVERS SINGLE	BLOCK OF 4
729	3c Century of Progress ...	25.00	40.00
728-29	Century of Progress	40.00	60.00
730	1c APS Sheet of 25	200.00	
730a	1c APS Imperf.	25.00	40.00
730a-31a(1)	1c APS Imperf	40.00	60.00
731	3c APS sheet of 25	200.00	
731a	3c APS single	30.00	45.00
732	3c NRA	30.00	45.00
733	3c Byrd	35.00	50.00
734	5c Kosciuszko	30.00	45.00
1934			
735	3c Nat'l Ex. sheet of 6 ...	85.00	
735a	3c Nat'l Ex. single	25.00	40.00
736	3c Maryland	20.00	30.00
737	3c Mothers of America	20.00	30.00
738	3c Mothers of America	20.00	30.00
739	3c Wisconsin	12.00	18.00
740	1c Yosemite	12.50	18.00
741	2c Grand Canyon	12.50	18.00
742	3c Mt. Rainier	13.50	19.50
743	4c Mesa Verde	15.00	22.50
744	5c Yellowstone	15.00	22.50
745	6c Crater Lake	18.50	25.00
746	7c Acadia	19.50	25.00
747	8c Zion	18.00	25.00
748	9c Glacier Park	22.00	32.50
749	10c Smoky Mountains	28.00	40.00
750	3c APS Sheet of 6	95.00	
750a	3c APS single	28.00	40.00
751	1c Trans-Miss. sheet of 6 ..	75.00	
751a	1c Trans-Miss. single ...	15.00	22.50
Special Printing 1935			
752	3c Peace Commemoration ..	30.00	45.00
753	3c Byrd	30.00	45.00
754	3c Mothers of America	30.00	45.00
755	3c Wisconsin Tercentenary .	30.00	45.00
756	1c Yosemite	30.00	45.00
757	2c Grand Canyon	30.00	45.00
758	3c Mount Ranier	30.00	45.00
759	4c Mesa Verde	35.00	50.00
760	5c Yellowstone	35.00	50.00
761	6c Crater Lake	35.00	50.00
762	7c Acadia	35.00	50.00
763	8c Zion	38.00	55.00
764	9c Glacier Park	38.00	55.00
765	10c Smoky Mountains.....	40.00	60.00
766a	1c Century of Progress	30.00	45.00
767a	3c Century of Progress	30.00	45.00
768a	3c Byrd	30.00	45.00
769a	1c Yosemite	30.00	45.00
770a	3c Mount Rainier	35.00	50.00
771	16c Coat of Arms	45.00	65.00

SCOTT CAT.NO.	DESCRIPTION	SINGLE	PLATE BLOCK
772	3c Connecticut	9.50	13.50
773	3c Calif. Pacific Expo......	9.50	13.50
774	3c Boulder Dam	13.00	17.00
775	3c Michigan	9.00	14.00
1936			
776	3c Texas	9.00	14.00
777	3c Rhode Island	9.00	14.00
778	3c TIPEX sheet	30.00	
782	3c Arkansas...........	9.00	13.00
783	3c Oregon	10.00	14.00
784	3c Anthony	15.00	21.00
1936-37			
785	1c Army	7.00	10.00
786	2c Army	7.00	10.00
787	3c Army	7.00	10.00
788	4c Army	7.00	11.00

SCOTT CAT.NO.	DESCRIPTION	FIRST DAY COVERS SINGLE	PLATE BLOCK
789	5c Army	8.00	12.00
790	1c Navy	7.00	10.00
791	2c Navy	7.00	10.00
792	3c Navy	7.00	10.00
793	4c Navy	7.00	11.00
794	5c Navy	8.00	12.00
1937			
795	3c NW Ordinance	8.50	12.50
796	5c V. Dare	9.50	13.00
797	10c S.P.A. pane	8.25	
798	3c Constitution	8.50	12.50
799	3c Hawaii	9.50	13.00
800	3c Alaska	9.50	13.00
801	3c Puerto Rico	9.50	13.00
802	3c Virgin Islands	9.50	13.00
1938-1954			
803	½c Franklin	3.00	5.00
803EE	Electric Eye	7.50	17.50
804	1c G. Washington	3.00	5.00
804EE	Electric Eye	7.50	17.50
804b	1c pane of 6	cpl.pane	20.00
805	1½c M. Washington	3.00	5.00
805EE	Electric Eye	7.50	17.50
806	2c J. Adams	3.00	5.00
806EE	Electric Eye (Type I)	10.00	20.00
806EE	Electric Eye (Type II)	7.50	17.50
806b	2c pane of 6	cpl.pane	20.00
807	3c Jefferson	3.00	5.00
807EE	Electric Eye	7.50	17.50
807EE	Electric Eye Convertible	10.00	20.00
807a	3c pane of 6	cpl.pane	24.00
808	4c Madison	4.00	8.00
808EE	Electric Eye	12.50	25.00
809	4½c White House	5.00	11.00
809EE	Electric Eye	12.50	25.00
810	5c J. Monroe	5.00	11.00
810EE	Electric Eye	12.50	25.00
811	6c J.Q. Adams	5.00	11.00
811EE	Electric Eye	12.50	25.00
812	7c A. Jackson	5.00	11.00
812EE	Electric Eye	12.50	25.00
813	8c Van Buren	5.00	11.00
813EE	Electric Eye	12.50	25.00
814	9c Harrison	5.00	11.00
814EE	Electric Eye	12.50	25.00
815	10c Tyler	6.00	12.00
815EE	Electric Eye	12.50	25.50
816	11c Polk	6.00	12.00
816EE	Electric Eye	16.00	32.00
817	12c Taylor	6.00	12.00
817EE	Electric Eye	16.00	32.00
818	13c Fillmore	6.00	12.00
818EE	Electric Eye	16.00	32.00
819	14c Pierce	6.00	12.00
819EE	Electric Eye	16.00	32.00
820	15c Buchanan	8.00	18.00
820EE	Electric Eye	16.00	32.00
821	16c Lincoln	8.00	18.00
821EE	Electric Eye	19.00	37.00
822	17c Johnson	8.00	18.00
822EE	Electric Eye	19.00	37.00
823	18c Grant	8.00	18.00
823EE	Electric Eye	19.00	37.00
824	19c Hayes	9.00	20.00
824EE	Electric Eye	19.00	37.00
825	20c Garfield	9.00	20.00
825EE	Electric Eye	19.00	37.00
826	21c Arthur	9.00	20.00
826EE	Electric Eye	22.00	44.00

SCOTT CAT.NO.	DESCRIPTION	FIRST DAY COVERS SINGLE	PLATE BLOCK
827	22c Cleveland	9.00	20.00
827EE	Electric Eye	22.00	44.00
828	24c Harrison	9.00	20.00
828EE	Electric Eye	22.00	44.00
829	25c McKinley	9.00	20.00
830	30c Roosevelt	12.00	23.00
830EE	Electric Eye	28.00	55.00
831	50c Wm. Taft	20.00	32.00
831EE	Electric Eye	28.00	55.00
832	$1 W. Wilson	70.00	125.00
832c	$1 W. Wilson	45.00	75.00
833	$2 Harding	140.00	250.00
834	$5 Coolidge	225.00	425.00
803-34	Presidentials ½c-$5, 32 Vars	595.00	1150.00
803-31	Pres.½c-50c, 29 Vars	185.00	395.00
	1938		
835	3c Ratification	8.50	11.50
836	3c Delaware	8.50	11.50
837	3c NW Territory	8.50	11.50
838	3c Iowa Territory	8.50	11.50
	1939		
839	1c Washington coil	____	(pr.10.00)
840	1½c M. Washington coil	____	(pr.10.00)
841	2c J. Adams coil	8.00	(pr.11.00)
842	3c Jefferson coil	10.00	(pr.12.00)
843	4c Madison coil	10.50	(pr.12.50)
844	4½c White House coil	10.50	(pr.10.50)
845	5c Monroe coil	11.50	(pr 14.00)
846	6c J.Q. Adams coil	12.00	(pr.15.00)
847	10c Tyler coil	22.50	(pr.37.50)
848	1c Washington coil	____	(pr.12.00)
849	1½c M. Washington coil	____	(pr.12.00)
850	2c J. Adams coil	8.00	(pr.14.00)
851	3c Jefferson coil	8.00	(pr.14.00)
852	3c Golden Gate	8.00	15.00
853	3c World's Fair	8.50	15.00
854	3c Inauguration	8.00	15.00
855	3c Baseball	17.50	26.50
856	3c Panama Canal	8.00	15.00
857	3c Printing	8.00	15.00
858	3c 4 States	7.00	10.00
	1940		
859	1c Irving	3.00	6.00
860	2c Cooper	3.00	6.00
861	3c Emerson	3.50	7.00
862	5c Alcott	5.00	10.00
863	10c Clemens	10.00	25.00
864	1c Longfellow	3.00	6.00
865	2c Whittier	3.00	6.00
866	3c Lowell	3.50	7.00
867	5c Whitman	5.00	10.00
868	10c Riley	10.00	25.00
869	1c Mann	3.00	6.00
870	2c Hopkins	3.00	6.00
871	3c C.W. Eliot	3.50	7.00
872	5c Willard	5.00	10.00
873	10c B.T. Washington	10.00	25.00
874	1c Audubon	3.00	6.00
875	2c Dr. Long	3.00	6.00
876	3c Burbank	3.50	7.00
877	5c Dr. Reed	5.00	10.00
878	10c J. Addams	10.00	25.00
879	1c Stephen Foster	3.00	6.00
880	2c J.P. Sousa	3.00	6.00
881	3c Victor Herbert	3.50	7.00
882	5c E. MacDowall	5.00	10.00

SCOTT CAT.NO.	DESCRIPTION	FIRST DAY COVERS SINGLE	PLATE BLOCK
883	10c Ethelbert Nevin	10.00	25.00
884	1c Gilbert Stuart	3.00	6.00
885	2c James Whistler	3.00	6.00
886	3c A. Saint-Gaudens	3.50	7.00
887	5c D.C. French	5.00	10.00
888	10c F. Remmington	10.00	25.00
889	1c Eli Whitney	3.00	6.00
890	2c Samuel Morse	3.00	6.00
891	3c Cyrus McCormick	3.50	7.00
892	5c Elias Howe	5.00	10.00
893	10c Alexander G. Bell	15.00	40.00
859-93	Famous Amer.,cpl.35 Vars	165.00	375.00
894	3c Pony Express	6.75	10.00
895	3c Pan American Union	5.25	8.50
896	3c Idaho Statehood	5.25	8.50
897	3c Wyoming Statehood	5.25	8.50
898	3c Coronado Expedition	5.25	8.50
899	1c National Defense	5.00	8.00
900	2c National Defense	5.00	8.00
901	3c National Defense	5.00	8.00
899-901	Set on 1 cover	15.00	25.00
902	3c Emancipation	6.00	9.00

SCOTT CAT.NO.	**AIRMAILS**	SINGLE	BLOCK
C8	15c Map	250.00	.....
C10	10c Lindbergh	250.00	.....
C11	5c Beacon	195.00	.....
C12	5c Winged Globe	100.00	.....
C13	65c Zeppelin	4,950.00	.....
C14	$1.30 Zeppelin	3,850.00	.....
C15	$2.60 Zeppelin	5,350.00	.....
C16	5c Winged Globe	500.00	.....
C17	8c Winged Globe	65.00	95.00
C18	50c Zeppelin	600.00	.....
C19	6c Globe (first day of rate)	50.00	80.00
C20	25c China Clipper	65.00	95.00
C21	20c China Clipper	65.00	95.00
C22	50c China Clipper	70.00	110.00
C23	6c Eagle holding sheild	30.00	40.00
C24	30c Winged Globe	55.00	85.00
CE1	16c Great Seal, blue	30.00	40.00
CE2	16c Great Seal, red & blue	25.00	35.00

NOTE: CACHETED FIRST DAY COVERS AFTER 1941 & BOOKLET PANES, ARE CATALOGED WITH STAMP LISTINGS.

U.S. FIRST DAY COVER COLLECTIONS

ALL CACHETED AND UNADDRESSED

The following specially prepared collections have been carefully assembled using only attractive, unaddressed covers and are being offered at low, money-saving prices. An excellent opportunity to start your collection of these fascinating covers.

NEW PRICE DECREASES.

#A851 300 Different $300.00   400.00
#A852 200 Different $200.00   250.00
#A853 100 Different $99.00   110.00
#A854 50 Different.. $39.95   45.00

INAUGURATION COVERS

1929 Hoover 160.00	1945 Truman................. 140.00	1965 Johnson 8.00
1933 Roosevelt 70.00	1949 Truman................. 75.00	1969 Nixon 6.00
1937 Roosevelt 175.00	1953 Eisenhower 17.50	1972 Nixon 5.00
1941 Roosevelt 160.00	1957 Eisenhower 12.00	1974 Ford 5.00
1945 Roosevelt 160.00	1961 Kennedy 17.50	1977 Carter 5.00
		1981 Reagan(2) 6.00

FIRST DAY COVER ALBUMS

SEE SUPPLY SECTION AT BACK OF BOOK FOR DETAILS

SCOTT NO.	DESCRIPTION	PRICE
1971		
S1423	American Wool	195.00
S1424	MacArthur	50.00
S1425	Blood Donors	30.00
S1426	Missouri Statehood	31.00
S1427-30	Wildlife (4)	175.00
S1431	Antarctic Treaty	43.00
S1432	Bicent. Emblem	225.00
S1433	Sloan Painting	45.00
S1434-35A	Space KSC Cancel(2)	25.00
S1434-35B	Same Huntsville cancel(2)	25.00
S1434-35C	Same Houston cancel(2)	25.00
S1436	Dickinson	28.00
S1437	San Juan	28.00
S1438	Drug Abuse	28.00
S1439	CARE	28.00
S1440-43	Historic(4)	125.00
S1444-45	Christmas(2)	33.00
1972		
S1446	Lanier	16.00
S1447	Peace Corps	16.00
S1451A	Hatteras blk	150.00
S1452	Wolf Trap Farm	15.00
S1453	Yellowstone w/DC cancel	17.50
S1454	McKinley Park	15.00
S1455	Family Planning	15.00
S1456-59	Craftsman 4 FDC's	130.00
S1460-62, SC85	Olymics (4)	40.00
S1463	PTA	10.00
S1464-7	Wildlife (4)	125.00
S1468	Mail Order	25.00
S1469	Osteopathic Medicine	13.00
S1470	Tom Sawyer	40.00
S1471-72	Christmas (2)	100.00
S1473	Pharmacy	16.00
S1474	Stamp Collecting	95.00
S1474A	Stamp Col.Show Cancel	90.00
1973		
S1475	Love	70.00
S1476	Pamphleteer	70.00
S1477	Broadside	70.00
S1478	Postrider	70.00
S1479	Drummer Boy	70.00
S1480-83	Boston Tea Party(4)	60.00
S1483A	Boston Tea blk	20.00
S1484	Gershwin	25.00
S1485	Jeffers	22.00
S1486	Tanner	5.00
S1487	Cather	5.00
S1488	Copernicus	6.00
S1489-98	Postal People(10)	45.00
S1499	Harry S. Truman	35.00
S1500-02, SC86	Electronics(4)	35.00
S1503	Lynden B. Johnson	55.00
S1504	Black Angus	5.00
S1505	Chautaqua('74)	5.00
S1506	Kansas Wheat('74)	5.00
S1507-08	Christmas(2)	8.00
S1509	Crossed Flags	48.00
S1509A	Same w/cable car FDC	48.00
S1519	Crossed Flags coil	32.00
S1519A	Same w/cable car FDC	32.00
1974		
S1525	VFW	5.00
S1526	Frost	5.00
S1527	EXPO '74	5.00
S1528	Kentucky Derby	5.00
S1529	Skylab(4)	14.00
S1530-37	UPU(8)	28.00
S1538-41	Minerals(4)	12.00
S1541A	Mineral blk	6.00
S1542	Fort Harrod	5.00
S1543-46	Congress (4)	11.00
S1546A	Congress blk	5.50
S1547	Energy Conservation	6.00
S1548	Sleepy Hollow	4.00
S1549	Retarded Children	4.00
S1550-51	Christmas (2)	5.00
S1552	Christmas pre-cancel	4.75
S1550-52	Christmas combos all 3 values on 1 FDC with both cancels	7.25
1975		
S1297	Parkman strip of 4	8.00
S1297	Parkman line pair	11.00
S1553	Ben West artist	4.00
S1554	Dunbar	4.00
S1555	Griffith	4.00
S1556	Pioneer/Jupiter	6.50
S1557	Mariner	6.50
S1558	Collective Bargaining	6.00
S1559-62	Contributors(4)	22.00
S1563	Lex-Concord on 2 FDC's one Lex.,one Concord	9.00
S1563A	Same both cancels on one cover	40.00
S1563B	Concord FDC w/slogan "Shot Heard"	45.00
S1564	Bunker Hill	3.50
S1565-68	Uniforms(4)	18.00
S1568A	Uniforms blk	5.00
S1569-70	ASTP pair on 2 FDC's	5.50
S1570A	ASTP pair 1 FDC	4.75
S1571	IWY	4.50
S1572-75	Postal Bicent.(4)	14.00
S1575A	Postal Bicent.blk	4.50
S1576	Peace through law	3.75
S1577-78	Bank Commerce 1 FDC	3.50
S1578A	Bank Commerce 2 FDC's	4.75
S1579-80	Christmas(2)	23.50

Scott No.	Description	Price	Scott No.	Description	Price
1975-79 Americana Series			S1711	Colorado	3.50
S1581-85	1c,2c,3c,4c values (4)	8.00	S1712-15	Butterflies(4)	11.00
S1591	9c Assemble	3.50	S1715A	Butterflies blk	5.25
S1592	10c Justice	2.50	S1716	Lafayette	3.00
S1593	11c Printing Press	3.50	S1717-20	Skilled Hands (4)	11.00
S1594	12c Torch	3.50	S1720A	Skilled Hands blk	5.25
S1595a	Liberty Booklet Pane of 6	11.00	S1721	Peace Bridge	3.00
S1595d	Liberty Booklet Pane of 5	11.00	S1721A	Same combo Canada-US	
S1596	13c Eagle	3.50		stamp Ft. Erie cancel	6.00
S1597	15c Ft. McHenry	2.50	S1721B	Same Buffalo cancel	6.00
S1598a	15c Ft. McHenry Bklt pane of 8	7.00	S1721C	US-Canada stamps w/both FD	
S1599	16c Statue of Liberty	3.00		cancels Buffalo-Ottawa	11.00
S1603	24c North Church	4.50	S1721D	combo w/US #961 on 1 cover	4.50
S1604	18c Fort Nisqually	3.00	S1722	Herkimer	2.50
S1605	29c Lighthouse	3.25	S1722A	Herkimer unofficial Oriskany	4.50
S1606	30c School	3.00	S1722B	Combo Herkimer and Oriskany FD	
S1608	50c "Betty" Lamp	3.50		cancels 1 FDC	15.00
S1610	$1.00 Rush Lamp	5.95	S1723-24	Energy Conservation &	
S1611	$2.00 Kerosene Lamp	10.00		Development 2 FDC's	4.50
S1612	$5.00 Lantern	20.00	S1724A	Same 1 FDC	3.25
S1613	3.1c Guitar Coil(5)	4.25	S1725	Alta California	2.50
S1614	7.7c Saxhorn Coil	4.50	S1725A	Same combo w/#1373	3.50
S1615	7.9c Drum Coil	4.50	S1725B	Alta. 2 cancels, San Jose &	
S1615C	8.4c Steinway Coil	3.25		Exhibition Station	4.75
S1616	9c Assembly Coil	11.75	S1725C	Alta, Exhib. Sta. Pict. cancel	3.50
S1617	10c Justice Coil	3.50	S1726	Confederation	2.75
S1617L	10c Line Pair Coil	8.00	S1727	Talking Pictures	4.50
S1618	13c Bell Coil	6.00	S1737A	Same combo w/US #928	5.50
S1618C	15c McHenry Coil	3.00	S1728	Saratoga	2.75
S1619	16c Statue of Liberty Coil	3.00	S1728A	Slogan, unoff. FD	3.95
S1619L	16c Liberty Line Pair	4.75	S1728B	Same, both cancels	4.50
S1622	13c Ind. Hall	4.25	S1728C	Same combo w/US #644	16.00
S1623a	Vending Booklet, perf. 11	95.00	S1729-30	Christmas(2)	5.50
S1623c	Vending Booklet.perf. 10	57.50	S1729-30	Christmas prs on (2) Valley	
S1625	13c Ind. Hall Coil	22.00		Forge & Omaha cancels	7.50
1976			S1729A	Wash. stamps with US #645	
S1629-31	Spirit of 76(3)	7.00		combo	7.00
S1631A	Spirit of 76 strip	5.25	S1729B	Wash. stamp FD cancel	
S1632	Interphil 76	5.50		& 13c Eagle, SEPAD Pict. cancel	4.75
S1633-82	Fifty State Flags	325.00	**1978**		
S1633A	Original 13 Colonies		S1731	Carl Sandburg	3.00
	with slogan cancel	110.00	S1732-33	Capt. Cook (4) 2 Hawaii—2 Alaska	9.00
S1683	Telephone Cent.	4.25	S1732A	Se—tenant Pairs(2) 1 Hawaii – 1	
S1684	Aviation	4.50		Alaska	5.95
S1685	Chemistry	3.50	'S1732A	2 Combos, Hawaii w/#799, C55,	
S1686-89	4 Souvenir Sheets	110.00		Alaska w/#800 & C53	15.00
S1686a-89a	20 Single FDC's	110.00	S1733A	3 Combos, Hawaii w/Hawaiian	
S1690	Ben Franklin	4.50		stamps of 1894, #74-6	48.00
S1690A	US-Canada combo		S1733B	Set of 3 Combo Covers each with dif.	
	Philadelphia FDC	9.75		cachet, Hawaii # 80-2	48.00
S1690B	Same B. Franklin pictorial		S1733C	Unoff. HAPEX FDC	5.00
	cancel	8.00	S1734	Indian Head Penny	7.00
S1690C	combo with both stamps		S1735	"A" Stamp	2.75
	and both FD cancels	25.00	S1736a	"A"Booklet Pane of 8	5.75
S1691-94	Declaration(4)	18.00	S1737a	Roses Booklet	7.00
S1694A	Declaration strip	7.75	S1737A	Roses (set of 6)	15.50
S1695-98	Olympics(4)	11.50	S1743	"A" Stamp Coil Pr.	3.50
S1698A	Olympics blk	6.00	S1743L	"A" Line Pair	6.00
S1699	Clara Maass	3.50	S1744	Harriet Tubman	3.00
S1700	A.S. Ochs	3.50	S1745-48	Quilts FDC's(4)	9.00
S1701-03	Christmas 3 FDC's	9.00	S1748A	Quilt blk	4.50
1977			S1749-52	Dance (4)	9.00
S1704	Wash. at Princeton	3.00	S1752A	Dance Blk	4.50
S1705	Sound Recording	3.50	S1753	French Alliance	2.75
S1706-09	Pueblo Art(4)	11.00	S1753A	Same w/1010, 1097, 1690	4.75
S1709A	Pueblo Art blk	5.00	S1754	Dr. Papanicolaou	3.00
S1710	Lindbergh Flight	3.50	S1754A	Same w/1263	3.50
S1710A	Same Roosevelt Field 5/20		S1754B	Offic. Cancer Society FDC	4.50
	& French 5/21 cancels on one cover	22.00	S1755	Jimmie Rodgers	2.50
S1710B	Pioneers of Aviation		S1755A	Same w/1252	3.75
	Lindbergh set of 5	24.00			

Scott No.	Description	Price
S1756	George M. Cohan	2.50
S1757	CAPEX Souvenir sheet	6.00
S1757A	Same 8 Single FDC's	16.75
S1757B	Same se-tenant Blk of 8	11.50
S1758	Photography	2.75
S1758A	Combo w/1062	3.50
S1759	Viking Mission	3.00
S1759A	Combo w/1556-7	4.50
S1760-63	Owls (4)	9.00
S1763A	Owls blk	4.50
S1764-67	Trees (4)	9.00
S1767A	Trees blk	4.50
S1768-69	Christmas 2 Singles	4.50
S1769A	Christmas 2 Pairs Wash., & Holly, MI.	5.00
S1288c	Holmes Bklt	6.95
S1305E	Holmes Coil	3.00
S1305EL	Holmes, line pair	7.00

1979

Scott No.	Description	Price
S1770	Robert F. Kennedy	2.50
S1770A	Combo w/Scott 1246	3.50
S1771	Martin Luther King	2.75
S1772	Year of the Child	2.50
S1772A	Combo w/Scott 1342	3.50
S1773	John Steinbeck	2.50
S1774	Albert Einstein	2.50
S1774A	Combo w/Scott 1285 & 1070	3.50
S1775-78	Toleware(4)	10.00
S1778A	Toleware blk	3.75
S1779-82	Architecture (4)	10.00
S1782A	Architecture blk	3.75
S1783-86	Endangered Flora (4)	10.00
S1786A	Flowers blk	3.75
S1787	Seeing Eye Dog	2.50
S1788	Special Olympics	2.50
S1788A	Special Olympics w/Scott 1385 & 1549	3.75
S1789	John Paul Jones	2.50
S1790	Decathlon (pr.)	3.75
S1791-94	Summer Olympics (4)	10.00
S1794A	Summer Olympics blk	4.50
S1799-1800	Christmas'79 (2)	5.00
S1800A	2pr. w/North Pole & Wash. postmarks	4.50
S1801	Will Rogers	2.50
S1801A	w/Scott 975	3.75
S1802	Vietnam Veterans	2.50
S1802A	w/Scott 1421-2	5.00

1980 Americana Series Coils

Scott No.	Description	Price
S1811	1c Coil pr.	2.50
S1811L	1c w/line Pair	5.00
S1813	3.5c Violin pr.	2.50
S1813L	3.5.c Violin w/line pr.	4.50

1981

Scott No.	Description	Price
S1738-42	Windmills (5)	12.25
S1742a	Booklet pane (10)	9.50
S1795-98	Winter Olympics (4)	10.00
S1798A	Winter Olympics blk	3.75
S1803	W.C. Fields	2.50
S1804	Banneker	2.50
S1805-10	Nat'l Letter Week pairs (3)	7.00
S1810A	Same 3 pr. on 1 FDC	5.00
S1821	Perkins	2.50
S1821A	w/Scott 931/990/1082	4.50
S1822	Madison	2.50
S1823	Bissell	2.50
S1823A	Off. Am. Lung Assoc.	2.50

Scott No.	Description	Price
S1823B	w/Scott WX1	35.00
S1824	Keller/Sullivan	2.50
S1825	VA	2.50
S1825A	w/Scott 929/940/1320/1525	6.00
S1826	Galvez	2.50
S1827-30	Coral Reefs (4)	10.00
S1830A	Coral Reefs blk	3.75
S1831	Labor	2.50
S1831A	w/Scott 988/1082/1558	4.50
S1832	Wharton	2.50
S1832A	w/Scott 1436 & 1487	3.75
S1833	Learning	2.50
S1833A	w/Scott 869-73	14.00
S1834-37	Indian Masks(4)	10.00
S1837A	Indian Masks blk	3.75
S1838 41	Architecture (4)	10.00
S1841A	Architecture blk	3.75
S1842-43	Christmas '80(2)	5.00

1980-84 Great Americans

Scott No.	Description	Price
S1843A	1c Dorothea Dix	2.25
S1844	2c Igor Stravinsky	2.25
S1844A	3c Henry Clay	2.25
S1845	4c Carl Schurz	2.25
S1846	5c Pearl Buck	2.25
S1846A	10c Richard Russell	2.25
S1847	13c Crazy Horse	2.50
S1849	17c Rachel Carson	2.50
S1850	18c George Mason	2.50
S1851	19c Sequoyah	2.50
S1852	20c Ralph Bunche	2.50
S1853	20c Thomas Gallaudet	2.25
S1854	20c Harry Truman	2.25
S1858	30c Frank Laubach	2.75
S1859	35c Charles Drew	2.75
S1860	37c Robert Millikan	2.75
S1861	40c Lillian Gilbreth	2.95

1981

Scott No.	Description	Price
S1818	"B" Eagle	2.25
S1819	"B" Eagle, from bklt. pn	2.25
S1819a	"B" Eagle, booklet pane of 8	6.25
S1820	"B" Eagle, coil	2.25
S1820L	"B" Eagle w/line pr.	4.50
S1874	Everett Dirksen	2.25
S1875	Whitney M. Young	2.25
S1876-79	Flowers (4)	9.00
S1879A	Flowers blk	3.50
S1880-89	Wildlife (10)	22.50
S1889a	Wildlife booklet pane of 10	6.50
S1890	"Waves of grain"	2.25
S1891	"Shining sea",pr	2.25
S1893a	"Purple Mountains", booklet pane	5.50
S1894	Flag & Supreme Court	2.25
S1895	Flag & Supreme Court, coil	2.25
S1896	Flag & Supreme Court, from bklt pn.	2.25
S1896a	Flag & Supreme Court, booklet pane of 6	6.95
S1896b	Flag & Supreme Court, bklt. pn. of 10	8.50

1981-84 Transportation Series

Scott No.	Description	Price
S1896C	1c Omnibus, coil	2.25
S1896L	1c Omnibus w/line pair	4.50
S1897	2c Locomotive, coil	2.25
S1897L	2c Locomotive coil w/Line pair	4.50
S1897A	4c Stagecoach, coil	2.25
S1897AL	4c Stagecoach, coil w/Line pair	4.50
S1897B	3c Railroad Handcar, coil	2.25
S1897BL	3c Railroad Handcar coil w/Line pair	4.50

S1897C	5c Motorcycle, coil	2.25
S1897CL	5c Motorcycle w/line pair	4.50
S1897D	5.2c Sleigh, coil	2.25
S1897DL	5.2c Sleigh w/line pair	4.50
S1898	5.9c Bicycle, coil	2.25
S1898L	5.9c Bicycle coil w/line pr.	4.50
1899	7.4c Baby Buggy	2.25
1899L	7.4c Baby Buggy w/no. pair	5.75
S1900	9.3c Mail Wagon, coil	2.25
S1900L	9.3c Mail Wagon, coil w/line pr.	4.50
S1901	10.9c Hansom Cab, coil	2.25
S1901L	10.9c Hansom Cab, coil w/line pr	4.50
1902	11c Caboose	2.25
1902L	11c Caboose w/no. pair	5.75
S1905	17c Electric Car, coil	2.25
S1905L	17c Electric Car, coil w/line pr.	4.50
S1906	18c Surrey, coil	2.25
S1906L	18c Surrey w/line pr.	4.50
S1907	20c Fire Pumper, coil	2.25
S1907L	20c Fire Pumper, coil w/line pr	4.50
S1910	Red Cross	2.25
S1911	Savings & Loan	2.25
S1912-19	Space Achievements (8)	18.00
S1919A	Space Achievements blk.	7.00
S1920	Professional Management	2.25
S1921-24	Wildlife Habitat (4)	9.00
S1924A	Wildlife Habitat blk	3.50
S1925	Disabled Persons	2.25
S1926	Edna St. Vincent Millay	2.25
S1927	Alcoholism	2.25
S1928-31	Architecture (4)	9.00
S1931A	Architecture blk	3.25
S1932	Babe Zaharias	2.25
S1933	Bobby Jones	2.25
S1934	Coming Through the Rye	2.25
S1935	18c James Hoban	2.25
S1936	20c James Hoban	2.25
S1937-38	Yorktown/Virginia Capes	2.75
S1937	Yorktown	2.25
S1938	Virginia Capes	2.25
S1939	Madonna & Child	2.25
S1940	Christmas Toy	2.25
S1941	John Hanson	2.25
S1942-45	Desert Plants (4)	9.00
S1945A	Desert Plants,blk	3.25
S1946	"C" Eagle	2.25
S1947	"C" Eagle, coil	2.25
S1947L	"C" Eagle, coil w/line pair	4.50
S1948	"C" Eagle, from bklt. pane	2.25
S1948a	"C" Eagle, booklet pane of 10	7.95
1982		
S1949	Bighorned Sheep	2.25
S1949a	Sheep booklet pane of 10	7.95
S1950	F.D.Roosevelt	2.25
S1951	LOVE	2.25
S1952	Washington	2.25
S1953-		
2002	Birds and Flowers (50)	165.00
S2003	USA/Netherlands	2.25
S2004	Library of Congress	2.25
S2005	Consumer Ed., coil	2.25
S2005L	Consumer Ed. coil w/line pair	4.50
S2006-09	World's Fair(4)	9.00
S2009A	World's Fair, blk	3.25
S2010	Horatio Alger	2.25
S2011	Aging	2.25
S2012	Barrymores	2.25
S2013	Dr. Mary Walker	2.25
S2014	Intl. Peace Garden	2.25
S2015	Libraries of America	2.25
S2016	Jackie Robinson	2.25
S2017	Touro Synagogue	2.25

S2018	Wolf Trap Farm	2.25
S2019-22	Architecture (4)	9.00
S2022A	Architecture blk	3.25
S2023	St. Francis of Assisi	2.25
S2024	Ponce de Leon	2.25
S2025	Kitten & Puppy	2.25
S2026	Madonna & Child	2.25
S2027-30	Christmas Scenes (4)	9.00
S2030A	Christmas Scenes, blk	3.25
1983		
S2031	Science & Industry	2.25
S2032-35	Ballooning (4)	9.00
S2035A	Ballooning (blk)	3.25
S2036	USA/Sweden	2.25
S2037	Civilian Cons. Corps	2.25
S2038	Joseph Priestley	2.25
S2039	Volunteerism	2.25
S2040	German Immigrants	2.25
S2041	Brooklyn Bridge	2.25
S2042	Tennessee Valley Authority	2.25
S2043	Physical Fitness	2.25
S2044	Scott Joplin	2.25
S2045	Medal of Honor	2.25
S2046	Babe Ruth	2.25
S2047	N. Hawthorne	2.25
S2048-51	13c Olympics (4)	9.00
S2051A	13c Olympics, blk	3.25
S2052	Treaty of Paris	2.25
S2053	Mail Service	2.25
S2054	Metropolitan Opera	2.25
S2055-58	Inventors (4)	9.00
S2058A	Inventors, blk	3.25
S2059-62	Streetcars (4)	9.00
S2062A	Streetcars, blk	3.25
S2063	Madonna	2.25
S2064	Santa	2.25
S2065	Martin Luther	2.25
1984		
S2066	Alaska Statehood	2.25
S2067-70	20c Winter Olympics (4)	9.00
S2070A	20 Winter Olympics, blk	3.25
S2071	F.D.I.C.	2.25
S2072	Love	2.25
S2073	Carter Woodson	2.25
S2074	Conservation	2.25
S2075	Credit Union	2.25
S2076-79	Orchids (4)	9.00
S2079A	Orchids, blk	3.25
S2080	Hawaii Statehood	2.25
S2081	National Archives	2.25
S2082-5	20c Olympics (4)	9.00
S2085A	20c Olympics, blk of 4	3.25
S2086	20c Louisiana Exposition	2.25
S2087	20c Health Research	2.25
S2088	20c Douglas Fairbanks	2.25
S2089	20c Jim Thorpe	2.25
S2090	20c John McCormack	2.25
S2091	20c St. Lawrence Seaway	2.25
S2092	20c Preserving Wetlands	2.25
S2093	20c Roanoke Voyages	2.25
S2094	20c Herman Melville	2.25
S2095	20c Horace Moses	2.25
S2096	20c Smokey Bear	2.25
S2097	20c Roberto Clemente	2.25
S2098-101	20c American Dogs (4)	9.00
S2101A	20c American Dogs, blk of 4	3.25
S2102	20c Crime Prevention	2.25
S2104	20c Family Unity	2.25
S2105	20c Eleanor Roosevelt	2.25
S2106	20c Nation of Readers	2.25

Scott No.	Description	Price
Airmails		
SC79	Airmail	165.00
SC84	City of Refuge	14.00
SC87	Statue of Liberty	61.50
SC87A	Same w/LISDA cancel	40.00
SC89-90	Int. Airs (2)	11.00
SC91-92	Wright Brothers(2)	4.50
SC92A	Wright Brothers Pair	3.50
SC92B	Combo w/1710,C45,C68	4.75
SC92C	Wright Brothers Set of 6 FDC's Pioneers of Aviation	25.00
SC93-94	Octave Chanute (2)	4.65
SC94A	Chanute Pair	3.25
SC95-96	Wiley Post (2)	4.00
SC96A	Wiley Post Pair	3.15
SC97	Summer Olympics	4.00
SC98	Philip Mazzei	3.00
SC99	Blanche Scott	2.75
SC100	Glenn Curtiss	3.00
SC101-04	28c Summer Olympics (4)	10.00
SC104A	Summer Olympics, blk	6.75
SC105-08	40c Summer Olympics (4)	13.00
SC108A	Summer Olympics, blk	7.50
SC109-12	35c Olympics (4)	11.75
SC112A	Olympics, blk	7.25
Postage Dues		
SJ102-03	Postage Dues(2)	16.00
1983 Officials		
SO127-29	1c, 4c, & 13c values	2.25
SO127/30	1c & 17c values	2.25
SO132	$1 value	6.50
SO133	$5 value	19.95
SO135	20c value	2.25
Stationery		
SU569	Tennis	89.50
SU576	Liberty Tree	5.75
SU577	Non profit	3.50
SU578	2.1c Non Profit	6.00
SU579	2.7c Non profit	2.50
SU580	"A" envelope	2.50
SU581	Uncle Sam	2.50
SU582	Centennial	3.75
SU583	Golf	4.00
SU584-85	Energy Envelopes(2)	6.75
SU586	U.S.A.	2.50
SU587	Auto Racing	2.75
SU588	15c Re-valued	2.75

Scott No.	Description	Price
SU589	3.1c (w/1286A)Non Profit Env.	2.50
SU590	3.5c Non Profit	2.50
SU591	5.9c Non Profit	2.50
SU592	(18c)"B" Eagle	2.50
SU593	Star	2.50
SU598	America's Cup	2.50
SU598A	America's Cup w/1095 & 1207	3.50
SU598B	22 FDC's of Winners	45.00
SU599	Honey Bee	2.50
SU600	Blinded Veterans	2.25
SU602	Seal of the U.S.	2.25
SU603	Purple Heart	2.25
SU604	5.2c Non Profit	2.25
SU605	Paralyzed Vets	2.25
SU606	Business	2.25
SUX78	G.R. Clark	3.00
SUX78A	Clark Combo w/Scott 651	10.00
SUX79	Casimir Polaski	2.50
SUX80	Summer Olympics	3.00
SUX81	Iolani Palace	2.50
SUX82	Winter Oly-Skater	2.50
SUX83	Mormon Temple	2.50
SUX84	Rochambeau	2.50
SUX84A	Combo w/French & U.S. stamps, both cancels	14.00
SUX85	King's Mountain	2.50
SUX85	Golden Hinde	2.50
SUX87	Battle of Cowpens	2.50
SUX88	(12c)"B" Eagle	2.25
SUX89	Isaiah Thomas	2.25
SUX90	Battle of Eutaw Springs	2.25
SUX91	Lewis & Clark Expedition	2.25
SUX92	Non-denominated	2.25
SUX93	13c Morris	2.25
SUX94	Francis Marion	2.25
SUX95	La Salle	2.25
SUX96	Philadelphia Academy	2.25
SUX97	St. Louis Post Office	2.25
SUX98	Landing of Ogelthorpe	2.25
SUX99	Washington Post Office	2.25
SUX100	Olympic Yachting	2.25
SUX101	Maryland	2.25
SUX102	Torch	2.25
SUX103	13c Baraga Postal Card	2.25
SUX104	13c Rancho San Pedro	2.25
SUXC18	Summer Olympics	4.00
SUXC19	Trans-Pacific	2.50
SUXC20	Soaring	2.25
SUXC21	Olympic Speedskating	2.25
SUZ2	Official Post Card	2.25

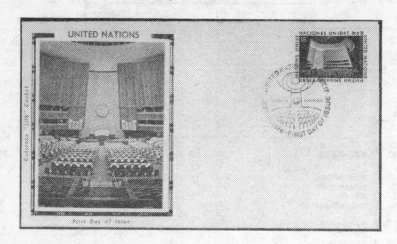

SCOTT CAT. NO.	DESCRIPTION	PRICE
1972		
S228	World Health Day	4.00
S229-30	Environmental(2)	7.25
S231	ECE	7.00
S232-3	United Nations Art(2)	7.50
1973		
S234-5	Disarmament(2)	17.50
S236-7	Drug Abuse(2)	17.50
S238-9	UN Volunteers(2)	8.00
S240-1	Namibia(2)	8.00
S242-3	Human Rights(2)	8.00
1974		
S244-5	I.L.O.(2)	17.50
S246	U.P.U. Cent	4.75
S247-48	United Nations Art(2)	23.00
S252-3	Population Year(2)	8.00
S254-5	Law of the Sea(2)	8.00
1975		
S256-7	Outer Space(2)	7.00
S258-9	I.W.Y.(2)	7.00
S260-2	UN 30th Anniv. set & sht(3)	20.00
S260-2A	Same San Franscisco	20.00
S263-4	Namibia(2)	7.50
S265-6	Peace Keeping)2)	8.00
1976		
S272-3	UN Associations(2)	5.00
S274-5	UNCTAD(2)	5.00
S276-77	Habitat(2)	5.00
S278-9	UN Postal Anniv.(2)	34.50
S280	Food Council	5.00
1977		
S281-2	WIPO(2)	5.00
S283-4	Water Conference(2)	5.00
S285-6	Security Council(2)	5.00
S287-8	Combat Racism(2)	6.00
S289-90	Atomic Energy(2)	5.00
1978		
S294-5	Smallpox(2)	5.25
S296-7	Namibia(2)	5.25
S298-9	ICAO(2)	5.25
S300-1	General Assembly (2)	5.25
S302-3	Tech. Cooperation(2)	5.25
1979		
S308-09	UNDRO(2)	6.00
S310-311	IYC(2)	24.00

SCOTT CAT. NO.	DESCRIPTION	PRICE
S312-13	Namibia(2)	4.50
S314-15	Justice(2)	4.50
1980		
S316-17	IEO(2)	4.50
S318-19	Decade Women(2)	4.50
S320-21	Peace Keeping(2)	5.25
S322-24	35th Anniversary(3) New York postmark	7.75
S322-24	35th Anniversary(3) San Francisco postmark	7.75
S325-40	Flags(16)	32.00
S341-42	Economic Council(2)	4.50
1981		
S343	Palestinian People	2.50
S344-45	Disabled Persons(2)	5.25
S346-47	Fresco(2)	5.25
S348-49	Sources of Energy(2)	5.50
S350-65	Flags(16)	38.50
S366-67	Volunteers(2)	5.25
1982		
S371-72	Human Environment(2)	5.50
S373	Space Exploration	2.50
S374-89	Flags(16)	38.50
S390-91	Nature Conservation(2)	5.25
1983		
S392-93	World Communications	6.50
S394-95	Safety at Sea	6.25
S396	World Food	2.25
S397-98	Trade	5.75
S399-414	Flags (16)	38.50
S415-16	Human Rights	6.50
1984		
S417-18	Population	6.50
S419-20	World Food Day	6.50
S421-22	World Heritage	6.75
S423-24	Refugees	6.75

UNITED NATIONS OFFICES ABROAD
Colorano "Silk" Cachets
"S" Preceding No. Indicates "SILK" Cachet
U.N. GENEVA SILKS

189

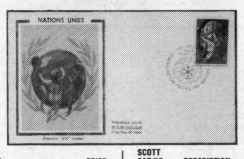

SCOTT CAT.NO.	DESCRIPTION	PRICE		SCOTT CAT.NO.	DESCRIPTION	PRICE
1972				S77-8	ICAO(2)	8.00
S24	World Health Day	5.25		S79-80	General Assembly(2)	8.00
S25-6	Environmental(2)	5.25		S81	Tech. Cooperation(1)	4.25
S27	ECE	4.00		**1979**		
S28-9	United Nations Art(2)	5.75		S82-83	UNDRO	10.00
1973				S84-85	Year of the Child	20.00
S30-1	Disarmement(2)	5.75		S86	Namibia	4.25
S32	Drug Abuse	5.75		S87-88	Justice(2)	8.00
S33	UN Volunteers	5.25		**1980**		
S34	Namibia	7.00		S89	IEO	4.25
S35-6	Human Rights(2)	5.75		S90-91	Women(2)	7.00
1974				S92	Peace Keeping	4.25
S37-8	I.L.O.(2)	11.00		S93-5	35th Anniversary(3)	12.75
S38-40	U.P.U. Cent.	7.50		S96-7	Economic Council(2)	7.25
S41-2	United Nations Art(2)	14.50		**1981**		
S43-4	Population Year(2)	12.50		S98	Palestinian People	3.75
S45	Law of the sea	7.50		S99-100	Disabled Persons(2)	8.00
1975				S101	Fresco	4.50
S46-7	Outer Space(2)	6.00		S102	Sources of Energy	4.25
S48-9	I.W.Y.(2)	9.00		S103-04	Volunteers	6.75
S50-2	UN 30th Anniv. set & sht(3)	22.00				
S53-4	Namibia(2)	13.00		**1982**		
S55-6	Peace Keeping(2)	12.00		S107-08	Human Environment	7.50
1976				S109-110	Space Exploration	7.75
S57	UN Associations	5.00		S111-112	Nature Conservation	8.00
S58	UNCTAD	5.00		**1983**		
S59-60	Habitat(2)	8.00		S113	World Communications	4.75
S61-2	UN Postal Anniv.(2)	36.50		S114-15	Safety at Sea	7.50
S63	Food Council	10.95		S116	World Food	5.00
1977				S117-18	Trade	8.85
S64	WIPO	4.75		S119-20	Human Rights	7.75
S65-6	Water Conference(2)	7.00		**1984**		
S67-6	Security Council	7.00		S121	Population	4.75
S69-70	Combat Racism	7.00		S122-123	World Food Day	7.50
S71-2	Atomic Energy (2)	7.75		S125-25	Heritage	7.50
1978				S126-27	Refugees	8.00
S74-5	Smallpox(2)	9.00				
S76	Namibia(1)	4.00				

U.N. VIENNA SILKS

SCOTT CAT.NO.	DESCRIPTION	PRICE		SCOTT CAT.NO.	DESCRIPTION	PRICE
1979				**1982**		
S7	IEO	6.50		S25-26	Human Environment	7.25
1980				S27	Space Exploration	4.00
S9-10	Women(2)	7.50		S28-29	Nature Conservation	7.25
S11	Peace Keeping	4.25		**1983**		
S12-14	35th Anniversary(3)	12.75		S30	World Communications	3.75
S15-16	Economic Council(2)	7.75		S31-32	Safety at Sea	7.50
1981				S33-34	World Food	8.50
S17	Palestinian People	3.25		S35-36	Trade	7.95
S18-19	Disabled Persons(2)	7.00		S37-38	Human Rights	8.50
S20	Fresco	4.00		**1984**		
S21	Sources of Energy	4.00		S39	Population	4.50
S22-23	Volunteers	7.25		S40-41	World Food Day	7.75
				S42-43	World Heritage	10.00
				S44-45	Refugees	8.50

SCOTT CAT.NO.	DESCRIPTION	PRICE
1973		
S566-7	Algonkian Ind.(2)	14.00
S568-9	Algonkian Ind.(2)	14.00
S570-1	Pacific Coast(2)('74)	14.00
S572-3	Pacific Coast(2)('74)	14.00
S574-7	Subarctic Ind.(4)('75)	15.00
S578-8[1]	Iroquois Ind.(4)('76)	15.00
S611	Monsignor de Laval	7.00
S612-4	Royal Mounties(3)	13.00
S615	Jeanne Mance	5.00
S616	Joseph Howe	5.00
S617	MacDonald's art	5.00
S618	Prince Edward Island	5.00
S619	Scottish Settlers	5.00
S620-1	Queens Visit(2)	13.00
S622	Nellie McClung	5.00
S623-4	Olympics(2)	27.00
S625-8	Christmas(4)	10.00
1974		
S629-32	Olympics(4)	44.00
S633	Winnipeg Cent.	4.00
S634-9	Letter Carriers(G)	15.00
S640	Agriculture College	4.00
S641	Alexander Bell	5.00
S642	World Cycling	5.00
S643	Mennonites	4.00
S644-7	Winter Olympics(4)	52.00
S648-9	U.P.U.Cent(2)	7.00
S650-3	Christmas(4)	10.00
S654	Marconi	4.00
S655	Merritt	4.00
1975		
S656-7	Olympics $1-$2(2)	115.00
S658-9	Literary(2)	5.00
S660-3	Churchment(4)	10.00
S664-6	Olympics(3)	16.00
S667	Calgary Centennial	4.00
S668	IWY	4.00
S669	Supreme Court Cent.	4.50
S670-3	Ships(4)	45.00
S674-9	Christmas(6)	13.00
S680	Canadian Legion	4.00
1976		
S681-3	Olympic Ceremonies(3)	16.00
S684-6	Olym. Art-Cultures(3)	11.00
S687-8	Olympic $1-$2(2)	45.00
S689	Olympics Innsbruck	3.75
S690	UN Habitat	3.75
S691	Ben Franklin	3.75
S692-3	Military College(2)	9.00
S694	Olympic Disabled	4.50

SCOTT CAT.NO.	DESCRIPTION	PRICE
S695-6	Literary(2)	7.00
S697-9	Christmas(3)	8.00
S700-3	Ships Part II(4)	24.50
1977		
S704	Queen's Jubilee	6.75
S732	Cougar	7.50
S733-4	Thomson's art(2)	5.00
S735	Governors General	3.50
S736	Order of Canada	3.50
S737	Peace Bridge	3.50
S738-9	Fleming & Bernier(2)	6.50
S740	Parlamentary Conf.	3.75
S741-3	Christmas(3)	7.50
S744-7	Ships Part III(4)	20.00
S748-51	Inuit Eskimos(4)	9.50
1978		
S752	Falcon	5.50
S753	CAPEX Stamp on stamp	4.50
S754-56	14c,30c & $1.25 CAPEX(3)	14.00
S756a	CAPEX Souvenir Sheet	11.50
S757-58	Commonwealth Games(2)	9.50
S759-62	Commonwealth Games(4)	9.50
S763-64	Capt.James Cook(2)	5.50
S765-66	Resource Dev.(2)	4.50
S767	National Exhib.	2.75
S768	Grey Nun	2.75
S769-72	Inuit Travel(4)	10.00
S773-5	Christmas(3)	8.00
S776-9	Ice Vessels(4)	10.00
S779A	Ice Vessel blk	5.00
1979		
S780	Quebec Winter Carnival	2.75
S813-14	Endegered Wildlife (2)	6.75
S815-16	Postal Code(2)	6.75
S817-18	Authors(2)	6.75
S819-20	Historic Colonies(2)	4.75
S821-32	Provinces & Territories(12)	40.00
S832a	Miniature Sheet of 12	17.00
S833	Kayak	2.50
S834	Women's Field Hockey	2.50
S835-8	Inuit Eskimos(4)	10.00
S839-41	Christmas(3)	7.75
S842	IYC	2.50
S843-6	Flying Boats(4)	12.00
1980		
S847	Arctic Islands	2.75
S848	Winter Oly.	3.25
S849-52	Arts(4)	11.75
S853-54	Wildlife(2)	5.25
S855	Int'l Flower Show	2.65
S856	Helping Hands	2.65
S857-8	"O Canada"(2)	5.75
S859	Diefenbaker	2.65
S860	Albani	2.65
S861	Willan	2.65
S862	Hanlan	2.65
S863-4	Sask. & Alberta(2)	5.25
S865	Uranium	3.25
S866-9	Inuit Spirits(4)	11.75
S870-2	Christmas(3)	8.50
S873-6	Military Aircraft(4)	11.75
S877	Lachapelle	2.65

SCOTT CAT.NO.	DESCRIPTION	PRICE	SCOTT CAT.NO.	DESCRIPTION	PRICE
1981			**1983**		
S878	Antique Instrument	3.25	S976	World Communications Yr.	3.25
S879-82	Feminists(4)	10.50	S977	Commonwealth Day	9.95
S883-84	Endangered Wildlife(2)	5.85	S978-79	Authors (2)	6.50
S885-86	Beatified Women(2)	5.25	S980	St. Johns Ambulance	3.25
S887-89	Painters(3)	8.50	S981-82	World Univ. Games (2)	6.00
S890-93	Canada Day(4)	10.50	S983-92	Canada Day, Forts (10)	32.95
S894-95	Botanists(2)	5.25	S993	Boy Scouts	3.25
S896	Floralies de Montreal	2.65	S994	Church Council	3.25
S897	Niagara-on-the-Lake	2.65	S995	Humphrey Gilbert	3.25
S898	Acadians	2.65	S996	Nickel	3.25
S899	Aaron Mosher	2.65	S997	Hanson	3.25
S900-02	Christmas(3)	7.85	S998	Labelle	3.25
S903-06	Aircrafts(4)	11.75	S999-1000	Locomotives (2)	6.50
S907	"A" Maple Leaf	3.25	S1001	37c Locomotive	3.50
1982			S1002	64c Locomotive	4.50
			S1003	Law School	3.25
S909-13	I.P.Y.E.	17.00	S1004-06	Christmas '83 (3)	10.75
S913a	I.P.Y.E. sheet	9.00	S1007-08	Armed Forces (3)	6.50
S914	Jules Leger	3.25			
S915	Terry Fox	3.25			
S916	Constitution	3.25			
S954	Salvation Army	3.25	**1984**		
S955-66	Canada Day, Paintings (12)	38.95	S1009	Yellowknife	3.25
S967	Regina	3.25	S1010	Year of the Arts	3.25
S968	Henley Regatta	3.25	S1011	Jaques Cartier	3.25
S969-72	Bush Aircraft (4)	14.50	S1012	Tall Ships	3.25
S973-75	Christmas, '82 (3)	10.75	S1013	Canadian Red Cross	3.25

UNITED NATIONS FIRST DAY COVERS (NEW YORK)

SCOTT CAT.NO.	DESCRIPTION	FIRST DAY COVERS INSC. BKL.	SINGLES	SCOTT CAT.NO.	DESCRIPTION	FIRST DAY COVERS INSC.BLK.	SINGLES
	Note: FDC's are supplied as one variety per cover. Example: #35-37 set will contain three covers.			86-87	4c & 8c International Bank	3.00	1.00
	1951				**1961**		
1-11	1c to $1, complete	245.00	120.00	88-89	4c & 8c International Court of Justice	3.00	1.00
1-11	as previous, uncacheted		70.00	90-91	4c & 7c International Monetary Fund	3.00	1.00
	1952			92	30c 30c Definitive Issue	5.00	1.30
12	5c United Nations Day	5.00	2.25	93-94	4c & 11c Economic Committee Latin America	5.00	1.50
13-14	3c & 5c Human Rights Day	7.75	3.00	95-96	4c & 11c Economic Committee Africa	4.25	1.10
	1953			97-99	3c,4c & 13c Children's Fund	4.75	1.80
15-16	3c & 5c Refugee Issue	11.50	3.25		**1962**		
17-18	3c & 5c U.P.U. Issue	11.75	3.50	100-01	4c & 7c Housing & Com. Development	3.50	1.00
19-20	3c & 5c Technical Assistance	9.00	2.50	102-03	4c & 11c Malaria Eradication	3.75	1.00
21-22	3c & 5c Human Rights Day	9.00	2.50	104-07	1c to 11c Definitives Issue	5.25	1.80
	1954			108-09	5c & 15c Memorial Issue	5.00	1.35
23-24	3c & 8c Food & Agriculture	9.25	3.00	110-11	4c & 11c Operation in the Congo	5.00	1.35
25-26	3c & 8c International Labor	11.25	3.25	112-13	4c & 11c Peaceful use of Outer Space	3.50	1.00
27-28	3c & 8c Geneva	18.75	5.25				
29-30	3c & 8c Human Rights	48.75	8.95		**1963**		
	1955			114-15	5c & 11c Science & Tech.	3.50	1.00
31-32	3c & 8c Int. Civil Aviation Org.	15.50	4.50	116-17	5c & 11c Freedom from Hunger	3.50	1.00
33-34	3c & 8c UNESCO	9.50	2.75	118	25c Temporary Exec. Authority	6.25	1.50
35-37	3c to 8c United Nations	12.25	3.50	119-20	5c & 11c Gen. Assembly Bldg	3.50	1.00
38	3c to 8c as above, souvenir sheet		125.00	121-22	5c & 11c 15th Anniversary	3.50	1.00
39-40	3c & 8c Human Rights Day	6.25	2.25	123-24	5c & 11c Maritime Org. (IMCO)	3.50	1.00
	1956			125-28	2c to 50c Definitives	10.25	3.50
41-42	3c & 8c Int. Telecomm.	8.25	2.25	129-30	5c & 11c Trade & Develop.	3.00	1.00
43-44	3c & 8c World Health Org	8.00	2.75	131-32	5c & 11c Narcotics Control	3.00	1.00
45-46	3c & 8c United Nations Day	3.50	1.00	133	5c Cessation Nuclear Testing	3.00	1.00
47-48	3c & 8c Human Rights Day	3.00	1.00	134-36	4c to 11c Educ. for Progress	3.50	1.20
	1957				**1965**		
49-50	3c & 8c Meteorological	3.00	1.00	137-38	5c & 11c U.N. Special Fund	3.00	1.00
51-52	3c & 8c Emergency Force	3.00	1.00	139-40	5c & 11c U.N. Forces in Cyprus	3.00	1.00
53-54	3c & 8c Em. Force, re-engraved		90.00	141-42	5c & 11c I.T.U. Centenary	3.00	1.00
55-56	3c & 8c Security Council	3.00	1.00	143-44	5c & 11c Intl. Cooperation Yr.	3.50	1.10
57-58	3c & 8c Human Rights Day	3.00	1.00	145	as above, souvenir sheet		3.25
	1958			146-49	1c to 25c Definitivs	10.50	4.00
59-60	3c & 8c Atomic Energy Agency	3.00	1.00		**1966**		
61-62	3c & 8c Central Hall	3.00	1.00	150	$1 Definitive	14.50	5.00
63-64	4c & 8c Definitives	3.00	1.00		**1965**		
65-66	4c & 8c Econ. & Social Council	3.00	1.00	151-53	4c to 11c Population Trends	3.25	1.10
67-68	4c & 8c Human Rights Day	3.00	1.00		**1966**		
	1959			154-55	5c & 15c World Federation (WFUNA)	3.25	1.00
69-70	4c & 8c Flushing Meadows	3.00	1.00	156-57	5c & 11c World Health Org.	3.25	1.00
71-72	4c & 8c Economic Comm. Eur.	4.25	1.20	158-59	5c & 11c Coffee Agreement	3.25	1.00
73-74	4c & 8c Trusteeship Council	3.00	1.00	160	15c Peace Keeping Observers	3.25	1.00
75-76	4c & 8c World Refugee Year	3.00	1.00	161-63	4c to 11c UNICEF	3.25	1.05
	1960				**1967**		
77-78	4c & 8c Palais de Chaillot	3.00	1.00	164-65	5c & 11c Development Prog.	3.25	1.00
79-80	4c & 8c Economic Comm. Asia	3.00	1.00				
81-82	4c & 8c 5th World Forestry Congress	3.00	1.00				
83-84	4c & 8c 15th Anniversary	3.00	1.00				
85	as above, souvenir sheet		6.00				

SCOTT CAT.NO.	DESCRIPTION	FIRST DAY COVERS INSC. BLK.	SINGLES
166-67	1½c & 5c Definitives	3.25	1.00
168-69	5c & 11c Independence . . .	3.25	1.00
170-74	4c to 15c EXPO '67,Canada	16.00	4.00
175-76	5c & 15c Int. Tourist Year . .	3.25	1.10
177-78	6c & 13c Towards Disarm .	3.25	1.10
179	36c Chagall Window, souv. sht		1.75
180	6c Kiss of Peace (Chagall Window)	1.75	.50
1968			
181-82	6c & 13c Secretariat	3.75	1.20
183-84	6c & 75c H. Starcke Statue	21.00	10.00
185-86	6c & 13c Industrial Develop .	3.75	1.20
187	6c Definitive	1.25	.70
188-89	6c & 20c World Weather Watch	4.50	1.30
190-91	6c & 13c Int. Yr.-Human Rights	5.75	1.40
1969			
192-93	6c & 13c Inst-Tng. Research .	3.75	1.25
194-95	6c & 15c U.N. Bldg.,Chile . . .	4.25	1.25
196	13c Definitive	3.00	.90
197-98	6c & 13c Peace-Int. Law . .	3.50	1.10
199-200	6c & 20c Labor & Develop .	5.25	1.50
201-02	6c & 13c Tunisian Mosaics .	4.50	1.10
1970			
203-04	6c & 25c Japanese Peace Bell	3.75	1.50
205-06	6c & 13c L. Mekong Delta Development	3.50	1.10
207-08	6c & 13c Fight Cancer	3.50	1.10
209-11	6c to 25c Peace & Progress .	8.75	2.50
212	as above, souvenir sheet . .		1.95
213-14	6c & 13c Peace, Just.&Prog.	4.25	1.25
1971			
215	6c Peaceful Uses Sea Bed .	2.15	.80
216-17	6c & 13c Support for Refugees	3.95	1.35
218	13c World Food Programme .	2.75	1.00
219	20c U.P.U. Building	3.50	1.10
220-21	8c & 13c Anti-Discrimination	3.75	1.35
222-23	8c & 60c Definitives	9.75	3.50
224-25	8c & 21c International Schools	4.50	1.40
1972			
226	95c Definitive	10.75	3.75
227	8c Non-Proliferation	1.75	.85
228	15c World Health Day	2.75	1.00
229-30	8c & 15c Environment	4.00	1.20
231	21c Econ. Comm.-Europe .	3.50	1.10
232-33	8c & 15c Art-Sert Ceiling . . .	4.00	1.20
1973			
234-35	8c & 15c Disarmament Decade	3.75	1.35
236-37	8c & 15c Stop Drug Abuse .	4.50	1.80
238-39	8c & 21c Volunteers Prog . .	4.50	1.80
240-41	8c & 15c Namibia	4.50	1.80
242-43	8c & 21c Human Rights . . .	4.50	2.00
1974			
244-45	10c & 21c ILO Headquarters .	4.50	2.00
246	10c Universal Postal Union . .	2.25	1.00
247-48	10c & 18c Brazil Peace Mural	4.25	1.40
249-51	2c to 18c Definitives	6.25	1.95
252-53	10c & 18c World Population Year	4.25	1.50
254-55	10c & 26c Law of the Sea . .	4.50	1.65
1975			
256-57	10c & 26c Peaceful Use of Space	4.50	1.65
258-59	10c & 18c Int'l. Womens Year	4.50	1.50

SCOTT CAT.NO.	DESCRIPTION	FIRST DAY COVERS INSC.BLK.	SINGLES
260-61	10c & 26c 30th Anniversary	5.75	1.80
262	As above, souvenir sheet . . .		1.80
263-64	10c & 18c Namibia	5.25	1.75
265-66	13c & 26c Peace-keeping . .	5.75	2.75
1976			
267-71	3c to 50c Definitives	18.25	9.00
272-73	13c & 26c World Federation .	7.85	2.00
274-75	13c & 31c Conference on T&D	5.95	1.95
276-77	13c & 25c Conference on Human Settlements	5.75	1.80
278-79	13c & 31c Postal Adminis . .	28.50	14.00
280	13c World Food Council . .	2.95	1.10
1977			
281-82	13c & 31c WIPO	8.60	2.95
283-84	13c & 25c Water Conference	5.75	1.80
285-86	13c & 31c Security Council .	8.25	2.95
287-88	13c & 25c Combat Racism . .	5.75	1.80
289-90	13c & 18c Atomic Energy . .	5.75	2.50
1978			
291-93	1c,25c & $1 Definitives . . .	17.50	7.65
294-95	13c & 31c Smallpox Eradication	8.65	1.95
296-97	13c & 18c Namibia	6.25	1.70
298-99	13c & 25c ICAO	7.45	1.85
300-01	13c & 18c General Assembly	5.25	1.60
302-03	13c & 31c TCDC	5.40	1.75
1979			
304-07	5c to 20c Definitives	11.00	3.75
308-09	15c & 20c UNDRO	7.25	1.95
310-11	15c & 31c I.Y.C.	20.00	10.00
312-13	15c & 31c Namibia	8.00	2.25
314-15	15c & 20c International Court of Justice	5.25	1.65
1980			
316-17	15c & 31c New Int'l Econ. Order	6.00	2.25
318-19	15c & 20c Decade for Women	5.75	1.95
320-21	15c & 31c Peace keeping . .	5.65	1.95
322-23	15c & 31c 35th Anniversary	5.65	1.95
324	As above, Souvenir Sheet . . .		2.25
325-40	15c Flags (16)	75.00	26.50
341-42	15c & 20c Economic & Social Council	5.25	1.65
1981			
343	15c Palestinian People	2.95	1.30
344-45	20c & 35c Disabled Persons .	9.60	3.75
346-47	20c & 31c Fresco	7.75	3.50
348-49	20c & 40c Sources of Energy	6.75	3.85
350-65	20c Flags(Geneva Cachet) (16)	199.95	89.95
	20c Flags (Engraved cachet) (16)	77.50	27.50
366-67	18c & 28c Volunteers	7.75	3.50
1982			
368-70	17c,28c & 40c Definitives . .	12.95	5.75
371-72	18c & 40c Environment	9.00	4.00
373	20c Space Exploration . . .	3.35	1.65
374-89	20c Flags (16)	77.50	27.50
390-91	20c & 28c Nature Cons	7.75	3.50
1983			
392-93	20c & 40c Wld. Comm.	9.00	4.00
394-95	20c & 37c Safety at Sea	9.00	4.00
396	20c World Food Program . . .	4.00	2.25
397-98	20c & 28c World Trade	7.75	3.50
399-414	20c Flags (16)	77.50	27.50
415-16	20c & 40c Human Rts	9.00	4.00

SCOTT CAT.NO.	DESCRIPTION	FIRST DAY COVERS INSC. BLK.	SINGLES
	1984		
417-18	20c & 40c Population . . .	9.00	4.00
419-20	20c & 40c Food Day	9.00	4.00
421-22	20c & 50c Heritage	9.50	4.25
423-24	20c & 50c Refugees	9.50	4.25
425-40	20c Flags (16)	77.50	27.50
	AIR POST FIRST DAY COVERS		
	1951		
C1-4	6c to 25c complete	69.95	37.00
	1957-59		
C5-7	4c to 7c, complete	3.75	1.25
	1963-64		
C8-12	6c to 25c, complete	9.25	3.25
	1968-69		
C13-14	10c & 20c, complete	7.25	2.50
	1972		
C15-18	9c to 21c, complete	9.25	3.25
	1974		
C19-21	13c to 26c, complete	10.00	4.00
	1977		
C22-23	25c & 31c, complete	10.00	4.00

U.N. FIRST DAY COVERS (GENEVA)

1969-70

SCOTT CAT.NO.	DESCRIPTION	FIRST DAY COVERS INSC. BLK.	SINGLES
1-14	5c to 10fr., complete	135.00	55.00
	1971		
15	30c Peaceful Uses Sea Bed . .	5.00	1.75
16	50c Support for Refugees . . .	5.25	1.50
17	50c World Food Programme .	6.00	2.00
18	75c U.P.U. Building	7.00	3.25
19-20	30c & 50c Anti-Discrim	6.50	3.00
21	1,10fr International School . .	7.00	3.25
	1972		
22	40c Definitive	4.00	1.60
23	40c Non Proliferation	5.00	2.00
24	80c World Health Day	5.00	1.95
25-26	40c & 80c Environment	9.50	4.00
27	1, 10fr Econ. Comm.-Europe .	8.00	2.80
28-29	40c & 80c Art-Sert Ceiling . .	9.00	4.00
	1973		
30-31	60c & 1,10fr Disarmament Decade	9.75	4.00
32	60c Stop Drug Abuse	5.00	2.00
33	80c Volunteer Program	5.75	2.50
34	60c Namibia	5.75	2.50
35-36	40c & 80c Human Rights . . .	8.50	3.25
	1974		
37-38	60c & 80c ILO Headquarters	7.75	3.00
39-40	30c & 60c Universal Postal Union	5.75	2.50
41-42	60c & 1fr. Brazil Peace Mural	10.00	3.75
43-44	60c & 80c World Population Year	9.50	3.85
45	1,30fr. Law of the Sea	8.50	2.75

SCOTT CAT.NO.	DESCRIPTION	FIRST DAY COVERS INSC. BLK.	SINGLES
	1975		
46-47	60c & 90c Peaceful Use of Outer Space	8.50	2.75
48-49	60c & 90c International Women's Year	8.75	3.00
50-51	60c & 90c 30th Anniversary	8.50	2.75
52	As above, souvenir sheet . . .	___	3.00
53-54	50c & 1,30fr. Namibia	7.95	2.75
55-56	60c & 70c Peace-keeping . . .	6.50	2.25
	1976		
57	90c World Federation	4.50	1.75
58	1,10fr. Conf. on Trade & Development	6.75	2.00
59-60	40c & 1,10fr. Conf. On Human Settlement	10.00	3.75
61-62	80c & 1,10fr. Postal Administration	30.00	16.00
63	70c World Food Council	4.75	1.65
	1977		
64	80c WIPO	4.75	1.65
65-66	80c & 1.10fr. Water Conference	12.25	4.50
67-68	80c & 1,10fr. Security Council	12.25	4.50
69-70	40c & 1,10fr. Combat Racism	9.00	3.00
71-72	80c & 1,10fr. Atomic Energy	10.00	4.00
	1978		
73	35c Definitive	2.25	1.20
74-75	80c & 1,10fr. Smallpox Eradication	12.75	4.75
76	80c Namibia	4.50	1.75
77-78	70c & 80c ICAO	10.25	3.95
79-80	70c & 1,10fr. General Assembly	18.50	6.95
81	80c TCDC	6.50	2.25
	1979		
82-83	80c & 1,50fr UNDRO	15.75	5.75
84-85	80c & 1,10fr I.Y.C.	20.00	10.00
86	1,10fr. Namibia	8.50	2.75
87-88	80c & 1.10fr. International Court of Justice	9.25	3.25
	1980		
89	80c New International Econ. Order	6.75	2.50
90-91	40c & 70c Decade for Women	10.00	4.25
92	1,10fr Peace-Keeping	9.00	2.75
93-94	40c & 70c 35th Anniversary	9.75	4.25
95	Same, Souvenir Sheet		4.25
96-97	40c & 70c Economic & Social Council	9.75	4.25
	1981		
98	80c Palestinian People	6.50	2.50
99-100	40c & 1,10fr Disabled Persons	15.00	5.50
101	80c Fresco	5.65	2.15
102	1,10fr Sources of Energy . . .	7.50	2.65
103-04	40c & 70c Volunteers	8.25	3.50
	1982		
105-06	30c & 1,00fr Definitives . . .	10.50	4.25
107-08	40c & 1,20fr Environment . .	12.00	4.50
109-10	80c & 1,00fr Space Exploration	13.25	4.95
111-12	40c & 1,50fr Nature Conservation	15.00	5.25

SCOTT CAT. NO.	DESCRIPTION	FIRST DAY COVERS INSC.BLOCK	SINGLES
1983.			
113	1,20fr Wld. Comm	7.50	2.65
114-15	40c & 80c		
	Safety at Sea	8.75	3.50
116	1,50fr World Food Prgm	9.85	3.30
117-18	80c & 1,10fr World Trade	13.25	4.95
119-20	20c & 1, 20fr Human Rts	12.50	4.50
1984			
121	1,20fr Population	7.25	2.50
122-23	50c & 80c Food Day	9.75	3.75
124-25	50c & 70c Heritage	8.75	3.50
126-27	35c & 1,50fr Refugees	15.00	5.25

U.N. FIRST DAY COVERS (VIENNA)

1979

SCOTT CAT. NO.	DESCRIPTION	INSC.BLOCK	SINGLES
1-6	50g to s10 Definitives	27.50	10.75
1980			
7	s4 New International Econ. Order	6.00	2.00
8	s2.50 Definitive	3.75	1.35
9-10	s4 & s6 Decade for Women	10.75	4.00
11	s6 Peace-Keeping	5.95	1.85
12-13	s4 & s6 35th Anniversary	11.00	4.25
14	Same, Souvenir Sheet		4.25
15-16	s4 & s6 Economic & Social Council	11.00	4.25

SCOTT CAT. NO.	DESCRIPTION	FIRST DAY COVERS INSC.BLOCK	SINGLES
1981			
17	s4 Palestinian People	4.25	1.75
18-19	s4 & s6 Disabled Persons	10.75	4.35
20	s6 Fresco	5.50	2.15
21	s7.50 Sources of Energy	9.00	2.50
22-23	s5 & s7 Volunteers	10.95	4.50
1982			
24	s3 Definitive	3.00	1.50
25-26	s5 & s7 Environment	10.50	4.00
27	s5 Space Exploration	4.45	1.85
28-29	s5 & s7 Nature Conservation	10.50	4.00
1983			
30	s4 World Communications	3.50	1.50
31-32	s4 & s6 Safety at Sea	8.50	3.50
33-34	s5 & s7 Food Program	10.00	3.85
35-36	s4 & s8.50 World Trade	10.50	4.00
37-38	s5 & s7 Human Rts	10.00	3.85
1984			
39	s7 Population	5.00	1.85
40-41	s4.50 & s6 Food Day	9.25	3.75
42-43	s3.50 & s15 Heritage	15.00	5.00
44-45	s4.50 & s8.50 Refugees	10.50	4.00

UNITED NATIONS STAMPS
COMPLETE UNUSED
AT REDUCED PRICES!

Buy complete, at a special savings, ALL the unused postage and air-mail sets of United Nations (New York) stamps from 1951 through 1984. These are in fine-very fine, never hinged condition and are offered to you at even less than our already discounted prices for individual year date sets.

#1-442, C1-23 1951 through 1984, complete unused,
439 varieties, including the 7 souvenir sheets $995.00

#1/442, C1-23 1951 through 1984 complete unused,
432 varieties, without the souvenir sheets $429.00

SCOTT CAT.NO.	DESCRIPTION		INSCRIP. BLOCKS OF 4	UNUSED SINGLES

BUY COMPLETE YEARS AND SAVE
NEW YORK

1-11	1951 Isues ......(11)	....	150.00	30.00
12-22	1952-53 Issues ....(11)	....	125.00	24.50
23-30	1954 Issues ....(8)	....	255.00	55.00
31/40	1955 Issues-No#38 ..(9)	....	165.00	32.00
41-48	1956 Issues ......(8)	....	31.00	7.50
49-58	1957 Issues ......(10)	....	13.75	2.50
59-68	1958 Issues ......(10)	....	7.75	1.50
69-76	1959 Issues .... (8)	....	17.50	3.75
77/87	1960 Issues-No#85 ..(10)	....	13.35	2.95
88-99	1961 Issues ......(12)	....	27.50	6.15
100-13	1962 Issues ......(14)	....	52.95	11.50
114-22	1963 Issues ......(9)	....	27.50	6.50
123-36	1964 Issues ......(14)	....	32.25	7.25
137/53	1965 Issues-#137-44, 146-49, 151-53 No#145 (15)	....	48.75	10.75
150/63	1966 Issues-#150, 154-63 ....(11)	....	38.95	8.75
164/80	1967 Issues-No#179(16)	....	35.25	7.75
181-91	1968 Issues ......(11)	....	96.75	19.95
192-202	1969 Issues ......(11)	....	24.25	5.65
203/14	1970 Issues-No#212(11)	....	28.50	6.75
215-25	1971 Issues ......(11)	....	32.95	7.75
226-33	1972 Issues ....(8)	....	37.75	9.00
234-43	1973 Issues ......(10)	....	26.25	5.95
244-55	1974 Issues ......(12)	....	39.75	8.75
256/66	1975 Issues-No#262(10)	....	40.00	8.15
267-80	1976 Issues ......(14)	....	.....	33.50
281-90	1977 Issues ......(10)	....	44.50	10.25
291-303	1978 Issues ......(13)	....	61.75	13.75
304-15	1979 Issues ......(12)	....	85.95	20.50
316/42	1980 Issues-No#324(26)	....	83.50	18.25
343-67	1981 Issues ......(25)	....	72.00	17.50
368-91	1982 Issues ......(24)	....	51.95	12.60
392-416	1983 Issues ......(25)	....	55.95	13.50
417-42	1984 Issues ......(26)	....	56.00	14.00
C1-C23	1951-77 Airmail Issues ....(23)	....	128.50	25.00

UNITED NATIONS (NEW YORK)

All U.N. issues will range between F-VF centering & will be never hinged.

SCOTT CAT.NO.	DESCRIPTION	INSCRIP. BLOCKS OF 4	UNUSED SINGLES

1, 6

2, 10, UX1-2

19-20

21-22

3, 11

4, 7, 9

1953

Scott	Description	Inscrip. Blocks of 4	Unused Singles
15-16	3c & 5c Refugee Issue	24.50	5.50
17-18	3c & 5c U.P.U. Issue	32.50	6.75
19-20	3c & 5c Technical Assistance	22.00	4.75
21-22	3c & 5c Human Rights Day	38.00	7.00

5

8

23-24   25-26   29-30

1951

1-11	1c to $1 Definitives	150.00	30.00

27-28

12

13-14

1952

12	5c United Nations Day	6.50	1.40
13-14	3c & 5c Human Rights Day	17.50	3.00

1954

23-24	3c & 8c Food & Agriculture	32.00	6.25
25-26	3c & 8c International Labor	48.00	12.00
27-28	3c & 8c Geneva	60.00	15.00
29-30	3c & 8c Human Rights Day	150.00	32.00

15-16

17-18

31-32

33-34

SCOTT CAT.NO.	DESCRIPTION	INSCRIP. BLOCKS OF 4	UNUSED SINGLES

35-38

39-40

1955

SCOTT CAT.NO.	DESCRIPTION	INSCRIP. BLOCKS OF 4	UNUSED SINGLES
31-32	3c & 8c Int. Civil Aviation Org.	75.00	15.00
33-34	3c & 8c UNESCO	30.00	5.50
35-37	3c to 8c United Nations	70.00	15.00
38	Same, Souvenir Sheet	____	575.00
38	Same, Unused, hinged	____	400.00
38	Same, Used Sheet	____	100.00
39-40	3c & 8c Human Rights Day	17.00	4.00

41-42

43-44

45-46

47-48

1956

SCOTT CAT.NO.	DESCRIPTION	INSCRIP. BLOCKS OF 4	UNUSED SINGLES
41-42	3c & 8c International Telecommunications	18.00	4.00
43-44	3c & 8c World Health Org.	18.00	4.00
45-46	3c & 8c United Nations Day	2.75	.45
47-48	3c & 8c Human Rights Day	1.75	.30

49-50

55-56

SCOTT CAT.NO.	DESCRIPTION	INSCRIP. BLOCKS OF 4	UNUSED SINGLES

51-52 (No Halo) 53-54 (Halo)

57-58

1957

SCOTT CAT.NO.	DESCRIPTION	INSCRIP. BLOCKS OF 4	UNUSED SINGLES
49-50	3c & 8c Meteorological Org.	1.60	.30
51-52	3c & 8c Emergency Force	1.60	.30
53-54	Same, Re-engraved	3.25	.65
55-56	3c & 8c Security Council	1.60	.30
57-58	3c & 8c Human Rights Day	1.60	.30

59-60 67-68

61-62 63-64

65-66

1958

SCOTT CAT.NO.	DESCRIPTION	INSCRIP. BLOCKS OF 4	UNUSED SINGLES
59-60	3c & 8c Atomic Energy Agency	1.60	.30
61-62	3c & 8c Central Hall	1.60	.30
63-64	4c & 8c U.N. Seal	1.60	.35
65-66	4c & 8c Economic & Social Council	1.95	.35
67-68	4c & 8c Human Rights Day	1.95	.35

69-70

71-72

SCOTT CAT.NO.	DESCRIPTION	INSCRIP. BLOCKS OF 4	UNUSED SINGLES

73-74   75-76

90-91   92

95-96

1959

69-70	4c & 8c Flushing Meadows .	2.65	.60
71-72	4c & 8c Economic Committee Europe	7.50	1.60
73-74	4c & 8c Trusteeship Council	5.25	1.00
75-76	4c & 8c World Refugee Year	3.25	.75

77-78   81-82   86-87

1961

88-89	4c & 8c Int. Court of Justice	2.65	.60
90-91	4c & 7c International Monetary Fund	2.65	.60
92	30c Abstract Flags	6.50	1.50
93-94	4c & 11c Economic Committee Latin America . .	8.50	2.00
95-96	4c & 11c Economic Committee Africa	4.25	.90
97-99	3c, 4c & 13c Childrens Fund	4.80	1.00

79-80   83-85

1960

77-78	4c & 8c Palais de Chaillot . .	2.85	.65
79-80	4c & 8c Economic Committee Asia	2.85	.65
81-82	4c & 8c 5th World Forestry Congress	2.85	.65
83-84	4c & 8c 15th Anniversary . .	2.85	.65
85	Same, Souvenir Sheet		12.50
86-87	4c & 8c International Bank .	2.85	.65

100-01   102-03

1962

| 100-01 | 4c & 7c Housing & Community Development . . | 4.10 | .95 |
| 102-03 | 4c & 11c Malaria Eradication | 5.75 | 1.25 |

88-89   93-94   97-99

104   105

SCOTT CAT.NO.	DESCRIPTION	INSCRIP. BLOCKS OF 4	UNUSED SINGLES

106

107

| 104-07 | 1c to 11c Definitives | 4.85 | 1.10 |

108-09

110-11

112-13

108-09	5c & 15c Memorial Issue	21.50	5.00
110-11	4c & 11c Operation in the Congo	15.00	3.00
112-13	4c & 11c Peaceful Use of Outer Space	4.75	1.10

114-15

116-17

121-22

118

119-20

1963

114-15	5c & 11c Science & Technology	5.65	1.35
116-17	5c & 11c Freedom From Hunger	5.25	1.25
118	25c UNTEA	7.50	1.75
119-20	5c & 11c General Assembly Building	5.25	1.25
121-22	5c & 11c Human Rights	5.65	1.35

BUY YEAR DATE SETS AND SAVE!

SCOTT CAT.NO.	DESCRIPTION	INSCRIP. BLOCKS OF 4	UNUSED SINGLES

123-24

125, UX3

126

127

128, U3-4

1964

| 123-24 | 5c & 11c Maritime Org. (IMCO) | 4.50 | 1.00 |
| 125-28 | 2c to 50c Definitives | 15.00 | 3.50 |

129-30

131-32

133

134-36

129-30	5c & 11c Trade & Development	4.25	.90
131-32	5c & 11c Narcotics Control	4.50	1.00
133	5c Cessation of Nuclear Testing	1.25	.25
134-36	4c to 11c Education for Progress	4.50	1.00

137-38

139-40

SCOTT CAT.NO.	DESCRIPTION	INSCRIP. BLOCKS OF 4	UNUSED SINGLES

141-42

143-45

1965

SCOTT CAT.NO.	DESCRIPTION	INSCRIP. BLOCKS OF 4	UNUSED SINGLES
137-38	5c & 11c U.N. Special Fund	3.50	.80
139-40	5c & 11c U.N. Forces in Cyprus	3.50	.80
141-42	5c & 11c I.T.U. Centenary	3.50	.80
143-44	5c & 15c International Cooperation Year	4.25	1.00
145	Same, Souvenir Sheet	——	2.25

146

147

148

149

150

151-53

SCOTT CAT.NO.	DESCRIPTION	INSCRIP. BLOCKS OF 4	UNUSED SINGLES
146-49	1c to 25c Definitive	32.50	7.00
149	25c Definitive-Flourescent	260.00	50.00

1966

SCOTT CAT.NO.	DESCRIPTION	INSCRIP. BLOCKS OF 4	UNUSED SINGLES
150	$1 Definitives	22.50	5.00

1965

SCOTT CAT.NO.	DESCRIPTION	INSCRIP. BLOCKS OF 4	UNUSED SINGLES
151-53	4c to 11c Population Trends	4.25	1.00

DON'T FORGET CRYSTAL MOUNT

SCOTT CAT.NO.	DESCRIPTION	INSCRIP. BLOCKS OF 4	UNUSED SINGLES

154-55

156-57

158-59

160

1966

SCOTT CAT.NO.	DESCRIPTION	INSCRIP. BLOCKS OF 4	UNUSED SINGLES
154-55	5c & 15c World Fed. (WFUNA)	4.25	1.00
156-57	5c & 11c World Health Org.	3.50	.80
158-59	5c & 11c Coffee Agreement	3.50	.80
160	15c Peacekeeping Observers	3.50	.75

161

162

163

SCOTT CAT.NO.	DESCRIPTION	INSCRIP. BLOCKS OF 4	UNUSED SINGLES
161-63	4c to 11c UNICEF	4.25	1.00

164-65

166

168-69

167

SCOTT CAT.NO.	DESCRIPTION	INSCRIP. BLOCKS OF 4	UNUSED SINGLES
	1967		
164-65	5c & 11c Development	3.50	.80
166-67	1½c & 5c Definitives	1.85	.40
168-69	5c & 11c Independence . . .	3.50	.80

170 171 173

174 172

| 170-74 | 4c to 15c Expo '67-Canada . | 18.75 | 4.00 |

175-76 177-178

179

180

SCOTT CAT.NO.	DESCRIPTION	INSCRIP. BLOCKS OF 4	UNUSED SINGLES
175-76	5c & 15c International Tourist Year	4.25	1.00
177-78	6c & 13c Towards Disarmament	4.25	1.00
179	36c Chagall Windows s/s . .		2.00
180	6c Kiss of Peace	1.35	.30

181-82 185-86

183-84 187, U5 190-91

188-89

	1968		
181-82	6c & 13c Secretariat	4.25	1.00
183-84	6c & 75c H. Starcke	80.00	16.00
185-86	6c & 13c Industrial Development	4.00	.95
187	6c Definitive	1.35	.30
188-89	6c & 20c Weather Watch . .	5.45	1.30
190-91	6c & 13c International Year— Human Rights	7.50	1.75

192-93 194-95

197-98 196

SCOTT CAT.NO.	DESCRIPTION	INSCRIP. BLOCKS OF 4	UNUSED SINGLES
	1969		
192-93	6c & 13c Inst. Tng., Research	4.00	.95
194-95	6c & 15c U.N. Building-Chile	4.75	1.10
196	13c Definitive	2.85	.65
197-98	6c & 13c Peace Through International Law	4.25	1.00

199-200

201

202

199-200	6c & 20c Labor & Development	5.45	1.30
201-02	6c & 13c Tunisian Mosaics	4.45	1.05

203-04

205-06

1970

203-04	6c & 25c Japanese Peace Bell	6.50	1.55
205-06	6c & 13c L. Mekong Delta Development	4.00	.95

207-08

209-10

211, 212

213-14

SCOTT CAT.NO.	DESCRIPTION	INSCRIP. BLOCKS OF 4	UNUSED SINGLES
207-08	6c & 13c Fight Cancer	4.00	.95
209-11	6c to 25c Peace & Progress	11.50	2.75
212	Same, Souvenir Sheet	———	2.25
213-14	6c & 13c Peace, Justice and Progress	4.00	.95

215

216-17

219

218

1971

215	6c Peaceful Uses Sea Bed	1.55	.35
216-17	6c & 13c Support Refugees	4.00	.95
218	13c World Food Programme	2.85	.65
219	20c U.P.U. Building	4.25	1.00

220

221

224-25

222, UC12

223

220-21	8c & 13c Anti-Discrimination	4.45	1.05
222-23	8c & 60c Definitives	11.50	2.75
224-25	8c & 21c International School	6.15	1.45

BUY YEAR DATE SETS AND SAVE!

SCOTT CAT.NO.	DESCRIPTION	INSCRIP. BLOCKS OF 4	UNUSED SINGLES

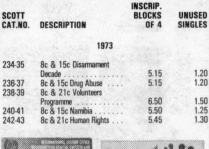

226   227

228   229-30

1972

226	95c Definitive	19.00	4.50
227	8c Non-Proliferation	1.85	.40
228	15c World Health Org.	3.85	.90
229-30	8c & 15c Environment	5.15	1.20

231   232-33

| 231 | 21c Economic Committee Europe | 4.95 | 1.15 |
| 232-33 | 8c & 15c Art-Sert Ceiling | 4.95 | 1.15 |

234-35

236-37

238-39

240-41   242-43

1973

234-35	8c & 15c Disarmament Decade	5.15	1.20
236-37	8c & 15c Drug Abuse	5.15	1.20
238-39	8c & 21c Volunteers Programme	6.50	1.50
240-41	8c & 15c Namibia	5.50	1.25
242-43	8c & 21c Human Rights	5.45	1.30

244-45   246

247-48

1974

244-45	10c & 21c ILO Headquarters	12.00	2.50
246	10c Universal Postal Union	2.45	.55
247-48	10c & 18c Brazil Peace Mural	7.50	1.75

249   250, U6

251   252-53   254-55

249-51	2c to 18c Definitives	7.00	1.60
252-53	10c & 18c World Population Year	5.95	1.40
254-55	10c & 26c Law of the Sea	7.00	1.60

DON'T FORGET CRYSTAL MOUNT

SCOTT CAT.NO.	DESCRIPTION	INSCRIP. BLOCKS OF 4	UNUSED SINGLES

256-57

258-59

260-62

263-64

265-66

1975

256-57	10c & 26c Peaceful Use of Space	13.50	2.50
258-59	10c & 18c International Women's Year	5.45	1.30
260-61	10c & 26c Anniversary	6.75	1.60
262	Same, Souvenir Sheet	—	3.25
263-64	10c & 18c Namibia	5.35	1.25
265-66	13c & 26c Peacekeeping	11.50	1.95

267

268

269

270

271

SCOTT CAT.NO.	DESCRIPTION	INSCRIP. BLOCKS OF 4	UNUSED SINGLES

272-73

274-75

276-77

278-79

280

1976

267-71	3c to 50c Definitives	20.95	4.50
272-73	13c & 26c World Federation	8.50	2.00
274-75	13c & 31c Conference on Trade & Development	9.50	2.20
276-77	13c & 25c Conference on Human Settlements	8.50	2.00
278-79	13c & 31c Postal Administration	—	24.50
280	13c World Food Council	2.85	.65

281-82

285-86

283-84

287-88

289-90

1977

281-82	13c & 31c WIPO	12.00	2.75
283-84	13c & 25c Water Conference	10.25	2.45
285-86	13c & 31c Security Council	10.25	2.25
287-88	13c & 25c Combat Racism	7.95	1.90
189-90	13c & 18c Atomic Energy	6.65	1.55

FOR YOUR CONVENIENCE IN ORDERING, COMPLETE YEAR DATE SETS ARE LISTED AT THE BEGINNING OF U.N. ISSUES.

SCOTT CAT.NO.	DESCRIPTION	INSCRIP. BLOCKS OF 4	UNUSED SINGLES

291

292

293

294-95

296-97

298-99

300-01

302-03

1978

Scott	Description	Blocks of 4	Singles
291-93	1c, 25c & $1 Definities	28.50	6.00
294-95	13c & 31c Smallpox Eradication	8.50	2.00
296-97	13c & 18c Namibia	5.75	1.35
298-99	13c & 25c ICAO	7.00	1.65
300-01	13c & 18c General Assembly	5.75	1.35
302-03	13c & 31c TCDC	9.50	2.25

304

305

306

SCOTT CAT.NO.	DESCRIPTION	INSCRIP. BLOCKS OF 4	UNUSED SINGLES

307

308-09

310-11

312-13

1979

Scott	Description	Blocks of 4	Singles
304-07	5c, 11c, 15c, & 20c Definitives	11.50	2.75
308-09	15c & 20c UNDRO	7.50	1.75
310-311	15c & 31c I.Y.C.	52.50	12.50
312-313	15c & 31c Namibia	9.50	2.30
314-315	15c & 20c Court of Justice	9.95	2.40

314-15

316-317

318-19

320-321

322-23

SCOTT CAT.NO.	DESCRIPTION	INSCRIP. BLOCKS OF 4	UNUSED SINGLES

325

326 Luxembourg
327 Fiji
328 Viet Nam

329

330 Suriname
331 Bangladesh
332 Mali

333

334 France
335 Venezuela
336 Salvador

337

338 Cameroun
339 Rwanda
340 Hungary

341-42

SCOTT CAT.NO.	DESCRIPTION	INSCRIP. BLOCKS OF 4	UNUSED SINGLES

343

344-45

346-47

348-49

350

351 Sri Lanka
352 Bolivia
353 Equatorial Guinea

354

355 Czechoslovakia
356 Thailand
357 Trinidad and Tobago

358

359 Kuwait
360 Sudan
361 Egypt

362

363 Singapore
364 Panama
365 Costa Rica

366-67

1980

Scott	Description	Blocks of 4	Unused Singles
16-17	13c & 31c Economics	14.50	1.90
18-19	15c & 20c Decade for Women	6.25	1.50
20-21	15c & 31c Peace-Keeping ..	8.25	2.00
22-23	15c & 31c Anniversary ...	8.25	2.00
24	Same, Souvenir Sheet	—	2.00
25-40	1980 World Flags, 16 Varieties	40.80	10.40
25-28	15c World Flags, 4 Varieties	10.40	2.60
29-32	15c World Flags, 4 Varieties	10.40	2.60
33-36	15c World Flags, 4 Varieties	10.40	2.60
37-40	15c World Flags, 4 Varieties	10.40	2.60
41-42	15c & 20c Economic and Social Council	10.00	1.50

SCOTT CAT.NO.	DESCRIPTION	INSCRIP. BLOCKS OF 4	UNUSED SINGLES
	1981		
343	15c Palestinian People	2.45	.55
344-45	20c & 35c Disabled Persons	8.15	1.95
346-47	20c & 31c Fresco	7.50	1.80
348-49	20c & 40c Sources of Energy	8.75	2.10
350-65	1981 World Flags, 16 varieties	42.00	10.40
350-53	20c World Flags, 4 vars. ...	10.50(16)	2.60
354-57	20c World Flags, 4 vars ...	10.50(16)	2.60
358-61	20c World Flags, 4 vars. ...	10.50(16)	2.60
362-65	20c World Flags, 4 vars. ...	10.50(16)	2.60
366-67	18c & 28c Volunteers Program	7.10	1.70

368

369

370

371-72

373

374

375 Malaysia
376 Seychelles
377 Ireland

378

379 Albania
380 Dominica
381 Solomon Islands

382

383 Swaziland
384 Nicaragua
385 Burma

386

387 Guyana
388 Belgium
389 Nigeria

390-91

SCOTT CAT.NO.	DESCRIPTION	INSCRIP. BLOCKS OF 4	UNUSED SINGLES
	1982		
368-70	17c, 28c, & 40c Definitives	8.75	2.15
371-72	20c & 40c Human Environment	6.60	1.50
373	20c Space Exploration	2.20	.50
374-89	World Flags, 16 vars.	32.40	8.00
374-77	20c World Flags, 4 vars. ...	8.10(16)	2.00
378-81	20c World Flags, 4 vars. ...	8.10(16)	2.00
382-85	20c World Flags, 4 vars. ...	8.10(16)	2.00
386-89	20c World Flags, 4 vars. ...	8.10(16)	2.00
390-91	20c & 28c Nature Conservation	5.10	1.20

392-93

394-95

396

397-98

399

400 Barbados
401 Nepal
402 Israel

403

404 Byelorussian SSR
405 Jamaica
406 Kenya

SCOTT CAT.NO.	DESCRIPTION	INSCRIP. BLOCKS OF 4	UNUSED SINGLES

407

408	Peru
409	Bulgaria
410	Canada

411

412	Senegal
413	Brazil
414	Sweden

415-16

1983

SCOTT CAT.NO.	DESCRIPTION	INSCRIP. BLOCKS OF 4	UNUSED SINGLES
392-93	20c & 40c World Comm. .	6.60	1.50
394-95	20c & 37c Safety at Sea .	6.25	1.45
396	20c World Food Program .	2.20	.50
397-98	20c & 28c Trade & Development	5.10	1.20
399-414	World Flags, 16 vars.	32.40	8.00
399-402	20c World Flags, 4 vars. . .	8.10(16)	2.00
403-06	20c World Flags, 4 vars. . .	8.10(16)	2.00
407-10	20c World Flags, 4 vars. . .	8.10(16)	2.00
411-14	20c World Flags, 4 vars. . .	8.10(16)	2.00
415-16	20c & 40c Human Rights .	6.60	1.50

417-18

419-20

421-22

423-24

1984

17-18	20c & 40c Population . . .	6.60	1.50
19-20	20c & 40c Food Day	6.60	1.50
21-22	20c & 50c Heritage	7.50	1.75
23-24	20c & 50c Future for Refugees	7.75	1.75

425

426	Pakistan
427	Benin
428	Italy

429

430	Papua New Guinea
431	Uruguay
432	Chile

433

434	United Arab Emirates
435	Ecuador
436	Bahamas

437

438	Bhutan
439	Central African Rep.
440	Australia

425-40	1984 World Flags, 16 varieties	32.40	8.00
425-28	20c World Flags, 4 vars. . .	8.10(16)	2.00
429-32	20c World Flags, 4 vars. . .	8.10(16)	2.00
433-36	20c World Flags, 4 vars. . .	8.10(16)	2.00
437-40	20c World Flags, 4 vars. . .	8.10(16)	2.00

SCOTT CAT.NO.	DESCRIPTION	INSCRIP. BLOCKS OF 4	UNUSED SINGLES	SCOTT CAT.NO.	DESCRIPTION	INSCRIP. BLOCKS OF 4	UNUSED SINGLES

AIR MAIL ISSUES

C1-2, UC5   C3-C4, UC1-2

1951

| C1-4 | 6c,10c,15c, & 20c ...... | 75.00 | 12.95 |

C5-6, UXC1, UXC3

C7, UC4

1957-59

| C5-7 | 4c,5c, & 7c .... | 3.35 | .75 |

C8, UXC4

C9, UC6, UC8

C10

C12

C11

1963-64

| C8-12 | 6c,8c,13c,15c, & 25c .... | 14.50 | 3.00 |

C13

C14

1968-69

| C13-14 | 10c & 20c .... | 6.75 | 1.60 |

C15, UXC8

C16, UC10

C17, UXC10

C18

1972

| C15-18 | 9c,11c,17c & 21c ...... | 12.00 | 2.75 |

C19, UC11

C21

C20, UXC11

1974

| C19-21 | 13c,18c, & 26c .... | 12.00 | 2.75 |

C22

C23

1977

| C22-23 | 25c & 31c .... | 11.75 | 2.8 |

SCOTT CAT. NO.	DESCRIPTION	MINT ENTIRE	FIRST DAY COVER	SCOTT CAT. NO.	DESCRIPTION	MINT ENTIRE	FIRST DAY COVER

ENVELOPES AND AIR LETTER SHEETS

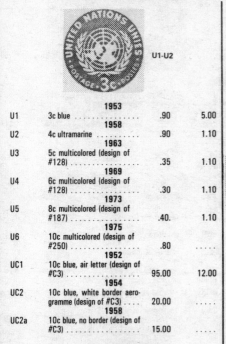

U1-U2

1953

U1	3c blue	.90	5.00

1958

U2	4c ultramarine	.90	1.10

1963

U3	5c multicolored (design of #128)	.35	1.10

1969

U4	6c multicolored (design of #128)	.30	1.10

1973

U5	8c multicolored (design of #187)	.40.	1.10

1975

U6	10c multicolored (design of #250)	.80	.....

1952

UC1	10c blue, air letter (design of #C3)	95.00	12.00

1954

UC2	10c blue, white border aerogramme (design of #C3)	20.00	.....

1958

UC2a	10c blue, no border (design of #C3)	15.00	.....

UC3

1959

UC3	7c blue	4.00	2.00

1960

UC4	10c blue on blue, letter sheet(design of #C7)	2.25	1.50

1961

UC5	11c blue on blue, letter sheet(design of #C1)	.95	1.50

1965

UC5a	11c blue on green, letter sheet (design of #C1)	1.75	.....

1963

UC6	8c multicolored (design of #C9)	.55	1.50

UC7

1958

UC7	13c shades of blue, letter sheet	.65	1.50

1969

UC8	10c multicolored (design of #C9)	.60	1.50

UC9

1972

UC9	15c shades of blue, letter sheet	.75	1.50

1973

UC10	11c multicolored (design of #C16)	.55	1.50

1975

UC11	13c multicolored (design of #C19)	.70	1.60

UC12	18c multicolored, aerograme (design of #222)	.90	1.60

UC13

1977

UC13	22c multicolored, aerogramme	1.10	1.70

1982

UC14	30c gray, aerogramme	.75	1.95

SCOTT CAT.NO. DESCRIPTION	MINT ENTIRE	FIRST DAY COVER	SCOTT CAT.NO. DESCRIPTION	MINT ENTIRE	FIRST DAY COVER

POSTAL CARDS

1952

UX1 2c blue on buff (design of #2) .... .35 2.20

1958

UX2 3c light olive brown on buff (design of #2) .... .95 1.75

1963

UX3 4c multicolored (design of #125) .... .25 .95

UX4

UX5-6

UX7 9c

UX8 13c

1969

UX4 5c blue & black .... .25 1.00

1973

UX5 6c multicolored .... .30 1.10

1975

UX6 8c multicolored .... .40 1.10

1977

UX7 9c multicolored .... .45 1.65

1982

UX8 13 multicolored .... .33 1.75

1957

UXC1 4c maroon on buff (design of #C5) .... .40 .75

1959

UXC2 4c & 1c (5c) (on UXC1) ... 1.35 90.00
UXC3 5c crimson on buff (design of #C6 .... 2.00 .95

UXC5-6

UXC7, UXC9

1963

UXC4 6c black & blue (design of #C8) .... .55 1.00

1965

UXC5 11c multicolored 1.00 1.40

1968

UXC6 13c yellow & green ...... .65 1.40

1969

UXC7 8c multicolored .... .40 1.15

1972

UXC8 9c multicolored (Design of #C15) .... .45 1.25
UXC9 15c multicolored .... .75 1.50

1975

UXC10 11c shades of blue (design of #C17) .... .55 1.75
UXC11 18c multicolored (design of #C20) .... .90 1.75

UXC12

1982

UXC12 28c multicolored .... .70 1.95

UNITED NATIONS — GENEVA — COMPLETE YEARS

		INSCRIP. BLOCKS OF 4	UNUSED SINGLES
1-14	1969-70 Issues (14)	225.00	45.00
15-21	1971 Issues (7)	68.95	14.95
22-29	1972 Issues (8)	65.75	12.95
30-36	1973 Issues (7)	59.50	12.95
37-45	1974 Issues (9)	66.75	15.50
46/56	1975 Issues (10) (no #52)	76.95	17.25
57-63	1976 Issues (7)	.....	33.50
64-72	1977 Issues (9)	73.50	16.75
73-81	1978 Issues (9)	71.75	16.50
82-88	1979 Issues (7)	113.50	24.75
89/97	1980 Issues (8) (no.#95)	53.75	13.00
98-104	1981 Issues (7)	37.75	8.65
105-12	1982 Issues (8)	35.95	8.50
113-20	1983 Issues (8)	39.95	9.00

GENEVA UNUSED STAMPS — Complete through 1983 at a Special Savings. #1-120, 120 Varieties (including the Souvenir Sheets).......... Only $235.00

SCOTT CAT. NO.	DESCRIPTION	INSCRIP. BLOCKS OF 4	UNUSED SINGLES	SCOTT CAT. NO.	DESCRIPTION	INSCRIP. BLOCKS OF 4	UNUSED SINGLES

UNITED NATIONS:
OFFICES IN GENEVA, SWITZERLAND
Denominations in Swiss Currency

1969-70

1-14	5c to 10fr Definitives	225.00	45.00

15

16

17

18

19

21

20

1971

15	30c Peaceful Uses Sea Bed	2.75	.60
16	50c Support for Refugees	9.50	1.80
17	50c World Food Programme	8.50	1.80
18	75c U.P.U. Building	12.00	2.25
19-20	30 & 50c Anti-Discrimination	12.50	2.75
21	1,10fr International School	27.50	6.50

SCOTT CAT.NO.	DESCRIPTION	INSCRIP. BLOCKS OF 4	UNUSED SINGLES

22

23

24

25-26

27

28-29

1972

SCOTT CAT.NO.	DESCRIPTION	INSCRIP. BLOCKS OF 4	UNUSED SINGLES
22	40c Definitive	3.35	.75
23	40c Non Proliferation	9.00	2.00
24	80c World Health Day	9.00	2.00
25-26	40c & 80c Environment	16.00	3.00
27	1,10fr Economic Committee-Europe	16.00	3.00
28-29	40c & 80c Art-Sert Ceiling	16.00	3.00

30-31

32

33

34

35-36

SCOTT CAT.NO.	DESCRIPTION	INSCRIP. BLOCKS OF 4	UNUSED SINGLES

1973

30-31	60c & 1,10fr Disarmament Decade	16.00	3.25
32	60c Drug Abuse	8.00	1.50
33	80c Volunteers	12.00	2.75
34	60c Namibia	15.50	3.75
35-36	40c & 80c Human Rights	11.00	2.50

37-38

43-44

39-40

45

1974

37-38	60c & 80c ILO Headquarters	15.00	3.50
39-40	30c & 60c U.P.U.	15.00	3.50
41-42	60c & 1fr Peace Mural	16.00	3.75
43-44	60c & 80c World Population Year	13.00	3.00
45	1,30fr Law of the Sea	11.25	2.50

46-47

48-49

50-52

53-54

55-56

SCOTT CAT.NO.	DESCRIPTION	INSCRIP. BLOCKS OF 4	UNUSED SINGLES
	1975		
46-47	60c & 90c Peaceful Use of Space	23.00	5.25
48-49	60c & 90c International Women's Year	12.50	2.50
50-51	60c & 90c 30th Anniversary	16.75	3.75
52	Same, Souvenir Sheet		3.00
53-54	50c & 1,30fr Namibia	15.75	3.65
55-56	60c & 70c Peace Keeping	13.25	3.00

57   58   59-60

61-62   63

	1976		
57	90c World Federation	10.00	2.25
58	1,10fr Conference — T. & D	11.75	2.75
59-60	40c & 1,50fr Conference — Human Settlement	15.75	3.65
61-62	80c & 1,10fr Postal Administration		25.00
63	70c World Food Council	6.75	1.50

64

65-66

71-72   67-68

69-70

	1977		
64	80c WIPO	7.25	1.65
65-66	80c & 1,10fr Water Conference	17.50	4.00
67-68	80c & 1,10fr Security Council	17.50	4.00
69-70	40c & 1,10fr Combat Racism	17.50	4.00
71-72	80c & 1,10fr Atomic Energy	17.50	4.00

73   74-75

76   77-78

79-80   81

	1978		
73	35c Definitive	3.75	.80
74-75	80c & 1,10fr Smallpox Eradication	19.50	4.50
76	80c Namibia	8.00	1.85
77-78	70c & 80c ICAO	15.75	3.75
79-80	70c & 1,10fr General Assembly	17.50	4.25
81	80c TCDC	10.75	2.40

SCOTT CAT.NO.	DESCRIPTION	INSCRIP. BLOCKS OF 4	UNUSED SINGLES	SCOTT CAT.NO.	DESCRIPTION	INSCRIP. BLOCKS OF 4	UNUSED SINGLES

82-83   84-85   98   99-100

86   87-88   89   101   102

1979

82-83	80c & 1,50fr UNDRO	30.00	6.25
84-85	80c & 1,10fr I.Y.C.	45.00	9.50
86	1,10fr Namibia	14.50	3.00
87-88	80c & 1,10fr Court of Justice	30.00	6.25

103-104

1981

98	80c Palestinian People	6.50	1.45
99-100	40c & 1,50 Disabled People	14.00	3.40
101	80c Fresco	5.65	1.35
102	1,10fr Sources of Energy ..	7.85	1.85
103-04	40c & 70c Volunteers Program	7.85	1.85

 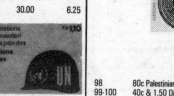

90-91   92

105-06   109-10

93   94

107-08   111-12

96-97

1980

89	80c Economics	10.40	2.25
90-91	40c & 70c Decade for Women	14.00	3.40
92	1,10fr Peace-Keeping	9.85	2.35
93-94	40c & 70c 35th Anniversary	11.50	2.75
95	Same, Souvenir Sheet	———	2.85
96-97	40c & 70c Economic & Social Council	11.00	2.65

1982

105-06	30c & 1,fr Definitives.....	7.65	1.85
107-08	40c & 1,20fr Human Environment	9.50	2.20
109-10	80c & 1,00fr Space Exploration	10.65	2.50
111-12	40c & 1,50fr Conservation	10.00	2.40

SCOTT CAT.NO.	DESCRIPTION	BLOCKS OF 4	UNUSED SINGLES

113

116

114-15

117-18

119-20

1983

113	1,20fr World Communications ...	8.25	1.85
114-15	40c & 80c Safety at Sea .	6.75	1.50
116	1,50fr World Food Program.....	8.25	1.85
117-18	80c & 1,10fr Trade & Development	10.00	2.35
119-20	40c & 1.20fr Human Rts .	8.75	2.00

122-123

121

124-25

126-27

121	1,20fr Population	5.85	1.35
122-23	50c & 80c Food Day	7.80	1.80
124-25	50c & 70c Heritage	5.85	1.35
126-27	35c & 1.50fr Future for Refugees	9.50	2.25

SEE SPECIAL OFFERS FOR STATIONERY AND POSTAL CARDS IN THIS SECTION

SCOTT CAT.NO.	DESCRIPTION	UNUSED ENTIRE	FIRST DAY COVER

AIR LETTER SHEETS & POSTAL CARDS

UC1

UX1   UX2

1969

| UC1 | 65c ultramarine & blue .... | 9.50 | 8.00 |

1969

| UX1 | 20c olive green & black ... | 2.20 | 2.00 |
| UX2 | 30c violet blue, blue, light & dark green .... | 3.00 | 3.00 |

UX3

UX4

1977

| UX3 | 40c multicolored .... | .80 | 2.35 |
| UX4 | 70c multicolored .... | 1.65 | 4.75 |

| SCOTT CAT.NO. | DESCRIPTION | INSCRIP. BLOCKS OF 4 | UNUSED SINGLES | SCOTT CAT.NO. | DESCRIPTION | INSCRIP. BLOCKS OF 4 | UNUSED SINGLES |

UNITED NATIONS:
OFFICES IN VIENNA, AUSTRIA
Denominations in Austrian Currency

1

2

3

4

5

6

7

8

1979

1-6	50g to s10 Definitives	36.50	7.75
7	s4 International Economic Order	110.00	4.75
8	s2.50 International Economic Definitive	3.65	.85

9-10

11

12-13   15-16

1980

9-10	s4 & s6 Decade for Women	21.00	4.25
11	s6 Peace-keeping	16.50	3.35
12-13	s4 & s6 35th Anniversary	14.75	3.50
14	Same, Souvenir Sheet	—	3.60
15-16	s4 & s6 Economic and Social Council	19.00	3.35

17

18-19

20   21

22-23

1981

17	s4 Palestinian People	3.85	.90
18-19	s4 & s6 Disabled Persons	9.50	2.30
20	s6 Fresco	5.65	1.35
21	s7,50 Sources of Energy	7.40	1.60
22-23	s5 & s7 Volunteers Program	11.00	2.50

SCOTT CAT.NO.	DESCRIPTION	INSCRIP. BLOCKS OF 4	UNUSED SINGLES

24

25-26

27

28-29

1982

24	s3 Definitive	2.15	.50
25-26	s5 & s7 Human Environment	7.75	1.85
27	s5 Space Exploration	3.45	.80
28-29	s5 & s7 Nature Conservation	7.75	1.85

30

33-34

31-32

35-36

37-38

1983

30	s4 World Comm	2.60	.60
31-32	s4 & s6 Safety at Sea	6.60	1.50
33-34	s5 & s7 World Food Program	7.75	1.85
35-36	s4 & s8.50 Trade and Development	7.75	1.85
37-38	s5 & s7 Human Rts	7.75	1.85

SCOTT CAT.NO.	DESCRIPTION	INSCRIP. BLOCKS OF 4	UNUSED SINGLES

39

40-41

42-43

44-45

1984

39	s7 Population	4.00	.95
40-41	s4.50 & s6 Food Day	7.60	1.75
42-43	s3.50 & s15 Heritage	10.75	2.50
44-45	s4.50 & s8.50 Future for Refugees	8.50	2.00

AIR LETTER SHEET & POSTAL CARDS

		ENTIRE	FIRST DAY COVERS

UC1

1982

| UC1 | s9 multicolored | 1.50 | 4.25 |

UX1

UX2

1982

| UX1 | s3 multicolored | .50 | 2.25 |
| UX2 | s5 multicolored | .80 | 3.50 |

UNITED NATIONS — VIENNA — COMPLETE YEARS

		INSCRIP. BLOCKS OF 4	UNUSED SINGLES
1-8	1979 Issues (8)	142.50	12.75
9-16	1980 Issues (7) (no.#14)	67.95	13.75
17-23	1981 Issues (7)	35.50	8.25
24-29	1982 Issues (6)	19.95	4.75
30-38	1983 Issues (9)	30.75	7.25

Vienna Unused Stamps — Complete through 1983 at a Special Savings, #1-38, 38 varieties including the Souvenir Sheet, only $44.50.

SCOTT CAT NO.	DESCRIPTION	UNUSED NH F	AVG	UNUSED F	AVG	USED F	AVG

CANAL ZONE

1904
U.S. Stamps 300, 319, 304, 306-07
overprinted

(overprint: CANAL ZONE / PANAMA)

4	1c blue green	50.00	40.00	35.00	25.00	30.00	20.00
5	2c carmine	50.00	40.00	35.00	25.00	30.00	18.00
6	5c blue.....................	170.00	140.00	125.00	90.00	95.00	65.00
7	8c violet black..............	310.00	240.00	220.00	150.00	145.00	120.00
8	10c pale red brown	285.00	215.00	200.00	135.00	145.00	120.00

1924-25
U.S. Stamps 551-54, 557,562,564-66, 569-71
overprinted

(overprint: CANAL ZONE)

Type 1. Flat Tops on Letters "A." Perf. 11

70	½c olive brown	1.50	1.25	1.20	.95	1.10	.80
71	1c deep green	2.65	2.15	2.00	1.50	.90	.60
72	1½c yellow brown	3.35	2.80	2.50	2.00	1.60	1.25
73	2c carmine	13.00	9.00	10.00	6.50	1.75	1.50
74	5c dark blue	32.50	25.00	25.00	17.50	13.00	9.00
75	10c orange	70.00	55.00	55.00	40.00	30.00	22.50
76	12c brown violet	65.00	50.00	50.00	35.00	32.50	25.00
77	14c dark blue	40.00	30.00	30.00	20.00	23.50	18.00
78	15c gray	75.00	60.00	60.00	45.00	42.00	32.50
79	30c olive brown	65.00	50.00	50.00	35.00	35.00	25.00
80	50c lilac	95.00	80.00	75.00	60.00	45.00	37.50
81	$1 violet brown.............	500.00	400.00	400.00	300.00	190.00	140.00

1925-28

U.S. Stamps 554-55, 557,564-66,623,567, 569-71, overprinted

(overprint: CANAL ZONE)

Type II. Pointed Tops on Letters "A."

84	2c carmine	50.00	40.00	40.00	30.00	12.00	8.50
85	3c violet	7.00	5.50	5.25	4.00	3.25	2.50
86	5c dark blue	7.25	6.00	5.50	4.25	3.35	2.60
87	10c orange	75.00	60.00	60.00	45.00	13.00	10.00
88	12c brown violet	45.00	35.00	35.00	25.00	18.00	13.50
89	14c dark blue	45.00	35.00	35.00	25.00	20.00	15.00
90	15c gray	14.00	11.00	11.00	8.00	5.00	4.00
91	17c black	8.50	7.00	6.50	5.00	3.95	3.00
92	20c carmine	13.00	10.00	10.00	7.50	5.25	4.00
93	30c olive brown	11.00	8.25	8.50	6.00	4.75	3.50
94	50c lilac...................	525.00	400.00	420.00	300.00	200.00	145.00
95	$1 violet brown.............	260.00	195.00	200.00	140.00	65.00	45.00

1926

Type II overprint on U.S. Stamp 627

96	2c carmine rose	9.50	7.25	7.50	5.25	5.25	4.00

SEE PAGE X FOR CONDITION DEFINITIONS

SCOTT CAT NO.	DESCRIPTION	UNUSED NH		UNUSED		USED	
		F	AVG	F	AVG	F	AVG

1927
Type II overprint on U.S. stamps 583-84, 591
Rotary Press Printing, Perf. 10

97	2c carmine	90.00	70.00	70.00	50.00	12.50	9.00
98	3c violet	15.00	11.00	12.00	8.00	5.50	4.00
99	10c orange	27.50	20.00	22.50	15.00	7.50	6.00

1927-31
Type II overprint on U.S. Stamps 632, 634-35, 637, 642
Rotary Press Printing, Perf. 11 x 10½

100	1c green	3.00	2.20	2.50	1.75	1.80	1.35
101	2c carmine	3.75	2.90	3.00	2.25	1.45	1.10
102	3c violet	10.00	7.75	8.00	6.00	2.75	2.00
103	5c dark blue	30.00	24.00	25.00	19.00	10.75	7.75
104	10c orange	30.00	24.00	25.00	19.00	10.75	7.75

105, 160 106 107 108, 161 109

110 111 112 113 114

1928 Builders Issue

105-14	1c to 50 cpl., 10 vars.	15.50	12.25	13.50	10.50	7.95	6.95
105	1c Gorgas	.27	.22	.22	.18	.15	.10
106	2c Goethals	.50	.40	.45	.35	.35	.25
107	5c Gaillard Cut	2.25	1.70	2.00	1.50	.95	.75
108	10c Hodges	.80	.60	.70	.50	.40	.30
109	12c Galliard	1.85	1.50	1.60	1.25	1.00	.75
110	14c Sibert	2.25	1.70	2.00	1.50	1.25	1.00
111	15c Smith	1.10	.90	.95	.75	.80	.60
112	20c Rousseau	1.35	1.10	1.20	.95	.80	.60
113	30c Williamson	2.30	1.80	2.00	1.50	1.35	1.00
114	50c Blackburn	3.50	3.00	3.00	2.50	1.10	.85

1933
Type II overprint on U.S. Stamps 720 & 695
Rotary Press Printing, Perf. 11 x 10½

115	3c Washington	4.95	3.85	4.25	3.25	.60	.50
116	14c Indian	8.00	6.00	7.00	5.00	3.25	2.50

117, 153

1934

117	3c Goethals	.35	.30	.30	.25	.17	.12

BUY COMPLETE SETS AND SAVE

SCOTT CAT NO.	DESCRIPTION	UNUSED NH F	UNUSED NH AVG	UNUSED F	UNUSED AVG	USED F	USED AVG
		1939					
		U.S. Stamps 803,805 overprinted					
118	½c red orange	.40	.35	.35	.30	.30	.25
119	1½c bistre brown	.45	.40	.40	.35	.40	.35

CANAL ZONE POSTAGE	122 Gaillard Cut — Before	123 After
	124 Bas Obispo — Before	125 After
	126 Gatun Locks — Before	127 After
	128 Canal Channel — Before	129 After
	130 Gamboa — Before	131 After
	132 Pedro Miguel Locks — Before	133 After
	134 Gatun Spillway — Before	135 After

120
Balboa — Before

121
Balboa — After

1939. 25th ANNIVERSARY ISSUE

SCOTT CAT NO.	DESCRIPTION	UNUSED NH F	UNUSED NH AVG	UNUSED F	UNUSED AVG	USED F	USED AVG
120-35	1c-50c cpl., Vars.	185.00	155.00	160.00	107.50	74.95	58.95
120	1c yellow green	.85	.70	.75	.60	.50	.40
121	2c rose carmine	1.10	.90	.90	.75	.60	.50
122	3c purple	.85	.70	.75	.60	.30	.25
123	5c dark blue	2.25	1.80	1.85	1.50	1.60	1.20
124	6c red orange	4.35	3.60	3.75	3.00	2.25	1.75
125	7c black	4.35	3.60	3.75	3.00	2.25	1.75
126	8c green	5.50	4.75	4.75	4.00	3.00	2.50
127	10c ultramarine	5.50	4.75	4.75	4.00	2.75	2.25
128	11c blue green	13.50	10.75	11.50	9.00	8.50	6.50
129	12c brown carmine	11.00	9.00	9.50	7.50	8.00	6.00
130	14c dark violet	12.50	10.00	10.50	8.25	6.75	5.25
131	15c olive green	21.00	16.75	18.00	14.00	6.75	5.25
132	18c rose pink	16.00	13.00	14.00	11.00	10.00	8.00
133	20c brown	23.00	19.00	20.00	16.00	5.50	4.25
134	25c orange	35.00	30.00	30.00	25.00	14.50	12.00
135	50c violet brown	40.00	35.00	35.00	30.00	5.75	4.50

NOTE: To determine the VF price for stamps issued from 1901 to 1940, add the difference between the Avg. and F prices to the F price. To determine the VF price on stamps issued from 1941 to date, add 15% to the F/NH or F (used) price (minimum .03 per item). All VF unused stamps from 1941 to date will be NH. From 1964 to date, all stamps will be F/NH.

136

137

138

139, 155, 164

140, 162

SCOTT CAT NO.	DESCRIPTION	PLATE BLOCK F/NH	F	UNUSED F/NH	F	USED F
		1946-49				
136-40	½c-25c cpl., 5 var.	.....	....	4.50	3.95	1.85
136	½c Major General Davis	4.50(6)	4.00(6)	.60	.50	.20
137	1½c Governor Magoon	4.75(6)	4.00(6)	.60	.50	.20
138	2c Theodore Roosevelt	1.75(6)	1.50(6)	.22	.18	.13
139	5c Stevens	5.00(6)	4.50(6)	.60	.50	.20
140	25c J.F. Wallace	18.00(6)	16.50(6)	2.75	2.50	1.25

141

142

143

144

145

1948

141	10c Map-Biological Area	22.50(6)	20.00(6)	2.50	2.25	1.50

1949.

142-45	3c-18c cpl., 4 Vars.	.....	.....	9.00	8.00	4.25
142	3c "Forty Niners"	12.00(6)	10.00(6)	1.50	1.25	.45
143	6c Journey-Las Cruces	15.00(6)	12.50(6)	1.60	1.35	.65
144	12c Las Cruces-Panama Trail	28.00(6)	25.00(6)	2.75	2.50	1.25
145	18c Departure-San Franscisco	33.00(6)	30.00(6)	3.65	3.40	2.10

146   147   148   149

150   152, 154   156   157   151

1951

146	10c Culebra Cut	40.00(6)	35.00(6)	3.75	3.50	2.00

1955

147	3c Panama Railroad Cent.	13.25(6)	12.50(6)	1.65	1.50	.60

1957

148	3c Gorgas Hospital	6.50	6.00	.90	.75	.40

1958

149	4c S.S. Ancon	4.25	4.00	.75	.60	.30

SCOTT CAT NO.	DESCRIPTION	PLATE BLOCK F/NH	F		UNUSED F/NH	F		USED F
		1958						
150	5c Theodore Roosevelt	4.50	4.25		.60	.55		.40
		1960						
151	4c Boy Scout Badge	6.50	6.00		.85	.80		.50
152	4c Administration Building	1.40	1.25		.27	.25		.18
	Coil Stamp. Perf. 10 Vertically (Design of 117)							
153	3c George W. Goethals	—	—		.19	.16		.15
	Coil Stamp. Perf. 10 Horizontally							
154	4c Administration Building	—	—		.25	.22		.18
	1962. Coil Stamp. Perf. 10 Vertically (Design of 139)							
155	5c John F. Stevens	—	—		.31	.28		.20
		1962						
156	4c Girl Scout Badge	4.50	4.25		.50	.45		.35
157	4c Thatcher Ferry Bridge	4.50	4.25		.45	.40		.30

158   159   163   165

		1968						
158	6c Goethals Memorial	2.65	. . . . .		.40	. . . . .		.18
		1971						
159	8c Fort San Lorenzo	3.50	. . . . .		.60	. . . . .		.30
	1975. Coil Stamps. Perf. 10 Vertically Design of 105, 108, & 140							
160	1c William C. Gorgas	—	—		.20			.10
161	10c Harry F. Hodges	—	—		.75			.15
162	25c John F. Wallace	. . . . .	. . . . .		5.00			1.10
		1976						
163	13c Cascadas Dredge	2.50	. . . . .		.55	. . . . .		.25
	1977. Rotary Press (Design of 139)							
164	5c John F. Stevens	1.75	. . . . .		.35	. . . . .		.18
		1978						
165	15c Locomotive	3.00	. . . . .		.70	. . . . .		.25

SCOTT CAT NO.	DESCRIPTION	UNUSED NH F	AVG	UNUSED F	AVG	USED F	AVG

AIR MAIL

AIR MAIL STAMPS

105 & 106 Surcharged

1929-31

25 CENTS 25

C1	15c on 1c green, Type I	19.00	15.00	16.00	12.00	9.25	7.00
C2	15c on 1c yellow green, Type II	210.00	160.00	175.00	125.00	120.00	90.00
C3	25c on 2c carmine	8.50	6.50	7.00	5.00	3.25	2.50

AIR MAIL

1929

☰10c

C4	10c on 50c lilac	19.00	14.00	15.00	11.00	12.00	9.25
C5	20c on 2c carmine	14.00	10.00	12.00	8.00	3.75	2.75

C6-14

C15

C16

C17

C18

C19

C20

1931-49

C6-14	4c -$1 cpl., 9 Vars.	34.50	27.95	31.95	23.95	9.75	8.00
C6	4c Gaillard Cut, red violet	1.15	.95	.95	.80	.80	.70
C7	5c Same, yellow green	.95	.80	.85	.70	.60	.50
C8	6c Same, yellow brown	1.30	1.10	1.15	.95	.60	.50
C9	10c Same, orange	1.50	1.30	1.30	1.10	.60	.50
C10	15c Same, blue	2.10	1.60	1.85	1.35	.50	.40
C11	20c Same, red violet	3.50	3.00	3.10	2.65	.50	.40
C12	30c Same, rose lake	4.50	4.00	4.75	3.50	1.15	1.25
C13	40c Same, yellow	4.50	4.00	4.75	3.50	2.00	1.50
C14	$1 Same, black	17.00	13.00	15.00	11.00	3.50	2.75

1939. 25th ANNIVERSARY ISSUE

C15-20	5c-$1 cpl., 6 Vars.	138.50	110.00	119.50	91.95	83.50	65.95
C15	5c Plane over Sosa Hill	6.50	5.00	5.50	4.25	4.25	3.75
C16	10c Map of Central America	6.50	5.00	5.50	4.25	4.00	3.50
C17	15c Scene near Fort Amador	6.75	5.25	5.75	4.50	2.25	1.50
C18	25c Clipper at Cristobal Harbor	29.50	24.00	25.00	20.00	16.50	12.50
C19	30c Clipper over Galliard Cut	22.50	16.75	19.00	14.00	11.00	8.50
C20	$1 Clipper Alighting	75.00	60.00	65.00	50.00	50.00	40.00

DON'T FORGET CRYSTAL MOUNT

SCOTT CAT NO.	DESCRIPTION	PLATE BLOCK F/NH	F	UNUSED F/NH	F	USED F

C21-C31, C34

C32

C33

C35

1951

C21	4c Globe & Wing, red violet	9.75(6)	9.00(6)	1.05	.95	.50
C22	6c Same, brown	9.75(6)	9.00(6)	1.05	.95	.40
C23	10c Same, red orange	15.00(6)	13.50(6)	1.65	1.50	.55
C24	21c Same, blue	95.00(6)	85.00(6)	12.00	11.00	3.75
C25	31c Same, cerise	115.00(6)	105.00(6)	12.00	11.00	3.50
C26	80c Same, gray black	67.50(6)	60.00(6)	8.00	7.00	2.25

1958

C27	5c Globe & Wing, yellow green	10.00	9.00	1.90	1.60	.65
C28	7c Same, olive	9.00	8.00	1.90	1.60	.55
C29	15c Same, brown violet	52.50	50.00	7.50	6.75	1.85
C30	25c Same, orange yellow	115.00	105.00	14.50	13.00	2.40
C31	35c Same, dark blue	100.00	90.00	14.50	13.00	2.40

1961

C32	15c Emblem Caribbean School	17.00	16.00	2.50	2.25	1.20

1962

C33	7c Anti-Malaria	5.75	5.00	1.05	.95	.60

1963 Design of 1951-58

C34	8c Globe & Wing, carmine	7.75	7.00	.95	.85	.45

1963

C35	15c Alliance Emblem	18.00	16.50	1.75	1.65	1.10

C36

C37

C38

C39

UNUSED CANAL ZONE
BOOKLET PANES OF 6

		F/VF NH	F/VF
71e	1c deep green	110.00	95.00
73a	2c carmine-perf. 11	135.00	110.00
101a	2c carmine-perf. 11x 10½	190.00	160.00
106a	2c Goethals	15.00	12.50
117a	3c Goethals	50.00	45.00
163a	13c Cascadas, pane of 4	4.00	3.75
C48a	10c Air-pane of 4	4.50	4.25
C49a	11c Air-pane of 4	4.00	3.50
C50a	13c Air-pane of 4	4.50	....

SCOTT CAT NO.	DESCRIPTION	PLATE BLOCK F/NH F	UNUSED F/NH F	USED F

C40

C41

C42-C53

1964. 50th ANNIVERSARY ISSUE

SCOTT CAT NO.	DESCRIPTION	PB F/NH	PB F	UNUSED F/NH	UNUSED F	USED F
C36-41	6c-80c cpl., 6 Vars	99.75	92.00	21.75	19.95	6.50
C36	6c Cristobal	4.75	4.00	.85	.75	.40
C37	8c Gatun Locks	4.50	4.25	.95	.85	.60
C38	15c Madden Dam	9.50	8.50	1.90	1.65	.60
C39	20c Gaillard Cut	12.00	11.00	2.50	2.25	.75
C40	80c Miraflores Locks	27.00	24.50	6.00	5.50	1.75
C41	80c Balboa	50.00	45.00	10.75	10.00	2.95

1965

SCOTT CAT NO.	DESCRIPTION	PB F/NH	PB F	UNUSED F/NH	UNUSED F	USED F
C42-47	6c-80c cpl., 6 Vars.	33.95	.....	6.50	.....	2.50
C42	6c Government Seal, green & black	3.25	.....	.45	.....	.15
C43	8c Same, rose red & black	3.50	.....	.60	.....	.15
C44	15c Same, blue & black	4.00	.....	.70	.....	.20
C45	20c Same, lilac & black	4.00	.....	.70	.....	.30
C46	30c Same, brown & black	5.50	.....	1.20	.....	.40
C47	80c Same, yellow & black	15.50	.....	3.25	.....	1.50

1968-76

SCOTT CAT NO.	DESCRIPTION	PB F/NH	UNUSED F/NH	USED F
C48	10c Government Seal, salmon & black	2.00	.40	.25
C49	11c Same, olive & black	2.25	.45	.25
C50	13c Same, green & black	4.00	.80	.35
C51	22c Same, blue & black	7.75	.90	.35
C52	25c Same, light olive & black	5.00	1.00	.35
C53	35c Same, salmon & black	8.50	1.40	.55

AIR MAIL OFFICIAL STAMPS

C7-14 Overprinted
1941-42. Overprint 19 to 20½mm Long.

OFFICIAL
PANAMA CANAL

SCOTT CAT NO.	DESCRIPTION	PB F/NH	PB F	UNUSED F/NH	UNUSED F	USED F
CO1-7	5c-$1 cpl., 7 Vars.	.....	.....	105.00	89.50	30.50
CO1	5c Gaillard Cut, light green	.....	.....	5.75	4.75	1.25
CO2	10c Same, orange	.....	.....	10.50	9.00	2.00
CO3	15c Same, blue	.....	.....	11.50	10.00	2.75
CO4	20c Same, deep violet	.....	.....	14.50	12.00	4.75
CO5	30c Same, rose lake	.....	.....	18.50	15.00	4.75
CO6	40c Same, yellow	.....	.....	19.00	17.00	7.00
CO7	$1 Same, black.	.....	.....	33.00	28.00	10.00

1947 Overprint 19 to 20½mm Long.

SCOTT CAT NO.	DESCRIPTION	PB F/NH	PB F	UNUSED F/NH	UNUSED F	USED F
CO14	6c yellow brown (on#C8)	.....	.....	10.50	9.00	3.75

SCOTT CAT. NO.	DESCRIPTION	UNUSED NH		UNUSED		USED	
		F	AVG	F	AVG	F	AVG

POSTAGE DUE STAMPS
1914
U.S. Postage Due Stamps J45-46, 49 overprinted

CANAL ZONE

J1	1c rose carmine	110.00	90.00	80.00	60.00	18.50	13.75
J2	2c rose carmine	275.00	225.00	210.00	160.00	60.00	45.00
J3	10c rose carmine	800.00	625.00	600.00	425.00	60.00	45.00

1924 Type I overprint on U.S. Postage Due Stamps J61-62, 65

J12	1c carmine rose	190.00	150.00	150.00	110.00	30.00	22.50
J13	2c deep claret	115.00	90.00	90.00	65.00	14.00	10.00
J14	10c deep claret	410.00	310.00	325.00	225.00	60.00	45.00

1925
Canal Zone Stamps 71,73,75 overprinted

POSTAGE DUE

J15	1c deep green	130.00	100.00	105.00	75.00	17.00	12.00
J16	2c carmine	45.00	35.00	35.00	25.00	6.50	4.75
J17	10c orange	50.00	40.00	40.00	30.00	11.00	8.75

1925 Type II overprint on U.S. Postage Due Stamps J61-62, 65

J18	1c deep claret	14.00	11.00	11.00	8.00	3.50	2.75
J19	2c deep claret	27.00	20.00	22.00	15.00	4.50	3.40
J20	10c deep claret	180.00	140.00	140.00	100.00	20.00	15.00

POSTAGE DUE

-1-

1929-30
107 surcharged

J21	1c on 5c blue	3.00	2.50	2.50	2.00	2.20	1.75
J22	2c on 5c blue	6.00	5.00	5.00	4.00	3.00	2.25
J23	5c on 5c blue	6.00	5.00	5.00	4.00	3.25	2.50
J24	10c on 5c blue	6.00	5.00	5.00	4.00	3.25	2.50

J25-J29

1932-41

J25-29	1c -15c cpl., 5 Vars.	4.10	3.50	3.35	2.75	2.60	2.35
J25	1c claret	.25	.20	.20	.16	.19	.15
J26	2c claret	.35	.30	.30	.25	.25	.20
J27	5c claret	.60	.50	.50	.40	.35	.30
J28	10c claret	1.60	1.40	1.35	1.10	1.25	1.00
J29	15c claret	1.55	1.35	1.25	1.00	1.10	.85

OFFICIAL STAMPS
1941
105,117,107,108,111,112, 114,139 overprinted "PANAMA" 10mm Long

OFFICIAL PANAMA CANAL

OFFICIAL PANAMA CANAL

		UNUSED		USED
		F/NH	F	F
O1/9	1c -50c (O1-2, 4-7, 9) 7 Vars	65.95	55.00	18.50
O1	1c yellow green	1.45	1.25	.40
O2	3c deep violet	3.00	2.50	.70
O3	5c blue	. . . . .	. . . . .	30.00
O4	10c orange	5.00	4.25	1.75
O5	15c gray	8.75	7.50	2.00
O6	20c olive brown	9.50	8.00	2.50
O7	50c rose lilac	35.00	30.00	7.50

1947

O9	5c deep blue	6.00	5.00	4.25

SCOTT CAT NO.	DESCRIPTION	UNUSED O.G. F	AVG	UNUSED F	AVG	USED F	AVG

CONFEDERATE STATES

1, 4
Jefferson Davis

2, 5
Thomas Jefferson

3
Andrew Jackson

6, 7
Jefferson Davis

6: Fine print
7: Coarse print

1861

1	5c green	310.00	245.00	240.00	175.00	150.00	110.00
2	10c blue	390.00	315.00	300.00	225.00	225.00	165.00

1862

3	2c green	975.00	775.00	750.00	550.00	925.00	650.00
4	5c blue	210.00	175.00	160.00	125.00	145.00	110.00
5	10c rose	1450.00	1150.00	1150.00	850.00	800.00	600.00
6	5c blue, London print	25.00	20.00	20.00	15.00	21.00	16.50
7	5c blue, Local print	31.50	25.00	24.00	18.00	27.50	20.00

8
Andrew Jackson

9

10, 11 (Die A)
Jefferson Davis

12 (Die B)

13
George Washington

14
John C. Calhoun

1863

8	2c brown red	110.00	85.00	85.00	60.00	325.00	240.00
9	10c blue(TEN)	1350.00	1050.00	1050.00	750.00	800.00	600.00
10	10c blue (with frame line)	5650.00	4450.00	4450.00	3200.00	2400.00	1600.00
11	10c blue (no frame)	25.00	20.00	20.00	15.00	22.00	16.00
12	10c blue, filled corner	27.50	22.00	21.50	16.00	23.00	17.00
13	20c green	75.00	60.00	60.00	45.00	350.00	265.00

1862

14	1c orange	245.00	195.00	190.00	140.00	. . . . .	. . . . .

CUBA
U.S. Administration

1899

**U.S. Stamps of
267,279,279B,
268,281,282C surcharged**

221	1c on 1c yellow green	8.75	7.00	6.75	5.00	.90	.65
222	2c on 2c carmine	8.75	7.00	6.75	5.00	.85	.60
223	2½c on 2c red	7.00	5.50	5.50	4.00	.90	.65
224	3c on 3c purple	19.50	14.00	14.00	10.00	2.75	1.75
225	5c on 5c blue	19.50	14.00	14.00	10.00	2.75	1.75
226	10c on 10c brown	48.50	38.50	36.50	27.50	12.00	8.50

SCOTT CAT NO.	DESCRIPTION	UNUSED O.G.		UNUSED		USED	
		F	AVG	F	AVG	F	AVG

Republic under U.S. Military Rule
Watermarked US-C

227	1c Columbus	5.00	4.25	4.25	3.25	.35	.25
228	2c Coconut Palms	5.00	4.25	4.25	3.25	.35	.25
229	3c Allegory,"Cuba"	5.00	4.25	4.25	3.25	.50	.40
230	5c Ocean Liner	8.75	7.00	6.75	5.00	.55	.45
231	10c Cane Field	25.00	20.00	19.00	14.00	1.25	.85

1902
229 Surcharged

HABILITADO
UN CENTAVO **1** OCTUBRE 1902

232	1c on 3c purple	3.95	3.15	3.45	2.65	1.30	.85

SPECIAL DELIVERY

1899; Surcharge of 1899 on U.S. E5

E1	10c on 10c blue	200.00	150.00	160.00	110.00	125.00	85.00

Republic under U.S. Military Rule
Watermarked US-C inscribed "Immediate"

E2
Special Delivery Messenger

E2	10c orange	80.00	60.00	65.00	45.00	18.50	13.50

POSTAGE DUE STAMPS   1899; Surcharge of 1899 on U.S. J38-39, J41-42

J1	1c on 1c deep claret	45.00	35.00	35.00	25.00	6.50	5.00
J2	2c on 2c deep claret	45.00	35.00	35.00	25.00	6.50	5.00
J3	5c on 5c deep claret	45.00	35.00	35.00	25.00	5.50	4.00
J4	10c on 10c deep claret	45.00	35.00	35.00	25.00	3.25	2.00

GUAM

1899

U.S. Stamps of 279,
267,268,272,280-82C,
284,275,276 overprinted

GUAM

1	1c deep green	50.00	38.00	44.00	32.50	40.00	30.00
2	2c carmine	50.00	38.00	44.00	32.50	40.00	30.00
3	3c purple	225.00	165.00	200.00	140.00	.....	.....
4	4c lilac brown	225.00	165.00	200.00	140.00	.....	.....
5	5c blue	65.00	52.50	60.00	45.00	.....	.....
6	6c lake	200.00	150.00	180.00	130.00	200.00	140.00
7	8c violet brown	180.00	140.00	160.00	125.00	.....	.....
8	10c brown (Type II)	105.00	78.50	92.50	67.50	.....	.....
10	15c olive green	225.00	165.00	195.00	140.00	.....	.....
11	50c orange	405.00	295.00	345.00	250.00	400.00	300.00
12	$1 black(Type II)	600.00	480.00	525.00	400.00	675.00	500.00

SPECIAL DELIVERY

1899

U.S. Stamp E5 overprinted   GUAM

E1	10c blue	275.00	215.00	215.00	160.00	.....	.....

SCOTT CAT NO.	DESCRIPTION	UNUSED O.G. F	AVG	UNUSED F	AVG	USED F	AVG

23, 24

HAWAII

25, 26

1864. Laid Paper

23	1c black	285.00	215.00	230.00	165.00	......	......
24	2c black	285.00	215.00	230.00	165.00	......	......

1865. Wove Paper

25	1c blue	285.00	215.00	230.00	165.00	......	......
26	2c blue	265.00	195.00	200.00	140.00	......	......

27-29, 50, 51
King Kamehameha IV

30
Princess Kamamalu

31
King Kamehameha IV

32, 39, 52C

33
King Kamehameha V

34
Mataia Kekuanaoa

1861-63

27	2c car. rose, horiz. laid paper	325.00	245.00	270.00	190.00	170.00	120.00
28	2c car. rose, vert. laid paper	325.00	245.00	270.00	190.00	170.00	120.00

1869. Engraved

29	2c red	105.00	85.00	85.00	65.00	......	......

1864-71

30	1c purple	15.00	12.00	13.00	10.00	12.75	10.00
31	2c vermilion	18.50	14.75	16.25	12.25	9.00	7.00
32	5c blue	105.00	85.00	85.00	65.00	30.00	22.50
33	6c green	38.50	30.00	33.00	25.00	11.00	8.50
34	18c rose	125.00	105.00	110.00	90.00	25.00	20.00

35, 38, 43
King
David Kalakaua

36, 46
Prince William
Pitt Leleiohoku

37, 42
Princess
Likeliko

40, 44, 45
King
David Kalakaua

1875

35	2c brown	11.50	9.50	9.50	7.50	3.75	2.75
36	12c black	77.50	60.00	68.50	48.50	38.50	28.50

41
Queen
Kapiolani

1882

47
Statue of King
Kamehameha I

48
King
William Lunalilo

49
Queen Emma
Kaleleonalani

52
Queen Liliuokalani

1882

37	1c blue	8.50	6.50	7.25	5.50	6.50	5.00
38	2c lilac rose	150.00	110.00	130.00	90.00	57.50	45.00
39	5c ultramarine	27.00	21.50	22.50	17.50	4.25	3.25
40	10c black	42.50	35.00	38.00	30.00	26.50	21.00
41	15c red brown	75.00	60.00	65.00	50.00	46.50	27.50

1883-84

42	1c green	4.00	3.25	3.50	2.75	2.65	2.15
43	2c rose	6.25	4.95	5.25	3.95	1.85	1.50
44	10c red brown	33.50	27.00	29.00	22.00	10.00	8.00

SCOTT CAT NO.	DESCRIPTION	UNUSED O.G. F	AVG	UNUSED F	AVG	USED F	AVG
45	10c vermilion	37.00	30.00	31.00	24.50	26.50	21.00
46	12c red lilac	115.00	95.00	100.00	80.00	55.00	40.00
47	25c dark violet	145.00	120.00	125.00	100.00	70.00	50.00
48	50c red	260.00	180.00	225.00	150.00	110.00	85.00
49	$1 rose red	350.00	280.00	300.00	225.00	120.00	95.00
		1890-91					
52	2c dull violet	6.50	5.25	5.75	4.25	2.35	1.75
52C	5c dark blue	160.00	125.00	130.00	95.00	115.00	85.00
	1893. Provisional Government. Red Overprint						
53	1c purple	8.25	5.00	5.50	4.25	5.25	3.75
54	1c blue	8.25	5.00	5.50	4.25	5.25	3.75
55	1c green	2.25	1.80	2.40	1.65	2.25	1.65
56	2c brown	9.75	7.95	8.75	6.95	10.50	7.50
57	2c dull violet	2.50	1.95	2.10	1.65	2.50	1.95
58	5c dark blue	12.50	10.50	11.00	9.00	14.00	11.00
59	5c ultramarine	8.00	6.50	7.00	5.50	7.00	5.50
60	6c green	15.50	12.50	14.00	11.00	16.75	13.00
61	10c black	11.25	9.25	10.00	8.00	8.25	6.25
62	12c black	11.50	9.25	10.25	8.00	10.25	8.00
63	12c red lilac	205.00	175.00	155.00	125.00	175.00	135.00
64	25c dark violet	41.50	34.00	36.50	30.00	28.50	22.00
	Black Overprint						
65	2c vermilion	80.00	65.00	70.00	55.00	57.50	45.00
66	2c rose	2.50	2.10	2.35	1.95	2.50	1.95
67	10c vermilion	17.25	13.75	15.00	12.00	28.50	22.50
68	10c red brown	9.00	7.25	8.00	6.25	8.50	6.25
69	12c red lilac	325.00	265.00	285.00	225.00	325.00	250.00
70	15c red brown	29.50	23.50	26.00	20.00	28.50	22.00
71	18c dull rose	33.00	26.00	29.50	22.50	40.00	31.50
72	50c red	75.00	60.00	67.50	55.00	67.50	55.00
73	$1 rose red	145.00	120.00	135.00	105.00	130.00	100.00

74, 80
Coat of Arms

75, 81
View of Honolulu

76
Statue of King
Kamehameha I

77
Star and Palm

78
S.S. "Arawa"

79
Pres. S.B. Dole

82
Statue of King
Kamehameha I

O1-6
Lorrin A. Thurston

		1894					
74	1c yellow	3.45	2.75	3.00	2.25	1.90	1.40
75	2c brown	3.65	2.90	3.20	2.50	1.30	1.15
76	5c rose lake	6.20	4.90	5.95	4.20	3.10	2.50
77	10c yellow green	7.25	5.75	6.50	5.00	7.25	5.75
78	12c blue	20.00	15.50	17.00	13.00	11.25	9.50
79	25c deep blue	21.00	16.50	18.50	14.00	18.00	14.00
		1899					
80	1c dark green	2.65	2.15	2.45	1.90	2.00	1.50
81	2c rose	2.85	2.25	2.60	2.00	1.90	1.50
82	5c blue	7.00	5.75	6.85	5.25	5.00	4.00
	1896. OFFICIAL STAMPS						
O1	2c green	40.00	30.00	35.00	25.00	24.50	18.00
O2	5c black brown	40.00	30.00	35.00	25.00	24.50	18.00
O3	6c deep ultramarine	40.00	30.00	35.00	25.00	24.50	18.00
O4	10c rose	40.00	30.00	35.00	25.00	24.50	18.00
O5	12c orange	40.00	30.00	35.00	25.00	24.50	18.00
O6	25c gray violet	40.00	30.00	35.00	25.00	24.50	18.00

REPUBLIC OF PALAU

Palau is a Strategic Trust of the United States; a designation granted by the United Nations after World War II. It is the first Trust Territory to be granted postal independence, which became effective November 1, 1982. The first stamps were issued March 10, 1983.

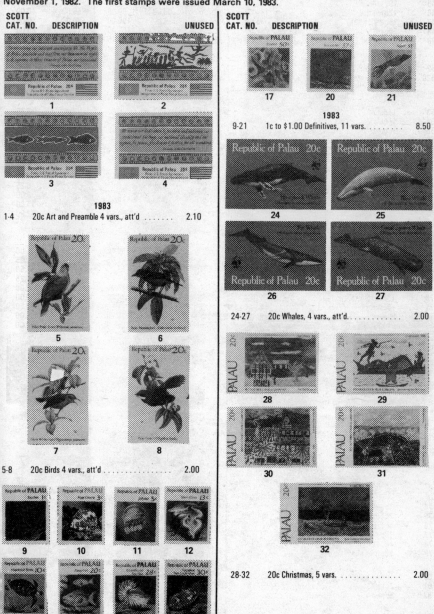

SCOTT CAT. NO.	DESCRIPTION	UNUSED

1983

1-4   20c Art and Preamble 4 vars., att'd 2.10

5-8   20c Birds 4 vars., att'd 2.00

1983

9-21   1c to $1.00 Definitives, 11 vars. 8.50

24-27   20c Whales, 4 vars., att'd............ 2.00

28-32   20c Christmas, 5 vars. 2.00

SCOTT CAT. NO.	DESCRIPTION	UNUSED

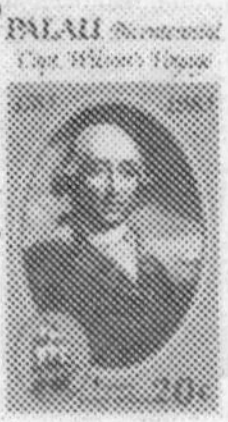

33

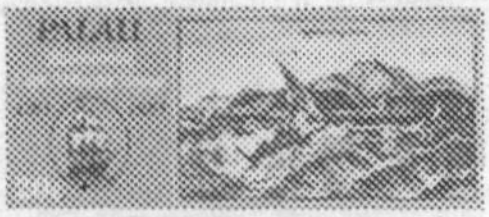

34

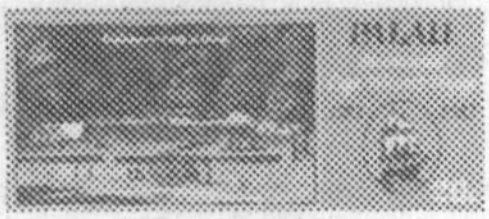

35

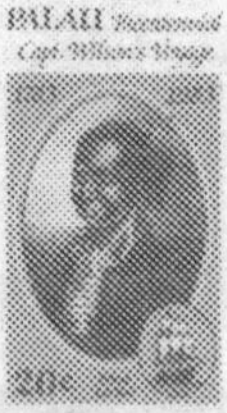

36

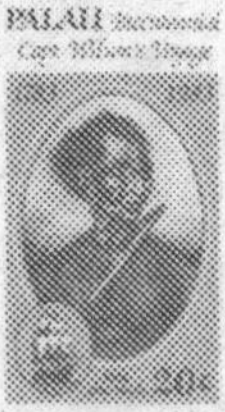

37

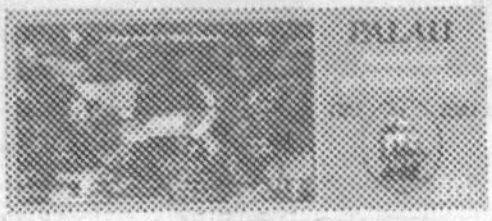

38

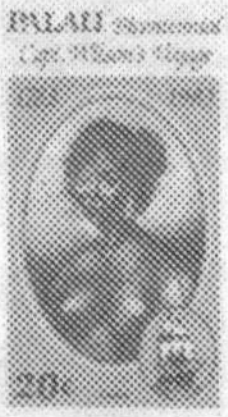

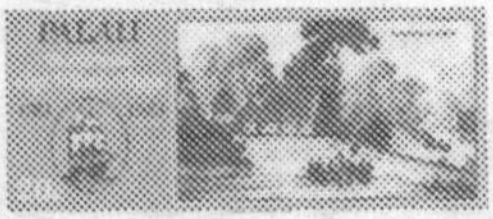

39

40

1984

33-40	20c When Different Worlds Meet, 8 vars., att'd	4.00

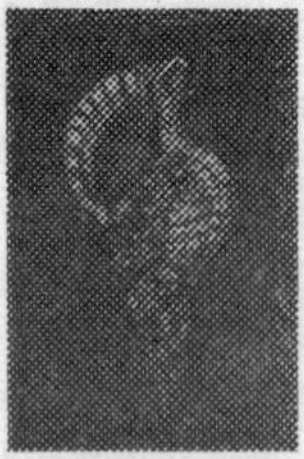

SCOTT CAT. NO.	DESCRIPTION	UNUSED

41

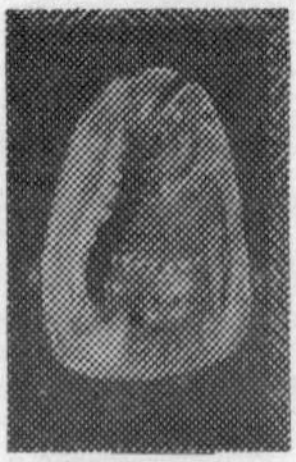

42

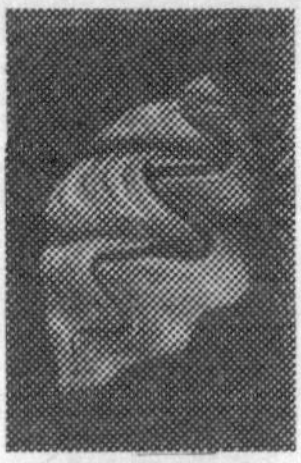

43

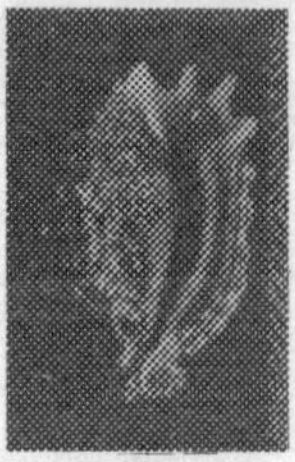

44

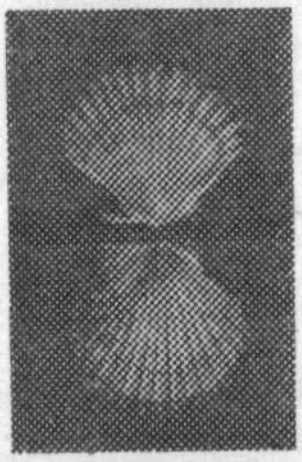

45

46

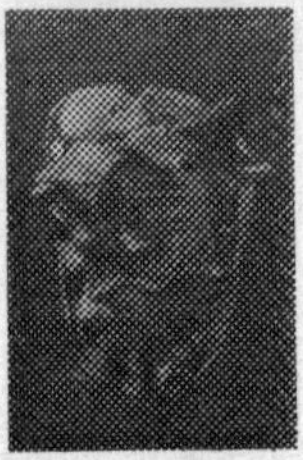

47

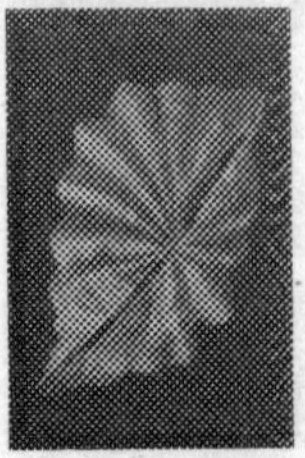

48

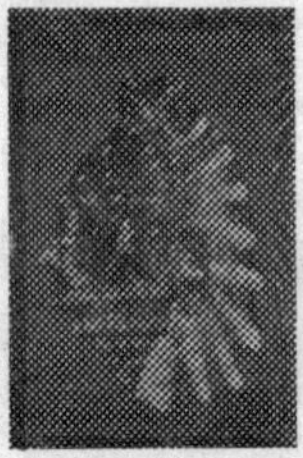

49

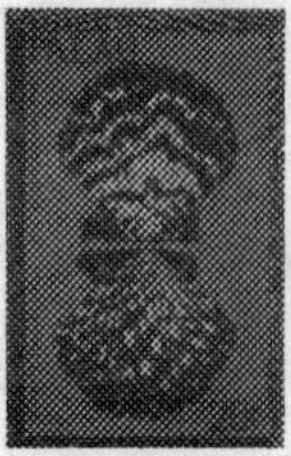

50

41-50	20c Seashells, 10 vars., att'd	5.00

SCOTT CAT. NO.	DESCRIPTION	UNUSED NH F	AVG	UNUSED F	AVG	USED F	AVG

PHILIPPINES

U.S. Stamps of various
issues overprinted

PHILIPPINES

1899
On 260. Unwatermarked

212	50c orange	625.00	575.00	525.00	375.00	350.00	250.00

On 279, 279d, 267-68, 281, 282C, 283, 284, 275
Double Line Watermark.

213	1c yellow green	6.75	5.00	6.00	4.50	1.65	1.25
214	2c orange red	3.40	2.30	2.60	2.00	.95	.75
215	3c purple	11.00	9.00	8.00	6.00	2.75	2.00
216	5c blue	11.00	9.00	8.00	6.00	2.30	1.80
217	10c brown(Type I)	30.00	23.00	28.00	19.50	7.75	5.75
217A	10c orange brown (Type II)	450.00	350.00	325.00	225.00	52.50	46.50
218	15c olive green	42.50	30.00	37.50	27.50	11.50	8.75
219	50c orange	215.00	175.00	150.00	110.00	57.50	45.00

1901
On 280, 282, 272, 276-78

220	4c orange brown	38.00	30.00	28.00	20.00	6.50	5.00
221	6c lake	39.50	28.50	34.00	25.00	10.50	7.75
222	8c violet brown	41.50	30.00	34.00	25.00	10.75	8.00
223	$1 black (Type I)	700.00	500.00	600.00	425.00	340.00	250.00
223A	$1 black (Type II)	3400.00	2500.00	3000.00	2250.00	1350.00	1000.00
224	$2 dark blue	1250.00	1000.00	900.00	650.00	400.00	300.00
225	$5 dark green	2250.00	1800.00	1700.00	1275.00	1100.00	775.00

1903-04
On 300-313

226	1c blue green	6.25	4.50	5.25	4.00	.75	.60
227	2c carmine	13.00	10.00	10.50	8.50	3.25	2.50
228	3c bright violet	100.00	75.00	80.00	65.00	17.00	12.50
229	4c brown	95.00	75.00	80.00	70.00	26.50	18.50
230	5c blue	20.00	14.75	16.50	13.00	2.50	1.95
231	6c brownish lake	90.00	75.00	83.50	70.00	21.00	15.00
232	8c violet black	60.00	50.00	46.00	35.00	16.50	12.50
233	10c pale red brown	39.00	29.00	32.50	24.50	4.50	3.50
234	13c brown violet	55.00	45.00	45.00	32.50	19.00	15.00
235	15c olive green	100.00	80.00	80.00	60.00	16.00	12.00
236	50c orange	245.00	190.00	190.00	140.00	50.00	40.00
237	$1 black	875.00	700.00	700.00	500.00	330.00	250.00
238	$2 dark blue	2500.00	1900.00	1850.00	1350.00	825.00	650.00
239	$5 dark green	3050.00	2350.00	2300.00	1650.00	1200.00	900.00

On 319

240	2c carmine	10.50	8.25	7.75	5.50	4.00	2.90

241, 261, 276, 285
290, 326, 340
Rizal

242, 262, 277
286, 291, 341
McKinley

243, 263, 278
287, 292, 342,
Magellan

244, 264, 279
287A, 293, 343
Legaspi

245, 265, 280
288, 294, 344
Lawton

246, 255, 266,
295, 345
Lincoln

SCOTT CAT. NO.	DESCRIPTION	UNUSED NH		UNUSED		USED	
		F	AVG	F	AVG	F	AVG

247,256,267 281,289,296 *Sampson*	248,257,268,282 289A,297,347 *Washington*	249,258,269 298,348 *Carriedo*	250,259,270,275 283,289C,299,349 *Franklin*	251-254,260,260A,271-274 284,289D,300-302,304,350-353 *Coat of Arms*

1906. Double line watermark. Perf. 12

SCOTT CAT. NO.	DESCRIPTION	F	AVG	F	AVG	F	AVG
241	2c deep green	.70	.55	.55	.40	.13	.10
242	4c carmine	1.15	1.00	1.00	.80	.13	.10
243	6c violet	3.05	2.45	2.45	1.95	.45	.35
244	8c brown	4.40	3.65	3.50	2.65	1.15	.90
245	10c blue	4.50	3.75	3.60	2.75	.28	.22
246	12c brown lake	7.75	6.25	6.00	4.50	3.50	2.65
247	16c violet black	8.75	7.50	6.25	6.00	.60	.50
248	20c orange brown	10.75	9.25	9.00	7.50	.90	.75
249	26c violet brown	9.25	7.75	7.50	6.00	5.40	4.15
250	30c olive green	9.25	7.75	7.50	6.00	3.00	2.25
251	1p orange	40.00	32.50	30.00	20.00	14.00	11.00
252	2p black	45.00	34.50	35.00	27.50	1.90	1.50
253	4p dark blue	130.00	110.00	115.00	80.00	22.00	17.00
254	10p dark green	295.00	240.00	225.00	175.00	90.00	75.00

1909-13

SCOTT CAT. NO.	DESCRIPTION	F	AVG	F	AVG	F	AVG
255	12c red orange	13.00	10.75	10.25	8.00	5.00	3.75
256	16c olive green	2.85	2.25	2.20	1.65	.65	.50
257	20c yellow	15.50	13.00	12.25	9.50	2.65	2.00
258	26c blue green	3.75	3.00	2.90	2.25	1.65	1.25
259	30c ultramarine	20.00	16.50	16.00	12.00	8.50	7.00
260	1p pale violet	47.50	38.50	36.50	27.50	7.25	5.50
260A	2p violet brown	155.00	115.00	120.00	100.00	3.40	2.50

1911-13. Single line watermark. Perf. 12

SCOTT CAT. NO.	DESCRIPTION	F	AVG	F	AVG	F	AVG
261	2c green	1.15	.95	.85	.70	.19	.15
262	4c carmine lake	6.50	5.25	5.00	3.75	.20	.15
263	6c deep violet	3.00	2.40	2.35	1.75	.19	.15
264	8c brown	12.50	10.50	10.00	8.00	.60	.45
265	10c blue	5.50	4.25	4.25	3.25	.25	.20
266	12c orange	3.75	2.95	3.00	2.25	.70	.55
267	16c olive green	4.25	3.50	3.35	2.50	.33	.25
268	20c yellow	5.00	4.25	4.25	3.50	.40	.30
269	26c blue green	5.25	4.25	4.00	3.00	.55	.40
270	30c ultramarine	6.00	4.75	4.75	3.50	1.25	.95
271	1p pale violet	35.00	28.00	26.50	20.00	1.00	.75
272	2p violet brown	51.50	41.50	39.50	30.00	1.60	1.25
273	4p deep blue	880.00	735.00	700.00	550.00	60.00	50.00
274	10p deep green	285.00	235.00	225.00	175.00	25.00	20.00

1914

SCOTT CAT. NO.	DESCRIPTION	F	AVG	F	AVG	F	AVG
275	30c gray	15.75	12.95	11.50	10.00	.85	.65

1914-23. Perf. 10

SCOTT CAT. NO.	DESCRIPTION	F	AVG	F	AVG	F	AVG
276	2c green	3.25	2.50	2.50	2.00	.27	.20
277	4c carmine	3.25	2.50	2.50	2.00	.27	.20
278	6c light violet	50.00	41.50	40.00	32.50	12.75	10.00
278a	6c deep violet	55.00	45.00	40.00	30.00	7.25	6.00
279	8c brown	45.00	35.00	35.00	25.00	8.75	7.50
280	10c dark blue	40.00	31.50	30.00	22.50	.45	.35
281	16c olive green	90.00	75.00	75.00	60.00	4.35	3.50
282	20c orange	30.00	25.00	25.00	20.00	1.65	1.25
283	30c gray	70.00	57.50	55.00	42.50	3.50	3.00
284	1p pale violet	140.00	110.00	110.00	85.00	3.75	3.25

SCOTT CAT. NO.	DESCRIPTION	UNUSED NH		UNUSED		USED	
		F	AVG	F	AVG	F	AVG

1918-26 Perf. 11.

285	2c green	28.00	20.00	19.00	15.00	3.75	3.00
286	4c carmine	42.50	32.00	30.00	24.50	3.00	2.50
287	6c deep violet	50.00	40.00	38.50	30.00	1.85	1.50
287A	8c light brown	265.00	215.00	225.00	165.00	40.00	35.00
288	10c dark blue	62.50	52.50	50.00	40.00	2.50	2.00
289	16c olive green	130.00	110.00	110.00	87.50	4.95	4.00
289A	20c orange	80.00	65.00	62.50	50.00	11.00	9.00
289C	30c gray	65.00	55.00	52.50	40.00	16.50	14.00
289D	1p pale violet	80.00	65.00	62.50	50.00	13.50	12.50

1917-25. Unwatermarked. Perf. 11.

290	2c yellow green	.30	.25	.25	.20	.10	.07
291	4c carmine	.25	.20	.20	.15	.10	.07
292	6c deep violet	.70	.55	.50	.40	.13	.10
293	8c yellow brown	.65	.55	.45	.35	.20	.15
294	10c deep blue	.45	.35	.35	.25	.13	.10
295	12c red orange	.95	.80	.75	.60	.21	.18
296	16c light olive green	57.50	47.50	47.50	37.50	.21	.18
297	20c orange yellow	.75	.60	.60	.45	.20	.15
298	26c green	1.10	.90	.85	.65	1.15	.95
299	30c gray	.95	.80	.80	.60	.21	.15
300	1p pale violet	50.00	40.00	40.00	30.00	1.60	1.15
301	2p violet brown	45.00	35.00	35.00	25.00	.90	.70
302	4p blue	30.00	25.00	25.00	20.00	.45	.35

303, 346
Dewey

319-325
Legislative Palace

1923-26

303	16c olive bistre	2.45	2.00	1.90	1.40	.30	.25
304	10p deep green	115.00	95.00	99.00	70.00	10.00	8.00

1926

319-25	2c-1p cpl., 7 vars.	70.00	65.00	60.00	55.00	40.00	25.00
319	2c green & black	.90	.80	.75	.65	.70	.60
320	4c carmine & black	1.00	.80	.75	.65	.90	.75
321	16c olive green & black	2.00	1.75	1.50	1.25	1.25	1.00
322	18c light brown & black	2.55	2.30	2.15	1.90	1.10	.90
323	20c orange & black	3.00	2.75	2.50	2.25	2.50	2.25
324	24c gray & black	2.50	2.15	2.00	1.65	1.65	1.45
325	1p rose lilac & black	65.00	60.00	55.00	50.00	35.00	30.00

1928. Coil Stamp. Perf. 11 vertically. Designs of 1917-26.

326	2c green	10.50	9.25	9.25	7.50	8.75	7.75

1925-31 Imperforate

340	2c green	.28	.25	.23	.20	.23	.20
341	4c carmine	.45	.40	.40	.35	.40	.35
342	6c deep violet	3.75	3.25	2.75	2.50	2.75	2.50
343	8c yellow brown	3.00	2.75	2.25	2.00	2.25	2.00
344	10c deep blue	3.75	3.25	2.75	2.50	2.75	2.50
345	12c red orange	5.50	5.00	4.25	3.50	4.25	3.50
346	16c olive bistre	4.25	3.75	3.25	3.00	3.25	3.00
347	20c yellow	4.25	3.75	3.25	3.00	3.25	3.00
348	26c blue green	4.25	3.75	3.25	3.00	3.25	3.00
349	30c gray	4.25	3.75	3.25	3.00	3.25	3.00
350	1p violet	12.50	11.50	10.50	9.50	10.50	9.50
351	2p violet brown	27.50	25.00	21.00	19.50	21.00	19.50
352	4p deep blue	67.50	62.50	55.00	50.00	55.00	50.00
353	10p deep green	215.00	195.00	180.00	165.00	180.00	165.00

SCOTT CAT. NO.	DESCRIPTION	UNUSED NH		UNUSED		USED	
		F	AVG	F	AVG	F	AVG

354

355

356

357*

358

359

360

*Although titled Pagsanjan Falls on the stamp through some error the picture is actually a view of Vernal Falls in Yosemite Park

1932

354	2c Mayon Volcano	1.30	1.20	1.10	.95	.65	.60
355	4c Manila Post Office	1.30	1.20	1.10	.95	.70	.65
356	12c Pier #7, Manila Bay	2.10	1.85	1.75	1.60	1.70	1.55
357	18c Pagsanjan Falls*	45.00	39.00	35.00	30.00	23.00	19.50
358	20c Rice Planting	2.00	1.75	1.75	1.50	1.40	1.25
359	24c Rice Terraces	2.50	2.25	2.25	2.00	1.50	1.35
360	32c Baguio Zigzag	2.50	2.25	2.25	2.00	1.50	1.35

302 surcharged

368	1p on 4p blue	4.00	3.50	3.00	2.75	.70	.65
369	2p on 4p dark blue	9.50	7.75	7.00	6.00	1.15	1.10

380

381

382

1934

380	2c Baseball Players	.90	.75	.70	.60	.35	.30
381	6c Tennis Player	1.00	.85	.75	.60	.85	.75
382	16c Basketball Players	1.50	1.25	1.25	1.00	1.20	1.00

383

384

385

386

387

388

389
390

SCOTT CAT. NO.	DESCRIPTION	UNUSED NH F	AVG	UNUSED F	AVG	USED F	AVG

391

392

393

394

395

396

1935

Scott	Description	NH F	NH AVG	Unused F	Unused AVG	Used F	Used AVG
383	2c Rizal	.13	.10	.11	.08	.10	.07
384	4c Woman & Caraboa	.12	.09	.10	.07	.10	.07
385	6c La Filipina	.33	.30	.25	.20	.13	.10
386	8c Pearl Fishing	.45	.40	.30	.25	.25	.20
387	10c Fort Santiago	.60	.55	.50	.40	.25	.20
388	12c Salt Springs	.45	.40	.35	.30	.30	.25
389	16c Magellen's Landing	.45	.40	.35	.30	.22	.20
390	20c "Juan de la Cruz"	.50	.45	.40	.35	.12	.10
391	26c Rice Terrace	.65	.60	.55	.50	.55	.50
392	30c Blood Compact	.65	.60	.55	.50	.55	.50
393	1p Barasoain Church	3.75	3.50	3.25	3.00	2.25	2.00
394	2p Battle of Manila Bay	7.75	7.00	6.50	6.00	2.25	2.00
395	4p Montalban Gorge	7.75	7.00	6.50	6.00	4.25	4.00
396	5p George Washington	18.50	16.00	14.00	12.00	2.75	2.50

402-404

408-410

397-401
"Temple of Human Progress"

Scott	Description	NH F	NH AVG	Unused F	Unused AVG	Used F	Used AVG
397-401	2c-50c cpl., 5 vars.	3.95	3.35	2.95	2.50	2.45	2.15
397	2c carmine rose	.40	.35	.30	.25	.22	.20
398	6c deep violet	.50	.45	.40	.35	.30	.25
399	16c blue	.60	.55	.45	.40	.35	.30
400	36c yellow green	1.10	.95	.85	.75	.65	.60
401	50c brown	1.45	1.25	1.10	.95	1.10	.95

1936

Scott	Description	NH F	NH AVG	Unused F	Unused AVG	Used F	Used AVG
402	2c Dr. Rizal, yellow brown	.25	.20	.20	.15	.22	.20
403	6c Same, slate blue	.35	.30	.30	.25	.25	.20
404	36c Same, red brown	.95	.90	.85	.75	.85	.75
408	2c Quezon, orange brown	.18	.15	.15	.12	.10	.07
409	6c Same, yellow green	.23	.20	.20	.15	.15	.10
410	12c Same, ultramarine	.40	.35	.30	.25	.30	.25

SEE PAGE X FOR CONDITION DEFINITIONS

SCOTT CAT. NO.	DESCRIPTION	UNUSED NH F	AVG	UNUSED F	AVG	USED F	AVG

1936-37
383-396 overprinted

COMMON-WEALTH   COMMONWEALTH

Scott	Description	NH F	NH AVG	Unused F	Unused AVG	Used F	Used AVG
411-20	2c-30c 10 vars.	6.75	6.15	5.50	5.00	3.65	3.15
411	2c rose	.16	.13	.13	.10	.10	.07
412	4c yellow green	1.30	1.20	1.10	.95	.75	.70
413	6c dark brown	.50	.45	.38	.35	.23	.20
414	8c violet	.60	.55	.50	.45	.45	.40
415	10c rose carmine	.43	.40	.38	.35	.13	.10
416	12c black	.43	.40	.38	.35	.13	.10
417	16c dark blue	.60	.55	.50	.45	.28	.25
418	20c light olive green	1.30	1.20	1.10	1.00	.85	.75
419	26c indigo	1.30	1.20	1.10	.95	.65	.60
420	30c orange red	.55	.50	.45	.40	.23	.20
421	1p orange & black	1.80	1.60	1.45	1.25	.50	.45
422	2p bistre & black	11.00	10.00	9.00	8.00	4.50	4.00
423	4p blue & black	33.50	30.50	27.50	25.00	4.50	4.00
424	5p green & black	4.00	3.75	3.25	3.00	2.25	2.00

425-430
Map of the Islands

431, 432
Coat of Arms

1937

Scott	Description	NH F	NH AVG	Unused F	Unused AVG	Used F	Used AVG
425-30	2c-50c cpl., 6 vars.	4.00	3.60	3.10	2.80	1.65	1.45
425	2c yellow green	.23	.20	.18	.15	.12	.09
426	6c light brown	.36	.33	.28	.25	.15	.12
427	12c sapphire	.38	.35	.33	.30	.15	.12
428	20c deep orange	1.00	.90	.80	.70	.23	.20
429	36c deep violet	1.15	1.00	.90	.80	.65	.60
430	50c carmine	1.25	1.15	1.00	.90	.45	.40
431	10p gray	7.50	6.75	6.25	5.50	3.30	2.95
432	20p henna brown	4.50	4.00	3.50	3.00	2.50	2.25

1938-40
383-396 overprinted
COMMON-WEALTH   COMMONWEALTH

Scott	Description	NH F	NH AVG	Unused F	Unused AVG	Used F	Used AVG
433-42	2c-30c, 10 vars.	5.85	5.25	4.75	4.15	3.15	2.65
433	2c rose	.16	.13	.13	.10	.10	.07
434	4c yellow green	1.00	.90	.80	.70	.70	.60
435	6c dark brown	.26	.23	.23	.20	.13	.10
436	8c violet	.26	.23	.23	.20	.18	.15
437	10c rose carmine	.21	.18	.18	.15	.13	.10
438	12c black	.21	.18	.18	.15	.18	.15
439	16c dark blue	.36	.33	.28	.25	.18	.15
440	20c light olive green	.36	.33	.28	.25	.18	.15
441	26c indigo	.65	.55	.50	.40	.45	.40
442	30c orange red	2.75	2.50	2.25	2.00	1.10	.95
443	1p orange and black	1.35	1.15	1.05	.95	.38	.35
444	2p bistre and black	6.25	5.75	5.50	5.00	1.40	1.25
445	4p blue and black	80.00	75.00	65.00	60.00	65.00	60.00
446	5p green and black	11.00	10.00	9.00	8.00	5.75	5.00

SCOTT CAT. NO.	DESCRIPTION	UNUSED NH F	AVG	UNUSED F	AVG	USED F	AVG
		1939-40 COMMEMORATIVES					
449-60	cpl., 12 vars	6.00	5.40	5.00	4.50	3.35	2.95

1939

384,298, 432 Surcharged
"First Foreign Trade Week, May 21-27, 1939"
and New Values

449	2c on 4c yellow green	.23	.20	.20	.15	.13	.10
450	6c on 26c blue green	.55	.50	.45	.40	.45	.40
451	50c on 20p henna brown	1.70	1.50	1.40	1.25	1.20	1.10

452-454

455-457

458-460

452	2c yellow green	.33	.30	.25	.20	.15	.12
453	6c carmine	.50	.45	.35	.30	.15	.12
454	12c bright blue	.55	.50	.45	.40	.15	.12
455	2c green	.20	.15	.16	.12	.13	.10
456	6c orange	.30	.25	.22	.20	.28	.25
457	12c carmine	.45	.40	.35	.30	.15	.12

1940

458	2c dark orange	.33	.30	.25	.20	.15	.12
459	6c dark green	.50	.45	.35	.30	.35	.30
460	12c purple	.70	.65	.55	.50	.35	.30

461,462

		UNUSED F/NH	F	USED F
		1941 Rotary Press Printing. Perf. 11 x 10½.		
461	2c Jose Rizal	.10	.07	.07
		Flat Plate Printing. Perf. 11.		
462	2c Jose Rizal	.21	.18	.15

This variety was issued only in booklet form; therefore, all copies have one or two straight edges.

FOR SELECTED PHILIPPINES PLATE BLOCKS, SEE NEXT PAGE

1944 Handstamped "VICTORY" overprint in violet.

464	2c apple green (on 461)	3.00	2.50	2.50	
469	6c carmine (on 453)	135.00	125.00	100.00	
473	10c carmine rose (on 415) ..	130.00	110.00	65.00	
480	16c dark blue (on 439)	150.00	130.00	110.00	
481	20c light olive green (on 440)	35.00	30.00	30.00	
482	30c orange red (on 420) ...	200.00	175.00	135.00	
483	30c orange red (on 442) ...	275.00	240.00	140.00	

DON'T FORGET CRYSTAL MOUNT

SELECTED PHILIPPINES PLATE BLOCKS
PLATE BLOCKS OF 4, EXCEPT AS NOTED

SCOTT CAT.NO.	DESCRIPTION	F	UNUSED AVG	SCOTT CAT.NO.	DESCRIPTION	F	UNUSED AVG
	1936 (30%)				**1938-40 (30%)**		
408	2c Pres. Quezon, orange brown (6)	1.20	1.00	438	12c Salt Spring (6)	1.50	1.35
409	6c Same, yellow green (6) ..	1.50	1.35		**1939 (30%)**		
410	12c Same, ultramarine (6) ..	2.85	2.65	452	2c Triumphal Arch, yellow green (6)	3.00	2.75
	1936-37 (30%)			453	6c Same, carmine (6)	3.75	3.50
				454	12c Same, bright blue (6) ..	4.50	4.00
411	2c J. Rizal (6)	1.20	1.00		**1940 (30%)**		
412	4c Woman & Carabao (6) ..	9.00	7.75	460	12c Quezon Taking Oath (6)	5.75	5.00
418	20c "J. de la Cruz"(6)	11.50	10.50		**1941 (20%)**		
	1937 (30%)			461	2c Jose Rizal	1.65	1.50
431	10p Coat of Arms, gray(6) ..	75.00	65.00				

NOTE: For Never Hinged prices, please add the percentage in parentheses to the appropriate condition price.

		UNUSED		USED
		F/NH	F	F
	1945			
	383-390, 392, 393 overprinted in black		**VICTORY** **COMMONWEALTH**	
485-94	2c-1p cpl., 10 vars	6.50	5.25	2.65
485	2c rose	.15	.12	.08
486	4c yellow green	.22	.18	.10
487	6c golden brown	.26	.22	.12
488	8c violet	.40	.35	.35
489	10c rose carmine	.30	.25	.18
490	12c black	.40	.35	.20
491	16c dark blue	.65	.50	.20
492	20c light olive green.....	.65	.50	.15
493	30c orange red	1.35	1.20	1.00
494	1p orange & black	2.50	2.00	.50
	431 & 432 **overprinted**		**VICTORY**	
495	10p gray	60.00	50.00	15.00
496	20p henna brown	52.50	42.50	19.50

497

	1946			
497	2c Jose Rizal	.15	.12	.07

SCOTT CAT. NO.	DESCRIPTION	UNUSED NH		UNUSED		USED	
		F	AVG	F	AVG	F	AVG

AIR POST STAMPS
1926. MADRID - MANILA FLIGHT ISSUE

290-95, 297-99, 301-04
overprinted

Perf. 11

C1	2c green	7.50	6.25	6.00	5.00	5.25	4.00
C2	4c carmine	8.50	7.25	7.00	6.00	6.25	4.75
C3	6c lilac	41.00	33.00	32.00	25.00	13.50	10.00
C4	8c orange brown	41.00	33.00	32.00	25.00	15.00	12.00
C5	10c deep blue	41.00	33.00	32.00	25.00	15.00	12.00
C6	12c red orange	48.00	41.00	38.00	30.00	22.50	18.00
C9	16c olive green	48.00	41.00	38.00	30.00	22.50	17.00
C10	20c orange yellow	48.00	41.00	38.00	30.00	22.50	17.00
C11	26c blue green	48.00	41.00	38.00	30.00	22.50	17.00
C12	30c gray	48.00	41.00	38.00	30.00	22.50	17.00
C13	2p violet brown	550.00	450.00	435.00	330.00	290.00	225.00
C14	4p dark blue	925.00	750.00	725.00	550.00	465.00	350.00
C15	10p deep green	1400.00	1150.00	1100.00	850.00	750.00	575.00

269 overprinted as above
Perf. 12

C16	26c blue green	2800.00	2400.00	2200.00	1700.00	......	

284 overprinted as above
Perf. 10

C17	1p violet	190.00	155.00	145.00	110.00	92.50	70.00

1928. LONDON ORIENT FLIGHT

290-95, 297-99, 303
1917-25 overprinted

Perf. 11

C18	2c green	1.50	1.20	1.10	.85	.80	.60
C19	4c carmine	1.50	1.20	1.10	.85	.95	.75
C20	6c violet	6.00	4.00	4.00	3.00	2.00	2.00
C21	8c orange brown	6.00	4.00	4.00	3.00	2.50	2.50
C22	10c deep blue	6.00	4.00	4.00	3.00	2.50	2.50
C23	12c red orange	7.75	6.50	6.25	5.00	4.00	3.00
C24	16c olive green	7.25	6.00	5.75	4.75	4.00	3.00
C25	20c orange yellow	7.50	6.25	6.00	5.00	4.25	3.00
C26	26c blue green	13.00	10.00	10.00	8.50	9.00	7.00
C27	30c gray	13.00	10.00	10.00	8.50	9.00	7.00

271 overprinted as above
Perf. 12

C28	1p lilac	65.00	50.00	53.50	40.00	53.50	40.00

1932. VON GRONAU ISSUE
354-60 overprinted

C29-35	2c-32c cpl., 7 Vars.	23.50	19.75	18.95	15.50	18.95	15.50

SCOTT CAT. NO.	DESCRIPTION	UNUSED NH		UNUSED		USED	
		F	AVG	F	AVG	F	AVG
C29	2c yellow green	.90	.75	.70	.60	.70	.60
C30	4c rose carmine	.95	.80	.75	.65	.75	.65
C31	12c orange	1.45	1.20	1.20	.95	1.20	.95
C32	18c red orange	7.25	6.25	6.00	5.00	6.00	5.00
C33	20c yellow	4.75	3.90	3.75	3.00	3.75	3.00
C34	24c deep violet	4.75	3.90	3.75	3.00	3.75	3.00
C35	32c olive brown	4.75	3.90	3.75	3.00	3.75	3.00

1922. REIN COMMMEMORATIVE

290-95, 297-99
overprinted

F.REIN
MADRID-MANILA
FLIGHT-1933

C36-45	2c-30 cpl., 10 Vars.	22.75	20.25	17.75	13.95	17.50	13.75
C36	2c green	.90	.75	.70	.60	.70	.60
C37	4c carmine	.95	.80	.75	.65	.75	.65
C38	6c deep violet	1.45	1.20	1.20	.90	1.20	.95
C39	8c orange brown	3.25	2.50	2.50	2.00	2.50	2.00
C40	10c dark blue	3.00	2.25	2.25	1.75	2.00	1.50
C41	12c orange	2.65	2.10	2.00	1.50	2.00	1.50
C42	16c olive green	2.65	2.10	2.00	1.50	2.00	1.50
C43	20c yellow	2.65	2.10	2.00	1.50	2.00	1.50
C44	26c blue green	2.90	2.35	2.25	1.75	2.25	1.75
C45	30c gray	3.65	3.10	3.00	2.50	3.00	2.50

1933
290,355-56, 358-60 overprinted

C46-51	2c -32c cpl., 6 Vars.	4.95	4.25	4.10	3.50	2.75	2.25
C46	2c green	1.15	1.00	.95	.80	.75	.60
C47	4c rose carmine	.21	.18	.18	.15	.19	.16
C48	12c orange	.85	.75	.70	.60	.30	.25
C49	20c yellow	.85	.75	.70	.60	.55	.45
C50	24c deep violet	.95	.85	.80	.70	.55	.45
C51	32c olive brown	1.25	1.10	1.10	.85	.60	.50

1935-39. COMMEMORATIVES

C52-58	cpl., 7 Vars	8.75	7.70	7.35	6.40	6.00	5.15

1935. TRANS-PACIFIC ISSUE
387 & 392 overprinted in gold

P.I.-U.S.
INITIAL FLIGHT

December-1935

C52	10c rose carmine	.65	.55	.50	.45	.50	.45
C53	30c orange red	1.10	.95	.90	.75	.90	.75

1936. MANILA-MADRID ARNACAL FLIGHT

291, 295, 298
Surcharged

MANILA-MADRID
ARNACAL
FLIGHT-1936

2 CENTAVOS 2

SCOTT CAT. NO.	DESCRIPTION	UNUSED NH		UNUSED		USED	
		F	AVG	F	AVG	F	AVG
C54	2c on 4c carmine	.20	.17	.17	.14	.15	.12
C55	6c on 12c red orange	.23	.20	.20	.17	.17	.14
C56	16c on 26c blue green	.70	.60	.60	.50	.45	.35

1939

298 & 431
Surcharged

FIRST
AIR MAIL EXHIBITION
Feb 17 to 19 1939
8 CENTAVO 8

| C57 | 8c on 26c blue green . . . . | 1.40 | 1.25 | 1.15 | 1.00 | .70 | .60 |
| C58 | 1p on 10p gray . . . . | 4.90 | 4.40 | 4.25 | 3.75 | 3.50 | 3.00 |

C59-C62
Moro Vinta & Clipper

		UNUSED			USED
		F/NH		F	F

1941

C59	8c carmine	1.50	1.25	.80
C60	20c blue	1.85	1.60	.65
C61	60c blue green	2.65	2.20	1.10
C62	21p sepia	1.25	1.10	.75

1944
C47 Handstamped "VICTORY"
overprint in violet

| C63 | 4c rose carmine . . . . | . . . . . | . . . . . | 1000.00 |

		UNUSED NH		UNUSED		USED	
		F	AVG	F	AVG	F	AVG

SPECIAL DELIVERY STAMPS

1901
U.S. E5 Surcharged *PHILIPPINES*

| E1 | 10c dark blue . . . . | 180.00 | 155.00 | 145.00 | 120.00 | 165.00 | 135.00 |

E2-E6
Special Delivery Messenger

1906 Double Line Watermark. Perf 12

| E2 | 20c deep ultramarine . . . . | 42.50 | 35.00 | 32.50 | 25.00 | 10.50 | 8.25 |

1911 Single Line Watermark. Perf.12

| E3 | 20c deep ultramarine . . . . | 30.00 | 26.50 | 25.00 | 20.00 | 3.00 | 2.65 |

1916 Single Line Watermark. Perf. 10

| E4 | 20c deep utlramarine . . . . | 200.00 | 175.00 | 155.00 | 130.00 | 45.00 | 38.50 |

1919 Unwatermarked. Perf. 11

| E5 | 20c ultramarine . . . . | 1.10 | .90 | .80 | .60 | .50 | .40 |

1925-31 Imperforate

| E6 | 20c dull violet . . . . | 23.00 | 20.00 | 17.50 | 15.00 | 17.50 | 15.00 |

SCOTT CAT. NO.	DESCRIPTION	UNUSED NH		UNUSED		USED	
		F	AVG	F	AVG	F	AVG

E5 overprinted   COMMONWEALTH

1939

| E7 | 20c blue violet .... | .75 | .65 | .60 | .50 | .60 | .50 |

1944. E7 Handstamped "VICTORY" overprint in violet

| E9 | 20c blue violet .... | 275.00 | ..... | 240.00 | ..... | 175.00 | ..... |

1945. "VICTORY" E7 overprinted in black

| E10 | 20c blue violet .... | 1.10 | ..... | 1.00 | ..... | .95 | ..... |

OFFICIAL SPECIAL DELIVERY STAMP

E5 overprinted   **O. B.**
1931

| E01 | 20c dull violet .... | 1.30 | 1.15 | 1.05 | .90 | .90 | .70 |

		UNUSED O.G.		UNUSED		USED	
		F	AVG	F	AVG	F	AVG

POSTAGE DUE STAMPS

1899

U.S. J38-44
overprinted

PHILIPPINES

J1	1c deep claret	5.85	4.65	5.00	4.00	3.00	2.00
J2	2c deep claret	6.75	5.50	6.00	5.00	3.00	2.00
J3	5c deep claret	11.00	8.75	9.75	8.00	4.75	3.50
J4	10c deep claret	20.50	15.00	16.25	14.00	7.75	6.00
J5	50c deep claret	195.00	165.00	190.00	150.00	110.00	85.00

1901

| J6 | 3c deep claret .... | 14.25 | 12.75 | 13.75 | 12.50 | 11.50 | 10.00 |
| J7 | 30c deep claret .... | 225.00 | 200.00 | 215.00 | 175.00 | 115.00 | 100.00 |

J8-J14
Post Office Clerk

SCOTT CAT. NO.	DESCRIPTION	UNUSED NH		UNUSED		USED	
		F	AVG	F	AVG	F	AVG

1928 Perf. 11

SCOTT CAT. NO.	DESCRIPTION	F	AVG	F	AVG	F	AVG
J8-14	4c-20c cpl., 7 Vars.	2.95	2.25	2.25	1.95	2.25	1.95
J8	4c brown red	.28	.25	.23	.20	.23	.20
J9	6c brown red	.45	.35	.35	.30	.35	.30
J10	8c brown red	.45	.35	.35	.30	.35	.30
J11	10c brown red	.45	.35	.35	.30	.35	.30
J12	12c brown red	.45	.35	.35	.30	.35	.30
J13	16c brown red	.50	.40	.40	.35	.40	.35
J14	20c brown red	.45	.35	.35	.30	.35	.30

1937

J8 Surcharged 3 CVOS. 3

SCOTT CAT. NO.	DESCRIPTION	F	AVG	F	AVG	F	AVG
J15	3c on 4c brown red	.45	.35	.35	.30	.20	.15

1944. J8-14 Handstamped "VICTORY" overprint in violet

SCOTT CAT. NO.	DESCRIPTION	F	AVG	F	AVG	F	AVG
J16	4c brown red	150.00	135.00	125.00	110.00	. . . . .	. . . . .
J18	8c brown red	110.00	100.00	97.50	85.00	. . . . .	. . . . .
J20	12c brown red	105.00	90.00	87.50	75.00	. . . . .	. . . . .

OFFICIAL STAMPS

1926

319-20, 322-23 overprinted   OFFICIAL

SCOTT CAT. NO.	DESCRIPTION	F	AVG	F	AVG	F	AVG
O1-4	2c-20c cpl., 4 Vars.	23.95	20.95	19.75	16.75	13.50	11.50
O1	2c green & black	4.00	3.50	3.25	2.75	2.60	2.20
O2	4c carmine & black	4.00	3.50	3.25	2.75	2.65	2.25
O3	18c brown & black	10.00	8.75	8.25	7.00	6.75	5.75
O4	20c orange & black	7.75	6.75	6.25	5.25	2.25	1.95

1931

290-95, 297-99, 303 overprinted   O.B.

SCOTT CAT. NO.	DESCRIPTION	F	AVG	F	AVG	F	AVG
O5-14	2c-30c cpl., 10 Vars.	5.25	4.25	4.00	3.50	2.50	1.95
O5	2c green	.18	.15	.15	.12	.10	.07
O6	4c carmine	.18	.15	.15	.12	.10	.07
O7	6c deep violet	.21	.18	.18	.15	.13	.10
O8	8c yellow brown	.21	.18	.18	.15	.13	.10
O9	10c deep blue	1.00	.90	.80	.70	.18	.15
O10	12c red orange	.60	.50	.45	.40	.30	.25
O11	16c light olive green	.60	.50	.45	.40	.15	.12
O12	20c orange yellow	.75	.65	.60	.50	.15	.12
O13	26c green	.95	.80	.75	.65	.75	.65
O14	30c gray	.75	.65	.60	.50	.60	.50

FOR YOUR CONVENIENCE IN ORDERING, COMPLETE SETS ARE LISTED BEFORE SINGLES

SCOTT CAT. NO.	DESCRIPTION	UNUSED NH		UNUSED		USED	
		F	AVG	F	AVG	F	AVG

1935

383-92 Overprinted O.B.

SCOTT CAT. NO.	DESCRIPTION	UNUSED NH F	AVG	UNUSED F	AVG	USED F	AVG
015-24	2c-30c cpl., 10 Vars.	3.35	2.85	2.85	2.25	2.25	1.75
015	2c rose	.14	.11	.11	.08	.10	.07
016	4c yellow green	.14	.11	.11	.08	.10	.07
017	6c dark brown	.18	.15	.15	.12	.10	.07
018	8c violet	.28	.25	.23	.20	.23	.20
019	10c rose carmine	.25	.22	.21	.18	.10	.07
020	12c black	.32	.28	.28	.25	.19	.16
021	16c dark blue	.32	.28	.28	.25	.23	.20
022	20c light olive green	.32	.28	.28	.25	.21	.18
023	26c indigo	.75	.65	.60	.50	.55	.45
024	30c orange red	.80	.70	.65	.55	.60	.50

1938

383 & 390 Overprinted O.B. COMMON-WEALTH

025	2c rose	.16	.13	.13	.10	.10	.07
026	20c light olive green	1.45	1.25	1.25	1.10	1.00	.85

1938-40
383-92 Overprinted O. B. COMMON-WEALTH | O. B. COMMONWEALTH

SCOTT CAT. NO.	DESCRIPTION	UNUSED NH F	AVG	UNUSED F	AVG	USED F	AVG
027-36	2c-30c cpl., 10 Vars.	4.40	3.65	3.40	2.95	2.95	2.40
027	2c rose	.16	.13	.13	.10	.10	.07
027a	No hypen var.	13.75	12.25	11.50	10.00	7.00	6.25
028	4c yellow green	.21	.18	.17	.13	.13	.10
029	6c dark brown	.35	.30	.30	.25	.10	.07
030	8c violet	.35	.30	.30	.25	.20	.15
031	10c rose carmine	.30	.25	.25	.20	.14	.11
032	12c black	.30	.23	.23	.20	.23	.20
033	16c dark blue	.50	.35	.35	.30	.17	.14
034	20c light olive green	.85	.70	.65	.55	.65	.55
035	26c indigo	.90	.75	.70	.60	.70	.60
036	30c orange red	.85	.70	.65	.55	.65	.55

1941

461 Overprinted

037	2c apple green	.11	.08	.10	.07	.10	.07

1946

497 Overprinted

044	2c sepia	.20	.16	.16	.13	.10	.07

UNUSED PHILIPPINES BOOKLET PANES OF 6

SCOTT CAT.NO.	DESCRIPTION	F/VF
290e	2c yellow green	22.50
291b	4c carmine	16.00
292c	6c violet	175.00
411a	2c rose	3.50
433a	2c rose	3.25
462b	2c apple green	1.65

SCOTT CAT.NO.	DESCRIPTION	UNUSED F/NH	F	USED F

JAPANESE OCCUPATION ISSUES

N1

N2

N3

N4

N5

N6

N7

1942-43

N1	2c apple green	.10	.07	.07
N2	12c black	.23	.12	.20
N3	16c dark blue	4.50	3.75	3.00
N4	5c on 6c brown	.21	.18	.12
N5	16c on 30c orange red . . .	.40	.35	.40
N6	50c on 1p orange & black .	.85	.70	.90
N7	1p on 4p blue & black . . .	75.00	60.00	50.00

N8

N9

N10-N11

1942

N8	2c on 4c yellow green . . .	3.75	3.00	2.50
N9	5c on 4c yellow green . . .	.60	.50	.40

1943

N10	2c on 8c carmine	.45	.40	.40
N11	5c on 1p sepia	.70	.60	.60

N12, N14, N29

N13, N16, N22

N15, N17, N21, N23

N18, N19, N24, N25

1943-44

N12-25	1c-5p cpl., 14 Vars.	11.50	9.50	8.00
N12	1c orange	.10	.07	.07
N13	2c green	10	.07	.07
N14	4c slate green	.10	.07	.07
N15	5c orange brown	.10	.07	.07
N16	6c red	.21	.18	.18
N17	10c blue green	.10	.07	.07

SCOTT CAT. NO.	DESCRIPTION	UNUSED F/NH	F	USED F
N18	12c steel blue	1.10	.90	.90
N19	16c dark brown	.10	.07	.07
N20	20c rose violet	1.15	.95	1.10
N21	21c violet	.45	.40	.40
N22	25c pale brown	.10	.07	.06
N23	1p deep carmine	.35	.30	.30
N24	2p violet	1.90	1.75	1.60
N25	5p dark olive	7.25	6.00	5.00

N26, N27   N28   N29-N31

1943

N26	2c carmine red	.30	.25	.25
N27	5c bright green	.30	.25	.25
N28	12c on 20c olive green	.45	.40	.40

Perf. 12

N29	5c light blue	.23	.20	.20
N30	12c orange	.23	.20	.20
N31	17c rose pink	.23	.20	.20

Imperforate Without Gum

N29a	5c light blue	.24	.21	.20
N30a	12c orange	.24	.21	.20
N31a	17c rose pink	.30	.25	.30

N32   N33   N34   N35-N36   N37-N39

1944. Perf. 12

N32	5c blue	.30	.25	.25
N33	12c carmine	.21	.18	.18
N34	17c deep orange	.21	.18	.18

Imperforate

N32a	5c blue	.30	.25	.25
N33a	12c carmine	.21	.18	.18
N34a	17c deep orange	.21	.18	.18

1944

N35	5c on 20c ultramarine	.65	.60	.60
N36	12c on 60c blue green	1.40	1.20	1.20

1945. Imperforate without Gum

N37	5c violet brown	.10	.07	.07
N38	7c blue green	.14	.11	.09
N39	20c chalky blue	.20	.17	.13

SCOTT CAT. NO.	DESCRIPTION	UNUSED F/NH	F	USED F

SEMI—POSTAL STAMPS

NB1-NB3

NB5-NB7

1942

NB1	2c + 1c pale violet	.25	.21	.21
NB2	5c + 1c bright green	.22	.18	.18
NB3	16c + 2c orange	18.00	15.25	10.50

1943. INDEPENDENCE SOUVENIR SHEET
Stamp designs of N29-31

NB4	5c-17c 3 vars., in 1 Souv. Sheet	21.00	17.50	1.75

1943. FLOOD RELIEF

NB5	12c + 21c blue	.20	.16	.16
NB6	20c + 36c rose	.17	.13	.13
NB7	21c + 40c violet	.20	.16	.16

1944. HEROES SOUVENIR SHEET
Stamp designs of N32-34

NB8	5c-17c 3 vars., in 1 Souv. Sheet	1.50	1.40	1.50

POSTAGE DUE STAMP

NJ1

1942

NJ1	3c on 4c brown red	17.00	15.00	7.50

OFFICIAL STAMPS

NO1

NO2, NO3

NO4

1943-44

NO1	2c apple green	.14	.11	.11
NO2	5c on 6c (on 413)	22.00	17.50	17.50
NO3	5c on 6c (on 435)	.35	.30	.30
NO4	16c on 30c orange red	.60	.50	.50

SEE PAGE X FOR CONDITION DEFINTITIONS

SCOTT CAT. NO.	DESCRIPTION	UNUSED F/NH	F	USED F

NO5

NO6

NO7

1944

N05	5c on 6c golden brown	.15	.12	.12
N06	20c olive green	.50	.40	.40
N07	1p sepia	1.25	1.10	1.15

BUY COMPLETE SETS AND SAVE

SCOTT CAT. NO.	DESCRIPTION	UNUSED OG F	AVG	UNUSED F	AVG	USED F	AVG

PUERTO RICO

1899

U.S. Stamps 279-79B, 281, 272, 282C overprinted

PORTO RICO

210	1c yellow green	10.50	8.00	9.50	7.00	2.75	2.00
211	2c carmine	9.50	7.00	8.50	6.00	2.25	1.65
212	5c blue	12.75	9.50	11.25	8.25	3.75	2.75
213	8c violet brown	45.00	40.00	40.00	30.00	23.50	17.50
214	10c brown (I)	30.00	22.00	28.00	20.00	9.00	6.75

1900
U.S. 279, 279B overprinted

PUERTO RICO

215	1c yellow green	7.85	5.85	6.85	5.00	2.75	2.00
216	2c carmine	7.85	5.85	6.85	5.00	2.75	2.00

POSTAGE DUE STAMPS

1899

U.S. Postage Due Stamps
J38-39, J41 overprinted

PORTO RICO

J1	1c deep claret	28.50	20.50	24.50	17.50	10.25	7.50
J2	2c deep claret	23.00	17.50	20.00	15.00	9.75	7.00
J3	10c deep claret	230.00	170.00	200.00	145.00	90.00	60.00

The Ryukyu Islands were under U.S. administration from April 1, 1945 till May 15, 1972. Prior to the General Issues of 1948 several Provisional Stamps were used.

SCOTT CAT.NO.	DESCRIPTION	UNUSED F/VF	AVG

RYUKYU ISLANDS

1, 1a, 3, 3a

2, 2a, 5, 5a

4, 4a, 6, 6a

7, 7a

1949. Second Printing

White gum & paper; sharp colors; clean perfs.

SCOTT CAT.NO.	DESCRIPTION	UNUSED F/VF	AVG
1-7	5s to 1y 7 Vars. Cpl.	35.50	31.95
1	5s Cycad	3.25	3.00
2	10s Lily	5.00	4.50
3	20s Cycad	5.00	4.50
4	30s Sailing Ship	5.00	4.50
5	40s Lily	3.25	3.00
6	50s Sailing ship	6.75	6.00
7	1y Farmer	9.25	8.50

1948. First Printing

Thick yellow gum; gray paper; dull colors ; rough perfs.

SCOTT CAT.NO.	DESCRIPTION	UNUSED F/VF	AVG
1a-7a	5s to 1y 7 Vars. Cpl.	460.00	400.00
1a	5s Cycad	4.50	4.00
2a	10s Lily	2.25	2.00
3a	20s Cycad	2.25	2.00
4a	30s Sailing Ship	4.75	4.25
5a	40s Lily	82.50	74.50
6a	50s Sailing Ship	3.50	3.00
7a	1y Farmer	385.00	340.00

8

9

10

11

12

13

1950

SCOTT CAT.NO.	DESCRIPTION	UNUSED F/VF	AVG
8-13	50s to 5y; 6 vars. cpl	87.50	79.95
8	50s Tile Roof	.30	.25
9	1y Ryukyu Girl	2.00	1.75
10	2y Shuri Castle	8.75	8.00
11	3y Dragon Head	55.00	52.00
12	4y Women at Beach	14.35	12.85
13	5y Sea Shells	11.25	9.75

NOTE: the 1950 printing of #8 is on toned paper and has yellowish gum. A 1958 printing exhibits white paper and colorless gum.

14

15

1951

SCOTT CAT.NO.	DESCRIPTION	UNUSED F/VF	AVG
14	3y Ryukyu University	55.00	50.00
15	3y Pine Tree	50.00	45.00

16, 16a-b, 17

18

1952

SCOTT CAT.NO.	DESCRIPTION	UNUSED F/VF	AVG
16	10y on 50s (No.8) Type II ..	10.50	9.00
16a	Same, Type I	45.00	42.00
16b	Same, Type III	50.00	45.00
17	100y on 2y (No. 10)	2400.00	2150.00
18	3y Government of Ryukyu ..	120.00	110.00

Type I — Bars are narrow spaced; '10' normal
Type II — Bars are wide spaced; '10' normal
Type III — Bars are wide spaced; '10' wide spaced

All Ryukyu Islands stamps will be UNUSED never hinged. From number 19 onward all issues will be F-VF. Prior to number 19 two grades are available.

SCOTT CAT.NO.	DESCRIPTION	UNUSED F-VF/NH

31   32   33

1954-55

31	4y Pottery	.80
32	15y Lacquerware	3.00
33	20y Textile Design	4.35

19   20   21

22   23   24

25   26

1952-53

19-26	1y to 100y 8 Vars., cpl. . .	38.35
19	1y Mandanbashi Bridge . . .	.25
20	2y Main Hall of Shuri Castle	.40
21	3y Shurei Gate.	.35
22	6y Stone Gate, Soganji Temple	1.95
23	10y Benzaiten do Temple . .	2.25
24	30y Altar at Shuri Castle . .	10.00
25	50y Tamaudun Shuri	10.50
26	100y Stone Bridge, Hosho Pond	15.00

34   35

36   37   38

1955

| 34 | 4y Noguni Shrine & Sweet Potato Plant . . . . | 10.00 |

1956

35	4y Stylized Trees	10.50
36	5y Willow Dance	1.50
37	8y Straw Hat Dance	2.50
38	14y Group Dance	2.75

27   28

39   40

| 39 | 4y Telephone . . . . | 17.95 |
| 40 | 2y Garland of Pine, Bamboo & Plum . . . . | 2.55 |

29   30

1953

27	3y Reception at Shuri Castle	11.00
28	6y Perry and Fleet	.95
29	4y Chofu Ota and Pencil . . .	9.00

1954

| 30 | 4y Shigo Toma & Pen . . . . . | 10.00 |

NOTE: F-VF means that centering will range between Fine & Very Fine

SCOTT CAT.NO.	DESCRIPTION	UNUSED F-VF/NH

41   42

1957

| 41 | 4y Map & Pencil Rocket ... | 1.40 |
| 42 | 2y Phoenix .... | .30 |

43

44-53

54

55

1958

| 43 | 4y Ryukyu Stamps ...... | 1.55 |

| 44-53 | ½c to $1.00, 10 vars., cpl., ungummed .... | 44.95 |

44	½c Yen, Symbol & Denom, orange	.25
45	1c Same, yellow green	.25
46	2c Same, dark blue	.35
47	3c Same, deep carmine	.35
48	4c Same, bright green	.60
49	5c Same, orange	1.50
50	10c Same, aquamarine	5.00
51	25c Same, bright violet blue .	3.50
51a	25c Same, bright violet blue (with gum)	5.00
52	50c Same, gray	18.75
52a	50c Same, gray (with gum) .	7.50
53	$1 Same, rose lilac	17.00

NOTE: Many shades, perf., and paper varieties exist on these issues.

SCOTT CAT.NO.	DESCRIPTION	UNUSED F-VF/NH
54	3c Gate of Courtesy	2.40
55	1½c Lion Dance	.25

56   57

1959

| 56 | 3c Mountains & Trees .... | 1.10 |
| 57 | 3c Yonaguni Moth .... | 1.30 |

58, 76   59, 77   60, 78

61, 79   62, 80   63

| 58-62 | ½c to 17c, 5 vars., cpl.... | 22.95 |

58	½c Hibiscus	.45
59	3c Moorish Idol	.90
60	8c Sea Shell	6.00
61	13c Dead Leaf Butterfly ...	3.50
62	17c Jellyfish	13.50
63	1½c Toy (Yakaji)	.65

64   65, 81

SCOTT CAT.NO.	DESCRIPTION	UNUSED F-VF/NH

66, 82   67, 83   68, 84

1960

| 64 | 3c University Badge | 1.20 |

DANCES II

| 65-68 | 1c-10c 4 vars., cpl. | 5.75 |

65	1c Munsuru	1.25
66	2½c Nufwabushi	2.20
67	5c Hatomabushi	1.15
68	10c Hanafubushi	1.45

72

73

| 72 | 3c Torch & Nago Bay | 6.75 |
| 73 | 8c Runners | 1.00 |

74   75

| 74 | 3c Egret & Sun | 6.00 |
| 75 | 1½c Bull Fight | 1.85 |

REDRAWN INSCRIPTION
1960-61

| 76-80 | ½c to 17c, 5 vars., cpl. | 9.25 |

76	½c Hibiscus	.50
77	3c Moorish Idol	1.10
78	8c Sea Shell	1.45
79	13c Dead Leaf Butterfly	1.45
80	17c Jellyfish	5.25

SCOTT CAT.NO.	DESCRIPTION	UNUSED F-VF/NH

84A   85

86   87

WITH "RYUKYUS" ADDED
1961-64

| 81-87 | 1c to $1.00. 8 vars., cpl. | 18.95 |

81	1c Munsuru	.25
82	2½c Nufwabushi	.35
83	5c Hatomabushi	.50
84	10c Hanafubushi	.85
84A	20c Shundun	1.20
85	25c Hanagasabushi	5.00
86	50c Nubui Kuduchi	5.00
87	$1 Kutubushi	7.00

88

90

89

92   91

1961

88	3c Pine Tree	2.00
89	3c Naha, Steamer & Sailboat	2.85
90	3c White Silver Temple	2.75
91	3c Boooks & Bird	2.75
92	1½c Eagles & Rising Sun	3.50

SCOTT CAT.NO.	DESCRIPTION	UNUSED F-VF/NH

93

94

95

97

96

93	1½c Steps, Trees & Building	1.20
94	3c GRI Building	1.60
95	3c Malaria Eradication	.95
96	8c Eradication Emblem	2.25
97	3c Children's Day	2.75

98

99

100

101

102

98-102	½c to 17c 5 vars., cpl. . . .	2.90
98	½c Sea Hibiscus	.30
99	3c Indian Coral Tree	.40
100	8c Iju	.60
101	13c Touch-Me-Not	.75
102	17c Shell Flower	1.10

DON'T FORGET CRYSTAL MOUNT

SCOTT CAT.NO.	DESCRIPTION	UNUSED F-VF/NH

103

105

104

103	3c Earthenware	6.00
104	3c Japanese Fencing	7.00
105	1½c Bingata Cloth	1.75

106

107

108

109

1963

106	3c Stone Relief	2.00
107	1½c Gooseneck Cactus . . .	.30
108	3c Trees & Hills	1.75
109	3c Map of Okinawa	2.50

110

111

112

113

SCOTT CAT.NO.	DESCRIPTION	UNUSED F-VF/NH
110	3c Hawks & Islands	2.20
111	3c Shioya Bridge	1.50
112	3c Lacquerware Bowl	5.00
113	3c Map of Far East	1.40

(114, 116, 117)

114

114	15c Mamaomoto	.90
115	3c Nakagusuku Castle Site	1.05
116	3c Human Rights	1.10
117	1½c Dragon	.45

118, 119, 120, 120a

121
1964

118	3c Mothers Day	.60
119	3c Agricultural Census	.60
120	3c Minsah Obi, pink	.85
120a	Same, carmine	1.45
121	3c Girl Scout & Emblem	.50

BUY COMPLETE SETS AND SAVE

SCOTT CAT.NO.	DESCRIPTION	UNUSED F-VF/NH

122, 122a   123

122	3c Shuri Relay Station	1.50
122a	3c Same, Inverted "1"	47.50
123	8c Antenna & Map	1.35

124   125
126   127

124	3c Olympic Torch & Emblem	.40
125	3c "Naihanchi"	.85
126	3c "Makiwara"	.80
127	3c "Kumite"	.80

128   129

| 128 | 3c Miyara Dunchi | .45 |
| 129 | 1½c Snake & Iris | .25 |

130   131

SCOTT CAT.NO.	DESCRIPTION	UNUSED F-VF/NH

132

133

1965

130	3c Boy Scouts	.85
131	3c Onoyama Stadium	.40
132	3c Samisen	1.00
133	3c Kin Power Plant	.40

134

135

| 134 | 3c ICY . . . . | .35 |
| 135 | 3c Naha City Hall . . . . | .35 |

136

137

138

139

1965-66

136	3c Chinese Box Turtle	.40
137	3c Hawksbill Turtle	.40
138	3c Asian Terrapin	.40

1965

| 139 | 1½c Horse . . . . | .20 |

BUY COMPLETE SETS
AND SAVE

SCOTT CAT.NO.	DESCRIPTION	UNUSED F-VF/NH

140

141

142

143

1966

140	3c Woodpecker	.25
141	3c Sika Deer	.25
142	3c Dugong	.25
143	3c Swallow	.25

144

146

147

145

144	3c Memorial Day	.25
145	3c University of Ryukyu . . .	.25
146	3c Lacquerware	.25
147	3c UNESCO	.25

148

149

| 148 | 3c Government Museum . . . | .25 |
| 149 | 3c Nakasone T. Genga's Tomb . . . . | .25 |

SCOTT CAT.NO.	DESCRIPTION	UNUSED F-VF/NH	SCOTT CAT.NO.	DESCRIPTION	UNUSED F-V/NH

150

151

152

153

154

155

150	1½c Ram in Iris Wreath . . .	.25

1966-67

151-55	5 Vars., cpl.	1.35
151	3c Clown Fish	.30
152	3c Young Boxfish	.30
153	3c Forceps Fish	.30
154	3c Spotted Triggerfish	.30
155	3c Saddleback Butterflyfish .	.30

156

157

158

159

160

161

1966

156	3c Tsuboya Urn	.30

1967-68

157-61	5 vars., cpl.	1.65
157	3c Episcopal Miter	.30
158	3c Venus Comb Murex	.30
159	3c Chiragra Spider	.30
160	3c Green Turban	.30
161	3c Euprotomus Bulla	.60

162

165

163

164

166

1967

162	3c Roofs & ITY Emblem . . .	.30
163	3c Mobile TB Clinic	.30
164	3c Hoja Bridge	.30
165	1½c Monkey	.25
166	3c TV Tower & Map	.25

SCOTT CAT.NO.	DESCRIPTION	UNUSED F-VF/NH

167

169

170

168

171

1968

167	3c Dr. Nakachi & Helper . . .	.30
168	3c Pill Box	.70
169	3c Man, Library, Book & Map	.45
170	3c Mailmen's Uniforms & 1948 Stamp	.45
171	3c Main Gate-Enkaku Temple	.75

172

173

174

175

176

177

172	3c Old Man's Dance	.45

SCOTT CAT.NO.	DESCRIPTION	UNUSED F-VF/NH

1968-69

173-77	5 vars., cpl.	4.40
173	3c Mictyris Longicarpus . . .	1.15
174	3c Uca Dubia Stimpson	.80
175	3c Baptozius Vinosus	.80
176	3c Cardisoma Carnifex	.95
177	3c Ocypode	.95

178

179

180

1968

178	3c Saraswati Pavilon	.65
179	3c Tennis Player	.60
180	1½c Cock & Iris	.20

181

182

183

184

1969

181	3c Boxer	.60
182	3c Ink Slab Screen	.70
183	3c Antennas & Map	.25
184	3c Gate of Courtesy & Emblems	.35

SCOTT CAT.NO.	DESCRIPTION	UNUSED F-VF/NH

185

186

187

188

189

1969-70

185-89	5 vars., cpl.	3.50
185	3c Tug of War Festival	.60
186	3c Hari Boat Race	.60
187	3c Izaiho Ceremony	.60
188	3c Mortardrum Dance	1.10
189	3c Sea God Dance	1.10

琉球郵便 ½c

[overprint]

190

191

192

193

SCOTT CAT.NO.	DESCRIPTION	UNUSED F-VF/NH

1969

190	½c on 3c (no.99) Indian Coral Tree	.25
191	3c Nakamura-Ke Farm House	.35
192	3c Statue & Maps	.45
193	1½c Dog & Flowers	.25

194

195, 195a

196, 196a

197, 197a

198, 198a

199, 199a

1970

194	3c Sake Flask	.75

195-99	5 vars., cpl.	3.50
195	3c "The Bell"	.75
196	3c Child & Kidnapper	.75
197	3c Robe of Feathers	.75
198	3c Vengeance of Two Sons	.75
199	3c Virgin & The Dragon	.75

195a-99a	5 vars., cpl., Sheets of 4	30.00
195a	3c Sheet of 4	6.35
196a	3c Sheet of 4	6.35
197a	3c Sheet of 4	6.35
198a	3c Sheet of 4	6.35
199a	3c Sheet of 4	6.35

200

201

SCOTT CAT.NO.	DESCRIPTION	UNUSED F-V/NH

202

203

| 200 | 3c Underwater Observatory | .75 |

1970-71

201	3c Noboru Jahana	.75
202	3c Saion Gushichan Bunjaku	2.00
203	3c Choho Giwan	.75

204

205

206

207

1970

204	3c Map & People	.45
205	3c Great Cycad of Une	.60
206	3c Flag, Diet & Map	1.10
207	1½c Boar & Cherry Blossoms	.30

208

209

210

211

SCOTT CAT.NO.	DESCRIPTION	UNUSED F-VF/NH

212

213

1971

208-12	5 Vars., cpl.	3.35
208	3c Low Hand Loom	.40
209	3c Filature	.40
210	3c Raincoat & Hat	.75
211	3c Rice Huller	1.25
212	3c Box & Scoop	.75
213	3c Water Carrier	.60

214

215

216

214	3c Old & New Naha	.50
215	2c Pinia Pulcherrima	.25
216	3c Madder	.25

217

218

219

1971-72

217	3c View from Mabuni Hill . .	.65
218	3c Mt. Arashi from Haneji Sea	.65
219	4c Yabuchi Is. from Yakena Port	.65

SCOTT CAT.NO.	DESCRIPTION	UNUSED F-VF/NH

1971

220	4c Dancer	.20
221	4c Deva King	.25
222	2c Rat & Chrysanthemums	.20
223	4c Student Nurse	.35

1972

224	5c Birds & Seashore	.60
225	5c Coral Reef	.60
226	5c Sun Over Islands	.60
227	5c Dove & Flags	1.15
228	5c Antique Sake Pot	1.00

SCOTT CAT.NO.	DESCRIPTION	UNUSED F-VF/NH

AIR MAIL STAMPS

1950

C1	8y Dove & Map, bright blue	80.00
C2	12y Same, green	27.50
C3	16y Same, rose carmine	25.00

1951-54

| C4-8 | 13y to 50y, 5 Vars, cpl. | 30.50 |

C4	13y Heavenly Maiden, blue	2.75
C5	18y Same, green	3.75
C6	30y Same, cerise	5.00
C7	40y Same, red violet	8.25
C8	50y Same, yellow orange	12.50

1957

| C9-13 | 15y to 60y 5 Vars., cpl. | 58.95 |

C9	15y Maiden Playing Flute, blue green	2.00
C10	20y Same, rose carmine	4.25
C11	35y Same, yellow green	13.00
C12	45y Same, reddish brown	18.00
C13	60y Same, gray	25.00

1959

| C14-18 | 9c to 35c, 5 Vars., cpl. | 39.95 |

C14	9c on 15y (no. C9)	2.00
C15	14c on 20y (no. C10)	2.50
C16	19c on 35y (no. C11)	5.75
C17	27c on 45y (no. C12)	14.00
C18	35c on 60y (no.C13)	18.50

改訂 ═══

[overprint]

9¢

C19-23   C24

SCOTT CAT.NO.	DESCRIPTION	UNUSED F-VF/NH

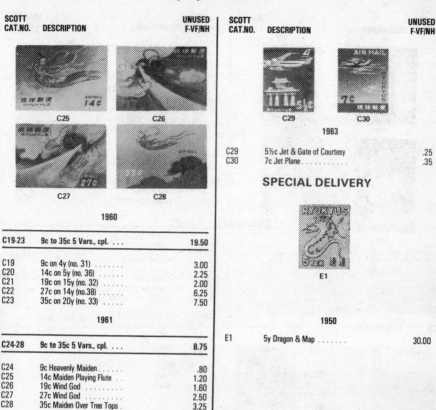

C25   C26

C27   C28

1960

C19-23	9c to 35c 5 Vars., cpl. ...	19.50
C19	9c on 4y (no. 31)	3.00
C20	14c on 5y (no. 36)	2.25
C21	19c on 15y (no. 32)	2.00
C22	27c on 14y (no.38)	6.25
C23	35c on 20y (no. 33)	7.50

1961

C24-28	9c to 35c 5 Vars., cpl. ...	8.75
C24	9c Heavenly Maiden	.80
C25	14c Maiden Playing Flute	1.20
C26	19c Wind God	1.60
C27	27c Wind God	2.50
C28	35c Maiden Over Tree Tops	3.25

SCOTT CAT.NO.	DESCRIPTION	UNUSED F-VF/NH

C29   C30

1963

C29	5½c Jet & Gate of Courtesy	.25
C30	7c Jet Plane	.35

SPECIAL DELIVERY

E1

1950

E1	5y Dragon & Map	30.00

SPECIAL OFFER!

50 Unused Ryukyu Island Issues

A terrific starter set of these colorful issues including many of the New Year's Issues, the **1964** Olympic Torch stamp, and the 3c Karate Issue all at more than 10% off individual prices.

A619 .... **Special Price $20.95**

SCOTT CAT NO.	DESCRIPTION	UNUSED OG		UNUSED		USED	
		F	AVG	F	AVG	F	AVG

1,2   3,5   4,6

Queen Victoria

1861. Perf. 14

| 2 | 2½p dull rose | 475.00 | 375.00 | 350.00 | 250.00 | 225.00 | 150.00 |

VANCOUVER ISLAND

1865. Imperforate.

| 4 | 10c blue | ..... | ..... | ..... | ..... | 1025.00 | 725.00 |

Perf. 14

| 5 | 5c rose | 425.00 | 325.00 | 340.00 | 240.00 | 215.00 | 150.00 |
| 6 | 10c blue | 425.00 | 325.00 | 340.00 | 240.00 | 215.00 | 150.00 |

7   8-18

Seal

BRITISH COLUMBIA

1865.

| 7 | 3p blue | 150.00 | 120.00 | 120.00 | 90.00 | 95.00 | 75.00 |

New Values Surcharged on 1865 design
1867-69 Perf. 14

8	2c brown	165.00	125.00	135.00	90.00	120.00	90.00
9	5c bright red	190.00	150.00	150.00	100.00	150.00	100.00
10	10c lilac rose	1625.00	1250.00	1250.00	950.00	.....	.....
11	25c orange	230.00	180.00	175.00	125.00	185.00	125.00
12	50c violet	800.00	650.00	575.00	425.00	.....	.....
13	$1 green	1350.00	1050.00	995.00	700.00	.....	.....

1869 Perf. 12½

14	5c bright red	1225.00	965.00	985.00	700.00	985.00	700.00
15	10c lilac rose	900.00	700.00	700.00	500.00	615.00	415.00
16	25c orange	875.00	600.00	575.00	400.00	445.00	320.00
17	50c violet	900.00	700.00	700.00	500.00	445.00	320.00
18	$1 green	1345.00	1045.00	1045.00	695.00	1100.00	800.00

CANADA

SCOTT CAT. NO.	DESCRIPTION	UNUSED O.G. F	UNUSED O.G. AVG	UNUSED F	UNUSED AVG	USED F	USED AVG

1, 4, 12	2, 5, 10, 13	7	8, 11	9
Beaver	Prince Albert	Jacques Cartier	Queen Victoria	

1851 Laid paper, Imperforate

1	3p red	......	......	......	......	825.00	600.00
2	6p grayish purple	......	......	......	......	1065.00	785.00

1852-55 Wove paper

4	3p red	2350.00	1975.00	1650.00	1300.00	255.00	180.00
4d	3p red (thin paper)	......	......	......	......	260.00	185.00
5	6p slate gray	......	......	......	......	975.00	750.00

1855

7	10p blue	......	......	......	......	1150.00	850.00

1857

8	½p rose	1220.00	935.00	900.00	625.00	510.00	385.00
9	7½p green	......	......	......	......	2400.00	1900.00

Very thick soft wove paper

10	6p reddish purple	......	......	......	......	2650.00	2175.00

1858-59 Perf. 12

11	½p rose	......	......	......	......	1000.00	750.00
12	3p red	......	......	......	......	585.00	410.00
13	6p brown violet	......	......	......	......	3750.00	2950.00

14	15	16, 17	18	19	20
Queen Victoria	Beaver	Prince Albert	Queen Victoria	Jacques Cartier	Queen Victoria

1859

14	1c rose	295.00	225.00	215.00	150.00	38.50	26.50
15	5c vermilion	410.00	310.00	295.00	200.00	22.50	15.00
16	10c black brown	......	......	......	......	2350.00	1800.00
17	10c red lilac	875.00	675.00	650.00	450.00	70.00	50.00
18	12½c yellow green	715.00	560.00	525.00	375.00	70.00	50.00
19	17c blue	950.00	750.00	700.00	500.00	115.00	85.00

1864

20	2c rose	575.00	450.00	425.00	300.00	225.00	160.00

NOTE: To determine the VF price for BNA stamps issued from 1851 to 1940, add the difference between the Avg. and F prices to the F price. To determine the NH price for issues prior to 1897, add 50% to the desired O.G. price.

SCOTT CAT. NO.	DESCRIPTION	UNUSED O.G.		UNUSED		USED	
		F	AVG	F	AVG	F	AVG

21   22, 23, 31   24, 32   25, 33

26   27   28   29, 30

Queen Victoria

1868-79 Wove paper, Perf. 12, unwkd.

21	½c black	70.00	50.00	60.00	40.00	40.00	30.00
22	1c brown red	575.00	390.00	475.00	300.00	60.00	40.00
23	1c yellow orange	1025.00	775.00	850.00	600.00	85.00	55.00
23a	1c deep orange	1025.00	775.00	850.00	600.00	90.00	60.00
24	2c green	525.00	390.00	425.00	300.00	50.00	35.00
25	3c red	1025.00	775.00	850.00	600.00	22.50	17.50
26	5c olive green (pf. 11½ x 12)	1025.00	775.00	850.00	600.00	130.00	90.00
27	6c brown	1025.00	775.00	850.00	600.00	60.00	40.00
28	12½c blue	600.00	450.00	500.00	350.00	70.00	50.00
29	15c gray violet	65.00	50.00	55.00	40.00	32.50	25.00
29b	15c red lilac	725.00	525.00	600.00	400.00	70.00	50.00
30	15c gray	75.00	55.00	65.00	45.00	35.00	25.00

1873-74 Wove paper. Perf. 11½ x 12, unwkd.

21a	½c black	.....	.....	.....	.....	50.00	35.00
29a	15c gray violet	.....	.....	.....	.....	225.00	150.00
30a	15c gray	.....	.....	.....	.....	180.00	125.00

1868-79 Wove paper. Perf. 12, wmkd.

22a	1c brown red	.....	.....	.....	.....	250.00	175.00
24a	2c green	.....	.....	.....	.....	250.00	175.00
25a	3c red	.....	.....	.....	.....	210.00	160.00
28a	12½c blue	.....	.....	.....	.....	250.00	175.00

1868 Laid Paper

31	1c brown red	.....	.....	.....	.....	2200.00	1550.00
33	3c bright red	.....	.....	.....	.....	475.00	300.00

34   35   36   37, 41   38, 42

39, 43   44   40, 45   46, 47

Queen Victoria

SCOTT CAT. NO.	DESCRIPTION	UNUSED O.G. F	AVG	UNUSED F	AVG	USED F	AVG
	1870-89 Perf. 12						
34	½c black	10.00	7.75	9.00	6.50	8.50	6.00
35	1c yellow	35.00	25.00	30.00	20.00	.95	.75
35a	1c orange	115.00	85.00	100.00	70.00	11.00	8.00
36	2c green	45.00	35.00	40.00	30.00	1.25	.95
36d	2c blue green	80.00	60.00	70.00	50.00	4.50	3.25
37	3c dull red	100.00	75.00	85.00	60.00	3.00	2.20
37c	3c orange red	95.00	72.50	80.00	60.00	2.35	1.75
38	5c slate green	345.00	270.00	300.00	225.00	22.50	16.00
39	6c yellow brown	250.00	200.00	225.00	175.00	20.00	14.00
40	10c rose lilac	450.00	350.00	400.00	300.00	60.00	40.00
	1873-79 Perf. 11½ x 12						
35d	1c orange	180.00	130.00	160.00	110.00	15.00	11.00
36e	2c green	245.00	180.00	215.00	150.00	20.00	15.00
37e	3c red	200.00	150.00	180.00	125.00	11.50	8.00
38a	5c slate green	.....	.....	.....	.....	35.00	25.00
39b	6c yellow brown	.....	.....	.....	.....	35.00	25.00
40c	10c pale rose lilac	.....	.....	.....	.....	175.00	135.00
	1888-93 Perf. 12						
41	3c vermilion	32.50	25.00	27.00	20.00	.55	.40
41a	3c rose carmine	430.00	335.00	375.00	275.00	10.00	6.50
42	5c gray	62.50	48.00	55.00	40.00	5.25	4.00
43	6c red brown	75.00	50.00	55.00	40.00	13.00	9.00
44	8c gray	75.00	50.00	55.00	40.00	5.50	4.00
45	10c brown red	225.00	150.00	175.00	125.00	42.50	30.00
46	20c vermilion	270.00	240.00	225.00	200.00	75.00	50.00
47	50c deep blue	485.00	360.00	425.00	300.00	42.50	30.00

NOTE: For N.H. prior to 1897 please add 50% to the desired condition price.

SCOTT CAT. NO.	DESCRIPTION	UNUSED NH F	AVG	UNUSED F	AVG	USED F	AVG

50-65
Queen Victoria in 1837 & 1897

	1897. JUBILEE ISSUE						
50	½c black	165.00	135.00	120.00	90.00	120.00	90.00
51	1c orange	17.50	14.00	12.50	9.00	10.50	8.00
52	2c green	25.00	20.00	18.00	13.00	16.50	12.50
53	3c bright rose	17.00	14.00	12.50	9.50	3.00	2.00
54	5c deep blue	55.00	45.00	40.00	30.00	28.00	20.00
55	6c yellow brown	295.00	225.00	220.00	150.00	215.00	150.00
56	8c dark violet	60.00	45.00	45.00	30.00	42.50	30.00
57	10c brown violet	145.00	110.00	110.00	75.00	110.00	75.00
58	15c steel blue	250.00	180.00	190.00	125.00	185.00	125.00
59	20c vermilion	295.00	225.00	215.00	150.00	210.00	150.00
60	50c ultramarine	365.00	300.00	260.00	200.00	210.00	150.00
61	$1 lake	1350.00	1050.00	1000.00	700.00	825.00	650.00
62	$2 dark purple	2750.00	2295.00	1925.00	1450.00	550.00	400.00
63	$3 yellow bistre	3150.00	2600.00	2250.00	1750.00	1300.00	1000.00
64	$4 purple	3150.00	2600.00	2250.00	1750.00	1300.00	1000.00
65	$5 olive green	3150.00	2600.00	2250.00	1750.00	1300.00	1000.00

SEE PAGE X FOR CONDITION DEFINITIONS

SCOTT CAT. NO.	DESCRIPTION	UNUSED N.H.		UNUSED		USED	
		F	AVG	F	AVG	F	AVG

66-73   74-84   85, 86

Queen Victoria   *Map Showing British Empire*

77: 2c Die I. Frame of four thin lines
77a: 2c Die II. Frame of thick line between two thin lines

1897-98

66	½c black	10.75	8.50	7.25	5.00	7.25	5.00
67	1c blue green	20.00	15.00	14.00	10.00	1.20	.95
68	2c purple	25.00	20.00	16.00	12.00	1.70	1.35
69	3c carmine	25.00	20.00	16.00	12.00	.50	.40
70	5c dark blue, bluish paper	123.00	97.50	91.50	66.50	7.00	5.00
71	6c brown	75.00	75.00	70.00	50.00	28.00	20.00
72	8c orange	200.00	165.00	145.00	110.00	11.50	8.50
73	10c brown violet	275.00	225.00	200.00	150.00	90.00	60.00

1898-1902

74	½c black	4.00	3.00	2.85	2.00	2.25	1.75
75	1c gray green	27.50	22.00	19.00	14.00	.20	.15
76	2c purple (I)	26.50	21.00	17.50	12.50	.20	.15
77	2c carmine (I)	35.00	30.00	22.50	17.50	.13	.10
77a	2c carmine (II)	35.00	30.00	22.50	17.50	.45	.35
78	3c carmine	40.00	35.00	37.50	22.50	.55	.45
79	5c blue, bluish paper	160.00	125.00	115.00	85.00	1.35	1.10
80	6c brown	190.00	155.00	135.00	100.00	40.00	30.00
81	7c olive yellow	95.00	75.00	65.00	45.00	18.00	13.00
82	8c orange	200.00	165.00	145.00	110.00	25.00	18.00
83	10c brown violet	310.00	250.00	225.00	165.00	20.00	14.50
84	20c olive green	600.00	475.00	445.00	325.00	100.00	75.00

1898. IMPERIAL PENNY POSTAGE COMMEMORATIVE

85	2c black, lavender & carmine	42.50	35.00	32.50	25.00	9.00	7.00
86	2c black, blue & carmine	42.50	35.00	32.50	25.00	9.00	7.00

1899
69 & 78 surcharged

87	2c on 3c carmine	17.00	13.50	11.00	8.00	7.00	5.00
88	2c on 3c carmine	19.00	15.00	12.00	9.00	5.00	4.00

King Edward VII

89-95

1903-08

89	1c green	28.00	22.50	19.00	14.00	.15	.12
90	2c carmine	28.00	22.50	19.00	14.00	.11	.08
90a	2c carmine, imperf.	65.00	55.00	45.00	35.00	45.00	35.00
91	5c blue, bluish paper	120.00	95.00	85.00	60.00	3.75	3.00
92	7c olive bistre	115.00	90.00	80.00	55.00	3.75	3.00
93	10c brown lilac	245.00	185.00	180.00	125.00	7.25	5.50
94	20c olive green	515.00	400.00	390.00	270.00	27.50	20.00
95	50c purple (1908)	1035.00	835.00	760.00	560.00	75.00	50.00

SCOTT CAT. NO. DESCRIPTION	UNUSED F	N.H. AVG	UNUSED F	AVG	USED F	AVG

96
Princess and Prince
of Wales in 1908

97
Jacques Cartier and
Samuel Champlain

98
Queen Alexandra
and King Edward

99
Champlain's Home
in Quebec

100
Generals Montcalm
and Wolfe

101
View of Quebec
in 1700

102
Champlain's Departure
for the West

103
Arrival of Cartier
at Quebec

1908. QUEBEC TERCENTENARY ISSUE

Scott	Description	Unused F	N.H. AVG	Unused F	AVG	Used F	AVG
96	½c black brown	10.00	8.25	6.75	5.00	6.75	5.00
97	1c blue green	20.00	15.00	14.00	10.00	6.25	5.00
98	2c carmine	23.50	18.00	17.00	12.00	2.00	1.50
99	5c dark blue	110.00	90.00	80.00	60.00	50.00	35.00
100	7c olive green	145.00	120.00	105.00	80.00	55.00	40.00
101	10c dark violet	240.00	180.00	175.00	120.00	115.00	85.00
102	15c red orange	275.00	225.00	195.00	145.00	145.00	110.00
103	20c yellow brown	300.00	245.00	215.00	165.00	200.00	150.00

104-134, 136-138, 184
King George V

1912-25

Scott	Description	Unused F	N.H. AVG	Unused F	AVG	Used F	AVG
104-22	**1c-$1 cpl., 18 Vars**	.....	.....	.....	.....	**43.95**	**34.50**
104	1c green	11.25	9.00	8.25	6.00	.10	.07
105	1c yellow (1922)	10.75	8.50	8.25	6.00	.15	.12
106	2c carmine	11.25	9.00	8.75	6.50	.10	.07
107	2c yellow green (1922)	10.25	8.00	7.75	5.50	.10	.07
108	3c brown (1918)	11.75	9.50	9.25	7.00	.10	.07
109	3c carmine (1922)	10.25	8.00	7.75	5.50	.10	.07
110	4c olive bistre (1922)	45.00	35.00	35.00	25.00	3.50	2.75
111	5c dark blue	160.00	130.00	120.00	90.00	.60	.45
112	5c violet (1922)	25.00	20.00	18.00	14.00	.60	.45
113	7c yellow ochre	35.00	28.00	26.00	18.00	2.25	1.75
114	7c red brown (1924)	35.00	28.00	27.00	19.00	9.50	7.50
115	8c blue (1925)	52.00	42.00	35.00	25.00	9.50	7.50
116	10c plum	215.00	175.00	165.00	125.00	2.00	1.50
117	10c blue (1922)	60.00	50.00	45.00	35.00	2.00	1.50
118	10c bistre brown (1925)	60.00	50.00	40.00	30.00	1.75	1.25
119	20c olive green	82.50	67.50	67.50	52.50	1.40	1.10
120	50c black brown (1925)	95.00	75.00	77.50	57.50	3.00	2.50
120a	50c black	155.00	120.00	120.00	85.00	3.75	3.00
122	$1 orange (1923)	215.00	175.00	165.00	125.00	9.50	7.50

SCOTT CAT. NO.	DESCRIPTION	UNUSED N.H. F	AVG	UNUSED F	AVG	USED F	AVG

Coil Pairs for Canada can be supplied at double the single price

1912 Coil Stamps. Perf. 8 Horizontally

123	1c green	130.00	105.00	100.00	75.00	42.50	35.00
124	2c carmine	130.00	105.00	100.00	75.00	42.50	35.00

1912-24 Perf. 8 Vertically

125-30	1c-3c cpl., 6 Vars.	190.00	155.00	142.50	103.50	18.95	14.95
125	1c dark green	18.00	14.00	14.00	10.00	.75	.60
126	1c yellow	13.00	10.00	10.50	7.50	8.25	6.00
126a	1c pair, imperf. between	32.00	27.00	23.00	18.00	.....	.....
127	2c carmine	32.00	25.00	22.50	15.00	.50	.40
128	2c green	16.00	12.50	12.50	9.00	.70	.60
128a	2c pair, imperf. between	37.00	31.00	27.50	21.00	.....	.....
129	3c brown	14.00	11.00	11.00	8.00	.80	.65
130	3c carmine	110.00	90.00	80.00	60.00	9.75	7.50
130a	3c pair, imperf. between	570.00	465.00	429.50	329.50	.....	.....

1915-24 Perf. 12 Horizontally

131	1c dark green	10.75	8.50	8.25	6.00	8.25	6.00
132	2c carmine	35.00	28.00	27.00	20.00	27.00	20.00
133	2c yellow green	155.00	115.00	118.00	83.00	118.00	83.00
134	3c brown	10.75	8.50	8.25	6.00	8.25	6.00

135
Quebec Conference of 1867

1917. CONFEDERATE ISSUE

135	3c brown	40.00	30.00	31.00	21.00	.65	.50

1924 Imperforate

136	1c yellow	80.00	70.00	60.00	50.00	60.00	50.00
137	2c green	80.00	70.00	60.00	50.00	60.00	50.00
138	3c carmine	35.00	30.00	27.50	22.50	30.00	25.00

1926   **2 CENTS**
109 Surcharged

139	2c on 3c carmine	95.00	75.00	75.00	55.00	80.00	60.00

109 Surcharged   **2 CENTS**

140	2c on 3c carmine	45.00	35.00	32.50	22.50	35.00	25.00

141
Sir John MacDonald

142
The Quebec Conference of 1867

143
The Parliament Building at Ottawa

144
Sir Wilfred Laurier

145
Map of Canada

SCOTT CAT. NO.	DESCRIPTION	UNUSED N.H. F	AVG	UNUSED F	AVG	USED F	AVG
1927. CONFEDERATION ISSUE							
141-45	1c-12c cpl., 5 Vars.	57.75	47.50	45.00	35.00	16.25	13.00
141	1c orange	5.75	4.75	4.25	3.25	.80	.70
142	2c green	3.15	2.60	2.50	2.50	.18	.15
143	3c brown carmine	17.50	14.50	12.75	9.75	6.50	5.00
144	5c violet	7.50	6.50	6.50	5.00	3.50	.275
145	12c dark blue	27.00	22.00	22.00	17.00	6.25	5.00

146	147	148
Thomas McGee	Sir Wilfred Laurier and Sir John MacDonald	Robert Baldwin and L.H. Lafontaine

1927. HISTORICAL ISSUE

SCOTT CAT. NO.	DESCRIPTION	UNUSED N.H. F	AVG	UNUSED F	AVG	USED F	AVG
146-48	5c-20c cpl., 3 Vars.	48.00	38.00	38.00	28.00	15.50	12.25
146	5c violet	7.00	5.50	5.50	4.00	3.50	2.75
147	12c green	15.00	11.50	12.00	8.50	6.00	4.75
148	20c brown carmine	29.00	23.00	23.00	17.00	7.00	5.50

George V

149-154, 160, 161

Mt. Hurd

155

156	157	158	159
Quebec Bridge	Harvesting Wheat	Fishing Schooner "Bluenose"	The Parliament Building at Ottawa

1928-29

SCOTT CAT. NO.	DESCRIPTION	UNUSED N.H. F	AVG	UNUSED F	AVG	USED F	AVG
149-55	1c-10c, 7 Varieties	102.75	90.50	89.50	67.75	30.50	24.95
149	1c orange	4.75	4.00	3.75	3.00	.30	.25
150	2c green	2.40	1.90	2.00	1.50	.11	.08
151	3c dark carmine	36.50	28.50	27.00	20.00	15.00	12.00
152	4c bistre	24.50	19.50	20.00	15.00	6.00	5.00
153	5c deep violet	11.50	9.00	9.25	7.00	2.75	2.50
154	8c blue	21.50	17.50	17.50	13.50	6.50	5.50
155	10c green	18.50	15.00	15.00	11.50	1.50	1.25
156	12c gray	29.50	23.50	21.00	15.00	9.00	7.00
157	20c dark carmine	55.00	45.00	40.00	30.00	11.50	9.50
158	50c dark blue	495.00	420.00	370.00	295.00	75.00	55.00
159	$1 olive green	575.00	475.00	450.00	350.00	75.00	60.00
1929 Coil Stamps. Perf. 8 Vertically							
160	1c orange	25.00	21.00	20.00	16.00	21.50	17.00
161	2c green	20.00	16.50	16.00	12.00	2.50	2.00

COMPLETE SETS ARE LISTED BEFORE SINGLES

SCOTT CAT. NO.	DESCRIPTION	UNUSED N.H. F	AVG	UNUSED F	AVG	USED F	AVG

2c Die I. Above "POSTAGE" faint crescent in ball of ornament. Top letter "P" has tiny dot of color.
2C Die II. Stronger and clearer crescent. Spot of color in "P" is larger.

162-172, 178-183
King George V

173
Parliament Library at Ottawa

174
The Old Citadel at Quebec

175
Harvesting Wheat on the Prairies

176
The Museum at Grand Pre, and Monument to Evangeline

177
Mt. Edith Cavell

1930-31

		UNUSED N.H. F	AVG	UNUSED F	AVG	USED F	AVG
162-72	1c-8c, 11 Varieties	81.95	68.00	65.50	52.75	29.00	24.75
162	1c orange	1.15	.95	.90	.75	.60	.50
163	1c deep green	1.90	1.70	1.60	1.35	.10	.07
164	2c dull green	1.75	1.40	1.35	1.10	.13	.10
165	2c deep red, die II	3.75	3.40	3.35	3.00	.10	.07
165a	2c deep red, die I	1.90	1.70	1.60	1.40	.18	.15
166	2c dark brown, die II	2.60	2.25	2.10	1.75	.13	.10
166b	2c dark brown, die I	6.75	5.75	5.50	4.50	5.00	4.50
167	3c deep red	2.60	2.25	2.10	1.75	.10	.07
168	4c yellow bistre	17.00	14.00	14.00	11.00	7.00	6.00
169	5c dull violet	9.75	7.75	8.00	6.00	6.00	5.00
170	5c dull blue	5.75	4.50	4.25	3.50	.18	.15
171	8c dark blue	28.50	23.00	23.00	18.00	12.00	10.00
172	8c red orange	11.75	9.75	9.50	7.50	5.00	4.25
173	10c olive green	14.00	11.00	11.50	8.50	1.70	1.40
174	12c gray black	25.00	19.50	17.75	12.75	7.00	6.00
175	20c brown red	50.00	39.00	37.00	27.00	.70	.60
176	50c dull blue	395.00	325.00	295.00	225.00	17.00	14.50
177	$1 dark olive green	395.00	325.00	295.00	225.00	48.00	25.00

Coil Pairs for Canada can be supplied at double the single price.

Coil Stamps Perf. 8½ Vertically

		UNUSED N.H. F	AVG	UNUSED F	AVG	USED F	AVG
178-83	1c-3c cpl., 6 Varieties	96.50	79.75	74.00	56.75	25.50	19.50
178	1c orange	19.00	15.50	14.50	11.00	13.00	10.00
179	1c deep green	11.00	9.00	9.00	7.00	5.50	4.50
180	2c dull green	9.25	7.75	8.50	6.00	4.00	3.00
181	2c deep red	21.50	18.00	15.50	12.00	3.25	2.75
182	2c dark brown	16.00	13.00	12.00	9.00	.70	.60
183	3c deep red	25.00	20.75	29.00	15.00	.45	.35

1931 Design of 1912-25 Perf. 12 x 8

		UNUSED N.H. F	AVG	UNUSED F	AVG	USED F	AVG
184	3c carmine	5.25	4.00	4.25	2.95	2.95	2.30

190
Sir George Etienne Cartier

192
King George V

193
Prince of Wales

194
Allegorical Figure of Britannia Surveying the British Empire

SCOTT CAT. NO.	DESCRIPTION	UNUSED N.H.		UNUSED		USED	
		F	AVG	F	AVG	F	AVG

1931

| 190 | 10c dark green . . . . | 13.75 | 11.75 | 11.00 | 9.00 | .15 | .12 |

1932

165 & 165a surcharged **3** ≡

| 191 | 3c on 2c deep red, die II . . . . | 1.85 | 1.60 | 1.50 | 1.25 | .15 | .12 |
| 191a | 3c on 2c deep red, die I . . . . | 4.00 | 3.25 | 3.00 | 2.50 | 2.35 | 2.00 |

1932. OTTAWA CONFERENCE ISSUE

192-94	3c-13c cpl., 3 Vars.	29.75	25.50	21.75	15.75	9.25	8.25
192	3c deep red	1.60	1.30	1.00	.75	.18	.15
193	5c dull blue	13.25	10.50	9.75	7.00	2.75	2.50
194	13c deep green	16.50	13.00	12.50	9.00	6.75	6.00

195-200, 205-207
King George V

201
The Old Citadel at Quebec

1932

195-201	1c-13c, 7 Vars.	163.50	137.50	137.50	109.00	14.00	12.00
195	1c dark green	1.15	1.00	1.00	.85	.10	.07
196	2c black brown	1.75	1.50	1.50	1.25	.10	.07
197	3c deep red	1.85	1.60	1.55	1.30	.10	.07
198	4c ochre	65.00	55.00	55.00	45.00	6.50	5.50
199	5c dark blue	9.50	8.00	8.00	6.50	.15	.12
200	8c red orange	33.00	25.00	27.50	20.00	4.50	3.75
201	13c dull violet	60.00	50.00	50.00	40.00	3.50	3.00

202
Parliament Buildings at Ottawa

203

204
S.S. Royal William

1933-34. COMMEMORATIVES

| 202/10 | (202-04, 208-10) cpl., 6 Vars. . . . . | 144.50 | 123.50 | 119.50 | 94.50 | 34.50 | 31.25 |

1933. POSTAL UNION ISSUE

| 202 | 5c dark blue . . . . | 14.50 | 13.00 | 11.50 | 10.00 | 3.25 | 3.00 |

1933. WORLD'S GRAIN EXHIBITION & CONFERENCE ISSUE

| 203 | 20c brown red . . . . | 65.00 | 55.00 | 55.00 | 45.00 | 16.00 | 14.50 |

1933. FIRST TRANS-ATLANTIC STEAMBOAT CROSSING COMMEMORATIVE

| 204 | 5c dark blue . . . . | 14.50 | 13.00 | 11.50 | 10.00 | 3.25 | 3.00 |

NOTE: To determine the VF price for BNA stamps issued from 1851 to 1940, add the difference between the Avg. and F prices to the F price. To determine the NH price for issues prior to 1897, add 50% to the desired O.G. price.

SCOTT CAT. NO.	DESCRIPTION	UNUSED N.H. F	AVG	UNUSED F	AVG	USED F	AVG

1933 Coil Stamps. Perf. 8½ Vertically

205	1c green	25.50	21.00	21.00	16.00	2.60	2.35
206	2c black brown	23.50	18.50	19.50	14.50	.85	.75
207	3c deep red	16.50	12.50	13.50	9.50	.45	.40

208

209

210

1934

208	3c Jacques Cartier	6.25	5.50	4.75	4.00	1.50	1.40
209	10c Loyalists Monument	50.00	40.00	40.00	30.00	9.50	8.50
210	2c N. Brunswick	4.25	3.25	3.25	2.50	3.25	3.00

211 212 213 214

215 216

1935

211-16	1c-13c cpl., 6 Varieties	41.50	37.50	31.00	27.00	16.00	14.50
211	1c Princess Elizabeth	.85	.75	.70	.60	.38	.35
212	2c Duke of York	1.60	1.45	1.25	1.10	.28	.25
213	3c George & Mary	4.35	4.00	3.65	3.25	.18	.15
214	5c Prince of Wales	9.75	8.75	7.75	6.75	5.00	4.75
215	10c Windsor Castle	10.75	9.75	8.50	7.50	3.25	3.00
216	13c Royal Yacht	16.50	15.00	12.00	10.00	8.00	7.00

217-222, 228-230
King George V

223

224

225

226

227

SCOTT CAT. NO.	DESCRIPTION	UNUSED N.H.		UNUSED		USED	
		F	AVG	F	AVG	F	AVG
217-25	1c-20c, 9 Varieties	93.75	74.95	74.95	56.50	4.95	4.65
217	1c green	.75	.65	.60	.50	.18	.15
218	2c brown	.85	.75	.70	.60	.10	.07
219	3c dark carmine	1.15	1.00	.95	.80	.10	.07
220	4c yellow	5.00	4.00	4.25	3.25	.55	.50
221	5c blue	5.00	4.00•	4.25	3.25	.18	.15
222	8c deep orange	5.00	4.00	4.25	3.25	2.50	2.25
223	10c Mounted Policeman	17.00	13.00	12.50	8.50	.21	.18
224	13c Conference of 1864	18.00	14.00	13.50	9.50	1.00	.90
225	20c Niagara Falls	46.00	37.50	38.00	30.00	.70	.60
226	50c Parliament Building	60.00	50.00	50.00	40.00	7.00	6.00
227	$1 Champlain Monument	135.00	110.00	110.00	85.00	14.50	11.00

1935-36 Coil Stamps. Perf. 8 Vertically

228	1c green	18.00	14.00	14.75	10.75	2.50	2.25
229	2c brown	15.00	11.50	12.25	8.75	1.05	.90
230	3c dark carmine	15.00	11.50	12.25	8.75	.40	.35

231-236, 238-240
King George VI

237

1937

231-36	1c-8c cpl., 6 Varieties	18.00	14.75	13.75	10.75	.95	.75
231	1c green	.70	.65	.60	.50	.10	.07
232	2c brown	.90	.80	.75	.65	.10	.07
233	3c carmine	1.20	1.05	.95	.85	.10	.07
234	4c yellow	5.50	4.50	4.25	3.25	.21	.18
235	5c blue	5.25	4.25	3.75	3.00	.10	.07
236	8c orange	5.50	4.50	4.25	3.25	.38	.35
237	3c Coronation	.43	.40	.38	.35	.13	.10

Coil Stamps. Perf. 8 Vertically

238	1c green	2.65	2.40	2.10	1.85	1.55	1.40
239	2c brown	3.85	3.50	3.15	2.75	.40	.35
240	3c carmine	5.50	4.50	4.50	3.50	.15	.12

242

244

246

247

241

243

245

248

1938

241	10c Memorial Hall	16.50	14.00	13.50	11.00	.18	.15
242	13c Halifax Harbor	21.00	17.50	17.50	14.00	.65	.60
243	20c Fort Garry Gate	45.00	37.50	37.50	30.00	.45	.40
244	50c Vancouver Harbor	90.00	75.00	75.00	60.00	7.25	6.50
245	$1 Chateau de Ramezay	225.00	165.00	160.00	135.00	15.25	8.50

SCOTT CAT NO.	DESCRIPTION	UNUSED N.H. F	AVG	UNUSED F	AVG	USED F	AVG
			1939				
246-48	1c-3c cpl., 3 Varieties	1.25	1.15	.95	.85	.35	.30
246	1c Princess Eliza. & Margaret	.45	.40	.33	.30	.18	.15
247	2c War Memorial	.45	.40	.33	.30	.13	.10
248	3c King George VI & Queen Elizabeth	.45	.40	.33	.30	.11	.08

249,255,263
278

250,254,264
267,279,281
King George VI

251,252,265
266,280

258, 259

260

257

253

256

261

262

1942-43. WAR ISSUE

		PLATE BLOCK F/NH	F	UNUSED F/NH	F	USED F
249-62	1c-$1, cpl., 14 Varieties	925.00	800.00	183.50	153.50	15.50
249-60	1c-20c, 12 Varieties	235.00	195.00	39.50	32.75	6.00
249	1c green	1.65	1.40	.35	.30	.07
250	2c brown	5.75	5.00	.70	.60	.07
251	3c dark carmine	5.75	5.00	.70	.60	.07
252	3c rose violet	3.00	2.50	.60	.50	.07
253	4c Grain Elevators	15.00	12.50	2.00	1.75	.70
254	4c dark carmine	3.00	2.50	.60	.50	.07
255	5c deep blue	9.00	8.00	1.75	1.50	.07
256	8c Farm Scene	17.50	15.00	3.25	2.75	.60
257	10c Parliament Buildings	35.00	30.00	5.00	4.00	.12
258	13c "Ram" Tank	42.50	35.00	7.25	6.00	4.00
259	14c "Ram" Tank	55.00	45.00	10.50	8.75	.30
260	20c Corvette	55.00	45.00	9.00	7.50	.30
261	50c Munitions Factory	190.00	160.00	40.00	32.50	2.25
262	$1 Destroyer	550.00	475.00	115.00	95.00	8.00

NOTE: To determine the VF price on stamps issued from 1941 to date, add 15% to the F/NH or F (used) price (minimum .03 per item). All VF unused stamps from 1941 to date will be NH. All F stamps issued after 1963 will be NH.

SCOTT CAT NO.	DESCRIPTION	PLATE BLOCK F/NH	F	UNUSED F/NH	F	USED F

Coil Stamps. Perf. 8 Vertically

263-67	1c-4c cpl., 5 Varieties	_____	_____	10.75	9.35	3.50
263	1c green	_____	_____	1.20	1.00	.65
264	2c brown	_____	_____	1.50	1.30	1.75
265	3c dark carmine	_____	_____	1.50	1.30	1.10
266	3c rose violet	_____	_____	3.00	2.50	.40
267	4c dark carmine	_____	_____	4.50	4.00	.25

268　　269　　270　　271

272　　273

1946. PEACE ISSUE

268	8c Farm Scene	11.50	10.00	2.50	2.25	.95
269	10c Great Bear Lake	17.50	14.50	2.50	2.25	.15
270	14c Hydro-Electric Power Station	30.00	25.00	5.25	4.25	.25
271	20c Reaper & Harvester	30.00	25.00	5.75	4.75	.20
272	50c Lumber Industry	175.00	150.00	30.00	25.00	2.50
273	$1 New Train Ferry	365.00	325.00	70.00	60.00	4.00

274　　275　　276　　277

1947-49. COMMEMORATIVES

274/83	(274-77, 82-83) cpl., 6 Vars.	6.85	6.25	1.50	1.35	.50
274	4c Alexander G. Bell	1.20	1.10	.28	.25	.12
275	4c Canadian Citizen	1.20	1.10	.28	.25	.12

1948.

276	4c Princess Elizabeth	1.20	1.10	.28	.25	.07
277	4c Parliament Building	1.20	1.10	.28	.25	.07

1948 Designs of 1942-43
Coil Stamps. Perf. 9½ Vertically

278-81	1c-4c cpl., 4 Varieties	_____		34.00	31.00	19.00
278	1c green	_____		4.25	4.00	3.00

SCOTT CAT. NO.	DESCRIPTION	PLATE BLOCK F/NH	F	UNUSED F/NH	F	USED F
279	2c brown	——	——	14.25	13.50	12.00
280	3c rose violet	——	——	8.00	7.25	2.50
281	4c dark carmine	——	——	10.25	9.00	3.00

282

283

1949.

282	4c Cabot's "Matthew"	1.20	1.10	.25	.22	.07
283	4c Founding of Halifax	1.20	1.10	.25	.22	.10

284, 289, 295, 297   285, 290, 298, 305, 309   286, 291, 296, 299   287, 292, 300, 306, 310   288, 293

King George VI

1949 (with "Postes-Postage")

284-88	1c-5c cpl., 5 Varieties	13.25	12.50	2.85	2.50	.38
284	1c green	1.00	.90	.18	.15	.07
285	2c sepia	1.60	1.50	.35	.30	.07
286	3c rose violet	1.75	1.60	.40	.35	.07
287	4c dark carmine	2.70	2.60	.60	.55	.07
288	5c deep blue	7.00	6.75	1.50	1.40	.12

1950 TYPE OF 1949
(without "Postes-Postage")

289-93	1c-5c cpl., 5 Varieties	30.95	27.25	3.45	3.00	2.00
289	1c green	.85	.75	.18	.15	.07
290	2c sepia	7.50	7.00	.45	.40	.18
291	3c rose violet	1.40	1.30	.31	.28	.07
292	4c dark carmine	1.95	1.75	.45	.40	.07
293	5c deep blue	21.00	18.00	2.25	2.00	1.75

294   301   302   303   304

294	50c Oil Wells, Alberta	120.00	110.00	23.50	21.00	1.75

Coil Stamps. Perf. 9½ Vertically

295-300	1c-4c cpl., 6 Varieties	——	——	20.50	19.95	4.65

SCOTT CAT. NO.	DESCRIPTION	PLATE BLOCK F/NH	F	UNUSED F/NH	F	USED F
	(without "Postes-Postage")					
295	1c green	——	——	.95	.90	.55
296	3c rose violet	——	——	1.15	1.05	.80
	(with "Postes-Postage")					
297	1c green	——	——	.48	.45	.35
298	2c sepia	——	——	2.50	2.40	2.50
299	3c rose violet	——	——	1.95	1.85	.30
300	4c dark carmine	——	——	14.75	14.50	1.10
301	10c Fur Resources	7.50	6.50	1.50	1.25	.10
	1951					
302	$1 Fishing	510.00	450.00	120.00	105.00	16.50
	1951-52 COMMEMORATIVES					
303/19	(303-04, 11-15, 17-19) cpl., 10 Varieties	48.00	46.50	9.00	8.25	3.50
303	3c Sir Robert L. Borden	1.90	1.80	.38	.35	.12
304	4c William L.M. King	1.90	1.80	.38	.35	.12
	(with "Postes-Postage")					
305	2c olive green	1.15	1.00	.25	.22	.07
306	4c orange vermilion	1.45	1.35	.33	.30	.07
	Coil Stamps. Perf. 9½ Vertically					
309	2c olive green	——	——	1.60	1.50	.90
310	4c orange vermilion	——	——	1.60	1.50	.90

311   312   313   314

311	4c Trains of 1851 & 1951	4.25	4.00	.95	.85	.15
312	5c Steamships	19.00	18.00	2.75	2.50	2.25
313	7c Stagecoach & Plane	9.25	9.00	1.85	1.75	.50
314	15c "Three Pence Beaver"	9.25	9.00	1.85	1.75	.45

315   316   317   318   319

315	4c Royal Visit	1.40	1.30	.30	.27	.07
	1952					
316	20c Paper Production	11.00	10.00	2.20	2.00	.07
317	4c Red Cross	1.40	1.30	.30	.27	.07
318	3c J.J.C. Abbott	1.40	1.30	.30	.27	.07
319	4c A. Mackenzie	1.90	1.75	.43	.40	.07

SCOTT CAT. NO.	DESCRIPTION	PLATE BLOCK F/NH	F	UNUSED F/NH	F	USED F

| | | 320 | 321 | 322 | 323 | 324 | 325-329, 331-333 |

1952-53

| 320 | 7c Canada Goose | 2.75 | 2.50 | .60 | .55 | .07 |
| 321 | $1 Indian House & Totem Pole | 120.00 | 115.00 | 27.50 | 25.00 | 1.10 |

1953-54 COMMEMORATIVES

| 322/50 | (322-24, 30, 35-36, 49-50) cpl., 8 Varieties | 13.95 | 12.75 | 2.95 | 2.75 | .55 |

322	2c Polar Bear	1.35	1.25	.23	.20	.10
323	3c Moose	1.45	1.35	.33	.30	.07
324	4c Bighorn Sheep	1.85	1.75	.38	.35	.07

| 325-29 | 1c-5c cpl., 5 Varieties | 5.60 | 5.25 | 1.20 | 1.05 | .30 |

325	1c violet brown	.55	.50	.13	.10	.07
326	2c green	.75	.65	.18	.15	.07
327	3c carmine rose	1.25	1.10	.28	.25	.07
328	4c violet	1.55	1.45	.33	.30	.07
329	5c ultramarine	1.95	1.85	.44	.40	.07

| | 330 | 334 | 335 | 336 | 337-342, 345-348 | 343 |

| 330 | 4c Queen Elizabeth II | 1.55 | 1.45 | .33 | .30 | .07 |

Coil Stamps. Perf. 9½ Vertically

331	2c green	—	—	1.60	1.50	1.45
332	3c carmine rose	—	—	1.60	1.50	1.35
333	4c violet	—	—	4.25	4.00	2.25

| 334 | 50c Textile Industry | 47.00 | 45.00 | 9.50 | 9.00 | .32 |

1954

| 335 | 4c Walrus | 2.55 | 2.45 | .43 | .40 | .07 |
| 336 | 5c Beaver | 2.60 | 2.50 | .60 | .55 | .07 |

| 337-43 | 1c-15c cpl., 7 Varieties | 15.25 | 14.20 | 3.20 | 2.95 | .55 |

337	1c violet brown	.55	.45	.13	.10	.07
338	2c green	.80	.70	.18	.15	.07
339	3c carmine rose	1.50	1.40	.28	.25	.07
340	4c violet	1.70	1.60	.33	.30	.07
341	5c bright blue	1.90	1.80	.44	.40	.07
342	6c orange	2.45	2.25	.53	.50	.12
343	15c Gannet	7.25	6.75	1.60	1.50	.12

SCOTT CAT. NO.	DESCRIPTION	PLATE BLOCK F/NH	F	UNUSED F/NH	F	USED F
	1954 Coil Stamps. Perf. 9½ Vertically					
345	2c green	――	――	.65	.60	.25
347	4c violet	――	――	1.75	1.65	.35
348	5c bright blue	――	――	2.40	2.25	.40

349	4c J.S.D. Thompson	2.50	2.25	.55	.50	.07
350	5c M. Bowell	2.50	2.25	.55	.50	.07

1955

351	10c Eskimo in Kayak	2.50	2.25	.55	.50	.07

SCOTT CAT. NO.	DESCRIPTION					
352/64	(352-61, 64) cpl., 11 Varieties	**1955-56. COMMEMORATIVES** 23.65	21.50	5.25	4.70	.95
352	4c Musk Ox	2.30	2.10	.50	.45	.07
353	5c Whooping Cranes	2.45	2.25	.55	.50	.08
354	5c Int'l. Civil Aviation Org.	2.40	2.20	.55	.50	.15
355	5c Alberta-Saskatchewan	2.40	2.20	.55	.50	.15
356	5c Boy Scout Jamboree	2.20	2.00	.55	.50	.12
357	4c R.B. Bennett	2.20	2.00	.44	.40	.07
358	5c C. Tupper	2.20	2.00	.50	.45	.10

1956

359	5c Hockey Players	2.20	2.00	.50	.45	.10
360	4c Caribou	2.20	2.00	.50	.45	.07
361	5c Mountain Goat	2.20	2.00	.50	.45	.07
362	20c Paper Industry	10.50	10.25	2.35	2.25	.10

SCOTT CAT. NO.	DESCRIPTION	PLATE BLOCK F/NH	F	UNUSED F/NH	F	USED F
363	25c Chemical Industry	13.00	12.50	3.00	2.85	.10
364	5c Fire Prevention	2.20	2.00	.50	.45	.07

365　　　　　　366　　　　　　　367　　　　　　368

1957. COMMEMORATIVES

365-74	cpl., 10 Vars.	29.75(7)	27.75(7)	8.35	7.75	5.85
365-68	cpl., 4 Vars., att'd	4.25	4.00	2.60	2.40	1.40
365	5c Fishing	———	———	.65	.60	.35
366	5c Swimming	———	———	.65	.60	.35
367	5c Hunting	———	———	.65	.60	.35
368	5c Skiing	———	———	.65	.60	.35

369　　　　　370　　　　　　371　　　　　　372　　　　　373　　　　　374

369	5c Loon	2.00	1.85	.44	.40	.07
370	5c D. Thompson, Explorer	2.20	2.00	.50	.45	.07
371	5c Parliament Building	2.00	1.80	.44	.40	.07
372	15c Posthorn & Globe	18.50	17.50	4.25	4.00	4.65
373	5c Coal Miner	1.70	1.55	.38	.35	.10
374	5c Royal Visit	1.70	1.55	.38	.35	.10

375　　　　　376　　　　　　377　　　　　　378　　　　　379

1958. COMMEMORATIVES

375-82	cpl., 8 Vars.	36.25	33.95	3.65	3.40	.80
375	5c Newspaper	8.50	8.00	.48	.45	.20
376	5c Int'l. Geophysical Year	8.50	8.00	.48	.45	.10
377	5c Miner Panning Gold	3.50	3.25	.48	.45	.10
378	5c La Verendrye, Explorer	3.00	2.75	.48	.45	.10
379	5c S. deChamplain & Quebec	6.50	6.25	.48	.45	.10

SCOTT CAT. NO.	DESCRIPTION	PLATE BLOCK F/NH	F	UNUSED F/NH	F	USED F

380

381

382

383

384

380	5c National Health	2.75	2.50	.48	.45	.08
381	5c Petroleum Industry	2.75	2.50	.48	.45	.08
382	5c Speaker's Chair & Mace	2.75	2.50	.48	.45	.10

1959. COMMEMORATIVES

383-88	cpl., 6 Vars.	17.50	16.50	2.95	2.60	.50
383	5c Old & Modern Planes	2.65	2.50	.53	.50	.10
384	5c N.A.T.O. Anniversary	2.40	2.25	.48	.45	.10

385

386

387

388

389

385	5c Woman Tending Tree	2.20	2.00	.48	.45	.08
386	5c Royal Tour	2.20	2.00	.48	.45	.08
387	5c St. Lawrence Seaway	6.50	6.25	.48	.45	.08
388	5c Plains of Abraham	2.70	2.50	.55	.50	.08

1960-62. COMMEMORATIVES

389-400	cpl., 12 Vars.	23.95	22.75	5.50	5.00	.85
389	5c Girl Guides Emblem	2.10	2.00	.48	.45	.07

390

391

392

393

394

395

FOR YOUR CONVENIENCE IN ORDERING, COMPLETE SETS ARE LISTED BEFORE SINGLE STAMP LISTINGS

SCOTT CAT. NO.	DESCRIPTION	PLATE BLOCK F/NH	F	UNUSED F/NH	F	USED F

396

397

398

399

400

Scott Cat. No.	Description	Plate Block F/NH	F	Unused F/NH	F	Used F
390	5c Battle of Long Sault	2.10	2.00	.48	.45	.07
	1961					
391	5c Earth Mover	2.10	2.00	.48	.45	.07
392	5c E.P. Johnson, Poetess	2.10	2.00	.48	.45	.07
393	5c A. Meighen	2.10	2.00	.48	.45	.07
394	5c Colombo Plan	2.10	2.00	.48	.45	.07
395	5c Natural Resources	2.10	2.00	.48	.45	.07
	1962					
396	5c Education	2.10	2.00	.48	.45	.07
397	5c Red River Settlement	2.10	2.00	.48	.45	.08
398	5c Jean Tallon	2.10	2.00	.48	.45	.07
399	5c Victoria, B.C. Centenary	2.10	2.00	.48	.45	.08
400	5c Trans-Canada	2.10	2.00	.48	.45	.10

401-409

1962-63

Scott Cat. No.	Description	Plate Block F/NH	F	Unused F/NH	F	Used F
401-05	1c-5c cpl., 5 Varieties	11.65	10.95	1.20	1.10	.30
401	1c deep brown	.60	.50	.13	.10	.07
402	2c green	6.75	6.50	.20	.17	.07
403	3c purple	1.55	1.45	.33	.30	.07
404	4c carmine	1.55	1.45	.30	.27	.07
405	5c violet blue	1.85	1.75	.35	.32	.07

1963-64 Coil Stamps. Perf. 9½ Horizontally

Scott Cat. No.	Description	Plate Block F/NH	F	Unused F/NH	F	Used F
406-09	2c-5c cpl., 4 Varieties	———	———	13.25	12.75	4.15
406	2c green	———	———	3.85	3.75	1.90
407	3c purple	———	———	2.85	2.75	1.00
408	4c carmine	———	———	3.35	3.25	1.00
409	5c violet blue	———	———	3.85	3.75	.50

SCOTT CAT. NO.	DESCRIPTION	PLATE BLOCK F/NH	UNUSED F/NH	USED F

410

411

412

413

1963-64. COMMEMORATIVES

410//35 (410, 12-13, 16-17, 31-35) 10 Vars.	18.25	4.85	.70

410	5c Sir Casimir S. Gzowski	1.90	.45	.08
411	$1 Export Trade	165.00	35.00	4.00
412	5c Sir M. Frobisher, Explorer	2.45	.55	.08
413	5c First Mail Routes	2.85	.65	.08

414, 430, 436

415

416

417

1963-64

414	7c Jet Takeoff	3.50	.75	.75
415	15c Canada Geese	19.50	4.50	.35

1964

416	5c World Peace	1.90	.45	.07
417	5c Canadian Unity	1.90	.45	.10

418
Ontario & White Trillium

429A
Canada & Maple Leaf

COATS OF ARMS & FLORAL EMBLEMS

419 Quebec & White Garden Lily
420 Nova Scotia & Mayflower
421 New Brunswick & Purple Violet
422 Manitoba & Prairie Crocus
423 British Columbia & Dogwood
424 Prince Edward Island & Lady's Slipper
425 Saskatchewan & Prairie Lily
426 Alberta & Wild Rose
427 Newfoundland & Pitcher Plant
428 Yukon & Fireweed
429 Northwest Territories & Mountain Avens

1964-66

418-29A cpl., 13 Vars.	32.00	6.00	2.00

418	5c red brown, buff & green	2.50	.50	.20
419	5c green, yellow & orange	2.50	.50	.15
420	5c blue, pink & green	2.50	.50	.15
421	5c carmine, green & violet	2.50	.50	.15
422	5c brown, lilac & green	3.50	.50	.15
423	5c lilac, green, bistre	2.50	.50	.15
424	5c pink, green & purple	2.50	.50	.15
425	5c sepia, orange & green	2.75	.50	.20
426	5c green, yellow & carmine	2.75	.50	.15
427	5c black, green & red	2.50	.50	.15
428	5c blue, red & green	2.50	.50	.20
429	5c olive, yellow & green	2.50	.50	.20
429A	5c blue & red	2.50	.50	.15

NOTE: To determine the VF price on stamps issued from 1941 to date, add 15 % to the F/NH or F (used) price (minimum .03 per item). All VF unused stamps from 1941 to date will be NH. All F stamps issued after 1963 until NH.

1964
Surcharged on 414

430	8c on 7c Jet Takeoff	3.00	.60	.50

431

432

434, 435

433

437

431	5c Charlottetown Conference	1.75	.40	.07
432	5c Quebec Conference	1.60	.37	.07

SCOTT CAT. NO.	DESCRIPTION	PLATE BLOCK F/NH	UNUSED F/NH	USED F
433	5c Queen Elizabeth's Visit ...	1.60	.37	.08
434	3c Christmas	1.30	.25	.07
435	5c Christmas	1.95	.35	.07

Jet type of 1964

436	8c Jet Takeoff	2.75	.55	.30

1965. COMMEMORATIVES

437-44	Varieties	12.25	2.65	.65
437	5c I.C.Y.	1.50	.35	.10

438	5c Sir Wilfred Grenfell	1.50	.35	.10
439	5c National Flag	1.50	.35	.10
440	5c Sir Winston Churchill ...	2.25	.50	.10
441	5c Inter-Parliamentary	1.50	.35	.10
442	5c Ottawa, National Capitol..	1.50	.35	.10

443, 444

445

446

443	3c Christmas	1.20	.25	.07
444	5c Christmas	2.10	.30	.07

SCOTT CAT. NO.	DESCRIPTION	PLATE BLOCK F/NH	UNUSED F/NH	USED F

1966. COMMEMORATIVES

445-52	8 Varieties	10.50	2.45	.60
445	5c Alouette II Satellite	1.50	.35	.10
446	5c LaSalle Arrival	1.50	.35	.07

447   448

447	5c Highway Safety	1.50	.35	.10
448	5c London Conference	1.50	.35	.07

449

450   451, 452   453

449	5c Atomic Reactor	1.50	.35	.10
450	5c Parliamentary Library ...	1.50	.35	.07
451	3c Christmas	.90	.18	.07
452	5c Christmas	1.50	.30	.07

1967. COMMEMORATIVES

453/77	(453, 69-77) cpl., 10 Vars.	15.50	3.25	.75
453	5c National Centennial	1.50	.35	.08

454   455   456, 466

457, 467   458, 468   459-60F, 468A-B, 543, 549

Stamps shown: 461, 462, 463, 464, 465, 465A, 465B

Regional Views & Art Designs

1967-72. Perf. 12 except as noted.

460 & 460C printed by British American Bank Note Co.
460F printed by Canadian Bank Note Co.

460 Original Die. Weak shading lines around 6. Perf. 12½ x 12.
460C Reworked Plate. Lines strengthened, darker. Perf. 12½ x 12.
460F Original Die. Strong shading lines, similar to 468B, but Perf. 12 x 12.

SCOTT CAT. NO.	DESCRIPTION	PLATE BLOCK F/NH	UNUSED F/NH	USED F
454-65B	1c $1, cpl., 17 Vars.	190.00	37.25	2.60
454-64	1c-20c, 14 Vars.	49.50	6.50	1.35
454	1c brown	1.00	.10	.07
455	2c green	1.75	.12	.07
456	3c dull purple	2.00	.20	.07
457	4c carmine rose	3.00	.25	.07
458	5c blue	1.75	.25	.07
459	6c orange, pf. 10	5.25	.50	.08
459B	6c orange 12½ x 12	4.50	.45	.08
460	6c black, 12½ x 12	3.00	.35	.08
460C	6c black, 12½ x 12	3.25	.45	.08
460F	6c black, pf. 12	6.00	.55	.15
461	8c "Alaska Highway"	5.50	.75	.40
462	10c "The Jack Pine"	3.75	.65	.07
463	15c "Bylot Island"	7.50	1.50	.10
464	20c "The Ferry, Quebec"	6.00	1.25	.10
465	"The Solemn Land"	13.50	2.50	.10
465A	50c "Summer Shores"	37.00	7.50	.20
465B	$1 "Imp. Wildcat No 3"	105.00	22.00	1.00

1967-70. Coil Stamps

SCOTT CAT. NO.	DESCRIPTION	PLATE BLOCK F/NH	UNUSED F/NH	USED F
466-68B	3c-6c cpl., 5 Vars.		5.75	3.40

Perf. 9½ Horizontally

466	3c dull purple		2.25	1.25
467	4c carmine rose		1.25	.95
468	5c blue		2.25	1.10

Perf. 10 Horizontally

468A	6c orange		.50	.15
468B	6c black		.45	.15

NOTE: See #543-50 for similar issues.

Stamps shown: 469, 470, 471, 472, 473

1967

469	5c Expo '67	1.50	.35	.10
470	5c Women's Franchise	2.25	.50	.08
471	5c Royal Visit	1.50	.35	.08
472	5c Pan-American Games	1.50	.35	.08
473	5c Canadian Press	1.50	.35	.08

Stamps shown: 474, 475

Stamps shown: 476, 477

SCOTT CAT. NO.	DESCRIPTION	PLATE BLOCK F/NH	UNUSED F/NH	USED F
474	5c George P. Vanier	1.75	.40	.08
475	5c View of Toronto	1.50	.32	.08
476	3c Christmas	1.00	.21	.08
477	5c Christmas	2.45	.55	.15

SCOTT CAT. NO.	DESCRIPTION	PLATE BLOCK F/NH	UNUSED F/NH	USED F
484	5c G. Brown, Politician	1.75	.40	.15
485	5c H. Bourassa Journalist	1.75	.40	.12
486	15c W.W.I Armistice	14.50	3.00	2.00

NOTE: Beginning with #478, some issues show a printer's inscription with no actual plate number.

479

480

478

481

482

483

484

485

486

487

488

489

490

491

492

493

494

1968. COMMEMORATIVES

SCOTT CAT. NO.	DESCRIPTION	PLATE BLOCK F/NH	UNUSED F/NH	USED F
478-89 cpl., 12 Vars.		36.75	7.95	2.95
478	5c Gray Jays	7.50	1.75	.12
479	5c Weathermap & Instruments	1.75	.40	.08
480	5c Narwhal	1.75	.40	.08
481	5c Int.'l Hydro. Decade	1.75	.40	.08
482	5c Voyage of "Nonsuch"	1.75	.40	.15
483	5c Lacrosse Players	1.75	.40	.15

SCOTT CAT. NO.	DESCRIPTION	PLATE BLOCK F/NH	UNUSED F/NH	USED F
487	5c J. McCrae	1.60	.35	.10
488	5c Eskimo Family	1.25	.25	.07
489	6c Mother & Child	1.60	.35	.07

1969. COMMEMORATIVES

SCOTT CAT. NO.	DESCRIPTION	PLATE BLOCK F/NH	UNUSED F/NH	USED F
490-504 cpl., 15 Vars.		79.95	17.25	9.95
490	6c Game of Curling	1.75	.40	.15
491	6c V. Massey	1.75	.40	.07

SCOTT CAT. NO.	DESCRIPTION	PLATE BLOCK F/NH	UNUSED F/NH	USED F
492	50cA.deSuzor-Cote, Artist ..	28.00	6.00	3.75
493	6c I.L.O.	1.75	.40	.12
494	15c Vickers Vimy Over Atlantic...............	18.00	4.00	2.50

495   496   500

501   502, 503

497   498

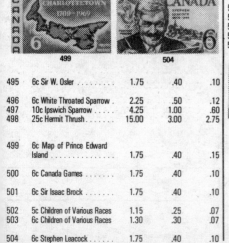

499   504

495	6c Sir W. Osler	1.75	.40	.10
496	6c White Throated Sparrow .	2.25	.50	.12
497	10c Ipswich Sparrow	4.25	1.00	.60
498	25c Hermit Thrush	15.00	3.00	2.75
499	6c Map of Prince Edward Island	1.75	.40	.15
500	6c Canada Games	1.75	.40	.10
501	6c Sir Isaac Brock	1.75	.40	.10
502	5c Children of Various Races	1.15	.25	.07
503	6c Children of Various Races	1.30	.30	.07
504	6c Stephen Leacock	1.75	.40	.10

SCOTT CAT. NO.	DESCRIPTION	PLATE BLOCK F/NH	UNUSED F/NH	USED F

505   506

507

1970. COMMEMORATIVES

505//31 (505-18, 31)15 Varieties		47.00(12)	24.50	20.95
505	6c Manitoba Cent.	1.50	.32	.07
506	6c N.W. Territory Centenary .	1.50	.32	.08
507	6c International Biological .	1.50	.32	.10

508   509

510   511

508-11	25c, 4 Vars., att'd	22.50	20.00	.....
508	25c Emblems	____	5.00	5.00
509	25c Dogwood	____	5.00	5.00
510	25c Lily	____	5.00	5.00
511	25c Trillium	____	5.00	5.00

512   513-14

515   516

SCOTT CAT. NO.	DESCRIPTION	PLATE BLOCK F/NH	UNUSED F/NH	USED F

Canada 6

517

518

512	6c H. Kelsey-Explorer	1.45	.32	.10
513	10c 25th U.N. Anniversary	6.00	1.25	.85
514	15c 25th U.N. Anniversary	8.25	1.75	1.25
515	6c L. Riel-Metis Leader	1.40	.32	.08
516	6c Sir A. Mackenzie-Explorer	1.40	.32	.07
517	6c Sir O. Mowat Confederation Father	1.40	.32	.10
518	6c Isle of Spruce	1.40	.32	.07

SCOTT CAT. NO.	DESCRIPTION	PLATE BLOCK F/NH	UNUSED F/NH	USED F
519-30	5c-15c, cpl., 12 Varieties	24.95(4)	6.50	3.35
519-23	5c cpl., 2 each 5 varieties	8.00(10)	.....	.....
519	5c Santa Claus		.40	.12
520	5c Sleigh		.40	.12
521	5c Nativity		.40	.12
522	5c Skiing		.40	.12
523	5c Snowman & Tree		.40	.12
524-28	6c cpl., 2 each 5 varieties	8.50(10)	.....	.....
524	6c Christ Child		.50	.12
525	6c Tree & Children		.50	.12
526	6c Toy Store		.50	.12
527	6c Santa Claus		.50	.12
528	6c Church		.50	.12

Note: We cannot supply blocks or pairs of the 5c & 6c Christmas designs in varying combinations of designs.

| 529 | 10c Christ Child | 3.00 | .65 | .60 |
| 530 | 15c Snowmobile & Trees | 7.35 | 1.75 | 1.75 |

Canada 15
519

Canada 5
520

Canada 5
521

Canada 5
522

Canada 5
523

6 Canada
524

6 Canada
525

6 Canada
526

6 Canada
527

6 Canada
528

Canada 10
529

Canada 15
530

531

532

534

533

535

536

Canada 7
537

Canada 7
538

Canada 6
539

| 531 | 6c Sir Donald A. Smith | 1.40 | .32 | .15 |

SCOTT CAT. NO.	DESCRIPTION	PLATE BLOCK F/NH	UNUSED F/NH	USED F
	1971. COMMEMORATIVES			
532/58	(532-42, 52-58) cpl. 18 Vars.	55.00	11.95	6.35
532	6c E. Carr-Painter & Writer .	1.40	.32	.07
533	6c Discovery of Insulin	1.50	.32	.07
534	6c Sir E. Rutherford - Physicist	1.50	.32	.07
535-38	6c-7c cpl., 4 Varieties . . .	6.75	1.50	.45
535	6c Maple Seeds	1.80	.40	.12
536	6c Summer Leaf	1.80	.40	.12
537	7c Autumn Leaf	1.80	.40	.12
538	7c Winter Leaf	1.80	.40	.12
539	6c L. Papineau-Polit. Reform.	1.40	.32	.15

540

541

542

543, 549

544, 550

540	6c Copper Mine Expedition . .	1.40	.32	.15
541	15c Radio Canada Int'l	18.00	4.00	3.00
542	6c Census Centennial	1.40	.32	.10
	1971-72			
543	7c Trans. & Communication .	4.50	.50	.10
544	8c Parlimentary Library	3.75	.45	.07
	1971. Coil Stamps. Perf. 10 Horizontally			
549	7c Trans. & Communication	_____	.65	.15
550	8c Parliamentary Library . . .	_____	.65	.08

562

553

552	7c B.C. Centennial	1.55	.35	.07
553	7c Paul Kane	5.00	1.00	.12

554-55

556-57

554-57	6c-15c cpl., 4 Varieties	12.50	2.75	2.35
554	6c Snow Flake, blue	1.40	.30	.07
555	7c same, green	1.55	.35	.07
556	10c Same, red & silver	2.50	.55	.60
557	15c Same, red blue & silver	8.00	1.75	1.75
558	7c P. Laporte	3.40	.35	.10

558

559

560

561

558	7c P. Laporte	3.40	.35	.10
	1972. COMMEMORATIVES			
559//610	(559-61, 82-85, 606-10) 12 Vars.	74.75(9)	17.25	15.25
559	8c Figure Skating	1.75	.40	.07
560	8c W.H.O.—Heart Disease . .	1.75	.40	.07
561	8c Frontenac & Ft. St. Louis	1.75	.40	10

562

563

SCOTT CAT. NO.	DESCRIPTION	PLATE BLOCK F/NH	UNUSED F/NH	USED F

1972-76. INDIAN PEOPLES OF CANADA

SCOTT CAT. NO.	DESCRIPTION	PLATE BLOCK F/NH	UNUSED F/NH	USED F
562-81 cpl, 20 Varieties		26.85(10)	10.55	2.85
562-63	8c 2 Vars, att'd	3.00	1.10	....
562	8c Buffalo Chase		.55	.15
563	8c Indian Artifacts		.55	.15
564-65	8c 2 Vars., att'd	3.00	1.10	....
564	8c Thunderbird Symbolism		.55	.15
565	8c Sun Dance Costume		.55	.15
566-67	8c 2 Vars., att'd	3.00	1.10	....
566	8c Algonkian Artifacts		.55	.15
567	8c Micmac Indians		.55	.15
568-69	8c 2 Vars., att'd	2.50	1.00	....
568	8c Thunderbird Symbolism		.50	.15
569	8c Costume		.50	.15
570-71	8c 2 Vars., att'd	2.20	.80	....
570	8c Nootka Sound House		.40	.15
571	8c Artifacts		.40	.15
572-73	8c 2 Vars., att'd	5.25	2.50	....
572	8c Chief in Chilkat Blanket		1.25	.15
573	8c Thunderbird-Kwakiutl		1.25	.15
574-75	8c 2 Vars, att'd	2.20	.80	....
574	8c Canoe & Artifacts		.40	.15
575	8c Dance-Kutcha-Kutchin		.40	.15
576-77	8c 2 Vars., att'd	2.20	.80	....
576	8c Kutchin Costume		.40	.15
577	8c Ojibwa Thunderbird		.40	.15
578-79	10c 2 Vars., att'd	2.50	1.00	....
578	10c Masks		.50	.15
579	10c Camp		.50	.15
580-81	10c 2 Vars., att'd	2.50	1.00	....
580	10c Iroquois Thunderbird		.50	.15
581	10c Man & Woman		.50	.15

NOTE: To determine the VF price on stamps issued from 1941 to date, add 15% to the F/NH or F (used) price (minimum .03 per item). All VF unused stamps from 1941 to date will be NH. From 1964 to date, all unused stamps will be F/NH.

SEE PAGE X FOR CONDITION DEFINITIONS

SCOTT CAT. NO.	DESCRIPTION	PLATE BLOCK F/NH	UNUSED F/NH	USED F

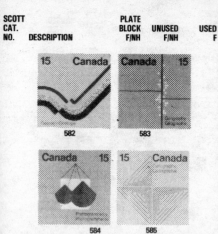

582   583

584   585

1972 EARTH SCIENCES

582-85	4 Vars., att'd	57.50(16)	14.00	
582	15c Geology	———	3.50	3.50
583	15c Geography	———	3.50	3.50
584	15c Photogrammetry	———	3.50	3.50
585	15c Cartography	———	3.50	3.50

NOTE: Plate Block Price is for a miniature pane of 16 Stamps

586   587   588   589

590   591   592   593,593b,593A
604,605

1973-76. DEFINITIVE ISSUE PERF. 12 x 12½

586-93A	1c-10c, 10 Vars.	19.25	3.95	2.95
586	1c Sir J. MacDonald	.35	.07	.07
587	2c Sir W. Laurier	.50	.10	.07
588	3c Sir R. L. Borden	.70	.15	.07
589	4c W. L. Mackenzie King	.90	.20	.07
590	5c R. B. Bennett	1.10	.25	.07
591	6c L. B. Pearson	1.30	.30	.07
592	7c L. St. Laurent	1.50	.35	.07
593	8c Queen Elizabeth blue	1.70	.40	.07
593b	8c Same, blue (pf. 13 x 13½)	10.00	2.00	2.00
593A	10c dark carmine (pf. 13 x 13½)	2.50	.50	.07

594,594a,594B   595,595a   596,596a

597,597a   598,598a,598B

599,599a,600

601

1972-74 Photogravure & Engraved. Perf 12½ x 12.

594-99	10c - $1, 8 Vars.	55.75	13.25	1.95
594	10c Forests	2.15	.50	.12
594B	10c Same	2.15	.50	.07
595	15c Mountain Sheep	3.15	.75	.15
596	20c Prairie Mosaic	4.15	1.00	.18
597	25c Polar Bears	5.25	1.25	.15
598	50c Seashore	10.50	2.50	.15
598B	50c Same	10.50	2.50	.13
599	$1 Vancouver Skyline	21.00	5.00	1.15

NOTE: #594-97 exist with 2 types of phosphor tagging. Prices above are for Ottawa tagged. Winnipeg tagged are listed on page 308.

#595 1st Design: Foreground has a screened effect.
#594B Revised: Foreground appears nearly solid.
#598 1st Design: Lighter colors. Surf at base of cliff partially dotted.
#598 B Revised: Deeper colors. Surf all dotted.
Plate block price is for blank corners.

SCOTT CAT. NO.	DESCRIPTION	PLATE BLOCK F/NH	UNUSED F/NH	USED F
	1976-77 Perf. 13.			
594a-99a	10c-$1, 6 Vars.	46.75	11.10	1.25
594a	10c Forests	2.15	.50	.10
595a	15c Mountain Sheep . . .	4.15	.95	.12
596a	20c Prairie Mosaic	5.25	1.25	.15
597a	25c Polar Bears	6.25	1.50	.12
598a	50c Seashore	10.50	2.50	.20
599a	$1 Vancouver Skyline . . .	21.00	5.00	.65
	1972. Lithographed & Engraved. Perf. 11			
600	$1 Vancouver Skyline	70.00	15.00	4.50
601	$2 Quebec Buildings	38.00	9.00	4.50
	1974-76. Coil Stamps			
604	8c Queen Elizabeth, blue . . . (pr .90)		.45	.07
605	10c Same, dark carmine . . . (pr 1.00)		.50	.10

606,607

608,609

610

611

612

614

613

	1972			
606-09	6c-15c cpl., 4 Varieties	12.35	2.70	1.75
606	6c 5 Candles	1.40	.30	.07
607	8c Same	1.75	.40	.07
608	10c 6 Candles	4.50	1.00	.70
609	15c Same	5.50	1.25	1.00
610	8c C. Krieghoff-Painter	3.80	.40	.12

	1973. COMMEMORATIVES			
611-28	18 Vars., cpl.	42.75	9.65	6.50

SCOTT CAT. NO.	DESCRIPTION	PLATE BLOCK F/NH	UNUSED F/NH	USED F
611	8c Monsignor De Laval	1.75	.40	.10
612	8c G.A. French & Map	1.75	.40	.10
613	10c Spectograph	2.15	.50	.50
614	15c "Musical Ride"	4.55	1.10	1.00

615

616

617

618

615	8c J. Mance- Nurse	1.75	.40	.10
616	8c J. Howe	1.75	.40	.10
617	15c "Mist Fantasy"-Painting	4.25	1.00	1.00
618	8c P.E.I. Confederation	1.75	.40	.10

619

620, 621

622

623, 624

SCOTT CAT. NO.	DESCRIPTION	PLATE BLOCK F/NH	UNUSED F/NH	USED F
619	8c Scottish Settlers	1.75	.40	.10
620	8c Royal Visit	1.75	.40	.15
621	15c Same	5.00	1.10	1.10
622	8c Nellie McClung	1.75	.40	.08
623	8c 21st Olympic Games	1.75	.40	.15
624	15c Same	5.00	1.10	1.10

625

626

627

628

SCOTT CAT. NO.	DESCRIPTION	PLATE BLOCK F/NH	UNUSED F/NH	USED F
625-28	6c to 15c, cpl., 4 Vars	8.45	1.95	1.40
625	6c Skate	1.40	.30	.07
626	8c Bird Ornament	1.75	.40	.07
627	10c Santa Claus	2.15	.50	.50
628	15c Shepard	3.60	.85	.85

629

630

631

632

BUY COMPLETE SETS AND SAVE

633

SCOTT CAT. NO.	DESCRIPTION	PLATE BLOCK F/NH	UNUSED F/NH	USED F
1974. COMMMEMORATIVES				
629-55	cpl., 27 Varieties	33.50(16)	12.50	6.50
629-32	8c, 4 Varieties, att'd	2.40	2.20	....
629	8c Children Diving		.55	.20
630	8c Jogging		.55	.20
631	8c Bicycling		.55	.20
632	8c Hiking		.55	.20
633	8c Winnipeg Centennary	1.75	.40	.08

634

635

636

637

638

639

640

641

SCOTT CAT. NO.	DESCRIPTION	PLATE BLOCK F/NH	UNUSED F/NH	USED F
634-39	8c, 6 Varieties, att'd	3.25(6)	3.00	....
634	8c Postal Clerk & Client		.50	.42
635	8c Mail Pick Up		.50	.42
636	8c Mail Handler		.50	.42
637	8c Sorting Mail		.50	.42

SCOTT CAT. NO.	DESCRIPTION	PLATE BLOCK F/NH	UNUSED F/NH	USED F
638	8c Letter Carrier	_____	.50	.42
639	8c Rural Delivery	_____	.50	.42
640	8c Agriculture Symbol	1.75	.40	.08
641	8c Antique to Modern Phones	1.75	.40	.08

642

643

644

645

646

647

648, 649

642	8c World Cycling Championship	1.75	.40	.08
643	8c Mennonite Settlers	1.75	.40	.08
644-47	8c, 4 Varieties, att'd	2.30	2.00	. . . .
644	8c Snowshoeing	_____	.50	.18
645	8c Skiing	_____	.50	.18
646	8c Skating	_____	.50	.18
647	8c Curling	_____	.50	.18
648	8c U.P.U. Cent.	1.75	.40	.10
649	15c Same	5.00	1.10	1.10

NOTE: To determine the VF price on stamps issued from 1941 to date, add 15% to the F/NH or F (used) price (minimum .03 per item). All VF unused stamps from 1941 to date will be NH. All stamps issued after 1963 will be NH.

650

651

652

653

650-53	6c to 15c, cpl., 4 Varieties .	8.50	1.90	1.30
650	6c Nativity	1.40	.30	.07
651	8c Skaters in Hull	1.75	.40	.07
652	10c The Ice Cone	2.20	.50	.45
653	15c Laurentian Village	3.60	.85	.80

654

655

656

657

654	8c G. Marconi-Radio Inventor.	1.75	.40	.0
655	8c W.H. Merritt & Welland Canal	1.75	.40	.0

1975. COMMEMORATIVES			
656-680 cpl. 25 Varieties . . . . . 133.00(18)		34.50	23.7
656	$1 " The Sprinter"	30.00	6.50	5.2
657	$2 "The Plunger"	65.00	15.00	12.0

658

659

658-59	8c, 2 Varieties, att'd	1.75	.80	. . .
658	8c L.M. Montgomery-Author	_____	.40	
659	8c L. Hemon-Author	_____	.40	

SCOTT CAT. NO.	DESCRIPTION	PLATE BLOCK F/NH	UNUSED F/NH	USED F

660

661

662

663

660	8c M. Bourgeoys-Educator . .	1.75	.40	.10
661	8c A. Desjardins-Credit Union	1.75	.40	.10
662-63	8c, 2 Vars., att'd	1.75	.80	. . . .
662	8c J. Cook & Church	____	.40	.32
663	8c S. Chown & Church	____	.40	.32

664

665

664

667

666

668

669

| 664 | 20c Pole Vaulter . . . . | 4.25 | 1.00 | 1.00 |
| 665 | 25c Marathon Runner . . . . | 5.50 | 1.25 | 1.00 |

SCOTT CAT. NO.	DESCRIPTION	PLATE BLOCK F/NH	UNUSED F/NH	USED F
666	50c Hurdler	9.50	2.25	1.65
667	8c Calgary Centenary	1.75	.40	.08
668	8c Int'l Women's Year	1.75	.40	.08
669	8c "Justice"	1.75	.40	.08

670

671

672

673

670-73	4 Vars., att'd	5.00	4.20	. . . .
670	8c W.D. Lawrence	____	1.05	.50
671	8c Beaver	____	1.05	.50
672	8c Neptune	____	1.05	.50
673	8c Quadra	____	1.05	.50

674

675

676

677

678

679

674-79	6c to 15c, cpl., 6 Vars . . .	8.15(4)	2.60	1.35
674-75	2 Vars., att'd	1.40	.60	. . . .
674	6c Santa Claus	____	.30	.07
675	6c Skater	____	.30	.07
676-77	2 Vars., att'd	1.75	.80	. . . .

SCOTT CAT. NO.	DESCRIPTION	PLATE BLOCK F/NH	UNUSED F/NH	USED F
676	8c Child	_____	.40	.10
677	8c Family & Tree	_____	.40	.10
678	10c Gift	2.20	.50	.35
679	15c Trees	3.25	.75	.75

680

681

682

683

| 680 | 8c Horn & Crest | 1.75 | .40 | .08 |

1976. COMMEMORATIVES

681-703 cpl., 23 Vars.	164.50(18)	39.50	26.50

681	8c Olympic Flame	1.75	.40	.10
682	20c Opening Ceremony	4.50	1.00	.75
683	25c Receiving Medals	5.50	1.25	1.25

684

685

686

684	20c Communication Arts	6.50	1.50	.90
685	25c Handicraft Tools	8.00	1.75	.95
686	50c Performing Arts	11.50	2.75	1.50

687

688

| 687 | $1 Notre Dame & Tower | 45.00 | 10.00 | 7.00 |
| 688 | $2 Olympic Stadium | 67.50 | 15.00 | 10.00 |

690

689

691

692

693

689	20c Olympic Winter Games	4.25	1.00	.85
690	20c "Habitat"	4.00	.95	.75
691	10c Benjamin Franklin	2.20	.50	.25
692-93	2 Vars., att'd	1.75	.80	.....
692	8c Color Parade	_____	.40	.18
693	8c Wing Parade	_____	.40	.18

BUY COMPLETE SETS AND SAVE

700-03	10c 4 Vars., att'd	2.20	2.00	.....
700	10c Northcote	_____	.50	.50
701	10c Chicora	_____	.50	.50
702	10c Passport	_____	.50	.50
703	10c Athabasca	_____	.50	.50

704

1977. COMMEMORATIVES

704/51	(704, 732-51) cpl., 21 Vars	39.25(14)	12.65	5.55
704	25c Silver Jubilee	5.25	1.25	1.25

705,781,781a   707,782,782b   708,783   709,784

710,785   711,711a,786   712

713, 713a, 716, 716a   714,715,729,730
789, 789a, 791, 792   790,797,800,806

1977-79 Definitives

Perf. 12 x 12½

705-27	1c to $2 cpl. 25 vars.	119.95(23)	29.95	9.65
705	1c Gentian	.35	.07	.07
707	2c West. Columbine	.50	.10	.07
708	3c Canada Lily	.65	.14	.08
709	4c Hepatica	.80	.17	.08

Left column stamp labels and table:

694

695

696

697

Canada 10
698

Canada 20
699

94	20c Olympiad-Phys. Disabled	5.25	1.25	1.25
95-96	8c 2 Vars., att'd	1.75	.80	.....
95	8c R.W. Service-Author	_____	.40	.12
96	8c G. Guevremont-Author	_____	.40	.12
97	8c Nativity Window	1.75	.40	.08
98	10c Same	2.20	.50	.18
99	20c Rondel	4.00	.95	.60

Canada 10
700

Canada 10
701

Canada 10
702

Canada 10
703

SCOTT CAT. NO.	DESCRIPTION	PLATE BLOCK F/NH	UNUSED F/NH	USED F
710	5c Shooting Star	.90	.20	.07
711	10c Lady's Slipper	2.20	.50	.10
711a	10c Same, pf. 13	2.20	.50	.10
712	12c Jewelweed, pf. 13 x 13½	2.45	.55	.10
713	12c Q.E. II, blue, white & black, pf. 13 x 13½	2.45	.55	.07
713a	12c Same, pf. 12 x 12½ .	_____	.55	.10
714	12c Parliament, pf. 13 . . .	2.45	.55	.07
715	14c Same, red & white, pf. 13	2.80	.65	.07
716	14c Q.E. II, red & gray, pf. 13 x 13½	2.80	.65	.07
716a	14c Same, pf. 12 x 12½ . .	_____	.65	.15

Note: 713a, 716a are from booklet panes. 713a will have one or more straight edges, 716a may or may not have straight edges.

717   718   719

720   721

723, 723A

724   725

Perf. 13½

717	15c Trembling Aspen	3.00	.70	.27
718	20c Douglas Fir	3.80	.90	.35
719	25c Sugar Maple	4.65	1.10	.45
720	30c Oak Leaf	5.25	1.25	.55
721	35c White Pine	5.85	1.40	.40
723	50c Main Street	9.25	2.25	.50
723A	50c Same, 1978 Lic. Plate .	8.25	2.00	.50
724	75c Row Houses	12.25	3.00	1.05
725	80c Hill Hugging Street	13.00	3.20	1.15

726

727

Perf. 13

SCOTT CAT. NO.	DESCRIPTION	PLATE BLOCK F/NH	UNUSED F/NH	USED F
726	$1 Fundy National Park . . .	14.50	3.50	1.25
727	$2 Kluane National Park . . .	26.50	6.50	2.75

1977-78 Coil Stamps. Perf. 10 Vert.

729	12c Parliament, blue, white & black	(pr 1.04)	.52	.10
730	14c Same, red & white	(pr 1.30)	.65	.10

732   733

734   735

1977

732	12c Cougar	2.45	.55	.10
733-34	2 Vars., att'd	2.45	1.10	. . .
733	12c Algonquin Park	_____	.55	.10
734	12c Autumn Birches	_____	.55	.10
735	12c Crown & Lion	2.45	.55	.10

736   737

736	12c Badge & Ribbon	2.45	.55	.10
737	12c Peace Bridge	2.45	.55	.10

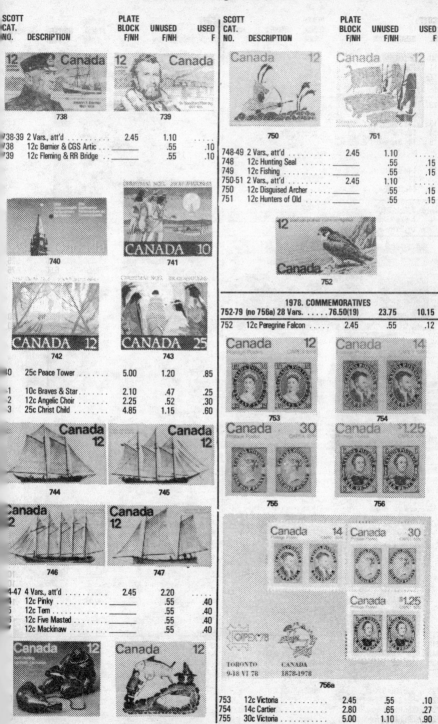

SCOTT CAT. NO.	DESCRIPTION	PLATE BLOCK F/NH	UNUSED F/NH	USED F
738-39	2 Vars., att'd	2.45	1.10	....
738	12c Bernier & CGS Artic	_____	.55	.10
739	12c Fleming & RR Bridge	_____	.55	.10

740

741

742

743

40	25c Peace Tower	5.00	1.20	.85
1	10c Braves & Star	2.10	.47	.25
2	12c Angelic Choir	2.25	.52	.30
3	25c Christ Child	4.85	1.15	.60

744

745

746

747

4-47	4 Vars., att'd	2.45	2.20	....
4	12c Pinky	_____	.55	.40
5	12c Tern	_____	.55	.40
6	12c Five Masted	_____	.55	.40
	12c Mackinaw	_____	.55	.40

748

749

750

751

SCOTT CAT. NO.	DESCRIPTION	PLATE BLOCK F/NH	UNUSED F/NH	USED F
748-49	2 Vars., att'd	2.45	1.10	....
748	12c Hunting Seal	_____	.55	.15
749	12c Fishing	_____	.55	.15
750-51	2 Vars., att'd	2.45	1.10	....
750	12c Disguised Archer	_____	.55	.15
751	12c Hunters of Old	_____	.55	.15

752

1978. COMMEMORATIVES

SCOTT CAT. NO.	DESCRIPTION	PLATE BLOCK F/NH	UNUSED F/NH	USED F
752-79	(no 756a) 28 Vars.	76.50(19)	23.75	10.15
752	12c Peregrine Falcon	2.45	.55	.12

753

754

755

756

756a

753	12c Victoria	2.45	.55	.10
754	14c Cartier	2.80	.65	.27
755	30c Victoria	5.00	1.10	.90

SCOTT CAT. NO.	DESCRIPTION	PLATE BLOCK F/NH	UNUSED F/NH	USED F
756	$1.25 Albert	21.50	5.00	2.25
756a	$1.69 Capex Sheet of 3	_____	6.75	.....

NOTE: 754, 756 & 756 were also issued in sheets of 50.

SCOTT CAT. NO.	DESCRIPTION	PLATE BLOCK F/NH	UNUSED F/NH	USED F
/65	14c Miners	_____	.65	.14
766	14c Tar Sands	_____	.65	.14
767	14c CNE 100th Anniversary	2.80	.65	.14

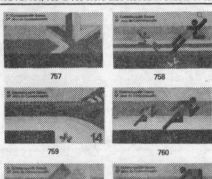

757　758　759　760　761　762

768

763　764

757	14c Games Symbol	2.80	.65	.15
758	30c Badminton Players	5.65	1.35	1.00
759-60	2 Vars., att'd	2.80	1.30	
759	14c Stadium	_____	.65	.14
760	14c Runners	_____	.65	.14
761-62	2 Vars., att'd	5.65	2.70	
761	30c Edmonton	_____	1.35	.80
762	30c Bowls	_____	1.35	.80
763-64	2 Vars., att'd	2.80	1.30	
763	14c Capt. Cook	_____	.65	.14
764	14c Nootka Sound	_____	.65	.14

769　770

771　772

768	14c Mere d'Youville	2.80	.65	.14
769-70	2 Vars., att'd	2.80	1.30	
769	14c Woman Walking	_____	.65	.14
770	14c Migration	_____	.65	.14
771-72	2 Vars., att'd	2.80	1.30	
771	14c Plane over Village	_____	.65	.14
772	14c Dog Team & Sled	_____	.65	.14

765　766

767

765-66	2 Vars., att'd	2.80	1.30	.....

773　774　775

776　777

SCOTT CAT. NO.	DESCRIPTION	PLATE BLOCK F/NH	UNUSED F/NH	USED F

778

779

773	12c Mary & Child w/pea . . .	2.25	.52	.12
774	14c Mary & Child w/apple . .	2.55	.60	.14
775	30c Mary & Child w/goldfinch	5.60	1.35	.90
776-79	4 vars., Att'd	2.65	2.48	. . . .
776	14c Robinson	_____	.62	.30
777	14c St. Roch	_____	.62	.30
778	14c Northern Light	_____	.62	.30
779	14c Labrador	_____	.62	.30

780

1979. COMMEMORATIVES

780/846	(780, 813-46) cpl., 35 vars.	.60.50(17)	25.50	12.75
780	14c Quebec Winter Carnival .	2.40	.55	.14

Types of #705-16

787

1979-83 Definitives. Perf. 13 x 13½

781-92	1c - 32c cpl. 14 vars.	.16.75(10)	4.50	1.15
81	1c Gentian	.35	.07	.0/
81a	1c Same, perf 12 x 12½ . . .	_____	.10	.10
82	2c Western Columbine . . .	.35	.07	.07
82b	2c Same, perf 12 x 12½ . . .	_____	.10	.10
83	3c Canada Lily	.45	.10	.08
84	4c Hepatica	.70	.15	.07
85	5c Shooting Star	.85	.18	.07
86	10c Lady's Slipper	1.50	.35	.10
87	15c Violet	2.00	.45	.35
89	17c Queen Eliz. green & black	2.55	.60	.07
9a	17c Same, perf 12 x 12½ . .	_____	.60	.10
0	17c Parliament Bldg. slate gm.	2.55	.60	.07
1	30c Queen Eliz. violet & black	3.45	.80	.08
2	32c Queen Eliz.	3.45	.80	.08

NOTE: 781a, 782b, 797 & 800 are from booklet panes and will have one or more straight edges. 789a may or may not have straight edges.

SCOTT CAT. NO.	DESCRIPTION	PLATE BLOCK F/NH	UNUSED F/NH	USED F

Perf. 12 x 12½

797	1c Parliament Bldg. slate blue	_____	.12	.12
800	5c Parliament Bldg. violet brn	_____	.15	.12

1979. Coil Stamps. Perf. 10 Vert.

806	17c Parliament Building, slate green	(pr 1.30)	.68	.10

813

814

817

818

815

816

819

820

813	17c Turtle	2.90	.68	.15
814	35c Whale	6.00	1.45	.95
815-16	2 vars., att'd	2.90	1.45	. . . .
815	17c Woman's Finger	_____	.68	.15
816	17c Man's Finger	_____	.68	.15
817-18	2 Vars., att'd	2.90	1.36	. . . .
817	17c "Fruits of the Earth" . .	_____	.68	.15
818	17c "The Golden Vessel" . .	_____	.68	.15
819-20	2 Vars., att'd	2.90	1.36	. . . .
819	17c Charles de Salaberry . .	_____	.68	.15
820	17c John By	_____	.68	.15

SCOTT CAT. NO.	DESCRIPTION	PLATE BLOCK F/NH	UNUSED F/NH	USED F

821 Ontario

PROVINCIAL FLAGS
822 Quebec
823 Nova Scotia
824 New Brunswick
825 Manitoba
826 British Columbia
827 Prince Edward Island
828 Saskatchewan
829 Alberta
830 Newfoundland
831 Northwest Territories

832 Yukon 1

832a	Sheet of 12 Vars., att'd ...	8.25	8.25	.....
Any	17c Single	_____	.68	.60

NOTE: When ordering singles, please use catalog number.

833

834

833	17c CK Championship	2.90	.68	.15
834	17c Field Hockey	2.90	.68	.15

835

836

837

838

835-86	2 Vars., att'd	2.90	1.36	....
835	17c Summer Tent	_____	.68	.15
836	17c Igloo	_____	.68	.15
837-38	2 Vars., att'd	2.90	1.36	....
837	17c The Dance	_____	.68	.15
838	17c Soapstone Figures	_____	.68	.15

839

840

841

842

839	15c Wooden Train	2.80	.65	.0
840	17c Horse Pull Toy	3.00	.70	.1
841	35c Knitted Doll	5.85	1.40	.8
842	17c I.Y.C.	3.00	.70	.1

843

844

845

846

843-44	2 Vars., att'd	3.00	1.40	...
843	17c Curtiss HS2L	_____	.70	.
844	17c Canadian CL215	_____	.70	.
845-46	2 Vars., att'd	6.25	3.00	...
845	35c Vickers Vedette	_____	1.50	.
846	35c Consolidated Canso	_____	1.50	.

847

848

849

850

SCOTT CAT. NO.	DESCRIPTION	PLATE BLOCK F/NH	UNUSED F/NH	USED F

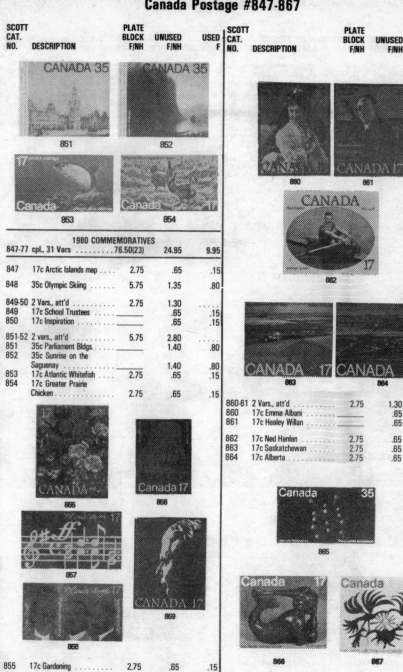

851 852 853 854

1980 COMMEMORATIVES

SCOTT CAT. NO.	DESCRIPTION	PLATE BLOCK F/NH	UNUSED F/NH	USED F
847-77	cpl., 31 Vars .... 76.50(23)		24.95	9.95
847	17c Arctic Islands map	2.75	.65	.15
848	35c Olympic Skiing	5.75	1.35	.80
849-50	2 Vars., att'd	2.75	1.30	.....
849	17c School Trustees	___	.65	.15
850	17c Inspiration	___	.65	.15
851-52	2 vars., att'd	5.75	2.80	
851	35c Parliament Bldgs.....	___	1.40	.80
852	35c Sunrise on the Saguenay		1.40	.80
853	17c Atlantic Whitefish	2.75	.65	.15
854	17c Greater Prairie Chicken	2.75	.65	.15

860 861 862 863 864 865 866 867

SCOTT CAT. NO.	DESCRIPTION	PLATE BLOCK F/NH	UNUSED F/NH	USED F
860-61	2 Vars., att'd	2.75	1.30	.....
860	17c Emma Albani	___	.65	.15
861	17c Healey Willan	___	.65	.15
862	17c Ned Hanlan	2.75	.65	.15
863	17c Saskatchewan	2.75	.65	.15
864	17c Alberta	2.75	.65	.15

855 866 857 869 862

SCOTT CAT. NO.	DESCRIPTION	PLATE BLOCK F/NH	UNUSED F/NH	USED F
855	17c Gardening	2.75	.65	.15
856	17c Rehabilitation	2.75	.65	.15
857-58	2 vars., att'd	2.75	1.30	.....
857	17c Bars of Music	___	.65	.34
858	17c 3 Musicians	___	.65	.34
859	17c John Diefenbaker	2.75	.65	.15
865	35c Uranium Resources ...	5.75	1.40	.75
866-67	2 Vars. att'd	2.75	1.30	.....
866	17c Sedna	___	.65	.15
867	17c Sun	___	.65	.15

SCOTT CAT. NO.	DESCRIPTION	PLATE BLOCK F/NH	UNUSED F/NH	USED F

868

869

868-69	2 Vars. att'd	5.75	2.80	....
868	35c Bird Spirit	_____	1.40	.75
869	35c Shaman	_____	1.40	.75

870

871

872

870	15c Xmas	2.55	.60	.10
871	17c Xmas	2.75	.65	.15
872	35c Xmas	5.60	1.35	.70

873

874

875

876

877

873-74	2 Vars., att'd	2.75	1.30	....
873	17c Avro Canada CF-100	_____	.65	.15
874	17c Avro Lancaster	_____	.65	.15
875-76	2 Vars., att'd	5.60	2.70	....
875	35c Curtiss JN-4	_____	1.35	.75
876	35c Hawker Hurricane	_____	1.35	.75
877	17c Dr. Lachapelle	2.75	.65	.15

878

	1981 COMMEMORATIVES			
878-906	cpl., 29 Vars.	51.95(19)	17.50	6.25
878	17c Antique Instrument	2.35	.55	.12

879

880

881

882

879-82	4 vars., att'd	2.35	2.20	....
879	17c Emily Stone	_____	.55	.16
880	17c Louise McKinney	_____	.55	.16
881	17c Idola Saint-Jean	_____	.55	.16
882	17c Henrietta Edwards	_____	.55	.16

883

884

885

886

883	17c Marmot	2.35	.55	.12
884	35c Bison	5.20	1.25	.65
885-86	2 vars., att'd	2.35	1.10	....
885	17c Kateri Tekakwitha	_____	.55	.15
886	17c Marie de l'Incarnation	_____	.55	.15

SCOTT CAT. NO.	DESCRIPTION	PLATE BLOCK F/NH	UNUSED F/NH	USED F

887

888

889

887	17c "At Baie St. Paul"	2.35	.55	.12
888	17c Self-Portrait	2.35	.55	.12
889	35c Untitled No. 6	5.00	1.20	.90

890

891

892

893

894

895

890-93	4 vars att'd	4.65(8)	2.20	____
890	17c Canada in 1867	____	.55	.15
891	17c Canada in 1873	____	.55	.15

SCOTT CAT. NO.	DESCRIPTION	PLATE BLOCK F/NH	UNUSED F/NH	USED F
892	17c Canada in 1905	____	.55	.15
893	17c Canada since 1949 ...	____	.55	.15
894-95	2 vars. att'd	2.35	1.10	.....
894	17c Frere Marie-Victorin ...	____	.55	.15
895	17c John Macoun	____	.55	.15

896

897

898

899

896	17c Montreal Rose	2.35	.55	.12
897	17c Niagara-on-the-Lake ...	2.35	.55	.12
898	17c Acadians	2.35	.55	.12
899	17c Aaron Mosher	2.35	.55	.12

900

901

902

900	15c Christmas Tree in 1781	2.35	.55	.10
901	15c Christmas Tree in 1881	2.35	.55	.10
902	15c Christmas Tree in 1981	2.35	.55	.10

SCOTT CAT. NO.	DESCRIPTION	PLATE BLOCK F/NH	UNUSED F/NH	USED F

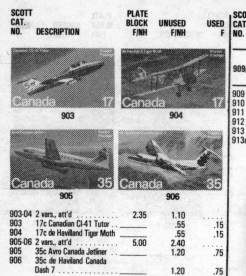

903　904

905　906

903-04	2 vars., att'd	2.35	1.10	
903	17c Canadian CI-41 Tutor		.55	.15
904	17c de Havilland Tiger Moth		.55	.15
905-06	2 vars., att'd	5.00	2.40	
905	35c Avro Canada Jetliner		1.20	.75
906	35c de Haviland Canada Dash 7		1.20	.75

907, 908

| 907 | (30c) "A" Maple Leaf | 3.80 | .90 | .08 |
| 908 | (30c) "A" Maple Leaf, coil | | .90 | .08 |

909　910

911　912

913

SCOTT CAT. NO.	DESCRIPTION	PLATE BLOCK F/NH	UNUSED F/NH	USED F
	1982 COMMEMORATIVES			
909/75	(909-16, 54-75) 30 vars., cpl	69.50(17)	24.50	7.65
909	30c 1851 Beaver	3.30	.75	.20
910	30c 1908 Champlain	3.30	.75	.25
911	35c 1935 Mountie	3.85	.85	.75
912	35c 1928 Mt. Hurd	3.85	.85	.75
913	60c 1929 Bluenose	6.60	1.50	1.10
913a	$1.90 Phil. Exhib. sheet of 5		4.75	

914　915

916

914	30c Jules Leger	3.30	.75	.18
915	30c Terry Fox	3.30	.75	.18
916	30c Constitution	3.30	.75	.18

NOTE: To determine the VF price on stamps issued from 1941 to date, add 15% to the F/NH or F (used) price (minimum .03 per item). All VF unused stamps from 1941 to date will be NH. All stamps issued after 1963 will be NH.

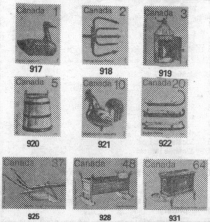

917　918　919

920　921　922

925　928　931

SCOTT CAT. NO.	DESCRIPTION	PLATE BLOCK F/NH	UNUSED F/NH	USED F
	1982-83 HERITAGE ARTIFACT DEFINITIVES			
917	1 c Decoy	.35	.07	.07
918	2c Fishing Spear	.35	.07	.07
919	3c Stable Lantern	.40	.08	.07
920	5c Bucket	.60	.13	.08
921	10c Weathercock	1.20	.25	.10
922	20c Skates	2.20	.50	.15
925	37c Plow	3.80	.90	.....
928	48c Cradle	4.65	1.10	.....
931	64c Stove	6.25	1.50	.....

CANADA

CANADA 60

923, 923a, 941, 942, 945, 946, 947, 950, 951

929

935

938

CANADA

	1982-83 Definitives			
923	30c Maple Leaf, blue & red, pf 13x13½	3.30	.75	.08
923a	As above, pf 12x12½		.75	.....
924	32c Maple Leaf, red on tan pf. 13x13½	3.50	.80	.08
929	60c Ontario Street	6.60	1.50	.75
935	$1.50 Waterton Lakes	16.50	3.75	1.95
938	$5 Point Pelee	55.00	12.50	.....
941	5c Maple Leaf, violet	_____	.12	.08
941A	8c Maple Leaf, dk. blue		.20	.08
942	10c Maple Leaf, green		.25	.08
945	30c Maple Leaf, red, pf 12x12½		.75	.10
946	32c Maple Leaf, brown on white, pf 12x12½		.80	.08
947	32c Maple Leaf, red on tan, pf 12x12½	—	.80	.08
950	30c Maple Leaf, coil	_____	.75	.08
951	32c Maple Leaf, coil	_____	.80	.08

NOTE: 941, 941A, 942, 945 & 946 are from booklet panes and will have one or more straight edges; 923a and 947 are from booklet panes, the middle strip of which is perforated completely

Canada 30

954

954	30c Salvation Army	3.30	.75	.08

956 Quebec
957 Newfoundland
958 Northwest Territories
959 Prince Edward Island
960 Nova Scotia
961 Saskatchewan
962 Ontario
963 New Brunswick
964 Alberta
965 British Columbia
966 Manitoba

CANADA 30

955 Yukon Territories

966a	Sheet of 12 vars., att'd	9.00	9.00	.....
Any	30c Single	_____	.75	.15

Regina

CANADA 30

967

968

967	30c Regina	3.30	.75	.10
968	30c Henley Regatta	3.30	.75	.10

30 Canada

30 Canada

969

970

60 Canada

60 Canada

971

972

969-70	2 vars., att'd	3.30	1.50	.....
969	30c Fairchild FC-2W1	_____	.75	.15
970	30c de Haviland Canada Beaver	_____	.75	.15
971-72	2 vars., att'd	6.60	3.00	.....
971	60c Noorduyn Norseman	_____	1.50	.65
972	60c Fokker Super Universal		1.50	.65

SCOTT CAT. NO.	DESCRIPTION	PLATE BLOCK F/NH	UNUSED F/NH	USED F

973   974   975

973	30c Joseph, Mary & Infant .	3.30	.75	.08
974	35c Shepherds	3.85	.85	.12
975	60c Wise Men	6.60	1.50	.65

1983 COMMEMORATIVES

| 976-1008 | Cpl., 33 Vars. . . . . | 89.95(20) | 30.75 | . . . . . |

976   977

| 976 | 32c World Comm. Year . . . . | 3.40 | .80 | .08 |
| 977 | $2.00 Commonwealth Day . | 21.00 | 5.00 | . . . . . |

978   979

978-79	2 Vars., att'd	3.40	1.60	. . . . .
978	32c Laure Conan	_____	.80	.12
979	32c E.J. Pratt	_____	.80	.12

980

| 980 | 32c St. John Ambulance . . . | 3.40 | .80 | .12 |

SCOTT CAT. NO.	DESCRIPTION	PLATE BLOCK F/NH	UNUSED F/NH	USED F

981   982

| 981 | 32c University Games . . . . | 3.40 | .80 | .12 |
| 982 | 64c University Games . . . . | 6.25 | 1.50 | . . . . |

983 Ft. Henry

984 Ft. William
985 Ft. Rodd Hill
986 Ft. Wellington
987 Ft. Prince of Wales
988 Halifax Citadel
989 Ft. Chambly
990 Ft. No. 1 Pt. Levis
991 Ft. at Coteau-du-Lac

992 Ft. Beausejour

| 992a | 32c Forts, pane of 10 . . . . | _____ | 7.50 | . . . . |
| Any | 32c Single . . . . | _____ | .80 | .50 |

993

994

995

993	32c Boy Scouts	3.40	.80	.12
994	32c Council of Churches . . .	3.40	.80	.12
995	32c Humphrey Gilbert	3.40	.80	.12

SCOTT CAT. NO.	DESCRIPTION	PLATE BLOCK F/NH	UNUSED F/NH	USED F

996

997

998

996	32c Nickel	3.40	.80	.12
997	32c Jesiah Hensen	3.40	.80	.12
998	32c Fr. Antoine Labelle	3.40	.80	.12

999

1000

1001

1002

999-1000				
	2 vars., attd	3.40	1.60	....
999	32c Toronto 4-4-0	....	.80	.15
1000	32c Dorchester 0-6-0	....	.80	.15
1001	37c Samsen 0-6-0	3.80	.90	....
1002	64c Adam Brown 4-4-0	6.25	1.50	....

1003

| 1003 | 32c Law School | 3.40 | .80 | .12 |

SCOTT CAT. NO.	DESCRIPTION	PLATE BLOCK F/NH	UNUSED F/NH	USED F

1004

1005

1006

1004	32c City Church	3.40	.80	.12
1005	37c Family	3.80	.90	....
1006	64c County Chapel	6.25	1.50	....

1007

1008

1007-08				
	2 vars., att'd	3.40	1.60	....
1007	32c Can. & Br. Reg	——	.80	.15
1008	32c Winn. & Dragoons	——	.80	.15

1009

1010

1984

| 1009 | 32c Yellowknife | 3.25 | .75 | .12 |
| 1010 | 32c Year of the Arts | 3.25 | .75 | .12 |

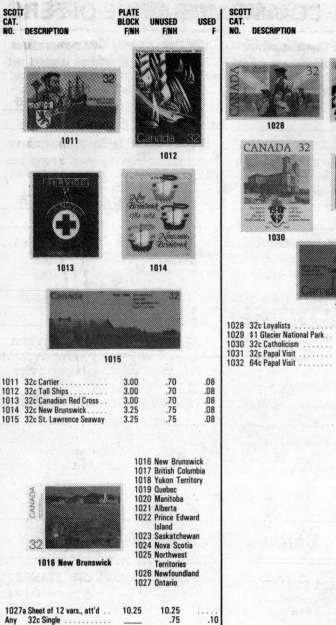

SCOTT CAT. NO.	DESCRIPTION	PLATE BLOCK F/NH	UNUSED F/NH	USED F

1011

1012

1013

1014

1015

SCOTT CAT. NO.	DESCRIPTION	PLATE BLOCK F/NH	UNUSED F/NH	USED F
1028	32c Loyalists	3.25	.75	.08
1029	$1 Glacier National Park	10.75	2.50	1.25
1030	32c Catholicism	3.25	.75	.08
1031	32c Papal Visit	3.25	.75	.08
1032	64c Papal Visit	6.50	1.50	.75

1028

1029

1030

1031

1032

SCOTT CAT. NO.	DESCRIPTION	PLATE BLOCK F/NH	UNUSED F/NH	USED F
1011	32c Cartier	3.00	.70	.08
1012	32c Tall Ships	3.00	.70	.08
1013	32c Canadian Red Cross	3.00	.70	.08
1014	32c New Brunswick	3.25	.75	.08
1015	32c St. Lawrence Seaway	3.25	.75	.08

1016 New Brunswick

1016 New Brunswick
1017 British Columbia
1018 Yukon Territory
1019 Quebec
1020 Manitoba
1021 Alberta
1022 Prince Edward Island
1023 Saskatchewan
1024 Nova Scotia
1025 Northwest Territories
1026 Newfoundland
1027 Ontario

1027a	Sheet of 12 vars., att'd	10.25	10.25	.....
Any	32c Single	___	.75	.10

CANADA COMMEMORATIVE OFFERS

70 Unused Canada Commemoratives
70 unused commemoratives issued between 1947 and 1963 at a special price.
SAVE $6.45
A723 .... $23.95

70 Unused Canada Commemoratives
70 unused commemoratives issued between 1964 and 1969 at a special price.
SAVE $6.65
A724 .... $27.50

105 Unused Canada Commemoratives
105 unused commemoratives issued between 1970 and 1974 at a special price.
SAVE $9.60
A725 .... $47.50

135 Unused Canada Commemoratives
135 unused commemoratives issued between 1975 and 1979 at a special price.
SAVE $9.45
A726 .... $87.50

380 Unused Canada Commemoratives
A combination of the four offers listed above. Save over $48.50 on individual prices.

A728 .... $170.00

120 Used Canada Commemoratives
120 used commemoratives isssued between 1947 and 1967 at a special price.
SAVE $4.31
A729 .... $9.95

110 Used Canada Commemoratives
110 used commemoratives issued between 1968 and 1974 at a special price.
SAVE $4.47
A730 .... $11.95

90 Used Canada Commemoratives
90 used commemoratives issued between 1975 and 1979 at a special price.
SAVE $6.25
A731 .... $11.95

320 Used Canada Commemoratives
A combination of the three offers listed above. Save 40% off individual prices.

A733 .... $29.95

Note: For Commemorative
Plate Block Offers

SEE NEXT PAGE

CANADA COIL OFFERS

20 UNUSED CANADA COIL STAMPS
20 Unused Canada Coil Stamps issued between 1937 and 1976. Save $5.50 off individual prices.

A738   **SPECIAL PRICE** $17.95

45 USED CANADA COIL STAMPS
45 Used Canada Coil Stamps issued between 1912 and 1976 at a substantial discount over individual prices. Save $9.92

A739   **SPECIAL PRICE** $28.95

SCOTT CAT. NO.	DESCRIPTION	BLANK CORNER BLOCKS F/NH	UNUSED F/NH	SCOTT CAT.NO.	DESCRIPTION	BLANK CORNER BLOCKS F/NH	UNUSED F/NH

CANADA PHOSPHOR TAGGED ISSUES

Overprinted with barely visible phosphorescent ink.

1962-63

SCOTT CAT. NO.	DESCRIPTION	BLANK CORNER BLOCKS F/NH	UNUSED F/NH
337p-41p	1c-5c Queen Elizabeth . . . (5)	70.00	16.00
401p-05p	1c-5c Queen Elizabeth . . . (5)	15.50	1.95

1964-66

434p-35p	3c + 5c 1964 Xmas . . . (2)	22.00	4.50
443p-44p	3c + 5c 1965 Xmas . . . (2)	5.25	.75
451p-52p	3c+5 1966 Xmas . . . . (2)	5.25	.75

1967

453p	5c National Centenary . . . (1)	2.50	.50

1967-72. QUEEN ELIZABETH

454p1-58p1	1c-5c Type I . . . . . . (5)	13.50	2.50
454p2-58p2	1c-5c Type II (no 456)(4)	10.00	1.10
459p1	6c org perf. 10 . . . . (1)	5.25	.85
459bp1	6c org. pf. 12½ x 12 . . . (1)	5.50	.65
460p1	6c black-Type I . . . . . (1)	4.25	.75
460cp2	6c black-Type II . . . . . . (1)	4.25	.55
460Fp1	6c black-Type I . . . . . . (1)	5.75	.55
460Fp2	6c black-Type II . . . . . . (1)	5.75	.55

Note: Type I has tagging between stamps. Type Ii has tagging down middle of stamps.

462p-65p	10c,15c,20c,25c Views . (4)	42.75	8.65

1967-69

476p-77p	3c + 5c 1967 Xmas . . . (2)	4.00	.95

SCOTT CAT.NO.	DESCRIPTION	BLANK CORNER BLOCKS F/NH	UNUSED F/NH
488p-89p	5c + 6c 1968 Xmas . . . (2)	3.65	.70
502p-03p	5c + 6c 1969 Xmas . . .)2)	3.75	.75

1970

505p	6c Manitoba . . . . (1)	1.75	.40
508p-11p	25c Expo '70 . . . . . . (4)	24.00	. . . . .
513p-14p	10c + 15c U.N. . . . . . . (2)	21.00	4.25
519p-30p	5c-15c 1970 Xmas . . . (12)	. . . . .	7.25

1971

541p	15c Radio Canada . . . . . (1)	42.50	8.00
543p	7c Queen Elizabeth . . . . . (1)	4.25	.70
544p	8c Queen Elizabeth . . . . . (1)	3.00	.55
550p	8c Queen Eliz., Coil . . . . . (1)	pr 1.20	.60
554p-57p	6c-15c 1971 Xmas . . . (4)	15.75	3.15

1972

560p	8c W.H.O. . . . . (1)	1.95	.45
561p	8c Frontenac . . . . (1)	1.95	.45
562p-63p	8c Indians . . . . (2)	5.50	pr 1.20
564p-65p	8c Indians . . . . (2)	5.50	pr 1.20
582p-85p	15c Sciences . . . . (4)	57.50(16)	. . . . .
594pw-97pw	10c-25c Pictorials Winnipeg Tagged . . . . . . (4)	43.50	8.50

Note: See regular listing (#596-98) for Ottawa tagged

606po-09po	6c-15c Xmas, Ottawa Tagged . . . . (4)	13.65	3.00
606pw-09pw	6c-15c Xmas, Winnipeg Tagged . . . . (4)	14.00	3.35
610p	8c Winter Scene . . . . . . (1)	4.00	.45

SCOTT CAT. NO.	DESCRIPTION	PLATE BLOCK F/NH	UNUSED F/NH	USED F	SCOTT CAT NO.	DESCRIPTION	PLATE BLOCK F/NH	UNUSED F/NH	USED F

SEMI-POSTAL STAMPS

B1-3

B4

Canada 8+2 B7

Canada 10+5 B8

B5

B6

Canada 15+5 B9

Canada 8+3 B10

Canada 10+5 B11

Canada 20+5 B12

1974-76

| B1-12 | cpl., 12 Vars. | 36.95 | 8.65 | ..... |

1974

B1-3	8c + 2c to 15c + 5c,cpl., 3 Vars.	9.50	2.20	.....
B1	8c + 2c Olympic Emblem	2.20	.50	.50
B2	10c + 5c Same	3.75	.90	.90
B3	15c + 5c Same	4.20	1.00	1.00

1975

B4-6	8c + 2c to 15c + 5c, cpl., 3 Vars.	9.50	2.20	.....
B4	8c + 2c Swimming	2.20	.50	.50
B5	10c + 5c Rowing	3.75	.90	.90
B6	15c + 5c Sailing	4.20	1.00	1.00

B7-9	8c + 2c to 15c + 5c, cpl., 3 Vars.	9.50	2.20	.....
B7	8c + 2c Fencing	2.20	.50	.50
B8	10c + 5c Boxing	3.75	.90	.90
B9	15c + 5c Judo	4.20	1.00	1.00

1976

B10-12	8c + 2c to 20c + 5c, cpl., 3 Vars.	10.55	2.50	.....
B10	8c + 2c Basketball	2.20	.50	.50
B11	10c + 5c Gymnastics	3.75	.90	.90
B12	20c + 5c Soccer	5.25	1.25	1.25

SUPPLIES

Don't forget that Harris offers a complete line of albums, supplies, and accessories for all your stamp collecting needs. See our supply section in the back of the catalog.

SCOTT CAT. NO.	DESCRIPTION	UNUSED NH F	AVG	UNUSED F	AVG	USED F	AVG

AIR POST STAMPS

C1   C2   C3   C4

1928

C1	5c brown olive	16.00	12.75	13.50	10.50	4.25	3.50

1930

C2	5c olive brown	70.00	55.00	60.00	47.50	30.00	25.00

1932

C3	6c on 5c brown olive	9.50	7.75	8.00	6.50	4.00	3.25
C4	6c on 5c olive brown	23.50	18.50	20.00	15.00	17.00	13.00

C5   C6

1935

C5	6c red brown	3.85	3.25	3.25	2.75	1.65	1.40

1938

C6	6c blue	3.60	3.00	3.00	2.50	.35	.30

C7, 8   C9

		PLATE BLOCK F/NH	F	UNUSED F/NH	F	USED F

1942-43

C7	6c deep blue	25.00	21.00	4.75	4.00	1.20
C8	7c deep blue	4.75	4.00	.95	.80	.15

1946

C9	7c deep blue	4.50	4.00	.95	.80	.15

SCOTT CAT NO.	DESCRIPTION	PLATE BLOCK F/NH	F	UNUSED F/NH	F	USED F

AIR POST SPECIAL DELIVERY

CE1, CE2   **1942-43**   CE3, CE4

CE1	16c ultramarine	18.09	16.25	4.00	3.50	2.50
CE2	17c ultramarine	22.00	20.00	4.75	4.25	3.75
	1946					
CE3	17c ultramarine (Circumflex "A")	42.00	36.50	9.50	8.00	10.00
	1947					
CE4	17c ultramarine (Grave "/")	42.00	36.50	9.50	8.00	10.00

AIR POST OFFICIAL STAMPS

1949
C9 overprinted
O.H.M.S.

CO1	7c blue	90.00	75.00	18.00	15.00	4.85

1950. C9 overprinted G

CO2	7c blue	125.00	110.00	28.00	25.00	23.00

		UNUSED NH F	AVG	UNUSED F	AVG	USED F	AVG

SPECIAL DELIVERY STAMPS

E1   E2   E3   E4

	1898						
E1	10c blue green	95.00	75.00	80.00	60.00	12.75	10.00
	1922						
E2	20c carmine . . . . /	105.00	85.00	90.00	70.00	12.50	11.00
	1927						
E3	20c orange	17.50	12.50	15.00	10.00	13.00	12.00
	1930						
E4	20c henna brown	105.00	85.00	90.00	70.00	21.00	19.00

SCOTT CAT NO.	DESCRIPTION	PLATE BLOCK F/NH	F	UNUSED F/NH	F	USED F

E5   E6   E7, E8   E9

1933

| E5 | 20c henna brown | ..... | ..... | 65.00 | 50.00 | 21.50 |

1935

| E6 | 20c dark carmine | ..... | ..... | 15.00 | 12.00 | 8.00 |

1938-39

E7	10c dark green	55.00	42.00	10.00	8.00	3.50
E8	20c dark carmine	.....	.....	50.00	42.50	40.00
E9	10c on 20c carmine (#E8)	75.00(6)	60.00(6)	10.00	8.00	8.00

E10   E11

1942

| E10 | 10c green | 23.50 | 20.00 | 4.75 | 4.00 | 1.65 |

1946

| E11 | 10c green | 16.00 | 13.00 | 3.50 | 3.00 | 1.15 |

SPECIAL DELIVERY OFFICIAL STAMPS

1950 E11 overprinted O.H.M.S.

| EO1 | 10c green | 175.00 | 150.00 | 40.00 | 30.00 | 25.00 |

1950 E11 overprinted G.

| EO2 | 10c green | ..... | ..... | 60.00 | 55.00 | 47.50 |

		UNUSED OG F	AVG	UNUSED F	AVG	USED F	AVG

REGISTRATION STAMPS

F1-F3

1875-88 Perf. 12

F1	2c orange	75.00	60.00	65.00	50.00	5.50	4.00
F1a	2c vermilion	90.00	70.00	80.00	60.00	13.50	10.00
F1b	2c rose carmine	170.00	130.00	150.00	110.00	60.00	45.00
F1d	2c orange, pf. 12 x 11½	300.00	240.00	260.00	200.00	50.00	37.50
F2	5c yellow green	110.00	85.00	95.00	70.00	5.00	3.75
F3	8c blue	525.00	390.00	450.00	325.00	350.00	260.00

SCOTT CAT. NO.	DESCRIPTION	UNUSED NH F	AVG	UNUSED F	AVG	USED F	AVG

POSTAGE DUE STAMPS

J1-J5

J6-J10

J11-J14

1906-28

J1	1c violet	10.50	8.75	8.00	6.25	4.00	3.50
J2	2c violet	15.50	13.50	12.50	10.50	1.10	.85
J3	4c violet	75.00	62.50	60.00	50.00	32.50	24.50
J4	5c violet	14.00	12.50	11.50	9.00	2.00	1.65
J5	10c violet	55.00	45.00	45.00	40.00	13.50	12.50

1930-32

J6	1c dark violet	11.00	9.50	9.00	7.50	7.25	6.00
J7	2c dark violet	8.00	7.00	6.50	5.50	1.50	1.25
J8	4c dark violet	16.25	14.25	13.50	11.25	7.25	6.00
J9	5c dark violet	16.25	14.25	13.50	11.00	7.00	5.75
J10	10c dark violet	120.00	100.00	95.00	75.00	12.00	10.00

1933-34

J11	1c dark violet	15.00	13.00	12.00	10.00	7.75	6.50
J12	2c dark violet	6.50	6.00	5.75	5.00	1.75	1.50
J13	4c dark violet	13.00	11.50	10.50	9.00	7.25	6.00
J14	10c dark violet	21.00	18.00	16.00	14.00	6.25	5.25

J15-J20

J21-J40

1935-65

J15	1c dark violet	.23	.20	.20	.17	.15	.12
J16	2c dark violet	.23	.20	.20	.17	.15	.12
J16B	3c dark violet	3.35	3.25	3.10	3.00	2.40	2.25
J17	4c dark violet	.40	.35	.35	.30	.15	.12
J18	5c dark violet	.55	.45	.50	.40	.40	.35
J19	6c dark violet	2.80	2.60	2.35	2.25	2.15	2.00
J20	10c dark violet	.70	.60	.60	.50	.15	.12

		PLATE BLOCK F/NH	UNUSED F/NH	USED F

1967. Perf. 12
Regular Size Design 20 mm x 17 mm

J21	1c carmine rose	1.95	.45	.45
J22	2c carmine rose	1.55	.35	.35
J23	3c carmine rose	1.55	.35	.35
J24	4c carmine rose	2.25	.50	.50
J25	5c carmine rose	16.00	3.50	3.00
J26	6c carmine rose	2.45	.55	.55
J27	10c carmine rose	2.45	.55	.55

SEE PAGE X FOR CONDITION DEFINITIONS

SCOTT CAT NO.	DESCRIPTION	PLATE BLOCK F/NH	UNUSED F/NH	USED F

1969-74. Perf. 12
Modualar Size Design 19½ mm x 16 mm

SCOTT CAT NO.	DESCRIPTION	PLATE BLOCK F/NH	UNUSED F/NH	USED F
J28	1c carmine rose ('70)	2.50	.50	.50
J29	2c carmine rose ('72)	.80	.17	.12
J30	3c carmine rose ('74)	.70	.15	.12
J31	4c carmine rose('69)	1.60	.35	.35
J32a	5c carmine rose ('69)	135.00	30.00	30.00
J33	6c carmine rose ('72)	1.35	.30	.22
J34	8c carmine rose ('69)	2.00	.40	.25
J35	10c carmine rose ('69)	3.00	.75	.40
J36	12c carmine rose ('69)	2.70	.60	.55
J37	16c carmine rose ('74)	3.35	.80	.50

1977-78
Perf. 12½ x 12

SCOTT CAT NO.	DESCRIPTION	PLATE BLOCK F/NH	UNUSED F/NH	USED F
J28a	1c carmine rose	.40	.07	.07
J31a	4c carmine rose	.95	.20	.15
J32	5c carmine rose	1.15	.25	.10
J34a	8c carmine rose	1.75	.40	.17
J35a	10c carmine rose........	2.15	.50	.15
J36a	12c carmine rose........	2.55	.60	.50
J38	20c carmine rose........	4.25	1.00	.45
J39	24c carmine rose........	5.00	1.20	.55
J40	50c carmine rose........	10.50	2.50	1.30

	UNUSED NH		UNUSED		USED	
	F	AVG	F	AVG	F	AVG

WAR TAX STAMPS

MR1,MR2   **MR3-MR7**

2c + 1c: Die I. Below large letter "T" there is a clear horizontal line of color.
Die II. Right side of line is replaced by two short diagonal lines and five dots.

1915

		F	AVG	F	AVG	F	AVG
MR1	1c green	9.25	7.75	7.00	5.50	.18	.15
MR2	2c carmine	9.25	7.75	7.00	5.50	.25	.20

1916. Perf. 12

		F	AVG	F	AVG	F	AVG
MR3	2c + 1c carmine (I)............	15.50	13.50	11.50	9.50	.15	.12
MR3a	2c + 1c carmine (II)...........	135.00	110.00	100.00	80.00	3.75	2.75
MR4	2c + 1c brown (II)	9.00	7.50	7.00	5.50	.15	.12
MR4a	2c + 1c brown (I)............	350.00	280.00	270.00	200.00	10.00	8.00

Perf. 12 x 8

		F	AVG	F	AVG	F	AVG
MR5	2c + 1c carmine	43.50	37.50	36.50	30.00	28.50	22.50

Coil Stamps. Perf. 8 Vertically

		F	AVG	F	AVG	F	AVG
MR6	2c + 1c carmine	130.00	110.00	100.00	80.00	5.50	4.50
MR7	2c + 1c brown (II)...........	19.00	16.00	14.50	11.50	.75	.60
MR7a	2c + 1c brown (I)............	140.00	120.00	110.00	85.00	4.00	3.75

NOTE: Coil Pairs of the above can be supplied at two times the single price.

SCOTT CAT NO.	DESCRIPTION	PLATE BLOCK F/NH	F	UNUSED F/NH	F	USED F

OFFICIAL STAMPS
1949-50
249,250,252,254, 269-273 overprinted
O.H.M.S.

SCOTT CAT NO.	DESCRIPTION	PLATE BLOCK F/NH	F	UNUSED F/NH	F	USED F
01	1c green	18.00	15.00	3.00	2.50	2.50
02	2c brown	170.00	140.00	23.50	20.00	15.00
03	3c rose violet	15.50	13.00	2.90	2.50	1.40
04	4c dark carmine	25.00	21.00	5.00	4.25	.75
06	10c olive	30.00	25.00	6.75	5.50	.65
07	14c black brown	52.50	39.50	10.00	8.50	2.25
08	20c slate black	105.00	90.00	25.00	21.00	3.00
09	50c dark blue green	1600.00	1400.00	375.00	325.00	225.00
010	$1 red violet	500.00	425.00	110.00	90.00	70.00

1950. 294 overprinted

SCOTT CAT NO.	DESCRIPTION	PLATE BLOCK F/NH	F	UNUSED F/NH	F	USED F
011	50c dull green	225.00	200.00	40.00	40.00	30.00

1950. 284-88 overprinted
O.H.M.S.

SCOTT CAT NO.	DESCRIPTION	PLATE BLOCK F/NH	F	UNUSED F/NH	F	USED F
012	1c green	2.75	2.50	.45	.40	.40
013	2c sepia	4.65	4.25	1.05	1.00	1.00
014	3c rose violet	8.00	7.00	1.35	1.25	.50
015	4c dark carmine	8.00	7.00	1.35	1.25	.15
015A	5c deep blue	15.50	14.50	2.60	2.35	1.75

1950. 284-88, 269-71, 294, 273 overprinted G

SCOTT CAT NO.	DESCRIPTION	PLATE BLOCK F/NH	F	UNUSED F/NH	F	USED F
016	1c green	1.50	1.35	.28	.25	.12
017	2c sepia	8.75	8.00	1.35	1.25	1.00
018	3c rose violet	7.25	6.50	1.35	1.25	.15
019	4c dark carmine	7.50	7.00	1.45	1.35	.15
020	5c deep blue	16.50	14.50	1.65	1.50	.90
021	10c olive	18.00	16.00	3.85	3.50	.45
022	14c black brown	55.00	50.00	11.00	10.00	2.15
023	20c slate black	130.00	110.00	30.00	25.00	1.10
024	50c dull green	65.00	55.00	13.50	12.00	6.00
025	$1 red violet	650.00	550.00	150.00	125.00	110.00

1950-51. 301, 302 overprinted G

SCOTT CAT NO.	DESCRIPTION	PLATE BLOCK F/NH	F	UNUSED F/NH	F	USED F
026	10c black brown	7.75	7.00	1.65	1.50	.20
027	$1 bright ultramarine	650.00	550.00	150.00	125.00	95.00

1951-53. 305-06, 316, 320-21 overprinted G

SCOTT CAT NO.	DESCRIPTION	PLATE BLOCK F/NH	F	UNUSED F/NH	F	USED F
028	2c olive green	2.60	2.40	.60	.55	.12
029	4c orange vermilion	6.75	6.25	1.55	1.45	.12
030	20c gray	14.50	13.00	3.25	2.85	.15
031	7c blue	19.50	18.00	5.25	4.50	1.00
032	$1 gray	130.00	110.00	30.00	25.00	10.00

1953. 325-29, 334 overprinted G

SCOTT CAT NO.	DESCRIPTION	PLATE BLOCK F/NH	F	UNUSED F/NH	F	USED F
033	1c violet brown	1.50	1.40	.33	.30	.10
034	2c green	1.85	1.70	.45	.40	.10
035	3c carmine rose	1.85	1.70	.45	.40	.10
036	4c violet	2.60	2.40	.65	.60	.10
037	5c ultramarine	2.60	2.40	.65	.60	.10
038	50c light green	45.00	40.00	8.75	8.00	1.25

1955. 351 overprinted G

SCOTT CAT NO.	DESCRIPTION	PLATE BLOCK F/NH	F	UNUSED F/NH	F	USED F
039	10c violet brown	4.65	4.25	1.10	1.00	.12

SCOTT CAT NO.	DESCRIPTION	PLATE BLOCK F/NH	F	UNUSED F/NH	F	USED F
		1955-56. 337,338,340,341,362 overprinted G				
040	1c violet brown	2.10	1.95	.45	.40	.35
041	2c green	2.75	2.50	.55	.50	.12
043	4c violet	8.00	7.50	1.90	1.80	.12
044	5c bright blue	3.25	3.00	.65	.60	.10
045	20c green	9.75	9.00	2.10	2.00	.17
		1961-62 Flying G overprinted on 334, 351, 362				
038a	50c light green	34.50	32.00	7.25	7.00	2.00
039a	10c violet brown	13.00	12.00	2.15	2.00	1.00
045a	20c green	52.50	50.00	8.25	7.50	.55
		1963. 401,402,404, 405 overprinted G				
046	1c deep brown	4.25	4.00	1.00	.95	1.20
047	2c green	3.75	3.50	.85	.80	.80
048	4c carmine	9.00	8.25	.95	.90	.90
049	5c violet blue	3.50	3.25	.55	.50	.50

SCOTT CAT NO.	DESCRIPTION	UNUSED NH F	AVG	UNUSED F	AVG
	CANADA COIL LINE PAIRS				
	1930-31				
178	1c orange	60.00	55.00	55.00	50.00
179	2c deep green	42.50	35.00	35.00	30.00
180	2c dull green	35.00	30.00	30.00	25.00
181	2c deep red	42.50	35.00	35.00	30.00
182	2c dark brown	57.50	50.00	50.00	45.00
183	3c red	85.00	77.50	77.50	70.00
	1933				
205	1c dark green	75.00	70.00	70.00	65.00
206	2c black brown	85.00	80.00	80.00	75.00
207	3c deep red	75.00	70.00	70.00	65.00

CANADA MINIATURE PANES

NOTE: The single prices listed are for mini-panes which range from Fine to Very Fine condition. All ordered panes will be supplied within that range.

338a	1961, 2c pane of 25 .... 5.00		443ap	1965, 3c pane 25 Xmas, tagged 10.00
338a	same, sealed pack of 2 .... 10.00		443ap	same, sealed pack of 2 .... 20.00
341b	1961, 5c pane of 20, pack of 1 .... 10.00		451a	1966, 3c pane of 25, Xmas 5.50
			451a	same, sealed pack of 2 .... 11.00
402a	1963, 2c pane of 25 .... 7.50		451ap	1966, 3c pane of 25, Xmas, tagged 6.50
402a	same, sealed pack of 2 .... 15.00		451ap	same, sealed pack of 2 .... 13.00
404b	1963, 4c pane of 25, pack of 1 .... 10.00			
405b	1963, 5c pane of 20, pack of 1 .... 11.00		457b	1967, 4c pane of 25, pack of 1 .... 25.00
405bp	1965, 5c pane of 20, tagged 55.00		458b	1967, 5c pane of 20, pack of 1 .... 40.00
			458bp	1967, 5c pane of 20, tagged 75.00
434a	1964, 3c pane of 25, Xmas 10.00			
434a	same, sealed pack of 2 .... 20.00		476a	1967, 3c pane of 25, Xmas 6.50
434ap	1964, 3c pane of 25, Xmas, tagged 18.00		476a	same, sealed pack of 2 .... 13.00
434ap	same, sealed pack of 2 .... 36.00		476ap	1967, 3c pane of 25, Xmas, tagged 8.00
			476ap	same, sealed pack of 2 .... 16.00
443a	1965, 3c pane of 25, Xmas 7.50			
443a	same, sealed pack of 2 .... 15.00			

CANADA BOOKLET PANES

(The figure in parentheses indicates number of stamps in pane)

SCOTT CAT NO.	DESCRIPTION		UNUSED NH			UNUSED	
			F	AVG		F	AVG
		1900					
77b	2c Victoria ....(6)		1375.00	1075.00		1075.00	900.00
		1903					
90b	2c Edward ....(6)		1900.00	1600.00		1500.00	1300.00
		1912-23					
104a	1c green ....(6)		60.00	50.00		45.00	35.00
105a	1c yellow ....(4)		115.00	95.00		90.00	70.00
105b	1c yellow ....(6)		105.00	85.00		80.00	60.00
106a	2c carmine ....(6)		65.00	55.00		50.00	40.00
107b	2c green ....(4)		110.00	90.00		85.00	65.00
107c	2c green ....(6)		550.00	525.00		400.00	375.00
108a	3c brown ....(4)		160.00	125.00		120.00	90.00
109a	3c carmine ....(4)		75.00	60.00		60.00	45.00
		1928					
149a	1c orange.............................(6)		42.50	32.50		35.00	25.00
150a	2c green ....(6)		42.50	32.50		35.00	25.00
153a	5c violet ....(6)		195.00	155.00		160.00	120.00
		1930-31					
163a	1c green ....(4)		250.00	195.00		200.00	150.00
163c	1c green ....(6)		80.00	55.00		60.00	45.00
164a	2c green ....(6)		80.00	55.00		60.00	45.00
165b	2c red ....(6)		30.00	27.00		27.00	22.50
166a	2c brown ....(4)		240.00	190.00		200.00	150.00
166c	2c brown ....(6)		60.00	50.00		47.50	40.00
167a	3c red ....(4)		60.00	50.00		47.50	40.00
		1932					
195a	1c green ....(4)		175.00	150.00		150.00	130.00
195b	1c green ....(6)		38.50	32.50		32.50	28.00
196a	2c brown ....(4)		175.00	150.00		145.00	125.00
196b	2c brown ....(6)		38.50	32.50		32.50	28.00
197a	3c red ....(4)		55.00	45.00		45.00	40.00
		1935					
217a	1c green ....(4)		130.00	110.00		110.00	90.00
217b	1c green ....(6)		45.00	40.00		40.00	35.00
218a	2c brown ....(4)		125.00	110.00		110.00	92.50
218b	2c brown ....(6)		45.00	40.00		40.00	35.00
219a	3c carmine ....(4)		45.00	40.00		40.00	35.00
		1937					
231a	1c green ....(4)		30.00	23.50		23.50	18.00
231b	1c green ....(6)		4.50	3.75		3.75	3.25
232a	2c brown ....(4)		30.00	25.00		25.00	20.00
232b	2c brown ....(6)		15.00	13.50		13.50	11.00
233a	3c carmine ....(4)		5.50	4.75		4.75	4.00

SCOTT CAT NO.	DESCRIPTION	UNUSED			DESCRIPTION	UNUSED	
		F/NH	F			F/NH	F
				1942-43			
249a	1c green ....(4)	9.00	8.00	252a	3c rose violet ...(4)	3.85	3.50
249b	1c green ....(6)	2.75	2.50	252b	3c rose violet ...(3)	2.85	2.50
249c	1c green ....(3)	2.25	2.00	252c	3c rose violet ...(6)	11.25	10.00
250a	2c brown ....(4)	9.00	8.00	254a	4c dark carmine .(6)	4.75	4.25
250b	2c brown......(6)	7.50	6.50	254b	4c dark carmine .(3)	3.75	3.50
251a	3c dark carmine .(4)	3.60	3.25				

SCOTT CAT NO.	DESCRIPTION	UNUSED F/NH	F
1949-51			
284a	1c green .... (3)	.65	.55
286a	3c violet .... (3)	1.50	1.40
286b	3c violet .... (4)	1.85	1.60
287a	4c dark carmine ...... (3)	13.75	13.00
287b	4c dark carmine ...... (6)	14.50	13.00
306a	4c vermilion .... (3)	3.75	3.40
306b	4c vermilion .... (6)	3.25	2.75
1953			
325a	1c violet brown ...... (3)	.85	.75
327a	3c carmine rose ...... (3)	1.55	1.40
327b	3c carmine rose ...... (4)	2.25	2.00
328a	4c violet .... (3)	1.85	1.60
328b	4c violet .... (6)	2.75	2.50
1954			
336a	5c Beaver .... (5)	3.00	2.75
337a	1c violet brown ...... (5)	.85	.75
340a	4c violet .... (5)	2.25	2.00
340b	4c violet .... (6)	7.75	7.25
341a	5c bright blue ...... (5)	2.50	2.25
1962-63			
401a	1c deep brown ...... (5)	5.00	4.50
404a	4c violet .... (5)	5.50	5.00
405a	5c violet blue ...... (5)	5.50	5.00
1967-70			
454a	1c brown .... (5)	.75	
454b	1c(1),6c(4)	2.50	
454c	1c(5),4c(5)	2.50	
455a	2c(4),3c(4)	2.50	
457a	4c carmine rose ...... (6)	2.00	
457c	4c carmine rose ...... (25)	10.00	
458a	5c blue .... (5)	7.25	
458c	5c blue .... (20)	9.50	
459a	6c orange .... (25)	11.50	
460a	6c black, die 1, perf. 10 .... (25)	22.00	
460b	6c black, die I, perf. 12½ x 12 ...... (25)	22.00	
460d	6c black, die II, perf 12½ x 12 ...... (4)	6.00	
460e	6c black, die II, perf. 10 .... (4)	9.00	

SCOTT CAT NO.	DESCRIPTION	UNUSED F/NH
1968		
488a	5c '68 Xmas .... (10)	4.00
488ap	5c '68 Xmas, tagged .. (10)	5.00
1969		
502a	5c '69 Xmas .... (10)	4.00
502ap	5c '69 Xmas,tagged ... (10)	5.00
1971-72		
543a	7c(3),3c(1),1c(1)	4.50
543b	7c(12),3c(4), 1c(4)	10.00
544a	8c(2), 6c(1), 1c(3)	2.50
544ap	Same as 544a, tagged	2.50
544b	8c(11), 6c(1), 1c(6)	7.50
544bp	Same as 544b, tagged	7.50
544cf	8c(5), 6c(1), 1c (4)	3.25
544cp	Same as 544c, tagged	3.25
1974-76		
586a	1c(3), 6c(1)c 8c(2)	.85
586b	1c(6), 6c(1), 8c(11)	4.00
586c	1c(2), 2c(4), 8c(4)	2.25
1977-79		
716bf	14c red & gray (716a)(25) .	17.50
781b	1c(2-781a); 12c(4-713a) ..	2.50
782a	2c(4-782b); 14c(3-716a) ..	2.50
789b	17c green & black (25)	17.00
797a	1c(1-797); 5c (3-800)	
	17c(2-780a)	2.00
1982 - 83		
923b	30c (20-923a)	12.00
941a	5c(2-941); 10c(1-942); 30c(1-945)	1.25
946b	5c(2-941); 8c(1-941A); 32c(1-946)	1.50
947a	32c(25-947)	17.95
992a	32c Forts (10)	7.50

NOTE: 941a comes with slogans on top or on bottom

		F/NH	F
1946			
C9a	7c Airmail .... (4)	3.25	3.00

NEWFOUNDLAND

SCOTT CAT NO.	DESCRIPTION	UNUSED OG F	AVG	UNUSED F	AVG	USED F	AVG

1,5,12A,15A,16,19

2,11,17

3,11A

4,12,18

6,13,20

7,14,21

8,22

9,10,15,23

1857. Imperforate. Thick Paper.

1	1p brown violet	120.00	95.00	90.00	65.00	95.00	70.00
2	2p scarlet vermilion	......	......	......	......	5100.00	4500.00
3	3p green	575.00	475.00	425.00	325.00	425.00	325.00
4	4p scarlet vermilion	......	......	......	......	3350.00	2650.00
5	5p brown violet	400.00	300.00	300.00	200.00	325.00	225.00
7	6½ scarlet vermilion	3000.00	2500.00	2200.00	1700.00	2150.00	1700.00
8	8p scarlet vermilion	500.00	395.00	365.00	265.00	365.00	265.00

1860. Thin Paper.

11	2p orange	500.00	400.00	375.00	275.00	375.00	275.00
11A	3p green	120.00	90.00	90.00	60.00	100.00	70.00
12	4p orange	3500.00	3000.00	2500.00	2000.00	1150.00	850.00
12A	5p violet brown	125.00	95.00	95.00	65.00	175.00	125.00
13	6p orange	4000.00	3500.00	2950.00	2400.00	750.00	550.00

1861-62. Thin Paper.

15A	1p violet brown	235.00	180.00	175.00	120.00	170.00	120.00
17	2p rose	290.00	210.00	215.00	140.00	225.00	150.00
18	4p rose	70.00	50.00	55.00	35.00	80.00	60.00
19	5p reddish brown	70.00	50.00	55.00	35.00	80.00	60.00
20	6p rose	30.00	22.50	23.00	15.00	50.00	35.00
21	6½p rose	105.00	80.00	80.00	55.00	200.00	140.00
22	8p rose	100.00	75.00	75.00	50.00	275.00	200.00
23	1sh rose	60.00	45.00	45.00	30.00	140.00	100.00

24, 38
Codfish

25, 26, 40
Seal

27
Prince Albert

28, 29
Queen Victoria

30
Fishing Ship

31
Queen Victoria

1865-94. Perf. 12

24	2c green	75.00	60.00	60.00	45.00	27.00	20.00
24a	2c green (white paper)	75.00	60.00	60.00	45.00	27.00	20.00
25	5c brown	510.00	400.00	425.00	310.00	300.00	225.00
26	5c black	290.00	220.00	235.00	175.00	160.00	120.00
27	10c black	250.00	200.00	200.00	150.00	100.00	75.00
27a	10c black (white paper)	190.00	150.00	160.00	120.00	50.00	37.50

SCOTT CAT NO.	DESCRIPTION	UNUSED OG		UNUSED		USED	
		F	AVG	F	AVG	F	AVG
28	12c pale red brown	250.00	190.00	200.00	150.00	125.00	100.00
28a	12c pale red brn. (white paper)	50.00	37.50	40.00	30.00	40.00	30.00
29	12c brown	62.50	47.50	50.00	37.50	50.00	37.50
30	13c orange	105.00	80.00	85.00	65.00	85.00	65.00
31	24c blue	42.50	32.50	35.00	25.00	35.00	25.00

32, 32A, 37　　　33-36, 39
Prince of Wales　　Queen Victoria

1868-94

32	1c violet	50.00	40.00	40.00	30.00	35.00	25.00
32A	1c brown lilac, re-engraved	60.00	50.00	50.00	40.00	40.00	30.00
33	3c vermilion	335.00	260.00	275.00	200.00	110.00	80.00
34	3c blue	300.00	220.00	245.00	170.00	17.00	12.00
35	6c dull rose	17.00	13.00	14.00	10.00	14.00	10.00
36	6c carmine lake	20.00	15.50	16.00	12.00	16.00	12.00

1876-79 Rouletted.

37	1c brown lilac	75.00	65.00	60.00	50.00	40.00	30.00
38	2c green	75.00	65.00	60.00	50.00	40.00	30.00
39	3c blue	260.00	195.00	220.00	150.00	14.00	10.00
40	5c blue	165.00	125.00	135.00	95.00	14.00	10.00

41-45　　　　　46-48　　　　　49-52　　　　　53-55
Prince of Wales　　Codfish　　Queen Victoria　　Seal

1880-96 Perf. 12.

41	1c violet brown	18.50	14.50	16.00	12.00	14.00	10.00
42	1c gray brown	18.50	14.50	16.00	12.00	14.00	10.00
43	1c brown (Reissue)	40.00	30.00	35.00	25.00	35.00	25.00
44	1c deep green	9.25	7.25	8.00	6.00	5.00	3.50
45	1c green (Reissue)	13.00	10.00	11.50	8.50	11.00	8.50
46	2c yellow green	18.50	14.50	16.00	12.00	16.00	12.00
47	2c green (Reissue)	37.50	26.50	30.00	22.00	27.50	20.00
48	2c red orange	12.50	8.50	10.00	7.00	8.50	6.00
49	3c blue	25.00	18.00	22.00	15.00	7.50	5.00
51	3c umber brown	25.00	18.00	22.00	15.00	7.50	5.00
52	3c violet brown (Reissue)	57.50	42.00	50.00	35.00	42.50	30.00
53	5c pale blue	210.00	150.00	185.00	125.00	10.50	8.00
54	5c dark blue	105.00	75.00	95.00	65.00	9.00	7.50
55	5c bright blue	30.00	22.00	26.00	18.00	7.50	6.00

56-58　　　　　59
Newfoundland Dog　　Schooner

SCOTT CAT NO.	DESCRIPTION	UNUSED OG		UNUSED		USED	
		F	AVG	F	AVG	F	AVG

1887-96

56	½c rose red	9.75	7.25	8.50	6.00	8.00	5.50
57	½c orange red	40.00	27.00	32.50	22.50	32.50	22.50
58	½c black	9.50	6.50	8.00	5.50	8.00	5.50
59	10c black	70.00	55.00	60.00	45.00	55.00	40.00

60
Queen Victoria

1890

60	3c slate	13.50	10.25	11.50	8.50	1.20	.95

61 *Queen Victoria*   **62** *John Cabot*   **63** *Cape Bonavista*   **64** *Caribou Hunting*   **65** *Mining*   **66** *Logging*

67 *Fishing*   **68** *Cabot's Ship*   **69** *Ptarmigan*   **70** *Seals*   **71** *Salmon Fishing*

72 *Seal of Colony*   **73** *Coast Scene*   **74** *King Henry VII*

SCOTT CAT NO.	DESCRIPTION	UNUSED NH		UNUSED		USED	
		F	AVG	F	AVG	F	AVG

1897. CABOT ISSUE

61-74	1c-60c cpl., 14 Vars	365.00	310.00	265.00	210.00	175.00	142.00
61	1c deep green	3.75	3.00	2.75	2.00	2.60	2.00
62	2c carmine lake	4.00	3.25	3.00	2.25	2.60	2.00
63	3c ultramarine	6.75	6.00	4.75	4.00	2.60	2.00
64	4c olive green	8.50	7.50	6.00	5.00	4.75	4.00
65	5c violet	10.50	9.00	7.50	6.00	4.75	4.00
66	6c red brown	8.25	7.00	6.50	5.50	5.25	4.50
67	8c red orange	22.00	18.00	16.50	12.50	9.50	8.00
68	10c black brown	26.50	22.50	19.00	15.00	8.00	7.00
69	12c dark blue	32.00	27.00	23.00	18.00	9.50	8.00
70	15c scarlet	32.00	27.00	23.00	18.00	9.50	8.00
71	24c gray violet	32.00	27.00	23.00	18.00	12.00	10.00
72	30c slate	60.00	50.00	45.00	35.00	35.00	25.00
73	35c red	115.00	100.00	85.00	70.00	65.00	55.00
74	60c black	22.00	18.00	16.00	12.00	12.00	10.00

SCOTT CAT NO.	DESCRIPTION	UNUSED NH F	UNUSED NH AVG	UNUSED F	UNUSED AVG	USED F	USED AVG

60a surcharged in black

ONE CENT
a

		ONE CENT b		ONE CENT c			
75	1c on 3c gray lilac, Type a	24.00	19.00	17.00	12.00	17.00	12.00
76	1c on 3c gray lilac, Type b	160.00	120.00	110.00	75.00	110.00	75.00
77	1c on 3c gray lilac, Type c	775.00	625.00	550.00	400.00	550.00	400.00

78 Edward, Prince of Wales	79, 80 Queen Victoria	81, 82 King Edward VII	83 Queen Alexandra	84 Queen Mary	85 King George V

1897-1901 ROYAL FAMILY ISSUE

78-85	½c-5c cpl., 8 Vars	99.95	77.95	75.95	55.95	22.50	17.50
78	½c olive green	5.25	4.25	4.00	3.00	4.00	3.00
79	1c carmine rose	6.00	5.00	4.50	3.50	4.00	3.00
80	1c yellow green	4.50	3.50	3.50	2.50	.40	.30
81	2c orange	6.00	5.00	4.50	3.50	4.00	3.00
82	2c vermilion	11.50	9.00	9.00	6.50	.75	.60
83	3c orange	8.00	7.00	6.00	5.00	.65	.50
84	4c violet	30.00	23.50	23.50	17.00	6.00	5.00
85	5c blue	35.00	25.00	25.00	18.00	4.00	3.00

86
Map of Newfoundland

1908

86	2c rose carmine	32.50	26.00	25.00	18.50	1.80	1.50

87 King James I	88 Arms of the London & Bristol Company	89 John Guy	90 Guy's Ship, the "Endeavor"	91 View of the Town of Cupids	92, 92A, 98 Lord Bacon

Type I. "Z" of "COLONIZATION" is reversed.
Type II. "Z" is normal.

93, 99 View of Mosquito Bay	94, 100 Logging Camp	95, 101 Paper Mills	96, 102 King Edward VII	97, 103 King George V

SCOTT CAT NO.	DESCRIPTION	UNUSED NH		UNUSED		USED	
		F	AVG	F	AVG	F	AVG

1910 JOHN GUY ISSUE
Lithographed. Perf. 12

87	1c deep green, Perf. 12 x 11	3.25	2.75	2.75	2.00	1.60	1.25
87a	1c deep green	6.75	5.50	5.25	4.00	3.00	2.25
87b	1c deep green, Perf. 12 x 14	5.00	4.25	3.75	3.00	2.25	1.80
88	2c carmine	6.75	5.50	5.25	4.00	1.25	.95
88a	2c carmine, Perf. 12 x 14	6.75	5.50	5.25	4.00	1.25	.95
88c	2c carmine, Perf. 12 x 11½	165.00	130.00	130.00	95.00	.....	.....
89	3c brown olive	17.50	13.50	14.00	10.00	14.00	10.00
90	4c dull violet	21.00	16.00	16.50	12.00	16.50	12.00
91	5c ultramarine, Perf. 14 x 12	12.50	9.75	9.50	7.00	4.25	3.50
91a	5c ultramarine	15.00	12.50	11.50	9.00	4.75	4.00
92	6c claret (I)	110.00	85.00	85.00	60.00	80.00	55.00
92A	6c claret (II)	38.50	30.00	30.00	22.50	27.50	20.00
93	8c pale brown	65.00	50.00	50.00	35.00	50.00	35.00
94	9c olive green	65.00	50.00	50.00	35.00	50.00	35.00
95	10c violet black	70.00	55.00	55.00	40.00	55.00	40.00
96	12c lilac brown	70.00	55.00	55.00	40.00	55.00	40.00
97	15c gray black	65.00	50.00	50.00	35.00	50.00	35.00

1911 Engraved. Perf. 14

98	6c brown violet	28.00	21.00	22.00	15.00	22.00	15.00
99	8c bistre brown	70.00	55.00	55.00	40.00	55.00	40.00
100	9c olive green	65.00	50.00	50.00	35.00	50.00	35.00
101	10c violet black	105.00	90.00	80.00	65.00	80.00	65.00
102	12c red brown	75.00	60.00	60.00	45.00	60.00	45.00
103	15c slate green	75.00	60.00	60.00	45.00	60.00	45.00

104	105	106	107	108	109
Queen Mary	King George	Prince of Wales	Prince Albert	Princess Mary	Prince Henry

110	111	112	113	114
Prince George	Prince John	Queen Alexandra	Duke of Connaught	Seal of Colony

1911. ROYAL FAMILY ISSUE

104-14	1c-15c cpl., 11 Vars.	350.00	295.00	295.00	215.00	275.00	195.00
104	1c yellow green	4.00	3.15	3.00	2.25	.30	.25
105	2c carmine	4.00	3.15	3.00	2.25	.30	.25
106	3c red brown	37.50	28.00	28.00	20.00	23.00	16.00
107	4c violet	37.50	28.00	28.00	20.00	22.00	15.00
108	5c ultramarine	14.50	11.00	11.50	8.00	2.25	1.75
109	6c black	32.00	25.00	25.00	18.00	25.00	18.00
110	8c blue (paper colored)	90.00	70.00	70.00	50.00	70.00	50.00
110a	8c blue (paper normal)	95.00	75.00	75.00	55.00	75.00	55.00
111	9c blue violet	36.00	28.00	28.00	20.00	28.00	20.00
112	10c dark green	52.00	42.00	40.00	30.00	40.00	30.00
113	12c plum	52.00	42.00	40.00	30.00	40.00	30.00
114	15c magenta	50.00	40.00	38.00	28.00	38.00	28.00

SCOTT CAT NO.	DESCRIPTION	UNUSED NH F	UNUSED NH AVG	UNUSED F	UNUSED AVG	USED F	USED AVG

115, 117, 118, 120, 122, 124-126   116, 119, 121, 123

1919. TRAIL OF THE CARIBOU ISSUE

Scott	Description	NH F	NH AVG	Un F	Un AVG	Used F	Used AVG
115-26	1c-36c cpl., 12 Vars.	275.00	225.00	225.00	173.95	180.00	150.00
115-19	1c-5c, 5 Varieties	21.50	17.25	17.25	13.50	4.25	3.95
115	1c green	2.85	2.25	2.25	1.75	.45	.40
116	2c scarlet	3.75	3.00	3.00	2.25	.55	.50
117	3c red brown	4.00	3.25	3.25	2.50	.30	.25
118	4c violet	5.50	4.50	4.50	3.50	1.90	1.50
119	5c ultramarine	6.50	5.50	5.25	4.25	1.90	1.50
120	6c gray	37.00	29.00	30.00	22.50	22.50	20.00
121	8c magenta	26.00	22.00	21.00	17.00	18.00	14.00
122	10c dark green	16.50	13.00	13.50	10.00	5.25	4.25
123	12c orange	55.00	45.00	45.00	35.00	40.00	30.00
124	15c dark blue	36.00	28.00	30.00	22.00	25.00	20.00
125	24c bistre	55.00	45.00	45.00	35.00	43.00	33.50
126	36c olive green	42.50	35.00	35.00	27.50	35.00	27.50

1920

Scott	Description	72 surcharged TWO CENTS F	AVG	70 & 73 surcharged THREE CENTS F	AVG	F	AVG
127	2c on 30c slate	10.75	8.50	8.50	6.50	8.50	6.50

Bars 10½ mm. apart

128	3c on 15c scarlet	300.00	250.00	250.00	200.00	250.00	200.00

Bars 13½ mm. apart

129	3c on 15c scarlet	17.00	13.00	14.00	10.00	14.00	10.00
130	3c on 35c red	17.00	13.00	14.00	10.00	14.00	10.00

131   132   133   134   135   136

137   138   139   140   141

142   143   144

SCOTT CAT NO.	DESCRIPTION	UNUSED NH		UNUSED		USED	
		F	AVG	F	AVG	F	AVG

1923-24 PICTORIAL ISSUE

SCOTT CAT NO.	DESCRIPTION	F	AVG	F	AVG	F	AVG
131-44	1c-24c cpl., 14 Varieties	188.50	150.00	150.00	115.00	142.95	105.00
131-37	1c-8c, 7 Varieties	30.75	25.75	21.50	20.00	16.50	12.75
131	1c gray green	2.75	2.25	2.10	1.85	.35	.30
132	2c carmine	2.75	2.25	-2.10	1.85	.30	25
133	3c brown	2.75	2.25	2.10	1.85	.30	.25
134	4c brown violet	3.75	3.25	2.85	2.50	2.25	1.75
135	5c ultramarine	6.25	5.50	5.00	4.25	3.25	2.50
136	6c gray black	8.00	6.50	6.50	5.00	6.50	5.00
137	8c dull violet	6.25	5.25	5.00	4.00	4.50	3.50
138	9c slate green	35.00	27.50	30.00	22.50	30.00	22.50
139	10c dark violet	6.25	5.25	-5.00	4.00	2.50	2.00
140	11c olive green	8.50	7.50	7.00	6.00	7.00	6.00
141	12c lake	8.75	8.00	7.25	6.25	7.25	6.25
142	15c deep blue	15.00	11.75	12.00	9.00	12.00	9.00
143	20c red brown	13.50	10.50	11.00	8.00	10.00	7.00
144	24c black brown	80.00	60.00	65.00	45.00	65.00	45.00

145, 163, 172
Map of
Newfoundland

146, 164, 173
S.S. Caribou

147, 165, 174
Queen Mary and
King George

148, 166, 175
Prince of Wales

149, 167, 176
Express Train

150, 168, 177
Newfoundland Hotel
St. John's

151, 178
Town of
Heart's Content

152, 155
Cabot Tower,
St. John's

153, 169, 179
War Memorial
St. John's

154, 158
Post Office,
St. John's

156, 170, 180
First Airplane to Cross
Atlantic Non-Stop

157, 171, 181
House of Parliament,
St. John's

159, 182
Grand Falls,
Labrador

1928 TOURIST PUBLICITY ISSUE
Unwatermarked. Thin paper, dull colors

SCOTT CAT NO.	DESCRIPTION	F	AVG	F	AVG	F	AVG
145-59	1c-30c cpl., 15 Varieties	125.00	105.00	110.00	88.50	91.95	73.50
145	1c deep green	2.75	2.00	2.50	1.75	1.00	.80
146	2c deep carmine	3.25	2.50	2.75	2.00	1.00	.80
147	3c brown	3.75	3.00	3.25	2.45	.55	.45
148	4c lilac rose	4.25	3.50	3.75	3.00	2.75	2.00
149	5c slate green	7.50	6.50	6.50	5.50	4.25	3.50
150	6c ultramarine	5.75	4.75	5.00	4.00	5.00	4.00
151	8c light red brown	8.00	7.00	7.00	6.00	6.00	5.00
152	9c myrtle green	9.50	8.25	8.25	7.00	7.25	6.00
153	10c dark violet	9.50	8.25	8.25	7.00	6.00	5.00
154	12c brown carmine	7.00	6.00	6.00	5.00	5.00	4.00
155	14c red brown	9.50	8.25	8.25	7.00	6.00	5.00
156	15c dark blue	10.00	8.75	8.75	7.50	8.25	7.00
157	20c gray black	7.50	6.50	6.50	5.50	5.50	4.50
158	28c gray green	35.00	27.00	30.00	22.50	30.00	22.50
159	30c olive brown	9.50	8.25	8.25	7.00	8.25	7.00

SCOTT CAT. NO.	DESCRIPTION	UNUSED NH F	AVG	UNUSED F	AVG	USED F	AVG

1929

136 surcharged in red

THREE CENTS

| 160 | 3c on 6c gray black . . . . | 6.00 | 4.75 | 5.25 | 4.00 | 5.25 | 4.00 |

1929-31 Tourist Publicity Issue
Types of 1928 re-engraved.
Unwatermarked. Thicker paper, brighter colors

163-71	1c-20c cpl., 9 Varieties	142.95	115.95	123.50	96.50	85.75	62.50
163	1c green	2.60	2.10	2.25	1.75	.75	.60
164	2c deep carmine	3.00	2.40	2.50	2.00	.35	.30
165	3c deep red brown	3.60	2.70	3.00	2.25	.35	30
166	4c magenta	4.60	3.60	4.00	3.00	1.50	1.25
167	5c slate green	5.50	4.50	4.75	3.75	1.70	1.40
168	6c ultramarine	15.50	12.00	13.50	10.00	13.50	10.00
169	10c dark violet	5.75	4.75	5.00	4.00	2.25	1.90
170	15c deep blue	45.00	35.00	40.00	30.00	35.00	25.00
171	20c gray black	65.00	55.00	55.00	45.00	35.00	25.00

1931 Tourist Publicity Issue
Types of 1928 re-engraved, watermarked, coat of arms.
Thicker paper, brighter colors.

172-82	1c-30c cpl. 11 Varieties	250.00	200.00	217.50	168.95	157.95	118.50
172	1c green	3.75	3.00	3.25	2.50	1.50	1.25
173	2c red	4.35	3.60	3.75	3.00	1.55	1.30
174	3c red brown	4.75	4.00	4.00	3.25	1.50	1.25
175	4c rose	7.00	6.00	6.00	5.00	2.50	2.00
176	5c greenish gray	15.50	12.00	13.50	10.00	12.50	9.00
177	6c ultramarine	29.00	24.00	25.00	20.00	23.00	18.00
178	8c light red brown	29.00	24.00	25.00	20.00	23.00	18.00
179	10c dark violet	19.00	15.00	16.50	12.50	12.50	9.00
180	15c deep blue	52.00	42.00	45.00	35.00	40.00	30.00
181	20c gray black	52.00	42.00	45.00	35.00	13.50	10.00
182	30c olive brown	48.00	38.00	42.00	32.00	35.00	25.00

SCOTT
CAT
NO.   DESCRIPTION

| | UNUSED NH | | UNUSED | | USED | |
| | F | AVG | F | AVG | F | AVG |

183, 184, 253
Codfish

185, 186
King George

187
Queen Mary

188, 189
Prince of Wales

190, 191, 257
Caribou

192
Princess Elizabeth

5c. Die I. Antlers equal in height.
Die II. Antlers under "T" higher.

193, 260
Salmon

194, 261
Newfoundland Dog

195, 262
Northern Seal

196, 263
Trans-Atlantic Beacon

197, 265
Sealing Fleet

198, 199, 266
Fishing Fleet

208
The Duchess of York

209, 259
Corner Brook Paper Mills

210, 264
Loading Iron Ore,
Bell Island

1932-37 RESOURCES ISSUE Perf. 13½

Scott No.	Description	NH F	NH AVG	Unused F	Unused AVG	Used F	Used AVG
183-99	1c-48c cpl., 17 Varieties	109.50	93.50	94.50	76.50	70.95	56.50
183-91	1c-5c, 9 Varieties	25.75	21.95	21.95	18.50	5.95	4.65
183	1c green	2.40	2.00	2.00	1.65	.80	.70
184	1c gray black	.50	.45	.40	.35	.15	.12
185	2c rose	2.40	2.00	2.00	2.00	.40	.35
186	2c green	1.75	1.50	1.50	1.25	.15	.12
187	3c orange brown	1.75	1.50	1.50	1.25	.30	.25
188	4c deep violet	7.25	6.25	6.25	5.25	2.25	1.75
189	4c rose lake	1.20	1.00	.95	.85	.20	.15
190	5c violet brown	8.25	7.25	7.00	6.00	1.85	1.50
191	5c deep violet (II)	1.75	1.50	1.50	1.25	.15	.12
191a	5c deep violet (I)	10.75	9.50	9.00	8.00	.75	.65
192	6c dull blue	17.50	14.50	15.00	12.00	15.00	12.00
193	10c olive black	2.00	1.75	1.75	1.45	.90	.80
194	14c black	5.00	4.25	4.25	3.50	4.25	3.50
195	15c magenta	5.00	4.25	4.25	3.50	4.25	3.50
196	20c gray green	5.00	4.25	4.25	3.50	1.40	1.25
197	25c gray	5.25	4.25	4.75	4.00	3.75	3.00
198	30c ultramarine	37.50	30.00	32.50	25.00	32.50	25.00
199	48c red brown	11.00	9.50	9.50	8.00	6.50	5.50

1932 Perf. 13½

Scott No.	Description	NH F	NH AVG	Unused F	Unused AVG	Used F	Used AVG
208-10	7c-24c cpl., 3 Varieties	9.50	8.25	8.50	7.00	6.95	5.70
208	7c red brown	2.35	2.00	2.10	1.75	2.10	1.75
209	8c orange red	2.35	2.00	2.10	1.75	1.50	1.25
210	24c light blue	5.50	4.75	4.75	4.00	3.75	3.00

NOTE: To determine the VF price for stamps issued from 1847 to 1940, add the difference between the Avg. and F prices to the F price. To determine the NH price for issues prior to 1897, add 50% to the appropriate O.G. price.

SCOTT CAT NO.	DESCRIPTION	UNUSED NH F	AVG	UNUSED F	AVG	USED F	AVG

211 *Plane & Dog Sled*

1933 LAND & SEA OVERPRINT

211	15c brown	11.50	9.50	10.00	8.00	10.00	8.00

212
Sir Humphrey Gilbert

213
Compton Castle, Devon

214
The Gilbert Arms

215
Eton College

216
Token to Gilbert from Queen Elizabeth

217
Gilbert Commissioned by Queen Elizabeth

218
Gilbert's Fleet Leaving Plymouth

219
The Fleet Arriving at St. John's

220
Annexation of Newfoundland

221
Coat of Arms of England

222
Gilbert on the "Squirrel"

223
1624 Map of Newfoundland

224
Queen Elizabeth I

225
Gilbert Statue at Truro

1933. SIR HUMPHREY GILBERT ISSUE

Scott No.	Description	Unused NH F	AVG	Unused F	AVG	Used F	AVG
212-25	1c-32c cpl., 14 Varieties	203.50	174.50	170.00	140.00	160.00	135.00
212-20	1c-10c, 9 Varieties	66.95	60.50	54.00	47.95	49.00	43.50
212	1c gray black	1.75	1.65	1.40	1.25	1.05	.95
213	2c green	1.80	1.70	1.50	1.30	1.05	.95
214	3c yellow brown	2.50	2.30	2.00	1.80	1.70	1.50
215	4c carmine	2.50	2.30	2.00	1.80	.80	.75
216	5c dull violet	3.25	2.85	2.60	2.35	1.70	1.50
217	7c blue	17.25	15.75	14.25	12.75	14.25	12.75
218	8c orange red	14.75	13.25	11.75	10.25	11.75	10.25
219	9c ultramarine	14.75	13.25	11.75	10.25	11.75	10.25
220	10c red brown	12.50	11.50	10.25	9.00	8.00	7.00
221	14c black	27.00	21.50	23.00	18.00	23.00	18.00
222	15c claret	29.00	24.00	25.00	20.00	25.00	20.00
223	20c deep green	15.00	13.50	12.50	10.00	10.25	8.00
224	24c violet brown	38.00	31.00	33.00	26.00	32.00	26.00
225	32c gray	35.00	30.00	30.00	25.00	30.00	25.00

SCOTT CAT NO.	DESCRIPTION	UNUSED NH F	AVG	UNUSED F	AVG	USED F	AVG

226-229
Windsor Castle and King George

230-232
King George VI and Queen Elizabeth

1935. SILVER JUBILEE ISSUE

Scott No.	Description	NH F	NH AVG	Unused F	Unused AVG	Used F	Used AVG
226-29	4c-24c cpl., 4 Varieties	16.00	14.75	14.00	12.75	12.75	11.50
226	4c bright rose	1.80	1.65	1.55	1.40	1.00	.90
227	5c violet	2.05	1.90	1.80	1.65	1.50	1.35
228	7c dark blue	3.35	3.10	3.25	3.00	3.25	3.00
229	24c olive green	10.00	9.00	8.25	7.50	7.75	7.00

1937. CORONATION ISSUE

Scott No.	Description	NH F	NH AVG	Unused F	Unused AVG	Used F	Used AVG
230-32	2c-5c cpl., 3 Varieties	3.50	3.15	2.95	2.50	2.95	2.50
230	2c deep green	.90	.80	.70	.60	.70	.60
231	4c carmine rose	.90	.80	.70	.60	.70	.60
232	5c dark violet	2.00	1.75	1.75	1.50	1.75	1.50

3c DIE I: Fine Impression
DIE II: Coarse Impression

233

234

235

236

237

238

239

240

241

242

243

1937 LONG CORONATION ISSUE

Scott No.	Description	NH F	NH AVG	Unused F	Unused AVG	Used F	Used AVG
233-43	1c-48c cpl., 11 Varieties	49.95	43.50	45.95	33.75	39.50	33.50
233	1c Codfish	.60	.55	.50	.45	.40	.35
234	3c Newfoundland Map, Die I	2.50	2.25	2.20	2.00	.80	.75
234a	3c Same, Die II	2.00	1.75	1.85	1.60	.65	.60
235	7c Caribou	2.75	2.50	2.50	2.25	2.45	2.25
236	8c Paper Mills	2.75	2.50	2.50	2.25	2.45	2.25
237	10c Salmon	6.75	6.00	5.75	5.00	5.75	5.00
238	14c Newfoundland Dog	5.75	5.00	4.75	4.00	4.75	4.00
239	15c Northern Seal	6.75	5.50	5.25	4.50	5.25	4.50
240	20c Cape Race	4.75	4.00	4.00	3.25	4.50	3.25
241	24c Bell Island	5.50	4.75	4.75	4.00	4.75	4.00
242	25c Sealing Fleet	5.75	5.00	5.00	4.25	5.00	4.25
243	48c Fishing Fleet	6.75	6.00	6.00	5.00	5.00	4.25

SEE PAGE X FOR CONDITION DEFINITIONS

SCOTT CAT NO.	DESCRIPTION	UNUSED NH F	AVG	UNUSED F	AVG	USED F	AVG

245, 254
King George VI

246, 255
Queen Elizabeth

247, 256
Princess Elizabeth

248, 258
Queen Mary

1938 ROYAL FAMILY. Perf. 13½

245-48	2c-7c cpl., 4 Varieties	10.50	8.50	8.95	7.00	2.65	2.25
245	2c green	2.60	2.10	2.25	1.75	.25	.20
246	3c dark carmine	2.60	2.10	2.25	1.75	.30	.25
247	4c light blue	3.25	2.75	2.75	2.25	.25	.20
248	7c dark ultramarine	2.60	2.10	2.25	1.75	2.00	1.75

249

252

1939-41

249-52	cpl., 4 Vars.	5.75	4.95	4.95	4.15	4.95	4.10

1939. ROYAL VISIT COMMEMORATIVE

249	5c violet blue	1.75	1.50	1.50	1.25	1.50	1.25

2

249 SURCHARGED

▲ **CENTS** ▲

250	2c on 5c violet blue	1.90	1.65	1.65	1.40	1.65	1.40
251	4c on 5c violet blue	1.75	1.50	1.50	1.25	1.50	1.25

1941. GRENFELL ISSUE

252	5c dull blue	.65	.60	.60	.50	.55	.45

		PLATE BLOCK F/NH	F	UNUSED F/NH	F	USED F	

1941-44 RESOURCES ISSUE
Designs of 1931-38. Perf. 12½

253-66	1c-48c cpl., 14 Varieties	. . . . .	. . . . .	21.75	18.50	14.65	
253	1c dark gray	1.40	1.25	.30	.25	.12	
254	2c deep green	1.50	1.40	.35	.30	.10	
255	3c rose carmine	2.25	2.00	.50	.45	.10	
256	4c blue	4.00	3.50	.80	.75	.13	
257	5c violet	3.75	3.25	.80	.75	.18	
258	7c violet blue	6.00	5.25	1.40	1.20	1.10	
259	8c red	5.50	4.75	1.30	1.10	.95	
260	10c brownish black	8.25	7.25	1.30	1.10	.75	
261	14c black	12.00	9.75	2.40	2.00	1.75	
262	15c rose violet	12.50	10.00	2.40	2.00	1.75	
263	20c green	12.50	10.00	2.10	1.75	1.50	
264	24c deep blue	15.00	12.50	2.75	2.25	2.00	
265	25c slate	15.00	12.50	2.75	2.25	2.00	
266	48c red brown	23.50	20.00	3.85	3.25	3.00	

SCOTT CAT NO.	DESCRIPTION	PLATE BLOCK F/NH	F	UNUSED F/NH	F	USED F

267

268

269

270

	1943-47 COMMEMORATIVES					
267-70	cpl., 4 Vars.	18.75	15.25	3.35	2.75	2.10
267	30c Memorial University	13.00	11.00	2.10	1.75	1.45
	1946					
268	2c on 30c Memorial Univ.	2.50	2.00	.50	.45	.45
	1947					
269	4c Princess Elizabeth	2.50	2.00	.45	.40	.10
270	5c Cabot in the "Matthew"	1.80	1.50	.40	.35	.25

		UNUSED NH F	AVG	UNUSED F	AVG	USED F	AVG

AIR POST STAMPS

C2

C3

		1919					
C2	$1 on 15c scarlet	475.00	375.00	335.00	250.00	335.00	250.00
C2a	Same, without comma after "post" .	550.00	450.00	400.00	300.00	400.00	300.00
		1921					
C3	35c red	335.00	260.00	250.00	175.00	250.00	175.00
C3a	Same, with period after "1921" ...	335.00	260.00	250.00	175.00	250.00	175.00

C6, C9
Airplane and Dog Team

C7, C10
First Transatlantic Airmail

C8, C11
Routes of Historic Transatlantic Flights

		1931. Unwatermarked					
C6	15c brown	16.50	13.00	13.25	10.00	13.25	10.00
C7	50c green...................	33.00	25.00	28.00	20.00	28.00	20.00
C8	$1 blue	115.00	90.00	95.00	70.00	95.00	70.00
		Watermarked Coat of Arms					
C9	15c brown	12.50	9.75	10.00	7.50	10.00	7.50
C10	50c green...................	55.00	45.00	45.00	35.00	45.00	35.00
C11	$1 blue	150.00	120.00	125.00	95.00	115.00	85.00

SCOTT CAT NO.	DESCRIPTION	UNUSED NH F	UNUSED NH AVG	UNUSED F	UNUSED AVG	USED F	USED AVG

C12

1932 TRANS ATLANTIC FLIGHT

| C12 | $1.50 on $1 blue .... | 725.00 | 600.00 | 600.00 | 475.00 | 600.00 | 475.00 |

C13   C14   C15   C16

C17   C18   C19

1933. LABRADOR ISSUE

C13-17	5c-75c cpl., 5 Varieties	265.00	220.00	225.00	185.00	225.00	185.00
C13	5c "Put to Flight"	21.50	18.00	18.50	15.00	18.50	15.00
C14	10c "Land of Heart's Delight"	31.00	26.00	27.00	22.00	25.00	20.00
C15	30c "Spotting the Herd"	52.00	42.00	45.00	35.00	45.00	35.00
C16	60c "News from Home"	87.50	72.00	75.00	60.00	75.00	60.00
C17	75c "Labrador, The Land of Gold"	90.00	75.00	80.00	65.00	80.00	65.00

1933. BALBO FLIGHT ISSUE

| C18 | $4.50 on 75c bistre .... | 925.00 | 825.00 | 800.00 | 700.00 | 800.00 | 700.00 |

1943

| C19 | 7c St. John's .... | .70 | .60 | .60 | .50 | .60 | .50 |

POSTAGE DUE STAMPS

J1-J7

1939 Unwatermarked, perf. 10½ x 10.

J1-6	1c-10c cpl., 6 Varieties	29.50	25.50	25.00	21.25	25.00	21.25
J1	1c yellow green	2.90	2.40	2.50	2.00	2.50	2.00
J2	2c vermilion	5.00	4.50	4.25	3.75	4.25	3.75
J3	3c ultramarine	5.75	5.00	4.75	4.25	4.75	4.25
J4	4c yellow orange	7.50	6.50	6.50	5.50	6.50	5.50
J5	5c pale brown	5.00	4.25	4.25	3.50	4.25	3.50
J6	10c dark violet	5.00	4.25	4.25	3.50	4.25	3.50

SCOTT CAT NO.	DESCRIPTION	PLATE BLOCK F/NH	F	UNUSED F/NH	F	USED F
		1946-49				
J1a-4a	1c-4c cpl., 4 Varieties	. . . . .	. . . . .	31.00	19.75	18.50
		Unwatermarked, perf. 11.				
J1a	1c yellow green	27.50	22.50	4.00	3.50	3.50
		Unwatermarked, perf. 11 x 9				
J2a	2c vermilion	33.50	27.00	5.00	4.50	4.00
J3a	3c ultramarine	42.00	35.00	5.50	5.00	5.00
J4a	4c yellow orange	60.00	50.00	9.25	8.00	7.00
		1949				
		Type of 1939, watermarked, perf. 11				
J7	10c dark violet	57.50	50.00	9.25	8.00	8.00

NEW BRUNSWICK

	UNUSED O.G. F	AVG	UNUSED F	AVG	USED F	AVG

Crown of Great Britain Surrounded by Heraldic Flowers of the United Kingdom

1-4

1851 PENCE ISSUE. Imperforate.

		UNUSED O.G. F	AVG	UNUSED F	AVG	USED F	AVG
1	3p red	2000.00	1500.00	1500.00	1000.00	400.00	300.00
2	6p olive yellow	4350.00	3700.00	3150.00	2500.00	800.00	600.00
3	1sh bright red violet	. . . . .	. . . . .	. . . . .	. . . . .	3000.00	2500.00
4	1sh dull violet	. . . . .	. . . . .	. . . . .	. . . . .	3000.00	2500.00

6	7	8	9	10	11

1860-63 CENTS ISSUE.

		UNUSED O.G. F	AVG	UNUSED F	AVG	USED F	AVG
6	1c Locomotive	28.00	20.00	24.00	16.00	23.00	15.00
7	2c Queen Victoria, orange	15.00	11.00	12.50	8.50	12.50	8.50
8	5c Same, yellow green	15.00	11.00	12.50	8.50	12.50	8.50
9	10c Same, vermilion	35.00	25.00	30.00	20.00	30.00	20.00
10	12½c Ships	65.00	47.50	55.00	37.50	55.00	37.50
11	17c Prince of Wales	42.50	32.50	35.00	25.00	35.00	25.00

NOVA SCOTIA

2-7
*Royal Crown and Heraldic
Flowers of the United Kingdom*

1851-53 PENCE ISSUE.
Imperf. Blue paper

		UNUSED OG		UNUSED		USED	
	DESCRIPTION	F	AVG	F	AVG	F	AVG
1	1p Queen Victoria	2000.00	1500.00	1500.00	1000.00	425.00	300.00
2	3p blue	800.00	600.00	600.00	400.00	150.00	100.00
3	3p dark blue	1050.00	800.00	800.00	550.00	150.00	100.00
4	6p yellow green	3900.00	3200.00	3200.00	2400.00	465.00	325.00
5	6p dark green	7000.00	5800.00	5500.00	4300.00	975.00	700.00
6	1 sh reddish violet	......	......	......	......	3200.00	2500.00
7	1sh dull violet	......	......	......	......	3200.00	2500.00

8-10

11, 12
Queen Victoria

13

1860-63 CENTS ISSUE
White or Yellowish paper. Perf. 12

		F	AVG	F	AVG	F	AVG
8	1c black	8.50	6.50	7.00	5.00	7.00	5.00
9	2c Lilac	11.00	9.00	9.00	7.00	8.00	6.00
10	5c blue	400.00	295.00	300.00	225.00	9.00	7.00
11	8½c green	8.50	6.50	7.00	5.00	20.00	15.00
12	10c vermilion	11.00	9.00	9.00	7.00	9.75	7.00
13	12½c black	35.00	25.00	30.00	20.00	30.00	20.00

PRINCE EDWARD ISLAND

| | 1, 5 | 2, 6 | 3, 7 | 4 | 8 |

Queen Victoria

SCOTT CAT NO.	DESCRIPTION	UNUSED OG		UNUSED		USED	
		F	AVG	F	AVG	F	AVG

1861 PENCE ISSUE. Perf. 9

1	2p rose	500.00	400.00	375.00	275.00	190.00	130.00
2	3p blue	950.00	750.00	700.00	500.00	380.00	275.00
3	6p yellow green	1350.00	1050.00	1075.00	725.00	550.00	400.00

1862-65 PENCE ISSUE. Perf. 11 to 12

4	1p yellow orange	38.00	28.00	32.00	22.00	30.00	20.00
5	2p rose	10.50	8.00	8.50	6.00	8.50	6.00
6	3p blue	13.00	10.50	10.50	8.00	10.50	8.00
7	6p green	90.00	65.00	75.00	50.00	75.00	50.00
8	9p violet	60.00	45.00	50.00	35.00	50.00	35.00

| | 9 | 10 |

Queen Victoria

1868 PENCE ISSUE

9	4p black	13.25	10.50	10.75	8.00	22.50	15.00

1870 PENCE ISSUE

10	4½p brown	67.50	52.50	55.00	40.00	55.00	40.00

| | 11 | 12 | 13 | 14 | 15 | 16 |

Queen Victoria

1872 CENTS ISSUE

11	1c brown orange	8.50	6.50	7.00	5.00	10.00	7.00
12	2c ultramarine	16.00	11.75	13.00	9.00	30.00	20.00
13	3c rose	24.00	18.00	22.00	14.00	21.00	14.00
14	4c green	8.50	6.50	7.00	5.00	15.00	10.00
15	6c black	8.50	6.50	7.00	5.00	15.00	10.00
16	12c violet	8.50	6.50	7.00	5.00	27.50	20.00

SEE PAGE X FOR CONDITION DEFINITIONS

The UNITED STATES Stamp Identifier

SHOWS YOU HOW TO DISTINGUISH BETWEEN THE RARE AND COMMON UNITED STATES STAMPS THAT LOOK ALIKE

What does "Grill with points up" mean? "Single line watermark?" How can I tell whether my 15¢ "Landing of Columbus" stamp of 1869 is worth $1,750 (Type I) or $850 (Type II)?

At one time or another, every collector of United States stamps asks questions like these. For very often, it is a minute difference in design that determines not only whether a stamp is Type I, II, or III, but whether it is a great rarity or just another common variety. The different varieties of the 1¢ Franklin design of 1851-56, for example, range in price from $37.50 to $95,000.00. So it pays to know how to tell the correct types of your stamps! To enable you to do so easily and quickly is the purpose of this U.S. STAMP IDENTIFIER.

Other seemingly identical, but actually different United States stamps may be told apart by differences in perforations, watermarks, grills or methods in printing. These terms are fully explained in the glossary at the back of this IDENTIFIER. And charts are included which make it easy for you to quickly identify the most troublesome of U.S. stamps — the hard-to-classify regular issues of 1908 to 1932.

NOTE: The illustrations and catalog numbers used herein are from the Standard Postage Stamp Catalogue, by special permission of the publishers, Scott Publications, Inc.

FIRST UNITED STATES POSTAGE ISSUE OF 1847

1   2

Original Issue of 1847

948   *1947 "Cipex" Souvenir Sheet*

3   4

Reproductions of 1875

The first stamps of the United States Government - the 5¢ and 10¢ designs shown to the left above -were placed in use in July 1847, superseding the Postmasters' Provisionals then being used in several cities. In 1875, official reproductions (right above) were made from newly engraved printing plates.

In the original 5¢ design, the top edge of Franklin's shirt touches the circular frame about at a level with the top of the "F" of "FIVE", while in the 1875 reproduction it is on a level with the top of the figure "5."

In the original 10¢ design, the left edge of Washington's coat points to the "T" of "TEN," and the right edge points between the "T" and "S"

of "CENTS". In the reproductions, the left and right outlines of the coat point to the right edge of "X" and to the center of the "S" of "CENTS" respectively. Also, on the 1875 reprints, the eyes have a sleepy look and the line of the mouth is straighter.

The 1947 "Cipex" Souvenir Sheet, issued on the hundredth anniversary of United States stamps, features reproductions of the two original designs. Stamps cut out of the souvenir sheet are, of course, valid for postage. However, no difficulty in identification should be encountered since the 1947 reproductions are light blue (5¢) instead of the original red brown, and brownish orange (10¢) instead of the original black.

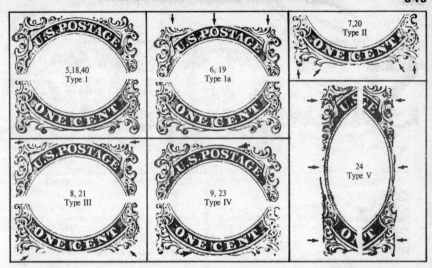

TYPE I
5,18,40

Type 1a
6, 19

7,20
Type II

8, 21
Type III

9, 23
Type IV

24
Type V

TYPE I has the most complete design of the various types of this stamp. At the top and bottom there is an unbroken curved line running outside the bands reading "U.S. POSTAGE" and "ONE CENT". The scrolls at bottom are turned under, forming curls. The scrolls and outer line at top are complete.

TYPE Ia is like Type I at bottom but ornaments and curved line at top are partly cut away.

TYPE Ib (not illustrated) is like Type I at top but little curls at bottom are not quite so complete nor clear and scroll work is partly cut away.

TYPE II has the outside bottom line complete, but the little curls of the bottom scrolls and the lower part of the plume ornaments are missing. Side ornaments are complete.

TYPE III has the outside lines at both top and bottom partly cut away in the middle. The side ornaments are complete.

TYPE IIIa (not illustrated) is similar to Type III with the outer line cut away at top or bottom, but not both. 8A, 22.

TYPE IV is similar to Type II but the curved lines at top or bottom (or both) have been recut in several different ways, and usually appear thicker than Type II.

TYPE V is similar to Type III but has the side ornaments partly cut away. Type V occurs only on perforated stamps.

TYPE OF THE 3c WASHINGTON DESIGN OF 1851-60

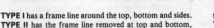

10, 11, 25, 41
Type I

26
Type II

26a
Type IIa

TYPE I has a frame line around the top, bottom and sides.
TYPE II has the frame line removed at top and bottom, while the side frame lines are continuous from top to bottom of the plate.
TYPE IIa is similar to Type II, but the side frame lines were recut individually, hence are broken between stamps.

TYPES OF THE 5¢ JEFFERSON DESIGN OF 1851-60

12, 27—29
Type I

30, 30A, 42
Type II

TYPE I is a complete design with projections (arrow) at the top and bottom as well as at the sides.

TYPE II has the projections at the top and bottom partly or completely cut away.

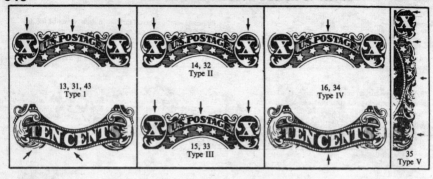

13, 31, 43
Type 1

14, 32
Type II

15, 33
Type III

16, 34
Type IV

35
Type V

TYPE I has the "shells" at the lower corners practically complete, while the outer line below "TEN CENTS" is very nearly complete. At the top, the outer lines are broken above "U.S. POSTAGE" and above the "X" in each corner.

TYPE II has the design complete at the top, but the outer line at the bottom is broken in the middle and the "shells" are partially cut away.

TYPE III has both top and bottom outer lines partly cut away: that is, similar to Type I at the top and Type II at the bottom.
TYPE IV has the outer lines at the top or bottom of the stamp, or at both places, recut to show more strongly and heavily.
TYPES I, II, and IV have complete ornaments at the sides and three small circles or pearls (arrow) at the outer edges of the bottom panel.
TYPE V has the side ornaments, including one or two of the small "pearls," partly cut away. The outside line over the "X" at the right top has also been partly cut away.

TYPES OF THE ISSUE OF 1861

Shortly after the outbreak of the Civil War in 1861, the Post Office demonetized all stamps issued up to that time in order to prevent their use by the Confederacy. Two new sets of designs, consisting of the six stamps shown above plus 24¢ and 30¢ demoninations, were prepared by the American Bank Note Company. The first designs, except for the 10¢ and 24¢ values, were not regularly issued and are extremely rare and valuable. The second designs became the regular issue of 1861. The illustrations at the left below show the first (or un-issued) designs, which were all printed on thin, semi-transparent paper. The second (or regular) designs are shown at the right. See page 155 for grilled varieties.

55 63

63 shows a small dash (arrow) under the top of the ornaments at the right of the figure "1" in the upper left hand corner of the stamp.

3¢ 1861 PINK (Scott's #64)—It is impossible to describe a "pink" in words, but it might be helpful to remember that this stamp is usually rather heavily inked, and has a tinge of blue or purple which makes it stand out from the various shades of rose to red brown sometimes mistaken for it.

56 64-66, 74

64, 66 and **74** show a small ball (arrow) at each corner of the design. Also, the ornaments at the corners are larger than in A25a.

57 67, 75, 76

67, 75 and **76** have a leaflet (arrow) projecting from the scrolled ornaments at each corner of the stamp.

58, 62B

58, 62B has no curved line below the row of stars and there is only one outer line of the ornaments above them.

68

68 has a heavy curved line below the row of stars (arrow), and the ornaments above the stars have a double outer line.

59   69

69 has an oval and scroll (arrow) in each corner of the design. **59** has no such design and the corners are rounded.

62

62 does not have the row of dashes or spot of color present in **72**.

72

72 has a row of small dashes between the parallel lines of the angle at the top center of the stamp. There is also a spot of color (arrow) in the apex of the lower line of the single.

TYPES OF THE 15¢ "LANDING OF COLUMBUS" DESIGN OF 1869

118: Type I

119: Type II

118, TYPE 1 has the central picture without the frame line shown in Type II.
119, TYPE II, has a frame line (arrows) around the central picture; also a diamond shaped ornament appears below the "T" of "POSTAGE."

129, TYPE III (not illustrated) is like Type I except that the fringe of brown shading lines which appears around the sides and bottom of the picture on Types I and II has been removed.

TYPES OF THE 1870-71 AND 1873 ISSUES

The stamps of the 1870-71 issue were printed by the National Bank Note Company. The similar issue of 1873 was printed by the Continental Bank Note Company. When Continental took over the plates previously used by National, they applied the so-called "secret marks" to the designs of the 1¢ through 15¢ denominations, by which the two issues, can be distinguished as shown below. The illustrations at the left show the original designs of 1870-71; those at the right show the secret marks applied to the issue of 1873.

ISSUE OF 1870-71	ISSUE OF 1873	ISSUE OF 1870-71	ISSUE OF 1873

134, 145   156

156 has a small curved mark in the pearl at the left of the figure "1".

135, 146   157

135 and **146** are red brown. Type **157** is brown and in some copies has a small diagonal line under the scroll at the left of the "U.S." (arrow).

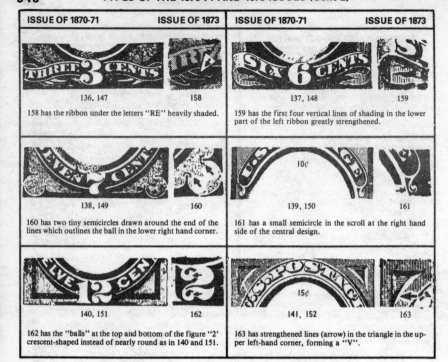

ISSUE OF 1870-71	ISSUE OF 1873	ISSUE OF 1870-71	ISSUE OF 1873
136, 147	158	137, 148	159

158 has the ribbon under the letters "RE" heavily shaded.

159 has the first four vertical lines of shading in the lower part of the left ribbon greatly strengthened.

| 138, 149 | 160 | 139, 150 | 161 |

160 has two tiny semicircles drawn around the end of the lines which outlines the ball in the lower right hand corner.

161 has a small semicircle in the scroll at the right hand side of the central design.

| 140, 151 | 162 | 141, 152 | 163 |

162 has the "balls" at the top and bottom of the figure "2" crescent-shaped instead of nearly round as in 140 and 151.

163 has strengthened lines (arrow) in the triangle in the upper left-hand corner, forming a "V".

RE-ENGRAVED DESIGNS OF 1881-82

The 1¢, 3¢, 6¢ and 10¢ denominations of the 1873 & 1879 issues, shown above, were re-engraved in 1881-82. The new plates resulted in the four variations described below. The background shading lines in all four of these stamps appear stronger and more heavily inked than the earlier designs.

1¢

206

206 has strengthened vertical shading lines in the upper part of the stamp, making the background appear almost solid. Lines of shading have also been added to the curving ornaments in the upper corners.

6¢

208

208 has only three vertical lines between the edge of the panel and the outside left margin of the stamp. (In the preceding issues there were four such lines.)

3¢

207

207 has a solid shading line at the sides of the central oval (arrow) that is only about half the previous width. Also a short horizontal line has been cut below the "TS" of "CENTS".

10¢

209

209 has only four vertical lines between the left side of the oval and the edge of the shield. (In the preceding issues there were five such lines.) Also, the lines in the background have been made much heavier so that these stamps appear more heavily inked than previous issues.

TYPES OF THE
REGULAR ISSUES OF 1890-98

Two varieties of the 1980-93 issue

1890-93. This issue, printed by the American Bank Note Company, consists of a 1¢, 2¢, 3¢, 4¢, 5¢, 6¢, 8¢, 10¢, 15¢, 30¢ and 90¢ denomination.

Two varieties of the 1894-98 issue

1894-98. This issue — and all subsequent regular United States issues — were printed by the Bureau of Engraving and Printing, Washington, D.C. In more recent years, starting in 1943, some commemorative issues were printed by private firms. The 1894-98 "Bureau" issue is similar in design to the issue of 1890 but triangles (arrows) were added to the upper corners of the stamps and there are some differences in denominations.

2¢ "CAP ON 2" VARIETY
OF 1890

Cap on left "2"   *Cap on right "2"*

Plate defects in the printing of the 2¢ "Washington" stamp of 1890 accounts for the "Cap on left 2" and "Cap on both 2s" varieties illustrated above.

TYPES OF THE
2¢ WASHINGTON DESIGN
OF 1894-98

The triangles in the upper right and left hand corners of the stamp determine the type.

248-250, 265
Type I

251, 266
Type II

252,
267, 279B
Type III

TYPE I has horizontal lines of the same thickness within and without the triangle.
TYPE II has horizontal lines which cross the triangle but are thinner within it than without.
TYPE III has thin lines inside the triangle and these do not cross the double frame line of the triangle.

10¢ WEBSTER DESIGN OF 1898

282C
Type I

283
Type II

TYPE I has an unbroken white curved line below the words "TEN CENTS".
In **TYPE II** the white line is broken by the ornaments at a point just below the "E" in "TEN" and the "T" in "CENTS" (arrows).

$1 PERRY DESIGN OF 1894-95

261, 276
Type I

261A, 276A
Type II

In **Type I** the circles around the "$1" are broken at the point where they meet the curved line below "ONE DOLLAR" (arrows).
Type II shows these circles complete.

2¢ COLUMBIAN "BROKEN HAT"
VARIETY OF 1893

As a result of a plate defect, some stamps of the 2¢ Columbian design show a noticeable white notch or gash in the hat worn by the third figure to the left of Columbus. This "broken hat" variety is somewhat less common than the regular 2¢ design.

231   *Broken Hat variety, 231C*

4¢ COLUMBIAN BLUE ERROR — Collectors often mistake the many shades of the normal 4¢ ultramarine for the rare and valuable blue error. Actually, the "error" is not ultramarine at all, but a deep blue, similar to the deeper blue shades of the 1¢ Columbian.

Perforation	Watermark	Other Identifying Features	(1¢)	(2¢)	(3¢)	(4¢)	3¢ thru $1 denominations	8¢ thru $1 denominations
PERF. 12	USPS	White paper	331	332			333-42	422-23
	USPS	Bluish gray paper	357	358			359-66	
	USPS	White paper	374	375	405	406	376-82 407	414-21
COIL 12	USPS	Perf. Horizontal	348	349			350-51	
	USPS	Perf. Vertical	352	353			354-56	
	USPS	Perf. Horizontal	385	386				
	USPS	Perf. Vertical	387	388			389	
IMPERF.	USPS		343	344			345-47	
	USPS	Flat Plate	383	384	408	409		
	USPS	Rotary Press				459		
	Unwmkd.	Flat Plate			481	482-82A	483-85	
	Unwmkd.	Offset			531	532-34B	535	
COIL 8½	USPS	Perf. Horizontal	390	391	410	411		
	USPS	Perf. Vertical	392	393	412	413	394-96	
PERF. 10	USPS							460
	USPS				424	425	426-30	431-40
	Unwmkd.	Flat Plate			462	463	464-69	470-78
	Unwmkd.	Rotary Press			543			
COIL 10	USPS	Perf. Horiz. — Flat			441	442		
	USPS	Perf. Horiz. — Rotary			448	449-50		
	USPS	Perf. Vert. — Flat			443	444	445-47	
	USPS	Perf. Vert. — Rotary			452	453-55	456-58	
	Unwmkd.	Perf. Horizontal			486	487-88	489	
	Unwmkd.	Perf. Vertical			490	491-92	493-96	497
PERF. 11	USPS			519				
	USPS					461		
	Unwmkd.	Flat Plate			498	499-500	501-07	508-18
	Unwmkd.	Rotary Press			*544-45	546		
	Unwmkd.	Offset			525	526-28B	529-30	
Perf. 12½	Unwmkd.	Offset			536			
11 x 10	Unwmkd.	Rotary			538	539-40	541	
10 x 11	Unwmkd.	Rotary			542			

¢Design of #544 is 19 mm. wide x 22½ mm. high. #545 is 19½ to 20 mm. wide x 22 mm. high.

22mm — Size of Flat Plate Design — 18½-19mm

Stamps printed by rotary press are always slightly wider or taller on issues prior to 1954. Measurements do not apply to booklet singles.

HOW TO USE THIS IDENTIFICATION CHART

Numbers referred to herein are from Scott's Standard Postage Stamp Catalog. To identify any stamp in this series, first check the type by comparing it with the illustrations at the top of the chart. Then check the perforations, and whether the stamp is single or double line watermarked or unwatermarked. With this information you can quickly find out the Standard Catalog number by checking down and across the chart. For example, a 1¢ Franklin, perf. 12, single line watermark, must be Scott's #374.

During the years 1912 through 1920, the 2¢ Washington design pictured below was issued and re-issued with slight variations which give rise to the many different types of this stamp. Certain of these types, as you will see by consulting a catalog of United States stamps, are far more valuable than others. The several variations in actual design are pictured and described below. For perforation, watermark and printing variations, see the handy identification chart on the preceding page.

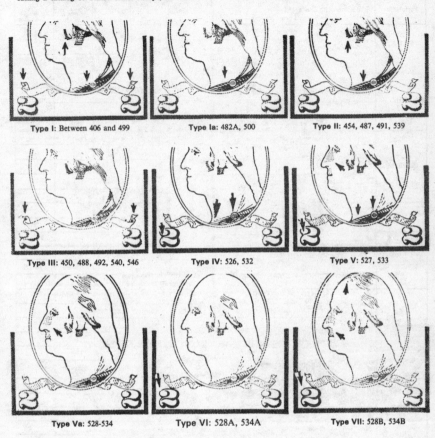

Type I: Between 406 and 499

Type Ia: 482A, 500

Type II: 454, 487, 491, 539

Type III: 450, 488, 492, 540, 546

Type IV: 526, 532

Type V: 527, 533

Type Va: 528-534

Type VI: 528A, 534A

Type VII: 528B, 534B

TYPE I — The ribbon at left above the figure "2" has one shading line in the first curve, while the ribbon at the right has one shading line in the second curve. Button of toga has a faint outline. Top line of toga, from button to front of throat, is very faint. Shading lines of the face, terminating in front of the ear, are not joined. Type I occurs on both flat and rotary press printings.

TYPE Ia — Similar to Type I except that all of the lines are stronger. Lines of the toga button are heavy. Occurs only on flat press printings.

TYPE II — Ribbons are shaded as in Type I. Toga button and shading lines to the left of it are heavy. The shading lines in front of the ear are joined and end in a strong vertically curved line (arrow). Occurs only on rotary press printings.

TYPE III — Ribbons are shaded with two lines instead of one; otherwise similar to Type II. Occurs on rotary press printing only.

TYPE IV — Top line of toga is broken. Shading lines inside the toga button read "GID". The line of color in the left "2" is very thin and usually broken. Occurs on offset printings only.

TYPE V — Top line of toga is complete. Toga button has five vertical shaded lines. Line of color in the left "2" is very thin and usually broken. Nose shaded as shown in illustration. Occurs on offset printings only.

TYPE Va — Same as Type V except in shading dots of nose. Third row of dots from bottom has four dots instead of six. Also, the overall height of Type Va is ⅓ millimeter less than Type V. Occurs on offset printings only.

TYPE VI — Same as Type V except that the line of color in the left "2" is very heavy (arrow). Occurs on offset printing only.

TYPE VII — Line of color in left "2" is clear and continuous and heavier than in Types V or Va, but not as heavy as in Type VI. There are three rows of vertical dots (instead of two) in the shading of the upper lip, and additional dots have been added to the hair at the top of the head. Occurs on offset printings only.

TYPES OF THE 3¢ WASHINGTON DESIGN OF 1908-20

Type I: Between 333 and 501

Type II: 484, 494, 502, 541

TYPE I. The top line of the toga is weak as are the top parts of the shading lines that join the toga line. The fifth shading line from the left (arrow) is partly cut away at the top. Also the line between the lip is thin. Occurs on flat and rotary press printings.

TYPE II. The top line of the toga is strong and the shading lines that join it are heavy and complete. The line between the lips is heavy. Occurs on flat and rotary press printings.

Type III: 529

Type IV. 530, 535

TYPE III. The top line of the toga is strong, but the fifth shading line from the left (arrow) is missing. The center line of the toga button consists of two short vertical lines with a dot between them. The "P" and "O" of "POST-AGE" are separated by a small line of color. Occurs on offset printings only.

TYPE IV. The shading lines of the toga are complete. The center line of the toga button consists of a single unbroken vertical line running through the dot in the center. The "P" and "O" of "POSTAGE" are joined. TYPE IV occurs only in offset printings.

TYPES OF THE 2¢ WASHINGTON DESIGN OF 1922-29

Type I: Between 554 and 634

TYPE 1 has thin hair lines at top center of head.

TYPE II has three heavy hair lines (arrow) at top.

Type II: 599A, 634A

ORIGINAL

REVISED

BOOKLET SINGLE

ORIGINAL has the vertical bar of the "¢" symbol pointing to the left part of the "E" of "POSTAGE". In the necktie area, there are complete downward sloping hatch lines which touch the right hand side of the tie. (1288, 1305E)

REVISED has the vertical bar of the "¢" symbol pointing to the center of the "E" of "POSTAGE". In the tie, the downward sloping hatch lines are almost eliminated while the lines angling upward do not touch the lower right hand side of the tie. The third line from the bottom is very short, leaving a colorless spot. (1288D, 1305I)

BOOKLET SINGLE has the vertical bar of the "¢" symbol pointing more toward the "G" of "POSTAGE". The necktie is 4½ millimeters long and is straightened down the center of the robe. The overall design size is smaller both vertically and horizontally. All copies have at least one straight edge. (1288B)

BOOKLET PANES are small sheets of stamps sold by the Post Office in booklet form. Most United States postage and airmail panes consist of a block of 6 stamps, or 5 stamps plus a label, that is straight-edged on all four sides but perforated between the stamps as illustrated. Booklet panes are usually collected unused, with the tab, or binding edge, attached.

Above: "sidewise coil".

Right: "endwise coil".

COIL STAMPS are stamps which come in long rolled strips, especially for use in vending machines, automatic affixing machines, etc. They have straight edges on two opposite sides and perforated edges on the other two sides. If the straight edges run up and down, the stamps are called "endwise coils"; if they run from side to side, they are called "sidewise coils". Coils are generally collected in singles, pairs or strips of four.

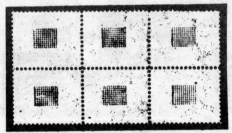

Block of six showing grill marks

GRILLS are raised impressions made in a stamp by pointed metal rollers, resembling the impressions made in a waffle by a waffle iron. The theory behind the grills used on the United States postage issues of 1867-71 was that the cancelling ink would soak into the broken fibers of the paper, thus preventing the stamp from being washed clean and used over again. If the grill impression is made from behind, so that the points show on the face of the stamp, the grill is said to be "points up". If done the opposite way, the grill is said to be "points down". Grills are further classified as "Grill A", "Grill B", etc., according to the type and size of the grill marks on the stamp. It should be remembered that a complete grill is not always found on any one stamp. Major varieties with grills are 79-101, 112-122 and 134-144.

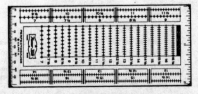

Perforation Gauge

PERFORATIONS around the edges of a stamp are measured by the number of perforation holes in a space of two centimeters, as "Perf. 11", "Perf. 12", etc. This sounds complicated but actually collectors use a simple measuring device called a perforation gauge which readily gives this information about any stamp. Where a stamp is identified by only one perforation number, it is perforated the same on all four sides; if two numbers are shown (e.g., Perf. 11 x 10½), the first number indicates the top and bottom; the second the sides.

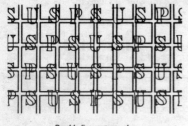

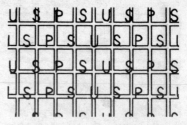

Double line watermark
PERIOD OF USE
Postage 1895-1910

Single line watermark
PERIOD OF USE
Postage 1910-1916

WATERMARKS are faint markings impressed into the paper during manufacture to help detect counterfeiting. Practically all United States postage stamps issued between the years 1895-1916 are watermarked "USPS" (United States Postal Service), either in single line or double line letters, as illustrated. Before 1895 and since 1916, all postage issues, except for Scott's #519 and some copies of the $1 "Presidential"—an error—are unwatermarked.

To see a watermark, place the stamp on a "watermark detector" and add a few drops of watermark fluid. The watermark—if there is one—will usually show clearly. From the illustrations it can be seen that frequently only a part of a letter will appear.

HOW TO DISTINGUISH BETWEEN FLAT, ROTARY AND OFFSET PRINTINGS.

FLAT PLATE means printed from flat metal plates or engravings.

ROTARY PRESS means printed from plates that are curved to fit around a cylinder. In the curving process, the designs of the stamp stretch slightly in the direction that the plate is curved, so that rotary press stamps issued prior to 1954 are always either slightly wider or slightly taller than the same designs printed from flat plates. Also, on rotary printings, one or more ridges have been forced into the paper to keep it from curling, and these usually show across the back of the stamp. No such ridges are found in flat press stamps.

Left: *rotary press issue slightly taller than corresponding flat press design.*
Right: *rotary press stamp slightly wider than the stamp design printed from flat plates.*

OFFSET is a method of printing in which the plate transfers or "offsets" the design onto a rubber blanket which, in turn, transfers it to the paper. On stamps printed from flat press or rotary press plates (that is, engraved stamps), a relatively large amount of ink is deposited on the paper, giving the stamps a "rough" feeling. If you run a fingernail or metal edge lightly across the lines on such stamps, you can actually feel the ridges of ink. Offset stamps, on the other hand, have a smooth or "soapy" feeling. The ink lies down uniformly on the surface of the paper, and no ridges can be felt.

SPECIAL PRINTINGS are reprints, either from the original or from new engravings, of stamps previously issued. They are usually printed in limited quantities and for specific purposes, and can almost always be distinguished from the originals by differences in color perforations, gum, type of paper, etc. The largest single groups—the Special Printings of 1875—consist of a complete set of all designs issued up to that date. They were prepared for display by the government at the Philadelphia Centennial Exposition of 1876. Another good example of a Special Printing is the 1947 "CIPEX" souvenir sheet, shown at the front of this U.S. IDENTIFIER, which was printed as a souvenir of the Centenary International Philatelic Exposition held in New York in May, 1947.

H.E. Harris & Co., Inc. ® *Everything for the Stamp Collector*

America's Finest Albums and Supplies

MASTERWORK ® Albums

WORLD-WIDE, UNITED STATES AND CANADA
LOOSE-LEAF ALBUMS
PLUS BEGINNER'S ALBUMS

Harris publishes albums to accommodate every size stamp collection. Loose-leaf albums for world-wide collections include the "top-of-the-line" Two-Volume Standard and the Citation ("World's Largest" one-volume album). For smaller collections, the Senior Statesman, Statesman, and beginner's Traveler are available. Collectors of United States stamps have a choice of the luxury Classic or the Liberty album, both loose-leaf. Young beginners can also start with the softbound Adventurer (world-wide) or American Treasury (U.S. stamps). New supplements are published in January of every year to keep the loose-leaf albums up-to-date. The complete album line is described in the following pages. Harris albums are available from stamp dealers, hobby shops, and variety stores, or by mail from Harris.

Accessories to Increase Hobby Enjoyment

- **COVER ALBUMS • STOCK BOOKS • GAUGES • TONGS**
- **MAGNIFIERS • COIN SUPPLIES • BLANK ALBUMS**
- **MUCH, MUCH MORE**

Harris sells the finest supplies and accessories for stamps, First Day Covers, coins, and bank notes. Look through these pages to find the supplies that suit your particular collecting interests. Stock books to hold loose stamps, conventional magnifying glasses and several illuminated magnifiers, hinges and Harris Crystal Mount are all listed along with many other helpful items. Your dealer may have some of these supplies; they are all available from H.E. Harris & Co., Inc., Box O, Boston, Mass. 02117.

The Incomparable *Harris*
FIRST DAY
COVER ALBUM

Handsome and Durable
Loose-Leaf Album for
All Your Covers

only $**21.95**

This beautiful library-style album protects and displays your highly prized covers in sparkling clear vinyl pages. Each page is divided into two 4" pockets that hold two covers. By inserting them back-to-back, 80 covers may be mounted in each 20-page album! The durable two-post binder makes it simple to add extra pages. The dark brown simulated leather binder is gold stamped.

H139   Harris First Day Cover Album (U.S. & Foreign covers) $21.95

AND

When It's Time to Add More Pages...

W139   20 pages, 4" deep vinyl pockets (U.S. & Foreign covers) . . 11.95

H.E. Harris & Co. Inc. ® *Everything for the Stamp Collector*

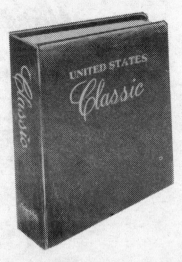

The Famous

Harris

UNITED STATES CLASSIC ALBUM

Only **$39⁹⁵**

NO Supplement needed until January 1986

A luxurious loose-leaf album for every collector who wants the BEST, with all the features required by knowledgeable collectors

The Harris Classic Album is a fine alternative to the big specialized United States albums now on the market. Years in the making, the Classic offers all the features demanded by the advanced U.S. collector and by the general collector of U.S. stamps who wants to start with the largest and finest album on the market. No expense has been spared to make the Harris Classic first in its field.

• 100% Complete - every space illustrated: Postmaster Provisionals, Regular Postage, Air Post, Special Delivery, Certified Mail, Registration, Air Post Special Delivery, Postage Due, Parcel Post, Special Handling, Parcel Post Postage Due, Officials, Newspaper, Offices Abroad, Hunting Permits, and Confederate States. Pages for Coil Pairs and Souvenir Sheets.

• Uncrowded 9-1/8" x 12" pages, printed one side only on cream-colored heavy stock. More spacious, artistic page arrangement than any other album.

• Rich brown two-post binder, in simulated leather-like vinyl, with color-coordinated vinyl interior.

• Complete through December 1983, no supplement needed until January, 1985.

You will not need the X113 Series of Supplements listed below if you are buying a new Classic.

H113	Harris U.S. Calssic Album	$39.95
W113	Bordered Blank Pages, pkg. of 64 extra pages	4.95
F113	Binder Only (Leather Like Vinyl)	20.00
F116	Velour Suede-Textured Binder	14.00
Y113	Velour Suede-Textured Slipcase for F116 Binder	11.95
X113W	1984 Supplement	3.95
X113U	1983 Supplement	3.95
X113T	1982 Supplement	3.95
X113S	1981 Supplement	3.95
X113R	1980 Supplement	3.95
X113	Booklet Pane section - 96 pages	6.95

"America's best selling album for U.S. stamps"

UNITED STATES
LIBERTY®
ALBUM

BEAUTIFUL
LOOSE-LEAF
ALBUM
100%
ILLUSTRATED

still only **$15.95**

"America's Best Buys"

Without a doubt, the Harris Liberty is the most popular album for collectors of U.S. stamps. There are over 2,700 illustrations on pages that are printed on one side only, and on extremely high quality white paper. Spaces are included for U.S. definitives, commemoratives, airmails, special delivery, postage dues and hunting permit stamps. This comprehensive album also includes spaces for Confederate State stamps, and the United Nations (complete). Rugged blue and green vinyl loose-leaf binder allows for maximum expansion. 416 pages. No supplement needed until January, 1986.

H108 U.S. LIBERTY ALBUM .... only $15.95
F108 U.S. LIBERTY ALBUM, binder only 10.00

Expand Your Liberty Album with Blank Pages

Blank pages with matching borders allow for expansion. 64 sheets (128 pages). Each package of blank pages contains 550 gummed titles.

W120Z 64 bordered, unillustrated extra pages $4.95

ILLUSTRATED SUPPLEMENTS PUBLISHED YEARLY

H.E. Harris & Co., Inc. ® *Everything for the Stamp Collector*

The ULTIMATE for PLATE BLOCK COLLECTORS

UNITED STATES PLATE BLOCK ALBUMS
(ALSO FOR ORDINARY BLOCKS)

STILL ONLY
$39.95

UNRIVALED LOOSE-LEAF ALBUM FOR U.S. PLATE BLOCKS IN TWO HANDSOME VOLUMES

A comprehensive two-volume set for plate block collectors.

Large capacity albums, each with matching brown and gold vinyl binder. Each stamp is illustrated and the pages are printed on one side only. Important and informative descriptions are included for each issue.

VOLUME A . . . 480 pages for over 730 plate blocks. Starts with the 1901 Pan-American Exposition issue and provides spaces for Commemorative, Air Post, Air Post Special Delivery, Special Handling and Certified Mail Plate Blocks, 1901-63 complete; Regular Postage and Special Delivery 1922-62. A special section, "Features of Plate Block Collecting" furnish the collector with all the basic background information necessary for enjoying this collecting specialty.

VOLUME B . . . over 400 pages for more than 400 plate blocks. Starts in 1964 where Volume A stops and brings your collection up to date. Illustrated supplements are published yearly.

H122	U.S. PLATE BLOCK ALBUM, Volumes A & B, complete	$39.95
H120	U.S. PLATE BLOCK ALBUM, Volume A	21.95
H121	U.S. PLATE BLOCK ALBUM, Volume B — No supplement needed until January 1986	21.95
F119	BINDER ONLY, for either Volume A or B	10.00

W120Z Bordered unillustrated pages for Harris Plate Block Album, set of 64 sheets (128 pages) with 550 gummed titles 4.95

ILLUSTRATED SUPPLEMENTS PUBLISHED YEARLY

new from Harris!
CANADA PLATE BLOCK ALBUM
$21.95

SAVE $3.95 WHEN YOU BUY BOTH SINGLES & PLATE BLOCK ALBUM!

H161

The Ultimate Album for Canadian Plate Block Collectors!

No effort has been spared to bring you the finest Canada plate block album! It's the perfect companion to the Harris singles album, and like its mate will require no supplement until January of 1986. There are 416 pages in this all-new album for Canada-only plate blocks. Pages for commemoratives and definitives from the 1942 War Issue to date are included, plus all the categories listed here:

- Semi-Postals, complete
- Air Post, complete
- Air Post Special Delivery, complete
- Air Port Officials, complete
- Special Delivery, complete
- Special Delivery Officials, complete
- Officials, complete

H161	Harris Canada Plate Block Album	$21.95
F161	Harris Canada Plate Block Binder	10.00

H162	Both Albums (H160 and H161) Special Price	39.95
	SAVE $3.95	

The very finest . . .
designed by collectors for collectors

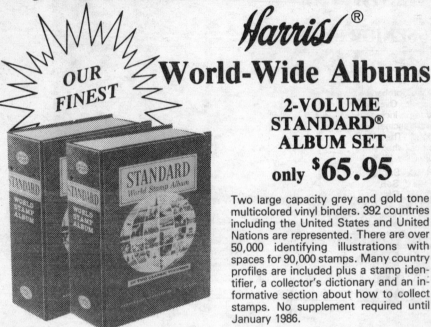

OUR FINEST

Harris® **World-Wide Albums**

2-VOLUME STANDARD® ALBUM SET

only $65.95

Two large capacity grey and gold tone multicolored vinyl binders. 392 countries including the United States and United Nations are represented. There are over 50,000 identifying illustrations with spaces for 90,000 stamps. Many country profiles are included plus a stamp identifier, a collector's dictionary and an informative section about how to collect stamps. No supplement required until January 1986.

H100	Two-Volume Standard Loose-Leaf Album, set. . .	$65.95
F100	One Standard Binder Only	14.00
W152	Glassine interleaves, 100 per package	4.95

CITATION®
Holds More Than 70,000 Stamps!

Only $55.95

Single volume with 47,000 illustrations and spaces for over 70,000 stamps. 350 stamp-issuing countries. A wealth of geographical and historical information included as well as a stamp dictionary, and a stamp identifier. Vinyl binder of burnished gold on maroon. No supplement required until January 1986.

H101	Citation Loose-leaf Album Only	$55.95
F101	Citation Binder, cpl., each	16.00
W152	Glassine interleaves, 100 per package	4.95

H.E. Harris & Co., Inc. ® *Everything for the Stamp Collector*

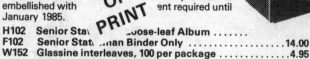

Harris ®

SENIOR STATESMAN®

ONLY $39.95

A comprehensive world-wide album with over 925 pages. Over 23,000 i ~~~~~~ ns for over 45,000 stamps including ~~~~~~ de country profiles with fascinating ~~~~~~ ographical information. The strik ~~~~~~ en vinyl binder is embellished with ~~~~~~ ent required until January 1985.

OUT OF PRINT

H102	**Senior Sta~~~~~~oose-leaf Album**	. . . .
F102	**Senior Stat~~~~~~an Binder Only**	. . . . .14.00
W152	**Glassine interleaves, 100 per package**	. . . . .4.95

America's Most Popular Low-Priced Album

STATESMAN® ALBUM

$21.95

Sturdy blue and gold vinyl binder with spaces for over 20,000 stamps. Over 390 countries represented with over 9,500 illustrations. Includes country profiles, collector's dictionary, stamp identifier, and spaces for colorful coats of arms and world flags. 440 pages. No supplement required until January 1986.

H103	**Statesman Deluxe Loose-leaf Album**	. . . . .only $21.95
F103	**Statesman Binder Only**	. . . . .10.00

AMBASSADOR® ALBUM

Ambassador world-wide loose-leaf album with spaces for over 10,000 stamps.

$15.95

H104	Ambassador Album only	. . . .$15.95
F104	Ambassador Vinyl Binder only	. . . .$10.00

TRAVELER ALBUM®

$9.95

NOT ILLUSTRATED: Loose-leaf beginners album with bright red coated linen binder. Over 4,000 illustrations. Includes helpful hints section, and geographic outlines.

H105	**Traveler Album**	. . . .$9.95
F105	**Traveler Binder Only**	. . . . .6.00

Build your very own personalized collection of topical stamps — also great for country specialties.

HARRIS TOPICAL and SINGLE COUNTRY ALBUMS
$21.95

Stamps shown not included. Pages you receive will be lightly dot ruled (quadrilled) to guide you in placing stamps.

Topical and Single-Country Albums custom-made for your special interest! Brown padded 3-ring binders have the look of leather; emblem of topic is gold-stamped on the cover; the title is gold-stamped on the spine. Fifty pages of heavy quality card stock, faintly dot ruled. The name of the topic or country is printed at top of each page. Binders 10½" x 11½"; pages 8½" x 11". Complete 50-page album, $21.95 each.

TOPICS		COUNTRIES	
Animals	H002	Australia-New Zealand	H050
Art	H003	British Comm.	H085
Automobiles	H080	Bohemia-Moravia	H070
Birds	H004	China	H053
Cats	H005	Egypt	H074
Dogs	H007	France	H054
Fish	H009	Germany	H055
Flowers	H010	Great Britain	H056
Horses	H011	Israel	H058
Kennedy	H025	Japan	H059
Olympics	H017	Poland	H063
Railroads	H018	Ryukyu Is.	H084
Scouts	H021	Russia	H066
Ships	H022	South Seas	H082
Space	H023	Spain	H069
Sports	H024	Sweden	H064
Stamps on Stamps	H077	Switzerland	H065
Stamps of War	H076	Turkey	H067
		United States	H071
		United Nations	H086
		Vatican City	H068

Extra pages and binders available for any title

Extra pages for any title, pkg. of 25 (use "W" prefix plus number) $10.00

Extra binders, any title (use "F" prefix plus number) $14.00

SOFTBOUND BEGINNERS ALBUMS

U.S. AMERICAN TREASURY

Only $6.00

A fine introductory album for United States stamps. Spaces for hundreds of the most popular stamps, with interesting historical information about many stamps.

H196 American Treasury $6.00

ADVENTURER WORLD ALBUM

Only $6.00

A fine softbound world-wide album for beginners. Same pages as the more expensive Traveler above. Bright illustrated cover. Includes pages for U.S. Stamps.

H195 Adventurer Album $6.00

ALL-PURPOSE BINDER

Create your own album using any Harris pages $6.00

- Simulated leather maroon vinyl binder, with "Postage Stamp Album" on spine in gold.
- 2-post construction, accepts Harris Speedrille or blank album pages or any Harris album pages.
- Lets you make your own custom album on any subject.

F130 .... $6.00

U.S. AMERICAN TREASURY KIT

Only $9.95

Wonderful starter kit contains the album described above plus a collection of 65 U.S. stamps, hinges, and Presidents and U.S. flag seals. This is our newest U.S. kit and is becoming very popular for its large album and low price.

L196   Treasury Kit $9.95

ADVENTURER WORLD KIT

Only $9.95

This kit includes Adventurer world album plus a collection of world wide stamps, hinges, magnifier, and world flags.

L195   Adventurer Kit $9.95

UNITED STATES & POSSESSIONS, UNITED NATIONS, CANADA & PROVINCES

MASTERWORK® WORLD-WIDE SUPPLEMENTS

Your older Harris Masterwork®
Album Need Never Go Out of Date

HARRIS SUPPLEMENTS FOR ALL *Harris/* WORLD-WIDE LOOSE-LEAF ALBUMS

still only $5.95

1984 MASTER SUPPLEMENT	X100W	$5.95
1983 MASTER SUPPLEMENT	X100U	5.95
1982 MASTER SUPPLEMENT	X100T	5.95
1981 MASTER SUPPLEMENT	X100S	5.95
1980 MASTER SUPPLEMENT	X100R	5.95
1979 MASTER SUPPLEMENT	X100P	5.95
128 Speed-rille Pages—Preruled Expansion Pages	W150	$4.95
128 Bordered Nonillustrated Extra Pages	W151	4.95
100 Glassine Interleaves—Fits All Harris L.L. Albums	W152	4.95

CANADA SUPPLEMENTS
$2.95

Canada 1983-84	X160W	$2.95
Canada 1982-83	X160U	2.95
Canada 1981-82	X160T	2.95
Canada 1980-81	X160S	2.95
Canada 1979-80	X160R	2.95
Canada 1978-79	X160P	2.95
Canada 1977-78	X160N	2.95
Canada 1976-77	X160M	2.95
Canada 1975-76	X160L	2.95

UNITED NATIONS SUPPLEMENTS
$2.95

U.N. 1983-84	X165W	$2.95
U.N. 1982-83	X165U	2.95
U.N. 1981-82	X165T	2.95
U.N. 1980-81	X165S	2.95
U.N. 1979-80	X165R	2.95
U.N. 1978-79	X165P	2.95
U.N. 1977-78	X165N	2.95
U.N. 1976-77	X165M	2.95
U.N. 1975-76	X165L	2.95

PLEASE NOTE: SUPPLEMENTS PRIOR TO THOSE LISTED ARE OUT OF PRINT

H.E. Harris & Co., Inc. ® *Everything for the Stamp Collector*

MASTERWORK® UNITED STATES SUPPLEMENTS

FOR HARRIS LOOSE-LEAF U.S. LIBERTY ALBUMS
$2.95

1984	X108W	$2.95
1983	X108U	2.95
1982	X108T	2.95
1981	X108S	2.95
1980	X108R	2.95
1979	X108P	2.95
Bordered Pages	W120Z	4.95

FOR HARRIS U.S. PLATE BLOCK ALBUM
$3.95

1984	X109W	$3.95
1983	X109U	3.95
1982	X109T	3.95
1981	X109S	3.95
1980	X109R	3.95
1979	X109P	3.95
Through Mid-1978	X109N	3.95
Through Mid-1977	X109M	3.95
Through Mid-1976	X109L	3.95
Bordered pages	W120Z	4.95

For Our Finest U.S. Album
The U.S. CLASSIC SUPPLEMENT
$3.95 each

1984	X113W	$3.95
1983	X113U	3.95
1982	X113T	3.95
1981	X113S	3.95
1980	X113R	3.95
Booklet Pane Section	X113	6.95
Blank Pages for Classic	W113	4.95
Glassine Interleaves, pkg. of 100	W152	4.95

PLEASE NOTE: SUPPLEMENTS PUBLISHED IN JANUARY OF EACH YEAR.

Extra Binders for Your Growing Collection

FOR WORLD-WIDE COLLECTIONS

F100 Standard Binder Only $14.00
F101 Citation Binder Only 16.00
F102 Sr. Statesman Binder Only 14.00
F103 Statesman Binder Only 10.00
F104 Ambassador Binder Only 10.00
F105 Traveler Binder Only 6.00

FOR UNITED STATES COLLECTIONS, PLUS PLATE BLOCKS & CANADA

F113 Classic Binder vinyl edition $20.00
F116 Classic Binder velour edition 14.00
F108 Liberty Binder (blue) 10.00
F119 Plate Block Binder (brown) 10.00
F117 Independence Binder................................ 6.00
F160 Canada Binder (green)............................. 10.00
F161 Canada Plate Block Binder (green) 10.00

H.E.Harris & Co., Inc. ® *Everything for the Stamp Collector*

Extra Pages for All Harris Loose-Leaf Albums. 4 Styles.

Pages designed for the collector who prefers complete freedom and flexibility in creating specialty sections for your album that reflect your particular interests. The ideal way to expand certain countries or to create sections for specialties such as First Day Covers, Postal Cards, Souvenir Sheets, Revenues, etc.

Speed-rille ® ALBUM PAGES
For World-Wide Albums

Speed-rille® are the ONLY pages preruled with tiny guide lines which divide the sheet into equal sections, automatically allowing you to make neat and attractive arrangements with all sizes and shapes of stamps—no measuring or guessing. Easy instructions included. 128 pages—64 sheets printed on both sides—plus 850 dry-gummed identifying titles for countries of the world; borders match Harris world-wide albums; pages fit all Harris albums.

W150 . . . . Only $4.95

BLANK PAGES
WITH DOUBLE BORDERS
For World-Wide Albums

For all Harris Masterwork Albums. 128 pages—64 sheets with borders on both sides—plus 850 dry-gummed identifying titles for countries of the world and for U.S. and foreign specialties, such as "First Day Covers," "Air Post Stamps," etc.

W151 . . . . Only $4.95

BLANK PAGES
FOR HARRIS MASTERWORK® U.S.
Liberty, U.S. Plate Block & Canada Albums

128 pages—64 sheets with borders on one side only—plus more than 550 matching dry-gummed titles for United States and its Possessions, United Nations, Canada and its Provinces and specialty titles such as "Booklet Panes," "First Day Covers," etc.
TRIPLE BORDERS

W120Z . . . . Only $4.95

BLANK PAGES
FOR HARRIS U.S. CLASSIC ALBUM

64 sheets with borders on one side only. Rich cream-colored heavy stock with borders that match the Harris Classic Album.

W113 For U.S. Classic . . . . Only $4.95

A real problem-solver

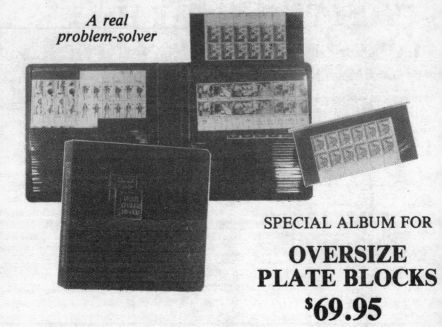

SPECIAL ALBUM FOR

OVERSIZE PLATE BLOCKS
$69.95

A top-quality Allsyte album for jumbo multi-stamp plate blocks or strips, like the Gershwin issue (6 plate numbers, 12 stamps) or Postal People (5 plate numbers, 20 stamps). convenient flip style. Rugged 12″ x 12¼″ black binder stamped in gold; fifty big 10½″ x 5″ acetate packets with removable black inserts, to hold 100 blocks back-to-back.

H650 Oversize Plate Block Album $69.95

BUREAU SOUVENIR CARD ALBUM

$69.95

This beautiful album provides a fine protective home for your souvenir cards. Each page frames your Bureau card beautifully.
Souvenir cards are issued by the U.S. Postal Service or the Bureau of Engraving and Printing as souvenirs of important philatelic gatherings.

H157	Complete Album 1939-1981	$69.95
F157	Binder only	29.95
W157F	Souvenir Card Pages, 1980	5.95
W157G	Souvenir Card Pages, 1981	5.95
W157H	Souvenir Card Pages, 1982	5.95
W158	Souvenir Card Album blank pages	.5.95

Display and Protect Your Mint Sheets

OUR FINEST PEERLESS MINT SHEET ALBUM
$37.95

Rich Blue Imitation Leather Binder—100 Pages

Specially designed to store and protect mint sheets; consists of 100 big transparent pocket pages, size 11″ x 11″, of high quality, clear glassine stock. Pages are open at the top and side, closed at the bottom; thus mint sheets may be easily inserted or removed, yet will not fall out when the album lies flat or is held in the normal vertical position. Binder is made of blue imitation leather.
H133 PEERLESS MINT SHEET ALBUM $37.95

MINT SHEET BOOK
$4.95

Economical Cardboard Cover
An economical book designed to store and protect mint sheets, 48 sheets stored back to back. The glassine pocket pages, size 9-3/8″x 10¾″, are open at the top and right-hand side but closed at the bottom; thus the sheets may easily be inserted or removed, yet will not fall out.
H140 MINT SHEET BOOK $4.95

PLATE STRIP OR MINT BLOCK FILES

A perfect way to store your extra plate strips or mint blocks. Each paper bound booklet comes with a good supply of glassine pocket pages to protect your stamps. Plate Strip File measures 5″ × 11″; Mint Block File measures 5¼″ × 4¼″.

Y765 Plate Strip File $3.95
Y764 Mint Block File 1.95

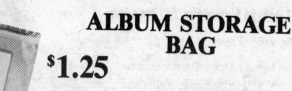

ALBUM STORAGE BAG
$1.25

Professionally safeguard your collection against humidity, dust, and grime. An important accessory, these heavy-duty plastic ALBUM STORAGE BAGS are ideal for moving and storage. Seals and unseals instantly. Lines on the outside on which to label and organize contents.

Y759 Album Bag $1.25

CRYSTAL MOUNT®
PROTECTS STAMPS BEST
$3.50

Don't mount stamps with hinges when you want to protect the gum on the back of a stamp. Harris acetate Crystal Mount protects stamps and displays them beautifully. All really valuable stamps need the protection of these mounts. Crystal Mount is ecnomical; it comes in long flat tubes that can be cut to fit stamps. Gummed strip on back mounts them in your album.

Y741 SMALL 1 1/16" high for U.S. regular issues and horizontal commemoratives.
Y742 INTERMEDIATE 1 5/32" high, for U.S. "Famous Americans".
Y743 MEDIUM. 1 5/8" high, for U.S. vertical commemoratives.
Y744 LARGE. 2¼" high, for extra-large stamps.
Y745 BLOCKS AND PLATE BLOCKS OF FOUR, 2¾" high.
Y746 COVER SIZE. 3 7/8" high.
Y747 JUMBO. 4¼" high, for extra-large plate blocks and oversize covers.
Y749 ASSORTED SIZES. A generous amount of all seven sizes.

Crystal Mount® , per pkg. (State number when ordering) ...$3.50

ANOTHER FINE HARRIS PUBLICATION

HOW TO COLLECT STAMPS
$2.50

An indispensable reference work for every stamp collector. 19-page World-Wide Stamp Identifier; Big 13-page Map Section; Foreign Numerical Tables; U. S. Stamp Identifier. Plus How to Get Stamps; Famous Rarities; How to Organize a Stamp Club; History of Stamps; guide to Accessories, etc.

29000 HOW TO COLLECT STAMPS.....................................$2.50

H.E. Harris & Co., Inc.® *Everything for the Stamp Collector*

HANDY STOCK BOOK

Big 9x6'' Pages **$4.50**

The Handy Stock Book contains 10 pages of durable tag stock capable of holding more than 400 single stamps. The top pocket of each sheet is wide enough to hold blocks of 4. The book is bound in extra-heavy leatherette cover stock with plastic spiral binding which permits the book to lie flat when open.

Y802 Handy Stock Book **$4.50**

STAMP COLLECTORS STOCK BOOK **$2.50**

Contains five tough manila stock sheets, size 4¼'' x 7¼'', with a durable paperboard cover. Best buy ever in a small pocket stock book.

Y801 Stamp Collectors Stock Book **$2.50**

STAMP STOCK BOOK FITS SAFETY DEPOSIT BOX **$12.95**

A great new idea! Neat stock book designed especially for the stamps you keep in the bank! A full 12'' high but only 4½'' across. Flawlessly constructed of heaviest quality material. Eight pages hold stamps on both sides; 10 rows of glassine pockets per page; glassine interleaves between pages. Fits easily into safety deposit box!

Y810 Bank Stock Book **$12.95**

STAMP COLLECTORS INVENTORY RECORD **$9.95**

A convenient little book, ideal for keeping an "at a glance" record of your stamp collection. You can make entries for the catalog no., condition, cost, and value of each stamp. This attractive six-ring binder measures 4-1/4'' x 6-3/8'', is made of durable vinyl, and is gold stamped. Refills available. Also available in softcover, pocket-size version.

Y763 Inventory Record, binder with 48 sheets **$9.95**
Y762 50 Sheet Refill Pack for above **2.95**
Y761 Inventory Record, softcover with
    24 pages (non-refillable) **2.95**

Harris
STAMP COLLECTING KITS
"The gift that keeps on giving"

The best introduction to the exciting hobby of stamp collecting is to start with a complete collecting kit. Each kit contains everything needed to start a lifetime of enjoyment with America's favorite hobby. Choose one for your children ... as a gift for someone special ... or to start in the stamp hobby yourself!

UNITED STATES KIT
for the beginning collector of United States Stamps

LIBERTY® KIT
$29.95

Contains the fabulous Harris LIBERTY loose-leaf album. Also 100 all-different U.S. stamps, stamp hinges, magnifier, seals of state flags, Portraits of U.S. Presidents, U.S. stamp map, stamp tongs, perforation gauge. Handsome Gift Box.

L108   Liberty Kit
Complete—Gift Boxed . . . .**only $29.95**

H. E. Harris & Co., Inc.® *Everything for the Stamp Collector*

Harris World-Wide Kits

CITATION® KIT
$69.95

America's Finest Stamp Kit. Has everything you need; the world's largest capacity stamp album... Big valuable stamp collection... All accessories. Kit contains: CITATION Loose-Leaf Stamp Album (See complete description elsewhere). 500 World-Wide Stamps (includes stamps from many countries on six continents); 16 Freak Stamps; 23 World Menagerie Stamps; 31 Stamptacular Stamps; 150 Flags of the World; 124 Coats of Arms of the World; U. S. Presidents Seals; 50 U. S. State Flags; "The Stamp Finder" (indispensable guidebook for determining the country to which any stamp belongs); "How to Collect Stamps"; Pocket Stock Book; magnifying glass; stamp tongs; perforation gauge; 600 stamp hinges and big 22" x 34" World Stamp Map.

L101   Citation Kit
Complete (Not Boxed)........$69.95

SENIOR STATESMAN® KIT

Ideal kit to make stam~ collecting more fun than ever! ~~~ s our elegant Senior Sta⁺ ~~~~ ⌐ver 300 genuine post~ ~~~ '00 hinges, magnifier, st~ ~~~ ~np tongs, 150 Flags of ~~~ ~4 Coats of Arms, U. S. St⁺ ~gs, Portraits of U. S. Presidents, World Stamp Map.

L102 Senior Statesman Kit
Complete (Not Boxed).......

All albums in Harris World-Wide kits include spaces for United States stamps.

More World-Wide Kits from Harris

THE STATESMAN® KIT
$29.95

This perfect medium-price kit is attractively packaged in a handsome gift box. Contains the big, profusely illustrated Statesman loose-leaf album; over 300 all-different postage stamps from all parts of the world; 600 stamp hinges; powerful stamp magnifier; richly colored Flags and Coats of Arms of the World; U.S. State Flags; handsome portrait collection of U.S. Presidents in color; metal stamp tongs; handy Stamp Wallet and World Stamp Map.

L103 Statesman Kit
Complete—Gift boxed $29.95

THE TRAVELER® KIT
$16.95

Features the famous Traveler loose-leaf Album. You'll also find over 200 different world-wide postage stamps, stamp hinges, magnifier, Flags and Coats of Arms of many nations, U.S. State Flags and portraits of U.S. Presidents.

L105 Traveler Kit
Complete—Gift boxed $16.95

All Albums in world-wide kits include spaces for United States stamps.

NEW!
ADVANCED COLLECTING KITS

The best introduction to the hobby of stamp collecting. Each kit contains everything needed to start a lifetime of enjoyment with America's favorite hobby. Every kit handsomely boxed and you save dollars over the price of items when purchased individually!

ADVANCED U.S. STAMP COLLECTOR KIT $99⁹⁵

SAVE $38.07 —$138.02 if items purchased individually

1 Our finest U.S. Classic album — 100% illustrated and complete for the advanced collector. Interleave sheets, blank pages, tongs, perf. gauge, magnifier, 4 pkg. of Crystal Mount, rare stamp sheets, U.S. map, 2000 hinges included plus 60 mint regular issue stamps (1917-'74) and 25 mint coil stamps (pre-1971).
L150

ADVANCED WORLD—WIDE KIT $99⁹⁵

SAVE $21.65 — $121.60 if items purchased individually

2 Two large capacity Standard albums for stamps from around the world plus world flags, coats of arms, state flags and presidents seals. There's a stock book, magnifier, perf gauge, world map, stamp hinges, tongs, rare stamp sheet, U.S. map, stamp finder, "how to collect" book and 850 world wide stamps. Also included is a package of 200 U.S. stamps and 23 world menagerie, 16 oddities and 31 stamptacular stamps.
L151

U.S. ADULT KIT $69⁹⁵

SAVE $18.41 — $88.36 if items purchased individually

3 Our fabulous loose-leaf Liberty album and interleave sheets, magnifier, 2000 stamp hinges, tongs, perf gauge, pkg. of assorted size Crystal Mount, state flags and president seals, U.S. map, rare stamp sheet included. Stamps included — 45 used regular early issues, 80 used regular 1938-74', 40 used coils pre-1975 and 30 used special delivery/postage dues.
L152

ADULT WORLD-WIDE KIT $69⁹⁵

SAVE $17.23 — $87.18 if items purchased individually

4 America's Finest Stamp Kit. Citation Loose-Leaf Stamp Album, 500 World-Wide Stamps, 16 Freak Stamps, 23 World Menagerie Stamps, 31 Stamptacular Stamps, 150 Flags of the World, 124 Coats of Arms of the World, U.S. Presidents Seals, 50 U.S. State Flags. "The Stamp Finder" guidebook, "How to Collect Stamps." Pocket stock Book, magnifying glass, stamp tongs, perforation gauge, 600 stamp hinges and World Stamp Map.
L153

SCOTT CATALOGS
$20 each

Scott world-wide catalogs list stamps of the entire world in four convenient volumes. The Scott numbers and identification of stamps are used everywhere and a Scott catalog is needed by every serious collector. Prices are given for both unused and used stamps. We ship the latest issue when you order.

Y865 Volume 1: United States, United Nations,
and British Commonwealth of Nations $20.00

Y866 Volume II: Countries of the World, A-F 20.00

Y867 Volume III: Countries of the World, G-O 20.00

Y869 Volume IV: Countries of the World, P-Z 20.00

THE SCOTT SPECIALIZED
UNITED STATES CATALOG
$20

The Scott United States specialized catalog is a treasure trove of information on all classes of United States stamps including revenues, postal stationery, postal cards, etc. Detailed identification of every variety of issue, differences in dies, everything the advanced collector, dealer, and specialist needs to know about United States stamps. Prices for first day covers, blocks, plate blocks, and much more. Big, clear oversized illustrations.

Y868 Scott U.S. Specialized Catalog, Latest Edition.........$20.00

THE SCOTT INTERNATIONAL ALBUM
The finest album the philatelic world has ever known!

If you're a serious world-wide collector, there is only one album for you. The comprehensive one: Scott's International. It's the ultimate world-wide album.

The Scott International is a full philatelic library with over 13,000 spacious pages for almost 200,000 world issues. Every space is illustrated or identifies each stamp; pages are chemically neutralized to protect your stamp treasures from deterioration.

Start with one or more jumbo binders ($20.00 each) and purchase exactly the pages you want, when you want them. The full library is separated into 24 parts. You purchase pages separately, so you can start wherever you want and build your own album set.

For the sophisticated collector there is no other choice. The International is the most treasured album in the world of stamp collecting.

Each Scott International section includes a title page describing the contents and blue leatherette strip printed with part number in silver, to mount on spine of binder.

HARRIS CRYSTAL MOUNT® $^{\$}$**3.50**pkg.

is your best choice of a quality clear acetate mount for your finest blocks, stamps and covers. One package at $3.50 mounts many. See inside back cover for sizes and ordering information.

H.E. Harris & Co., Inc. ® *Everything for the Stamp Collector*

SCOTT INTERNATIONAL BINDERS

Hinged post construction, blue reinforced binding, silver lettering. Each jumbo binder holds 400 pages.

F200Y Binder, each $20.00
F201Y International Slipcase $20.00

INTERNATIONAL ALBUM PAGES

(When a part has an "A" and a "A1" section, both sections are required to cover the time period stated in the listing.)

W200A-1	Part 2, 1940-1949, pages only, A-Jam	$36.00
W200A-2	Part 2, 1940-1944, pages only, Jap-Z	36.00
W200B-1	Part 3B, 1949-1955, pages only K-Z	36.00
W200D	Part 5, 1960-1965, pages only	$36.00
W200D-1	Part 5A, 1960-1965, pages only	36.00
W200E-1	Part 6A, 1965-1968, pages only	36.00
W200F	Part 7A 1968-1971, pages only, A-K	36.00
W200F-1	Part 7B, 1968-1971, pages only, L-Z	36.00
W200G	Part 8A 1971-1973, pages only A-Lie	36.00
W200G-1	Part 8B, 1971-1973, pages only, Lux-Z	36.00
W200J	Part 10, 1974-1975, pages only	36.00
W200M	Part 13, 1977-1978, pages only	36.00
W200N	Part 14, 1978, pages only	36.00
W200P	Part 15, 1979, pages only	36.00
W200R	Part 16, 1980, pages only	36.00
W200S	Part 17, 1981, pages only	36.00
W200T	Part 18, 1982, pages only	36.00

Harris Customers Please Note: Only 17 of the 24 Scott album page sections are listed here. These are all that are currently available. Scott has set no reprint date for the missing sections. Please order carefully and order only those listed here. Thank you.

Blank Pages For All Scott Specialty Albums

These pages fit the single-country Scott Specialty Album series which are the ultra-complete albums for the most exacting specialist.

W322A Border "A" Blank Pages, 40 Sheets 6.95

W325 Border "A" green quadrille-ruled pages, 40 sheets 6.95

MAGNIFIERS

FINE QUALITY READING GLASSES

Choice of 2 Sizes
Both are 5x Magnification

Clear lenses of the highest quality mounted in wide chromium plated brass rims...solid black ebonite handles.

Y774 Reading Glass 3″ lens 7.95
Y775 Reading Glass 4″ lens 10.95

FOLDING POCKET MAGNIFIER

Lenses of good magnifying power which fold back into their own handles for pocket carrying.

Y751 Folding Magnifier, 1″ lens
4x Magnification $4.95

Y752 Folding Magnifier, excellent quality, 1¼″ lens, 3.5x
Magnification $7.95

Y753 Folding Magnifier, good quality, 1¾″ lens, 3x Magnification $2.95

STAND MAGNIFIER
$24.95

Leaves
Both Hands
Free

These adjustable ball-jointed magnifiers leave both hands free to examine stamps. A really superb magnifier for the most discriminating collector. Generous 2″ diameter lens, 2x magnification. Rugged all-metal construction to last a lifetime. Lens swivels to any angle and locks in place with thumb screw.
Y772 Stand Magnifier $24.95

BIG 4-INCH MAGNIFIER

With High-Power Extra Lens Built Right In

$29.95

Lights Up Viewing Area

**EXTRA
5X
LENS**

The wide field lens of this magnifier lets you view an area the size of a paperback book page all at once, and a built-in light shines a powerful beam on the viewing area. The big 3-power lens is 4" in diameter. A unique bifocal feature gives you an extra 5-power lens set right into the big lens, so you can get ultra-close magnification at a glance. Satin black plastic case is 10" long with thumb-operated light switch. Uses 2 "C" batteries, included. Magnification is 2.5x overall and 5x in bifocal area.

Y798 Bifocal Magnifier..............$29.95

Press to light

Electro-Optix
MAGNIFIER/ILLUMINATOR

BOS

BOSTON

5X LIGHTED POCKET MAGNIFIER WITH CASE

$14.95

Light-up pocket magnifier has 5-power lens 7/8" in diameter. Shines a bright beam of light on your work; eliminates shadows and dark areas. Push-button switch at top for easy one-hand use. Rugged 2x2" rigid plastic frame; soft plastic case. Uses 2 "AAA" batteries, included. 5x magnification.

Y797 Scanner Magnifier $14.95

ELECTRO-OPTIX LIGHTED STAND MAGNIFIER

$24.95

Highest quality magnifier/illuminator. Distortion-free 3" lens, two-position switch for brilliant momentary or fixed light. Perfect for examining stamps, coins, maps, fine print, etc. Attractive charcoal-and-bone-colored impact-resistant plastic housing. Operates on 2 "C" cells, not incl. A superior instrument! 3x magnification.

**Y807 Electro-Optix Illuminated
    Magnifier** $24.95

H.E.Harris & Co. Inc. ® *Everything for the Stamp Collector*

Basic Needs for Every Collector

PRE-FOLDED EASY-MOUNT STAMP HINGES
$2.49

These are the popular quality Universal Hinges—conveniently folded and ready for immediate application. Real time savers and a great aid to the collector in mounting stamps more neatly.

Y738 2,000 Universal Folding Hinges $2.49

IDEAL STAMP TONGS
$2.25

Always use tongs to handle stamps. These are made of high quality, flexible steel, nickel-plated.

Y781   4¼" Ideal Tongs **$2.25**

STAMP DRYING BOOK
$9.95

The new and easy way to dry stamps that have been washed. No more drying stamps in stacks of newspapers or other makeshifts. The ingenious combination of satin-smooth and blotting pages allows stamps to dry smooth and clean, yet prevents moisture from going through from one page to another. Contains ten large size pages and can be used over and over again for thousands of stamps.

Y871 Stamp Drying Book **$9.95**

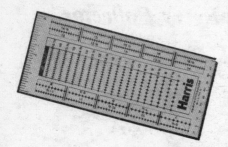

PERFECTO GAUGE
$1.95

Measures stamps from Perf. 7 to Perf. 16½ including intermediate half perfs. Two scales enable you to measure loose and mounted stamps.

Y783 Perforation Gauge $1.95

STAMPLIFT
Eliminates Soaking $10.95

Ingenious stamp accessory allowing quick, easy removal of old hinges and restoration of hopelessly stuck-down mint stamps to former condition without destroying original gum. Substantially made of green and ivory plastic. Requires no chemicals.

Y811 Stamplift $10.95

GLASSINE ENVELOPES
SORT AND FILE YOUR STAMPS

Made of finest quality glassine paper, carefully selected for optimum transparency and durability. Buy them by the hundred or thousand.

		per 100	per 1000
Y701	No. 1 Size (1¾" x 2-7/8")	$2.25	$19.95
Y701A	1½ Size (2-1/6" x 3½")	2.50	22.95
Y702	No. 2 Size (2-5/16" x 3-5/8")	2.75	24.95
Y703	No. 3 Size (2½" x 4¼")	3.00	26.95
Y704	No. 4 Size (3¼" x 4-7/8")	3.25	29.95
Y704A	No. 4½ Size (3-1/8" x 5-1/16")	3.95	34.95
Y705	No. 5 Size (3½" x 6")	4.95	44.95
Y706	No. 6 Size (3¾" x 6¾")	5.95	54.95
Y707	No. 7 Size (4-1/8" x 6¼")	6.95	59.95
Y708	No. 8 Size (4½" x 6-5/8")	7.95	69.95
Y709	No. 9 Size (4" x 8-7/8")	9.95	89.95
Y710	No. 10 Size (4-1/8" x 9½")	10.95	95.95
Y711	No. 11 Size (4½" x 10-3/8")	11.95	99.95

Stamp Maps add to the pleasure of collecting!

**WORLD
STAMP
MAP**

This magnificent World Stamp Map enables you to locate nearly every stamp-issuing country in the world. It is 22"x34", printed on heavy paper in brilliant colors. It is profusely illustrated with photographs of stamps from the world over. A collection of 100 all-different genuine postage stamps match the stamps illustrated! With stamps mounted, your Stamp Map becomes a beautiful decoration, a unique "conversation piece." Shipped rolled in a protective tube. MAP SHIPPED SEPARATELY.

Y725 World Stamp Map with Collection of 100 Stamps (cpl.)..............$4.95
Y725A World Stamp Map only 2.00
WC23426 World Stamp Collection only 4.00

**UNITED
STATES
STAMP
MAP**

Rediscover the history and culture of the U. S. with the exciting, decorative Harris U. S. Stamp Map. It pictures 75 United States Stamps, positioned in or near the states and areas of the country whose people and places are commemorated by the stamps. The map is 22"x34", printed on heavy paper in rich tones of turquoise, beige, and brown. Can be decorated with the actual U. S. stamps to make a colorful display. Shipped in protective tube. MAP SHIPPED SEPARATELY.

Y726 U.S. Map with Matching Collection of 75 different special-quality
U.S. Stamps (cpl.) $4.95
Y726A U.S. Stamp Map only 2.00
UC15028 U.S. Stamp Collection only 4.00

H.E. Harris & Co., Inc. ® *Everything for the Stamp Collector*

THREE MILLION DOLLARS WORTH!
RARE STAMPS
Reproduced on full color Perforated Sheet $1.95

Many of the world's rarest stamps have been locked away in bank vaults for over a generation, but you can study them and learn about them with this philatelic master-piece! The Harris research and art departments have recreated 50 of these stamps, worth over $3,000,000, on a beautiful 17" x 18" sheet. The 1847 Mauritius errors are included, the 1856 British Guiana and the 1918 U.S. 24¢ inverted Jenny. All reproductions are oversize; each accompanied by identifying data and current estimated market value. Reproductions are perforated and gummed for mounting.

Y730A $3,000,000 Rare Stamp Sheet $1.95

ENHANCE YOUR ALBUMS WITH SEALS

A fun collection of perforated gummed seals and at a very low price! Many Harris albums have spaces to mount A through D seals.

79¢
each sheet

A. PRESIDENTS OF THE UNITED STATES. Color portraits of our Presidents, painted especially for Harris. Add interest to the U. S. pages in your album.
Y-723A Presidents of the U.S. .... .79

B. U. S. STATE FLAGS. Flags of our 50 States in beautiful colors.
Y-724A 50 U. S. State Flags .... .79

C. FLAGS of the WORLD. Printed in true colors, these flags of many different countries will fit spaces provided in all of the most popular albums.
Y-722A Flags of the World .... .79

D. COATS OF ARMS. Handsome Coats of Arms of many nations, printed in brilliant true colors.
Y-721A Coats of Arms .... .79

E. WONDERS OF THE WORLD. 24 seals picturing famous places and buildings.
Y732 World Wonders .... .79

F. WILD WEST SEALS. 24 seals. Beauiful color paintings of famous guns and portraits of noted gunslingers.
Y720 Wild West Seals .... .79

A-F SEALS COMPLETE. Save 37% when you order all six seal packages listed above:
Y720, Y721A — 24A, Y732 ....3.00

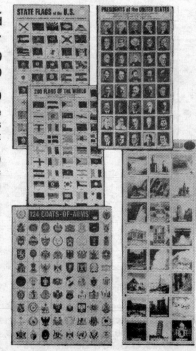

CLASSIC 8"x10" STAMPRINTS™
Prints Reproduce Rare United States Stamps in Color

U. S. No. C15
Graf Zeppelin Airmail

U. S. No. 2
1847 Washington

U. S. No. 1
1847 Franklin

U. S. No. 122
1869 Lincoln

1847 Issues
9x12 Album Page

U. S. No. C3a
1918 Airmail Invert

U. S. No. 295a
Pan-American Invert

These unique and beautiful stamp prints (suitable for framing) are replicas of the original stamps, enlarged to 8"x10" and handcrafted to show the intricate detail of the engraver's art. The quality of these reproductions, printed on extremely fine, durable stock, makes them collectibles in their own right. Well-known philatelic writer, Herman Herst, Jr., has rated them as "magnificent and faithful reproductions." You may order these classic prints now, in a Limited Edition, through H.E. Harris & Co., Inc.

Set includes: 1918 Curtiss "Jenny" Invert; the 1847 imperforates, 5c Benjamin Franklin and 10c George Washington; the 90c Abraham Lincoln of 1869; and the 2c Pan Am Invert of 1901. And finally a big 6"x 13" reproduction of the $2.60 Graf Zeppelin stamp.

Y850	Graf Zeppelin Airmail 1930 (6"x 13")	$2.95
Y851	"Jenny" Airmail Invert 1918	2.95
Y852	Lincoln 1869	2.95
Y853	Washington 1847	2.95
Y854	Franklin 1847	2.95
Y855	Pan-American Invert 1901	2.95
Y856	Complete Set of All Six	12.95

W138 Special 9"x12" album page, with 5c Franklin and 10c Washington 1847 stamps in the colors of the originals, on parchment-like stiff paper, with story behind the first U.S. 1847 General Issue **$1.50**

HARRIS COIN FOLDERS $2.50 each

The Harris coin folders are 8½ x 11", with openings for coins punched in heavy card stock. Covers are rich blue finely-textured stock, printed in white and decorated with brilliant metallic silver embossed coin designs (copper for pennies). Presidential Series provides a dated space for each mint variation of each year, and the quantity minted of each coin. Blank spaces are provided for future issues. Each folder is 2 pages.

2150 Lincoln Memorial Cents, 1959 to Present $2.50
2155 Jefferson Nickels, 1951 to Present 2.50
2160 Roosevelt Dimes, 1965 to Present 2.50
2165 Washington Quarters, 1965 to Present 2.50
2170 Kennedy Half-Dollars, 1964 to Present 2.50
2175 Eisenhower/Anthony Dollars, 1971 to Present.................2.50

COLLECT 1 COIN FOR EACH YEAR $2.50 each

These 8½ x 11" blue folders have openings punched for one coin per year, disregarding mint mark variations. Each space is dated, with blank spaces for future years. Cents begin with first Lincoln penny issued in 1909, nickels with first Buffalo nickel, and dimes with the first "Mercury" dime. Rich metallic coin design.

2185 Cents, 1909 to Present $2.50
2190 Nickels, 1913 to Present 2.50
2195 Dimes, 1916 to Present 2.50

BLANK CREATE-A-COLLECTION
COIN FOLDERS $2.50 each

With these folders, you may assemble any collection you wish. The 8½ x 11" blue folders with metallic coin design have openings for many coins, but no dates printed.

2220 Cents ......$2.50   2235 Quarters ...$2.50
2225 Nickels .....2.50   2240 Half-Dollars .2.50
2230 Dimes ......2.50   2245 Dollars 2.50

WORLD COIN ALBUM

Increase your collecting pleasure by using our 3-ring loose-leaf album with clear vinyl pages for coins. You can see both sides of the coins. Each page has 28 pockets—14 small and 14 large and spaces for printed descriptions of coins from Harris approvals (or your own), or for additional coins.

H168 World Money Album with 3 pages $16.95
F168 World Money Binder alone 12.00
W168 World Coin Pages, pkg. of 5 . . . . 6.50
L168 Coin Kit incl. H168 album
and 15 coins 19.95

WORLD BANK NOTE ALBUM

Display your banknotes in this luxurious album! The binder is a rich brown padded simulated leather, with "Bank Notes of the World" stamped in gold on the cover. Oversize three-ring binder mechanism provides room for plenty of pages, with pockets of varying sizes of bank notes.

H131 Banknote Album with 6 Pages $16.95
L131A Complete Harris Bank Note Album Kit, with 6
pages and 5 World-Wide Bank Notes 19.95
F131 Bank Note Binder Only 12.00

6 VINYL BANK NOTE ALBUM PAGES $6.50pkg

Clearview Vinyl Pages are transparent so that you can see both sides of your Bank Notes without removing them.

W700A single pocket, pages $6.50
W701A 2 pocket horizontal, pages 6.50
W702A 2 pocket vertical, pages 6.50
W703A 3 pocket horizontal, pages 6.50
W704A 4 pocket: 2 large, 2 small, pages 6.50
W705A 4 pocket horizontal, pages 6.50
W706A Assorted, pages 6.50

**STANDARD CATALOG OF
WORLD PAPER MONEY** $39.95

By Albert Pick. A must for the serious collector. Full 1,088 pages features 300 countries and covers from 1974 through 1979. This catalog has detailed descriptions and over 26,000 notes listed by date with over 7,000 original photographs. Available in hard cover only.

Y879 World Paper Money $39.95

APPLICATION FOR HARRIS CREDIT PLAN

Fill out and sign: Please read important information on back. Include $15 down payment if you are sending an order with your application.

Harris

CREDIT PLAN

Rank _____ SS# _____

Time in Service _____

Pay grade _____

Name of
Commanding Officer _____

Please fill in the following:

IMPORTANT: Form must be completely filled out in order to be considered for Membership

Optional—Check only if desired

Name:
☐ Mr.
☐ Mrs. _____
☐ Miss
☐ Ms.

Date: _____

Residence Address: _____   Soc.Sec. No. _____

City/State/Zip _____

My Telephone Number: _____

Employer Name: _____   Phone No. _____

Address: _____   Postion _____

City/State/Zip _____

Date of Birth: _____   No. of Dependents _____

★ ★

If Response is None, Please Indicated None

Name of My Bank: _____

Type of Account _____   Acct. No. _____

Address of Bank: _____

City/State/Zip _____

	Exp. Date	Acct. No.	Bank Name and Address
VISA or Chargex:			
Master Card:			
American Express:			
Diners Club:			

Name & Address of Landlord or Mortgage Bank: _____

_____   Acct. No. _____

Bank w/Installment Loan: _____

_____   Acct. No. _____

List 2 places where you now have current charges:

Name & Address: _____

_____   Acct. No. _____

Name & Address _____

_____   Acct. No. _____

New members must be 18 years of age or older.

Please mail this application to: H.E. HARRIS & CO., INC., BOX X, BOSTON, MASS. 02117

BE SURE TO READ, SIGN AND RETURN THE AGREEMENT ON REVERSE SIDE.

H.E. HARRIS & CO., INC. CREDIT PLAN AGREEMENT

1. In consideration of H.E. HARRIS & CO., INC. extending credit to me under its Harris Credit Plan, I agree to the following terms and conditions: I can avoid incurring a FINANCE CHARGE by paying the New Balance in full provided that such payment is received within 28 days of the Closing Date shown on the Periodic Statement. If I do not timely pay the entire New Balance a FINANCE CHARGE will be computed monthly on the Previous Balance after applying payments and credits (Adjusted Balance Method). No FINANCE CHARGE will be added for a billing period in which there was no Previous Balance or during which payments or credits equal or exceed the Previous Balance. I may at any time pay the total amount owing (New Balance) on the account. Each month I have the option of paying the New Balance, 1/8 of the New Balance or any amount in-between. Minimum monthly payment will be no less than $15.00. Each payment received by H.E. Harris & Co., Inc. shall be applied to merchandise and services as follows: First to unpaid FINANCE CHARGE, then to any unpaid Previous Balance and then to new purchases.

2. I may pay the Minimum Payment Due shown on the periodic statement. If I avail myself of this option, I will incur and pay a FINANCE CHARGE. The FINANCE CHARGE is applied to the Previous Month's Balance after deducting payments, credits and returns (Adjusted Balance Method). The FINANCE CHARGE is determined by multiplying the appropriate Periodic Rate by the balance subject to FINANCE CHARGE shown in the table below.

	MONTHLY PERIODIC RATE	ANNUAL PERCENTAGE RATE
All states, U.S. territories and Canada	.75%	9.00%

3. If I default in making any required payment in full when due, H.E. Harris & Co., Inc. may declare the unpaid New Balance immediately due and may charge collection costs and attorney's fees to the extent permitted by law.

4. Subsequent purchases may be added to my account from time to time provided my account is in good standing.

5. I understand and agree that this Credit Agreement and the disclosures contained herein is not a commitment by H.E. Harris & Co., Inc. to extend credit.

6. On all first purchases on new accounts a minimum down payment of $15.00, with approved credit, will be required.

7. H.E. Harris & Co., Inc. is authorized to investigate my credit record and to verify my credit, and to report to proper persons and bureaus my performance of this Agreement.

8. H.E. Harris & Co., Inc. reserves the right to change generally for all customers, from time to time, the terms of this Agreement in accordance with applicable law and on notice to me by postage prepaid of such change or changes.

9. I, the buyer, have read this Agreement and agree to its terms and conditions acknowledge receipt of a copy thereof.

10. A copy of your rights under the Federal Truth In Lending Act will be mailed to you upon acceptance into the Harris Credit Plan.

H.E. HARRIS & CO., INC.

By *Wesley Mann*

_____   _____
Signature   Seller's Approval

PLEASE KEEP THIS COPY

H.E. HARRIS & CO., INC. CREDIT PLAN AGREEMENT
CUSTOMER COPY

1. In consideration of H.E. HARRIS & CO., INC. extending credit to me under its Harris Credit Plan, I agree to the following terms and conditions: I can avoid incurring a FINANCE CHARGE by paying the New Balance in full provided that such payment is received within 28 days of the Closing Date shown on the Periodic Statement. If I do not timely pay the entire New Balance a FINANCE CHARGE will be computed monthly on the Previous Balance after applying payments and credits (Adjusted Balance Method). No FINANCE CHARGE will be added for a billing period in which there was no Previous Balance or during which payments or credits equal or exceed the Previous Balance. I may at any time pay the total amount owing (New Balance) on the account. Each month I have the option of paying the New Balance, 1/8 of the New Balance or any amount in-between. Minimum monthly payment will be no less than $15.00. Each payment received by H.E. Harris & Co., Inc. shall be applied to merchandise and services as follows: First to unpaid FINANCE CHARGE, then to any unpaid Previous Balance and then to new purchases.

2. I may pay the Minimum Payment Due shown on the periodic statement. If I avail myself of this option, I will incur and pay a FINANCE CHARGE. The FINANCE CHARGE is applied to the Previous Month's Balance after deducting payments, credits and returns (Adjusted Balance Method). The FINANCE CHARGE is determined by multiplying the appropriate Periodic Rate by the balance subject to FINANCE CHARGE shown in the table below.

	MONTHLY PERIODIC RATE	ANNUAL PERCENTAGE RATE
All states, U.S. territories and Canada	.75%	9.00%

3. If I default in making any required payment in full when due, H.E. Harris & Co., Inc. may declare the unpaid New Balance immediately due and may charge collection costs and attorney's fees to the extent permitted by law.

4. Subsequent purchases may be added to my account from time to time provided my account is in good standing.

5. I understand and agree that this Credit Agreement and the disclosures contained herein is not a commitment by H.E. Harris & Co., Inc. to extend credit.

6. On all first purchases on new accounts a minimum down payment of $15.00, with approved credit, will be required.

7. H.E. Harris & Co., Inc. is authorized to investigate my credit record and to verify my credit, and to report to proper persons and bureaus my performance of this Agreement.

8. H.E. Harris & Co., Inc. reserves the right to change generally for all customers, from time to time, the terms of this Agreement in accordance with applicable law and on notice to me by postage prepaid of such change or changes.

9. I, the buyer, have read this Agreement and agree to its terms and conditions acknowledge receipt of a copy thereof.

10. A copy of your rights under the Federal Truth In Lending Act will be mailed to you upon acceptance into the Harris Credit Plan.

HOW TO WRITE YOUR ORDER
Please use the Order Blank

1. Print name and address information complete-including Zip code.

2. Specify quantity, country, description of items, catalog number, and choice of condition.

3. Check whether stamp is used or unused.

4. Fill in retail price of each item.

5. Massachusetts residents only, must add 5% sales tax.

6. Figure postage, handling, and insurance from chart on this page.

7. Make payment in U.S. funds to H.E. Harris & Co., Inc. Canada residents should write "U.S." after numerical dollar amount on check, or purchase money order in U.S. funds. If paying in Canadian funds, add 20% to total order.

Example:

QTY	Country & Catalog Number also specify single, plate block, etc.	Condition	UNUSED	USED	H.E.H. PRICE	LEAVE BLANK
1	U.S. 651	AVG		✓	1.65	
1	U.S. 660	F, NH	✓		9.75	
1	U.S. 743 Pl. Block	VF, NH	✓		60.00	
1	Philippines 411-20	AVG	✓		5.00	
1	H108 Liberty Album				15.95	
TOTAL ALL PAGES					92.35	
MASS. RESIDENTS ADD 5% SALES TAX						
INSURANCE, POSTAGE AND HANDLING					2.25	
TOTAL AMOUNT					94.60	

30-DAY MONEY-BACK GUARANTEE. All stamps, albums and supplies are sold by Harris on a 30-day money-back guarantee. You must be pleased or you may return any item for credit or refund. (Please enclose original order and indicate replacement or refund.)

NOTE ON CONDITION. When ordering from this catalog, specify the condition and list the price from the appropraite column in this catalog. If you do not specify condition, we will send stamps with average centering before 1940, fine centering after 1940, and fine/never hinged after 1964.

WANT LISTS: Harris fills want lists for United States, British North America, and foreign stamps. Please do not use want lists for inexpensive stamps that can be ordered outright from our regular listings. But if you are looking for elusive scarce stamps that are hard to find in stock, please let Harris have your want lists. You should have a charge account with Harris, or a Visa, Master Card or American Express account to use our want list service.

INSURANCE, POSTAGE, AND HANDLING CHART

Charges include delivery, insurance, and handling. They defray only part of the guaranteed charges-we absorb the rest. Delivery of your order is guaranteed.

IF ORDER TOTALS		$10.00 or under	$10.01— $99.99	Over $100.00
Stamps only		1.00	1.50	2.25
Mixed stamps and supplies— Less than $5.00 in supplies		1.75	2.25	3.00
Supplies, albums, & mixed orders other than above	U.S.	1.75	3.00	4.75
	Canada	2.75	5.50	7.75

All Canada Customs must be paid by the customer. Actual postage and handling to all foreign countries will be billed.

H.E. HARRIS & CO., INC., Box O, Boston, Mass. 02117
MINIMUM CASH ORDER—$5.00   CHARGE—$15.00 Date _____

Prices in this Spring-Summer 1985-Edition are effective through September 30, 1985

Harris Credit Plan or Credit Card Number

Charge my purchase to:
- ☐ MasterCard
- ☐ VISA
- ☐ Chargex
- ☐ American Express
- ☐ HCP

INTERBANK NO.   EXP. DATE   MONTH YEAR

DCB03

Signature _____

Name _____
(PLEASE PRINT OR TYPE)

Street _____

City/State/Zip _____

Phone (in case of question about order) ( )_____
Moved since your last order? If so, please give your old address:

Street _____

City/State/Zip _____
All adjustment inquiries must be accompanied by this order blank.

Qty.	Country & Catalog Number also specify single, plate block, etc.	Condition	UNUSED	USED	H.E.H. PRICE	LEAVE BLANK
TOTAL ALL PAGES						
Mass. Residents Add 5% Sales Tax						
Insurance, Postage and Handling (See Chart—preceding page)						
TOTAL AMOUNT (Must total $5 or more)						
Canadian Residents Paying in Canadian Funds must add 20% (See note/Terms and Information)						
TOTAL ENCLOSED						

Order Blank, Page 2.

Qty.	Country & Catalog Number also specify single, plate block, etc.	Condition	UNUSED	USED	H.E.H. PRICE	LEAVE BLANK
	TOTAL OF THIS PAGE					

CHARGE YOUR ORDER Read and sign credit agreement on preceding pages and attach to order with $10.00 down payment.

H.E. HARRIS & CO., INC., Box O, Boston, Mass. 02117

MINIMUM CASH ORDER—$5.00   CHARGE—$15.00 Date _____

Prices in this Spring-Summer 1985-Edition are effective through September 30, 1985

Harris Credit Plan or Credit Card Number

INTERBANK NO.   EXP. DATE   MONTH   YEAR

Charge my purchase to:
- ☐ MasterCard
- ☐ VISA
- ☐ Chargex
- ☐ American Express
- ☐ HCP

DCB03

Signature _____

Name _____
(PLEASE PRINT OR TYPE)

Street _____

City/State/Zip _____

Phone (in case of question about order) (   ) _____

Moved since your last order? If so, please give your old address:

Street _____

City/State/Zip _____

All adjustment inquiries must be accompanied by this order blank.

Qty.	Country & Catalog Number also specify single, plate block, etc.	Condition	UNUSED	USED	H.E.H. PRICE	LEAVE BLANK

TOTAL ALL PAGES		
Mass. Residents Add 5% Sales Tax		
Insurance, Postage and Handling (See Chart—preceding page)		
TOTAL AMOUNT (Must total $5 or more)		
Canadian Residents Paying in Canadian Funds must add 20% (See note/Terms and Information)		
TOTAL ENCLOSED		

Order Blank, Page 2.

Qty.	Country & Catalog Number also specify single, plate block, etc.	Condition	UNUSED	USED	H.E.H. PRICE	LEAVE BLANK
		TOTAL OF THIS PAGE				

CHARGE YOUR ORDER Read and sign credit agreement on preceding pages and attach to order with $10.00 down payment.

H.E. HARRIS & CO., INC., Box O, Boston, Mass. 02117
MINIMUM CASH ORDER — $5.00   CHARGE — $15.00 Date _____

Prices in this Spring-Summer 1985-Edition are effective through September 30, 1985

Harris Credit Plan or Credit Card Number

MONTH   YEAR

INTERBANK NO.   EXP. DATE

Charge my purchase to:
- ☐ MasterCard
- ☐ VISA
- ☐ Chargex
- ☐ American Express
- ☐ HCP

DCB03

Signature _____

Name _____
(PLEASE PRINT OR TYPE)

Street _____

City/State/Zip _____

Phone (in case of question about order) ( )_____
Moved since your last order? If so, please give your old address:

Street _____

City/State/Zip _____
All adjustment inquiries must be accompanied by this order blank.

Qty.	Country & Catalog Number also specify single, plate block, etc.	Condition	UNUSED	USED	H.E.H. PRICE	LEAVE BLANK

TOTAL ALL PAGES		
Mass. Residents Add 5% Sales Tax		
Insurance, Postage and Handling (See Chart—preceding page)		
TOTAL AMOUNT (Must total $5 or more)		
Canadian Residents Paying in Canadian Funds must add 20% (See note/Terms and Information)		
TOTAL ENCLOSED		

Order Blank, Page 2.

Qty.	Country & Catalog Number also specify single, plate block, etc.	Condition	UNUSED	USED	H.E.H. PRICE	LEAVE BLANK
	TOTAL OF THIS PAGE					

CHARGE YOUR ORDER Read and sign credit agreement on preceding pages and attach to order with $10.00 down payment.

NOTES

NOTES